JUN   2004

B MEAD, M.
Banner, Lois
Intertwined lives :
Margaret Mead, Ruth

P9-CIU-080

WITHDRAWN

JUN - 2001

ALSO BY LOIS W. BANNER

Elizabeth Cady Stanton: A Radical for Woman's Rights (1980)

American Beauty (1983)

In Full Flower: Aging Women, Power, and Sexuality (1992)

Women in Modern America: A Brief History (1974; 3rd ed., 1995)

Finding Fran: History and Memory in the Lives of Two Women (1998)

INTERTWINED
LIVES

INTERTWINED LIVES

MARGARET MEAD, RUTH BENEDICT, *and* THEIR CIRCLE

LOIS W. BANNER

Alfred A. Knopf   New York   2003

ALAMEDA FREE LIBRARY
2200-A Central Avenue
Alameda, CA 94501

THIS IS A BORZOI BOOK
PUBLISHED BY ALFRED A. KNOPF

Copyright © 2003 by Lois W. Banner

All rights reserved under International and Pan-American Copyright Conventions.
Published in the United States by Alfred A. Knopf, a division of Random House, Inc.,
New York, and simultaneously in Canada by Random House of Canada Limited,
Toronto. Distributed by Random House, Inc., New York.

www.randomhouse.com

Knopf, Borzoi Books, and the colophon are registered trademarks
of Random House, Inc.

Grateful acknowledgment is made to the following for permission to reprint
previously published material:

The Edna St. Vincent Millay Society: Poem "First Fig"
by Edna St. Vincent Millay. From *Collected Poems*, HarperCollins.
Copyright © 1992, 1950 by Edna St. Vincent Millay. All rights reserved.
Reprinted by permission of Elizabeth Barnett, literary executor.

HarperCollins Publishers Inc.: Excerpt from *Blackberry Winter* by Margaret Mead.
Copyright © 1972 by Margaret Mead. Reprinted by permission of
HarperCollins Publishers Inc.

Houghton Mifflin Company: Excerpt from *An Anthropologist at Work:
Writings of Ruth Benedict*, edited by Margaret Mead. Copyright © 1959
by Margaret Mead. Renewed 1987 by Mary Catherine Bateson. All rights reserved.
Reprinted by permission of Houghton Mifflin Company.

Special Collections, Vassar College Libraries: Excerpts from the papers of Ruth Benedict.
Reprinted by permission of Special Collections, Vassar College Libraries.

Library of Congress Cataloging-in-Publication Data

Banner, Lois W.
Intertwined lives : Margaret Mead, Ruth Benedict, and their circle /
Lois W. Banner.—1st ed.
p.   cm.
Includes bibliographical references and index.
ISBN 0-679-45435-7
1. Mead, Margaret, 1901–1978.   2. Benedict, Ruth, 1887–1948.   I. Title.

GN20 .B36 2003
306'.092–dc21   2002040659

Manufactured in the United States of America
First Edition

For John and Jill, for the past and the present;
For Owen, Christina, and Victoria, for the future;

And to John Laslett, with love.

Contents

Acknowledgments

I FIRST BECAME INTERESTED in Ruth Benedict and Margaret Mead nearly twenty years ago, when I began teaching courses in feminist theory and the history of the women's movement and realized the importance of these two women to twentieth-century feminism. I wrote a preliminary paper on Mead, but I gave up the project when I learned that large portions of both the Benedict Papers, at Vassar College, and the Mead Papers, at the Library of Congress, were restricted until their close friends and associates had died.[1] That is, in fact, the usual practice with such collections.

I returned to the venture a decade later, as men's studies began, women's studies turned to the study of gender, and lesbian and gay studies emerged. Mead's and Benedict's writings, I realized, contained a past version of these new trends; charting their lives seemed even more important to me than it had ten years before. As I worked on this book, the restricted material in both the Benedict and Mead Papers—amounting to hundreds of letters and documents—opened to scholars; the process culminated with the large body of Mead papers that was opened between December 2000 and November 2001, the centenary year of her birth. Indeed, my study is the first biographical account of the lives of these two women to draw on all their papers.

Because Benedict's papers don't contain the extensive materials regarding her ancestry and childhood that exist for Mead, I visited Norwich, New York, the seat of Chenango County, where Benedict spent many of her early years. I found new material on her in the Norwich Public Library, the Norwich First Baptist Church, the Chenango County Court House, and the Chenango County Historical Society, including a diary her mother kept at the ages of sixteen and seventeen. I am the first scholar to use the papers of Benedict's sister, Margery Fulton Freeman, in the special collections of Occidental College, Los Angeles, and those of Geoffrey Gorer at the University of Sussex, in England. Nearly every archive I consulted contained material not yet investigated by scholars, including the Robert H. Lowie Papers at Berkeley, the Léonie Adams–William Troy Papers and the Karen Horney Papers at Yale, and the revealing oral interview with Louise Rosenblatt, Mead's college roommate, in the Oral History Project at Columbia University.

Many individuals have generously shared documents and other archival materials with me. Desley Deacon provided me with Xerox copies of material in the file in the Elsie Clews Parsons Papers in the Rye, New York, Historical Society pertaining to the course Benedict took with Parsons in 1919. Carleton Mabee sent me Xerox copies of his interviews with Elizabeth Mead Steig, Mead's sister, and with Karsten Stapelfeldt, the husband of Eleanor Pelham Kortheuer, a close friend of both Mead's and Benedict's. Philip Sapir shared with me letters from his father, Edward Sapir, to Ruth Benedict. Dorie Jackson of the Norwich Public Library brought to my attention the special edition of the *Chenango Telegraph* for July 4, 1896, written and produced by women in the community; and members of the vestry of the Norwich First Baptist Church granted me access to the manuscript records of the church. I especially thank Dale Storms, director of the Chenango County Historical Society, who found manuscripts and other materials concerning Benedict and her Shattuck and Fulton families in the collections there.

In working on this book, I became close to the group of scholars studying Mead and Benedict. I celebrate the biography of Mead written by Jane Howard, as well as those of Benedict by Judith Modell and Margaret Caffrey, and the work on Benedict and Mead by Hilary Lapsley.[2] I have found these books invaluable guides, and although my interpretations may differ from theirs, I thank Modell, Lapsley, and especially Margaret Caffrey for conversations I have had with them.

For reading all or portions of my manuscript, I thank historians Desley Deacon, Richard Fox, Helen Horowitz, Lawrence Levine, Rosalind Rosenberg, and Alice Wexler; gay and lesbian studies specialists—and historians—Alice Echols and Joanne Meyerowitz; and anthropologists Nancy Lutkehaus and Gerald Sullivan. I thank Nancy for her kindness and help all along the way, and I also thank Cynthia Hogue and Susan McCabe for tutoring me in the reading of poetry and Jennifer Terry for our conversations. My debts to Dolores Janiewski of Victoria University in Wellington, New Zealand, are many, for she read the Reo Fortune Papers, located at her university, for me, and persuaded me to coedit a collection of scholarly articles on Benedict and Mead with her, a collection to be published by Johns Hopkins University Press as *Reading Benedict / Reading Mead: Feminism, Race, and Imperial Visions.* I also thank the commentators on my paper on Benedict at the Organization of American Historians convention in Los Angeles, April 2001—Daniel Horowitz and Mari Jo Buhle—and those on my Mead paper at the convention of the American Anthropological Association in December 2001—Richard Handler and Kamala Wisweswaran.

I am indebted to the archivists at all the manuscript collections I consulted, especially to Nancy MacKechnie and Dean Rogers of Vassar College and Mary Wolfskill at the Library of Congress. Unfailingly gracious, Mary has been a model of fair-mindedness to everyone using the Mead Papers. I am grateful to Patricia Francis of the Library of Congress for helping me through the thickets of those papers. Mary Catherine Bateson's openness to scholars investigating her mother's life and her own fine intellect are invaluable to all of us who work on Benedict and Mead. I thank her very much for permission to publish material from both her mother's papers and Ruth Benedict's.

My thanks to my son, Gideon Banner, for his knowledge of Shakespeare and his research skills; to my sister, Lila Myers, for helping me with plant imagery; and to my daughter, Olivia, for her computer, her fax machine, and her editing skills. I thank my brother-in-law, Peter Laslett, of Cambridge University, for helping me find Gregory Bateson's Half Moon and sharing with me his knowledge of it before his untimely death. I thank my USC colleague Mauricio Mazon for sharing his understanding of psychiatry with me; Ellen DuBois, Devra Weber, and Lila Karp for their insights; and the members of the Silverlake community in Los Angeles, especially Adele Wallace and Jeannette Melley, for their support.

My thanks to Anne Marie Kooistra, Victoria Vantoch, Sarah Laslett, Lynn Sacco, and Belinda Lum for their research assistance, and to the University of Southern California for its generosity in providing me with research support and leave. As always, my agent, Nikki Smith, and my editor, Jane Garrett, have been outstanding. My deepest appreciation goes to my brother, John Wendland, and my sister-in-law, Jill Felzan, for opening their home and hearts to me during the many months I spent in Washington, D.C., doing research at the Library of Congress. I have dedicated this book to them and to their children, Owen, Christina, and Victoria. My love and my thanks to my husband, John H. M. Laslett, a major historian in his own right, for putting up with my maneuvers to take vacations at places where "my" archives were located and with my constant conversation about Benedict and Mead, as well as for his emotional support and critical skills.

PROLOGUE

The Sibyls

Rome, 1926

I N September 1926, Margaret Mead and Ruth Benedict met in Rome to attend the International Congress of Americanists. It was a conference of specialists on Native Americans, a disorganized conference, they thought, and somewhat boring, except for Benito Mussolini's "comic opera" entrance to address the meeting—he arrived with a blare of trumpets and guards in medieval uniforms. So Mead and Benedict spent a lot of time sight-seeing. Mead remembered their visiting the grave of John Keats late one afternoon and becoming so absorbed in paying tribute to a poet they revered that they forgot the time; they were locked in the cemetery and had to ring the bell for the porter to let them out. She also remembered viewing the five Sibyls Michelangelo painted on the Sistine Chapel ceiling, his rendition of the mythical priestesses of Apollo who supposedly dwelt throughout the ancient Mediterranean world. Those figures were important to Benedict; she wanted Mead to see them.[1]

That visit to the Sistine Chapel intrigues me, for it offers an entry into understanding the relationship between Benedict and Mead. They had met in New York City four years before, in the fall of 1922, in the introductory course in anthropology at Barnard College. Mead was a student in the class, and Benedict, fifteen years older and a Ph.D. candidate in anthropology at Columbia University across the street, was the teaching assistant. Some two years later they became lovers. They met in Rome in 1926 three months after Mead returned to Europe in June from her first fieldwork trip, a study of adolescent girls in Samoa that would make her famous.

Introspective and insecure, Benedict sometimes retreated to a fantasy world she had created as a child, a world dominated by Michelangelo's Sibyls. It was located in what Benedict called her "delectable mountains." She borrowed the term from John Bunyan's *Pilgrim's*

Progress, where it's the name for the earthly Eden in mountains on the road to the Celestial City that Bunyan's pilgrim travels. The weather in Benedict's world was always warm and sunny; its inhabitants were always idle. They never worried or quarreled; Benedict called them her "beautiful people." They moved as though in a pageant, walking at a slow, even pace. Or they skimmed the ground, serene and graceful, like the sinuous figures in William Blake's lithographs. They sometimes sat on the ground or in chairs, looking like Michelangelo's Sibyls. Benedict was twelve when she introduced the Sibyls into her fantasy world; they took it over so completely that she had difficulty as an adult remembering what her fantasy figures looked like before then.[2]

No matter their importance to Benedict, Mead didn't like the Sibyls; after looking at them in the chapel, she called them "outsized demagogues." Mead was usually empathetic, but she could be a petulant child with Benedict. Seemingly unconcerned, Benedict responded in a mischievous tone: "I knew you wouldn't like them." Yet humor can conceal anxiety, and Benedict had reason to be anxious. For their disagreement over the Sibyls escalated into a full-blown quarrel, a quarrel so furious that Mead described it not only as "violent" but also as one of the few serious arguments in their twenty-five-year friendship. What caused the disagreement? Hadn't Mead seen reproductions of Michelangelo's Sibyls? Didn't she know about Benedict's fantasy world?

In their letters and writings, neither Benedict nor Mead answers this question. "This isn't a detective story." Mead made that statement with regard to Benedict's life in *An Anthropologist at Work*, her selection of Benedict's poems, letters, and writing that she wove together with her own biographical sketches of her friend and published in 1959, a decade after Benedict's death.[3] Yet her use of the word "this" to refer to her version of Benedict's life suggests that other biographers might discover other stories through detective work. Whether consciously or not, Mead peppered her writings with clues, clues about loves and hates, dreams and obsessions. Investigating the lives of these two women is first and foremost an exercise in detection.

People who knew Benedict described her as calm, sometimes shy, with an expressionless demeanor, although her haunting beauty and the slight smile that flickered over her face made her intriguing: she had a "Mona Lisa" smile, people said. (The shyness and the smile are apparent in photographs of her.) As early as her college years, she described her composure as a "mask" she put on to hide the emotional turmoil inside her. Mead was more open; she had a reputation as a gossip. Nonetheless, she concealed much. During the year she spent as a college freshman at DePauw University in Indiana, she took a course in "history as past ethics" taught by a Methodist minister, a "fiery-eyed enthusiast" who convinced her that one didn't need to tell the whole truth all at once.[4] Moreover, she had the ability to put negative memories out of her mind—or to recast those memories as positive. She remembered that when she and her younger brother were children a nurse locked him in a closet. But her memory wasn't accurate. She had been locked up, she later learned, not he.[5]

This is not to say that Mead's biographical writings about Benedict—or her own autobiographical writings—are untrue. She doesn't, however, always reveal the whole story. She had to maintain a delicate balance between telling the narrative of her life and not offending friends or relatives or risking public embarrassment. She possessed a powerful, intuitive mind. She arranged data in new combinations, engaging in the re-visioning that lies at the heart of the scholarly enterprise. She engaged in the same reconfigurings in her personal life. Just as she created networks of friends and colleagues, she generated multiple explanations in scholarly analysis and with regard to her private behavior. Her daughter, Mary Catherine Bateson, remembered that when she was a child her mother usually provided "a multiplicity of rationales for her arrangements."[6] And like all of us, she had a point of view about the people and events in her life and a healthy desire to justify her behavior. Take a look at the autobiographies of other eminent women in our national past—Elizabeth Cady Stanton, Margaret Sanger, Eleanor Roosevelt. Those memoirs are much less revealing than Mead's.

As anthropologists, Benedict and Mead considered themselves scientists. Accuracy was their standard. Yet while often focused on theory, on using data to arrive at a level of abstraction, they ran the risk, like all theorists, of stressing part of their material and not its entirety. Both were passionate, committed to their own arguments, hoping to find scientific truth. Yet they realized the relativity of scholarly interpretations, that there can be alternative approaches to any point of view. They knew that reality can lie in the eye of the beholder.[7] Both were modernists, schooled in Proust, Yeats, Pound, and Woolf. They knew the modernist theories about varying realities; they applied those theories in the poetry they wrote. They knew the challenge that scientists such as Albert Einstein and Max Planck had issued to Newtonian science; they lived in an era steeped in Freud. They were engaged in the difficult attempts to create cross-disciplinary linkages among the sciences, the social sciences, and the humanities and to incorporate female modernity into their lives: the combination of careers, a freer sexuality, and a companionate marriage that defined the modern New Woman. Moreover, they were intellectuals trying to bridge the gap between academics and the public as well as reformers trying to change the world through their writings, and both projects require clear and absorbing narration. All these factors colored their lives, their work, and their dispute over Michelangelo's Sibyls.

WHAT DO THE SIBYLS LOOK LIKE? Massive in size, each is seated on a bench that resembles a throne. Each has a book of prophecy in her hands. Each faces an Old Testament prophet across a scene taken from a major event of Old Testament history—the Creation of Adam and Eve, the flood, Noah's drunkenness. Those scenes point to the birth of Christ and to his Resurrection, for the Sistine Chapel is dedicated to the Virgin Mary and, according to medieval legend, the Sibyls had predicted the birth of Christ, thereby becoming major figures from classical antiquity for the Christian era. Their massive bodies are masculinized, with muscular arms and twisted torsos underscoring their energy and strength. But they also display the gender blending typical of Michelangelo's figures, a blending that has led homosexual writers to claim him as one of their own, for the Sibyls have breasts and rounded bodies. The term "bisexual" might describe them best.[8] And as women with masculine features, they might also be seen as precursors of the "mannish" lesbian of the Euro-American imagination of the turn into the twentieth century, a figure that haunted that age.

BENEDICT LIKED THE monumentality of the Sibyls, but Mead didn't. Strong-willed and argumentative, Mead had, as anthropologist Ray Birdwhistell put it, "such a masculine mind." Yet she valued femininity—grace and charm, compassion and dependency—and she had a taste for domesticity. It wasn't simply a masquerade on her part to hide her same-sex inclinations and to avoid being identified as a "mannish" lesbian. She felt her femininity sincerely, and she enjoyed it. She was tiny, five feet two inches in height, weighing less than a hundred pounds in 1926. She was feminine in appearance. "I never played the male role in any relationship," she declared.[9]

Yet she was insulting when she called the Sibyls "outsized demagogues," and more insulting still when we remember that in September 1926 she and Benedict were in Mussolini's fascist Italy. The dictator may have seemed comic to the anthropologists at the conference, but his young Blackshirt guards were everywhere in Rome—symbolizing masculine power in the imperial city. By calling the Sibyls "outsized demagogues," Mead implied that Benedict was too much for her to handle. When they first met in Rome, Mead was struck by Benedict's new short haircut and by how white her hair had become during Mead's year away; she looked as if she were wearing a silver helmet.[10] Benedict resembled an Amazon—one of those mythic warrior women of antiquity who battled men. In the early twentieth century "Amazon" denoted a militant feminist or a career woman; it also meant a "mannish" lesbian. Benedict, five feet eight inches tall, had a large and athletic body: she was "fleet of foot," with "large capable hands." She was also a vigorous swimmer, and she found catharsis in chopping up logs for firewood.[11] Moreover, she had a sense of herself as both masculine and feminine. Mead's use of the term "outsized demagogues" to describe the Sibyls implied a criticism of Benedict.

"When you meet a human being," wrote Sigmund Freud, "the first distinction you make is 'male or female.' "[12] Postmodern theorists of gender regard "male" and "female" as constructed categories, creations of a Western dualistic mentality that separates black from white, reason from emotion, human beings from nature. Yet Benedict and Mead used those words in their work and in defining themselves. A biography of them can't be written without referring to "male" and "female." Indeed, a main purpose of this book is to chart the impact of what I call the "geography of gender" on their lives. By that term I mean the complex terrain of gender and sexuality that they negotiated during their lives—political, social, professional, familial, or individual.

My "geography of gender" also involves the psychological road they traveled in determining their sexual identities. I present those identities as more fluid than fixed until each reached a crisis point in her life in the early 1930s and took a stand. In my analysis, I have been especially influenced by the approaches of psychologist Beverly Burch and queer theorist Judith Halberstam. Both contend, as Halberstam puts it, that identity is a "process with multiple sites for becoming and being."[13] Or, according to Burch, identity formation is part of a life process in which sexual orientation can be fixed or change over time—responding to biological inclination, position on the life cycle, historical currents, medical and group definitions, or the influence of people and events.[14]

My "geography of gender" also has a historical component. In the 1890s, the women's movement and its demands for equality—in law, the workforce, the professions, voting—split the modern era open.[15] Those demands, sometimes voiced in an antimale rhetoric, generated a backlash in the form of a strident masculinity evident in the romanticization of male violence and war and the popularity of a new cult of virility around sports like football and bodybuilding. Historians have noted strong trends toward "feminization" around the turn of the century, countered by a "masculinization" in areas such as literature and art, the academic and scientific realms, and culture more broadly considered. Reform Darwinism and evolutionary progressivism contested conservative Darwinism and evolutionary traditionalism. Racism, homophobia, and misogyny flourished. Male writers and artists populated their works with female demons—witches, Medusas, mermaids.[16] Meanwhile, a new celebration of domesticity and motherhood appeared. These forces—the women's movement, the backlash against it, and the celebration of motherhood—flowed through the twentieth century and were manifested in multiple ways in the lives and writings of Benedict and Mead.

ON THAT SEPTEMBER DAY in 1926 when Ruth and Margaret quarreled over Michelangelo's Sibyls, it wasn't certain that they would be able to maintain their romance—or their friendship. Both were married, if unhappily: Ruth to Stanley Benedict, a prominent biochemist at New York's Cornell Medical College; Margaret to Luther Cressman, a part-time Episcopal priest studying for a Ph.D. in sociology at Columbia. Their friendship had already survived Margaret's brief affair with Edward Sapir, an older, eminent linguist and anthropologist. Then on her voyage by boat from Samoa to Europe by way of Australia in the late spring of 1926, Margaret fell for yet another man—a young New Zealand graduate student in psychology and anthropology named Reo Fortune, who was on his way to take up a fellowship at Cambridge University. Luther Cressman, Reo Fortune, Ruth Benedict: whom would Margaret choose? The answer wasn't clear, as she traveled around Europe during the summer with Cress-man and then with Fortune, until Ruth ordered her to come to the conference in Rome.

Both Ruth and Margaret espoused free-love doctrines that called for sexual experimentation and prohibited jealousy, but both also believed in marriage and feared compromising their careers. There was the age difference between them and their shared conviction that a woman was fulfilled through having a child. Ruth had failed to conceive a child. She regarded Margaret as her lover, but she also thought of her as a daughter and a brilliant protégée. And as angry as Ruth was with Margaret over her love involvements, she didn't want to lose her.

There they were in the Sistine Chapel on that September day, hot and tired, craning their necks and straining to see the murky Sibyls some forty feet overhead—the ceiling hadn't been cleaned in centuries. They were torn between conflicting loves, unhappy with their husbands, and not yet certain what direction to take in anthropology.[17] It was all part of the grand-opera mode in which Mead lived her life, dramatic and overblown, creating plots that she played out, as though she were both the writer and the heroine of sensational literary fictions, or a producer of organizations and epic situations. Benedict, averse to publicity, kept a low profile. Yet in her own way she too was a diva: manipulative and demanding adulation, disliking some people no less passionately than she cared about others, but also generous and able to inspire. And like Mead she could soar above everyone, reaching the high notes and producing ideas that reflected and defined an era.

In the 1930s psychologist Abraham Maslow studied with Benedict at Columbia University. Deeply impressed by her, he used her as a model in his theory of self-actualization, which proposes that everyone has the potential to achieve a transcendent self.[18] It was a tribute to a woman who had overcome a difficult childhood, a hearing disability, and a tendency toward severe depression through self-analysis and sheer grit. Something similar might be said of Mead. Underneath her Pollyanna optimism and her soaring ambition lay insecurities. It isn't easy to be told as a child that you have special gifts and then have to prove it as an adult. That insecurity of hers, which she downplayed in her autobiography as much as she emphasized Benedict's, can be seen in a lifelong tendency toward neuritis in her right arm and toward small, debilitating accidents—a broken leg, broken glasses, a sprained ankle. Yet she thought up impossible mountains to climb and then she climbed them, again and again, moving fast, putting her body on the line, sometimes teetering on the edge of a breakdown but never falling over the brink.

Benedict and Mead lived together only twice: during the summer of 1928 in New York, and during the mid-1940s in Washington, D.C., where both had wartime jobs. They never coauthored a published work. Neither of their manuscript collections contains a photograph of the two of them together: so strong was their desire to conceal the depth of their friendship. Yet each read and criticized the other's work. When apart, they kept in touch through letters and phone calls. When Benedict died unexpectedly in 1948 of a heart attack at the age of sixty-one, Mead was bereft. Benedict had been her closest female friend for most of her adult life—her mentor and lover, her mother and daughter, her alter ego.

In 1926 the disagreement over the Sibyls brought them close to a breakup. Margaret had insulted the figures that Ruth loved, her "beautiful people." Margaret was defensive about Reo and troubled about Ruth, who threatened to break with her. Still, they resolved the quarrel, moving beyond it to create one of history's most famous friendships. Despite ups and downs in the years ahead, their commitment to each other held. This book is the story of that friendship, in all its pleasure and pain and startling originality, and of the circle—of family, friends, colleagues, lovers, and ideas—that sustained them.

IN THE SCORES OF LETTERS that Benedict and Mead wrote to each other from 1922 on, as well as in journals and other writings, neither used the term "lesbian" to refer to herself or to the other. By the 1930s Mead occasionally used "lesbian" to refer to other women, but Benedict didn't. Rather, they used "homosexual" or "heterosexual." Both sometimes used the terms "invert" and "pervert," although Benedict used the latter term mostly ironically. In a letter to Mead in 1935 she called herself an "androgyne." To refer to individuals who were sexually attracted to both genders, they used the term "mixed type," not "bisexual." Mead didn't use that word in her writings until 1938, in the friend-of-the-court brief she filed in Bali for her friend Walter Spies, on trial for sodomy with Balinese boys. Benedict never used the word.[19] In this book I follow their practice, although I also use the term "lesbian" in accordance with present-day usage. I conclude that Benedict became what we call "lesbian," while I treat Mead's position as more ambiguous. I am aware of the debates over word usage within the lesbian, gay, and feminist communities. I hope that I have made a contribution to that debate through exploring the terminology used by two major women intellectuals. Why they used the words they did will become clearer over the course of my narrative.[20]

In writing this book, I read everything that Benedict and Mead wrote and much of the work of others they mentioned in their writings, letters, and journals. I plumbed the historical contexts to their lives, and I investigated their childhoods. For I believe, as they did, that one's early years are crucial to the construction of the adult self. In the process I have produced a dual biography, a story of two lives lived separately but deeply intertwined. Benedict and Mead both believed that the comparative anthropology of several societies offered insights into all of them; similarly, comparing the biographies of two individuals can shed light on each of them. And I delved into the published writings and manuscript collections of their friends and associates, to understand not only the interconnections between their own lives but how they extended the circle of friendship, desire, devotion, and difference to other lives.

PART I

Ancestry

CHAPTER I

Pioneering Women and Men

P URITAN MORALISM, Revolutionary idealism, the movement
west—these major themes of the American experience resonate
in the backgrounds of Benedict and Mead. The ancestors of
both came from the British Isles in the early years of colonization:
Benedict's from England, Mead's from there and from Ireland and
Scotland as well. Benedict had forebears among the Pilgrims on the
Mayflower in 1620 and among followers of Roger Williams, the dissenting Baptist preacher who founded the Rhode Island Colony in
1636. Mead traced branches of her family to English Puritans who
founded the Massachusetts Bay Colony in 1630 and to Scottish Pres-
byterians who immigrated to America in the late seventeenth century
after the Stuart Restoration brought the reestablishment of Anglicanism in Great Britain and the outlawing of nonconforming religions.
With a typical dramatic flourish, Mead recounted that Presbyterian
forebears of hers hid in caves on the Scottish coast to elude soldiers of
the crown before they sailed to America.[1]

Both women had male ancestors who fought in the American Revolution; Mead claimed no fewer than seven and Benedict six. For the
most part these men were farmers who temporarily took up soldiering
and who returned to farming once the war ended. Mead's ancestor
Josiah Fogg from New Hampshire achieved a higher rank than most:
commissioned a lieutenant colonel, he assumed the title of major once
he went back home. Benedict especially honored the Revolutionary
patriotism of her paternal great-great-grandfather, Samuel Fulton. A
Baptist minister in Nova Scotia, he proposed a toast to George Washington at a public banquet in Halifax in 1799 that so enraged the loyal-

ist majority who had immigrated there from New England that he was charged with sedition. To avoid arrest, he fled from Canada to upstate New York. Finding a congregation in the city of Poughkeepsie that needed a minister, he took the post and stayed.

In the decades after the Revolution, forebears of both Benedict's and Mead's went west. They were farmers, businesspeople, doctors, and ministers—mostly middle class. Some of them carried on the dissenting traditions of their forebears by becoming abolitionists, reformers, and women's rights advocates. From the 1870s on, some of the women among them graduated from college and then taught school before marrying; some of those women participated in the culture of female romantic friendships that was a key experience of Victorian women. And these elements of Mead's and Benedict's backgrounds—migration, dissent, moralism, and female bonding—played a role in shaping them as adults.

IN 1801, three years after Benedict's paternal Fulton great-great-grandfather fled from Nova Scotia to Poughkeepsie, her maternal Shattuck ancestors migrated from Connecticut to upstate New York. They settled as farmers near the town of Norwich, some forty miles northeast of Binghamton, in a territory recently opened to Anglo settlement. Benedict honored their adventuring spirit as well as her maternal lineage among them by describing them as traveling west in the dead of winter, through rugged forests, on a bobsled, "with a cow tied behind to give milk to the babies." They participated, she wrote, in "the rugged individualism of American pioneer life, giving zest and initiative to human existence."[2]

Those Shattuck and Fulton families living in upstate New York didn't meet for some seventy years, until in 1876 a grandson of the Nova Scotia rebel, another Samuel Fulton, moved to Norwich with his wife and children after years spent as a homeopathic physician in Michigan. Buying the practice of a Norwich doctor who had retired, he hung out his shingle, established himself in the community, and along with his family attended the same Baptist church as the Shattucks. It was there that Samuel's nineteen-year-old son, Frederick—who would become Ruth Fulton's father—met the sixteen-year-old Bertrice Shattuck—who would become Ruth's mother. According to family legend, they fell in love at first sight.

They waited ten years to marry—until Bertrice graduated from

Vassar College and taught for a year at a girls' school in Ohio and Frederick graduated from Colgate University and the New York City Homeopathic College, becoming a homeopathic physician like his father. Frederick established a practice in New York City, and he and Bertrice married and settled there. Ruth was born a year later, in 1887. Margery, their second daughter, was born a year and a half after Ruth. Shortly after Margery's birth, however, Frederick tragically died of Bright's disease (kidney failure), leaving Bertrice with two young children to support.

Returning to her parents' farm, Bertrice taught in the Norwich public high school; demonstrating a significant independence, in 1895 she took a teaching position in a high school in St. Joseph, Missouri. Two years later she became lady principal (dean of girls) at Pillsbury Academy in Owatonna, Minnesota, and in 1899 she accepted a position as head of circulation at the Buffalo Public Library in Buffalo, New York. She remained there until she retired, some eleven years later. In her moving she took along her daughters and her older, unmarried sister, Hetty, who cared for Ruth and Margery while Bertrice worked. They spent summer vacations at the Shattuck farm in Norwich. Bertrice never remarried.

Margaret Mead, for her part, condensed decades of the migrations of her ancestors by way of New England and Pennsylvania into one broad sweep when she wrote that forebears of hers journeyed "across the ocean [from England] to the prairies from Kentucky to Ohio."[3] In fact, some went farther west, to Illinois and Wisconsin. In the 1800s forebears of hers migrated to the Western Reserve territory, where two of her great-great-grandfathers helped found the town of Winchester, Ohio. One of their sons, a Methodist circuit rider and a justice of the peace, was the father of Martha Ramsey Mead, Margaret Mead's paternal grandmother and the mother of Edward Mead, Margaret's father. After Martha's husband died when Edward was six, she took up schoolteaching. Like Bertrice Shattuck, also a schoolteacher, she didn't remarry, and again as in the case of Bertrice, an unmarried sister lived with her and helped with housekeeping and child care.

Emily Fogg, Margaret Mead's mother, was the daughter of Foggs in Chicago whose ancestors had migrated there from New England via upstate New York. Mostly well-to-do, related to the Fogg who provided the funds for the Fogg Museum at Harvard, they were Unitarians, abolitionists, and women's rights advocates. James Fogg, Emily's grandfather, was a Free-Soil candidate from Buffalo for the House of

Representatives in 1852 and then the founder in Chicago of a whole-sale seed company with sales throughout the Midwest. After he died his son James, Emily's father, took over his business. Emily attended Wellesley College for two years before enrolling in 1894 in the new University of Chicago. She met Edward Mead in a class there. A graduate of Methodist DePauw University in Indiana, he was a doctoral student in economics.

After Emily graduated from the University of Chicago, she taught for several years in a private girls' school near New York City and then entered the doctoral program at Bryn Mawr—at a time when women with Ph.D.'s were rare. Edward finished his Ph.D. at the University of Pennsylvania. In 1900 he was appointed to the faculty of the university's Wharton School of Commerce and Finance, and he and Emily married. Margaret, their first child, was born a year later. They had three more children: Richard, born in 1904; Elizabeth, in 1909; Priscilla, in 1911. Another child, Katherine, was born in 1905, a year after Richard, but she died six months after her birth.

Like Bertrice Shattuck moving around the country with her daughters and her sister, Margaret Mead's family moved a lot, although they stayed near Philadelphia. Edward wanted to live close to his work at the university, but Emily wanted to be in Hammonton, New Jersey, fifty miles south of Philadelphia, where she was doing her dissertation on an Italian immigrant community. They compromised by buying a large house in Hammonton and living there in the fall and spring and in rented houses in Philadelphia in the winter. During the summer they went on vacation to the Jersey shore or to Nantucket Island, off the coast of Massachusetts. They moved as often as four times a year. They didn't worry about schools for their children because Martha Mead, Edward's mother, now in her sixties and a retired schoolteacher, moved in with them after Margaret was born, and she taught the children at home. In 1910 they sold the house in Hammonton and bought a farm in Bucks County, Pennsylvania, near the village of Holicong. They settled down there until Margaret entered high school in nearby Doylestown, where they rented a house for a time.

BENEDICT AND MEAD were both proud of their pioneering heritages. Those ancestries encouraged their adventuring as anthropologists, furthered their friendship, and bolstered their adult efforts to challenge gender conventions and forge careers at a time of substantial discrimination against women in the professions. During the early twentieth century many individuals among the Anglo majority in the United States revered such backgrounds, given the huge "new" immigration of people from Eastern Europe and the Mediterranean in that era. As "Old Americans," Benedict and Mead had clout. At conferences Mead sometimes introduced herself as a tenth-generation American.[4] Benedict identified herself in *Current Biography* as an "Old American" and wrote that "all the arguments are on the side of the Founding Fathers who urged no discrimination on the basis of race, creed or color."[5]

California educator Roger Revelle, a friend of Mead's, characterized her as "thoroughly American." She took pride in her long family history in the United States, he stated; "she felt like she was a product of this country in a very profound way."[6] Benedict, in noting her ancestors' migration to upstate New York in winter on a bobsled with a cow tied behind, had praised their pioneering spirit and their maternalism; Mead implicitly did the same when she wrote that Indians had attacked a wagon train carrying ancestors of hers going west and spared "only a blue-eyed mother and her blue-eyed baby."[7] Mead knew that the harsh U.S. government treatment of the Native Americans and the Anglo incursions on their land had provoked their violence. Yet she was proud of her family for settling in frontier regions and she was especially proud of their women, whom she regarded as heroic in leaving kith and kin to face unknown dangers, including childbirth, in the unsettled West. Mead's "blue-eyed" mother with a "blue-eyed baby," the Madonna with her child, was a symbol critical of the male violence of the massacre, not of Indian culture.

Mead saw the immigrants to the United States as connected in a broad way, beginning with the Native Americans. The accepted view of her day was that the American Indians weren't indigenous to the American continent but rather had slowly migrated into it from Siberia over a land bridge that had once existed at the Bering Strait. Drawing from that hypothesis, she regarded them as part of a migratory stream that included Anglos like her ancestors and continued on to embrace the more recent immigrants from Germany, Eastern Europe, Scandinavia, and the Mediterranean. Mead thought of herself as "Old American," but she also identified herself as part of that broader immigrant stream.[8]

Benedict was more critical of her ancestors than Mead, for she felt a sense of alienation from mainstream society that Mead didn't share.

She celebrated her frontier heritage, but she was ambivalent about her Puritan ancestry—those Pilgrims on the *Mayflower* and the Baptists in Rhode Island. Like many intellectuals in the 1920s she criticized the Puritans for moral repression and a commercial mentality that led to nineteenth-century Victorianism and modern materialism, while she denounced the sexual Puritanism of her Baptist upbringing. She wrote in her journal that she had been "born of the Puritan distrust of the senses, of its disgust at the basic manifestations of life." In *Patterns of Culture* she called the Puritan divines of the seventeenth century "psychopathic neurotics" who had put women to death as witches in Salem.[9] As for Mead, in *Growing Up in New Guinea*, which she wrote during the economic crisis of the Depression, she criticized the Puritans for their competitive materialism and their repression of sexuality. In *And Keep Your Powder Dry*, which she wrote partly to inspire national confidence during World War II, she praised them for their moral determination and their practicality.

In 1948, in a eulogy, Mead separated Benedict from her Puritan ancestors to locate her roots among the "yeoman" farming families in upstate New York from which she was also descended. "Yeoman" is an old English term, denoting the virtue of closeness to the land—as in Thomas Jefferson's yeoman farmers, his natural nobility in his plan for a virtuous democratic nation. Mead maintained that Benedict's background gave her a sense of security and distinction that recent immigrants often lacked. "Her firm sense of her sturdy yeoman antecedents was a refuge, which she particularly recognized, from the uncertainties and incompatible leanings that accompany more recent migrations or shifting urban backgrounds."[10]

Mead further declared that her friend's connection to the land enhanced her sensitivity as an anthropologist because it gave her a special bond with the tribal people she studied, people who also lived close to nature. Mead could have applied this statement to herself as well. Like Benedict living on her grandfather's farm in upstate New York during her childhood, Mead spent much of her childhood close to nature, first in the community of Hammonton, New Jersey, and then on the farm in Buckingham, Pennsylvania. Both Benedict and Mead liked city life; each had her primary residence in New York City during much of her adult life. Yet both also loved the rhythm of the seasons, the sounds and smells of the outdoors. In the 1920s both wrote poetry, and both set their verse in the landscapes of their childhood. Benedict wrote about "haws," "surfeited bees," "the gold broken stubble" of

November, and the "bleak long winter" in upstate New York. Mead wrote about "pinewoods" and "daisies on a cowpath." Such words and phrases are farm America to the core.[11]

As adults, both Benedict and Mead decorated their homes with furniture inherited from their families, not with artifacts from their fieldwork. As a curator at the American Museum of Natural History for over fifty years, Mead collected artifacts for the museum when she went on field trips, but she furnished her apartments with family antiques: she described her various living rooms as replicas of her mother's living room when she was a child. She appreciated "the table my grandmother started housekeeping on and my brother used to pound with his Latin book."[12]

The few photos of Benedict's homes reveal a taste for the straight lines of colonial and craftsman design and the sinuosity of Victorian curves and patterned Oriental rugs. They point to a personality both controlled and passionate, both rational and emotional. They reflect her identification with her family lineage and with the history of the nation. That identification of Mead's and Benedict's gave them the security to assume critical stances, while it reminded them of the force of tradition, that the past matters in planning for the future. They flirted with socialism, adopted Deweyian liberalism, and saw their anthropology as furthering social reform as well as scientific understanding—with Benedict's sense of alienation from the mainstream and Mead's sense of belonging to it coloring their work.

Neither of them wore bohemian garb or styles based on the clothing of tribal or folk peoples. They went to Greenwich Village for parties and poetry readings, but they didn't dress like Village radicals. Mead liked clothing that was frilly and feminine; she loved wearing hats, small ones, "with a bit of whimsy—a rose perched up front perhaps."[13] Even in the field, studying tribal cultures, she wore skirts, and in public she often wore white gloves, as did most ladies before the 1960s. Benedict preferred more tailored attire, dresses and fitted suits in soft shades of grayed blue and green that matched her sense of constraint and the ambiguity of her smile, with a frilly blouse, so that she looked both professional and feminine. Benedict's graduate students remembered her as possessing "the gracious manners and tone of a well-bred woman."[14] In the 1950s, when femininity was especially in vogue, Mead wore dresses by the Italian designer Fabiani that were bell-shaped, with small waists and full skirts held out by layers of ruffled taffeta, a style fashionable in that decade.[15]

BENEDICT'S AND MEAD'S ancestors were connected not only to seventeenth-century colonization, eighteenth-century revolution, and the nineteenth-century movement west, but also to dissent. Puritanism, Presbyterianism, Methodism, Baptism, Unitarianism—the religions of Mead's and Benedict's ancestors—had all originated as protesting faiths, and those religions continued to embrace dissent as they broke into sects, regrouped into denominations, and became major forces behind the reform movements of the nineteenth century. Indeed, the family trees of Benedict and Mead contain striking numbers of reformers, abolitionists, and women's rights advocates. Given this background, it's not surprising that both women felt an imperative toward social reform as adults.

Among Benedict's ancestors, the patriotic Samuel Fulton who had fled from Nova Scotia to escape arrest had a number of reform-minded descendants. The most prominent among them was his grandson Justin Fulton, the brother of Samuel Fulton the homeopath and thus Ruth's great-uncle. Like his grandfather, Justin Fulton was a Baptist minister. He was famed for his preaching, first at the huge Tremont Temple in Boston and then at a church in Brooklyn, New York. He honored the abolitionists through a laudatory biography he wrote of the Boston abolitionist Timothy Gilbert. He also wrote a book on women in which he supported the women's rights movement, so long as women weren't given the vote, deferred to their husbands, and took full responsibility for housework and for raising their children.[16]

Samuel Fulton, Justin's brother, carried on his family's dissenting tradition in his medical practice. Regular doctors bled their patients and had them take purgatives, attempting to release from the body the evil humors that they thought caused illness, while homeopaths prescribed small doses of minerals and herbs to stimulate the body's natural power to heal. Homeopathy was introduced in the United States in New York City from Germany in 1825, and it flourished in upstate New York, where it meshed with antebellum reform movements such as abolitionism and women's rights, which were strong in the region.[17] According to Samuel Fulton's obituary in the Norwich newspaper, he was dedicated to social improvement. He "earnestly" supported "everything which, in his opinion, tended to the better development of the interests of the village." He was also president of the county homeopathic society for many years.[18]

Ruth Benedict spent much of her childhood at the farm in Norwich owned by her maternal grandfather, John Shattuck. Deeply pious, he was a deacon of the Norwich Baptist Church and head of its Sunday school for many years. Yet financial matters preoccupied him. Like many farmers in upstate New York, he specialized in dairy farming, and by the 1880s increasing mechanization and the appearance of large-scale operations had undermined the profitability of the smaller dairy farms. To survive as a farmer, Shattuck periodically increased his mortgage to buy more land and livestock. He also introduced rigorous sanitary procedures in his production of milk and butter. Widely copied by farmers in the region, those procedures were viewed as having staved off a threat from the new oleomargarine industry.[19] Shattuck was twice elected president of the state dairy farmers' association.

Involved with his farm and his church, Shattuck didn't have much time for reform activities, although he had supported abolitionism when young. When older, he upheld his church's policy of admitting African-Americans as members: Norwich had a small black community dating to the antebellum era when slavery still existed in New York State.[20] His obituary in the local newspaper praised him for backing higher education for women. That support mostly involved encouraging three of his four daughters—Hetty, Bertrice, and Myra—to go to college. Still, in an era in which about 1 percent of individuals—whether male or female—in the eligible age group went to college, his daughters' attendance was remarkable: of the four, only Myra didn't attend school beyond high school.[21]

With regard to the Foggs in Chicago, James Fogg, Margaret Mead's grandfather, was, like John Shattuck, preoccupied with his business affairs, as head of the wholesale seed business that he inherited from his father. Given the volatility of the farm economy, however, making a profit selling seeds wasn't easy. He provided his family with an affluent lifestyle and a large house on Chicago's exclusive North Shore, but he suffered from chronic emotional depression and, according to his daughter Fanny, he wasn't much of a businessman. Like John Shattuck the dairy farmer, he didn't have time to participate in reform activity, although in his youth he had wanted to be a reformer and politician like his father, a Free-Soil candidate for the House of Representatives from Buffalo before he opened the seed business.[22]

For the most part, to find reformers in Benedict's and Mead's families one must look to the women. That gendered pattern of reform

involvement wasn't unusual. Men working to provide economic support for their families while their wives and daughters engaged in
reform activity when not doing housework or caring for children—that
pattern has often been typical of reform movements in the United
States. Moreover, in the nineteenth century many of the women in
Benedict's and Mead's families—like John Shattuck's daughters—
attended girls' academies and colleges and then taught school. They
thereby participated in one of the nineteenth century's most successful
reforms: the opening of secondary and higher education to women.
That educational experience motivated many women college graduates
to take up reform and women's rights; those movements allowed them
to have unofficial careers outside the home, at least until they married.

AMONG JOHN SHATTUCK's four daughters, Hetty, the eldest, went
to Vassar for a year. After she dropped out she came home and helped
with the housework before becoming Bertrice's housekeeper. Mary,
third in birth order, graduated from the Boston School of Oratory and
then taught at girls' academies in Ohio and Virginia before marrying.
Myra, the youngest daughter, remained at home to care for her parents
as they aged. Bertrice, the middle child between Hetty and Mary, was
the best student and the most ambitious of the four sisters. She set her
sights on Vassar, putting off her engagement to Fred Fulton until she
completed her education. When it became apparent that her father,
who was struggling with mortgage payments, couldn't pay her
expenses, she earned the money to pay for them herself. She taught at
a high school near Norwich for several years and, once at Vassar, she
worked part-time in the library.[23]

Ella Fulton, Ruth Benedict's aunt and the only daughter of Samuel
Fulton the homeopath, had the most success in education among
Benedict's female relatives in Norwich. Ella's mother became an
invalid in later life, and Ella cared for her until she died in 1899. Then
she made up for lost time. Returning to Michigan, where her family
had lived, she completed a B.A. degree at Kalamazoo College. After
she graduated she was hired as an instructor there, then appointed a
professor, and finally chosen to be dean of women. Resigning that
position after a number of years, she studied in Germany, did graduate
work at the University of Chicago, and finished her career as dean of
women at the University of North Dakota. She never married.[24]

A number of Margaret Mead's female relatives also attended college and then taught school. That was the case with Emily and Fanny Fogg, the daughters of James Fogg, the Chicago seed merchant. After Emily completed two years at Wellesley, James Fogg's seed business went bankrupt. Like Bertrice Shattuck, Emily then earned the money to pay for college herself, graduating from the new University of Chicago in 1896 and then teaching at a girls' school near New York City. Her sister, Fanny, two years younger, attended college for a year and then taught at a girls' school in Tacoma, Washington, before moving back to Chicago to teach until she married.

These women forebears of Benedict's and Mead's who attained college degrees and then taught school were part of a group of middle-class young women who did so. They responded to their own desires for achievement, the rhetoric of the women's rights movement, the opening of colleges to women, and a huge demand in the growing nation for teachers in elementary and secondary schools. Even when physician Edward Clarke launched his famous attack on female undergraduates in 1871, charging that serious study would ruin their reproductive organs and turn them into "hermaphrodites," college women like Bertrice Shattuck paid no heed. The standard epithets calling college women "Amazons" and "mannish maidens" didn't stop them either.[25] Such women wanted knowledge and training for careers. They realized that by teaching they could save money for marriage or for their education. They also realized that the volatile U.S. economy—or the death of a husband—could bankrupt families and wipe out their savings. Most of the advice books for girls in that era recommended that they get some education before marrying so that they could support themselves if they had to.[26]

The percentage of women in the eligible age group who attended college in the nineteenth century was small—about 1 percent. Yet the percentage of men in the eligible age group who attended college wasn't much higher. And the percentage of college students who were women was sizable—and growing. By 1870 college enrollments were 21 percent female; by 1880, 32 percent; by 1910, nearly 40 percent.[27] Moreover, precollege teaching was feminizing in that era. By 1850 women dominated elementary teaching; by 1890 they were becoming a majority of high school teachers. Indeed, by the late nineteenth century so many women college graduates taught school for a year or two, often at private academies for girls, after they graduated and before they married that the experience became a near rite of passage for them. Sheltered middle-class young women moved away from home to make independent lives, finding their jobs through friendship networks at their colleges or through teacher-placement agencies.[28] In Benedict's family those women included Ella Fulton going to Michigan and North Dakota; Bertrice Shattuck to Ohio, Missouri, and Minnesota; and Mary Shattuck to Ohio and Virginia. In Mead's family they included Emily Fogg (Mead) going to New York City; and Fanny Fogg (McMaster) to the state of Washington.

Still, none of these women became lawyers or doctors. And those who married for the most part didn't work outside their homes for pay once they married. They respected the "breadwinner" ethic of the day that decreed that a husband should support his family unaided.[29] A Vassar alumnae report for 1910 lists the employment record of the thirty-three members of Bertrice Shattuck's graduating class of 1885 in the twenty-five years intervening. Almost all spent the first year or two after graduation teaching school—or in training for a professional career. Once they married, however, they became homemakers. Only the nine who never married or who were widowed continued with careers—one as a doctor, a second as a visiting nurse, a third as a journalist and head of her own advertising agency, and five as schoolteachers and school administrators. These nine, however, constituted nearly 30 percent of the class. The report doesn't list the participation of these graduates in reform and women's rights organizations, even though the founders and leaders of such organizations were often women with college degrees.[30]

Attending college and participating in reform activity wasn't characteristic of all the women in Benedict's and Mead's families. Both Benedict's grandmothers—Joanna Shattuck, the wife of the dairy farmer, and Harriet Fulton, married to the homeopathic physician—raised their children and then became invalids as they aged. Extant sources don't reveal what troubled them, but such invalidism, whether due to illness or to emotional distress, wasn't unusual among middle-class women in the nineteenth century. Before Harriet married Samuel Fulton, however, she seemed bent on career achievement. Raised in Ann Arbor, Michigan, she attended a female academy there and then taught at the preparatory school for the University of Michigan. When she married Samuel she gave up schoolteaching, raised her children—and then broke down. After her death her daughter, Ella, was the one to achieve a brilliant career.

In the case of Margaret Mead, her maternal grandmother in Chicago, Elizabeth Fogg, the wife of the seed merchant, mostly remained at home, raising five children. Yet she was a woman of spirit, remembered by her granddaughters as wearing purple and smoking cigars. According to Mead, who disliked her, she had a "blithe childish irresponsibility" and a love of "frivolous" literature. After her husband died, she ran off with a young man.[31] Martha Ramsay Mead, Margaret Mead's paternal grandmother from Winchester, Ohio, was no less independent—if more career-minded. She had a college degree and a career in education. As a teacher she was a reformer: she studied the writings of progressive educators like Friedrich Froebel and applied their ideas in her teaching. Spending her time on her profession, her son, and the local Methodist church, however, she wasn't indignant about gender inequality and she wasn't a women's rights activist. Nor was Elizabeth Fogg, although when female relatives of hers in Chicago became involved in women's organizations in the Progressive era she attended meetings along with them.

THE PARTICIPATION OF Benedict's Fulton and Shattuck female relatives in reform activities is revealed in a special edition of the *Chenango Telegraph* for the Fourth of July, 1896. (The *Chenango Telegraph* covered all the towns in Chenango County, for which Norwich is the county seat.) Local women wrote and edited the special edition, which documents the existence of many women's organizations in the area, including women's church groups, a women's civic improvement society, local chapters of the Women's Christian Temperance Union (WCTU), the Young Women's Christian Association (YWCA), the Daughters of the American Revolution (DAR), and a small, but vocal, woman suffrage group.

Both Bertrice Shattuck, Benedict's mother, and Ella Fulton, Benedict's aunt, wrote articles for the special edition. In her article Ella lists the successes of the women's rights movement, exhibiting a militant, even antimale, stance. She begins with a tribute to Emma Willard, founder in 1821 of what was to become the famed Emma Willard School in Troy, New York—among the first women's academies in the nation. She provides statistics on the growing participation of women in the workforce. She extols women philanthropists and reformers. She praises the women's symphony orchestra of Boston, explaining that men were playing its wind instruments because few women had as yet mastered them. She burlesques masculine behavior. "A maiden lady in Newburg," she writes, "keeps a parrot which swears and a monkey which draws tobacco. She says between the two she doesn't miss a husband very much."

Bertrice Shattuck's article is different. It's mostly a description of St. Joseph, Missouri, to which she moved with her daughters and her sister Hetty in 1895 to take up a position teaching high school. She focuses on the city's religious life, expressing surprise at the strength and variety of the churches in the city. She notes that the city has a Southern flavor, since Kentuckians who came from Virginia were its original settlers, but Northerners and Southerners are ending their animosities as they realize that they are "citizens of a common country and servants of one Master." She praises the interdenominational missions of the city's churches in the immigrant district of the city, with its few churches and many saloons, especially the establishing of a day nursery and a kindergarten by the YMCA and the YWCA working together.

By 1896 the woman suffrage movement in New York State was at a high point, and the women's special edition of the Chenango newspaper reflected the organizational enthusiasm generated by that movement. Bertrice and her sisters were pious Baptists, and they participated in the heightened sensitivity to the cause of women through the women's missionary society of their church. In 1891, before moving to St. Joseph, Bertrice became vice president of the missionary society, with her oldest sister, Hetty, its secretary. The members of the society made quilts and sold them to raise money; they went door-to-door soliciting contributions. They sent the money they raised to the national Baptist board coordinating overseas missions and the one overseeing domestic missions to the Indians of the Southwest and Asian immigrants in San Francisco. At their meetings they read aloud the reports of those boards about "our sisters with black, red, and yellow skins." They researched and wrote papers that they read at the meetings: Myra Shattuck gave a paper on the Indians of North America. Ruth and her sister, Margery, became participants in the society when they were initiated into a "baby band."[32]

Like the Shattuck women in Norwich, the Fogg women in Chicago became involved in reform, especially in the late 1880s, with the appearance of the Progressive movement in their city. In 1888 Margaret Mead's wealthy great-aunt Fanny Fogg Howe paved the way by participating in the founding of the Chicago Women's Club, an organization central to women's reform activities in the city. Howe became a close associate of Jane Addams at Hull House, and she eventually chaired the Illinois State Board of Charities. She provided a model for the younger women in the family, including her namesake, Fanny Fogg, Margaret Mead's aunt, who taught school before she married and, once married, took up volunteer work at both the Chicago Women's Club and Hull House. Margaret Mead remembered sitting on the floor of Hull House as a child, reading case records while she waited for her aunt. When Fanny Fogg was certain that she wouldn't have children, she accepted a paid position as a caseworker for the Chicago Juvenile Protective Association.

Emily Fogg Mead, Margaret Mead's mother, followed the example of the women of her family in Chicago by working as a volunteer for reform organizations once she married and had children. Despite her husband's recurring financial problems, she didn't attempt to find paid work: she respected the breadwinner ethic. When she died in 1950, at the age of seventy-eight, her obituary in the *New York Times* described her as a widely known civic leader. She was an officer of the Pennsylvania state branches of the American Association of University Women, the YWCA, and the woman suffrage organization. She was also active in the Women's Trade Union League and after World War I in the newly founded American Civil Liberties Union and the Women's International League for Peace and Freedom.[33] She wrote a Master's essay but never completed her Ph.D.

Just as Margaret Mead's female forebears among the Chicago Foggs were involved in reform and women's rights activities in Chicago, Mead's mother was a leader in women's organizations in Pennsylvania. Mead grew up with women's rights sentiments all around her. She went with Emily Fogg Mead to women's meetings; she helped her mother print and distribute pamphlets; she heard her give speeches and engage in debates; and she saw her mother's name in the newspapers. Yet Mead's paternal grandmother, Martha, who cared for her and taught her at home, didn't join Emily in those activities. After a lifetime of professional work, she relished the creative parts of domesticity—cooking, sewing, caring for children. Martha's passivity toward women's rights and her enjoyment of domesticity influenced Margaret as much as her mother's activism.

In the case of Ruth Benedict, the attitude of the women in her family toward women's rights and careers for women was equally complex. She was the niece of a militant women's rights supporter and the daughter of a moderate—both women with careers in education. Ella Fulton never married, while Bertrice Fulton glorified marriage and motherhood and raised her daughter to anticipate having a career in a woman's profession like religious missions, social work, or school-teaching—until she married. Ruth Benedict, like Margaret Mead, was critical of organized feminism throughout her adult life. Still, growing up in a family with a tradition of educated women working as school-teachers and reformers influenced her, as a similar family tradition influenced Margaret Mead.

MEAD'S AND BENEDICT'S family backgrounds reflect another theme in the history of the United States, one involving female friend-ship—and love between women. The rise of industrial capitalism by the mid-nineteenth century brought many middle-class men out of the home, workshop, and family farm into the arena of business and left their wives and daughters at home, creating a space where female friendships flourished. The separation between home and work encouraged women to join together in reform endeavors, and thus to enter male public space, while the single women among them some-times lived together in what were known as Boston marriages. Deaths during the Civil War and men's greater propensity to move to the frontier produced a gender imbalance, with more women than men in some regions of the Northeast, while continuing high rates of death in childbirth and Victorian strictures against sexuality made some women hesitant to marry. The term "Boston marriage" was derived from the close relationship between the two central female characters in Henry James's novel *The Bostonians* (1886). According to Mead, as late as the 1900s Boston marriages weren't unusual, even in rural Pennsylvania where she spent much of her childhood.[34]

Middle-class women's sphere of activity and friendship extended to girls, who were allowed to have close, even passionate, relationships with other girls. Such friendships were viewed as an innocent out-growth of the emotionality of adolescence and as a way of preparing girls for the emotional bonding both of the adult female community and of marriage. Moreover, they deterred seduction by males and pos-sible pregnancy at a time when the age of first marriage was rising, cre-ating a large group of young women and men outside the bonds of matrimony.[35] Girls were expected to have a "best" friend or a "bosom" friend; such relationships were often called "smashes" or "crushes." "Soul mate" and "kindred spirit" were analogous to those terms, although they weren't entirely synonymous with them, since they could also apply to friendships between men—and between women and men. Young men, too, had loving relationships with each other in this era, although, according to historian E. Anthony Rotundo, for the most part their intense friendships didn't continue beyond marriage.[36]

All these terms were related to the nineteenth-century vogues of spiritualism and Romanticism. The former held that the dead and the living could form special bonds; a vast expansion of interest in it resulted from the deaths of young men on the battlefield during the Civil War. Romanticism was a reaction to the rationalism of the Enlightenment, and it was encouraged by the emotionalism of the periodic waves of religious revivalism that swept the United States from the Great Awakening of the eighteenth century to the Civil War and beyond. The Romantic movement encouraged a passionate emotionality that could be expressed through sexuality or be channeled into spirituality or a drive for material or creative achievement. Middle-class Victorians also kept their passion in check through sentimentality, a feminized and domesticated form of emotion that was evident in the popularity, for example, of Valentine's Day cards, decorated with hearts, flowers, and cherubs, and containing simple, formulaic verse, with the formerly demonic Cupid now a chubby infant.[37] And that age glorified friendship, which was valued as uplifting. Ralph Waldo Emerson celebrated friendship in an 1841 essay on the subject. "The moment we indulge our affections [in friendship]," he wrote, "the earth is metamorphosed, there is no winter and no night."[38]

Yet the arbiters of middle-class morality didn't seem to realize that close bonding between girls might lead to genital sexuality, or that some young women might not become sufficiently attracted to men to make the transition to heterosexual desire. Middle-class Victorians regarded men as more highly sexed than women. Still connecting sex to procreation, they identified the sex act with the male sex organ. Moreover, the prohibition against masturbation was intense, and practices like oral sex were beyond respectable thought. Respectable members of the middle class often called homosexuality "the crime that cannot be named." Men, it was thought, went to prostitutes to indulge in "perversions."[39]

But physical affection between girls wasn't frowned on. In 1905 Mary Wood-Allen, head of the social purity department of the national WCTU, observed that girls "go about with their arms around each other, they loll against each other, and sit with clasped hands by the hour. They fondle and kiss." What might be called a culture of "smashing" was particularly strong at single-sex girls' schools. In 1898 a graduate student at Clark University studying with psychologist G. Stanley Hall, the day's foremost expert on "adolescence," sent a questionnaire on friendship and love to individuals associated with a number of colleges. Ninety-one questionnaires were returned. To a question about "first love," forty-nine respondents, or more than one-half, replied with reports of same-sex love. One woman, age nineteen, wrote of having been infatuated with female teachers. Another, age thirty-three, wrote that at fourteen her first experience of falling in love was with another girl. "It was insane, intense love, [and it had] the same quality and sensations as my first love with a man at eighteen." A third woman, age thirty-five, described her experience at a women's college. "When I was a freshman in college I knew at least thirty girls who were in love with a senior. Some sought her because it was the fashion, but I know that my own homage and that of many others was sincere and passionate." When she was a senior, she became the adored being. "I was the recipient of languishing glances, original verses, roses, and passionate letters written at mid-night and three in the morning."[40]

Did Benedict's and Mead's female relatives who attended and taught at single-sex schools participate in a culture of smashing there? For the most part no documentation exists for these women—except for Benedict's and Mead's mothers. At Vassar, Bertrice Shattuck's college, and at Wellesley, which Emily Fogg attended, smashing flourished. Bertrice kept her distance from it, but Emily participated in it enthusiastically.

Opened in 1865, Vassar was among the first women's colleges in the nation. It was conservative in approach: its course of study, focused on ethics and the classics, copied that of the men's colleges; its goal was to produce better wives and mothers—and perhaps teachers. Daily attendance at chapel was required, and its presidents were male, as were its full professors, although its initial faculty included a sizable number of graduates of women's seminaries. Astronomer Maria Mitchell was on the faculty, and she brought women's rights reformers like Lucy Stone to the campus to speak, although woman suffrage activities were otherwise discouraged—and Mitchell believed that women shouldn't be given the vote until they had proved that they could succeed as teachers and other professionals in fields such as medicine and law.[41]

Smashing was important at Vassar. The college had such a reputation for it that the Yale student newspaper commented on it in 1873, and the Cornell student newspaper reprinted the Yale comment:

> When a Vassar girl takes a shine to another, she straightway enters upon a regular course of bouquet sendings, interspersed with tinted notes, mysterious packages of "Ridley's Mixed Candles," locks of hair perhaps, and many other tender tokens, until the object of her attentions is captured, the two become inseparable, and the aggressor is considered by her circle of acquaintances as—smashed.

In 1882 Alice Stone Blackwell, the daughter of well-known reformers and woman suffrage advocates Lucy Stone and Henry Blackwell, confided to a relative that Maria Mitchell had told her that the teachers at Vassar found smashing a "pest." "It kept the girls from studying & sometimes made a girl drop behind her class year after year," Blackwell wrote. It replicated romantic courtship with young men; it produced the same infatuations, obsessions, jealousies, and betrayals. "If the 'smash' is mutual, they monopolize each other & 'spoon' continually, & sleep together & lie awake all night talking instead of going to sleep."[42]

From Vassar's beginnings, the students were encouraged to think of the college as a family and the other students as "sisters." Classes had special relationships: freshmen with juniors, sophomores with seniors. Men were permitted on campus only on Sundays; the female students escorted each other to parties and dances, with some of them slicking down their hair and wearing male clothing to play the part of young men. But they weren't permitted to wear pants: even when Vassar women played the male roles in school plays, they wore long black skirts.[43] Yet partly because of Vassar's reputation for smashing, the opening of women's colleges like Smith and Wellesley, with more modern curricula and, in the case of Smith, ties to nearby male colleges, brought a serious decline in applications to Vassar. By 1885, the year Bertrice Fulton graduated, her class had only thirty-three members.

Bertrice Shattuck's copy of the Class Day Book for her graduating class documents the culture of smashing at Vassar. That year's baccalaureate address by Samuel Caldwell, Vassar's president, which was reprinted in the graduation book, focuses on it. The speech begins with a tribute to friendship. "It is written on the soul and all the life as well that God designed us for each other, for acquaintance, for friendship, for love." Caldwell repeats standard sentiments about the benefits of friendship, sentiments expressed in texts on friendship from the ancient Greeks to the one by Ralph Waldo Emerson. He states: "We see in our friend a second self." And "during the often troubled period of youth, a friend can provide security." Abruptly changing his tone, however, he excoriates romantic friendships between young women, calling them "crazes" that are "fleeting" and "unsubstantial." "They are born of imagination, of young impulse, of temporary fancy, and have not truth enough in them to keep them alive." Yet he confesses that they are "not unknown within these walls."

In addition to Caldwell's sermon, Bertrice's Class Day Book also contains predictions for each student's future written by a class "Sibyl"; the predictions identify smashes in the class. The Sibyl foresees a double wedding for Anna Lester and Clara Hiscock, even though such marriages to men would be surprising, since they would be "such a contradiction of the views of the young ladies in question." The prediction for Edith Lowry involves her intense friendship with Mary Ricker. Foreseeing that Edith will marry but that her husband will die, the Sibyl predicts that Edith will then go to Mary for comfort, "as of old," and the two of them will become "as inseparable as during that last week of Senior Vacation." The Sibyl describes Elizabeth Deming and Elizabeth Dunning as being "hopelessly entangled during their college course."

How did Bertrice Shattuck react to the culture of smashing at Vassar? The evidence suggests that she avoided it, since she remained committed to Fred Fulton and became engaged to him in her senior year. Margery Fulton, Ruth's sister, maintained that their mother, who was older than her classmates and who didn't have much money, felt out of place.[44] Yet more than age and lack of money may have produced Bertrice's alienation. The Sibyl's prediction for her in the Class Day Book isn't positive. Bertrice was the only engaged member of the class, and the Sibyl states that she has "saved" the class from the "ignominy" of not having anyone engaged before graduation. Yet while predicting outstanding achievements for most of the other graduates, the Sibyl foresees only that Bertrice will "cling" to the title of "Mrs. Fulton" throughout her life. Still, Bertrice accepted the romantic friendships in her class, since she sent her daughters to Vassar and, according to Margery, told them "exalted tales of college friendships" when they were children.[45]

What about Emily Fogg, Margaret Mead's mother? What was her experience of smashing at Wellesley? In contrast to Vassar, at Wellesley the administration encouraged women's rights and was committed to hiring an all-woman faculty. A student group worked for women's rights, and a weekly column in the school newspaper provided news about the women's movement nationwide. A woman professor of mathematics took students to visit the home of Lucy Stone and Henry Blackwell, located near the college, so that they could learn about a marriage based on gender equality. Emily Fogg strongly supported women's rights. Referring to herself and her school friends, she wrote in an autobiographical memoir: "I can feel the joy we felt when we found an article in a scientific magazine showing female superiority among the insects."[46]

The culture of smashing was strong at Wellesley. In later life, Emily wrote two brief, unpublished memoirs, in which she described her experience of it. Her first passionate friendship with another student occurred during her freshman year, when a sophomore lavished attention on her and "petted" her as though she were a child. The second involvement, more intense, occurred during her sophomore year, when she and a classmate fell deeply in love. They took long walks and talked about their lives. At the time Emily didn't think of the relationship as homosexual because she didn't know that a same-sex orientation could exist, much less what erotic practices might be involved. However, since there was a "slight stigma" on crushes, the students involved in them kept them secret. Yet because the students at Wellesley were so deeply committed to one another, Emily wrote, the absence of men at the college didn't bother them.[47]

After Emily Fogg left Wellesley because her father could no longer afford it, she worked for several years and then entered the University of Chicago in 1894. She was attracted to its many educational innovations and its commitment to women's rights, with women constituting nearly 40 percent of its undergraduates and 25 percent of its graduate students. Alice Freeman Palmer, its first dean of women, had been president of Wellesley when Emily Fogg was there; she was the most prominent woman academic in the nation after M. Carey Thomas, the president of Bryn Mawr.

Emily majored in sociology. A number of the faculty members in

that department were affiliated with Jane Addams's Hull House, where
they taught courses and learned from Addams. They advocated communitarian and pacific values, which they associated with women.
Albion Small, Thorstein Veblen, John Dewey—all were influenced by
their colleague Lester Ward, who stood Darwinian theory on its head
by arguing that women, not men, were the original humans and that
men were a more recent and inferior product of evolution.[48] Still,
there is little evidence of a culture of female smashing at the University
of Chicago. With male students present, heterosexuality was in force,
and women students didn't become as emotionally involved with one
another as at the women's college.

The women at coeducational colleges did form strong friendships
with one another: female sororities as well as male fraternities were
founded at a number of them during this era. Yet many of those coeducational schools were established partly to bring young women and
men together in a setting that might facilitate courtship and marriage.
Indeed, the literature promoting coeducational colleges attacked
single-sex women's institutions for fostering premature "sexual tension" and "unnatural" and diseased sexuality.[49] The Victorians valued
romantic friendships between young women and those between young
men, but there was growing concern that they might undermine heterosexual marriage.

Born in 1871, Emily Fogg reached maturity in the 1890s, when
what has been called the first-wave women's rights movement—that of
the nineteenth and early twentieth centuries—was reaching a high
point. In her memoirs Emily identifies Olive Schreiner's *The Story of an
African Farm* (1883) as the text that transformed her into a passionate
advocate of women's rights. That novel, written by the South African
author who traveled to London to become a close friend of Havelock
Ellis and other leftist intellectuals and writers, became an international
best-seller. It was the first of a number of popular works written by
women from the 1880s to the First World War that inspired women
toward women's rights and feminism.[50] In addition to *The Story of an
African Farm*, these works included Charlotte Perkins Gilman's *Women
and Economics* (1898), Elsie Clews Parsons's *The Family* (1906), and
Ellen Key's *Love and Marriage* (1911).

Technically a story of seduction and abandonment, *The Story of an
African Farm* in fact explodes the trope. Its heroine, Lyndall, refuses to
marry the man who has exploited her sexually, even though he is
wealthy and handsome and repeatedly proposes marriage. But she

doesn't love him. She refuses to enter a marriage that for her would be based only on sexual attraction and satisfying the dictates of conventional morality. Even when the issue becomes legitimizing her child by him, she won't marry him. In the stirring second half of the novel, Lyndall displays a deep anger against women's position and the way women were raised, how they were taught from their earliest years to become not only dependent wives but also sexual objects for men. She dies with the shame of having borne an illegitimate child.

Schreiner was best known for her stance in her nonfiction works that women needed to be employed outside the home to be truly independent. In this novel, however, she implies that the entire gender system must be overturned to achieve equality between women and men, as her female characters display masculine assertiveness and her men can be feminine. When the male protagonist, a gentle man in love with Lyndall, dresses as a woman so that he can nurse her as she is dying, he finds that he likes to cross-dress, to acknowledge the femininity he possesses. Schreiner explains: "We [men and women] are all of the same compound, mixed in different proportions."[51]

Still, Schreiner believed that what mattered most for women was a noble love for a man. That love should involve a coming together based on a spirituality that Lyndall can find neither with her seducer-turned-suitor nor with the gentle man who nurses her, for she isn't in love with either of them. This neo-Romantic idea of love as an elemental force with a deeply spiritual side would influence Benedict and Mead, women with roots in both the traditional nineteenth century and the modern twentieth century.

What Emily Fogg made of Schreiner's ideas is difficult to determine. Her memoirs, in addition to Margaret Mead's later writings about her, indicate that she accepted the position of her generation of women's rights reformers, which included the belief that women were morally superior to men and that men should give up the "double standard"—under which they had sex with impunity while women were expected to remain virtuous—and take up women's "single standard" of marital faithfulness. The belief in men's immorality, in addition to male attacks on the campaigns for prohibition and women's rights, led some women's rights activists to avoid marriage and adopt an antimale stance.[52] Emily Fogg Mead didn't go that far, but she had difficulties with her husband's aggressive masculinity and his extramarital affairs.

Indeed, why Emily Fogg married Edward Mead is something of a puzzle, since she waited until she was thirty to do so and he turned out to be a near disaster as a husband. Perhaps he was gentle and romantic in their early years together, and she convinced herself that she had found with him the "one true love" advocated by Olive Schreiner. Perhaps she thought she could craft a marriage with him like that between Lucy Stone and Henry Blackwell, in which they worked together for women's rights—and had only one child. Perhaps Emily's model was Alice Freeman Palmer, who after marrying a Harvard professor and giving up the presidency of Wellesley, became a consultant on higher education issues before becoming dean of women at the University of Chicago—and who had no children.

Emily Mead was a leader of women's rights organizations in Pennsylvania while she bore five children, although her relationship with Edward was rocky. Yet how could it have been otherwise? In her memoirs she reveals that she cut off her emotions after she left Wellesley and that she married not out of love but because she thought that she should. In those memoirs, she remembers having been emotionally free as a child, but she wonders if she had any emotions at all as an adult.

THERE WERE DIFFERENCES between Benedict's and Mead's childhoods. Bertrice Shattuck had a college degree and lived in several regions of the country, and John Shattuck was an innovative dairy farmer and president of the state dairy association. Neither of them, however, had the sophistication or the sense of entitlement of Mead's parents, both of whom had graduate degrees, and especially of her mother, born to a family that was part of the reform elite of Chicago. Benedict's natal family was evangelical Baptist; Mead's was freethinking and atheist. Mead's family had money, despite her father's occasional financial shortfalls. They had servants, and a tenant farmer ran their farm. In contrast, Benedict's grandfather had regular financial difficulties, and he ran his farm himself, with the help of seasonal farmhands. Bertrice had difficulty supporting her daughters: well-to-do friends paid for Ruth's and Margery's education at a private girls' high school in Buffalo and at Vassar. Intellectuals and women's rights advocates were guests at the Meads' home; local residents and Baptist church members came to the Shattuck farmhouse. When Bertrice was lady principal at Pillsbury Academy in Owatonna, she was invited to the homes of the city's elite, but that doesn't seem to have been the case when she was a high school teacher in St. Joseph, Missouri, and a librarian in Buffalo, New York.

Benedict and Mead honored their family heritages and wrote with affection about their childhoods. Yet both those childhoods were difficult. Each woman was ambivalent about her mother, and each had problems with her father. Emily Fogg Mead was emotionally distant, while Edward Mead was overbearing. Benedict's father died when she was eighteen months old; he then became a fantasy figure in her imagination whom she constructed as she wanted him to be. Bertrice Fulton, like Emily Mead, was emotionally distant, for she was preoccupied with her work and with mourning a dead husband. She turned her despair over Fred Fulton's death into what Benedict called a "cult of mourning."

Behind the admirable records of personal achievement and reform involvement of the members of Benedict's and Mead's childhood families lies another reality, one filled with conflict and anger, in which some family members don't measure up to the positive descriptions I have provided. That negativity underlying the family tales of love and achievement of the Shattucks and the Fultons, the Foggs and the Meads was as important in the making of Benedict and Mead as their classic American ancestries rooted in migration, revolution, reform— and communities of women.

PART II

Backgrounds

CHAPTER 2

Apollo and Dionysus

Ruth Benedict's Childhood

IN 1935, at the age of forty-eight, Ruth Benedict wrote a brief memoir, mostly about her childhood, which she titled "The Story of My Life." Comprising twenty printed pages, it was the only extended memoir of her life that she wrote. Yale social psychologist and psychoanalyst John Dollard, a friend of hers and Mead's, was promoting a life-history mode of social analysis based on analyzing the lives of representative members of a society as a way of understanding the larger structure. Exploring his approach, Benedict and Mead wrote brief memoirs of their early lives.[1] Benedict's is both a self-analysis and a compelling tale, in which she portrays herself as a disturbed girl painfully coming to terms with life and with a difficult family. It seems to draw from the dark world of the Dobu and Kwakiutl tribal societies that she focused on in *Patterns of Culture*, published in 1934, and from Sigmund Freud's portrayal of human behavior as motivated by irrational forces that were produced in childhood and buried deep in the unconscious.[2]

Yet darkness isn't Benedict's only mood in the memoir: there is happiness in it, too. As a child she lived in cities, with their urban excitement. Even Norwich was a center for the railroad and the farm economy of its region of upstate New York. It had streets lined with large Victorian houses, an opera house, and thriving drug and piano factories; the city center is only three miles from the site of the Shattuck farm. Yet the city—and the farm—are located in a long, narrow valley, verdant and filled with farms in Benedict's childhood. The valley is bordered by high, forested hills. Majestic and brooding, those hills dominate the landscape; they were Benedict's "delectable mountains," the site of her fantasy world.[3]

Tall and well coordinated, Benedict was a natural athlete, and she loved to swim and to dance. She could take a sensuous delight in her body and in nature: Mead appreciated that side of her, which was a part of her appeal. In her better moods, according to Mead, she found pleasure "in apple blossoms after rain"; she found it thrilling when "four black crows flapped westward every sunset."[4] Even as a child she wrote poetry. She also memorized verse: as she and her sister did the dishes each evening, they sometimes learned poems from the handwritten copies that Ruth made from poetry collections and placed on a rack above the sink. Benedict remembered memorizing Percy Bysshe Shelley's "Ode to the West Wind" and "To a Skylark" and William Cullen Bryant's "To a Waterfowl" and "Thanatopsis."[5]

These are poems in which the poet takes his lesson from and celebrates the natural world. Bryant's two poems describe death as a process of nature by which one joins all of humanity and the world of nature in a cycle of decay and regeneration. Shelley's "Ode to the West Wind" asks the wind to lift him from his worldly despairs. His "To a Skylark" exalts the skylark for reaching its song to the lofty spheres of heaven while remaining true to home. A sense of the divine as a universal force is in these poems, and of heaven as a place of peace."[6] Yet nature can be as menacing as it is bountiful in them, and death as much eternal darkness as release. In winter, in Shelley's ode, the seeds lie in the earth, "Each like a corpse within its grave."

Still, in "The Story of My Life" the one line of poetry that Benedict notes she remembers writing as a teenager is hopeful, not despairing, as it describes a spring prelude to an April snowstorm: "Through numberless days of sunshine and spring the sun had made love to the earth, and lovely, lovely had been the days." The line contains the kind of sexual-spiritual metaphor to be found in the Romantic poets—or in the Old Testament Song of Solomon—a tribute to the "sacred marriage" of earth and heaven, the goddess and the young god, the lover and the beloved. Benedict ended "The Story of My Life" with this line of poetry, on a happy note, one filled with sensuality and the joy of living, part of a glorious spring. Yet an April snowstorm takes over, just as despair would become a dominant motif of Benedict's later life.

As an adult Benedict suffered from severe depressions that were punctuated by emotional highs. In public she hid her internal turmoil through the blank expression on her face, the mask that she wore; in private she retreated into the fantasy world of her "delectable mountains"—or into elaborate suicide fantasies, in which she visualized the reactions of each of her friends if she were to take her life.[7]

In childhood her symptoms of emotional distress were, if anything, more severe. As a very young child she sometimes ran away from the farmhouse to the distant fields on the farm. She had attacks of vomiting, beginning when she was three years old and occurring every six weeks for a number of years. She had tantrums so severe that she sometimes had to be restrained, and she sometimes vomited at the end of them. As an adult Benedict called her rages and depressions her "devils"; as a child she called her tantrums her "naughty times." In the diary she kept in 1897, when she was ten, she records being embarrassed when her fifth-grade teacher criticized children's tantrums as "wooden swearing," for she thought she was being singled out for blame. She describes "wooden swearing" as slamming doors and kicking and upending furniture.[8]

Ruth had other emotional problems as a child. She was often withdrawn, and she didn't like being touched. She tried not to show pain: "At five I remember jumping off a beam in the barn and fainting with a sprained ankle. But I crawled into the hay afterward to try to prevent anyone's finding me and seeing my pain." She never cried in front of others: "It was a final humiliation which was devastating to me." At the age of six she decided to conceal her private thoughts and feelings from everyone. She went to a favorite retreat of hers in the haymow. As she recalled, in that space, hidden in the hay, "it came to me with a brilliant flash of illumination that I could always without fail have myself for company, and that if I didn't talk to anyone about the things that mattered to me no one could ever take them away." Still, she had "exposure" dreams, "minutely detailed experiences of bursting into tears in a room filled with attentive well-known faces." Moreover, she never forgot an incident in which she smashed a playmate's doll to bits. For years after she felt guilty about smashing the doll, although she couldn't remember why she had done it.[9]

There was also her fantasy world. At first it involved an imaginary playmate with whom she explored, in her imagination, "hand in hand the unparalleled beauty of the country over the hill."[10] When she was five, her mother became so annoyed over her running away that she made Ruth stay in her room until she explained her behavior. After a day in her room, Ruth told her mother about her imaginary world and how in running away she was trying to reach it. In response, Bertrice took her to the top of the hill and showed her that Uncle George's farmhouse, not the world of her fantasy friend, was on the other side. Bertrice's strategy worked. Disillusioned by learning that her fantasy world didn't exist, Ruth stopped running away from home.

But she didn't stop creating fantasies. Instead, she invented a new one out of the life of Christ. Her pious mother couldn't object to that. Such refiguring wasn't difficult for Ruth, for as a girl she was as religious as the rest of her family. She went to Sunday school and to prayer meetings; she read the Bible repeatedly, as her mother had when she was a child. Ruth's favorite Bible passages were those about the life of Christ. "Christ was a real person to me," she wrote. In the summer of 1898, when she was eleven, she was baptized by immersion in the tank of water across from the altar in the local Baptist church—a large structure dating from the 1890s, with stained-glass windows and a pipe organ. The church is still there today, with the large baptismal tank in the same place. "Jesus will wash away my sins," Ruth wrote in her diary. "I am the Lord's and he is mine."[11]

After moving to Buffalo with her family when she was twelve, she secularized her fantasy world. She located it in her "delectable mountains" and modeled its inhabitants after figures in drawings by William Blake, the Romantic visionary, and then after Michelangelo's Sibyls. In addition, she substituted her dead father for the figure of Christ. As might be expected, she mixed Christ and her father up in her mind; indeed, Beatrice so revered her husband after he died that Ruth's sister Margery thought that the Christ in the painting in the farmhouse kitchen—one that depicted him being sentenced by Pontius Pilate to crucifixion—was actually her father.[12] Benedict, in her answers to Mead's questionnaire about dreams for Mead's 1927 project on dreaming, described her fantasy world in some detail. "My father used to stand and welcome me, but he never touched me. I remember beautiful sounds and odors and a soft bed or couch, but I do not think I ever developed any plots about the things that happened to me there." "From the time of adolescence," she continued, "I always turned to this fantasy world as a way of creating an atmosphere where there were no petty distractions or vexations, where affections were of noble proportions, effortlessly loyal and not at the mercy of ragged nerves. The only part I played was just in being there."[13] What were the "petty distractions" and "vexations" in her childhood? Why did they prompt her to create a serene, asexual world?

LIKE A DETECTIVE searching for clues, like Freud in his case studies sifting through his patients' memories of childhood events to explain their neuroses, in "The Story of My Life" Benedict explored her memories of her childhood to find the cause for her difficult behavior. Above all, she tried to remember an experience so traumatic that it could explain everything. In doing so, according to Mead, she used the Freudian theory of trauma, the belief that a key event in childhood can be so overwhelming that it triggers personality disorders. That approach to understanding human personality was, according to Mead, very popular in the 1930s.[14]

To begin with, Benedict considered possible physiological causes for her emotional distress. She noted her inability to hear in one ear, a hearing loss that her doctors traced to a bout of measles when she was three. Combined with her shyness and occasional stuttering, her weak hearing undoubtedly contributed to her sense of alienation from others, of existing in a separate world. Yet Margery, for one, downplayed Ruth's weak hearing. She maintained that Ruth had no difficulty hearing in conversations one on one and that in theaters she heard the actors if she sat in the front rows. She noted that Stanley Benedict, during his courtship with Ruth, didn't realize that she had a hearing problem—an oversight that may reveal more about Stanley than about Ruth. Margery also thought that in many situations Ruth's failure to respond resulted not from her weak hearing but from her tendency to become so absorbed in what she was doing that she blocked out distractions. Ruth herself remembered using her weak hearing when she was a child as an excuse to pretend not to hear when someone called her.[15]

Benedict further suspected that a hormonal imbalance might have caused her problems, especially the vomiting. That speculation also is plausible. By the mid-1930s, when she wrote her memoir, it had been known for some time that hormones play a role in body functioning, although exactly how they operate was still unknown. Her vomiting attacks match the symptoms of a rare childhood illness that pediatricians in the 1890s called "cyclic vomiting" and that today is known as chronic vomiting syndrome. It involves regular spells of vomiting—spells that generally occur before the age of puberty, when the eating disorders of bulimia and anorexia nervosa usually begin. Even today the cause of chronic vomiting syndrome remains obscure, although medical researchers concur that it is connected to emotional instability and to whatever causes migraine headaches. As an adult, Mead noted, Benedict suffered from "violent sick headaches." As Ruth speculated, a hormonal imbalance might have caused her spells of vomiting.[16]

Yet neither her weak hearing nor her hormones seemed to Benedict a sufficient explanation for her neurotic behavior as a child. Turning to her family as a possible source, she focused on conflicts in it. They weren't hard to find. In the first place, even though she was the older child in her family, she had been jealous of Margery, and she had directed her tantrums so frequently against her sister that Bertrice worried she might hurt her. Yet Ruth thought that her mother preferred Margery, "a cherubically beautiful child with no behavior problems"—and in her memoir Margery agreed. Going to the opposite extreme, Bertrice sometimes treated her daughters, so close in age, like twins. She dressed them alike and enrolled them in the same class in school, even though Ruth disliked competing with Margery, a dutiful student who often got better grades than she and who demanded that they be in the same class.

There was also tension among the adults in the Shattuck family on the farm, especially among the four Shattuck sisters. Her aunts, Benedict wrote, often had loud arguments. "It was a particular grievance of mine that my family stomped on their heels." "Some fracas would be going on," she wrote, and using a powerful metaphor, "something within me was murdered." By contrast, the playmate in her first fantasy world lived in a family with "a warm, friendly life without recriminations and brawls." That the Shattuck sisters didn't get along is perhaps understandable, for their ages spanned twenty-three years. Hetty, the eldest, was born in 1851; Myra, the youngest, in 1874.[17]

Among Ruth's quarreling aunts, Hetty was the most difficult—and she served as Bertrice's homemaker and child tender during the years that Bertrice and her daughters moved around the country. According to Margery, Hetty was deeply pious and personally domineering, with no interest in her sister's children. Hetty's obituary in the Norwich newspaper praises her for her piety, her attention to detail, and her success in teaching a Sunday school class of adolescent boys—testimony to her toughness and to what the obituary calls her "executive ability."[18] Margery described her as a stern disciplinarian incapable of showing love. When Hetty died in 1900, Margery and Ruth were glad to be rid of her. In her memoir Margery describes herself as crying so hard at Hetty's funeral that the adults became worried about her. But they didn't know that she was crying for joy that Hetty was gone, not out of sorrow over her death.[19]

Ruth was different from her aunts. She described them as prosaic and lacking in aesthetic sensitivity, while she was artistic, responding to color and shape, texture and smell. They were oblivious to the grandeur of the tall, dark hills that border the Norwich valley. They "did not watch for the four black crows that flapped westward every sunset." She noted further that they didn't like "praying and processions with candles, both of which filled me with bliss. They did not want to put on their best dresses and watch the evening come on."[20] When Ruth sat on the steps of the farmhouse shelling peas, she sometimes summoned up her fantasy world. If someone called her to come inside, disturbing her daydream, she might have a tantrum.

What role did her father's Fulton family play in her childhood? Did her feminist aunt Ella influence her? Ruth doesn't refer to any of the Fultons in "The Story of My Life," even though Samuel Fulton the homeopath specialized in the "diseases" of women and children and was known for his skill at diagnosis.[21] He probably diagnosed Ruth as suffering from chronic vomiting syndrome and treated her with homeopathic remedies. In her memoirs, however, Margery portrays Samuel as bumbling and acerbic and Harriet, his wife, as domineering and sharp-tongued. According to Margery, Harriet and Ella were very close, and they were contemptuous of the men in their family. They made Samuel's life miserable—and they weren't nice to Fred. As for "Grandma" Harriet Fulton's invalidism and Ella's caring for her, Margery sarcastically called Ella's efforts "noble" and "dauntless."[22]

However, Margery didn't tell the whole story, a story that is revealed in Samuel's and Harriet's wills, filed in the Chenango County Courthouse in Norwich. When Samuel died in 1896, he left his sizable estate (mostly in insurance bonds) to Harriet, with bequests of one thousand dollars each to Ruth and Margery after Harriet died. In Harriet's will, Ella was left the Fulton money with twenty-five dollar bequests to Ruth and Margery. When Harriet died soon after Samuel, Ella inherited the Fulton estate and used the money to pay for her college and graduate school.[23] With two children to support and a very low salary in Buffalo, Bertrice struggled to get by; she could have used the Fulton inheritance. Ella's making off with it must have rankled, perhaps compromising her militant feminism in Ruth's eyes.

Ruth's favorite relative in Norwich was her grandfather John Shattuck, the pious church deacon and farmer, known for the sanitary measures he introduced into dairy farming. Indeed, his obituary lauds him for keeping "good and clean" throughout his life.[24] In "The Story of My Life," Ruth describes him as an aged patriarch with a long white beard, whom she dearly loved. When one of her tantrums began, he had only to leave the farmhouse, silently disapproving, and she would snap out of it. Yet despite his control over Ruth, he wasn't able to stop his daughters from quarreling. Benedict had two vivid memories of him. The first one involved her going to a distant field where he was cutting hay, thus violating her promise to her mother to stay near the farmhouse. When Ruth confessed her disobedience to her grandfather, he replied that if Bertrice didn't ask about it they wouldn't tell her. "It was a high point in my life," Ruth wrote. "I had a secret with Grandfather, and I could see that he liked it as well as I did."[25]

The second memory involved Ruth's grandfather leading the family in prayers every morning in the farmhouse and always asking God to guide them toward "the light that shineth more and more unto the perfect day."[26] John Shattuck's Baptist faith was evangelical, focused on the individual attaining a personal sense of God's grace and the assurance of salvation after death through belief in his son, Jesus Christ. It was also Calvinist in approach, built on the Puritan doctrine of original sin and its strict moral code. Yet more than any other Protestant denomination, the Baptists preserved a millennial sense of the possibility of perfection on earth, based on the prediction in the Book of Revelation that Christ will reign on earth for a thousand years before the Final Judgment. That was John Shattuck's "perfect day" in his daily prayers. The millennial urge was evident in the extensive missionary outreach of the Baptist Church, including the women's missionary society in Ruth's Norwich church. It was also evident in Ruth's favorite passage in *Pilgrim's Progress*, written by John Bunyan, who helped found the Baptist Church in England, when the pilgrim on his journey to heaven reached the "delectable mountains" along the way.[27]

Like Ruth, John Bunyan was a depressive; like him, Ruth in her own way was an ecstatic visionary, who never lost her Baptist belief in millennial possibilities, even when she lost her Christian faith and had to envision the features of perfection on an imperfect earth. Her favorite poets—Blake, Keats, Shelley, Yeats—all had a visionary side. Mead, in her foreword to Benedict's 1940 book on race, wrote that Benedict meant the book to be "a handbook for those who carried a pilgrim's staff in their hands on the steep journey into an unknown land."[28]

In Ruth's Baptist church, religious activities, including missionary society programs and prayer meetings, occurred throughout the week. Sunday services culminated in a ritual drawn from revivalist practice in which the minister invited those who felt the spirit of God to come to the altar to confess their sins and to receive God's blessing. Children weren't baptized until they were ten or eleven and could testify publicly to their Christian faith. Rather than simply sprinkling water over their heads—the practice in most Protestant denominations—the minister immersed them in a large tank of water beside the church altar, in a ritual that bore a resemblance to birth—or drowning—as the individual being baptized died in Christ, shedding the old self, to emerge as reborn, united with Christ in the community of sanctified believers. When Ruth was baptized by immersion at the age of eleven, she felt reborn.[29] Now she was assured of God's grace, through his son, Jesus Christ. Emotional by nature, the young Ruth was passionate about Christ.

Among Ruth's family members on the Shattuck farm, her grandmother Joanna was frail, with translucent skin. Ruth later described her in the poem "Of Graves":

> My grandmother was slim and white,
>   And idle as can be,
> And sometimes in the bright sunlight
>   She'd shiver suddenly.
>
> She always laughed a little laugh
>   And nodded down to me:
> "The rabbit nibbled at the grass
>   Will someday cover me."
>
> And days I shiver swift and strange,
>   This is what I see:
> Sunlight and rabbit in the grass.
>   And peace possesses me.[30]

Joanna Shattuck was a chronic invalid; perhaps bearing four daughters over twenty-three years wore her out. Perhaps she had children over such a long span—including two daughters probably born just before the onset of menopause—because her "patriarchal" husband wanted a son. Margery remembered her grandmother Joanna as so unassuming and deferential to her husband that she seemed an extension of him. Both Ruth and Margery remembered her furtively kissing them as they passed her in the halls of the farmhouse.

WHAT ABOUT BENEDICT's mother and father? What influence did they have on her? Bertrice obviously was important to Ruth. She was a single parent, the final authority in the family; she ended Ruth's "running away" simply by showing her that her fantasy world didn't exist. Yet when they were children, neither Ruth nor Margery liked her. Both found her meticulous and controlled, without much ability to love. Ruth thought that Bertrice, like her sisters, was prosaic and lacked aesthetic sensitivity. During Ruth's childhood she seemed driven by duty and a need for constant activity. Ruth resented her coming home exhausted from teaching, with little energy for her daughters. For her part, Margery thought that Bertrice didn't understand the volatile, creative Ruth.[31]

The diary Bertrice kept in 1876 and 1877, when she was sixteen and seventeen, reveals that, like Ruth, she suffered from periods of depression. She deals with them by praying and reading the Bible; they lessen after she falls in love with Fred Fulton ("the handsomest man I ever saw"), and he begins to court her. Still, the moods don't disappear. She complains to her diary that she is always cast as the sourpuss old maid in school plays. During her senior year in high school she is chosen as a speaker in a debate on women's rights, but she is excused from it when she suffers an attack of nerves—"almost dissolving myself in my silly fashion."[32] Given this moodiness, her fixation on Fred Fulton after his death becomes more understandable. So does her constant activity, for such behavior isn't unusual on the part of a chronic depressive coping with the impulse to retreat from life.

Victorian mourning was extensive, with elaborate funeral rituals and bereaved family members wearing black for months. Yet Bertrice's mourning for her husband was extravagant even in light of those conventions, for it went on for years. Despite her self-discipline, any mention of Fred or their marriage could bring a "tragic look" into her eyes. Ruth and Margery dreaded that look. In addition, on the anniversary of Fred's death every year, Bertrice engaged in a fit of weeping after she went to bed. That weeping produced in Ruth "an excruciating misery with physical trembling of a peculiar involuntary kind which culminated periodically in rigidity like an orgasm."[33] Ruth's extreme reaction suggests that fear and guilt were mixed up with sexuality in her mind.

Ruth identified her father with Christ, substituting him for Christ in her fantasy world. What was he actually like when he was alive? Letters he wrote to Bertrice before they married indicate that Ruth had him wrong. He wasn't serene and Christlike. In those letters he is agitated, even paranoid. He is unsure about his future; he feels threatened by destructive individuals and forces.[34] Bertrice confides to her diary that something is wrong with Fred, although she adds that it isn't proper for her to reveal what is troubling him, even in this private record. She mentions, however, that Fred's father, Samuel Fulton the homeopath, was so determined that Fred become a physician that he held an all-night prayer meeting over his son until he agreed to go to medical school.[35] Fred carried out his promise, but he seems to have internalized whatever anger he felt against his father over doing so. His obituaries suggest that after becoming a doctor he became so obsessed with his medical duties and the research on cancer he undertook that he became physically run down and susceptible to the illness that killed him.[36]

After reviewing the conflicts in her childhood family, Benedict had reached the end of her memory. Yet nothing she had remembered thus far seemed powerful enough to her to be the traumatic event for which she was searching, the event that might explain her neurotic behavior. Then, several months before she wrote "The Story of My Life," her aunt Myra told her a story about her father's death that she seized on as her "clue." In Myra's tale, Bertrice brought Ruth into the parlor of the Shattuck farmhouse where Fred's body was lying in an open casket. Weeping hysterically over the body, Bertrice made Ruth promise again and again that she would never forget her father.

Benedict herself never remembered this scene, although she accepted Myra's story as true. To confirm it, she remembered her reaction to a painting in the Museum of Fine Arts that she had seen on a visit to Boston at some point after her marriage. The painting was El Greco's portrait of Fray Felix Hortensio Paravicino; she thought the figure looked like her father as he lay dying. Versed in literature and art, Benedict often looked at her experiences through the lens of a poem, novel, or painting. In the late 1920s she even taught a course on the history of art in Columbia's extension program. It's not surprising that she identified her father with El Greco's cleric. The figure in the painting is thin, with the luminous skin of El Greco's figures. Seeing that portrait triggered a memory of her father as he lay dying and suggested to her even before Myra told her the story of her mother's weeping over her father's corpse that her emotional problems were related to his death. When Myra confirmed that suspicion, Benedict seized on her aunt's account as her traumatic event. With that event in hand, she wrote "The Story of My Life."

BENEDICT'S BIOGRAPHERS HAVE accepted her explanation that her mother's hysteria over her father's death caused her emotional difficulties. Indeed, a large psychological literature, beginning with Freud's 1917 "Mourning and Melancholia," concludes that the death of a parent can have a decisive emotional impact on a child. The child's ego, Freud reasoned, internalizes the lost loved one and then punishes itself for the pain that has been inflicted, in the process sometimes punishing anyone emotionally close to the bereaved child. John Bowlby, considered authoritative on the subject of children and emotional loss, agrees that a child who loses a parent may demonstrate extreme anger—or withdraw into shyness and depression. In his *Existential Psychotherapy*, Irvin Yalom contends that anxiety over death is the major factor in all human development.[37]

Yet it was her mother's grieving, Ruth believed, and not her father's death, that troubled her. For she romanticized death: she wasn't afraid of it. As an adult she expressed the wish that she had lived in ancient Egypt. That society, with its mummies and pyramid tombs, was fixated on death, and women had unusual authority in it for the ancient world. Even as a child Benedict liked to see corpses in caskets, with calm, composed faces. Such an attitude may seem strange to us today, with our avoidance of death, but when Benedict was a child life expectancy was still low and rural families still laid out corpses in front parlors before burial. She probably saw many dead bodies when she was a child; they were, like her father, at peace. Her Christian relatives told her that the dead who were believers went to heaven, where they lived with Christ and the angels. Thus to die young, as her father had, was a blessing. Why would she mourn a father who was so chosen?[38]

And why would she fear death? When she was nine years old her mother gave her a book of stories of the lives of noble Romans that included the suicide of Cato. When emperor Julius Caesar defeated the republican forces Cato led and he faced imprisonment, Cato, a Stoic, killed himself to preserve his honor, which was a central Roman virtue. Cato's suicide didn't seem to trouble Ruth's mother, who had been educated in the classics at Vassar, but when a neighboring servant girl committed suicide, Ruth's family condemned the girl. Ruth refused to accept their judgment. On this occasion, as on others, she made up her own mind. She was, after all, the firstborn in her family, independent in her own way. She demanded attention through her tantrums; she liked being different from the rest of her family.[39]

The story of Cato and his noble death is rooted in tranquility, in a Stoicism with no fear of death. Similarly, Ruth's fantasy world, with her "beautiful people" in her "delectable mountains," was tranquil, a secularized heaven without sexuality, just as in the Christian afterlife. That characteristic became more pronounced, Benedict noted in Mead's dream-research questionnaire, after she read W. H. Hudson's *A Crystal Age*, a science fiction romance published in 1887 that influenced her design for her world. Hudson's novel is about a community of celibate people dressed in white who live in a white, crystalline world. All are the children of one woman who rules them and who is both a "Sibyl" and a "Christ" who suffers for their sins. The hero of the novel stumbles into this world after falling into a ravine. Eventually he kills himself when he realizes that the woman he has fallen in love with—as well as everyone else there—has no interest in sex. Before then, he is entranced by "their angelic women and mild-mannered men with downy, unrazored lips."[40]

The moral of the story seems to be either the superiority of an ungendered world to a gendered one or the power of sex for good or ill. In the late nineteenth century writers used the translucent crystal to symbolize spiritual regeneration as well as the gender transformation that some believed homosexuality involved.[41] And the appearance of Hudson's characters—androgynous, wearing white, living in a white world—matched Ruth's re-visioning of her dead father as feminized and Christlike and as standing at the entry to her fantasy world but never touching her, with beautiful sounds and odors and a "soft bed or couch" in the background. Perhaps she fantasized such a scenario as a way of avoiding sexual feelings. Or did she construct her fantasy world as the mirror opposite of the real one, where a frightening sexuality was present?

In "The Story of My Life" Benedict rejects any sexual experience of her own as her traumatic event. When she wrote her memoir, Freud's libido theory was in eclipse. American neo-Freudians like Benedict's friend Karen Horney rejected Freud's theories of the primacy of childhood sexuality and the Oedipus complex; in 1938 Benedict wrote a review of Horney's *The Neurotic Personality of Our Time* praising her for that stance.[42] Yet the power of sexuality persists in Benedict's memoir and in her journal entries. In "The Story of My Life" she calls her mother's hysterical crying over her father's corpse her "primal scene," using Freud's term for a child's presumed first sight of parents having sex. In a journal fragment she describes her tantrums as attacking her "like sword thrusts from the outside."[43] In this context her reaction to her mother's weeping by experiencing involuntary physical trembling culminating in "rigidity like an orgasm" sounds less like an ecstatic response to passion than a paralysis caused by fear.

In *Patterns of Culture* Benedict adopted the terms "Apollonian" and "Dionysian" from Friedrich Nietzsche's *The Birth of Tragedy* to describe the Pueblo Indians as Apollonian and the Plains Indians as Dionysian. She also used the Apollo/Dionysus distinction to describe her internal self. Her fantasy world was the world of her father, and it was Apollonian—ordered and rational. The world of her mother, "the world of confusion and explosive weeping," was Dionysian. Nietzsche viewed the dualism between Apollo and Dionysus as the basis for Greek drama, which grew out of rites of the worship of Dionysus. The Apollo/Dionysus dualism also symbolized to him the human conflicts between reason and emotion, birth and death, creation and destruction. "The Apollonian spirit," wrote Nietszche, "wrests man from his Dionysiac self-destruction." As Kay Jamison expressed it in her study of the relationship between creativity and the manic-depressive syndrome, which she defines as involving a range of highs and lows varying from individual to individual: "The integration of these deeper, truly irrational forces with more logical processes can be a torturous task, but if successful, the resulting work often bears a unique stamp, a 'touch of fire.' "[44]

Dionysus was a god of joyful living as well as of destruction, and he could inspire: ever since Plato artistic creativity has been seen as a fire, a Daemon of divine inspiration. Late-nineteenth-century aesthetic and decadent authors found true freedom by taking Dionysus to an extreme. Even Nietzsche wrote in *The Birth of Tragedy*: "How shall man force nature to yield up her secrets, but 'by unnatural acts'?" In

Patterns of Culture Benedict defined Dionysianism in positive terms, using an aphorism from William Blake: "The path of excess leads to the palace of wisdom."[45]

Benedict rarely revealed the daydreams or night dreams that related to her internal Dionysian self. But when she did they were often horrible, as were her "exposure" dreams, in which she burst into tears in a room filled with the caring faces of people who loved her. She also described to Mead a dream she had as an adult in which she was enclosed in a shroud and felt "scissors cold against my skin as the cloth was slit down the back." Then there was a dream she had shortly before she and Stanley separated in 1930, in which she was "being served with a mess of new ground meat, and I was picking over it in an agony to find some hint of the beauty of the living body that had been brought to this—some bit of the soft skin on the cheek, or the rounded arm. I awoke, sobbing."[46]

Above all, there was her henhouse dream. According to Mead, as an adult Benedict sometimes had difficulty finishing a lecture because "before her eyes there would move a procession of eidetic figures of bedraggled, half-human creatures, struggling like dust-covered fowl into a poultry house, fit only for the food of more glorious beings." The word "eidetic" locates the dream in imagination, not hallucination: Benedict didn't see those creatures, but a vivid image of them came into her mind.[47] In "The Procession of Idiots," a daydream that she recorded for Mead's dream-research project, she described having the same vision when she was a child. It came into her mind as she lay in bed drowsy, before falling asleep. It took place in the henhouse at her grandfather's farm, where she witnessed a horrible procession:

> A procession of draped individuals whose faces she could not see were passing into the door of her grandfather's henhouse. They were families, each of them a unit, with children, six to ten in each group, with the children arranged in order of height and the parents out of proportion in the lead and rear of their off-spring. Then she is in the henhouse. The figures take up positions in back of the high rows of hen boxes, and they stand woodenly behind the boxes. Three individuals of the procession seat themselves on the boxes, with three standing in front of them and three taller standing behind. She looks into the faces of the nine individuals: they are all idiots with deformed and hideous bodies.[48]

As a child Benedict was revolted by the henhouse, "that dark and smelly and lice-infected place." Henhouses, filled with droppings, are often dirty, but given the cleanliness of her grandfather's farm, the condition of his henhouse seems curious. Hens are a metaphor for females, as in the term "henpecked" to describe husbands dominated by wives. Roosters control hens, with one rooster impregnating many hens. Benedict's family on the Shattuck farm was composed of women dominated by her grandfather, an older, "patriarchal" male, and they took their frustrations out on each other. Was the henhouse dream a metaphor for Benedict's experience of her family as not functioning well, as "deformed"? Was it a metaphor as well for her internal self—revealing a sense of deep inadequacy, a soul in considerable pain?

The poetry that Benedict wrote in the 1920s can be interpreted, like her fantasy world, as another form of dreaming drawn from her imagination. Her poetry is often elegiac, sometimes filled with pain. Grounded in the tradition of women's lyric poetry since Sappho, it also draws from the irony and agony of the dramatists and metaphysical poets of the seventeenth century that male modernists like T. S. Eliot rediscovered—as did female poets like Louise Bogan and Léonie Adams, close friends of Benedict's. Her poetry has a Puritan austerity, mixed with the majesty of the Old Testament and the fire of John Webster and John Donne. Sometimes—although not often—the gentleness of early American poetry is in it, with hemlocks, fringed gentian flowers, and rabbits.[49] Influenced by Symbolists like William Butler Yeats, she sometimes explored symbols relating to a spiritual world beyond reality, and she examined her fears and tried to understand that part of her self still lost in childhood.[50]

Her poetry contains male monsters—Behemoth and Leviathan from the biblical Book of Revelation; the Minotaur and Orion from classical mythology. The man-eating Minotaur, half-bull and half-man, lived in the labyrinth on the island of Crete and devoured maidens as well as youths; Orion was a giant hunter who tried to rape Artemis before her scorpion killed him and Zeus consigned him to the constellation of stars that bears his name. In addition to the occasional monsters, Christ is a major figure in Benedict's poetry. Yet her Christ is Jesus dying on the cross, not Christ the gentle shepherd. Romantic poets used the suffering Christ as a symbol of the agony of artistic production; male homosexual and lesbian poets used him as a symbol of their personal suffering. For Yeats the figure was a symbol of the Hermetic Order, a mystical sect to which he belonged. Ruth Fulton had merged herself with Christ through her baptism, while she identified her father with Christ in her fantasy world. And Christ was related to Dionysus, in his guise as the young nature god associated with trees who in ancient times was killed every winter and revived every spring. Dionysus and Apollo—emotion and reason—were important to Ruth, as she engaged in a lifelong struggle to control her emotionality through sheer force of will.[51]

Given Benedict's childhood behavior, the possibility of sexual abuse can't be ignored. Her fear of being touched, her asexual fantasy world, her vomiting, her rage against her sister, the episode in which she smashed a friend's doll—these behaviors fall into ones catalogued by experts as characteristic of a child being abused.[52]

Nothing physically out of line may have occurred. "Abuse" can be solely emotional. In her study of the work of Karen Horney, Marcia Westkott argues that although Horney rejected Freud's theory of childhood sexuality, she identified parental mishandling of children as the major problem of childhood. In particular, she excoriated parental sexualization of daughters, including behaviors ranging from incest to teaching girls to regard their bodies as unclean and themselves as inferior to boys. Such abuse, according to Westkott, often results in a child displaying "frozen watchfulness." "A sexualizing experience," writes Westkott, "does not have to be violent or physically abusive to promote . . . the attitude of 'frozen watchfulness' clinicians find in abused children."[53] One might describe the masklike expression on Benedict's face as "frozen watchfulness." Benedict used the term "murder," as in "something within me was murdered," to refer to the impact on her of the quarreling in her family. She later referred to Mary Wollstonecraft's need as an adolescent to "save her soul alive" after her father's abuse of her when she was a child.

The subject of incest was of major interest to both the anthropologists and the literary modernists of Benedict's day. In his early work, Freud contended that older male relatives had molested the female hysterics who were his first patients, although he recanted that interpretation, concluding that those women fantasized the abuse. In *Totem and Taboo* (1918), however, he theorized that the incest prohibition had been introduced in prehistory out of guilt after a "primitive horde" of sons killed their father to gain sexual access to the women of the tribe, who were their mothers and sisters. Like Freud, most anthropologists focused on the prohibition, not the act. Benedict did too, writing in *Patterns of Culture* about the universal incest taboo that extended beyond the immediate family and wasn't always intended solely "to prevent inbreeding, as in the United States." (Margaret Mead was unusual in stressing the act, calling it a "grisly horror" in a 1965 encyclopedia entry on incest.)[54]

Late-nineteenth-century aesthetic and decadent writers—early modernists—regarded incest as a sexual perversion that, like sodomy or sadomasochism, symbolized their belief that to become completely free, individuals had to transgress all prohibitions, whether in thought or deed, as in William Blake's path of excess leading to the palace of wisdom. Given these resonances, Benedict could hardly have avoided considering the possibility of incest in her own childhood.

"The problem with regard to sexuality in the raising of children in the United States," she wrote in 1938, "is not whether or not the child's sexuality is consistently exploited," but whether children are taught behavior they must later unlearn. "The child is sexless," Benedict wrote, but "the adult estimates his virility by his sexual activities."[55] The statement might be interpreted as an indictment of adults sexually exploiting children—or of raising them with Puritan attitudes about sex that they have to overcome as adults. Benedict wrote that she was "born of the Puritan distrust of the senses, of its disgust at the basic manifestations of life." In her answers to Mead's dream-research questionnaire, she indicated that she didn't masturbate as a child.

In "The Story of My Life," Benedict described how her aunt Mary, her mother's second-youngest sister, made her play a game that involved her hiding and then Mary trying to find her and hug her. Ruth hated that game because she didn't like to be touched and her aunt knew it. Then there was her memory of "the big scene of the kind." That scene involved her great-uncle Justin Fulton, the famed Baptist minister, who often visited the Norwich farm. On one occasion he offered Ruth and her sister fifty cents for a kiss. Ruth fled from him, screaming in terror, hiding underneath the sewing machine. In the 1890s such machines were operated by foot, using a treadle, and the space between the machine and the treadle wasn't covered. Hiding there, Ruth would have been exposed.[56]

In addition to the tracts her uncle Justin wrote about abolitionism and woman's rights, he also wrote one about female sexuality. In it he argued that women's sexuality is dangerous to men, since in the Garden of Eden Eve accepted the apple from the serpent—the devil in disguise—and gave it to Adam, thus causing him to sin. The argument that Eve brought sin into the world had been standard in ministers' sermons in the early nineteenth century to justify women's subordination, but Justin Fulton took it to an extreme. As a result of Eve's action, Fulton contended, the devil controls all women. Because of this satanic control, they can't stop themselves from becoming temptresses whom men can't resist.[57] To present-day sensibilities, Fulton's argument sounds like a rationalization for male sexual exploitation of women— blaming the victim for the crime. Benedict called her uncle Justin "cocksure." Drawn from the word "cock," meaning rooster (or the male sex organ), the term, relating to the behavior of roosters in a hen-house, designates a highly masculine man who flaunts his virility.

As a child Benedict had another sexual experience involving a grown man. At the school she attended for two years in Owatonna, Minnesota, where her mother was lady principal, the school janitor made "wonderful" purple title pages for her papers. Ruth describes this man in her memoir as "good looking" and as her favorite adult in Owatonna. When they were alone he stroked her hair, and she liked that. She was ten years old. According to Benedict, he was later fired for "soliciting" girls. In her memoir she writes about her experience with the janitor dispassionately, as though this man's behavior wasn't unusual.

Did Bertrice leave Minnesota and a well-paid position because of him? Given Ruth's physical and emotional difficulties, it seems curious that Bertrice kept moving. And when she went from Owatonna and Pillsbury Academy to Buffalo and the public library, she accepted a sizable pay cut. In Owatonna she had been well-off financially, and she was welcomed into the homes of the city's elite. In Buffalo she and her children lived in a tiny apartment in her sister Mary's house, and they had difficulty getting by. She may have feared the impact of the depression of the 1890s on her employment future, but the evidence for that supposition isn't conclusive. In that decade Pillsbury Academy still had a lot of students and a large endowment; it didn't begin to decline until ten years later.[58] Did Ruth's experience with the janitor prompt Bertrice to move again?

THERE ARE DISCREPANCIES between Ruth's diary, written when she was ten and eleven years old, and her memoir, written when she was forty-eight. In the diary she doesn't dwell on her emotional difficulties, except for reporting her tantrums and expressing guilt over them. She records no episodes of vomiting; they may have ended by then. She seems alternately happy playing with Margery and their girlfriends and in despair over her sister's better grades in school. She exhibits no hostility to her mother or her aunt. She describes a charming scene one autumn day in which she and her mother, sister, and aunt rake up leaves in their yard and she and her sister cover their mother and aunt with leaves and then, with all of them laughing, roll on top of the pile. She records how, late one night, when she was restless with a high fever, her mother took her into her bed and comforted her until she fell asleep.

Ruth exhibits deep piety in the diary. She describes her baptism with fervor. She reports that her mother often reads stories about religious missionaries to her and then announces that she intends to become a missionary to the "heathen" when she grows up. She mentions that the school janitor is drawing pictures for her, but she reports nothing more about him. She notes one Sunday that the minister at church has preached a sermon on adultery and that, as usual, she doesn't understand what he is talking about. She isn't unhappy to move to Buffalo, explaining that her mother received the offer of employment at the public library because the man who was its head had lived next door to them in St. Joseph, Missouri, and they had become friendly with him.

Soon after they arrived in Buffalo, Ruth wrote in her diary that she was bored with keeping it. After several more entries she stopped writing in it. Thus there isn't a precise record of the years in Buffalo when she experienced puberty, with its emotional and sexual impacts. During these years she attended St. Margaret's Episcopal School for Girls, one of those same-sex schools at which romantic friendships existed. Yet something occurred during these years to prompt Ruth to introduce Michelangelo's Sibyls into her fantasy world. Perhaps she borrowed them from the "Sibyl" who made predictions in her mother's graduation yearbook from Vassar, or from the "Sibyl" that was the title of the yearbook at Pillsbury Academy, or from W. H. Hudson's Sibyl in *A Crystal Age*. Perhaps she saw illustrations of Michelangelo's Sybils in an art book. Throughout the nineteenth century they were symbols of female inspiration and intuition. They are powerful figures, both masculine and feminine, able to stop an intruder. Did Ruth intend them as symbolic protection? Perhaps they were related to a series of painful operations on her adenoids that Ruth underwent during these years to improve her hearing. Or were they related to her awakening sexuality during puberty? Did the Sibyls combine the genders in a way that appealed to her?

After Ruth and her family moved to Buffalo, her tantrums became more frequent. At her wits' end, Bertrice determined to stop them. Taking Ruth to her bedroom, Bertrice lit candles, opened the Bible, and had Ruth kneel by the bed and pray to God again and again to stop the tantrums. Bertrice's intervention worked. Twelve years previously, by the side of Fred Fulton's corpse in the parlor, she had presumably made Ruth promise that she wouldn't forget her father. Now she created a similar scene. The bed, the candles, the Bible, her mother's pleas—all that deeply impressed Ruth, still a Christian believer. Her tantrums ended, but her depressions began. That's the story Benedict tells in "The Story of My Life," but it's only partly correct. Her tantrums modulated into depression, but she still had outbursts of anger—and unwanted emotional highs.

Benedict feminized her father and turned him into Christ. He may have been her Apollonian figure, the imaginary person who represented a calm male presence in her life, but her mother, the family breadwinner, played the masculine role in her childhood family. In a journal fragment from the late 1920s, Ruth called herself masochistic. "I guess Freudians would say that what I wanted was to return to my mother's womb," she wrote.[59] Perhaps she wanted to be reborn as someone who had come to terms with the gender crossing in her family, with a feminized father and a masculinized mother. Her relationships with the female members of her family were conflicted, while she idealized her grandfather and her father, the primary males in her childhood. How to reconcile the masculine and feminine sides of herself was a central issue in her life.

As she matured into adolescence, Benedict gave up her tantrums to become more like the composed father figure of her fantasy. She expanded her ability to concentrate into creating an emotionless, "mask-like" expression on her face, behind which she hid her internal self. The "Mona Lisa" smile indicated both gentleness and the confusion at the center of her being—as well as a rueful reaction to her inability at times to hear, according to Mead. Friends of Benedict's noted that she had a sense of humor, but according to Mead she sometimes laughed loudly at situations that no one else found funny.[60] That behavior sounds like her emotions breaking through. To the young Benedict, however, her mask was a way to hide from the world and to control herself. And it was in keeping with her sense of alienation, of being like "a stranger in a strange land." She took that description from Moses' explanation in the Book of Exodus about why he is leading the Israelites out of Egypt, back to their native land. The Jews are "strangers in a strange land," and they want to go home.[61] The description also related to Ruth's feelings about ancient Egypt, about her favorite land of death. She had to find her way to it to become a whole person; she had to embrace her depressions—her death—in order to live.

Yet such features as her "mask," her feeling like "a stranger in a strange land," and her wish that she had been born in ancient Egypt may have been related to a sense of sexual difference on her part. Expressing such difference from the norm in terms of hiding behind a "mask" or as feeling like a stranger in one's land of birth have been typical of individuals with a same-sex orientation in the history of the United States. Mead provided a clue to what Benedict meant by these phrases in one of her musings on her friend's life. "When Ruth Benedict asked the question, 'Would I have been happy in another country—Egypt perhaps?' she was making an assumption about a part of herself that was innate and significant."[62] The "part of herself that was innate and significant" could be seen as her homosexual sense of self.

In "The Story of My Life" Benedict stated that a daydream she had of an Egyptian sphinx before she wrote the memoir symbolized her sense that she had finally found peace in midlife. "I was alone on a great desert that was dominated by a magnificent Egyptian sphinx. Nothing can describe the wisdom and irony of that sphinx's face, and I went to it and buried my face in its paws and wept and wept—happily and with confidence."[63] With the head of a woman and the body of a male, the sphinx is a bisexual being. In Greek mythology the figure is portrayed as a malevolent female who devours the travelers who can't answer the riddle about the nature of humans that she poses to anyone entering the road she controls. In Egyptian legend, however, the sphinx represents masculine rationality and royal power and is benevolent.[64]

Despite her physical and emotional difficulties, Benedict was tough. In her brief biography of Mary Wollstonecraft she described Wollstonecraft as having survived a difficult childhood. "It is only the very spirited who survive mentally, the very strong who are clean thereafter."[65] The independence and force of Benedict's personality are apparent during her difficult childhood. The self-direction is there in her creating a fantasy world and refusing to give it up when her mother objected to it. It is there in her refusal to regard suicide as evil. She may have been victimized—by abuse, by death, by her own emotionality—but she fought back.

She even rejected a key feature of her family's Christianity. She and her sister, like many devout Christians, said the Lord's Prayer every night at bedtime. She disliked the phrase "forgive us our debts" in that prayer, for she understood the phrase to mean that anything "sinful" she had done would be forgiven, and she thought that was wrong. She thought she should be held accountable for her sins. "I do not remember what sin I had on my conscience the night I first got out of bed and said the prayer over again omitting the 'forgive us our debts.'" (Her "sin" may have been her tantrums, her "naughty times"; it may have been something else.) Yet she didn't omit it because she was punishing herself, for she didn't feel guilty about her sins. She noted that she felt "no Puritan load on my conscience about my unforgiven sins."

Yet it's doubtful that she felt no guilt. She expresses guilt over her tantrums in her childhood diary; guilt is there in her reaction to her mother's weeping; she must have felt guilt over her father's death and her mother's unhappiness. One can't believe in the doctrine of original sin and the repressive moral code of a Puritan religion without feeling guilt, and guilt is a negative, self-accusatory emotion that can lead to depression—or self-overcoming. As a girl Ruth faced the negativity of her Calvinist faith. Wise beyond her years, she never discussed her omission of the phrase about forgiveness with anyone; she realized that her devout relatives would have insisted that she reinsert it because she was blaspheming God by leaving it out. Her independent self prevailed. "I hadn't discovered any authority over and above the fact that it didn't seem right to me."[66]

Yet she began to say the phrase "forgive us our debts" again when she was twelve years old. That was when she experienced menarche and introduced the Sibyls into her fantasy world. Several years later she began to attend St. Margaret's Episcopal School for Girls, where she encountered a culture of female romantic friendships. In that environment and in the series of female environments she entered after St. Margaret's—first, Vassar College, and then social work and high school teaching in girls' schools—she continued her project of understanding herself as sexual and intellectual, emotional and spiritual, male and female.

CHAPTER 3

"The Young-Eyed Cherubim"
Margaret Mead's Childhood

IN HER AUTOBIOGRAPHICAL WRITINGS, Margaret Mead relates two versions of her childhood. The first is positive, in keeping with her celebration of her "Old American" ancestry. The second, like Benedict's, is negative. The positive approach dominates a brief memoir Mead was commissioned to write in the early 1970s for a volume of autobiographies of eminent psychologists—a commission that testifies to her reputation in the field of psychology. The negative version dominates the brief, unpublished account of her life, entitled "Life History," that she wrote in 1935 for John Dollard—a companion piece to Benedict's "The Story of My Life."[1] The negative approach is also evident in the drafts of *Blackberry Winter*—and in the published version. Rhoda Métraux, Mead's partner during the last decades of her life, shaped the published version from the drafts that Mead wrote. In editing Mead's rough prose into an elegant text, Métraux didn't always eliminate the negativity. Mead once said that she wasn't certain what Rhoda left in from the drafts and what she took out.[2] Sometimes reading like a stream-of-consciousness narrative, the drafts contain information that isn't in the published version, especially with regard to her childhood.

In her various memoirs, however, Mead doesn't adopt Benedict's approach in "The Story of My Life" of looking for a traumatic event in her childhood to explain her adult personality. Commenting in 1950 on the writing of autobiography, Mead criticized the "trauma" approach as too rigid. Without mentioning Benedict's memoir by name, Mead used it as an example of the flaws in that method. Under the theory of trauma, she wrote, "if your father died when you were two, everything was fitted into the background of your having lost your father at two."[3] In letters and statements to others, Mead sometimes identified the death of her sister Katherine when she was five as a traumatic event that had a major impact on her, but she didn't dwell on it in her autobiography.

A public figure of note, Mead wanted to write a memoir that would last. She also wanted young people to read it, for in the 1970s, when she was writing *Blackberry Winter,* she had positioned herself as an intermediary between the younger, rebellious generation and their more conservative elders, and she wanted both groups to know about her parents' progressive child-rearing techniques—how they had raised her several generations ahead of her time. Yet in a draft introduction to the autobiography that was omitted from the final version, Mead suggested that organizing it in terms of her parents' child-rearing practices wasn't her original plan. Rather, she had initially intended to chart the development of her sexual identity and to end "a forty-year silence on the subject."[4] Draft chapters on her childhood focus on her participation in the culture of romantic friendships between girls, although much of that material was eliminated from the published version.

In her autobiography Mead recast the classic form of male autobiography, the heroic journey narrative of overcoming difficulties through individual self-creation—a narrative immortalized by Benjamin Franklin in his autobiography about rising from poverty to fame—by describing her parents' influence on her and then demonstrating how her path to success fulfilled her early promise, as she turned every opportunity that came her way to her advantage. And she also honored her identity as a woman and the traditional female narrative that culminated in marriage and motherhood by ending her memoir with the birth of her daughter and then with her feelings as a grandmother. Through this theme of motherhood she also concealed her free-love behavior and her sexual involvements with women—as well as with men other than her husbands. Her friendship with Ruth Benedict is part of the narrative of *Blackberry Winter,* but her presentation of their friendship in that work has neither the passion nor the complexity of her discussion of it in *An Anthropologist at Work,* written nearly two decades previously, before her years with Rhoda Métraux.

Yet in both texts Mead focused on Benedict's reclusive, depressed side, while depicting herself as an energetic and outgoing optimist, blessed with the good luck often possessed by males in the heroic tradition of autobiography. That good fortune brought her to Barnard College and Ruth Benedict in 1922 and put her on the same ship with Reo Fortune returning from Samoa to Europe in 1926 and at the same location in New Guinea with Gregory Bateson in 1932. The interpretation of herself as an optimist and her life as blessed by fate isn't inaccurate, just as her portrayal of Benedict as depressed isn't false. These representations, however, are part of a more complex story. Just as Benedict had a sensual, athletic, and optimistic side, Mead could be discouraged and fearful of life.

IN MEAD'S POSITIVE VERSION of her family, her parents—and her paternal grandmother, who helped raise her—were outstanding mentors who taught her skills that proved indispensable to her later work as an ethnographer. Influenced by progressive educators who recommended that children receive instruction in crafts, Mead's mother always found craftspeople where they lived to teach her children their crafts: weaving, printmaking, basketry, wood carving, even carpentry. Knowing these crafts helped Mead to understand the craft production of the tribal societies she studied. As a child, she sometimes took painting lessons with local artists; she had a talent for drawing that was helpful in doing fieldwork, as when she copied native designs. Her elders also trained her in observation, a technique key to fieldwork; in teaching her science, Martha Mead had her catalogue the plants in each area in which they lived. Moreover, Margaret kept the family list of addresses and phone numbers up-to-date, planned family celebrations for birthdays and Christmas, and kept a record of the development of her two younger sisters. And her grandmother told her tales about Winchester, Ohio, Martha's native town, stories involving a complex kin network to which Martha belonged. Learning about that network helped Mead to understand the kinship arrangements of the tribal societies she studied.[5]

In Mead's positive version of her family her parents were brilliant intellectuals who made the academic world familiar to her from her earliest years. Her first toys, a wooden snake and a monkey, came from a string of wooden animals that students at the University of Pennsylvania had given to economics professor Simon Patten as a joke, to parody his lectures on Darwin and evolution. Her first playmates were children of her father's colleagues who lived near her family in an area where faculty of the University of Pennsylvania resided; to Margaret, famous academics were friends of her parents who came to their home for parties and dinners. Even when her family was alone at the dinner table they debated ideas and discussed a variety of intellectual topics— current events, literature, social problems.

When Mead was a child, her family and their friends recognized her potential; in the positive version of her childhood her parents nurtured her genius and expected her to achieve as an adult. In 1970, with her enthusiasm expanding into exaggeration, she told a reporter that she had been a precocious child raised by enlightened parents "seven decades ahead of my time."[6] Given this background, she had no qualms about becoming an academic. She was able to write a master's essay in psychology and a Ph.D. dissertation in anthropology at the same time, while adjusting to her first marriage and working part-time. That performance as a young adult was a preview of her versatility and speed as a mature anthropologist; both in her view were partly products of the way she was raised.

In the positive version of her family, her father was an outstanding mentor. A superb listener, he taught her to learn from others by listening to what they had to say. He carried a notebook in which he jotted down interesting remarks others made. He also taught Margaret how to deliver an effective speech: look individuals in the eye, he said; find ideas they can easily understand; don't pitch your remarks above the intellectual level of your audience. Moreover, he had a photographic memory, as did both she and her mother; he had learned the French needed for his doctoral dissertation in ten days. Edward Mead believed that there was no excuse for procrastinating in writing up research. "An article that had to be written," according to him, "had to be written quickly."[7]

He pioneered in adult education by founding an evening extension program in business for the Wharton School, with branches especially in the coal-mining regions of Pennsylvania, to provide education for workingmen who couldn't attend classes during the day. The project grew out of his missionary zeal to educate working-class young men because he had identified with working-class boys in his high school. His program was one of the first of its kind in the nation.

In Mead's positive version of her family, her mother was a model reformer who taught her children egalitarian attitudes toward race and ethnicity. Holding views advanced for that age, she believed that culture, not biology, shaped racial and ethnic behavior. Emily Fogg Mead's abolitionist family in Chicago held those attitudes, as did members of the progressive sociology department with whom she studied at the University of Chicago, with its ties to Hull House and the immigrant communities of Chicago. These connections influenced Emily to embark on a Ph.D. dissertation on the Italian community of Hammonton, New Jersey, composed of immigrants from the economically depressed farming regions of southern Italy who had settled in the unpromising New Jersey pine barrens. Given their poverty and lack of education, if they were able to succeed, any immigrant group could.

Emily never completed the dissertation, but her master's essay, published by the United States Bureau of Labor, is an impressive study of the economy, religion, culture, and family life of the Hammonton Italians. Margaret dedicated *The Changing Culture of an Indian Tribe* (1932) to Emily, calling her mother's master's essay "one of the pioneer studies of culture contact in the United States."[8] Basing it on statistical surveys, interviews with community members, and observations at events such as festivals and weddings, Emily demonstrated the success of the Italians in reclaiming the sandy soil of the pine barrens to grow crops and in establishing a stable society. Indeed, the second generation had begun the movement upward in the class structure characteristic of successful immigrant groups in the United States. Above all, Emily praised the Hammonton Italians for establishing a strong family life. "The home life of the Italians, like that of the Jews," she wrote, "has much for Americans to emulate."[9]

Emily's liberal views continued. She insisted that her children honor the family's black female servants by addressing them as "Mrs.," even though their neighbors laughed at them for doing so. Forbidden by Emily to use the term "nigger," when they chanted the counting rhyme "Eenie, meenie, miney, moe," they had to finish it with "catch a pigeon [not a nigger] by the toe." She countered local slanders against blacks as lazy or oversexed by relating the story of how a white man who was disliked in the community had raped a black woman whom everyone esteemed.[10] She thus substituted white men for black men as potential sexual predators, thus rejecting the national mythology to recognize a truer reality.

In the positive version of her upbringing, Mead even praised her family's frequent moving. For example, she claimed that through overseeing the family packing she learned organizational skills. Through meeting new children in new environments she learned flexibility. She had her first experience in "comparative sociology," she maintained, when she encountered the different ways the children in the places she lived played games like prisoner's base or run, sheepy, run.[11] Moreover, her family's frequent moving resulted in a continual turnover in servants, mostly German, Irish, and Polish women from immigrant communities near where they lived. In Bucks County they also had African-American servants, who came from a small group of local blacks descended from slaves who had come to the area by way of the Underground Railroad and stayed; indeed, the Mead farm had been a station on the path from slavery to freedom in Canada. In her class book for her junior high school graduation, Mead displayed her characteristic enthusiasm by stating that she had lived in sixty houses and eaten food made by over one hundred cooks.[12] Having become friends with servants from many ethnicities, Mead felt that she had learned about the relativity of cultures and the need for racial and ethnic tolerance.

In Mead's positive account of her childhood, her parents' marriage was loving and happy, in keeping with the romantic family tale that her father had told her mother he intended to marry her the first time they met in the class at the University of Chicago. Edward called Emily "Emmy-tiny"; she was five feet tall; he was six feet. When Margaret learned to talk, she called her mother "tiny wife." On a bookshelf in their living rooms they always placed their copy of *The Rubáiyát of Omar Khayyám*, the popular collection of love poems written by a Persian mystic. Edward and Emily had given the book to each other during their courtship, and on the flyleaf each had written an inscription in Greek.[13] As an intellectual comrade, Emily helped Edward with his scholarly work, especially by correcting the page proofs of his articles. If Emily said, "The third page is three lines short," he would answer, "Well, fill them in."[14]

In 1901, the year Margaret was born, Emily even followed Edward's lead as a professor of business by writing an article praising modern advertising for its educational and aesthetic value. According to Emily, advertising was spiritual and uplifting, while it produced energetic and efficient men and women knowledgeable about the newest business products. It provided women involved with children and housework at home with an opening to the outside world. It also familiarized the masses with more economical ways of living, with its information about new, less expensive products. However, there was a downside: Emily didn't like shady medical advertising, circulars that littered the ground around mailboxes, and signs that desecrated beautiful scenery.[15]

In educating their children, Edward and Emily followed the ideas of Martha Mead. As a progressive educator, she criticized public schools for regimenting children into grades, teaching them a fixed curriculum, and including neither crafts nor practical skills in their studies. Because of these deficiencies, Martha taught Margaret and her siblings at home. In fact, she had such an aversion to regimenting children in teaching them that she engaged her grandchildren in formal study for only an hour or two a day and left them to their own devices for the rest of the time. When Margaret went to public school in Swarthmore, Pennsylvania, in the fourth grade, her elders pressured the school administration into introducing the Gary Plan, developed in Gary, Indiana, and popular among progressive educators.[16] Under it, students studied in learning groups at their own pace, not in grades.

Mead's positive version of her childhood served to honor her parents. It also answered critics who questioned her anthropological ability and her attitudes on race; those critics appeared long before Derek Freeman published his attack on her Samoan research in 1983.[17] In response to critics who questioned her racial attitudes, she detailed the egalitarian beliefs her mother had taught her. In response to critics who questioned her ability to learn languages and do fieldwork so quickly—spending less than a year in nearly every society she studied—she suggested that her elders had taught her how to observe and to keep records; that she, as well as her mother and father, had a photographic memory; and that she had learned fieldwork techniques from her mother's sophisticated work on the Hammonton Italians. Because of this upbringing, she could do fieldwork more quickly than other anthropologists. She could master a language and a culture in less than a year, and she could do ethnographies of seven cultures in ten years, more than any other anthropologist of her generation.

The positive version also functioned as an educational tool to display her reform positions, such as her support for progressive education and for communal child rearing. Her family wasn't exactly communal, but it included her mother and father, three siblings, a grandmother, and a series of servants. Moreover, she contended that being raised in a family that wasn't completely nuclear taught her how to be flexible. In her later career critics attacked her for being overly argumentative, even abrasive, but in her autobiographical writing she presented herself as reconciling differences. Because of her closeness to her two younger sisters and to the aging Martha Mead, she bridged three generations. Her family, she asserted, ratified that blending of ages by its flexible, optimistic attitude. "Everything we did was related comparatively to the past, vigorously to the present, and hopefully to the future." Her family's lack of rigidity also encouraged fluid thinking. She never thought in dualisms, she claimed. Although she overstated the case, she did come to regard gender as a fluid category. Having a child relate only to a mother and a father, she contended, is "one of the roots of thinking in dichotomy," of holding to a rigid either/or attitude.[18] The structure of her family made her a more holistic person, she concluded.

A SECOND, more negative version of Mead's childhood is also in the drafts of *Blackberry Winter,* as well as in the published version. Indeed, a point-counterpoint between optimism and pessimism and between praise and criticism constitutes one of the fascinations of the published memoir, which is by turns controlled and sprawling, focused and hazy. The many flaws that Mead reveals in her upbringing undermine the stated purpose of the memoir, to illustrate how that upbringing produced her adult success. But that purpose may have been added after the project was under way, when she gave up the theme of describing the development of her adult sexual identity.

Her title, *Blackberry Winter,* reflects her bifurcated approach. It is drawn from the farm term for the time of year when, after rising temperatures herald the advent of spring, a cold spell briefly appears. (In farming communities that cold spell is often associated with blackberries, for without the frost that accompanies the cold the blackberry vines may not produce berries. Mead was familiar with the process because the Italians in Hammonton grew blackberries for market.) Yet optimism is never absent from Mead's memoir. Just as frost produces lush berries on blackberry vines, the negativities of her childhood, she suggests, produced a richer outcome in her midlife. That optimistic attitude, the notion that failure breeds success, that every cloud has a silver lining, is quintessentially American as well as vintage Mead.[19] Moreover, the "blackberry winter" image of Mead's memoir seems a reply to the conclusion of Benedict's "The Story of My Life," in which Benedict cited a line of poetry she wrote as a teenager describing the beauty of the spring before an unexpected April snowstorm brought a blight on the land. Mead's "blackberry winter," in contrast, doesn't end bleakly; the cold spell of her childhood was needed to produce a rich harvest of blackberries—a successful, fulfilling life.

The memoir's alternation between optimism and pessimism is apparent in its opening, which sets the tone of the work. In the first paragraph of the published prologue Mead describes life as a journey that is bound to turn out right if an individual works hard and takes advantage of opportunities. Yet she immediately contradicts herself by asserting that "the ship itself may go down at any time during the voyage."[20] In the beginning pages of the first chapter, each positive memory is connected to a negative one. A positive description of the house in Hammonton, celebrating its warmth and family joy, is preceded by a scene in which neighbors bang at the door to tell the Meads that their chimney is on fire and followed by one in which Margaret's beloved grandmother suffers a heart attack. A joyful description of Margaret dancing in the wind is followed by her plunging her hands into a hornets' nest, provoking the hornets to sting her all over her body.[21]

In the negative version of her childhood her father is a bully, with a loud voice and a habit of yelling for Margaret's mother, expecting her to drop whatever she is doing and obey him. He spends hours on the telephone talking to male cronies. He isn't interested in others beyond what he can learn from them; he is often undependable and sarcastic. He is critical of social planning and progressive reform, and he harbors racist attitudes. As an academic, his work is didactic, without much complexity, and he pays little attention to the ideas of other scholars. Obsessed with concrete process, wanting to make a lot of money, he is more an entrepreneur than an academic. His business ventures are sometimes crackpot, as when he tries to rescue a pretzel factory from bankruptcy and their house is filled with barrels of pretzels.[22]

He could be contradictory. He called Margaret "Punk" and then "the original Punk" when her brother was born. He left much of the parenting of Margaret and her sisters to his wife and mother, devoting his attention to Richard, a sickly child whom he overprotected. He expected Margaret to do better than her brother in school, although he expressed regret that, with her gifts, she wasn't a boy. He regarded intellectualism as "feminine," and he implied that only science mattered and that humanists were second-rate. Yet that attitude suggested that even though she was female Margaret could become an intellectual and an academic.

Edward and Emily were freethinkers and atheists, although Edward, whom Martha had brought up a Methodist, recited Bible passages all the time. At the age of eleven, influenced by the adult daughter of the local Episcopal priest, who had become her close friend, Margaret rebelled against her parents by joining her friend's Episcopal church. The morning of her baptism her father embarrassed her by galloping on his horse down the road shouting: "Going to be baptized." For a year or so after the baptism, he threatened to have her "unbaptized" whenever she did anything he didn't like, enjoying a joke that made her furious.[23]

Edward often enforced discipline suddenly, as when he sent Margaret away from the table at dinner because her neck wasn't clean. In the negative version of her childhood she resented such intrusions, as well as his using money to control her. When she was in college he periodically threatened to stop paying her expenses. At her graduation from Barnard, he mortified her by grasping her Phi Beta Kappa key, which she was wearing on a chain around her neck, and announcing: "That cost me ten thousand dollars, and it's worth it." In 1928, when Mead was doing fieldwork among the Manus of the Admiralty Islands off the coast of New Guinea, Ruth Benedict had lunch with Edward Mead to try to persuade him to pay for college for Margaret's sister Priscilla. After experiencing his stubbornness, Benedict wrote to Mead: "My congratulations, Margaret, I don't see how you ever grew up!"[24]

At base, Edward Mead was a hypermasculine male typical of the late-nineteenth-century era of imperialism, violence in sports, and the "robber baron" mentality in business. He was an enthusiast for corporate capitalism. Alluding to Henry Wadsworth Longfellow's *Hiawatha* in one of his books, he described the business mergers then being formed as "like the trees in the primeval forest . . . wide and deep in the necessities of mankind."[25] Edward was a man's man, happiest with male cronies. Aside from his scholarly work, he read little but Westerns, and he read them again and again. Despite his Methodist upbringing, he could be vulgar in speech, infuriating his wife. He was unfaithful to her when he was away from home, teaching his evening classes or promoting his business ventures. He contemplated leaving Emily for a "red-haired" woman and then decided against it when he realized the expense of supporting both her and his family. That seemed to cure him of infidelity: he bought the farm in Bucks County as compensation for that affair. "Mother always used to grit her teeth and say she knew and hadn't forgotten why that farm had been bought," Mead remembered.[26]

Edward sometimes dressed like an Edwardian dandy, in a frock coat with a cravat around his neck and a stickpin in the cravat.[27] He didn't like the morality and etiquette of middle-class women, and he could be contemptuous of his wife's "stylish and serious" friends. Margaret Mead recalled: "He once bought a couple of heifers from a friend of Mother's and named them after this rather pompous woman and her secretary. After that, he delighted in pointing out their names and milk yields on the chart in the dairy shed."[28] In those days of less frequent bathing than today, without the use of deodorants, body odor could be discernible. When Edward didn't like the way a woman smelled, he had no hesitation in scolding her and making a scene.[29]

He had a streak of violence in him. When Margaret was a child, he sometimes frightened her by holding her so tightly that it hurt. "The sense of uncontrolled and feared aggression [from him] was strong," she remembered.[30] In conversations much later in life, after they had reached an accommodation bordering on friendship, he told her that she was the only child he had wanted and that the other children hadn't been planned. In later life, Mead asserted that she was tough enough to protect herself from her father but that she had always worried about her two younger sisters.[31] (With regard to her father's sexual performance, Mead stated that he was abrupt, lacking in sophistication—although she didn't disclose the source for this assertion.) Still, she was attracted to him as a child. He often talked about the beauty of her hands and held them, and, she observed, "I think they were highly libidinized."[32]

Mead could be sympathetic toward her father, as when she speculated that his aggressive masculinity troubled him. "He was always attracted by a kind of rough, much rougher sort of life than Mother thought, and at the same time he didn't want to be allowed to live it"; he married Emily, Mead asserted, because he thought she could rein him in.[33] Mead concluded that many men of his generation felt the same pull between immorality and virtue. She realized that when he was a boy his mother and his aunt, who cared for him while Martha Mead worked, competed for his attention. He was accustomed to having women serve him, and he expected his wife to do the same. Margaret further conjectured that his difficult behavior resulted from guilt over his father's death when he was six.[34]

Mead mastered her father early in her life. She learned not to trust his promises, and she figured out how to counter his manipulations around money by ignoring them or by manipulating him in return.

When Franz Boas was reluctant to approve her going to the South Seas to do her first fieldwork, she maneuvered her father into paying her way by suggesting that Boas was trying to take over his parental role; Edward gave her the money to retain his sense of control over her. She often challenged him directly, for she came to realize that he relished debate and didn't respect people who didn't fight back.[35]

As an adult, Mead had many of her father's characteristics. Like him she did her work quickly, producing not only ethnographies but also scholarly and popular articles at breakneck speed. She could be harsh, just like him. She prided herself on her femininity, but she could take on his brusque masculine style. As she grew older and entered academic and professional circles controlled by men, she silenced them by being tougher than they. She sometimes answered the phone like her father, simply saying "Mead here" and launching into what she had to say.[36]

As an adult she had a habit of showing up at the apartments of close friends when she was recovering from a broken leg or a sprained ankle and was between marriages and expecting them to take her in until she recovered. None could refuse her. Her fame, her neediness, her loyalty captivated them. Her friend Eleanor Pelham Kortheuer (whom everyone called Pelham) remembered one occasion when Mead was staying with her and Ruth Benedict came to visit. Ruth smiled ruefully at Pelham behind Margaret's back as Margaret continually talked on the phone, sometimes using a "tough drill sargeant's voice." Ruth silently sympathized with Pelham, but she was loyal to Margaret, as they all were.[37] She was drawn in by her insecurities, her glittering personality, her mental and verbal brilliance, and the dramas she created. And Ruth must have realized that if she said anything it probably wouldn't do any good, anyway.

IN *BLACKBERRY WINTER*, Mead's portrait of her mother is more positive than that of her father. To begin with, she praises Emily's gentleness. Her mother, Mead remembered, had a radiant smile that no one who met her ever forgot. "Her vehemence," Mead explains, "was reserved for the causes she supported."[38] Yet Mead also describes her mother as often grim, as obsessively neat, and as without much capacity for personal pleasure. She wore plain, austere clothing; she wouldn't accept presents because she felt that extra money should be spent on worthy causes, not on personal indulgence. In 1933, on her field trip to the Tchambuli in New Guinea with Reo Fortune, Mead wrote to Benedict that she was enjoying a stray kitten that had wandered into their house. But she kept thinking that her pleasure in the animal was wrong. "Mother was always so firm about how really wrong and anti-suffrage it was to care specially about a given animal what with all the suffering that was in the world."[39]

Emily didn't learn how to cook until she was sixty, but when Margaret was growing up she insisted that plain food, without sauces or butter, be served at meals. She held liberal attitudes about race and ethnicity, but she treated her cooks and maids so harshly that they often quit. She eventually espoused socialism, and in 1917 she hung a large red hammer and sickle in the window of their house in honor of the Bolshevik Revolution.[40] Yet she drew a distinction between the elite reformers with whom she identified and the common people, who in her opinion lacked manners and breeding. After all, she had been raised on Chicago's North Shore, in a family with ties to Chicago's elite. When her mother invoked class privilege, Mead considered her a snob.

Emily's snobbery was intricate; it included interdictions on chewing gum, ice cream sodas, cheap paperbacks, and trips to Coney Island. Emily allowed Margaret and her siblings to play with the local children in Bucks County, but she restricted their contacts with the Italian children in Hammonton. She drew distinctions between "ordinary people," "people with some background," and "fine people." People in the first two categories were anti-Catholic, anti-Semitic, and racist. The "fine people"—mostly women—were sophisticated and liberal, and they did reform work.[41]

Moreover, Emily Mead was uncomfortable with her body and with sensuality. In an unpublished memoir, she wrote that when her daughters dirtied the bathroom or left clothes on the floor she thought about the dance hall actresses of her youth who flaunted their bodies on the stage and had affairs. She hated those thoughts because they reminded her of her passionate feelings when she was young. "I have wondered sometimes whether I had any emotions, and yet I can remember being ardent and intense when young."[42] Mead's sister Elizabeth claimed that Emily didn't want any more children after Margaret was born but that she didn't use birth control and so she submitted to her husband and bore the rest of them. She had wanted a career, not five children. Emily confessed in a memoir that she had never enjoyed sex.[43]

In fact, there were contradictions in her teachings about sex. She talked openly about rape, as in her story of the black woman raped by a white man. In other areas, however, she was reticent. She expected Margaret to marry and have children and she taught her to call her vagina her "little body," saying that it needed protection because babies came from it. In line with that teaching, when Margaret was a teenager she wore a strong, reinforced corset, one like "armor plate," so that she wouldn't damage her breasts and female organs when playing games like baseball. In later years Margaret gave up playing sports and even exercising her body. When Emily became incensed on hearing a rumor that Margaret had been intimate with a friend of her brother's—a rumor Margaret denied—Margaret stopped telling her mother anything about her personal life.[44]

Edward and Emily's marriage had problems from the start. A more sensitive man might have been able to draw out Emily's sensual side, the "intensity" she had experienced when she was young. A less conflicted woman, someone more at ease with her sensuality and not so devoted to a militant women's rights stance that could become anti-male, might have been better able to deal with Edward. And they were separated by social class. Edward came from a rural, middle-class Methodist background; Emily's was upper middle class, urban, and Unitarian. Mead depicted Edward as stereotypically masculine, while Emily seems to have been a stereotypical suffragist, putting principle above human relationships too often. Margaret may have connected Emily's coldness to her work on behalf of women, and that may partly explain why she developed negative feelings about feminism.

WHAT ABOUT MARTHA MEAD? Edward's mother moved in with his family soon after Margaret was born, and she remained with them for the next twenty-seven years, until she died in 1928. Unlike Benedict's difficult aunt Hetty, her childhood caretaker, Martha was warm and generous—a perfect grandmother, in Margaret Mead's eyes. In her autobiographical writings, Mead never criticizes her. Martha seems to have been shrewd enough not to intrude on major family decisions, and although a devout Methodist, she kept her religious beliefs to herself. She sometimes tried to broker the dissension between Edward and Emily; when Edward threatened to leave Emily for the other woman, Martha declared that if he left she would stay with Emily. She denounced racism, nativism, and anti-Semitism as strongly as Emily: Christ and his mother were Jewish, Martha said, and to her that proved the equality of Jews.[45] Like her son, however, Martha was stubborn, and she sometimes came into conflict with her daughter-in-law, who hadn't wanted her to live with them in the first place. Emily felt that Martha's catering to Edward forced her to serve him too.[46]

Only five feet tall, Martha was as tiny as her daughter-in-law, whom she resembled in appearance. Although Margaret's sister Elizabeth remembered Martha as dogmatic and a poor teacher, Margaret's memory was the opposite.[47] Margaret found her grandmother loving and dependable; in that behavior Martha was preferable to Emily, who smiled her loving smile but was cold and distant; who fought for women's rights and called herself a socialist—and yet was elitist. In the family, Martha chose Margaret as her confidante, while Margaret turned to her grandmother. In *Blackberry Winter* Mead asserted that Martha was the most decisive influence in her life; in "Life History" she stated that she wished that she had been named Martha, not Margaret.[48]

Margaret liked her grandmother's femininity. Following her women's rights principles, Emily had Margaret wear bloomers and boy's clothing, dressing her like her brother in "coats with brass buttons and round stiff berets." Margaret didn't like that clothing. In contrast, Martha wore dresses that made her look dainty and feminine, and Margaret wanted to look like her. "My grandmother gave me my ease in being a woman," she asserted. "She was unquestionably feminine— small and dainty and wholly without masculine protest or feminist aggrievement." Emily marveled that Margaret didn't resent having been born female, but Martha thought that girls were quicker to develop than boys—a belief that helps explain why Margaret's father expected her to do better in school than her brother.[49]

After many years of teaching, Martha was tired of working and enthusiastic about the creative aspects of domesticity: baking, handicrafts, caring for children. She made such activities seem as fulfilling to Margaret as her mother's research on the Italians in Hammonton and her reform involvements. Like her son, Martha was critical of Emily's elitism, although her reaction to it was subtle, emerging for example in a disagreement with Emily over what books Margaret should read. With the exception of Emerson, Emily didn't think much of American writers. She wanted Margaret to read the great English novelists of the nineteenth century—Thackery and Austen, Eliot and Dickens. Martha liked the American authors Henry Wadsworth Longfellow and James Whitcomb Riley, but Emily considered them "crass" and "sentimental."

In this debate, as in others, Margaret took her grandmother's side. A voracious reader of fiction, she enjoyed literature both high and low. She picked up her grandmother's taste for folksy, sentimental writing, while she secretly read books the servants read, like the romantic novels of Marie Corelli, the best-selling novelist of the age. She later decided that such books were valuable because they reflected culture at its most representative level. "When mother sniffed about Grandma's 'taste' I sniffed back internally and set my face against the snobbery of the academic world. . . . Words like vulgar and sentimental got thrown around, but I didn't really care."[50]

This taste for commonality, this identification with ordinary people, was important to Mead's later career as a lecturer and analyst of American culture. It also nourished a sentimental streak in her, a way in which in her public lecturing she could sound like a cracker-barrel philosopher, speaking folk wisdom, the descendant of James Whitcomb Riley—with an insight into the vernacular imagination and the ethical optimism of the nineteenth century. In school and at home Mead read the classics—Greek drama, Shakespeare, Milton, the nineteenth-century English novelists. But she wasn't the same kind of intellectual as Benedict: she didn't read George Santayana and Nietzsche for pleasure, and she didn't have the same abstract mind as her friend. Both her mother and father were social scientists, focused on empirical approaches. Mead absorbed that influence.

And there was her grandmother, with her taste for popular literature and her dislike of Emily's elitism. Honoring this side of her family and of herself, Mead began the prologue to *Blackberry Winter* with a quote from, of all possible sources, a popular homily that, printed and framed, hung on the wall of the local doctor's office "like a flowered valentine." The quotation read: "All things work together for good to them that love God." And she often repeated other favorite sayings of her grandmother: "Get the distaff ready, and God will send the flax" and "The harder you're hit, the higher you bounce." Mead liked such optimistic aphorisms—folk wisdom that fueled American energy—and given her photographic memory, her head was full of them. She kept them out of her academic writing, but they appear in her popular work. "You'll never be able to write a word," her childhood friend Alice Thwing said to her when she was sixteen. "It would be nothing but a mass of quotations."[51]

IN THE LATE 1920S Ruth Benedict put together a collection of her poetry for publication and titled it "Winter of the Blood." The title had a number of meanings: her advancing age, with menopause ahead; the difficulties in her relationships with both her husband, Stanley, and Margaret Mead. It also referred to Fanny Blood, the youthful lover of the eighteenth-century feminist Mary Wollstonecraft, about whom Benedict had written a brief unpublished biography. The title seems to be echoed in Mead's title *Blackberry Winter.*

In fact, given the closeness between Benedict and Mead as well as the biographical accounts Mead wrote about her friend before writing her own autobiography, the similarities and differences between their lives must have been in Mead's mind as she turned to the task of chronicling her own life. The similarities between them went beyond living on farms and being the eldest daughters in conflicted families that moved a lot and were proud of their colonial and Revolutionary heritages, of being "Old Americans." They extended to areas of fantasy and reality, spirituality and sexuality, and even the experience of family death when they were young.

The death of her father when she was eighteen months old left a deep impression on Benedict; the death of Mead's sister Katherine when she was five had a similar impact on Mead. Sometimes Mead regarded that death as the central event in her childhood. Her parents had allowed her to name Katherine; the baby, who slept in her room, had died in that room, according to Mead's friend Patricia Grinager.[52] That was difficult enough, but Margaret wasn't permitted to mourn her sister—just as Ruth hadn't been permitted to mourn her father when he died. "I wasn't allowed to go to the funeral or see the baby. They had a drawing made from a cast afterwards that they kept and her eyes weren't open and I didn't like that."[53]

For a long time after Katherine died Margaret searched for her, even though she knew she was dead. Then she searched for a twin—a companion so like herself that she could never be lost. She fantasized that gypsies had stolen that twin. "Sometimes I went searching for my lost twin in old deserted buildings, and I would peer through the dusty cobwebbed windows to see if the gypsies were camping inside." She imagined that after she married she herself would bear twins, a boy and a girl. "I remember their names, Florence and Floyd and Roland and Rolanda."[54]

Young children dealing with loss sometimes make up fantasies about playmates or a twin; Margaret's fantasies resemble Ruth's about a playmate with whom she roamed the Norwich hills. Margaret's day-dreams, however, went further, leading her to worry that she might lose her identity. She feared that gypsies would kidnap her as well as her twin and that her family wouldn't be able to reclaim her because as she grew older and her body changed they wouldn't recognize her. Then she cut her arm on a piece of glass, and she decided that the problem was solved, for the resulting scar gave her a permanent mark by which she could always be identified. Her fantasy became more positive. The gypsies still kidnapped her, but she learned a great many languages and skills while with them. Then she returned home, more perfect than before, and her family recognized her because of the scar. In an alternate set of daydreams, however, she was adopted by a family with gentler, less perplexing parents, ones that she liked better than the ones she had.[55]

Katherine's death affected the entire family. Stunned by unexpected loss, everyone became disoriented; Edward and Emily became more estranged than before. It is likely that Edward's infidelities began then, especially since he formed a close relationship with the male doctor who treated Katherine. Finding Emily cold and unemotional, the doctor was critical of her, giving Edward justification for turning to other women. In a draft of *Blackberry Winter*, Mead describes the doctor as a "hostile rival and critic of my mother's."[56]

Given Mead's optimism and her ability to repress negative memories, it's difficult to determine the long-term effect of Katherine's death on her. Mead contended that her sister Elizabeth, born five years after Katherine died, served as a substitute for her. "I got my major identity crisis settled before I was six," she declared in the positive version of her childhood. But she never entirely explained away her behavior during kindergarten—a progressive one, with arts and crafts—which she entered not long after Katherine died. Each day she had to be dragged away from her teacher, kicking and screaming, away from "the school I preferred to home."[57] Whatever her positive feelings about her family—and those feelings were strong—there was a negative side.

WHEN SHE WAS IN COLLEGE, Mead wrote short stories, many of them drawn from episodes in her childhood. In fact, she considered a career as a writer of fiction, although her writing instructor at Barnard called the stories of hers that he read "trite and conventional."[58] Her efforts seemed limited even to her in comparison with those of her college apartment mate, Léonie Adams, already a rising star in New York poetry circles when they were at Barnard. "I had no taste for failing gloriously," Mead wrote, or "for spending my life trying to write the great American novel."[59]

No matter their defects, Mead's stories provide insight into their author. In the first place, they challenge Mead's portrayal of herself as invariably upbeat, as never remaining depressed for more than ten minutes.[60] Filled with danger, involving rape, marital infidelity, and hints of incest, they seem related to a darker side of herself—one in which she hadn't mastered her father and in which males were menacing and to be feared. They don't contain the monsters or the classical allusions of Benedict's stories and poetry; even when Mead wrote dark lyric poetry in the 1920s, she was rarely as gloomy—or as learned—as Benedict. One of her stories, however, contains a character she called "the young-eyed cherubim." He might be seen as representing a suffering Christ.[61]

In "The Blind Woman," the blind Mrs. Sackville doesn't stop a gang of village toughs from abducting her half-witted female servant, even though she hears them in the act and realizes that they will rape the girl. She worries about her motives in remaining silent, about the violence and sexuality at the core of her self. In "The Young-Eyed Cherubim," an eight-year-old boy is attracted to his "beautiful and lustful" mother. The "village toughs" threaten to beat him up until he tells them about her extramarital affair. They tell his father and, furious with his wife, the father beats her with the boy's toy train. To punish her son, the mother describes her sexual encounters to him, feeding his "sense of sin with new and degrading experiences." When he reaches adolescence, the boy enters a monastery to expiate his guilt. Yet like the title character in Oscar Wilde's *The Picture of Dorian Gray*, he still looks angelic despite his experience of evil. The title of Mead's story comes from the lines in Shakespeare's *The Merchant of Venice* in which the angels sing to "the young-eyed cherubins."[62]

Mead also focused on marital discord and perverse sexuality in her story titled "Lassitude." In that story the teenage Millie suspects that her father is unfaithful to her mother when he goes away from home on business trips. When her mother sobs in her father's absences, Millie comforts her by sleeping with her in her bed. Lying next to her mother, she is drawn to her soft white arms, as though she has taken her father's place in her parents' marital relations. Then, like Mrs. Sackville in "The Blind Woman," Millie's mother goes blind, and Millie accidentally spies on her father looking at pornographic pictures and hears him gloating over his wife's loss of sight: "Now there'll be no more prying and spying so a man can't call his soul his own." Sensing that Millie is angry with him, he tries to placate her. She avoids his touch, however, for it both attracts and repels her. Confused by her feelings, Millie is unable to confront him. Thus the story's title: "Lassitude."

Mead asserted that she wrote her stories partly out of fascination with local scandals that her high school classmates in Doylestown gossiped about and from which she derived most of her plots. Both "The Blind Woman" and "The Young-Eyed Cherubim" were based on real incidents in the local community. Mrs. Sackville of "The Blind Woman" was modeled after a leader of the community who didn't stop village toughs from raping her servant. The father in "The Young-Eyed Cherubim" was modeled after a local man who did beat his wife with his son's toy train when he discovered that she had been unfaithful.[63]

What about "Lassitude"? Mead never identified its source, although it seems drawn from her own experience. Her father did have extramarital affairs when he was away during the week, teaching in his extension schools or promoting his business projects. Mead's mother didn't lose her sight, but she often seemed blind to her husband's indiscretions. There isn't any evidence that Edward Mead read pornography, although he was a masculine man who may have liked erotica. Like her other stories, "Lassitude" implies that Mead disliked male violence. Yet women have power in Mead's stories, as well as perverse desire: Mrs. Sackville in "The Blind Woman," the mother in "The Young-Eyed Cherubim."

Set in the locales in which she grew up, Mead's stories reflect themes of betrayal and violence underneath the harmony of American communities—themes characteristic of realist novels like Edith Wharton's *Ethan Frome* and Theodore Dreiser's *An American Tragedy*. They also reflect the Freudianism popular in the 1920s, especially Freud's theories of the primacy of the libido and the Oedipus complex—with the young-eyed cherub involved with his mother and Millie in "Lassitude" with her mother and father. Mead read Freud as early as high school, and his ideas were popular at Barnard when she was a student there.[64] Yet she also explored her own psyche in her stories, trying as she matured to understand through fictional re-creation her feelings about her family and herself.

LIKE BENEDICT'S CHILDHOOD, Mead's was far from easy, and its difficulties affected her as an adult. She had a lifelong fear of exposure, of being found out. When she picked a flower in a park as a small child and her mother made her show the flower to a policeman, she was afraid he was going to arrest her, although he only smiled. "That little exercise in fear of those in power was enough to last me all my life," she later wrote. After she returned from Samoa, she was terrified that Franz Boas was going to reject what she had written about Samoan adolescents, although he only suggested that she be more precise in differentiating sexual from romantic love among them. Even in her forties, when the assistant director of the American Museum of Natural History left an urgent message for her to see him one day, she became frightened that he was going to fire her. The old fear, she wrote, came over her and "clutched" at her stomach, although as it turned out he only wanted to ask her to serve on an advisory committee for a science book club.[65]

She also had a fear of disaster and of disgrace, as when people "zip the Pullman sheets into their dresses and can't get them out," or the locks on bathroom doors don't work, or the flush toilet overflows. That fear produced a lifetime "style of awareness and watchfulness."[66] In doing her fieldwork, she had a fear of failure. "There is a euphoria when one reaches the field," she wrote. Then after a few weeks the fear arises that the researcher can never understand the native society, that it is too complex to figure out. "That has been," she confessed, "a nightmare that has never ceased to haunt me."[67]

Her unpublished stories reveal a concern about rape, and the "armored" corset she wore seems designed as much for protection as for support. In *A Rap on Race*, her conversation with James Baldwin, she told him that she had a lifetime fantasy of being a black woman raped by a white man, like the admired black woman in her childhood community. In "Life History" she referred to her childhood fear of rape. She traced it to having undergone menarche at the age of twelve and developing an adult female body at too young an age, before she was ready to handle the attention she received from men. Men in public places—even the boys in school—began staring at her, frightening and embarrassing her. Walking through the village store was agony, as the men lounging on each side of the aisle looked her up and down.[68] Then there were the "village toughs" who were central characters in

"The Blind Woman" and "The Young-Eyed Cherubim." They were hostile to women, dangerous to them.

Margaret also feared the masculinity in herself. Sexologists in that era defined a female homosexual as a "mannish" woman who not only acted like a man but also had the "soul" of a man. Mead preferred feminine and frilly clothing; she didn't want to be a boy. She wrote in a draft of *Blackberry Winter* that "the thought of having one of those vague masculinizing diseases" filled her "with horror."[69] Yet she appreciated strong, masculine women. She had a reproduction of the Venus de Milo in her bedroom as a child—the famed female figure from antiquity who, broad-shouldered and with a large waist, was a model of beauty for her age—while on a wall of her bedroom hung a print of Guido Reni's *Aurora*. In that seventeenth-century painting, popular in the early twentieth century, a masculinized goddess of the dawn leads a chariot driven by her feminized lover, Tithonus, with a sturdy group of female "hours" alongside. A large cherub dominates the center of the painting.[70]

Like Benedict, Mead sometimes had a nervous stomach. In a medical history she compiled for her doctor in 1948, she noted that she had frequent attacks of indigestion between the ages of ten and twelve. When she was confirmed in the Episcopal Church, she had a violent attack of vomiting. Throughout her college years she had attacks of indigestion.[71] As for other physical ailments, during college and after, Mead suffered from neuritis in her right arm; as an adult she often had accidents—spraining her ankle, breaking her leg.

Mead also claimed that she, like Benedict, saw eidetic visions. She usually controlled them, but sometimes she couldn't; she called the controlled ones "dramatic" and the uncontrolled ones "obsessive." When Jean Houston guided her through a series of them in the interview she did with her toward the end of Mead's life, Mead moved from drama to obsession to drama, beginning with a vision of women winnowing in rice fields, and then moving to horrible scenes of early hospitals with prostitutes serving as nurses. But she managed to get that imagery under control, and she finished by seeing Florence Nightingale with a lamp, the virtuous woman who brought cleanliness and trained nurses to English hospitals. In her regular life, Mead's most frequent obsessive visions and dreams were of dead babies; those visions and dreams began when she was a student at Barnard.[72]

She disliked being alone. She rarely went to restaurants or plays by herself; when traveling she stayed with friends. She didn't go on fieldwork trips alone; the trip to Samoa was one of the few times she did so, and even then she tried to persuade another female graduate student to accompany her. This need for others may have resulted from her ebullient personality, which flourished in front of an audience and in having someone to debate—or from having been raised in a family with so many people in it, with someone always there for company.[73] Her dislike of being alone could also indicate a fear of exposure, of losing herself.

Mead was always active, but that activity sometimes seems like frenzy. "Be lazy, go crazy," she wrote to Benedict.[74] She had the ability to do many things at once—but she often seems on a manic high and sometimes on the edge of a breakdown: mania, she once said, was her characteristic emotional expression; she thought she would die talking at the top of her lungs.[75] Benedict engaged in suicidal fantasies and went to bed, mired in depression; Mead kept busy. Perhaps by doing so she was escaping—from Katherine's death, her father's caprice, the tensions at home. Margaret's first husband, Luther Cressman, minced no words in disparaging the Mead family. They displayed little affection, he said. Their home was filled with tension; they seemed to him "unintegrated." After spending Christmas Day in 1926 with her family, Margaret wrote to Reo Fortune that "twenty-four hours of my family have left me worn out. My family all love and hate like individuals unrelated to each other."[76]

There is also the watercolor Mead's sister Elizabeth painted in 1935 of the farmhouse in Bucks County, which is reproduced in *Blackberry Winter*. Their grandmother is in the center of the painting, with Priscilla and Elizabeth at Martha's sides. It isn't an affectionate piece. The season is winter; the trees have no leaves; the figures are stern and emaciated, wearing drab clothing, standing at a distance from the house. The painting seems to foreshadow the fates of Margaret's siblings. The overprotected Richard struggled to free himself from his father and the powerful women of his childhood family to attain a modest career as a college professor of business, like his father. The beautiful Priscilla competed with Margaret by trying for a career in anthropology and then giving it up for marriage. The gentle Elizabeth differentiated herself by becoming an artist. Both sisters married famous men who overshadowed them: Elizabeth married William Steig, the cartoonist and children's book author; Priscilla married Leo Rosten, the humorist and writer of Hollywood screenplays. In the end, ill and with a conflicted marriage, suffering from a long-term glandular dysfunction, Priscilla committed suicide. For her part, Elizabeth had emotional lows that may explain the austere "blackberry winter" aspect of her painting.[77]

Like Benedict, Mead was tough. Whether she was born that way, because she was the first child, or because she modeled herself after her powerful parents, she developed a strong personality. From dealing with those parents, often in conflict, she learned the art of manipulation, how to play them off against each other. She also defied them. Joining the Episcopal Church was an act of rebellion, as was her always claiming a room for herself away from the rest of the family in each of their houses—at the top of the house, sometimes in the attic. She characterized her room playfully in her memoir in the series of autobiographies of psychologists as combining "the charms of godmothers and wicked fairies." She described it in *Blackberry Winter* as making her feel safe from "intrusion and loss."[78]

Ruth's tantrums were outbursts of rage; Margaret's were controlled, as when she stormed out of the dining room to her bedroom when her father dressed her down—and banged every door on the way. Her strength made her a stable force in the family. Along with her grandmother she served as family confidante; eventually, she contended, everyone in the family came to her with their problems. "My grandmother used to spend an hour a day brushing my hair, and she spoke of poor Emily and Eddie and whatever was worrying her about them, and I came to think of them as my children."[79] By the age of ten Margaret was a sober child; even as an adult she didn't respond well to jokes. She didn't like board games—especially chess.[80] But she lived her life as though it were a secret escapade or a game of chance.

After the birth of Elizabeth when Margaret was eight, Emily suffered a nervous breakdown and spent the next year in a rest home. The family moved to Swarthmore to be near her. At that point, Margaret took over much of Elizabeth's upbringing (and later that of Priscilla), in addition to her roles as keeper of the family records and overseer of family moving. She liked organizing the lives of others; she traced her enjoyment in being a producer of events—and lives—to having taken on that role in her family. With unsuspecting irony, she wrote that when she was a child, she thought of herself as "without any particular gifts of beauty or performing skills of any kind," and noted, "the role of stage managing others appealed to me."[81]

Mead came to consider herself as both an adult and a child because that combination drew from her particular qualities of maturity and childishness and because her grandmother treated her that way. The

rest of the family, especially her sisters, picked up the same attitude.
"In a sense I treat adults as children in the sense that they need protection," Mead told Jean Houston.[82] She continued to play a parental role
for her family and friends throughout her life. She remained a mother
to her younger sisters: she oversaw their education, found men for
them to date, gave them advice. She had a genius for friendship, for
soothing hurts, and for inspiring individuals with her enthusiasm for
life. She also had a childlike quality in keeping with her tiny body that
attracted people to her, as someone who needed to be protected.

She also could be free and easy, seeming without a care in the
world. When she was romantically involved with Edward Sapir, he
wrote her a poem comparing her to Ariel, the androgynous good spirit
in Shakespeare's *The Tempest* who is captive to Prospero and wants to
be free. In the poem Sapir cautioned her to take care that her ambition
didn't reach too far, that in trying for difficult goals she didn't destroy
herself.

> *Of the heedless sun are you an Ariel,*
> *Rising through cloud to a discovered blue. . . .*
> *Reckless, be safe. The little wise feet know*
> *Sun-ways and clouds and sudden earthen aim,*
> *And steps of beauty quicken into flame*
> *Wherein you burn up wholly in arrest.*[83]

Mead answered him in a poem in which she told him that he was
wrong. No matter how often "she tattered her frocks" and "her skipping ropes got caught in trees," her joy in life would allow her to
achieve what she wanted. She wasn't like Phaëthon, who burned up
when he got too close to the sun, for the dryads—the nymphs of the
forest—watched out for her, and her very striving, her willingness to
"fling a rope so high," would enable her to reach the stars. She could
live life without limits because, as the homily on the wall of the doctor's
office said, "All things work together for good to them that love God."
Her answer to Sapir's poem went:

> *She used to skip when she was small*
> *And all her frocks she tattered,*
> *But mother gently gathered up*
> *The dishes that she shattered.*

Her skipping rope got caught in trees
And shook the blossoms down,
But her skip was so lighthearted
That the dryads could not frown.

And when at last she tore a star
Out of the studded sky,
God only smiled at one whose glee
Could fling a rope so high.[84]

As much as she mothered others, they also mothered her. And she had the capacity to dream dreams for everyone, not just for herself. She inspired Ruth Benedict to do her best work, just as Benedict inspired her. In their creative friendship lay a major source for each woman's success. The two women were both similar and different, and the interplay of their personalities brought them together. But one must be wary of accepting Mead's version of their friendship in which she was an optimist and Benedict was a depressive. Benedict may have felt that her upbringing "murdered" her soul; she may have suffered from shyness, weak hearing, and depression. But no less than Mead she was determined to succeed and willing to take risks to come out ahead. And Mead also had a difficult and yet hopeful childhood, one that inspired her and kept her running, away from failure and toward fame, to tear a star out of a "studded sky."

PART III

Searching for Self

CHAPTER 4

"Smashing"

Female Romantic Friendships

IN 1908, WHEN Margaret Mead was seven, she met a young woman on a train to Philadelphia and was "strangely attracted" to her. Four years later, that woman reentered Margaret's life when she appeared at the Mead farmhouse in Bucks County. She was there with her widowed father, the priest of the local Episcopal church, and they were recruiting members for the church. Her name was Lucia; she was the companion and housekeeper for her father. Mead's grandmother politely invited them in for tea, and Margaret found Lucia as appealing in this second meeting as in the first. She began visiting Lucia at the rectory where she lived with her father, and she found there, with Lucia, a place that contained "the things I felt were lacking at home."[1]

In the drafts of her autobiography Mead thus begins the story of her friendship with the woman she called Miss Lucia, "the most humanly sensitive person I had ever known;"[2] it was Lucia who influenced her to profess the Episcopal faith. The story of their relationship introduces her other female friendships in her childhood and adolescence and foreshadows her relationship with Ruth Benedict. Both Benedict and Mead participated in the culture of romantic friendships between girls that was central to the Victorian system of gender socialization. In fact, Mead's description of that culture in the drafts of her autobiography is one of the most comprehensive ever written. Recent scholars have questioned the culture's extent and influence, but Mead's narrative amply demonstrates its power to shape lives, while revealing its complex structure that encouraged intimate relations between girls while guiding them into marriage.[3]

Mead located the source of her childhood drive toward loving girls and women in popular-culture representations, especially in novels. Writing her autobiography in the 1970s, when theories of personal relationships drawn from the theater were in vogue, Mead described those representations as part of "scripts" from which individuals learned "roles." Or she borrowed Benedict's term "pattern" from *Patterns of Culture* to indicate the cultural forms that mold the individual personality. With regard to her childhood friendships she wrote: "It was the culturally standard idea that came first and the people who came later; I was role playing and looking for others to play the role."[4] Recent analysts of romantic friendships between girls in the Victorian era find their source in the relationships between sisters or between mothers and daughters. Yet Mead's feelings about her mother were ambivalent, and her two sisters who lived beyond infancy weren't born until she was eight and then ten years old. She thought that the culture around her, not her family, shaped her drive toward making intimate female friends.[5]

Limited information exists about Ruth Benedict's experience of the culture of romantic friendships between girls until she attended single-sex schools: St. Margaret's Episcopal School for Girls in Buffalo between 1903 and 1905 and Vassar College between 1905 and 1909. At both schools a culture of "smashing" existed—and it lingered on at Barnard when Mead went there in the early 1920s. Indeed, as Havelock Ellis and other contemporary sexologists pointed out and as Benedict's and Mead's mothers had discovered a generation before, romantic friendships between girls were very popular at female single-sex institutions in that era.

ACCORDING TO MEAD, the cultural script that she followed in her childhood required her in the first place to find a favorite teacher, like the kindergarten teacher she clung to at the end of the school day. Yet between kindergarten and junior high Margaret had difficulty finding a favorite teacher because her grandmother mostly taught her at home. When the Mead family lived in Swarthmore, Margaret went to public school in the fourth grade, and she became attached to her teacher because they both liked the poetry of James Whitcomb Riley. In high school she thought she'd found her ideal in her Latin teacher, until she became disillusioned when she realized that the teacher didn't know much Latin. When Margaret attended a girls' school after high school for a year to improve her French, the teacher she chose as her favorite was actively homosexual and afraid to become involved with a student.[6]

For the most part, Lucia played the mentor role for Margaret during her early adolescence. In a draft chapter of *Blackberry Winter,* Mead described their relationship. She portrayed it as sentimental, not passionate, although she seemed to indicate some eroticism in it when she wrote that she was "strangely attracted" to Lucia on the train and that she persuaded her "delicious" Miss Lucia to participate in her favorite friendship ritual of pledging devotion in the ravine behind the farmhouse.[7] Tree-lined and hidden from view, with a brook running through it, the ravine was a special place of Margaret's for fantasy play. She took Lucia there in the dead of winter to tell her that she had begun menstruating, that she had now become a woman.[8] Moreover, in converting to Lucia's Episcopal faith, she shared with her friend the rich ritual of the Anglican Church. In Sunday services, priests, acolytes, and the choir dressed in vestments process down the aisle, carrying the cross, the scepter, and sometimes a censer containing smoldering incense, with its fumes wafting over the congregation. Communion, the rite of sanctification through eating the wafer and drinking the wine symbolizing Christ's body and blood, is the high point of every service; the liturgy draws passages from Scripture to symbolically reenact Christ's crucifixion and his resurrection, the divine guarantee of God's love and salvation to believers.

This near medieval, esoteric setting reflects the traditionalism and mysticism of the High Church movement, which, originating in England in the 1830s, introduced elements of Catholicism into Anglicanism. Margaret liked the aesthetic appeal of the ceremony, its rich fabrics and pageantry, its traditionalism rooted in the romance of medieval lore, the sense it gave of union with the divine. She liked the Episcopal emphasis on love, not guilt, on human goodness, not human depravity. She also liked secrets and leading a double life. "Being high church in those days was rather like being a crypto member of a secret society," she wrote. "There were burning issues, making the sign of the cross, candles on the altar." Margaret would remain a devout Episcopalian for the rest of her life.[9]

Margaret also identified with Lucia during Lucia's engagement to be married. Margaret was ecstatic when Lucia became engaged and deeply upset when she broke it off. She remembered Lucia telling her about ending the engagement as one of the worst moments of her life. In actuality, Margaret's behavior mimicked that of the heroine of a favorite novel of hers, *The Little Colonel at Boarding School*, who identifies even more strongly with her romantic friend at the boarding school they attend when that girl becomes engaged.[10] Margaret's emotional merging with Lucia reflected her culture's belief that a female friendship could be as absorbing as a romance with a man. Yet Margaret expected her friend to marry, just as she expected to marry. That was the culmination of the plots of the romance novels she read; even her freethinking parents expected her to marry. Lucia's breaking her engagement threatened the Victorian gender system at a time in Margaret's life when she accepted it. In this system, if women didn't marry, gender completion in heterosexuality—essential to an ordered society—was broken. While waiting for marriage, a girl could have romantic friendships with other girls. It was also important that she have an older female mentor, to provide guidance through the trying adolescent years. That person functioned as an idealized mother—or sister—free from family tensions. A model educator, she grew out of the Socratic and Sapphic tradition of older mentors inspiring their students by their example.[11]

ACCORDING TO MEAD, the cultural "script" for relationships in her childhood dictated that in addition to a favorite teacher she find a "best friend" her own age. Yet when Margaret lived on the farm in Bucks County and her grandmother taught her at home, she had great difficulty finding a "best friend" because the only girls available were unsophisticated farm girls who lived near her and who had neither her ambition nor her knowledge of life. And because they didn't read novels, they didn't know the requirements of proper romantic behavior. They were bewildered by the friendship rituals she got from novels, like pledging eternal devotion in the ravine behind the farmhouse.

Margaret read novels written for girls; both the moralistic Elsie Dinsmore tales and the secular Little Colonel series were favorites of hers. In the latter books adolescent female homoeroticism is a major subtext, as a group of girls from throughout the nation form a circle around Lloyd Sherman, the "Little Colonel," who is the granddaughter of a Kentucky planter. They wear friendship rings and feel a deep sentimentalized affection for one another. They don't, however, "fall in love" with one another; that intense emotional experience occurs at the single-sex boarding schools they attend, where they form "crushes" and "smashes" with their schoolmates—safely away from home. Although overt sexuality isn't described in the novels, there's always an erotic edge to these schoolgirl romances, as when the heroine of *The Little Colonel at Boarding School* identifies with her engaged "crush."

Margaret also read series of novels written for boys, like the Motorboat Boys and the Boy Engineers, in which young male protagonists solve mysteries through using engines and tools.[12] From those books she learned about adventuring and taking risks close to home, as she did about adventuring on a global scale from Sir Walter Scott's stories about Scotland, Rudyard Kipling's about imperial India, and Robert Louis Stevenson's about pirates and kidnapped children. And she read *St. Nicholas Magazine,* the era's most popular magazine for children. Margaret's "script" for relationships can be found in its stories in which girls engage in romantic friendships with each other and find favorite female teachers to admire. In these stories, in line with the emergence of the independent New Woman of the 1890s, they behave like tomboys—until they marry.[13]

When Margaret went to junior high school at the Buckingham Friends School and then to the public high school in Doylestown, she made female "best friends" easily. Sarah Slotter was one. Even though the other students called her Sally Meat Axe, Mead found her "intense, enormously intelligent, exciting." Margaret had sleepovers with Sally, and they stayed awake all night talking.[14] Another "best friend" was Marjorie Barber. She wasn't intelligent, but she was beautiful: Margaret was attracted to beautiful people throughout her life. When Margaret was home from school one month because she was sick, Marjorie wrote her love notes. In those notes Marjorie refers to herself as "dimples" and to Margaret as "sweetheart," "darling," "dearest," and "dearest one." She is "tickled to pieces" when she finds a note from Margaret on her school desk. She wants to know all Margaret's thoughts and feelings. She writes that "Lois" told her she was going to visit Margaret and she intends to come along. But they can't see Margaret together because she would be too jealous. "I'll talk to your mother or anybody there while she [Lois] sees you."[15]

Margaret's erotic friendships with girls in junior high and high school didn't stop with Sarah Slotter and Marjorie Barber. There was also Ruth Carver. In 1915 Margaret wrote to Alice Thwing that she wasn't as crazy about Ruth as she once had been. For her part, Ruth wrote Margaret letters of devotion for some years, calling her "Peggy, my precious." When Margaret was at Barnard, Ruth begged her to come home for a visit. "If I'm not inducement enough," she writes, "Jane is irresistible." And more girls were involved. "Catherine Evans does satisfy that feminine weakness in me that loves a little bundle of soft clothes and blankets," wrote Ruth. She confided to Margaret that she even "went off into the woods with Mary Swartzlander for supper the other night." She chided Margaret for not writing and complained that she had been forced into some "peculiar friendships" to get any news about her.[16]

Yet such erotic relationships among middle-class girls couldn't exist free of imperatives to marry men. The popular romance novels of the day made romantic love between a man and a woman an adventure of its own, one that usually ended in marriage. Some romance novelists, like the hugely popular Marie Corelli, whose novels Margaret borrowed from the servants and read in secret, focused on sensationalized settings and themes. Corelli set her novels in science fantasy and exotic oriental locales, created a mood of fin de siècle decadence, and filled them with hermetic lore, pseudoscientific formulas, and a Romantic belief in the artist as savior of mankind. They contain a good deal of gender ambiguity, a dislike of militant women's rights advocates, and a focus on women's power over men through femininity. They also refer negatively to that "hermaphroditic production, a mannish woman."[17]

The romance novels that Margaret read influenced her both directly and subtly. When the Mead family lived on the farm in Bucks County, Margaret became best friends with a girl named Lillian, who lived on a nearby farm. For a time Margaret insisted that everyone call her "Stina," after Christina in Charlotte Yonge's *Dove in the Eagle's Nest*, a novel set in a castle in the Alps in fifteenth-century Austria.[18] A typical romance heroine, Christina resists a villainous noble before marrying the heroic male who rescues her; devoutly Christian, she influences the nobles by her example. Yonge's novel, like those of Corelli, suggests that femininity contains hidden power. Margaret was more bold at the age of twelve when a friend of her brother's tried "clumsily" to seduce her and she scared him off by using a stream of invectives she remembered from the scene in Sir Walter Scott's *Rebecca* in which the villain corners Rebecca in a castle tower and she curses him and threatens to throw herself off the parapet unless he leaves her alone.[19] Like many heroines of romance, Rebecca eventually marries the gentle man who rescues her.

The most important feature of the "cultural script" that guided girls away from female friendships and toward marriage, according to Mead, was the requirement that from early childhood they have a boyfriend. In fact, a standard episode in the day's literature for girls is the heroine's realization that she loves the boy who has been her comrade throughout her childhood. In Louisa May Alcott's *Little Women*— the most popular girls' novel of the age—Jo March comes too late to that realization about Laurie, her next-door neighbor, for he has decided to marry her sister. Lloyd Sherman, the Little Colonel, comes to it just in time, as her male childhood comrade prepares to leave her.

According to Mead, a girl didn't have to spend much time with her childhood boyfriend; what mattered was that she had one. In Hammonton, Margaret chose an Italian boy from the immigrant community her mother was studying because he made it easy by sending her a valentine one Valentine's Day. In high school her boyfriend was a boy who, although crippled by polio, was an accomplished piano player and the pitcher on the local baseball team. That relationship was more serious. The two of them, along with several other boy-girl couples, ate lunch together every day. Their loving behavior prompted one of the teachers to threaten to get a screen to shield herself from their "sticky sentimentality."[20]

In the nineteenth-century system of gender socialization, boyfriends coexisted with girlfriends in a balance that exists in a pale imitation today. Margaret might flirt with her high school boyfriend, but she had sleepovers with Sarah Slotter and received love notes from Marjorie Barber. Still, the emotional nexus between boyfriends and girlfriends is apparent in those notes, in which Marjorie alternates between expressing desire for Margaret and expressing desire for boys. At the same time that she calls Margaret "sweetheart" and "dearest" and expresses jealousy of "Lois," she complains that "Jack" isn't paying her any attention, although "Ted" seems interested, despite his annoyance when she gave "Hawley" a rose. She congratulates Margaret on her success with "Mr. Cressman's brother." Luther Cressman, to whom Margaret became engaged during her senior year in high school, was the brother of her math teacher. She met him when he was visiting his brother. He was a senior at Pennsylvania State University, four years older than she.

Before Luther appeared, Mead asserts, she had no sexual interest in boys. Indeed, in her draft chapter on childhood friendships, she distinguishes between child and adult desire. The first, according to Mead, is "sentimental" and "romantic"; the second is physical and insistent: Mead called it "passion." The argument draws from Freud's theory of a period of latent sexuality between childhood and adolescence—Mead saw latency as important to successful maturation.[21] Her high school boyfriend was a sentimental attachment, and other male confederates of hers were simply friends: in high school Julian Gardy was her chum, but he was Lillian's boyfriend, not hers. Together they founded afterschool clubs in which they held debates and played charades. When they were older, they played kissing games, such as post office and spin the platter. Yet those games weren't sexual, Mead contended, because they hadn't reached the age "when passion replaces romance." As if to emphasize her innocence, she stated that in high school she prayed for girls who smoked because she thought they would become prostitutes.[22]

Mead's contention that she felt only "romance" and not "passion" as an adolescent becomes more comprehensible in light of nineteenth-century definitions of sexuality, for the middle class in that age held spirituality to be even more important than sexuality in intimate relations. To the Victorians, true love required a sense of merging, an emotional "soul communion." It was a secularized religious ecstasy, a Romantic emotionalism validating the individual personality and disciplining it into marriage, a merger that was the ultimate sacrifice of self to guarantee self-worth. Sentimentality—eroticism sublimated through style—regulated passion's dangerous intensity. The spirituality and the sentimentality are evident in behavior that Mead engaged in with her high school boyfriend, behavior that influenced her in later life. Every night at eight o'clock, each of them went to an open window in their bedrooms, thought of the other, and whispered endearments. It didn't matter that they weren't together; the emotion was what counted.[23]

Mead stated that she derived this nightly ritual from two popular contemporary novels: *The Brushwood Boy*, by Rudyard Kipling, and *Peter Ibbetson*, by George Du Maurier. In each book the hero and heroine can't be together, but they meet in dreams. In *The Brushwood Boy* they wander over magical landscapes in their dreams; in *Peter Ibbetson* they attend the salons of avant-garde artists and social elites. In both novels, their dreams are more satisfying than reality. Mead contended that Kipling's formula in *The Brushwood Boy* for what he called "true" dreaming always worked when she used it: you lie on your back, put your hands behind your head, and imagine where you want to be. When you go to sleep, you will be there. Following that formula, she maintained, she had vivid and complex dreams that were like novels, with fulfilling plots.[24]

These two novels drew from the romantic convention that true love is as satisfying when lovers are apart as when they are together. That convention was a staple of the courtly love tradition, which endowed passionate love with mystical transcendence. The seventeenth-century metaphysical poet John Donne wrote in "Present in Absence" that "hearts of truest mettle" could find "affections ground / Beyond time, place, and all mortality." The Romantic poets of the early nineteenth century, devoted to passionate emotion, brought the appeal of separation into the modern era, and Emerson wrote in his essay on friendship: "Let the soul be assured that somewhere in the universe it should rejoin its friend, and it would be content and cheerful alone for a thousand years." The heartache and pleasure of yearning for a lost love was a theme in the mystical love poetry of two favorites of Mead's—Omar Khayyám and Rabindranath Tagore—who searched for God, always absent and always present, within the self. It was enshrined in grand opera and its "Liebestod" theme, the consummation of love through death as the ultimate expression of passion. Renowned lovers throughout history who died because of their love exemplified that theme: Antony and Cleopatra, Tristan and Isolde, Romeo and Juliet.[25]

In this view of love, imagined meetings could be as satisfying as actual ones. With *Peter Ibbetson* in mind, Margaret and her high school sweetheart expressed their "desire" every night through a communion of their souls. Yet that novel gave her more than just a recipe for romance; it showed that even though lovers were separated, they could remain connected through transcendent feelings. The message of the book, Mead wrote, was "one more thread in the bright tapestry of the belief that love could be eternal, and conquering all separations, either on earth or in heaven."[26] That idea would later become important in her relationship with Ruth Benedict.

Yet the sublimation Margaret practiced with her boyfriend doesn't necessarily mean that she wasn't engaging in "sex" with her female romantic friends. Havelock Ellis, the contemporary authority on sexual behavior, realized the ambiguity of childhood sexuality in this era when he wrote that when children of the same sex slept in the same bed they often "unintentionally" generated "sexual irritation" in each other—"which they fostered by touching and kissing." He defined "sexual irritation" as "pudential turgescence with secretion of mucus and involuntary twitching of the neighboring muscles": he seems to describe an orgasm. Yet he didn't think that this behavior was homosexual; he called it "the often precocious play of the normal instinct." He contended that most individuals become ashamed of it, easily forget it, and become heterosexual.[27]

However one defines the behavior that Ellis described, he suggests that children engaging in sex play had limited definitions into which to fit it. Emily Fogg Mead wrote in her memoir that she didn't regard her romantic friendships at Wellesley as "homosexual" because she didn't know that such an identity existed. It's possible that her daughter also didn't. In *Blackberry Winter* and its drafts Mead doesn't use the term "homosexual" to refer to her early romantic friendships with girls; it's only when she arrived at Barnard in the fall of 1920 that she introduces the term "homosexual" in connection with her female friendships—to claim that they weren't.

Did Mead engage in physical intimacy with her adolescent female romantic friends? Did she and Sarah Slotter do more than talk when they had sleepovers? In *Coming of Age in Samoa* she referred to "the casual homosexual practices which are the usual manifestations of associations between two young persons of the same sex." In *Sex and Temperament in Three Primitive Societies* she referred to the historical era when girls embraced each other, caressed each other's hair, arranged each other's clothing, and slept in the same bed, "comfortably and without embarrassment."[28] Those sources suggest that Mead's romantic friendships with girls were at the very least homoerotic in nature. Beyond that, however, the record is obscure.

WHY DID MARGARET become engaged to Luther Cressman? In a draft of her autobiography she maintained that it was her variation on the standard adolescent rebellion against the older, parental generation. Both her parents were freethinkers; her mother was a socialist. The only way she could rebel against them was by taking traditional stands. They were atheists; she became an Episcopalian. Her mother, an advocate of women's rights, avoided domesticity; she liked it. Her parents hadn't married until they were nearly thirty; she became engaged during her senior year in high school, despite their objections because she was only seventeen.[29] And the older Luther, a college man, was sophisticated in her eyes. One of six brothers, he liked women, and he liked to listen to them talk.[30] Resembling the gentle Laurie of *Little Women* and the boyfriend of the "Little Colonel," he was a larger-than-life character come into her life. Becoming engaged to him fulfilled her childhood dreams; he was, in fact, attractive to women.

Luther was the opposite of her masculine father, and he would father her well. He was also easily influenced. Margaret persuaded him to convert from Presbyterianism to Episcopalianism and to study for the ministry. And Luther gave her the security of having a fiancé while she conducted the rest of her life. Margaret liked to lead a dramatic, unconventional life, but she also liked to put it in order. Modeling herself after Miss Lucia and the minister's wife who was the protagonist of a number of sentimental novels by Charlotte Yonge, she had decided to marry a minister, have six children, and solve all the parish problems. She also persuaded Luther that they should wait to have full sexual relations until they married. Margaret's problem with him was that as she matured she outgrew him. In a draft of her autobiography she maintained that they had simply followed their culture's "script" for relationships when they became engaged, but she didn't include that judgment in the published version.[31]

One wonders, however, about the independence of someone so careful to follow the patterns her culture dictated—which was how Mead presented herself as a child and an adolescent in the draft chapters of *Blackberry Winter.* The argument implied that her bisexual sexual drive was a product of cultural expectations rather than an innate drive within herself. Mead didn't want to be considered abnormal. She wanted to be truly female—and truly American. In her draft chapter "Love and Friendship" she wrote that the path to marriage dictated by her society could result in beautiful weddings that met a girl's every expectation, although over time the marriage might end up in "encrusted" wedding photos of brides and grooms on bedside tables: the scene suggests failed sexuality. Besides, the commitment to monogamy that American society wanted could just as easily lead a woman to a woman as a partner as to a man. Thus she tied her nontraditional sexual orientation to a traditional source: the sentimental culture of nineteenth-century America. That was the culture of her Mead grandmother and of the poetry of James Whitcomb Riley and Henry Wadsworth Longfellow. According to this version of Mead's life, same-sex romantic friendships were as American as an apple for the teacher or a valentine for a best friend.[32]

Mead also implied in this analysis that the path to adult sexual identity could be rocky. What happened to the young woman who married but was confused by shifting her affections from a female to a male? What if she continued to desire women after she married? By the late nineteenth century, sexologists like Havelock Ellis exposed to public view the homoeroticism of the Victorian system of sexual socialization, and moral arbiters condemned romantic friendships between girls. Ellis viewed those friendships as a normal stage of life for girls on the road to heterosexual maturity—although their widespread existence at single-sex girls' schools gave him pause. Other cultural spokesmen didn't share his equanimity. Many now condemned such relationships as leading to homosexuality; some had done so since the 1870s, when Smith College was founded partly in reaction to the culture of smashing at Vassar.

Confused by their physical desire, caught in the transition between two sex systems—Victorian and modern—what should young women like Benedict and Mead do? How to resolve that dilemma concerned both of them for many years.

WITH REGARD TO Ruth Benedict and the culture of romantic friendships between girls, the record is much scantier than that for Margaret Mead. Neither "Story of My Life" nor her childhood diary mentions any search on her part for boyfriends, favorite teachers, or even best friends as she grew up—until she began attending St. Margaret's Episcopal School for Girls in 1903. Before then she immersed herself in books and fantasies. She kept aloof from other children, with her sister Margery her friend and antagonist. When she lived in Minnesota and attended Pillsbury Academy, however, she became close to a group of girls who were her classmates. According to Ruth's diary for 1897–1898, they formed clubs such as a "Sunshine Sewing Society," and they played the game of house, a perennial favorite among girls, in which they cooked, cleaned, and cared for their dolls as babies. (In her draft chapter "Love and Friendship" for *Blackberry Winter,* Mead identified the game of house as a key ritual socializing girls to marriage and motherhood.) In those games, Ruth took on the role of the mother.[33] By the age of eleven she had reached her full adult height of five feet eight inches. She must have towered over her friends, with her height giving her a special authority.

In Ruth's diary and in "The Story of My Life" she noted the books she read—some the same books that Mead read in the 1910s. They included Sir Walter Scott's *Lady of the Lake* and his *Ivanhoe*; Louisa May Alcott's *Eight Cousins*; and *St. Nicholas*, the children's magazine that Mead later read. Throughout her childhood Ruth read the Bible; her favorite Bible story was the story of Ruth, her namesake. The literature that Benedict read supports Mead's hypothesis that cultural representations led girls to form romantic friendships with other girls and then to marry.

Scott's *Lady of the Lake*, an epic poem set in the Highlands of Scotland, involves violent clans battling each other. A brutal man threatens the heroine and a gentler one rescues her. Alternately glorifying and condemning male violence, *Lady of the Lake* locates a woman's freedom in holding out for the right husband. Louisa May Alcott in *Eight Cousins* finds society's main problem in class divisions and greed; her heroine rejects wealthy suitors to marry a virtuous man. Alcott criticizes romantic friendships between girls, identifying them with the self-indulgent newly rich of the Gilded Age. When the fashionable Miss Bliss offers herself as a "bosom friend" to the heroine, the heroine replies that she doesn't want one.[34]

The story of Ruth, Benedict's favorite Bible story, deemphasizes the romance plot to focus on a relationship between two women, Ruth and her mother-in-law, Naomi. The death of Ruth's husband has left the two women paupers. Burdened with an older woman, Ruth may lose any chance for remarriage and financial security, but she refuses to abandon Naomi. She speaks the famous words of devotion to her, not to Boas, the landowner she marries: "Wither thou goest, I will go and where thou lodgest, I will lodge: thy people shall be my people, and thy God my God." The story of Ruth and Naomi was the major historical example to Victorian women of a devoted friendship between women; more recently it has been claimed as a founding text of the lesbian literary tradition.[35]

In 1903 Ruth and Margery entered St. Margaret's, an elite school for girls. Located in a refurbished mansion in the elite residential section of Buffalo, it was small, with five teachers and a hundred students.[36] One of those students was Mabel Ganson, a year ahead of Ruth. As the married Mabel Dodge, she would become famous for her pre–World War I salon in Greenwich Village; remarried in the 1920s and known as Mabel Dodge Luhan, she would establish a famed artist's community in Taos, New Mexico. Possessing great flair, Mabel stood out even in high school. Ruth and Mabel weren't close, but Ruth was friends with a girl whose older sister was Mabel's friend. Ruth sensed that Mabel, like herself, was different: "I remember knowing that she lived for something I recognized, something different from those things for which most people around me lived."[37]

What did Mabel live for? According to her biographer, she was then devoted to "beauty." Oscar Wilde's visit to Buffalo in 1882 had inspired a continuing vogue for aestheticism in the city, and Mabel embraced it. She took private art lessons from the art teacher at St. Margaret's, a painter named Miss Clark, who wore "artistic neckties of soft silk," lived for "intense experience," and constantly looked for "beauty."[38] Miss Clark gave drawing and painting classes to all the students at St. Margaret's one afternoon a week. Ruth would have been in one of her classes.

In her autobiography, Luhan describes St. Margaret's. Small and intimate, the school had "close, overwarm rooms." Several faculty members were alluring. Every morning Miss Tuck, the school's "mysterious" headmistress, delivered a moral homily to the students, with "underlying wicked enchantment." Mabel fell in love with Miss Moore, the English teacher: "My thoughts went to her constantly and I memorized her, the tones in her dusky rolls of hair and the look in her eyes." The other students called Mabel's feelings about Miss Moore a "crush."[39]

Mabel was also romantically involved with a girl who lived near her and who allowed Mabel to fondle her breasts. We don't know if Ruth engaged in such behavior, although her brief remarks about St. Margaret's in "The Story of My Life" indicate that she was aware of the culture of smashing there. She writes that the "youngest Becker daughter" was "one of the first of those people to be romantically devoted to me." The youngest Becker daughter may have been Ruth's friend who was the sister of Mabel's friend. There is also Ruth's statement that Mabel "lived for something I recognized, something different from those things for which most people around me lived."[40] The statement may indicate a dawning appreciation of the aestheticism that Mabel espoused, but it also sounds like someone becoming aware of an alternate sexual identity.

In her English class during her senior year at St. Margaret's, Ruth wrote a paper on Longfellow's long epic poem *Evangeline*, a favorite text for high school English classes in that era. In her paper, Ruth rewrote the poem as a narrative in her own words.[41] *Evangeline* deals with the resettlement of the Acadians, the French population of Nova

Scotia, throughout the British colonies during the French and Indian War. Evangeline, an Acadian woman, searches for her fiancé, Gabriel, after they are separated during the resettlement. For years she travels the North American continent looking for him, eventually winding up in Philadelphia as a charity worker among the poor. In making her rounds, she stumbles across him, destitute and dying from yellow fever. He dies in her arms.[42]

There is a striking episode of female bonding in Longfellow's poem. Traveling on the far reaches of the frontier, Evangeline meets a Shawnee woman near the Ozark Mountains. Longfellow portrays this native woman, to whom Evangeline is attracted, as dangerous to her quest for Gabriel: she is a "Circe" and a "snake." Evangeline quickly leaves her to continue on her quest.[43] In Ruth's version, however, the episode with the Shawnee woman is the key to the story. She titles that section of her narrative "A Blessed Incident," for the two women become close when they realize that each has lost a lover and that the men may have deserted them. They spend a night talking; they reach a state of spiritual love, in which "all things seemed transitory, passing— love, sorrow, fear—and we had outgrown all!" Ruth's Evangeline doesn't go to Philadelphia and become a charity worker. Her quest ends with the Shawnee woman.

In a poem Benedict later wrote—and dedicated to Mead—she called herself "this Gabriel." The name referred to the archangel Gabriel who is God's special messenger and to the Gabriel for whom Evangeline searched. In finding Mead, Benedict found her soul mate: the Shawnee woman episode in her "Evangeline" suggests that her life partner might be female, not male. And "Evangeline" was one of Ruth's early stories that she kept. That indicated, according to Mead, that it was important to "themes of her early experience."[44] The theme that it elucidates, of course, concerns romantic friendships with girls. And like the Sibyls of Greek legend, the Shawnee woman was connected to nature and to ancient traditions of prophetic women. In a sense, Ruth's meeting with the Shawnee woman was prophetic of her future. For she later studied the Plains Indians, a grouping that included the Shawnees; as an anthropologist she specialized in the Indians of the Southwest and of the Plains.

When Ruth entered Vassar in 1905, the college was flourishing. To recover from the doldrums of Bertrice Shattuck's day, the administration had constructed new buildings, modernized the curriculum, hired well-trained faculty, and combined traditionalism with change. Woman suffrage activities were still forbidden on campus and attendance at chapel was required, but the college had achieved a reputation for outstanding teaching and for student involvement in progressive reform. When Ruth was at Vassar, over 50 percent of the student body belonged to the Vassar branch of the College Settlement Association, a coalition formed by the Eastern women's colleges to support settlement houses. Under Vassar's new pragmatism, romantic friendships flourished.[45]

Besides, the faculty was embattled over gender. Female professors, three-quarters of the faculty, were angry that men chaired many of the departments. The faculty men were angry that the several women who chaired departments refused to hire men. Two of those women, Laura Johnson Wylie in English and Lucy Maynard Salmon in history, lived with female partners in Poughkeepsie. Wylie's partner, Gertrude Buck, who was younger than she, was the only other full professor in the English department; they were so close that they considered adopting a child. Both Wylie and Buck, along with Lucy Salmon, participated in women's reform and suffrage activities in Poughkeepsie. The third female professor who chaired a department, Laura Washburn in psychology, lived with her mother and never married. Believing so strongly in women's equality with men that she refused to join separate women's organizations, she was renowned for having demanded entry into a men's smoker at a psychology convention and, once inside, lighting up a cigar.[46]

Ruth Fulton majored in English; Wylie and Buck were teachers of hers. Wylie, a specialist in English literature, was the first woman to receive a Ph.D. in English from Yale, and Yale published her dissertation. Buck, with a Ph.D. from the University of Michigan, specialized in drama and the theater. Wylie and Buck were known for their "democratic" or "social" theory of reading, which they developed separately and together. In it they implicitly challenged male critics of their day who, influenced by the male heroic tradition in that era of imperialism, found "great" male authors to extol. In contrast, Wylie and Buck viewed readers as the real critics. They challenged readers to become more adept by exploring the historical, social, and biographical milieus behind texts and their authors. They preferred texts that increased social awareness, and they liked authors like Shelley and Whitman who extolled the common man and progressive social change. Buck even took the populist position that any book had value, so long as it influenced readers.[47]

Wylie and Buck weren't militant feminists. They didn't assign women's rights texts in their courses. In analyzing the writing of George Eliot, Wylie mentioned neither Eliot's gender nor any feminist themes in her work: Wylie's focus was on humanity, not women. As progressive reformers, Wylie and Buck upheld the romantic organicism of the day that exalted nature, the common man, and solidarity between social classes. They saw democratic education and leadership by elite reformers as the way to effect social change. Such a point of view was popular among liberal intellectuals and reformers like Jane Addams and John Dewey; Buck had studied with Dewey at the University of Michigan. That point of view would influence Benedict's—and Mead's—mature thought.[48]

Wylie and Buck taught Ruth how to write a critical essay by combining philosophical detachment with poetic intuition in an informal, ironic style. They also taught her the importance of imagination in any intellectual project. Nietzsche and Santayana, favorite authors of Ruth's, also made that point, which dates back to Romantics like Coleridge and Shelley. Dorothy Lee, an anthropologist trained by Benedict who taught at Vassar, contended that Wylie and Buck's reading of texts in terms of their cultural backgrounds was crucial to Benedict's mature theory that culture shapes individuals. Their work also prefigured the later reader-response school of literary criticism. A direct link from them to that school existed through Louise Rosenblatt, Mead's roommate at Barnard College, who became a professor of literature at Brooklyn College and one of the creators of reader-response theory, and who did graduate work with Benedict at Columbia in the late 1920s.[49]

A number of Ruth's essays were published in the *Vassar Miscellany*, the college literary magazine. Several criticized Wylie and Buck's "democratic" theory of reading, without mentioning it by name. Approving Matthew Arnold's distinction between "high" and "low" art, Ruth praised the complexity of Chaucer, while criticizing the sentimentality of popular romance writer Mary J. Holmes.[50] Other essays of hers dealt with the struggle of individuals touched by insanity to achieve self-control—a topic with resonance in her own life. In an essay on the Fool in Shakespeare's *King Lear*, she interpreted the character as the rational part of Lear's self who tries to force the mentally troubled king to face reality, although the Fool himself is flawed because he has stifled his emotions. In an essay on the English essayist

Charles Lamb, a chronic depressive whose sister in a manic fit stabbed their mother to death, Ruth concluded that Lamb coped with the horrors in his life by concentrating on nature and friendships and writing his narratives of Shakespeare's plays for children.

Ruth also wrote an essay on Euripides' *The Trojan Women*. In that play, the imprisoned Trojan women mourn the deaths of their husbands and sons in the Trojan War and await their fates as slaves and concubines to the victorious Greeks. Ruth focused on the daughter of the defeated king of Troy, the visionary Cassandra, whom men have treated brutally. Because she rejected Apollo's sexual advances, the god decreed that she would make prophecies that no one would believe. The Greek warrior Ajax has raped her; King Agamemnon of Mycenae has chosen her as his concubine. She has gone insane. In her mad scene she sings, in Ruth's words, "the marriage song of her shame" with "inspired abandon."[51]

Drawing on Nietzsche, Benedict concluded that personal salvation lies in suffering, for the experience of pain has a "splendor and beauty" that can inspire self-understanding. Many Western male heroes—Dionysus, Odysseus, even Christ—went to hell and lived through it. They fought their dragons and won, strengthened by the experience. A woman has to find a similar path. Singing with an "inspired abandon," Cassandra combines the inspiration of intuition with the emotion of letting go in what Ruth calls the "terrible unity" that is Euripides' solution to the suffering of the Trojan women. Ten years later, in "The Bo-Cu Plant"—a mystery/horror story about suffering and death that she wrote during World War I—Ruth's heroine fights back against masculine power through murderous rage; in her "Mary Wollstonecraft," Wollstonecraft reacts to her father's abuse of her as a child by re-creating herself as a revolutionary. Eventually, however, Ruth returned to the heroic martyr theme, with success in life a matter of self-control and acceptance of one's fate.

In an essay on Walt Whitman, Ruth praised his self-reliant individuals, who have "manly and courageous instincts" along with "loving perceptions." Whitman celebrated an athletic masculinity, but he also praised gender crossing. Ruth applauded lines of his that blend male and female:

> *Curious what is more subtle*
> *Than this which ties me to the man or woman that*
> *looks in my face,*

Which fuses me into you now, and pours my meaning into
    you.[52]

What about Whitman's homosexuality? In her essay Ruth seems
enthusiastic about it at first. She praises Whitman for including in his
poetry everything that fostered a "deep and essential beauty," including "physical nature in all its manifestations and functions." Then she
equivocates, attributing his writing about "physical nature" to "the
excesses of an intoxication of enthusiasm." In other words, he was too
explicit about sex. "He did not see," she asserts, "that their very poetry
may lie in our instinct of secrecy regarding them." She derived that
idea from Aestheticist writers like Walter Pater, who viewed "concealment" as producing a richer art by introducing ambiguity.[53] It also
reflected Ruth's internalizing her culture's prohibitions about sex to
the point that she regarded concealing her sexuality as instinctive. She
already wore a "mask" before the world.

The point about concealment also reflected Ruth's struggle to
understand Symbolist poetry. Symbolists like Yeats envisioned a world
beyond the visible world, accessible through intuition. Ruth praised
Symbolism, calling it a modernism that preserved "the sane, healthy,
half revelation, half concealment whose essentials are reverence and
the sense of unity." Spirituality was disappearing in modern society.
Symbolism was a "reverential search after the highest truth, an
acknowledgment of the broad unity of things";[54] it drew on the Christian mysticism familiar to her. Using allusion and metaphor, Symbolist
poets broke reality apart, challenging the realist emphasis on the visible world.[55]

In addition to the Symbolists, Ruth read Santayana and Nietzsche.
Santayana was a rationalist, cool and detached. He praised imagination
and intuition, but he stressed mental discipline. Nietzsche opted for
more emotionality.[56] Ruth admired Nietzsche, as did many contemporary feminists, for his bold attacks on middle-class morality and his call
for the self-realized individual, the *Übermensch*, or overman. With
regard to women, Nietzsche defined nature and intuition as female,
drawing on the feminization of abstract qualities in Western imagery
to counter the misogyny of his statements like that advising men to
tame women with a whip. And Nietzsche, like Whitman, celebrated
friendship: "The friend should be the festival of the earth to you and
an anticipation of the overman," he wrote. "I teach you the friend in
whom the world stands completed, a bowl of goodness." When Mead

went to Samoa, Benedict sent her a copy of Nietzsche's *Thus Spake Zarathustra*, to celebrate their friendship and to firm up her resolve.[57]

During her college years Ruth also read the Aestheticist writers Algernon Swinburne, Walter Pater, and John Addington Symonds, major figures in the Platonic revival of the late nineteenth century that rediscovered Plato's dialogues—and their emphasis on same-sex love. In her freshman year, Ruth read Pater's famous conclusion to *The Renaissance*, and it affected her deeply, as it did many writers of her generation. For Ruth, as for the others, the important passage was the one about living for transformative moments that concluded: "To burn with a hard, gemlike flame, to maintain this ecstasy, is success in life." Both Santayana and Nietzsche advised living for the moment, but Pater illuminated the concept with the metaphor of flames and burning, elemental images of creativity and destruction which suggested that only a revolution against convention could produce individual transformation. They echoed the flame of homosexual love in Plato's *Symposium;* they validated Blake's and Nietzsche's briefs for "perverse" experience; they foreshadowed Edna St. Vincent Millay's candle burning at both ends, which became the watchword of Mead's generation of the 1920s.[58]

Using her own words for transformation, Ruth wrote that Pater's lines gave her soul back to her.[59] They allowed her to think of becoming a poet; they offered spiritual illumination in a secular path. They opened up to her the Aestheticist thinkers and their belief that freedom lay in forbidden behavior. They allowed her to conceive of crossing over her gender to take on a male persona. Pater's "gemlike flame" referred to alchemy's fire and its philosopher's stone, major artifacts of the European mystical tradition, that could change base metals into gold—as well as transforming everything into its opposite.[60]

Yet Pater's "gemlike" flame was hard, not soft. In his writings Nietzsche praised virility, the warrior virtue. Drawing on the standard belief that women possess intuition and not reason, Santayana wrote in *The Life of Reason* that "there is something mysterious and oracular about a woman's mind which inspires a certain instinctive deference and puts it out of the question to judge what she says by masculine standards. She has a kind of sibylline intuition."[61] Ruth read *The Life of Reason* in college. Given Santayana's dismissal of women as philosophers, the logical position for her to take was to assume a male persona, to counter men by joining them. How could she be a real philosopher otherwise? As Margaret Mead later wrote: "Where 'logic' is regarded as male, and 'intuition' as female, little girls with a capacity for logical thought may be pushed toward inversion [homosexuality] as a preference."[62] These issues of gender and sexuality raised by the poets and philosophers that Ruth read take on additional meaning when viewed in the context of the culture of smashing at Vassar.

In 1905, when Ruth Fulton entered Vassar, the culture of romantic friendships was as strong as in her mother's day. Freshmen were initiated into it through a reception given by the sophomores to which each sophomore invited a freshman "date," then sent her flowers, called for her in the evening, and at the dance "filled her dance card like the most devoted swain."[63] This mirroring of heterosexual behavior reached an apogee when the classes of 1903 and 1904 held a "wedding ceremony" to celebrate their closeness. In her 1905 survey of Vassar social life, Mary Crawford wrote that after spring vacation the Vassar "mutual admiration of sorority" was at its height, as "every night between dinner and chapel the seniors withdraw to the steps of Rockefeller Hall and sing their class song, with the sophomores below to adore them."[64]

The spring celebration of friendship continued with May Day, when students picked flowers and arranged them in baskets to place outside the doors of special friends. It culminated in the Daisy Chain at graduation, when twenty sophomores chosen by the seniors carried a large chain of daisies woven by the sophomore class. "Adoring" sophomores invented the ritual in the 1890s to honor the seniors. "There was a danger in women's colleges," wrote Julia Schwartz in *Vassar Studies*, of a student developing "an abnormal devotion to her own sex."[65]

By the time Ruth graduated in 1909, the prophecy in the yearbook for each graduate, made by a class Sibyl in her mother's day, had been shortened to a description of the graduate in one or two lines. Ruth was literary editor of the yearbook; she probably wrote many of the descriptions and edited the rest. In about one-third the graduate is characterized as masculine. Katherine McMartin is "a man, without fantasticalities"; Donalda Cameron Rise is "a fiery man, very proud and positive." Margery Fulton, on the other hand, is defined in female terms as "Clearly a Superior Woman." Ruth's characterization is different. She is "A salad: for in him we see / Oil, vinegar, pepper and saltness agree." Ruth Fulton at Vassar wasn't sweet and feminine; she crossed over gender lines to become both salt and pepper. "Salad," derived from Elizabethan usage, referred to the freshness of youth.[66] Such use of words and symbols with multiple meanings seems to fore-shadow Ruth's later poetry and suggests that she wrote this description herself.

Putting on plays was a favorite activity at the women's colleges, and Vassar was known for its productions. A student organization, Phi-laletheis, oversaw them, and both Ruth and Margery belonged to it. Shakespeare's comedies were a staple; in Ruth's junior year *As You Like It* was produced and in her senior year *Much Ado About Nothing*. Margery was on the crew for both plays. Gender crossing is a major issue in these plays, as their female protagonists take on masculine characteristics for a time. Beatrice of *Much Ado* at first refuses to marry; she "fathers herself" and wishes that she were a man. Rosalind in *As You Like It* avoids an arranged marriage by escaping into the forest, Shakespeare's space free from social convention. But the forest can be dangerous. Fearing rape, Rosalind puts on male clothing. As a man she is called Ganymede, the name of the young man in classical mythology who was Zeus's first homosexual partner and in Shakespeare's day the name for boys who were passive partners in sex with adult men.[67]

Beatrice and Rosalind are coupled with Benedick and Orlando. Once the men fall in love, they are feminized. Benedick shaves his beard, puts on perfume, and paints his face. Once Orlando sees Ros-alind, he loses any sense of being male, becoming "a quintain, a mere lifeless block.[68] Both plays end with the marriage of their male and female protagonists, who return to their regular gender. Before that resolution, however, Shakespeare suggests that each gender possesses elements of the other.

In the Vassar production of *Much Ado*, Inez Milholland played Benedick. (Milholland is famed in women's history for having dis-obeyed the prohibition against woman suffrage meetings at Vassar by holding one in a graveyard and for riding a white horse at the head of a woman suffrage parade in Washington, D.C., in 1913.) In the gradua-tion yearbook she is captioned as "fascinating—but a trifle dangerous for household use." In playing Benedick she wore male clothing, for by Ruth's day the prohibition against wearing trousers in plays had been ended, and she underwent the new and "elaborate coaching in the matter of using legs suddenly liberated," learning to walk across the stage with bold male movements and to sit with her knees "well apart."[69]

After Ruth graduated, she wrote a letter of appreciation to Shakespeare professor Florence Keys, to whom her class dedicated its senior yearbook. In her salutation, she addressed Keys as "My Dear," indicating some affection between them. After the salutation Ruth wrote: "I wonder how unprepared you are for that heading in a letter of mine?" In other words, she thought that Keys liked her but she didn't know how much. The body of the letter, extolling Keys's teaching, replicates the tribute in the yearbook and suggests that Ruth wrote both.[70]

Wanda Neff's novel *We Sing Diana* (1928) contains a description of the culture of smashing at Vassar in the 1900s. In the novel a student who is repulsed by its homoeroticism describes how it functions. Students develop crushes on teachers and on one another. So many freshmen adore Miss Godwin, an English teacher who is a "mannish" lesbian wearing "strictly tailored clothes, and mannish felt hats, shoes, and ties," that she is called the "Freshman Disease." When a student develops a crush on the narrator of the novel and suggests that they engage in physical intimacy, she is horrified. Yet she can't escape the culture of smashing. She takes a walk in the countryside, and she overhears two girls talking passionately to each other. She watches them lying in a field, passionately kissing; she realizes that they are the star literature student and the star science student at the school.[71]

Neff set her novel at Vassar in the 1910s, when the college culture of smashing was still strong there. However, Louise Rosenblatt, Margaret Mead's college roommate at Barnard, asserted that Neff based its central characters on Mead and her friends at Barnard in the early 1920s. Neff was an instructor in the English department when they were students there; she was also a faculty advisor in the apartment building in which they lived. She spied on them. She was certain they were lesbians, and she hated lesbians. They discovered to their dismay that she was writing a novel about them. Rosenblatt ended her narrative at that point, except for an assertion that they weren't lesbian.[72]

The issues of women's rights and race were also important at Vassar when Benedict was there. The writings of Charlotte Perkins Gilman, the major women's rights theorist of the day, were popular: Inez Milholland introduced Gilman's *Women and Economics* to the campus, and it became the "Bible" of the students. Gilman was present at the woman suffrage meeting in the graveyard; Margery and Ruth were probably there, too.[73] In *Women and Economics* Gilman maintained that to become independent, women needed to work for pay outside the home, while she criticized men for their aggressiveness, both in sexual relations and in war. An evolutionary optimist, she anticipated an egalitarian future. Yet she excoriated "perversions," calling them "lower forms" and "erratic phases" on the evolutionary progress to monogamous marriage.[74]

The question of race became significant to Ruth Fulton in her senior year when Booker T. Washington came to speak on campus and students from the South protested when a group of Northern students had lunch with him. Reacting to that incident, Benedict wrote a paper, "Racial Types in Shakespeare's Plays." By "racial types" she meant nationalities as well as races, following the standard usage of the day. In her paper Ruth praised Shakespeare for using "racial types" to heighten the drama of his plays, not to illustrate the superiority of one race over another. Discussing Othello, she challenged the view that his "Moorish passion of jealousy" was like that of primitive "savages," not modern men. In her view it was stronger than that of the "colder northern races," but it was the same emotion. What amounted in her day to a progressive attitude about race foreshadowed her later views on the subject.[75]

By the time Ruth graduated from Vassar she seemed to have her depressions under control. She had participated in many activities in college: she was class vice president during freshman year; in subsequent years she chaired the Bible study group, belonged to literary clubs, and was literary editor of the senior yearbook. Along with Margery she was elected to Phi Beta Kappa; both sisters spoke at graduation. Soon after that event, Margery married a Presbyterian minister, moved to a parish in Pasadena, California, with him, and soon had several babies. Ruth put off finding a husband while she spent the year after graduation touring Europe with two classmates and a chaperon; the wealthy father of one of her companions paid her way. After returning from Europe she went back to Buffalo to become a visitor for the city's charitable society, a forerunner to a modern social work agency. Yet a few years later, she confronted directly the imperative of her culture that she marry and have children.

ONE CAN PARTLY IDENTIFY Benedict's views about gender as a young adult in the papers she wrote in her courses at Vassar. One can do the same for Mead from drafts of *Blackberry Winter*, although her detailed story of the development of her sexual identity stops at the point when she became engaged to Luther Cressman. In a draft chapter Mead states that she learned about prostitution, rape, and venereal disease from conversations among her elders at home, about illegitimacy from Dickens's *Bleak House*, and about abortion from a short story in a magazine. Her last reference in her writings to her early reading about sexuality concerns *The Affairs of Anatol*, a series of dialogues written by Viennese author Arthur Schnitzler. Mead asserted that the book shocked her.[76] Indeed, to a young woman who prayed for female classmates who smoked, fearing they might become prostitutes, Schnitzler's portrayals of a hedonistic bachelor who seduces and abandons women, of women who are sensual and uncommitted, and of prostitutes who are real people with ambitions and desires must have been shocking—and informative.

How did Mead learn about homosexuality? She later stated that anyone who read Greek and Latin texts in school couldn't miss the homosexuality in them. She also stated that her liberal views about sex came partly from French writers.[77] She may have read Théophile Gautier's *Mademoiselle de Maupin* (1835), a novel about gender crossing that circulated secretly among college women in these years and that influenced writer Willa Cather and Bryn Mawr president M. Carey Thomas, both lesbian in orientation. The characters in Gautier's novel are sexually ambiguous, and some turn out to be the opposite gender from what they first seem to be. The heroine dresses as a man to go to male places like taverns and find out what men really think of women when they are alone together. The novel ends with a production of Shakespeare's *As You Like It* in which the female protagonist of the novel, dressed as a man, cross-dresses as a woman to play Rosalind—and then cross-dresses as a man for the scenes in the forest.[78]

Did Benedict and Mead read the sexologists? Their writings were the obvious source in this era from which to learn about homosexuality. There were many of them—doctors, scientists, and self-appointed experts in Europe and the United States who from the 1870s on attempted to define human sexuality and sexual identity. In the process they named the categories of "homosexual," "hermaphrodite," "transvestite," "invert," and "bisexual." Moral censors tried to confine the circulation of their writings to doctors, but the many published editions of their works in the United States indicate a large underground market. Havelock Ellis's *Sexual Inversion*, the best-known writing in the genre, was published in 1901 in Philadelphia after it was banned in England—and vice agents in the United States didn't seize it. Mead later noted that she read Havelock Ellis—as did Benedict. *Sexual Inversion* was the first volume he wrote of his *Studies in the Psychology of*

Sex, a compendium of all the expert opinion on the subject of sexuality that Ellis could find. In *Sexual Inversion*, itself an encyclopedic work, Ellis discusses the ideas of the other sexologists on homosexuality, providing an introduction to all of them.[79]

Ellis lists the classic homosexual literature, including *Mademoiselle de Maupin*. He notes the same-sex relationships of ancient Greece and the same-sex orientation of Michelangelo. He reprints the famous letter Walt Whitman wrote John Addington Symonds denying his homosexuality, and he asserts that, like Symonds, he doesn't believe Whitman. He reports that many men and women of high intellectual and artistic achievement have been homosexual. Yet the debate he details is confusing. The traditional view was that homosexuality meant passive behavior in the male sex act, as in Ganymede submitting to Zeus. That view lay behind the sodomy laws, which criminalized sex acts, not identities, and which had been on the books in every state since the colonial period, often including in their provisions prohibitions on bestiality and oral sex as well as anal intercourse. Karoly Maria Benkert (pseudonym Kertbeny) however, coined the term "homosexuality" in 1869 and defined it as an identity in which an individual desires members of his or her own sex. But what was that identity? Was it innate in humans or acquired through cultural experience?

Many sexologists, following German neuropsychiatrist Richard von Krafft-Ebing, catalogued homosexuality as a dangerous perversion produced by evolutionary degeneration. Havelock Ellis disagreed, viewing it as a genetic anomaly, like being color-blind. Still others, like Magnus Hirschfeld, were influenced by the day's scientific discoveries that the fetus initially isn't gendered and that a number of primitive organisms are hermaphrodites to conclude that each gender possesses attributes of the other and that humans may be "bisexual" in sexual orientation at birth. Hirschfeld, himself homosexual, was a leader of the homosexual rights movement in Germany and a doctor in Berlin who founded the world's first sex clinic, where he counseled both homosexuals and heterosexuals, dispensed birth control, assembled one of the world's largest collections of material on sexuality, and, by the 1920s, did sex change operations. Hitler closed his clinic and destroyed his records in 1933. Hirschfeld reached the radical conclusion that human genitalia, anatomy, and psychology are so mixed up in individuals that no two people are alike in their sexual identity. In his clinic, he reported, he encountered heterosexual women who preferred homosexual men as partners and homosexual men who preferred heterosexual women.[80]

In the writings of even the radical sexologists, however, bisexuality was an ambiguous concept. It could refer to individuals who were attracted to both sexes or to individuals who united both sexes within themselves, in what some sexologists called a "third sex." This idea of homosexuals as a different order of beings from heterosexuals persisted from the time that Karl Heinrich Ulrichs first advanced it in the 1870s, when he defined same-sex-oriented individuals as possessing different "souls" (internal selves) from heterosexuals—souls that were masculine in the case of women and feminine in the case of men. Most sexologists agreed that homosexuality involved an internal gender crossing, which many called "inversion." This crossover raised the possibility that any male who exhibited feminine characteristics or any female who exhibited masculine ones was on the road to becoming homosexual. Such distinctions reinforced the notion of a division between male and female that was fundamental to mainstream thought.

The most complex thinker among the sexologists was Sigmund Freud. Drawing a distinction between sexual aim as a diffuse drive and sexual object as a specific one, he cut loose from the distinction between homosexuality and heterosexuality as innate predispositions, proposing that humans were born with a diffuse sexual drive—he called it "polymorphous perversity." Although true maturity, in his view, involved making a transition to heterosexuality, the diffuse drive could persist throughout life, go into a remission that was temporary, or constitute an episode on the way to heterosexuality. It might reappear late in life. It could fluctuate between a heterosexual object and a homosexual one. However, echoing the standard belief, Freud wrote that "character-inversion" was a regular feature of the constitution of women oriented to their own gender, although that wasn't the case among homosexual men.[81]

Sexologist Edward Carpenter was an English writer—and homosexual—widely read in the United States. He asserted that most sexologists considered inversion central to homosexuality. "The only theory which has at all held its ground in this matter [the definition of sexual identity]," he wrote, "is that in cases of sex inversion, there is a mixture of male and female." His "mixture" in the case of women involved a definite persona, in which the female invert had "emotions along mas-

culine lines and the outer body feminine."[82] Although Carpenter
maintained that homosexual men were superior beings because they
combined the genders, he didn't like assertive homosexual women.
Thus he participated in constructing the "mannish lesbian."

Further confusing a complex debate, the sexologists avoided the
term "lesbian" because of its imprecise usage: among female homosexuals it sometimes meant all lesbians and sometimes the partner who
took the active role in sex.[83] Moreover, the sexologists didn't use the
word "gender" as we do today, to identify the social self in distinction
to the biological self. Rather, they used the term "sex" to mean both.
Thus they conflated the social with the biological, ratifying the belief
that "male" and "female" were bedrock identities, breached at the risk
of bringing on inversion. Finally, the endocrinologists, who by the
1900s had discovered the sex hormones, maintained that only men
produced male hormones and women female ones. Thus they provided additional support for separating male from female and regarding homosexuals as inverts.[84]

In mainstream culture, the attitude toward homosexuality in this
age of gender conflict wasn't positive. Most doctors in the United
States, for example, based their thinking about homosexuality on the
most negative passages in Krafft-Ebing and Ellis about evolutionary
degeneracy causing the orientation. Describing the prevailing negativity about homosexuality, Margaret Mead pointed to the sodomy laws
and to the ban against receiving homosexuals in respectable society.
She remembered a constant stream of covert jokes and phrases when
she was young calling homosexuals unreliable and depicting them as
"forgers, thieves, embezzlers, cowards, traitors, turncoats." She noted
the negative impact of the 1895 trial of Oscar Wilde, in which Wilde,
famous in the United States through his lecture tours, was revealed as
having engaged in sex with young male prostitutes. After that, she
maintained, male homosexuals in the United States were often called
"Oscar Wildes."[85]

An additional point needs to be highlighted. Hirschfeld, Freud, and
Ellis all concluded that human sexuality is fluid at birth and that
humans don't acquire a precise sexual identity until adolescence, until
their bodies develop secondary sexual characteristics—breasts, pubic
hair, beards, the full-grown genitalia. At that point, they agreed, the
awakening sex urges are often directed toward one's own sex. When
the transition to heterosexuality takes place in subsequent years, the
other impulse remains latent, though easily brought to the surface,

where it can become dominant. But the process could be confusing. According to Hirschfeld, "The diagnosis of homosexuality is not at all easy. Some people think they are homosexuals without being so. More frequently people think they aren't homosexual when they are. Even in the case of educated homosexuals, self-awareness often begins only in their mid-twenties, after reading educational material."[86] Both Hirschfeld and Ellis agreed that the only way individuals could be certain they were homosexual was if they had a complete aversion to sex relations with the opposite sex. Otherwise, they stood in-between.

In order to understand Benedict's and Mead's journeys to self-understanding, it is important to keep in mind the opinions of the experts of their day about sexual identity. Evidence from the two women's letters and their writings indicates that they were familiar with this body of knowledge, confusing as it was. They also read poets, philosophers, anthropologists—and feminists—who had opinions on these issues. They had to put these varying points of view together with their own feelings and experiences. The process of doing so would occupy them for many years—until each indicated her solution in the mid-1930s in the masterpiece she wrote: Ruth Benedict in *Patterns of Culture* and Margaret Mead in *Sex and Temperament in Three Primitive Societies*.

CHAPTER 5

"*Mary Wollstonecraft*"

Ruth Benedict and Early Twentieth-Century Feminism

URING THE YEAR that Ruth Benedict toured Europe after graduating from Vassar in 1909, her mood was upbeat. In her letter to Florence Keys, her Shakespeare teacher—which she wrote from Italy that fall—she referred to her own "youthful, unquenchable optimistic spirit." On viewing the Swiss Alps bathed in "sunset magic," she had a Pateresque experience of the ecstasy of a transformative moment of time. "That hour," she wrote, "is mine forever."[1] She and her companions, along with their chaperon, lived with families in Italy, Germany, and Switzerland, and she liked the experience. By the end of the trip, however, as she faced returning home, she became depressed. Reaching London, she went to the National Portrait Gallery to find portraits of women "who had saved their souls alive." She found such a woman in a painting of Mary Wollstonecraft, the late-eighteenth-century English writer, already renowned as the first modern feminist.[2]

Ruth never forgot the woman in that painting, with her "sad" but "steady" brown eyes and the "gallant poise of her head."[3] The memory of Wollstonecraft sustained her during the next ten years, as she coped with the issue of marrying and having a career, read her favorite philosophers and the new feminists and New Moralists, dealt with her continual lows and occasional highs, and tried to figure out the meaning of her self in terms of Dionysus and Apollo, reason and emotion, and male and female, engaging in the quest for identity that was as modern as T. S. Eliot and as ancient as St. Augustine. Her quest was rendered more pressing by the horrors of World War I, which deeply affected her. Trying to become a writer, in 1916 Benedict wrote a brief mystery/horror story, "The Bo-Cu Plant"; in 1918 she wrote a brief biography of Mary Wollstonecraft. Although she didn't publish either work, both were responses to World War I that reflected issues in her own life and foreshadowed important themes in her later work.

AFTER RETURNING FROM EUROPE, Ruth spent an unhappy year as a district visitor for the Charitable Organization Society of Buffalo and three years teaching at private girls' high schools in Los Angeles and Pasadena: one at the Westlake School for Girls in West Los Angeles; two at the Orton School for Girls in Pasadena. She went to Southern California with her mother, who retired from the Buffalo public library to help Margery with her infants, and Ruth and Bertrice moved in with Margery and her family. Ruth's depression only worsened; she didn't find relief in the warm climate and lush vegetation of Southern California. Ruth started keeping a journal, and her entries reflect her despair. At the end of her first year in Pasadena she wrote: "I've just come through a year in which I have not dared to think; I seemed to keep my grip only by setting my teeth and playing up to the mask I had chosen." "My real me," she continued, "was a creature I dared not look upon—it was terrorized by loneliness, frozen by a sense of futility, obsessed by a longing to stop. The mask was tightly adjusted."[4]

Ruth kept trying to achieve Pater's moments of transcendence. She was able to do so, but she couldn't extend them into a permanent state, Pater's "hard, gemlike flame." Her depression always returned. She saw herself as Goethe's Faust, standing on top of a mountain and surveying the world below: "I can stand on the dizzy heights and behold the nations of the world. But the instinctive thought that comes to crown the experience is just, 'if only, if only everything might stop with this.'" Emotional highs came upon her without warning, to turn quickly into lows. "A morning in the library, an afternoon with someone I really care about," she wrote, "a day in the mountains, a goodnight time with the [Margery's] babies, can almost frighten me with happiness." "But," she continued, "then it is gone and I cannot see what holds it all together. What is worthwhile? What is the purpose? I only wanted my feelings dulled. I wanted to be just placidly contented when I saw the full moon hang low over the ocean."[5]

Ruth's periods of elation and depression were regular enough that one suspects a physiological cause—as with the chronic vomiting of her childhood. Yet she had specific discontents. She was jealous of her sister's happiness as a wife and mother, and she didn't like Margery's minister husband, whom she found overbearing. She felt oppressed working in the feminized occupations of social work and schoolteaching: both had long hours and low pay. As a schoolteacher she liked her students, but she didn't like proctoring study hall or chaperoning them. Like many women college graduates of her generation, she didn't possess the enthusiasm of the pioneering generations of graduates, who were determined to prove that women could graduate from college and succeed at careers. By the early twentieth century, that goal had been realized. Ruth read Charlotte Perkins Gilman, but her struggle was more for self-realization than for women's rights.[6]

Still pious, she organized a missionary society at her brother-in-law's church, but she didn't become involved in the large women's rights community in Los Angeles or in the campaigns for woman suffrage in California.[7] The philosophers and poets she read didn't help her any longer. There were so many of them, each with differing advice—in her journal she listed Christ, Buddha, Browning, Keats, Spinoza, Whitman, even Theodore Roosevelt, with his widely publicized opinion that unmarried women college graduates were committing "race suicide." Expressing a modern point of view, she asserted that the "answers" given by philosophers that had once satisfied her were no more than "attitudes taken by different temperaments."[8] Disillusioned with intellectualism and careers, Ruth found there wasn't much left for her to do but to marry.

The romance novels she had read as a girl, as well as her family and the larger society, recommended marriage. Yet despite her discontents, Ruth hesitated to take the step. In fact, the entries in her journal suggest that she had to persuade herself to do it. Important in her decision was her seeming inability to make any lasting women friends during these years. In 1912 she wrote in her journal in extravagant language borrowed from Emerson about her "longing for friendship, a 'blanching vertical eye-glare' of loneliness." Blinding in its intensity, with its vertical, phallic—or vulval—"eye-glare," her longing affected even her sexual self. She explored the ancient tale of Theseus and Ariadne as a

metaphor for her predicament. Trapped in the labyrinth by the Minotaur, Theseus is rescued by Ariadne, a Cretan princess, who gives him
a string to lead him out. Ruth wrote that she felt like Theseus, trapped
in the labyrinth, with no Ariadne to guide her out.[9] The simile
expressed her sense of herself as a bifurcated being, both male and
female, and one trapped in a labyrinth—even then a metaphor for the
contradictions of the internal self. And the Minotaur? That seems a
reference to the emotions that she controlled with difficulty. Or did
the reference to Ariadne refer to an actual woman, to a lover that she
had lost? A letter to Ruth from Stanley Benedict during these years
mentions someone named Jean, with whom she went to a ranch to pick
pears and to listen to Beethoven and Mozart.[10] The sensuality of these
activities—their association with leisure and pleasure—suggests that
Ruth escaped from her regular life with a female companion, but Stanley's reference is the only hint of such episodes.

The only close female friends Ruth mentions in her journal during
these years were a group of unmarried, older women in Pasadena,
most of whom taught school with her and whom she found very
dreary. They spent their time with her mourning over not being married. The most unpleasant one took Ruth to her room and opened a
trunk to show her the cookbooks that she had collected for her marriage. She took them out of the trunk one by one and lovingly stroked
them. To Ruth the experience was dismal; she found this woman so
unattractive that she couldn't imagine a man desiring her and so "pad-
locked with reticence" that she had become "thick-coated with man-
nerisms."[11] In other words, her lack of sexual experience with men had,
in Freudian fashion, caused her to develop physical tics.

Bertrice and Margery teased Ruth about her "course in old
maids."[12] Both had experienced the culture of smashing at Vassar: it
was time for Ruth to find a man. Indeed, Ruth's "old maids" might
drive any woman into marriage; they're so stereotypical that they seem
constructions of her imagination designed to convince herself that
unmarried women weren't exciting, that the inspirational Miss Clark,
the art teacher at St. Margaret's, or Florence Keys, her Shakespeare
professor at Vassar, were few and far between.

Ruth was so uncertain about marriage that she had to go through
an epiphany to decide to marry. Drawing from the Darwinian biology
of her age—which influenced even feminist writers—she wrote that
the desire to have children was "stored up in us as a great battery
charged by the accumulated instincts of uncounted generations."

"When there are no children," she concluded, "unless the instinct is somehow employed, the battery either becomes an explosive danger or at best the current rapidly falls off, with its consequent loss of power."[13] In other words, she now decided that her failure to marry and become a mother was causing her emotional highs and lows. To arrive at this position, she concluded that she couldn't discipline herself into contentment on her own because only men had enough self-confidence to do it. Something innately female was the problem. "Does this sense of personal worth, this enthusiasm for one's own personality," she wrote, "belong only to great self-expressive souls? Or may I perhaps be shut from it by eternal law because I am a woman?" She felt imprisoned in her female self—and then she broke free by embracing her female side wholeheartedly. She suddenly yearned for "a great love, a quiet home, and children." She rhapsodized that "a woman has one supreme power—to love."[14]

She now praised women who had been muses to famous poets, rather than poets themselves. Referring to Dante's female spiritual guide, Beatrice, in *The Divine Comedy*—and perhaps to her own mother, Bertrice—she wrote, "do we care whether Beatrice formed clubs or wrote a sonnet?" She continued, "In the quiet self-fulfilling love of Wordsworth's home, do we ask that Mary Wordsworth should have achieved individual self-expression?" Through marriage and motherhood, she decided, she could find the contentment she hadn't found in a career. She went so far as to express a desire to have a male child through whom she could vicariously experience career success. Her renewed decision to marry was also a way of leaving Margery's home and of getting away from her brother-in-law and the schoolteachers. "In a world that holds books and babies and canyon trails," she wrote, "why should one condemn one's self to live day-in, day-out with people one does not like?"[15]

In a reference in her journal to the person she had been in college, Ruth mourned giving up her masculine side to embrace her biological self. That statement may be the key to the extravagant language in her journal and to the cautionary tale of the old maids.

We thought once, in college perhaps, that we were the artificers of our own lives. We planned our usefulness in social work, in laboratories, in schools. And all the time we did not yet know we were women—we did not know that there lay as certain a moral hindrance to our man-modeled careers as to a man-modeled costume of shingled hair and trousers.[16]

What did Ruth mean by a "man-modeled costume of shingled hair and trousers"? She didn't mean the dress of college women in general: in the 1900s they wore white shirtwaist blouses and dark skirts and jackets; they didn't wear trousers. And they didn't shingle their hair; they kept it long and arranged it in a pompadour. The students who dressed in male clothing for the dances and the plays and who slicked back their hair to make it appear short wore the "man-modeled" costume. What was the "moral hindrance" to such cross-dressing? It was that sexologists connected that dress to the "mannish lesbian."

That person existed in women who cross-dressed or adopted aspects of masculine appearance and behavior, whether for self-realization or protection, or because of a tradition dating to George Sand in the nineteenth century and before, or because they copied the dress of the "mannish lesbians" described by the sexologists. Conservative commentators expanded this figure beyond all reality: she smoked, she liked sports, she carried a gun. They placed on her their fears of the militant suffragists who, they thought, wanted to overturn the binary gender order that they considered crucial to personal and social stability. In one of her guises, the "mannish woman" became the Amazon, the legendary ancient warrior woman who supposedly cut off a breast to more easily draw her bow and who was a symbol of the independent New Woman.[17]

Havelock Ellis expressed these fears in a passage in *Sexual Inversion* about the danger of women leaving the home for work. Marriage is decaying, he wrote, and "the sexual field of women is becoming restricted to trivial flirtation with the opposite sex, and to intimacy with their own sex. Having been taught independence of men, a tendency develops for women to carry this independence still further and to find love where they find work." Moreover, he concluded, a special danger lay in the reality that "the congenital anomaly occurs with special frequency in women of high intelligence who, voluntarily or involuntarily, influence others."[18]

Such negativity about independent women was enough to persuade any young woman who didn't like her work and who was confused about her sexual identity to marry. Stanley Benedict was waiting for Ruth. She probably didn't love him; in her letters to him she consistently put him off. But he was persistent, and he was the only man interested in her. He was the brother of two sisters who had been at Vassar with her. She met him in Buffalo; he visited her in Pasadena. By 1912 she was twenty-five years old, nearly an "old maid." Like her revered father, Stanley was a scientist doing research on cancer in New York. The similarity was uncanny. By marrying Stanley, she might find her way to the father figure of her fantasy world and end her depressions. And she could join the stream of radical and literary young men and women going to New York, which was emerging as the nation's literary and artistic center.

Ruth's grandfather died in 1912 and left the Shattuck farm to her aunt Myra. Ruth went back to Norwich, intending to help Myra manage it. When Stanley appeared soon after she arrived, she maneuvered him into proposing. The narrative of his proposal, transcribed in her journal, reads like any in the romance novels she had read as a girl. They walked along a path in the woods and sat down under a tree. Ruth told Stanley that she loved him.

> He had been lying on the ground. He sat up and moved toward me, and said with a tenderness and awe I had never heard before, "Oh, Ruth, is it true?" And then he put his arms around me, and rested his head against me. In the long minute we sat there, he asked in the same hushed voice, "Ruth, will you marry me?" And I answered him, "Yes, Stanley." After that we did not speak.[19]

A year later she married Stanley and moved with him to New York City. She had given in to convention, and yet she managed to maintain some independence. Following advanced ideas about marriage, she persuaded Stanley to agree that if either of them wanted a divorce, the other wouldn't object.[20] Even her taking Stanley's last name had a feminist dimension. She kept "Fulton" as a middle name to maintain her independence, signing her professional work Ruth Fulton Benedict. But according to Esther Goldfrank, a Columbia anthropologist who observed her closely, she was aware that "Benedict" could be the first name for a man. In Shakespeare's *Much Ado About Nothing*, produced at Vassar during Ruth's senior year, the male protagonist, feminized during the course of the play, is named Benedick. Benedict, meaning "he who is blessed," is also the source of the name of a monastic order. When Ruth said to Margaret Mead that "Benedict" was her "nom de plume,"[21] she hinted at the complexity of the name as a secret about her that was hidden in plain sight.

RUTH BENEDICT'S DECISION FOR marriage and motherhood and her marriage contract with Stanley reflected the impact on her of the feminist movement that appeared in the United States in 1910, as well as the "New Morality" or "free-love" movement with which it was sometimes associated. The feminist movement came into being in Europe in the 1900s. In contrast to the older women's rights ideology, which stressed gaining gender equality in law, politics, and the professions, the new feminism extolled marriage and motherhood, while often downplaying rights. It appealed to a generation of women wanting a fresh approach to their lives, one that focused on marriage and motherhood but also included education and careers.[22]

From today's perspective, the stance of the feminists of 1910 is confusing, since we think of feminists as demanding equal rights with men in the public sphere, not as focusing on maternalism and the home. Yet our present-day definition of the word "feminism" is a legacy of the radicalism of the 1970s, when, after a number of decades in which the use of the word "feminism" declined, militant women's rights advocates took it over to define their cause. They were unaware of the word's earlier connection to marriage and motherhood. In fact, in terms of today's word usages, the feminists of the second decade of the twentieth century should perhaps be called "postfeminists," for their position resembles that of the younger women of our own era who are critical of the feminist radicalisms of the 1970s.

The major spokeswoman of the new feminism was the Swedish writer Ellen Key, who combined radical and conservative positions on gender to offer an appealing compromise to a Euro-American world confused about women's roles. She wrote five books on women and marriage between 1909 and 1914, all translated into English and published by G. P. Putnam's Sons, a major New York publisher. By following Ellen Key, one could be both traditional and progressive at the same time.[23]

Key drew on evolutionary theory and late-nineteenth-century neo-Romanticism to glorify heterosexual love as a "divine" evolutionary force. "The power of a great love to enhance a person's value for mankind," Key wrote, "can only be compared with the glow of religious faith or the creative joy of genius." Her ideal love was so compelling, she asserted, that it could happen only once in a lifetime; its emotional force, expressed in a sense of merging, had to result in marriage. Motherhood had to be part of it, for having and raising a child was a biological imperative and a woman's greatest joy. A truly sensual woman, wrote Key, "with her whole being will desire a child."[24] Moreover, her ideal love could normally occur only between a man and a woman because of the "magnetism" of their difference. When achieved, it had the power to transform individuals into self-realized beings who, through bearing and raising exemplary children, could create a better society.

Key insisted that women must stay at home to raise their children, who were so crucial to social improvement that they couldn't be entrusted to others. Opposing Key, Charlotte Perkins Gilman advocated the building of apartment houses with professional kitchens and kindergartens attached to them and child care readily available so that women with children could be relieved of child rearing and domestic chores to be able to work and thus achieve independence through becoming financially self-sufficient. Yet Key, as usual, wasn't as conservative on this issue as she at first seems. She proposed that governments pay stipends to unmarried mothers to stay at home and raise their children, a proposal that laid the groundwork for early systems of state welfare to mothers and children.

Key's ideas appealed to Ruth Fulton. Although Ruth had decided to marry, she still wanted to work for social reform. Key made such service easy: by marrying her "true love" and raising exemplary children Ruth could contribute to creating a better future. Ruth hesitated to declare Stanley her "true love," although in the first glow of romantic love even an inappropriate person can seem ideal.

Key worried that finding one's "true love" might be difficult and that experimentation might be necessary to make certain that the choice was right. Thus she went so far as to advocate trial marriage, sensuality in marriage, and free divorce—radical positions for her era. Yet what she meant by sensuality could be confusing. She separated herself from the free-love advocates, whom she (inaccurately) charged with replacing marriage, spirituality, and true love with undisciplined sex. Favoring spiritual communion over physical love, she wrote that sensual love "enslaves, dissipates, and lessens the personality," while spiritual love "liberates, conserves, and deepens the personality." She went so far as to contend that "the more they grow cooler erotically the more sensitive women become."[25]

Key praised the women's rights movement for ending women's oppression in such areas as education and the law. She praised unmarried career women and celebrated women's friendships for providing "the finest vibration of admiration, inspiration, sympathy, and adoration." Key was unmarried, and most of her friends were women. Yet she excoriated militant suffrage advocates as "Amazons" and, echoing Charlotte Perkins Gilman, called lesbianism an "impure form of femininity." She contended that there had been "an overestimation of friendship" in the "feminine world" and too much talk about "Sapphic women."[26]

While defining men and women as innately different, Key also called for "new" women and men who possessed the characteristics of both sexes. Those characteristics, however, had to be kept separate, for it was dangerous to eliminate gender boundaries. "In genius," she wrote, "each guards his own sex with the finest attributes of the other." Her call for self-reliant women and men grew out of her advocacy of what she called "personality," by which she meant individuality, in the sense of Nietzsche's "overman" who rejects all bourgeois convention; Key was one of those early twentieth-century feminists who admired Nietzsche for the power of his rhetoric of independence. Borrowing from the sexologists, she called women whose personalities drew from both masculine and feminine a "third sex."[27]

Key also called for a "new man" who was sensitive and caring. No less than present-day men's studies scholars, she recognized that there were different masculinities—the aggressive imperialist and the gentle artist represented the extremes in her day.[28] She called the Romantic movement the "great regeneration"; an evolutionary optimist, she saw Romantic poets like Byron and Shelley, who celebrated emotion and passion and men with feminine qualities in their work while displaying such traits in their own lives, as the inspiration for a "new man" who was coming into being to match the "new woman." "Among young men," she wrote, "the erotic longing today is often as refined as among women."[29]

These themes in Key's thought came together in her biography of Rahel Varnhagen, the late-eighteenth-century Berlin salon hostess who numbered Goethe and Hegel among her devotees. Her biography influenced Ruth Benedict in writing her brief biography of Mary Wollstonecraft.[30] Key's Varnhagen is a heroic figure who overcomes the trauma of having been abused as a child by her father, "a cannibal breaking bones," to reach the heights of the intellectual society of Berlin. To do so, she re-created herself as "a glorious being, rushing forth in a Dionysiac train," and combining male rationality and female emotionality "in complete equilibrium." In having many love affairs, she acted in accordance with her "personality."[31] Then, when her "one true love" abandoned her, she married a young man she was fond of and settled down to a quiet domesticity. Key approved that decision, for he fit into her category of "new man." According to Magnus Hirschfeld, however, in the late nineteenth century the rumor in Berlin was that Varnhagen thought of herself as a homosexual male who desired women.[32]

Key's use of the word "personality" influenced Benedict. The word derived from the Greek word *prosopa*, which refers to the masks that actors wore onstage. In the Middle Ages Christian theologians used the Latin derivative *persona* to refer to the three figures of the God-head—Father, Son, and Holy Ghost—separate as personas but combined into a triune God, just as the soul of each human being in their view is also unique and at the same time connected to the divine. Thus "personality" had traditional Christian roots in the drive for ethical perfection and union with the divine as well as both ancient and modern secular roots in the notion of the self as a series of contrived performances, as a mask one puts on and off.

Both the religious and secular meanings were important to Ruth, as she slowly lost her Christian faith in a time when she continued to read modern poets like Yeats, for whom putting on a "mask" and becoming the person the mask implied was a central concept. By the 1920s the word "personality" took on even more complex meanings, as commercial advertisers, psychologists, and self-help advocates adopted it, while theologians continued to use it in a religious sense. Meantime, the traditional ideal of "character"—or maintaining a proper ethical stance—was replaced by a new therapeutic ideal of personality as the fully realized secular self, both reflecting and manipulating mass values.[33] "Personality" was an important word in these eras, when people were attempting to come to terms with modernity without losing the resonance of the traditional. It would become a central term for the culture-and-personality school in anthropology in which Benedict and Mead played a major role.

AS A THEORIST OF SEXUALITY, Ellen Key stood at the conservative end of a group of thinkers loosely linked together as the "New Moralists"; those theorists influenced Benedict and Mead. The term "New Moralism" sometimes served as a euphemism for free love, itself a complex ideology involving both a rebellion against the Victorian repression of sexuality and a continuation of its emphasis on spirituality. In the nineteenth century there had been free-love organizations and communities—Oneida is the best known—but they declined in the early twentieth century. Free love remained an ideology with texts and interpreters, however, and it influenced groups such as the young radicals in Greenwich Village before World War I and movements like that for birth control, but it wasn't institutionalized in the United States. Individuals who espoused it, like Benedict and Mead, read its texts, talked about it with others, and followed it on their own.

Its major interpreters were Havelock Ellis, in *The Art of Love* (1910), and Edward Carpenter, in *Love's Coming of Age* (1896).[34] World famous by the 1910s, Ellis wrote introductions to many of the works of the feminist writers of the day, including most of the English translations of Ellen Key's books. His praise for Mead's *Coming of Age in Samoa* appeared on its jacket cover and was considered important to its success among the general public. Ellis's wife, Edith, announced to him shortly after they married that she was lesbian, but they didn't divorce, for the New Moralists often downplayed sexuality to focus on spirituality as a central element in marriage. Thus Ellis had romances with other women, including Olive Schreiner and Margaret Sanger, and Edith had lesbian relationships. For his part, Edward Carpenter resigned a teaching position at Cambridge University and moved to the country, where he grew his own food, criticized the exploitation of workers under capitalism, lived with a male lover, and formed the Fellowship of the New Life. Ellis and other leading New Moralists belonged to it. Carpenter's *Love's Coming of Age* went through many editions before appearing in the Modern Library's "fifty-one best world books."[35]

In *The Art of Love*, Ellis agreed with Key that spirituality is crucial to any relationship and that marriage is necessary to "true love." Yet because in his view love is a synthesis of companionship and lust, he contended that friendship easily becomes erotic, while friendships entered through "the erotic portal" often possess a special intimacy. And because he believed that sexuality was a force flowing through the universe that needed to remain fluid to inspire reform, he thought monogamy absorbed too much energy. Thus marital partners should have sex with others. Above all, he contended that jealousy is the most harmful of the emotions: it had to be eliminated, for it made free love and thus universal reform impossible.

Influenced by Eastern mysticism, Carpenter agreed with Ellis that sexuality and love flowed through the universe, binding humans and nature together. He seconded Key's idea that a "true love" is a profound human experience—he called it "the deepest soul union." In a more pragmatic vein, he identified boredom as a major problem in marriage, and he counseled marital partners to practice variety, including "intimacies with outsiders" and "triune and other such relations." Carpenter studied the sex practices of other societies to find ways to improve Western marriage, and he found his means to improvement especially in the fertility ceremonies of ancient societies. Every society, he wrote, should have "the good sense to tolerate a Nature-festival now and then."[36]

These free-love ideas were important to Benedict. Her inability to commit to a goal for her life between 1909, when she graduated from college, and 1921, when she entered the Ph.D. program in anthropology at Columbia, reflected not only her chronic melancholia but also the contradictory positions of the feminists and the New Moralists. At first Benedict followed Key's imperatives toward love and marriage, although she also responded to Key's caution about being certain one has found one's true love, and she persuaded Stanley to agree to a marriage contract. When their marriage began to fall apart, Key's biography of Rahel Varnhagen—and the life of Mary Wollstonecraft—influenced Ruth to decide that a "peaceful domesticity" with Stanley was all she needed. When that compromise didn't work, she turned to the free-love ideas of Ellis and Carpenter—which Margaret Mead was also adopting by the early 1920s.

FOR THE FIRST YEAR after Ruth married Stanley, she was happy with him. She wrote of "this satisfying comradeship, this ardent delight, this transforming love."[37] Her initiation into heterosexual sex was a positive experience. In the unpublished poem "South Wind," she indicated her innocence and her fears of sex and Stanley's virile knowledge and his gentle approach:

> *I ran with the panic of virginity;*
> *But close, close,*

Resting his warm body at my back,
Wrapping his arms lingeringly across my breasts,
Without effort and without statement,
The south wind held me in his embrace. . . .

For the voluptuous wind
Was stronger than I was,
And older, and infinitely wiser,
And I knew he would compel me to learn his secret.[38]

Her new contentment with Stanley prompted her to question her religious beliefs further. He owned a cabin on a lake in New Hampshire where they spent summers; one summer early in their marriage they went to a Second Advent revival camp meeting held nearby. What Ruth discerned as the "crabbed Puritanism" of the people there appalled her. Through the emotionalism of the revival they may have found the "bonfire of love and delight" that she was searching for, but they seemed to her a "close-lipped people" for whom the universe "was about as rich and various as it is to a cat after mice." She now condemned her childhood religion as "a paralyzing, a limiting, a mocking finite, of the Infinite." She would have to find her path to ecstasy another way.

Ruth's memory of the intensity of her early relationship with Stanley long remained vivid; for years she clung to the illusion that they could re-create it. Stanley shared her love of philosophy; he could be empathic and amusing. Ruth liked spending summers at the cabin in New Hampshire—until he bought a motorboat and the noise of its engines shattered the silence. But once they settled into a domestic routine, he became rigid and demanding. His colleagues at Cornell Medical School found him austere, with a bad temper and a tendency to make harsh judgments. As he aged, one of those colleagues described him as looking like a "weathered sea captain." His mother was a published author and one of his sisters became president of Sweet Briar College, but he turned out to be a traditional male, obsessed with his work. He put up with Ruth's career, but he would have preferred a stay-at-home wife. Ruth's failure to conceive a child was disappointing to both of them.[39]

Stanley suffered from high blood pressure and chronic insomnia, and these conditions became worse when he accidentally inhaled gas he was experimenting with in his laboratory for use on the battlefield during World War I. He could be irritable and cranky. He couldn't stand noise, and he didn't like to go out in the evenings. Not surprisingly, he didn't like Ruth's mood swings. For her part, Ruth thought that what he really wanted was for her to become a carbon copy of himself. She wanted to discuss their problems; he wanted to forget them and to have peace and quiet. "The greatest relief I know is to have put something into words," wrote Ruth, "even to have him say cruel things to me is better than an utter silence about his viewpoint."[40] Stanley spent a lot of time on his hobby of photography, taking photographs and developing them in his darkroom at home.

Once married, they settled on suburban Long Island, and Ruth tried to be a housewife. But she soon found that role unbearable, and she persuaded Stanley to move to Greenwich Village, where they lived until he found city noises so disagreeable that they moved to the distant suburb of Bedford Hills. She then rented a room in the city, where she lived during the week: a radical act for the day. Once she achieved that independence, their marriage improved, although, like many spouses at odds, they derived a certain pleasure from blowups and reconciliations. Margaret Mead described their relationship as "always dependent on intensity as a medium."[41]

Yet Ruth was unable to leave Stanley: like Luther Cressman for Margaret Mead, he was a steadying anchor she relied on, so closely bound to her that he tolerated her independent life as long as she didn't tell him much about it. "With Stanley," wrote Mead, "silence is what is required."[42] The duration of their marriage resulted in part from bad timing: Ruth's sister, Margery, contended that when Ruth asked Stanley for a divorce early in their marriage he refused to give it to her; in 1931 Ruth was willing to give Stanley a divorce, but she didn't see the point of going through with it unless he asked for it—and he didn't. Ruth waxed and waned in her feelings about Stanley. In one journal fragment from the late 1920s she wrote that she closed herself off from him soon after they were married; in another she wrote that all she had ever wanted in life was for Stanley to love her. They didn't separate until 1930, nearly fifteen years after their marriage became rocky and after each of them fell in love with someone else.[43] They never divorced, and they remained friendly until Stanley died in 1936.

WHEN RUTH CAME TO New York City in 1914, pre–World War I radicalism was flourishing. Suffragists were marching, and so were labor union women on strike. Emma Goldman preached anarchism and birth control, and Greenwich Village radicals like Floyd Dell and Max Eastman spread socialism and free love through their journal, the *Masses*. The Armory Show had shocked the nation with abstract art by Picasso and Braque; the Provincetown Players were modernizing the theater; the poetry renaissance was heating up. Women's rights advocates of all persuasions met weekly for lunch and conversation at a Greenwich Village club called Heterodoxy, founded in 1912, where they shared their feminism and their life stories. They adopted Charlotte Perkins Gilman's arguments for careers for women and Ellen Key's for government support of unmarried mothers. They used Key's term "personality" to refer to women's need to develop individuality. Many were socialists. Most endorsed free sexuality and equal rights for women, while also wanting marriage, children, and Key's "great love." They criticized the women's rights advocates of the generation of Emily Fogg Mead as antisex and antimale.[44]

There's no evidence that Ruth participated in feminist organizations in these years, even when she lived in Greenwich Village and even though her high school classmate Mabel Dodge and her college classmate Inez Milholland were well-known feminists there. Dodge ran her salon; Milholland was a lawyer and a leader of the woman suffrage movement. Apparently, Ruth didn't contact them, although she seems to have gone to several meetings of Heterodoxy and to have disliked them: "No one who has subjected himself to a half dozen of its meetings," she asserted, "could have an iota of hope for it left." It seems she didn't like the self-involved nature of those meetings, the way in which individuals talked about their lives.[45] They did so to increase their feminist self-image, much like the "consciousness raising" of second wave feminists. Ruth, however, preferred to keep her personal life to herself; she also preferred organizations that included men.

In the summer of 1914, World War I broke out, and that conflagration left a lasting impression on Benedict, as it did on many writers of the day. The horrors of the war soon became apparent, as both armies retreated to huge trenches they dug, while the technologies of machine guns, poisonous gas, and airplanes with bombs inflicted death and terrible wounds. Massive offensives in 1916 on the part of both the Germans and the Allies produced staggering casualties and no gains for either side. Europe had been essentially at peace since the Napoleonic wars a century before; the West had seen nothing like the carnage of World War I since America's Civil War. The aggressive masculinity of the fin de siècle seemed to have gone amok. The world collapsed on August 1, 1914, wrote Gertrude Stein, "and the twentieth century was born."[46]

In response to the war and to the problems in her marriage, Ruth Benedict, with Stanley's help, wrote her mystery/horror story "The Bo-Cu Plant." The story begins with five male explorers meeting one evening in a mansion in London, "smoking oriental tobacco," and sharing tales of their adventures. One of them tells the story of the Bo-Cu plant, which grows on the banks of a tributary of the Amazon River. It has white flowers, with a large black spot on each petal; its scent can cause hallucinations "worse than anything in Dante." A lumber company has sent a group of surveyors to the region to assess cutting down a stand of mahogany for market, and one of them falls in love with a local Spanish woman named Nita. All is well until we learn that Nita's mother, dying in terrible agony at her birth and holding Nita responsible, placed a curse on her that she would never know sexual fulfillment in marriage. Nita and her lover marry; on their wedding night, when they retreat to their quarters, the bride turns into the devil, and the terrified husband kills her with an ax.[47]

Ruth and Stanley may each have harbored the fantasy of murdering the other: that's not unusual for spouses at odds. With the mother cursing the daughter, the story may also express hostility on the part of Ruth toward her mother. It also has a feminist dimension. With the demented, dying mother cursing the daughter and the daughter turning into a monster, it contains the ubiquitous female demons of turn-of-the-century literature—the mermaids and Circes associated with exotic flowers and poisonous plants in the art and novels of the period written by men—like the savage queen of the jungle, beautiful and menacing, at the center of Joseph Conrad's *The Heart of Darkness*. Women writers of the period, according to feminist analysts, turned those female demons into instruments of female power. Set in the Amazon, "The Bo-Cu Plant" evokes myths of female Amazons battling men, as Nita turns against her husband with fury.[48]

The story contains many male characters: the surveyors; the corporation behind them; the explorers in London; the devil who controls both the Bo-Cu plant and the women in the story. A benevolent male doctor narrates the story, but most of the men in it manipulate women and the environment. Even the male explorers in London smoke "oriental" tobacco and listen to a story about madwomen. Benedict describes them as well-to-do; two are non-Western men of color. Ah Sing is a "Chinaman from India"; Bollo is "an inky black prince from the upper Congo." They represent male imperialists differentiated not by race but by gender and class. Benedict wasn't yet ready to take on racist imperialism; she didn't become an antiracist crusader until she became close to Franz Boas, her mentor at Columbia and an intellectual leader in the movement for racial equality. Yet she had turned from the "masculine" orientation of her college years to her "feminine" side in marrying Stanley; in "The Bo-Cu Plant" she seemed to reject conventional masculinity even more.

Male imperialists, this interpretation implies, brought on World War I. In May 1917, Benedict wrote in her journal: "How useless to attempt anything but a steady day-by-day living with this tornado of world-horror over our heads."[49] Like Gertrude Stein and many writers of the period, she viewed World War I as having destroyed nineteenth-century optimism, its sense of inevitable progress expressed in the evolutionary enthusiasm of a neo-Romantic like Ellen Key. Ruth noted that in college she had studied Thomas Hobbes's *Leviathan* as an outdated relic of the past, for her teacher believed that all the problems of humanity had been solved: there wasn't a threatening Leviathan anywhere in sight. Yet that was no longer the case.[50] Leviathan and Behemoth, beasts of the Battle of Armageddon in the biblical Book of Revelation—an apocalyptic text from her Baptist childhood—appear in her poetry, just as the devil became the deus ex machina in her 1916 story. The brutal imagery of some of her poetry seems to be drawn partly from metaphors for the horror of war, as in her poem "Resurgam" (*resurgam* refers to resurrection):

> *This is the season when importunate rains*
> *Rutting the graves unearth slim skeletons*
> *We buried to corruption, and strong winds*
> *Whip from the ocean where no passing suns*
> *Strike nethermost, the bones we wept beside.*[51]

She also expressed her discontent about masculinity and the war in a poem about Rupert Brooke, the young English poet whose death early in the war became a transatlantic symbol of youth wasted in an inferno of destruction. He was one of her suffering Christ figures.

Brooke was famed on two continents for his beauty. On a tour of the
United States people stared at him on the streets, and he had created a
renowned free-love circle at Cambridge University. Ruth wrote:

> *Now God be thanked who took him at the hour*
> *Who let him die, flushed in an hour of dreaming. . . .*
>
> *We are wise now and weary. Hopes he knew*
> *Are perished utterly as a storm abated.*[52]

RESPONDING TO WHAT SEEMED the breakdown of Western values,
the women's movement divided further as feminists and women's rights
advocates took varying positions on the war. The mainstream women's
movement rallied behind the U.S. intervention on behalf of the Allies.
So did some of the feminists, although some took up pacifism and others attacked male aggression. Still others abandoned the separate cause
of women to embrace a new concept of "humanity" as the issue. "We
are being wrecked by an over-masculinized race," wrote Beatrice
Forbes-Robertson Hale in her survey of feminism. "Feminism only
comes of age when it develops into humanism."[53] Feminism, she was
convinced, needed to include men in its organizations and agendas.

These new directions in feminism influenced Benedict. With
women's increased participation in the workforce during World War I
and the passage of the woman suffrage amendment in New York State
in 1917, she decided that the women's rights movement had largely
succeeded. This conclusion may sound misguided today, after the
"second-wave" feminists of the 1960s and 1970s uncovered substantial
discrimination against women in laws, institutions, mores, and behavior, but Benedict—and Mead—reflecting a common sentiment in their
day, concluded that not much more needed to be done in agitating for
rights, at least not for middle-class women. Ellen Key had taken that
position even before the war.

Benedict called for a new women's movement focused on "personality," on attaining the creative individuality that Key—and Nietzsche—
had called for. "The ultimate objective, the high goal, remains an inward
affair, a matter of attitude," Benedict wrote. What women needed was
not a "semi-political party" but—using a religious metaphor—a "new
birth" to a new self. "We can hardly drag back from oblivion," she con-

tinued, "the vital questions that were life and death to us in the early summer of 1914"—questions that concerned suffrage and women's rights. To make the necessary changes, Ruth decided, women needed "heroines" to show them how to do it. "Just adventure through the life of one woman who has been profoundly stirred by a great restlessness," she wrote, "and you will comprehend more than from a library of theorizing."[54]

Young reformers in this era rejected pre–World War I progressive reform, with its focus on changing institutions and creating new ones, for they thought that progressivism had run its course when it failed to prevent World War I. Many also concluded that Western systems of ethics were bankrupt and that they needed to be reformulated around more spiritual and less materialistic goals. This context clarifies Benedict's individualistic impulse in creating heroines for women to follow in reshaping their lives: it was a nineteenth-century impulse in a cynical post–World War I world still fascinated by the individual personality. To reshape her interior self: that's what Benedict had been trying to do for many years.

Ruth decided to create heroines by writing brief biographies of Mary Wollstonecraft, Margaret Fuller, and Olive Schreiner and combining them into a volume she proposed calling "Adventures in Womanhood." It was a promising idea: biography became popular in the 1920s, and these three women were important writers whose lives extended from the eighteenth to the early twentieth centuries. Wollstonecraft represented the rational egalitarianism of the Enlightenment, Fuller the organic and gender-crossing strains of Romanticism, and Olive Schreiner the early twentieth century's neo-Romanticism and feminism. All of them called for independent, gender-balanced individuals; Wollstonecraft and Fuller both had romantic friendships with women when young and then married when older and had children. All three supported humanitarian reform and the advancement of women, although none was a militant women's rights advocate. All lived adventurous lives: Wollstonecraft went to Paris to observe the French Revolution of 1789; Fuller became a partisan in the Italian Revolution of 1848; Schreiner came from South Africa to London to join radical literary circles there.

When Houghton Mifflin turned down her proposal for the book, Benedict abandoned the project. She never wrote the biographies of Fuller and Schreiner. But her biography of Wollstonecraft elucidates her early thinking about women and gender. It is also autobiographical. Mead placed it at the end of *An Anthropologist at Work*, as though it were a reprise of Benedict's life. There's only one false note. Unlike Mary Wollstonecraft, Benedict didn't find contentment in marriage and a peaceful domesticity; in the end she found her real self in relationships with women.

BENEDICT'S WOLLSTONECRAFT IS heroic. She is adventurous and unbound by convention; her viewpoint is modern. She combines reason and emotion into a powerful tool to analyze her world and to reshape herself. She believes that "the first object of laudable ambition is to attain a character as a human being, regardless of the distinction of sex." Benedict downplays the dark side of Wollstonecraft that other biographers, beginning with her husband, William Godwin, have noted: her mood swings and depressions, her obsessiveness in love affairs.[55] What matters to Benedict is that Wollstonecraft didn't allow these negative traits to hold her back. Rather, overcoming them was central to her success.

Like Benedict, Wollstonecraft had a difficult childhood. Her alcoholic father beat her and her mother and sister. According to Benedict, she received the "arbitrary beatings and caresses of her father, his despotic whims." The terms "caresses" and "despotic whims" suggest that Benedict suspected that the abuse was sexual; she often quoted from Godwin's memoir in describing Wollstonecraft, but the terms "caresses" and "despotic whims" were her own. Present-day interpreters of Wollstonecraft who suspect that her father sexually abused her find only hints about it in her writings, but Benedict may have found the same hints. She also identified Wollstonecraft's mother as abusive to her children and implied that her sister replicated the family pattern by marrying an abusive husband.[56] After a childhood like Mary's, Benedict wrote, "it is only the very spirited who survive mentally, the very strong who are clean thereafter."

Wollstonecraft "saved her soul alive." How did she do it? She lived a passionate, self-reliant life. She realized that a "masculine Juggernaut" oppressed women, and she expressed her rage against it in *A Vindication of the Rights of Woman*, the first modern women's rights treatise.[57] Her father's abuse "filled her with contemptuous resentment," made her "color-blind to convention," roused her to "passion against the bondage of women," and fired her up to a "passionate

French Revolution faith in democracy." After her disastrous affair with the adventurer Gilbert Imlay, who deserted her after fathering her child, Wollstonecraft didn't pine after love, "a stalking intruder." In midlife she found a "quiet, pervading happiness" with William Godwin, the famed philosopher of rationality. "She was come at last into her tranquil maturity."[58]

Benedict's depiction of Godwin isn't positive: in what seems a caricature of Stanley, she described him as a "congealing of icy and solitary logical process." Yet Godwin was preferable to the other men in Wollstonecraft's life: her father, the alcoholic who abused her; Henry Fuseli, a married painter who rejected her; Gilbert Imlay, the rake who abandoned her. With marriage to Godwin, who maintained a separate apartment, she achieved a tranquil domestic life. In Benedict's view, that was enough. It was also what Ellen Key's Rahel Varnhagen had done.

In "Mary Wollstonecraft" Benedict discussed Mary's romantic friendship as a young woman with Fanny Blood. She recognized its eroticism: Fanny was Mary's "ruling passion," and Mary responded to Fanny's "looks in every nerve"—Benedict copied these phrases from Godwin's memoir. Yet she must have known from reading *Vindication* that Wollstonecraft was critical of sexual intimacy between women. Referring to girls in single-sex boarding schools and to women in London society, she wrote that "women are too generally familiar with each other, which leads to that gross degree of familiarity that so frequently renders the marriage state unhappy."[59]

In "Mary Wollstonecraft" Benedict indicted patriarchy as a "Juggernaut" and heterosexual love as a "stalking intruder." Yet she didn't address Godwin's criticism of Wollstonecraft in his memoir as too masculine, as Amazon in type. Benedict criticized the strident masculinity of her era and, like Ellen Key and others, suggested in "Mary Wollstonecraft" that the most realized personality combined reason and emotion, masculine and feminine. Yet that position was tricky: no feminist who, like Ellen Key and Olive Schreiner, called for a merging of masculine and feminine to create the emancipated woman wanted that woman to be too masculine.

Benedict had intended to include Margaret Fuller as the third subject in her proposed book of biographies, and Fuller's writings are revealing on this matter of the ideal female personality. In her major feminist work, *Women in the Nineteenth Century* (1845), she wrote that "male and female are perpetually passing into one another" and that "there is no wholly masculine man nor purely feminine woman." Yet she also wrote about women: "Were they free, were they wise fully to develop the strength and beauty of woman, they would never wish to be man, or man-like." Having made this judgment, Fuller had difficulty evaluating George Sand, the nineteenth-century French writer whose free behavior and cross-dressing made her a transatlantic symbol of the liberated Amazon. Fuller admired Sand, but she didn't like her practice of wearing male clothing and smoking cigarettes, for that behavior was too masculine. Fuller was able to praise Sand only after she read a positive evaluation of her by Elizabeth Barrett Browning—a model woman for her age once she married Robert Browning. Fuller now described Sand as "a large-brained woman and large-hearted man."[60]

When Houghton Mifflin rejected Ruth's book of biographies, she wasn't surprised. She herself had discerned a "falsetto note" in her writing.[61] Indeed, "Mary Wollstonecraft" has a melodramatic quality that reads like a holdover from "The Bo-Cu Plant." Once again, as so often in these years, Ruth abandoned a project midstream. Besides, she had tried social work again and had found, to her surprise, that now that she was older and more experienced she enjoyed it and was good at it. "I've called an organization into being that's doing good work," she wrote in her journal. "There are half a dozen positions I'm wanted in."[62] For a time she worked with the Red Cross on Long Island, then in the office at Lillian Wald's Henry Street Settlement. In 1919 she did interviews for the Carnegie Fund's Americanization Survey.[63] For a time she took courses in aesthetic dancing, and she envisioned herself as a professional dancer, moving gracefully in flowing robes, striking elegant poses.

Yet she still wanted to be an intellectual and a writer. She took several courses with John Dewey at Columbia; in the fall of 1919 she enrolled in a course on "Women and the Social Order," taught by Elsie Clews Parsons at the New School for Social Research, which was founded at the end of the war by dissenting academics and intellectuals, including Parsons and Dewey, who were angry at the incursions on free speech during the war at universities like Columbia and who wanted to create a more progressive educational environment; at this point it functioned mainly as an evening school for adults. Benedict seized the opportunity to study with Parsons, a prominent feminist who had given up a career as a social worker to combine writing with marriage and motherhood. In several recent books, Parsons had called

Benedict's grandparents—John Shattuck and Joanna Terry Shattuck.
Courtesy of Chenango County Historical Society

Ruth and Margery Fulton, Owatonna, Minnesota. Ruth is ten,
Margery eight and a half.
Special Collections, Vassar College Library

Benedict's graduation picture from St. Margaret's School, Buffalo.
Special Collections, Vassar College Library

Benedict at home in Bedford Hills, early 1920s.
Special Collections, Vassar College Library

Opposite: Ruth and Stanley Benedict at Lake Winnipesaukee,
New Hampshire, in the early years of their marriage.
Special Collections, Vassar College Library

Benedict, early 1920s. "Her beauty in eclipse." Photo probably taken by Stanley Benedict, an avid photographer.
Courtesy of the Institute for Intercultural Studies, New York City

Benedict, 1931. "Her beauty restored."
Special Collections, Vassar College Library

Benedict with two members of the Blackfoot tribe, 1939.
Special Collections, Vassar College Library

Benedict in her office at Columbia University, early 1940s.
Special Collections, Vassar College Library

Franz Boas.
Special Collections, Vassar College Library

Edward Sapir.
Special Collections, Vassar College Library

Geoffrey Gorer.
Library of Congress

for an end to social distinctions based on sex, race, and class: she ratified Ellen Key's message about the need to develop individuality and an independent personality, but she brought it into the modern era shorn of Key's glorification of romantic love.

Parsons saw friendship as a model for relationships and independence as a goal for both women and men.[64] Like Beatrice Forbes-Robertson Hale, she called for a new humanism that would include men and address the situation of both genders. She was ambivalent about the woman suffrage movement, since she feared that it would bring into power the kind of militant and antimale women whom she identified as leading the prohibition movement in particular. She criticized Heterodoxy in the course that Benedict took; she preferred organizations in which women worked together with men.[65] Disillusioned by the war and feminist support for it, Parsons had severed her ties with organized feminism to take up anthropology, becoming an expert on institutionalized homosexuality among the Indians of the Southwest.[66] Thirteen years older than Benedict, she seemed someone who could teach her a lot: Ruth's views on feminism were already similar to hers. Ruth signed up for Parsons's course with enthusiasm; by its end, however, she and Parsons would be hardly speaking.

AT FIRST PARSONS and Benedict got along. Parsons taught her course from sociological and feminist perspectives. She compared religion, kinship, marriage, and gender relations in a number of tribal societies, while relating her analyses to contemporary issues. She didn't confine her course content to the subject of women; she included male roles and behavior as well. This emphasis wasn't lost on Benedict, who had analyzed male behavior in "Mary Wollstonecraft" and "The Bo-Cu Plant" and whose anthropological writings would often focus on men.

In her course Parsons began by discussing the Pueblo Indians and their woman-centered institutions, under which descent is matrilineal, marital residence matrifocal, divorce easy, and society communal. She continued by examining other distinctive tribal societies, including the Australian ones with intricate kin arrangements and incest prohibitions and the Todas, a society on the Indian subcontinent that worshipped cows, regarded milk as sacred, and practiced polyandry. Parsons distributed written questions to her students asking why they were taking the course. In her answers Benedict stated that she hoped to learn ways of criticizing contemporary society through studying pre-state ones and of lessening her "blindness about conventions."

Parsons encouraged her students to apply what they were learning to the contemporary situation. In an answer to one of Parsons's written queries about how Pueblo women would view the "white" women who settled near them, Benedict was sympathetic to the Indian women and ambivalent about the white women. She wrote that the Indian women would be surprised that an Anglo married woman was expected to leave her kin to follow her husband and that she had no legal right to support from him if they separated, but that the air of independence of the married white women and their "loud-voiced ordering of everyone about the place" would disconcert them. Benedict already viewed women as both powerful and powerless—like her Anglo women following their husbands, yet taking command, or Mary Wollstonecraft, victimized by men while advancing the cause of women. In her answer to Parsons's question asking the students to define marriage, Benedict wrote that it was "any socially sanctioned sex relationship between man and woman."

The only paper Benedict wrote for the course that remains today is about contemporary marriage and sexuality, not about pre-state societies. Benedict derived her ideas in it directly from Parsons's work on the subject. She pours out her need for freedom. She writes that American society groups women into three categories: unmarried women, wives, and prostitutes. Those divisions, she declared, should be merged into one. All women should have the right to have sex whenever and with whomever they choose. Yet she still wanted some kind of "marriage arrangement"—in the sense of "long-standing and faithful intimacy between the sexes." She hadn't abandoned Ellen Key's notion of a perfect love. Echoing Edward Carpenter, she concluded that sexual freedom would strengthen her ideal of monogamy by relieving the boredom of having sex only with one person.

Ruth continued exploring these ideas in her journal. How can the human craving for sex be satisfied? she asked. Masturbation, she wrote, was one way. Citing Havelock Ellis, she asserted that "what's characteristically known as self-abuse" wasn't harmful, except when it violated "the law of moderation"; in other words, when it was too frequent. What about homosexuality? Varying her free-love position, she wrote that she couldn't entirely "swallow the solution in Plato's *Republic*."[67] Yet understanding Benedict here is tricky, for Plato's ideal society in that text included free love—but not homosexuality. Yet both in an article published in 1934, "Anthropology and the Abnormal," and in *Patterns of Culture* she would identify Plato as advocating homosexuality in the *Republic*. When a Dr. Weiss wrote her in 1943 pointing out her error, she acknowledged it. "Of course I should have mentioned the *Symposium* or *Phaedrus*, not the *Republic*," she wrote.[68] Did she make the same error in 1919? Did she mean to cite the *Symposium* or *Phaedrus*, not the *Republic*, in her journal? Was it free love that she rejected? Or did she reject homosexuality?

There is no indication of Parsons's reaction to Benedict's essay. Did she dispute Benedict's conclusions about love and marriage? Did she fail to understand her? In many ways they were similar. Both were feminists with little taste for organizations or militancy. Benedict didn't like feminist meetings; Parsons avoided making speeches and didn't march in suffrage parades. Both began their careers in social work, and both left that profession for anthropology. Both were controlled in style: Benedict put on her mask; Parsons was "always restrained," although in contrast to Benedict she was neither shy nor depressed.[69] But they differed in social class. Parsons, the daughter of one of the wealthiest men in New York, lived in mansions with servants taking care of her needs and had access to New York high society. That difference wasn't lost on Benedict. In her answer to Parsons's query about her background in Parson's questions about why the students were taking the class, she described herself as the daughter of farmers and as having lived in Pasadena among the "retired rich." Parsons was married and the mother of four children. Beautiful and statuesque, with a reputation for having lovers, she had everything Benedict wanted. It was a recipe for jealousy.

It's possible that Parsons wasn't a good teacher. In her twenty years as an anthropologist, this was the only class she taught. And Ruth didn't respond to her approach. Parsons focused on the details of cultures; Ruth liked the broad picture. Parsons didn't continue on at the New School for the spring semester that academic year; she steered Ruth to Alexander Goldenweiser, a Ph.D. from Columbia who was also teaching at the New School. The flamboyant Goldenweiser, the son of a famous Eastern European intellectual, made sweeping generalizations and had a flair for description, from the simple "red paint of Melanesia" to the complex "rise and fall of Gothic architecture in Europe."[70] Parsons communicated with her students by mail, having them send their work to her apartment on Park Avenue or her home in the wealthy suburb of Harrison, New York; Goldenweiser spent unlimited time with them. When he died, Benedict fulsomely praised him in print for bringing her into anthropology; she didn't mention Parsons.[71]

Sexual identity may have been an issue between them. In her readings for the class, Parsons assigned articles she had written on the Zuñi, including two on its berdache tradition. In that tradition males assumed women's occupations and dress. In her articles Parsons was sympathetic to it. In 1915 she described a gender-crossing "girl-boy" (katsotse) named Nancy as a "strong-minded woman" and as a "new woman, a large part of her male."[72] In several other books and articles, she was also sympathetic to homosexuality. She wrote that "for desire to cross gender boundaries one must turn to the fabled Amazons or to those buoyant spirits of the Renaissance by whom more than one aphorism of sex was questioned." Both the Amazons and the Renaissance women were predecessors, she suggested, to women in the contemporary women's rights movement. In 1916 she called for eliminating all sodomy laws, on the grounds of the right to privacy. She hinted that she had some experience of lesbianism: "From the charge of pederasty none who inspires both enmity and discipleship is secure."[73]

Yet she wasn't completely sympathetic to same-sex love. She defined it as originating mostly "from segregating sexes in barracks, or schools, or prisons, or by means of the endless conventional restrictions upon social intercourse between men and women." In other words, if men and women met on a regular and equal basis, "perversion" wouldn't occur. By 1922 her hostility had increased. Writing on the subject of sex for Harold Stearns's influential Civilization in the United States, she contended that if individuals didn't have heterosexual sex on a regular basis their drive might become "perverted." She wasn't completely certain of that, since "sex pathology" hadn't been studied with any statistical precision in the United States; still, she traced "the commonly observed spirit of isolation or antagonism between the sexes" as well as "the spirit of competition among individuals" to "homosexual masturbatory tendencies." That phrase referred to the belief, which Benedict had noted in her journal, that masturbating a lot could cause individuals, through fixating on their own sexuality, to become homosexual in inclination.[74]

Best-selling novelist Robert Herrick had an affair with Parsons. In 1932 he published The End of Desire, a roman à clef about the affair, after Parsons had ended it. Homosexuality is a central theme of the novel, with Parsons appearing, thinly veiled, as an expert in abnormal psychology. The character based on Parsons testifies as an expert witness in a trial of a "perverted" youth, and a teacher at her son's single-sex boarding school tries to seduce her son. Herrick's fictionalized Parsons has a nature "more finely endowed" than most people, and she needs to have "discriminating relationships" of "various colors." When she gives a public lecture on marriage in which she endorses the free-love views for which she is well known, numerous lesbian couples attend.[75]

Herrick may have fabricated the allegations of homosexuality; he was obviously hurting from Parsons's rejection when he wrote the novel. He stated elsewhere that he thought she liked men better than women.[76] Margaret Mead read *The End of Desire* soon after it was published; in a letter to Benedict she criticized Parsons for disliking women and for being confused about her sexual identity. "I would like to ask Elsie," she stated, "whether she hated women because she wished she was a man or hated them because she wasn't a woman and wished that she was."[77]

Whatever Benedict and Mead thought of her, Parsons was generous. Recognizing Benedict's potential, she didn't prevent her from entering the anthropology department at Columbia; she later funded her research. Benedict served as editor of the *Journal of American Folk-Lore*, funded by Parsons, who was an associate editor. She worked on a concordance of American Indian myths, again funded by Parsons. Yet their letters to each other are cold, mostly about the journal. Over the years they disagreed a lot; Boas mediated between them.[78] Their theoretical approaches differed, with Parsons focusing on cultural detail and on the diffusionist influence of Spanish and Mexican Indian cultures on the Pueblo Indians, while Benedict focused on dominant and deviant configurations in discrete cultures. In terms of the feminist movement, their feud may have been unfortunate, but their dislike of each other contributed to Benedict's initial interest in Margaret Mead, whom she saw as a potential ally in anthropology.

ENTERING THE GRADUATE PROGRAM in anthropology at Columbia seemed to solve Benedict's problem about what to do with her life. It held out a way for her to continue working for social reform through teaching, writing, and doing scholarship, and it offered her an intellectual community. Both Parsons and Goldenweiser, as well as other

Columbia anthropologists, published in popular intellectual journals. Goldenweiser brought the vision quest of American Indians to Benedict's attention as a possible dissertation topic; like the Indians who retreated from their regular society to find a spirit guide, Benedict also had visions in the form of eidetic daydreams. Through becoming a scholar she could use her ability to concentrate—to "shut up her ears"—to focus on the details of texts and cultures and by ordering them, order herself. She could journey to "other countries" to find an alternative one to the United States, where she felt like "a stranger in a strange land." She could become a scientist, challenging Stanley on his own ground; through teaching and writing books she could vicariously have the children that had been denied her. And in this new field of anthropology, in which exciting new knowledge was being created, she might find fame.

Religion, ethnicity, intellectualism, homosexuality, maternity, success—all Benedict's interests came together in the field of anthropology. Boas accepted her into the Columbia program and, aware of her age, he gave her credit for the courses she had taken at the New School so that she could finish a Ph.D. quickly. Benedict entered the program in 1921; Mead had entered Barnard the previous year. The stage was set for the two of them to meet in 1922 in Boas's introductory course in anthropology, with Benedict as the graduate student instructor and Mead as her student.

PART IV

From New York City to New Guinea

CHAPTER 6

DePauw University, Barnard College, and the Making of Margaret Mead

D URING WORLD WAR I, as Ruth Benedict adjusted to marriage, wrote stories, and reentered social work, Margaret
Mead was a student in junior high and high school. Young and
impressionable, she supported American intervention on behalf of the
allies. She rolled bandages at the Red Cross and gave four-minute
speeches selling war bonds to local groups. "I felt filled with the impact
of great historical decisions," she wrote, "in which Democracy would
triumph and the world be made safe from the Germans, who were her
enemies."[1] Speaking at her high school graduation, she endorsed
internationalism and an improved status for women as goals for war
and peace. After reading a magazine story in which German soldiers
raped a Belgian girl, she fantasized about leading a group of Spaniards
as spies in Germany. As a high school student, however, she was
involved with her studies, her friends, and, as a senior, with Luther
Cressman. Drafted into the army, he never left an artillery training
camp in Kentucky. The horror of World War I didn't shape Mead's
thinking in the way it did Benedict's.[2]

Once she had completed high school and a year of studying French
at a local girls' private school, Margaret expected to attend Wellesley
College, where her mother had gone. Instead, she spent her first year
of college in 1919 and 1920 at DePauw University in Indiana, her

father's alma mater. Experiencing one of his financial reversals and as capricious as ever, Edward Mead suddenly refused to pay for college for her, justifying his decision by having a doctor diagnose her as too small and fragile to handle college work. It was one of the only times in her life, Mead stated, that she had a "feminist fit."[3] In desperation, her mother suggested DePauw, correctly reasoning that Edward wouldn't refuse. Margaret didn't object; her parents and her grandmother had always praised the Midwest, where they had been raised, and she looked forward to being there.

Yet DePauw was a Methodist institution dominated by football and a fraternity/sorority system. This wasn't Emily Fogg's feminist Wellesley or her reform-minded University of Chicago. It wasn't Ruth Fulton's Vassar, with its intellectualism, ethic of social service, and devotion to Charlotte Perkins Gilman. Its student body was composed of upwardly mobile Midwesterners who were from the first generation of their families to go to college. In *Blackberry Winter* Mead described the male students as in training to be Rotarians and the female students as preparing to be their wives and members of garden clubs.[4]

Margaret didn't fit in. Everything about her was wrong: her Episcopalianism, her love of ideas, her Pennsylvania accent, her books of poetry, and the picture of Rabindranath Tagore, the Bengali mystical poet, on the wall of her dorm room. The female students at DePauw weren't used to difference, and Margaret committed the cardinal sin: she dressed differently. She liked color and pattern in her clothing; the DePauw women wore plain dresses, simply cut, many with middy collars made of lace. In the pictures in Margaret's yearbook you can see those students, dressed alike, in garb resembling a sailor's uniform: Mead called it a "Peter Thompson outfit." Taking the high ground, she wrote to her mother: "Many of the girls here are children whose only fame is in their clothes."[5]

The sorority women, in particular, found her appearance dowdy and her clothes out of style. The rumor got around that she wasn't especially bright when she arrived at her dormitory the weekend before school started wearing a wrinkled dress and rimless glasses and exhausted from the train ride from Pennsylvania to Indiana.[6] In the days after, Margaret went to sorority rush parties and didn't receive a bid. The sorority women shunned her on campus, since they were forbidden to speak to individuals going through rush—and they continued to avoid her once it had ended. To make matters worse, Margaret was an Episcopalian in a Methodist school. Because she didn't belong to an evangelical religion, she couldn't join the college YWCA, another student social center.

Yet DePauw had positive features. Margaret liked her classes, since the professors, who weren't expected to publish much, could spend a lot of time with her. She especially liked her required classes in religion, for their professors taught them from the perspective of the Social Gospel, the movement in Protestantism that, linked to progressive reform, focused on Christ's egalitarian teachings to promote social change. That message helped her to reconcile her mother's socialism—which seemed connected to her atheism—with her own Episcopal beliefs. Unlike Benedict, she wasn't rejecting a religion she experienced as repressive; she found security and spirituality in the Episcopal Church. She also liked her class in social ethics in which the "fiery-eyed" professor maintained that all the truth didn't have to be revealed at once.

The women in Margaret's dormitory were friendly: in fact, the culture of female romantic friendships wasn't entirely absent at coeducational DePauw. In letters to her family during the fall term, Margaret often referred to a Ruth, whom she described as "the sweetest thing that ever happened."[7] There was also Katharine Rothenberger, a resident in her dormitory who initially took pity on her and then fell under her spell. Margaret found the reserved Katharine elegant and desirable. She described her to Emily Mead: "She doesn't gloss over her reserve with an outer layer of apparent openness and familiarity, the way I do. One has to be brave and persistent to cross those deserts of ice and snow which she is." Appealing to Emily's elitism, she wrote: "She is a patrician from the top of her red-gold hair to the toe of her little pointed shoe." Margaret concluded: "You would love her."[8]

What went on between Margaret and Katharine is unclear, although Margaret later described her to Gregory Bateson as so secure in her Midwestern ideals that she was willing to try anything.[9] In a note between them that survives from that time, Katharine writes to Margaret that Hilda Jane has left her room and asks her to come and "tuck her in."[10] Yet she and Katharine acted in accordance with the system of gender socialization of Margaret's childhood, with its encouragement of both same-sex and heterosexual affection. The year after Margaret left DePauw for Barnard, Katharine wrote to her that she was as much in love with her as ever. She also described her boyfriend and confided: "I am on the verge of falling in love again. He is using the knock-down and drag-out method (which you said would be the only successful one)."[11]

Once Margaret's parents realized that she was isolated at DePauw, they urged her to withdraw, but she refused. The situation constituted an ethical challenge that she had to face, she declared, for the faults in the DePauw students reflected flaws in herself. That stance is impressive for someone in her late teens; it demonstrates the adult side of Mead, her unusual maturity at a young age, how she could face a crisis by standing her ground and fighting back. She decided to follow the advice of both her mother and father that she organize the unorganized dormitory students into a bloc of supporters.[12] Emily had years of experience in the politics of women's organizations and Edward in those of the university; both were shrewd about the strategy Margaret might use to win a place. "I never did believe in fraternities," Emily wrote to Margaret. "Get up your own group."[13]

Thus Margaret launched a campaign for popularity. She wrote award-winning scripts for college skits and festivals. In the fall carnival, she caused a stir by playing a "headless" lady in her dormitory's "haunted house," covering her head and body with a sheet, with bloody chicken brains on top of her head, while she carried a gory fake head in her arms.[14] Using skills she had learned in organizing family activities and clubs in high school, she held teas for students in her classes to form study groups loyal to her. Katharine's mother taught her what to wear. In the school's May Day celebration, for which she wrote the script, Margaret played the queen to Katharine's king. The morning of the event, she assembled baskets of flowers and delivered them to both friends and adversaries. Then she ran a successful campaign to elect Katharine student body vice president by pitting the sororities against one another. By the end of the school year, she was well known and respected—even by the sorority women.[15]

Margaret learned many lessons at DePauw. In experiencing discrimination, she later maintained, she learned what it was like to be a member of an oppressed minority. Minor confrontations often hurt the most, as when after she revamped her wardrobe a sorority member rudely grabbed the collar of the Peter Thompson dress she was wearing to see if it was an original or a copy. (It was an original.) The experience of being a member of a minority group, she stated, stood her in good stead when she became a student of the antiracist Franz Boas. She compared her experience at DePauw with that of the many Jews who were Boas students. They had grown up under the relative egalitarianism in Germany and the United States in the late nineteenth century, when anti-Semitism was at a low point, only to become pariahs by the century's end. All kinds of fighters, she wrote, are needed in the struggle to end discrimination—"both those who know at first hand the searing effects of discrimination and those who are shocked to the core by their encounters with the tragedies that are part of others' everyday experience."[16]

Through her campaign to be popular at DePauw, Margaret honed her understanding of group politics and of how to manipulate a situation to gain her ends. She had, indeed, become a producer of scenarios of no mean proportion, working both openly and behind the scenes. She even learned lessons from the sororities. They taught her the power of sisterhood, how young women who bond together gain strength and security through rituals and mutual support. She also learned that an inegalitarian environment could absorb her so completely that she mirrored its values. She could play a role dictated by the culture around her that wasn't healthy. A goal of her campaign for recognition was to receive a bid from a sorority, since, as she wrote her mother, "all the girls of any distinction or breeding here are in the sororities."[17]

She realized that the sororities were discriminatory, with each house selecting members on the basis of looks, dress, and background and the sororities rated against each other on a scale employing the same criteria. She wrote that a "blatant, strident artificiality" characterized the sororities. Yet she was elated when she was chosen for the literary honor society because belonging to it increased her appeal to the sororities; to keep in good repute with the administration each house pledged several students with outstanding grades. And she was overjoyed when a fraternity man asked her out, for the sororities functioned above all as dating and marriage bureaus, with the highest prestige going to their members who dated fraternity men. The dating system, however, distressed Margaret: she wanted to excel in her classes, but the men at DePauw usually didn't ask out women who got high grades.[18]

Mead's triumph at DePauw also resulted from her increasingly charismatic personality. No one ever described her as beautiful, but she could be irresistible. Her gaze was direct and riveting—like a laser beam, a friend later described it. She had such an ability to communicate with her eyes, another said.[19] She had her mother's engaging smile, and she had beautiful hair; people told her it shone. When speaking she used a lot of gestures; her tiny, childlike hands were fascinating: she thought that her father's holding them a lot when she was a child had libidinized them. "People thought that my hands had a special quality when they held them," she said, "the quality of my grasp or skin or whatever."[20] She had a lovely body, with slim legs; she touched people a lot; she moved close in conversations.

Her mind worked so quickly that it was fascinating to watch her think. And could she talk! "I never heard anyone talk before I met Margaret," stated her third husband, Gregory Bateson—the son of a famed biologist and a graduate of Cambridge University, used to brilliant conversation.[21] She could weave old ideas into new patterns, see possibilities others couldn't imagine, dream dreams for them they couldn't conceive. She could be childlike and maternal, playful and mature, sweet and dependent, needing mothering and able to give it. More than that, her body matched the 1920s ideal of beauty. Take a look at Mary Pickford and Clara Bow. Both are slim and tiny: the ideal woman of the 1920s was around five feet tall. Mead broke through the boundaries to women's achievement, but her appearance was located within those boundaries, and that limitation, ironically, was an advantage. The vitriolic public attacks against her didn't begin until she was middle-aged, when her body began to spread. Before then, she came to personify the flapper, a liberated icon for women in the 1920s.

In his famed description of Cleopatra, Plutarch wrote: "Her beauty was not incomparable," but "the attraction of her person, joining with the charm of her conversation . . . was something bewitching."[22] And Margaret could be bewitching. One hardly thinks of her as a vamp, but she could be seductive. Friends of Edna St. Vincent Millay described her as able, with a toss of her head, to change her looks from ordinary to beautiful.[23] Mead had that chameleon quality—in charm, if not in looks. By the time she was nineteen, she had conquered DePauw, and she would be equally magnetic at Barnard. Then it got out of hand, and Luther Cressman, along with Ruth Benedict, rescued her—for a time.

AFTER THE DIFFICULT YEAR at DePauw, Barnard seemed the college for Margaret. It had a reputation for radicalism, careerism, and urban sophistication—and sororities had been abolished in 1913 as undemocratic. During her first months at DePauw, when she had few friends, Margaret had cheered herself up by going to the library and reading reviews of Broadway plays. She realized that New York City was the intellectual center of the nation, and she wanted to be there. "I developed the sense, as did so many aspiring intellectuals," she wrote, "that the center of intellectual life was New York City, where Mencken and George Jean Nathan were publishing the *Smart Set*, where the *Freeman* and the *Nation*, and the *New Republic* flourished."[24] Luther was there as well, studying for the Episcopal priesthood at the General Theological Seminary. Although she hadn't seemed to pay much attention to him when she was at DePauw, she now wanted to be with him: at the very least he could save her from the perils of any hetero-sexual dating culture at Barnard and Columbia.

Elated by her triumph at DePauw and determined not to repeat the same mistakes, Mead hit Barnard like a whirlwind. During her first year, she attended classes, joined the debate team, wrote for the school newspaper, headed a Sunday-night discussion club, worked in Episco-pal groups, and taught Sunday school off campus. Free of DePauw conformity, she joined the Intercollegiate Socialist League: she may have disliked her mother's feminism, but she didn't completely reject her political beliefs. Margaret went to plays and lectures on and off campus—during her first year at Barnard, she claimed, she saw forty plays. She went to the opera, took a class in aesthetic dancing, and heard speakers such as her favorite Rabindranath Tagore. "I had a la-mentable tendency," Mead admitted, "to get interested in almost any-thing."[25] She spent time with Luther; she gave teas and went to teas. For Barnard's country fair in her first semester she dressed as a "sweet little girl" in a white dress with a blue crepe paper sash, and she carried the class mascot, a Maltese kitten, in a pink workbasket.[26]

Barnard was founded in 1889 as a college for the daughters of New York City's elites; it was the last of the Ivy League women's colleges—the so-called Seven Sisters—to appear. When it opened it wasn't iden-tified with feminism, but by the time Margaret arrived it was. Emily Putnam, a member of Bryn Mawr's first graduating class and dean of Barnard from 1894 to 1900, brought to the school her alma mater's emphasis on academic achievement and careers for women. Married after she was hired, Putnam was fired when she had a child. It's no wonder that in *The Lady*, a study of elite women throughout history, Putnam viewed men as having defined those women's roles. Margaret Mead rarely referred to feminist writers in her later work, but in *Sex and Temperament in Three Primitive Societies* she criticized Putnam for focusing too much on women in *The Lady* and failing to analyze male roles and behavior.[27]

Virginia C. Gildersleeve, a Barnard graduate who became dean in

1911 and remained in that position until 1947, continued Putnam's emphasis on academic achievement and careers for Barnard undergraduates. Unlike Putnam she never married: the rumor was that she was lesbian. Her emphasis on learning was evident in the banning of sororities after she arrived, in the many women professionals who spoke on campus, and in the small number of students involved in social service work during Mead's years at Barnard. As editor of the *Barnard Bulletin*, the school newspaper, in her senior year, Mead estimated that about 10 percent of the students were involved in social service. (The comparable figure for Vassar when Benedict went there was one-half.) Barnard students were careerists; religion and benevolence, the staples at Vassar, weren't a strong part of Barnard's profile.[28]

In 1920 Gildersleeve backed a faculty drive to require that all Barnard students take courses in psychology, sociology, and economics. With that requirement in place, no undergraduate college in the nation, including the all-male Columbia College, provided better training in the social sciences. Moreover, Barnard had an anthropology department, and that was rare among the women's colleges—and among colleges and universities in general. Gildersleeve's emphasis on achievement for women, however, had limits. Although Mead estimated that when she was a student at Barnard the faculty was half women, a listing of the faculty by rank in her graduation yearbook reveals that most of those women were assistant professors and lecturers. Gildersleeve had to keep Barnard in the good graces of the male administration at Columbia and the separate graduate school there.

Although political conservatism dominated the 1920s, many Barnard undergraduates had leftist inclinations when Mead was there. When she polled the students who had transferred to Barnard from other institutions for the *Barnard Bulletin*, they agreed that Barnard students were much more interested in current issues than the students at their previous schools. As editor of the paper, Mead featured leftist groups, including the Social Science Club, which in February 1923 sponsored a tour of the headquarters of the American Civil Liberties Union, the Anarchist Party, and the Workers Party. The tour ended with dinner at the Cooperative Cafeteria, where the profits were distributed among the workers.

The students at Barnard, like those at DePauw, found Mead different, although since most of them came from New York City while she came from Pennsylvania, they found her more Western than Eastern. Her apartment mate Deborah Kaplan, however, thought that she resembled an Eastern "Yankee," the legendary American whose innocent manner belied his shrewdness and who, as Constance Rourke described him, was a shape-shifter, able to take on a differing persona according to the situation.[29] Whatever Deb's suspicions, Margaret fit in, for the Barnard students, unlike those at DePauw, enjoyed difference. "I love, love, love, love it here," she wrote to her mother soon after she arrived.[30]

She made so many friends so quickly that she had difficulty keeping their names straight. "Names, names, names," she wrote her grandmother at the beginning of her second semester, "they gyrate, they dance, they scintillate before my weary eyes."[31] There were the students in her classes, those she worked with in campus activities, and those she recruited as dates for Luther's friends at his seminary. She organized others into a group called the Ash Can Cats from the students she lived with in an apartment in a large apartment building the college had purchased down the street from the campus. Drama teacher Minor Latham gave them the name "Ash Can Cats." The group wasn't large; it included about ten individuals by the time she graduated.[32] Yet it was very important to her: many of its members became her friends for life; many became close to Ruth Benedict.

The Ash Can Cats included Léonie Adams, the poet, and Deborah Kaplan, a high school classmate of Léonie's from Brooklyn. Eleanor Pelham Kortheuer had grown up around the corner from Barnard and was Episcopalian, like Margaret. They called her Pelham because of the several Eleanors in their group. Several students were assigned to their apartment, including Viola Corrigan, a Catholic with whom Margaret debated religion, and Mary Ann (Bunny) McCall, a stereotypical flapper with bobbed hair and short skirts who went to Princeton on the weekends. During Margaret's next two years, Leah Josephson Hanna, Eleanor Steele, and Hannah Kahn also became apartment mates—and Ash Can Cats. A number of Margaret's apartment mates and Ash Can Cats were Jewish, and Margaret liked that. She liked the creative spark of difference.

Hannah Kahn was the first among them to bob her hair. Because she then looked like a boy, they nicknamed her "David," after Michelangelo's statue of the Old Testament shepherd boy. Margaret and Léonie recruited Louise Rosenblatt for the apartment. The daughter of Jewish anarchists from Philadelphia, she was a student of literature who shared Margaret's radicalism and her love of ideas. Their group also included several students who lived at home and used their apartment when on campus. Eleanor Phillips was among this group, whom Margaret dubbed the "parasites"; she was ambivalent about the independent Eleanor, who was as opinionated as she and whom she described in her 1935 memoir as "possessive, acquisitive, snobbish, and excessively ambitious."[33]

From her arrival at Barnard, Margaret took charge; she had learned her lessons well at DePauw. Her energetic, outspoken manner attracted insecure young women to her. Even the gifted Léonie Adams was so shy that she often blushed when spoken to. Deb Kaplan went to Margaret for what sounds like training in how to influence others. Margaret advised her to be useful and amusing—and to use flattery whenever possible. Deb appreciated the advice, but she thought that when Margaret followed it herself she too often told others what they wanted to hear. It's no wonder that Deb described her as a Yankee.[34]

Margaret mothered her apartment mates, as she had mothered her two younger sisters. She gave them advice; she arranged their lives. She organized them into a family, with Léonie and herself the parents and the rest the "children." She saw herself as a producer, organizing the group around Léonie as she had organized the DePauw students around Katharine Rothenberger. The apartment mates who joined them in Margaret's second year were "grandchildren"; those who joined in her senior year were "great-grandchildren." Mead explained that she put these cross-generational family links together because she disliked grouping students by year in school—an idea she probably got from progressive educators by way of her grandmother Martha. The college family she created also resembled the sororities at DePauw.

Deciding that they should have experience with children, Margaret arranged for them to baby-sit children of faculty at night. That scheme also provided her with a quiet place to study away from her noisy roommates, once she put her charges to bed. She never forgot studying her assignments on baby-sitting nights for the introductory anthropology course with Benedict; she loved memorizing the complex kinship systems of Australian tribes and copying out Northwest Coast designs from pictures of the carvings of the Kwakiutl tribe that Franz Boas studied, "until I felt I had the feel of those marvelously dissected sharks and eagles in my fingertips."[35]

Like Margaret, her apartment mates became academic and extracurricular leaders. Because of their energy and cohesion, the group became a campus legend. They were drawn to grand gestures; one May Day, after dinner in the cafeteria, they sang the "Internationale" and then blew out red candles on a birthday cake. Naming their group seemed appropriate. An assistant dean who found their apartment strewn with clothing and empty gin bottles one day gave them their first name, "the mental and moral mess." She didn't know that Bunny McCall, the flapper, was responsible for the mess; they adopted the name "with a kind of wicked glee."[36] They replaced that name with another one they took from the insulting remarks of a conservative speaker at graduation one year about radicals at Barnard: "The Communist Morons." They liked Minor Latham's name, with its joking allusion to trash and to the contemporary Ashcan school of painters, who were realists with a radical edge. It became their lifelong name for their group.[37]

According to Louise Rosenblatt, their love of ideas and poetry kept them together, as did rituals they invented. They held feasts in restaurants off campus; after they finished eating, Léonie always read aloud Shelley's "Adonais," his tribute to Keats as the beautiful mythological Adonis beloved by both women and men, which Shelley wrote after Keats died from tuberculosis at the age of twenty-six. Margaret sometimes argued with the feisty Eleanor Phillips over doing this reading because she thought it was an insult to Shelley to read his poem about beauty when they were eating greasy pork chops in a cheap café. Eleanor replied that Shelley was always Shelley, no matter the occasion. When they went to Greenwich Village for dinner, they sometimes balanced a candle on its side and lit it at both ends, bringing to life the famous candle of Edna St. Vincent Millay's "First Fig" in *A Few Figs from Thistles:*

> *My candle burns at both ends;*
> *It will not last the night;*
> *But ah, my foes, and oh, my friends—*
> *It gives a lovely light!*[38]

Margaret and her apartment mates bobbed their hair, shortened their skirts, and learned to smoke, although they were serious about their studies and kept their distance from Bunny McCall's "flapper" behavior. They stayed up late talking about poetry and the theater, Freud and Marx, Sacco and Vanzetti. They applied Freudian ideas to each other. Agnes Piel, a student at the fringe of their group who was being psychoanalyzed, identified Léonie as masochistic and Margaret as "castrating" toward men. Margaret told Deb that she shouldn't marry her boyfriend because he was a "latent homosexual"; she accused Luther of having a "mother fixation" on her because he liked her breasts.[39]

According to Louise Rosenblatt, she, Léonie, and Margaret were especially close because of their radical views.[40] In *Blackberry Winter* Mead describes their radicalism as more emotional than ideological, but she made this judgment in the 1970s, long after she had abandoned the political radicalism of her youth. At Barnard, however, she belonged to the Intercollegiate Socialist League, supported the cooperative movement, marched in picket lines, and celebrated the communist May Day. When Margaret and Léonie shared the same room one year they put a sign on their door: "We don't believe in private property: please keep yours out!"[41]

As at most coeducational institutions in this era, a dating culture existed; it connected Barnard with Columbia College, although in *Blackberry Winter* Mead asserted that she and her friends refused to be controlled by it. If they had made plans with each other to go out, no one would cancel those plans if a man asked her out for the same time. "We learned loyalty to women, pleasure in conversation with women, and enjoyment of the way in which we complemented one another in terms of our differences in temperament, which we found as interesting as the complementarity that is produced by the difference of sex."[42] That sentence is startling; Mead's use of the term "temperament" relates to the theme about sexual orientation around which she originally intended to organize her autobiography but omitted in the published version.

In drafts of *Blackberry Winter*, Mead wrote about her romantic friendships with girls in her childhood but not about those she had at Barnard. Wanda Neff set the second half of *We Sing Diana* at Columbia University, portraying the school as infused with a heterosexual ethos after World War I. She described the Barnard women as wondering whether the "mannish" women on campus were "bisexual," thus suggesting that labeling their sexual identity had become an issue for young women. Indeed, in *Blackberry Winter* Mead suddenly raised "homosexuality" as a concern for herself and her Barnard friends. Contending that they were naive about sex, she stated that older, more sophisticated students explained the meaning of same-sex love to them. Avoiding any suggestion of homosexuality among them, she asserted that because of what the older students told them they worried that their past friendships with girls might have been "incipient examples."

Was Margaret physically involved with any of the Ash Can Cats? With the exception of Eleanor Steele, it seems doubtful, although Marie Eichelberger, Margaret's lifelong friend, suggested that Léonie might have been lesbian: in 1938 Marie wrote to Margaret that Ruth Benedict had suggested that she write her autobiography but that "like Léonie I can't because of the form of my attachments."[43] In later letters, Benedict referred to Léonie's "affair" with poet Louise Bogan. Bogan's biographers, however, dismiss the affair as an infatuation on the part of Léonie, who was involved with Edmund Wilson in the later 1920s and then married literary critic William Troy.[44] Pelham, who became close to Benedict (as did "David"), seemed to identify herself as heterosexual when she stated that she was so shy in college that Margaret found her men to date.[45] Surely she and the others understood, however, the multiple sexual meanings of Millay's candle burning "at both ends"—and that Michelangelo's David was an icon for lesbian women. On the other hand, most of Mead's college friends married, including Pelham and David. Bisexuality, not homosexuality, may have been the issue.

Yet the students at Barnard couldn't have avoided New York's ubiquitous male homosexual culture, for gay male prostitutes, the fabled "fairies" with dyed blond hair and wearing red ties, were readily visible in Greenwich Village and Times Square, districts where the restaurants and theaters that Mead and her friends went to were located. Performers who cross-dressed were standard on the vaudeville and nightclub stages. Moreover, Greenwich Village was known as a place where lesbians and male homosexuals gathered in nightclubs and cafés and where they lived. Huge drag balls, held in public halls like Madison Square Garden, functioned as "coming-out" rituals for young homosexual males, and the newspapers gave the balls front-page coverage. Mead's papers contain a circular for a ball held by the radical newspaper the *Liberator*. Its balls were known for the many homosexuals and cross-dressers in attendance.[46]

On one level this homosexual culture was open and acknowledged; on another it was concealed. Middle-class young women didn't write home about it, for outside sophisticated circles homosexuality was anathema. No respectable family would allow an individual suspected of it into their home.[47] Thus in writing about her Barnard experience in *Blackberry Winter*, Mead focused on her relationships with the Ash Can Cats and with Luther, while she concealed her romantic friendship with a classmate named Leone Newton. That relationship was connected to a "lesbian" circle in which Mead participated, one that existed at least from the beginning of her junior year and that continued until she graduated. She kept it a secret. Margaret was daring and she liked intrigue, but she didn't want to be exposed for scandalous behavior before she had even begun her adult life.

WHILE INVOLVED WITH her female friends at Barnard, Margaret was also engaged to Luther. When she first arrived in New York she seemed happy with him; she wrote to her mother that she was pleased that she had persuaded him to become more liberal: "He no longer boasts an inflexible moral code nor a single reactionary principle." She was enthusiastic about their relationship: "Luther and I have stood both the test of absence and the tests of nearness now, and we're more in love with each other than ever."[48] He lived downtown, near the General Theological Seminary he was attending, just above Greenwich Village. Late in life he confessed that he didn't see Margaret that often at the time: perhaps once or twice a week; hardly ever on the weekends.[49]

He did write her letters. They express passionate love—and concern over her health and her emotional state. At the beginning of her second year at Barnard he refers to the devils who were "rampaging around the things that were bothering you this summer," stating that he had told her "to tell the devils to go home." What those "devils" were he doesn't say. Just before Christmas that year, she announced her engagement to him at a tea for thirty-five friends, as though to make certain that everyone at Barnard knew about her heterosexual commitment. In the fall of her senior year Luther wrote to her that their love had forged them into "one complete being yet two distinct beings" and that he loved her "darling body" with a "fierce surging gentle love that satisfies, gratifies, completes, but never hurts you." Margaret had criticized him for not being playful, but his seriousness, he said, came from having to restrain himself in their intimacy "half realized and always held in check" by their agreement to forgo intercourse until marriage.[50]

No matter Margaret's engagement to Luther, by the end of her first year at Barnard she became intimate with a classmate named Leone Newton. The relationship lasted until she graduated. In *Blackberry Winter* and its drafts, Mead doesn't mention Leone—nor do any of the Ash Can Cats in later interviews—although Margaret kept notes and letters from her in her papers. Margaret's senior yearbook reveals that Leone was an outstanding student in science and, like Margaret, a leader in the class. She was a member of the student council and treasurer of the student association; one of their classmates described her as similar to Margaret in wanting to be "hot stuff." The graduation yearbook describes her as a "physics wit" and lists her address as the same building in which Margaret lived. She must have lived in a different apartment there.[51]

Leone's notes and letters to Margaret are sensual and playful, and they give the impression that she was deeply in love with her. Leone signed her correspondence "Lee" or "Peter"; Margaret called herself "Euphemia." They may have derived that name from the heroine of Charlotte Lenox's 1790 novel *Euphemia*, who has a romantic friendship with a woman.[52] Or it may have come from the late-sixteenth-century playwright John Lyly, known for his prose romance *Euphues*, written in a style of complex wordplay. Lyly's play *Gallathea*, a pastoral comedy that influenced Shakespeare in writing *As You Like It*, may also have influenced Margaret and Lee. In *Gallathea*, two female heroines dress in male clothing and hide in a forest to avoid unwanted marriages, as Rosalind does in *As You Like It*. In Shakespeare's play, men fall in love with the women in the forest, and, once Rosalind's disguise is revealed, they marry them. In *Gallathea*, however, the two women fall in love with each other and forget the men. The dilemma is resolved when Cupid transforms one of them into a man so that they can marry. The character Peter in the play is the servant of an alchemist who uses fire and the philosopher's stone to transform baser metals into gold. His activities mirror the play's resolution of gender confusion through gender transformation.[53]

Margaret and Lee shared a love of Shakespeare. In a note to Margaret ("Euphemia"), Lee wrote of her excitement over seeing Ethel Barrymore and Jane Cowl as rival Juliets in separate Broadway productions of *Romeo and Juliet*. Those productions took place in November 1922, the first semester of Margaret's senior year.[54] Elizabethan drama, with its gender bending and its cross-dressing, formed a fitting backdrop to this relationship, as it had to the pre–World War I romantic friendships at women's colleges. Mead herself pointed to that resonance when she wrote in 1974, in one of her *Redbook* columns, that "in Elizabethan England, where young boys played all the feminine roles on the stage, the device of having a boy playing the romantic role of a girl disguised as a boy fall in love with a man had almost infinite possibilities."[55] In her relationship with Leone Margaret, who had dressed as a "sweet little girl" in the Barnard fair in the fall of 1920, played the female part. A large grove of trees then stood in the center of the Barnard campus; called "the Jungle," it was symbolic of both bountiful nature and the threatening city outside the walls of the college. Margaret and Lee sometimes pinned notes to each other on trees in the grove, following the example of Rosalind and Orlando in *As You Like It* and the lovers in *Gallathea*. Margaret had produced and acted in *As You Like It* during her senior year in high school; the play was produced at Barnard in her senior year.[56]

The relationship between Margaret and Lee was passionate. "The warmest glow just raced through me when I found your letter on the 'tree' this morning," wrote Peter/Lee. "I seized it so hungrily that the 11-year-old William inquired if I was a 'feller.' He couldn't understand about a little wifelet." The relationship was also physical. Writing to Margaret, Peter/Lee expressed her passion in terms drawn from the language of both male and female lovemaking, reflecting the Victorian linking of male and female desire. "Today, in spite of having given my body, somewhere in that dim past, passionately, irrevocably, gladly—today I am an unmarked girl, dreaming slender dreams, fancying, timid—but tomorrow a woman seeking to surrender—or a master powerful, insistent, my loved one's face hot under my seeking lips."[57]

Their relationship was set in a lesbian circle, whose members included students named Billy and Eleanor. Billy may have been the class cheerleader: in the yearbook she is the only Billy in the class— aside from a Wilhemina from the South. Large and solid in her photo, Billy the cheerleader is spoofed as "the great Mlle Billy, with a sort of salt water taffy pulling style." Eleanor is hard to identify because of the several Eleanors among Margaret's friends. She may have been the feisty Eleanor Phillips, who never married, although she was more likely Eleanor Steele, who became a tragic figure in Margaret's life in the early 1930s when Margaret cared for her as she died from tuberculosis. When they were students at Barnard Eleanor called Margaret "little Angel Mother."[58]

In Margaret's lesbian circle, Lee and Billy sometimes paired off. Lee wrote to Margaret that she had spent a "perfect" day and night with Billy—"so big and strong and brave." She also hinted at having been intimate with Eleanor, as though a special bond connected the four of them. In her "Life History," Margaret distanced herself from her homosexual past, contending that Leone and Eleanor were the central couple in the group. Lee's letters suggest that the group met secretly. From the middle of her senior year Margaret was adamant that she and Leone had to end their relationship, although Leone resisted, begging Margaret to meet with them one more time. "There'll be just Billy and you and Eleanor and Vera and me and we can just dawdle and smoke and talk and be happy." She concluded with the telling statement that she would "receive her lessons in unselfishness very humbly."[59]

That spring Leone left New York and drove to San Francisco, where she found a job as a chemist in a laboratory at the University of California in Berkeley. But the breakup with Margaret and Margaret's marriage to Luther hurt. She missed Margaret terribly. "I want to hold you closely for one of our rare, rare moments," she wrote in a letter. And it was hard for Margaret to give up Leone. Even after she married Luther, she wrote poetry about her. One of those poems is about how difficult it was to keep their relationship secret:

> *Lovely lies, intricate lies*
> *Strangling me in your hair . . .*
>
> *Lambent lies, densely woven*
> *This be my only care*
> *That when I die, you may be*
> *True as your golden hair. . . .*
>
> *Beautiful lies with fair [abandon]*
> *You polish the edge of my soul*
> *Til hard and brittle. . . .*[60]

After several years in San Francisco, Leone came back to New York City and reentered Barnard. She took a course with Ruth Benedict, who wrote to Mead that Leone was involved with another student.[61] By the early 1930s she reappeared in Margaret's life again—and now she was married. After seeing Margaret, she wrote to her that she liked her even more than in college; what happened next remains unknown. Margaret told Gregory Bateson that Leone spent years unsuccessfully trying to be a lesbian and that she finally gave it up because it hadn't really satisfied her, and she married a man.[62] In "Life History," Margaret dismissed Leone as an oversexed, masculine type of woman who had led a hectic homosexual life in college with half a dozen students.[63]

MEAD'S EDUCATION AT Barnard was as crucial to her intellectual development as Benedict's at Vassar had been to hers. It wasn't her courses in the humanities that especially influenced Mead, although she graduated with a B.A. in English. Rather, those in the social sciences, especially psychology, were key. Barnard required its students to take courses in those disciplines, although Margaret, with academic parents in the social sciences, might have taken them anyway.[64]

The social science departments at Columbia were preeminent in the nation, and they were identified with empiricism and quantification, the dominant trends at the time in disciplines like sociology and psychology, which were undergoing the process of professionalization. Focusing inward on creating organizations and standards, they produced Ph.D.'s doing detailed monographic research, while they were pressured by conservative college presidents and boards of trustees as well as by businesses and governments wanting technical data from "objective experts." Historians of gender view these trends as a masculine response to the growing "feminization" of these disciplines, as in sociology large numbers of women entered social work, and in psychology women gained M.A.'s and Ph.D.'s and entered psychology departments in schools of education and served on testing staffs in hospitals and public agencies.[65]

In 1921, in an article on "intellectuals" in his famed compilation of articles on American thought and culture, critic Harold Stearns echoed male cultural commentators from George Santayana to Theodore Roosevelt in charging that "feminization" was destroying the intellectual establishment, the fabric of society, and the identity of men. William James's distinction between "tender-minded" idealism and "tough-minded" empiricism was in widespread use, as were the terms "hard" and "soft" to differentiate "masculine" sciences like physics and chemistry from "feminine" ones like sociology.[66]

At Columbia, as at other universities, the ties between the departments of sociology and psychology and the settlement houses forged in the progressive 1900s were severed by the 1920s, and practical training for a career in social welfare was transferred from the college to the professional schools. When Mead entered Barnard in 1920, training in what we call clinical psychology and in social work was available mainly at Teachers College or at the New York School of Philanthropy, which became the Columbia School of Social Work in 1940. Training in the departments of psychology and sociology—especially at the graduate level—was mostly experimental and quantitative, designed to foster scholarship, not activism.[67]

In her psychology courses, which she took at Teachers College as well as at Barnard, Mead learned how to do statistical surveys, graphs, and tables. She learned about short-term and long-term longitudinal studies. She learned sampling techniques and how to take case histories of individuals and to give a variety of tests, including the popular intelligence quotient (IQ) tests. Psychologist James McKeen Cattell of Columbia, a founder of the field of experimental psychology, had invented them; Edward L. Thorndike of Teachers College, a student of Cattell's and a pioneer in animal experimentation, was refining them. Trained by statisticians, Mead knew these techniques and used them in her fieldwork; she was a pioneer in doing so. In fact, her competence was recognized when, after she graduated, William Fielding Ogburn chose her as assistant editor of his *Journal of the American Statistical Association*.

Like many undergraduates, Margaret considered a number of majors: she almost switched to philosophy but, according to Louise Rosenblatt, she gave up the idea because she didn't see much future for women in that field. Aside from Minor Latham, Margaret's favorite professors at Barnard were William Fielding Ogburn in sociology and Harry Hollingworth in psychology. Both were critical of the growing scientism in their disciplines, and both included nonacademic theorists like Freud and Jung in their course readings.[68]

During World War I Ogburn did statistical surveys of social conditions, took graduate courses in anthropology with Boas, and underwent analysis. His best-known work, *Social Change with Respect to Culture and Human Nature*, contained his famous theory of cultural lag, his proposal that certain sectors of a society may change more quickly than others, as in instances of technology outdistancing general social development. In that book he referred to ethnographies done by anthropologists, criticized evolutionary thinking as hierarchical and racist, suggested that cultures shape their members from childhood on, and called for combining cultural and psychological interpretations into a new synthesis.[69] In other words, he anticipated a number of Benedict's and Mead's later ideas. Mead asserted that she had learned from him not to accept a biological explanation for a social phenomenon before analyzing it in cultural terms.[70] A model Southern gentleman from Georgia, Ogburn reveals hostility to women in his journal, but he treated his female students with great respect, becoming the "idol" of the Barnard campus and a close friend of Mead's. In 1926 he left Columbia for the University of Chicago. Once there, he became the nation's leading advocate of statistical analysis in scholarly methods, although he remained sympathetic to the humanities and to psychoanalysis, serving for a time as president of the Chicago Psychoanalytic Society.[71]

Harry Hollingworth, another of Margaret's favorite teachers at Barnard, was married to Leta Hollingworth, a professor of psychology at Teachers College renowned for her experiments disproving the scientific dogma that men were more "variable" in their abilities than women and thus inevitably superior in any endeavor. Harry Hollingworth called the variability thesis "the last foothold of the anti-feminists."[72] Both Leta and Harry marched in woman suffrage parades; Leta belonged to Heterodoxy and wrote about feminism in popular magazines. Mead doesn't seem to have taken any courses with Leta Hollingworth, but Harry talked about her work in his classes. That work included a well-known study of adolescence—in which she attacked lesbianism as a dangerous perversion. Accepting Freud's belief that humans are born desiring both sexes and that they mature into heterosexuality, Leta contended that older lesbians easily seduced adolescents, not yet fully heterosexual, into homosexual affairs. She condemned "violent crushes" at single-sex schools, recommended coeducation, and called for introducing courtship between boys and girls at a young age. Indeed, even William Fielding Ogburn called homosexuality a "psychosis."[73]

In her senior year at Barnard, Margaret also took the introductory course in anthropology with Franz Boas. He was there partly out of choice—he found the Barnard women better students than the male undergraduates at Columbia College—and partly because of his feud with Columbia president Nicholas Murray Butler, who isolated him there. Impressed by his knowledge and his critical skills, Margaret thought him the most brilliant teacher she had ever had.

Margaret kept her lecture notes from another Barnard course, one on ancient Greece. The notes include analyses of Plato's *Phaedrus* and *Symposium*, his dialogues about love and sexual identity. Discussing the relationships between men and boys, the instructor, following a standard contemporary interpretation, contended that such same-sex love was part of the Athenian "practice of virtue and philosophy" and that Plato downgraded whatever physical consummation was involved as an "earthly, coarse love." What mattered was spirituality: the soul remembers "her divine vision and is ever searching after it."[74]

Margaret wrote a paper for this class on the Athenian festival of Dionysus, which included a contest between male playwrights for the prize of best play. She didn't mention Nietzsche's analysis of Greek drama in terms of the Apollo-Dionysus dualism important to Benedict, nor did she refer to gender or sexuality in her paper, although she noted that in ancient Athens women were confined to their homes except for attending the plays and participating in certain festivals. Even in discussing Aeschylus's plays, some of which feature Cassandra and the Trojan War, Margaret didn't introduce gender as a category of analysis. Rather, she focused on the Athenian belief in the inevitability of retribution for hubris, or self-pride grown into the kind of arrogance that could result in the violation of ethical norms, as central to the violence and family disharmony in these plays.[75] Yet it was an analysis with relevance to her life, given the fact that her homosexual behavior violated her society's rules, and there might be reprisals if she was found out.

DURING MARGARET'S SENIOR YEAR, her relationships became even more complicated. Luther pressured her to marry him; Leone indulged the fantasy that she and Margaret could make their relationship public. Perhaps Margaret was engaging in the behavior Deborah Kaplan described, that of telling everyone what they wanted to hear. There was also Wanda Neff, the Barnard English instructor writing her novel about Margaret and her friends, living in their apartment building as a faculty advisor. She had them to dinner and hinted that she knew about their private lives. Neff knew a lot. In *We Sing Diana* the two students at Vassar that the narrator of the novel observes embracing in a field are the star literature student and the star science student; they seem modeled after Margaret and Leone. The English teacher described in the book as the "freshman disease" is probably modeled after Minor Latham, an expert on Shakespeare. It was known that she was lesbian; her partner was the doctor who ran the student health service.[76]

Did Mead learn that Neff was stereotyping Latham in her novel as a "mannish lesbian"? That was alarming, given the belief that older "mannish lesbians," especially older teachers with students, seduced vulnerable young women—a negative stereotype as venerable as the Sapphic one of female mentors guiding younger women to a successful maturity. The dramatic Latham was beloved at Barnard; the theater at the college is named after her. The Ash Can Cats had a "crush" on her. Margaret hardly wanted Latham's reputation destroyed. The summer after Margaret's graduation, one of her friends wrote to her that she was with a group of Barnard students who were trying to figure out what produced the "boyish-looking girl."[77] That remark was uncomfortably close.

Moreover, during her senior year Margaret's same-sex involvements went beyond her lesbian circle to include two other Barnard students. The first was Marie Bloomfield, sister of the eminent linguist Leonard Bloomfield and niece of the famed concert pianist Fannie Bloomfield-Zeisler.[78] Marie's parents had died when she was a child. Shy, awkward, and brilliant, she became an acolyte of the popular Margaret: she followed her around and made herself indispensable— running errands, straightening up Margaret's room. Margaret's second new involvement was with another Marie: Marie Eichelberger, an older student in the freshman class who was Marie Bloomfield's designated "little sister." Marie Eichelberger fascinated Margaret because she came to college "prepared to change every idea she had." When Eichelberger first looked at her across a room and their eyes met, Margaret knew that she had fallen in love with her; that's the story they always told. Like her "big sister" Marie Bloomfield, Marie Eichelberger made herself indispensable to Margaret by mending her clothes, cleaning her room, styling her hair, doing her nails.[79] In her "Life History," Mead asserted that Marie Bloomfield was insanely jealous of Louise Rosenblatt, Mead's roommate, although a more likely candidate was Marie Eichelberger, for one Marie seems to have copied the other.

Margaret was working her magic; it must have been a heady experience to have so many individuals in love with her. Yet underneath the glamour of multiple relationships and leading a secret life, something was wrong. For from the end of her first year at Barnard she suffered from neuritis in her right arm so severe that she learned to write with her left hand. She also suffered from attacks of nausea. In 1922 she began to have troubling dreams about dead babies. By her senior year she was smoking so heavily that a childhood friend who visited her remarked on it—and on how exhausted she looked.[80]

Why was she so anxious? Her classwork and extracurricular activities placed a good deal of pressure on her; it wasn't easy being, as one of her friends called her, "a pillar of the college." Her father, as capricious as ever, periodically threatened to cut off financial support. She stood up to him, but his threats bothered her. In "Life History" she stated that she developed a "conversion hysteria" from a "courtship shock" that brought back her childhood fear of rape. Did she regard her neuritis as the result of a "conversion hysteria"? Had Luther attempted to step over the boundary she had established in their sex life? She stated that despite what he had done she still intended to marry him and that she was aware of the incident in her childhood that lay behind the hysteria—but she didn't reveal what the incident was.

In 1948, as part of her therapy with Gotthard Booth, a Jungian analyst in New York whom she saw when her marriage to Gregory Bateson was falling apart, Margaret would undergo a handwriting analysis. Based on letters she wrote at various points in her life, the analysis is most detailed with regard to her college years, when it seems surprisingly perceptive. In her senior year, according to the analyst, she was close to a nervous breakdown. Confusion over her sexual orientation caused the problem. The analyst concluded that Margaret coped with her anxiety over whether she was heterosexual or homosexual by constructing a screen out of her many campus involvements behind which she hid her real self. Seeming in control of her emotions, she acted toward others like a domineering, yet caring, mother. As for her sexual orientation, she responded to men, but she felt hostility toward them; sometimes she preferred women. Basically, she wasn't sure what her sexual orientation was, and the confusion threw her into a panic.[81]

In early February 1923, Marie Bloomfield committed suicide. Just after Christmas break that year she was hospitalized with measles. When she recovered, Margaret checked her out of the hospital on a Friday and took her to her dormitory. She would have stayed with Marie over the weekend except that Leone Newton came down with an attack of hysterical blindness during an exam and she chose to nurse Leone, not Marie. In "Life History," Margaret wrote that she made Leone's "various little lesbian friends" leave her room; she took her out walking and to the movies; she calmed her down so that she recovered her sight. She didn't see Marie during that weekend. On Saturday afternoon several classmates visited Marie and read poetry with her. On Sunday she took a lethal dose of cyanide, which she stole from a science lab.[82]

No one blamed Margaret for Marie's death. During the previous month several of their friends had tried to talk Marie out of suicide;

Margaret didn't seem to have known about her intentions. Yet depression and death were central themes of the poetry that young women poets like Léonie Adams wrote after World War I. The Ash Can Cats identified with Keats and his death at an early age; they often quoted his famous line from "Ode to a Nightingale": "half in love with easeful Death." They liked Shelley's famous lines about death from *Adonais:* "Life, like a dome of many-colored glass, / stains the white radiance of eternity, / . . . Die, / If thou wouldst be with that which thou dost seek!" These lines may refer to actual death, or to the need for psychic annihilation and rebirth to reach transcendence. An adolescent depressive like Marie, however, could interpret them literally.

In a suicide note, she quoted the lines about "easeful death" from Keats. According to the *New York Times,* "she had become sick in mind, and had persuaded herself through something she had read that death was something to go to in ecstasy and exultation."[83] In *Blackberry Winter,* Mead reported her horror at finding Marie's body on the Monday morning following the weekend she had spent with Leone. Beside Marie's body was a copy of W. N. P. Barbellion's *Journal of a Disappointed Man.*[84] Why this book? Barbellion was the pen name of Bruce Frederick Cummings; the book described his suffering from a degenerative disease and ended with his suicide. It was an international bestseller; both women and men identified with the suffering of this feminized young man, who gave up his male lover to marry a woman before he died. Like Goethe's *Sorrows of Young Werther* more than a century before, the book inspired youthful suicides. Unfortunately, Marie Bloomfield was one of them.[85]

Marie's death had a major impact on Margaret, who felt guilty about it for the rest of her life, just as she felt guilt over her sister Katherine's unexpected death as a baby. She felt as though she shouldn't have chosen Leone, a tough person, over the vulnerable Marie. But she wasn't attracted to Marie the same way she was to Leone. Marie's death increased Margaret's need to try to solve everyone's problems; it left her with a deep fear of hurting anyone. She couldn't, for example, break with Marie Eichelberger even if she had wanted to—although Margaret sometimes felt smothered by Marie's obsessive assistance in personal matters and her worshipful adoration, she always appreciated Marie and depended on her to take care of her practical needs.

For the rest of her life Margaret felt a sense of impending doom if, faced with a crisis, she didn't address every possible outcome. Thus what may seem like scheming on her part can be interpreted in light of Marie Bloomfield's suicide as a frantic attempt to prevent calamity from occurring. In almost every circumstance, even when she was determined to have her own way, she tried to keep everyone happy. "By doing," she told Gotthard Booth, "I can prevent wounding."[86]

IT WAS IN THE FALL of her senior year that Mead took the introductory course in anthropology with Franz Boas, with Benedict as the teaching assistant. Each week Benedict met the students at the American Museum of Natural History, located at the western edge of Central Park at Seventy-ninth Street, a short subway or bus ride downtown from Columbia. The museum occupies a huge late-Victorian building built by wealthy New Yorkers to celebrate the city and impress its population, with its turrets and towers giving it the look of a castle. Inside were displays of artifacts demonstrating distinct cultural settings—like the extraordinary totem poles and masks collected by the expedition Boas sent in 1898 to the Pacific Northwest—or displays of beadwork and pottery from the Plains Indians and the Pueblos. And there, in the cavernous marble halls of the museum, began one of the most famous friendships between two women in history.

In her discussion section of the class, Benedict used the artifacts and displays in the museum to illustrate the week's readings and lectures. Yet after the first meeting, Mead was unhappy. The outstanding students in the lecture class, the ones who did the reading and sparked debate, weren't in her section. She was annoyed with herself for not paying more attention to her schedule.[87] Moreover, her first impression of Benedict wasn't positive. Shy, with weak hearing and a slight stutter, eager to impress her students in what was her first effort at teaching since her days in Pasadena, Benedict often asked students to repeat themselves. Mead was put off by her appearance. Benedict wore the same dress every day and what seemed to Mead an unstylish hat; her hair was mousy and unkempt. Mead didn't know that she wore that dress as an act of feminist rebellion against the male professors at Columbia, who always wore the same suit. Mead didn't realize that the hat, broad-beamed, with a large feather, was so fashionable that she hadn't seen the style yet. There would be years when Margaret dreamed about that hat.[88]

Mead's friends teased her about being in the weak discussion section. Unwilling to admit defeat, she decided to prove them wrong. It wasn't difficult to do. For Benedict began to intrigue her. Beneath the frumpy clothes, she had a tall, athletic body. Her "Mona Lisa" smile drew Mead in. When deeply engaged with her material she radiated intensity; her shyness disappeared and her beauty shone through. Then Mead realized that Benedict had talents as a teacher. She had a poetic way of presenting class materials and an ability to read herself into cultures that made them come alive. She drew interesting comparisons between cultures, and she joked about the material to inject life into Boas's dry, fact-packed lectures, as when she satirized the vision quest of the Crow Indians. She was a good storyteller.

Benedict's empathy with her students began to show through. "She had the rare gift of taking the inarticulate gropings of a student and illuminating it with a warmth that was like an accolade," wrote Mead. She used her weak hearing to bolster a student's confidence, as when she repeated questions in a manner "which made the questioner out to be much more intelligent than the original question." Boas's forbidding manner put off the students, and they didn't go to him for help; they went to Benedict, for she was often in the anthropology seminar room at Columbia with the door open, expecting them to consult her.[89]

Margaret wrote her grandmother that she was pleased she had waded through a dense tome on Stone Age man the summer before, for that reading allowed her to shine in the session when they analyzed the Paleolithic exhibits at the museum. Now she was glad that the bright students weren't in her section, for it was easy to get Benedict's attention. Other students began to share her revised opinion of Benedict. "We are all crazy about her," Mead wrote to her grandmother several weeks later.[90] Interest in Benedict spread among the student body. When it was discovered that she was married but lived alone during the week in a room near Columbia, a romantic rumor spread: she had an insane husband in an asylum outside New York.[91] The other students were jealous that they weren't in Mead's section. Demonstrating her powers of persuasion, Mead praised the class profusely and by the second semester its enrollment doubled.

Increasingly fascinated by Benedict, Mead found excuses to take the bus with her from Columbia to the museum and back again so that they could continue talking. She even rode the subway looking for her teacher, to strike up conversations. Their association deepened. "After a particularly exciting—and halting—explanation of the model of the Sun Dance in the Plains Indians Hall, I was brushed aside with inexplicable asperity when I asked for more references." But she persisted.

The next session, when Benedict gave her the reference in the form of a paper she herself had written, Mead understood her strange reaction. The paper was on the vision quest in the societies of the Plains Indians.[92]

Benedict made the next move when she invited Mead to attend the weekly seminar for anthropology professors and graduate students. She gave the paper at that seminar—an analysis of John Dewey's new *Human Nature and Conduct*. Yet it wasn't the content of Benedict's presentation that fascinated Margaret; rather, it was her style. Years later she wrote that she found Benedict's shyness and halting speech "devastating" on that occasion.[93] She wanted to protect her teacher in that professional setting, speaking to her peers, not just to undergraduates.

The feelings between Benedict and Mead developed slowly. Margaret had to sort out her relationships with Luther, Leone, and Marie Eichelberger. And as with Katharine Rothenberger, she had to be "brave and persistent" to cross Ruth's "deserts of ice and snow"—the emotional barrier that she constructed around herself, the mask that she wore. Yet Ruth later told Margaret that she had been curious about her even before they met. Ruth had seen her in the subway among a group of Barnard girls and, like so many others, she had been captivated by this tiny, radiant person. Ruth knew only that the name of the young woman on the subway was Margaret. And fascinated by Margaret's combination of fragility, strength, and intellectual determination, she had watched her walking across the Columbia campus, carrying a stack of heavy tomes that seemed to weigh down her body.[94]

Marie Bloomfield's death brought Ruth and Margaret closer together. Marie had been a student in Ruth's class; she, too, had been at the seminar where Benedict read her paper on Dewey's book, for Ruth had invited her as well as Margaret; she had ridden the subway with Margaret looking for Ruth. When Ruth heard the news about Marie, she invited Margaret to her apartment, soothed her with the story of Cato's suicide, and shared with Margaret her belief that suicide could be a noble act. Yet Benedict herself was upset by Marie's suicide. Without children of her own, she regarded her students as her children, and she was sorry for the unhappy Marie.[95] Sometimes regarding her barren womb as a symbolic rejection, she feared rejection by her students as well, and Marie's suicide fed into that fear. Yet here was Margaret Mead, a student leader with scores of friends, suddenly holding out the possibility of becoming her acolyte.

CHAPTER 7

"Unicorns at Sunrise"

Anthropology, Poetry, Gender, and Ruth Benedict

IN MARCH 1923, a month after Marie Bloomfield's suicide, Benedict suggested to Mead that she enter the Columbia Ph.D. program in anthropology. Ruth was persuasive—and shrewd. She revealed that she was a member of an informal "press committee" of anthropologists who were publicizing the subject in popular intellectual journals, thus appealing to Margaret's interest in writing.[1] She suggested that if Margaret wanted to follow her mother in studying an immigrant culture, she could do so in anthropology.[2] She stressed the need to document tribal societies, most with an oral tradition and no written records, before they disappeared under the impact of Westernization. Missionaries and explorers had investigated some of them, but their narratives were unreliable because most of them weren't trained scientists. Above all, Ruth saw doing these ethnographies as a crusade to preserve vital knowledge about humanity that was being lost, knowledge that could form the basis for a new science of society. She was honest about the small number of jobs in anthropology, which didn't have much of an academic presence. "Professor Boas and I," she said, "have nothing to offer but an opportunity to do work that matters."[3]

Then Ruth told Margaret a story about an aged chief of the Serrano Indians of Southern California, whom she had interviewed in doing fieldwork there the previous summer. The chief condemned the destruction of his culture by American commercialism. He didn't like buying food in tin cans at the government store; he didn't like going to the butcher for meat; he missed the excitement of the hunt. He had converted to Christianity, but he couldn't forget the magic of the old religion, when shamans "transformed themselves into bears before his very eyes." He described cultures as cups of clay. God gave every people a cup of clay from which they drank their life, he said. But the Serrano's cup was broken; their culture was destroyed.[4]

That cup of clay had meaning to Benedict, who brought to anthropology her knowledge of religion and myth. In Christianity, the Communion cup contains the wine symbolizing Christ's blood. In alchemy, the cup symbolizes the mother, as it does in Jung's and Freud's symbolism. God shaped Adam out of clay; the potters of the Southwest, mostly women, shaped their pots out of the clay of Mother Earth. The metaphor of the cup of clay had the rich resonance that Benedict liked. It anticipated her insight that cultures were integrated wholes; it came to symbolize her relationship with Margaret as a deep spiritual bond; it honored women as mothers and creators. In the immediate instance, it drew Mead into anthropology.

"I was a social science child," Mead later wrote. When she encountered Franz Boas and Ruth Benedict, "The basic ideas of the interdependence of race, language, and culture and the importance of the comparative method were already familiar to me." Social scientists like Thorstein Veblen, with whom her parents had studied at the University of Chicago, were already viewing cultures as individual entities, she asserted, disconnected from any concept of "race"; she was already conversant with Franz Boas's major contribution in that area. It was the intricate details of tribal cultures—details of kinship, language, design, and ritual—that formed anthropology's "revelatory" fascination to her, for in her opinion comparative sociologists slighted these details.[5] Through the metaphor of the cup of clay, she realized that intellect and imagination could be combined in anthropology in ways impossible in sociology and psychology, in line with Benedict's "exquisite response to literature and her disciplined appreciation of anthropological materials."[6]

Mead had already been admitted to the master's degree program in the psychology department at Columbia; she had intended to become a high school psychologist. But the prospect didn't excite her. She found courses at Teachers College boring, and she hadn't liked the aggressive males studying to be school administrators she had encountered in a course in educational psychology there that fall. Also, there was ethnic bias in the IQ tests that the Teachers College professors had developed.[7] As it turned out, Mead did both the M.A. in psychology and the Ph.D. in anthropology at the same time, and she criticized the IQ tests in her master's essay by using her mother's contacts in Hammonton to give IQ tests to three hundred Italian high school students and then correlating the results with the amount of English spoken in their homes. The more English spoken, the results showed, the higher the score.[8]

Mead remembered the adventure stories she had read as a child. She was still reading them: Mary Kingsley on her travels in West Africa; Edith Durham on hers in the Balkans. (Durham, it turned out, was the aunt of Gregory Bateson, who would become Mead's third husband.) When Benedict issued her invitation, Mead was reading a book by Mrs. Scoresby Routledge, a book about Routledge's adventures on Easter Island trying to solve the mystery of who had built its huge stone statues. Routledge failed: the last native who knew the secret of the builders had died just before she arrived. That failure graphically proved to Margaret the pressing need to do ethnographies of tribal societies before they disappeared.[9] She also realized the opportunity that had been offered her to study with Franz Boas, an eminent academic, and to attain the Ph.D. that had eluded her mother. She could combine a career with marriage, a goal of most New Women of the 1920s, and not hesitate in doing so—as Benedict had in her many years of indecision over what to do with her life.

The impulse to document tribal societies dominated Mead's career until World War II, when she turned toward contemporary issues and mostly stayed in the United States. In her writings before then—and even after—she stressed the need to record the details of tribal societies, for they were "priceless and irreplaceable samples of the different solutions which man has attempted to his problem of living." As a graduate student she woke up in the mornings, she later remembered, feeling a need to hurry, with the dreadful thought that "the last man on Raratonga may be dying this morning, and one more priceless experiment would be gone beyond recall."[10] As always, Mead was driven by the need to produce, to harness her energy to a worthwhile goal, to stop disaster from occurring.

Thus Margaret accepted Ruth's proposal to become a graduate student in anthropology. Luther didn't object; he now planned to study for a Ph.D. in sociology at Columbia and to leave the ministry. Ruth cemented Margaret's choice by giving her three hundred dollars—a considerable sum in those days—as a "no strings attached fellowship." She thus indicated her trust in Margaret's ability. Margaret realized that accepting the money implied attachment. By entering anthropology she chose to become closer to Ruth, who, after all, fit the role of favorite teacher from the cultural script of her childhood. In a letter thanking "Mrs. Benedict" for the money, Margaret called her a "fairy godmother."[11]

WHY DID RUTH recruit Margaret for anthropology? She didn't approach any other Barnard student. But she thought that Margaret was brilliant, and she wanted her for the field of anthropology—and for herself. She liked Margaret's warmth and the way she flattered her and made her feel special. She also liked Margaret's ability to soothe. She felt peaceful with Margaret, who rested her "like a padded chair and a fireplace."[12] That image suggests domestic tranquility, but it also suggests domination, for it was fathers who sat in armchairs in front of fireplaces. Often stymied in her relationship with Stanley, Ruth could hope for more authority with Margaret. She could play a masculine role with her, along with one of maternal caring: Margaret could be the child she wanted. And she was drawn to Margaret's optimism, energy, and determination to succeed. Margaret burned with Pater's "gemlike flame." In 1937, reflecting on Mead's lifetime of lovers, Ruth wrote: "And that's what you have and they want it. Such a fund of zest and determination will make life a different matter and they want it."[13]

Besides, by 1923 Benedict wanted a female lover. On New Year's Day that year she wrote a poem in her diary about desiring to "lie once with beauty, / Breast to breast."[14] Her relationship with Stanley was still difficult, although living alone in New York during the week and with him in Bedford Hills on the weekends helped. She told her sister, Margery, that when they got together it was like being on a second honeymoon.[15] She had also formed a frustrating friendship with anthropologist and linguist Edward Sapir, one of Boas's first Ph.D. students, who headed the Canadian government's bureau of ethnology in Ottawa. He and Benedict began to correspond when she sent him her dissertation and it impressed him; their friendship deepened when she sent him her poetry and he liked it. They saw each other when he came to New York, which he did a lot, for he felt isolated in Ottawa, which had neither a university nor much of an intellectual community.

Benedict and Sapir had a good deal in common. Both were drawn to theory; both had a tendency to depression; both wrote lyric poetry and wanted acclaim as public intellectuals. Sapir was unhappily married; his wife had been hospitalized several times for severe depression, and she had attempted suicide. For her part, Benedict appreciated the encouragement of this well-known scholar, although he sometimes treated her as a lackey, as when he asked her to type up his poetry or care for his children.[16] Short and jug-eared, Sapir looks unprepossessing in photographs. Yet Benedict was attracted to him, and several years later, Mead was too. His voice was low and rich, and he was animated in conversation, using many gestures. He was witty and a good mimic. That was enough for these academic women to fall for him— that, and his intelligence: his fellow anthropologists trained by Boas rated him the most brilliant among them.[17]

Benedict probably didn't have an affair with Sapir, who was a traditionalist when it came to sex and the family. His letters to Benedict, mostly about matters of form and word choice in her poetry, are more distanced than intimate. Florid in writing style, versed in psychoanalysis (although he was never analyzed), he nonetheless didn't open himself up. Benedict also kept her distance. Sapir chided her for her "apologetic, conditional style of utterance," described her poetry as "majestic" and "Puritan," and called her "a well-articulated rational type, to whom everything must 'mean' something in both thought and emotion."[18] Columbia anthropologist Ruth Bunzel, a friend of Benedict's and Mead's who studied with Sapir, called him abnormally innocent with regard to women.[19]

During the year that Ruth and Margaret met, Sapir was in New York because his wife was there for medical treatment. Ruth wrote in her diary that walking down a street with him gave her a thrill. Yet to be seductive wasn't easy for her. After seeing a production of Chekhov's *Three Sisters*, she commented in her diary that she didn't like the youngest sister's lack of reserve, her "childishness in her love affair."[20] The comment was unintentionally ironic, given her attraction to individuals like Margaret, who were playful and younger than she. Yet Ruth had difficulty dropping her mask. "Ruth in many ways expected the worst from people and steeled herself against it," Mead commented.[21] Esther Schiff Goldfrank experienced Ruth during those years as shy, introverted, and "aloof, nodding assent or smiling quizzically at some passing remark, unaggressive in manner, a person of few words."[22]

During that year Ruth spent time in the evenings in New York with a friend of hers from her undergraduate days at Vassar, an aspiring poet named Marguerite Arnold who wrote advertising copy to support herself. She and Ruth may have been lovers, although their relationship was as difficult as the ones Ruth had with Stanley and with Edward Sapir; in her diary she commented that Marguerite regarded her as "part of all that background she's trying to break away from."[23] Marie Eichelberger referred to Marguerite as Ruth's friend who would lock herself into a room and refuse to come out; Marguerite's published poems are about mental clinics and nervous breakdowns.[24] Yet despite Ruth's involvements with Stanley, Margaret, Marguerite, and Edward, she was still lonely and plagued by highs and lows. "I dread intense awareness," she wrote in her diary, "and yet it comes with such ghastly frequency."[25]

Ruth wrote in her diary that she wanted a "companion in harness."[26] That phrase implies commitment and the marital bond. Ruth wanted stability in her intimate life. She wanted fidelity with Stanley—and with a woman partner, too. She still desired an "Ariadne" to lead her out of the labyrinth of her emotions. At thirty-six she was no longer young. Whatever her rejection of homosexuality in her paper for Elsie Clews Parsons, she had changed her mind. She had decided that heterosexuality and homosexuality moved on "separate sets of wheels," that they drew from different parts of the self and that both drives needed to be fulfilled.[27] It was a brilliant compromise to offer Margaret, since it required her neither to give up Luther nor to make a public commitment of the sort that Leone Newton had wanted. Ruth and Margaret could be "companions in harness," faithful to each other while remaining married to men.

Yet Ruth didn't yet comprehend the complexities in Margaret's character. Margaret was so needy that spring, so willing to respond to Ruth's initiatives, as her personal life fell apart with the death of Marie Bloomfield and the loss of Leone Newton. Ruth didn't yet realize how mercurial Margaret could be. But she didn't immediately press a physical relationship on her. She was too afraid of increasing her own vulnerability, too afraid that if Margaret discovered the depths of her depressive self, she might reject her.[28] And even though Margaret was technically a student of Franz Boas's and not one of hers, there was still the student-teacher issue, the suspicion that older women teachers seduced their younger, vulnerable students even more readily than men did.

Benedict's phrase "companion in harness" also relates to the competitive sport of harness horseracing, and there was, indeed, competition in her professional life. By 1923 Franz Boas, the legendary founder of the academic field of anthropology, was in his sixties, and early students of his such as Edward Sapir were vying to succeed him as the leader of the field. The Columbia anthropologists were creating a new academic specialty. United in a common cause, few in number, they were close, like a family. But they were also divided, for they were brilliant, egocentric academics, each with his or her own approach. They formed strong friendships and strong animosities.

In particular, Benedict conflicted with Elsie Clews Parsons, who held a special position in the department because of her closeness to Boas and the substantial financial support she provided for the department. Parsons could be demanding and arrogant. Esther Goldfrank described her as "floating" over the department like a "queen."[29] She attracted the men in the department like moths to a flame. For a time she had a special relationship with Alfred Kroeber, Boas's first graduate student at Columbia, who chaired the anthropology department at Berkeley—an outpost of anthropology in the West. She was also a mentor to Gladys Reichard, another Ph.D. student, whom Benedict and Mead didn't like, even though Boas held her in high regard, since they found her boring and her empirical approach unimaginative.

In the spring of 1923 Benedict became angry with Parsons and Reichard when Boas gave the teaching position that opened up in the Barnard department to Reichard, reasoning that because she was single she needed the income more than the married Benedict. Yet Boas didn't abandon Benedict: he offered her the job editing the folklore concordance and then the *Journal of American Folk-Lore*. He knew that she enjoyed the detailed work of collating myths and editing papers, for those tasks calmed her and gave her a sense of control. He was willing to broker the disagreements between Benedict and Parsons; it's not surprising, however, that Benedict wanted to have, as Parsons had with Reichard, a "companion in harness."[30]

As an anthropologist, Mead could become Benedict's protégée. One thinks of the older Laura Wylie and the younger Gertrude Buck at Vassar, whose scholarship and lives were deeply intertwined. Like the relationship between Wylie and Buck, the one between Benedict and Mead would reinforce both their careers, increasing their self-confidence and deepening their individual approaches. And who was the driver of their team? That person was Franz Boas, who played an Olympian role in both their lives. Boas determined Benedict's career as an editor and placed Mead at the Museum of Natural History. It was his idea that Mead study the subject of adolescence on Samoa. He wrote laudatory prefaces for both *Coming of Age in Samoa* and *Patterns of Culture*—a favor he didn't extend to his male students.

For her part, Mead liked to have mentors. She was a brilliant performer and producer, but she also had a gift for being a student, for listening to others and absorbing what they had to say. She sometimes carried a notebook with her, as her father had, and she wrote down remarks others made. Until Benedict died, she consulted her about most professional matters. Yet Mead had other mentors. In the late 1920s she learned about the functionalist approach from British anthropologist A. R. Radcliffe-Brown; in the 1930s she learned about biology from Gregory Bateson and interdisciplinary networking from Lawrence Frank. And she liked to think of herself as the subordinate in a relationship, as the person who has the security of obeying and who doesn't make the rules. For someone as powerful as Mead, that self-image seems surprising. Yet she always contended that she alienated others not because she was overbearing but because she spoke too forcefully and fast and that, when others snapped at her because they couldn't follow her, she was often reduced to tears.[31]

Her friends disliked what they saw as her tendency to shift quickly from loving to raging, but Mead didn't see herself as controlling. "If I were a man," she asserted, "I would probably be one of those bantam fighters that fight in a way that they know they can't hurt anyone. I've always been so small I couldn't hurt anybody. I think of myself as being small and fighting back . . . and so I speak with the voice of someone who is David vis-à-vis Goliath."[32] In 1923, however, the contentious part of her career was in the future, as she prepared to become a student of Franz Boas and to take up her mission of documenting societies that were disappearing under the impact of modernization and the advancing force of the West.

WHAT IMMEDIATELY STOOD OUT about Franz Boas was his bizarre and compelling appearance. His white hair was leonine and his black eyes were piercing, but he had scars on his face, slashes that he wouldn't talk about but that everyone knew came from duels he had fought, as a young and impetuous college student in Germany, to defend his honor as a Jew against anti-Semitic slurs. By the 1920s his face was further marked by the effects of an operation he had undergone to remove a cancerous growth. On one side of his face he couldn't move his muscles, and his eye drooped. Cultural critic Lewis Mumford later described Boas's "gaping forehead," his "distorted mouth," and "the bulging eye that seemed to focus on one like a magnifying glass." Boas was, indeed, monstrous in appearance.[33] When being photographed, he turned the good side of his face to the camera.

His looks reflected the Herculean personality for which he was famous. Born a Jew in Germany, he attained a Ph.D. in physics and geography at the University of Kiel, did fieldwork among the Eskimos in Baffin Land, and worked as a curator at the ethnographic museum in Berlin before emigrating to the United States in 1886, at the age of twenty-eight. He came to the United States because of growing anti-Semitism in Germany and his belief in the promise of American democracy. He also wanted to join his uncle, Abraham Jacobi, a leader of the German Revolution of 1848 who had fled to New York City when the revolution failed, and who had become a leader of the German-Jewish community there. As a boy, Boas had been close to Jacobi, and he was engaged to the daughter of Jacobi's best friend, another 1848 émigré who lived in New York. He had met her when she and her family vacationed in Germany.

Ambitious, controlled, and demanding, Boas had a moralist's sense of right and wrong and an imperial desire, even as an academic, to conquer all kinds of territory. Alfred Kroeber called him "Daemonic."[34] Courtly and old-school European in manner, he had an aggressive masculine side; he was drawn to the Arctic because he identified with polar explorers like Robert Peary. Still, he used his powerful personality to further academic innovation and social reform, not business enterprise. His mother had founded a kindergarten in his home city of Minden, Germany; his uncle had been a revolutionary; his uncle's wife, Mary Putnam Jacobi, was the most eminent woman physician in the United States and a leader of women's rights and suffrage organizations in New York City.[35]

It took Boas ten years to find a permanent job in the United States, partly because of anti-Semitism and partly because, given his imperious personality, he easily clashed with his superiors—as he did with G. Stanley Hall, the opinionated president of Clark University, who hired him in 1889 to establish the first anthropology department in the nation and then forced him to resign in a dispute over policy. In 1896 his uncle used his wife's connections, as a Putnam, to New York elites to obtain a joint appointment for him to teach at Columbia and to serve as a curator at the American Museum of Natural History. In

1905, however, Boas resigned the curatorship because he clashed with Morris K. Jesup, the museum's president, over his failure to finish his report on the expedition he had sent to Siberia and the Northwest Coast to prove that the Native Americans had come from Asia to the American continent over the Bering Strait. (That expedition collected the Northwest totem poles and masks in the museum.) Subtle anti-Semitism probably also lay behind Boas's resignation. Yet he remained sufficiently friendly with the curators in the anthropology division—some of them former students of his—that they allowed him to use the museum's collections for his teaching, while they sometimes funded his students' fieldwork and hired them as curators.[36]

In his years at Columbia, Boas came into his own. Despite his problems at the museum—and with Columbia president Nicholas Murray Butler over Boas's neutral stand on World War I—he took anthropology in the United States in a new direction, establishing bridges to other academic disciplines and uncoupling it from its traditional connection to natural history and physical anthropology. With the help of early graduate students of his, such as Edward Sapir and Alfred Kroeber, he maneuvered control of the field away from museum curators, who focused on collecting artifacts, and into the hands of university professors, who focused on research. He made the Columbia department into a national center for the discipline. Between 1892 and 1926, of the forty-five Ph.D. degrees in anthropology granted nationwide, Boas oversaw nineteen. By 1930 individuals who had studied with Boas headed most of the anthropology departments in the United States.[37]

Influenced by the descriptive and empirical German science of the late nineteenth century, Boas launched a new "American anthropology" that he called "historical." By this he meant that the evolutionism of nineteenth-century anthropologists, who ranked societies from "primitive" to "civilized," with modern Western societies at the top, would be put on hold until individual societies were studied in depth. He proposed the technique of "salvage ethnology" to find the "ethnographic present" of those societies—which in practice meant reconstructing the historical past before the incursion of Westernization by interviewing the oldest members of a society about their original culture, as Benedict would do with the Serrano Indians. His historical anthropology also included limiting the older technique of analyzing a cultural element like totemism worldwide to analyzing it in adjacent societies or in societies similar enough that they could be grouped into a culture area, like the Pueblos or the Plains Indians. He called this technique "diffusion." Since the diffusion of cultural elements usually occurred over time, this technique was implicitly historical, as in Boas's study of the spread of the raven myth among the tribes of the Northwest Coast of the North American continent along the trading links those tribes developed over time.[38]

Both Benedict's and Mead's dissertations were diffusionist studies, although they were structural in approach, with a limited historical component. Benedict studied the vision quest among the North American Indians; Mead studied the techniques of building houses and canoes and of tattooing in a number of Polynesian societies. Both their dissertations were "library" studies, based on published research in libraries. To be credible Boasians, however, they had to go to the field. Thus Benedict studied the Serrano Indians even before she received her Ph.D., and Mead did the same with the Samoans, one of the Polynesian societies she had included in her dissertation.

Boas's schemes were grandiose. He attacked the evolutionists and proclaimed a new anthropology. He dispatched his expedition to prove that the American Indians came from Asia. He sent his early Ph.D. students among the Plains Indian tribes to construct grammars for languages that might die out, given the destruction of the buffalo herds on which those societies depended for a livelihood and around which they had constructed their cultures. He envisioned sending such teams throughout the world. He set up a center for Pan-American cultural cooperation and research, the International School of Mexico; he envisioned creating a center for the study of the Far East. He founded the *Journal of American Folk-Lore* and the *International Journal of American Linguistics*. He played a role in founding the American Anthropological Association and interdisciplinary organizations like the Social Science Research Council, established in 1924. By his death in 1942 he had published more than six hundred articles, drawn from all branches of anthropology: archaeology, linguistics, folklore, ethnology, and physical anthropology.

As a mentor, however, Boas could be difficult. He had a prodigious memory and was an astute critic, but his lectures were sometimes disorganized, and he could be gruff and dismissive. The department at Columbia was organized according to the hierarchical European model, with one full professor (Boas) and the other faculty members subordinate, and that structure increased Boas's power. He ordered his students around; he was involved in so many projects that he was often unavailable. He gave Mead a half hour's worth of instruction on how to do fieldwork before she went to Samoa; in the end she devised her approach herself.

Moreover, Boas was so focused on criticism that he had difficulty maintaining a position—or writing an overview of his own fieldwork on the Indians of the Northwest Coast. An empiricist at heart, he feared finding a new detail about the society he was studying that might invalidate his conclusions. According to Mead, in graduate courses he continually warned the students against "premature generalization," which he seemed to fear "like the plague."[39] Sapir complained about his dislike of generalizing: "I sometimes wonder if there is more to Boas than a stupendous capacity for work and a sustained quality of enthusiasm. He will never take a theory of some magnitude and see where it leads him."[40]

Yet his multifaceted work suggested a number of approaches: empiricism, diffusionism, structuralism, oral history, and the search for cultural regularities and laws. In 1920 he even approved a cautious use of Freud, although he found Freud dogmatic and his approach historically conditioned and not universal, as Freud claimed.[41] Despite his bent toward what he called "science," he didn't dismiss humanistic and aesthetic approaches: he began studying the Indians of the Northwest Coast after he became fascinated with their artistic production in carvings, masks, and totem poles. And by the mid-1920s he turned to the study of individual societies, suggesting that Mead focus on Samoa while supporting Benedict in her configurationist approach, based on analyzing individual societies.

His eclecticism allowed his students to take different directions without breaking with him. They disliked being called "Boasians," but sometimes they grouped themselves under that rubric. Robert Lowie extended Boasian historicism to argue that cultures had no patterns, that all were "things of shreds and patches." (The phrase comes from Gilbert and Sullivan's song describing a minstrel in *The Mikado*.) Paul Radin studied one Winnebago medicine man in depth, before taking up history and diffusionism; Alexander Goldenweiser did his diffusionist study of totemism among the Iroquois tribes before turning to writing textbooks and constructing theory. Clark Wissler devised the concept of culture regions among the Native American tribes, like the Pueblos and the Plains Indians; he later devised an "acculturation" approach focused on the process of Westernization. Alfred Kroeber posited that a "superorganic" force shaped societies; it was like Darwin's notion of evolution, with a cultural force replacing biology.[42]

Benedict and Sapir stood between these analysts, with Benedict focusing on "patterns" in societies and Sapir on individuals and their relationship to their society. Mead followed Benedict in using a configurationist approach, but more than any other anthropologist of her generation, she used a variety of methods, including sociological, psychological, humanistic, and even biological approaches. Mead may have had the last word on Boas when she wrote that he "saw the whole story of man, as spread out in a great panorama." She added that he then probed into "a problem now of language, now of physical type, now of art style—each a deep, sudden, intensive stab at some strategic point into an enormous untapped and unknown mass of information which he would someday master."[43]

There is a universalizing quality to Boas's work that is reflected in the work of his students, especially that of Benedict and Mead. When Mead wrote that Boas saw the whole story of man spread out in a vast panorama, she could have been writing about her mature work and that of Benedict, as they both took on multifaceted projects and became intellectuals and reformers of note. Franz Boas provided them with a model for constructing their careers, as each of them took a comprehensive path, unusual for women in the masculine academic and intellectual world of their day.

BOAS WAS AMONG the first academics in the United States to take a stand against the growing racism and nativism of the early twentieth century. In 1911 he published both *The Mind of Primitive Man* and *Changes in the Bodily Form of Descendants of Immigrants*. The former, a compilation of his articles, was the most comprehensive critique of racist social science published in the United States up to that time. The latter, a project in physical anthropology, involved a statistical study of the measurements of head sizes and head shapes of eighteen thousand immigrants and their children, in which Boas attempted to disprove the venerable cephalic index—the ratio (multiplied by 100) between the width and length of the head. (He had thirteen assistants doing the measuring.) That strange index, invented by nineteenth-century physical anthropologists in France, was believed to remain constant by race, including what we today call ethnicity. The courts, the government, and most scientists accepted it as the definitive proof of racial membership.

As a physical anthropologist Boas liked to do measurements. In the early 1920s he undertook a project measuring the width of the pelvic girdle among Italians in Philadelphia and Jews in New York City—and Emily Fogg Mead did measurements for him among the Italians in Hammonton.[44] Margaret Mead was influenced by this work, which moved away from the head and the brain to focus on the body; in the 1930s she became interested in measuring and theorizing about what were called "constitutional types of body size and build."

Boas attacked the prevailing racism in other ways. One was his democratization of the word "culture" to mean the totality of a society's customs and behaviors rather than the "superior" artistic production of its "elite." Traditionally, "culture" meant "civilization," as in referring to an individual as "cultured." But that equation supported the racist belief in the superiority of European civilization as the high point of evolution, which Boas rejected. Defining culture broadly and associating it with individual societies supported the idea of the relativity of cultures and challenged the biological, Darwinian model of development: semantically, "culture" was now as comprehensive as "nature" in a way that "society," which implied a focus on institutions, wasn't.

By 1900 ethnologists were being called "cultural anthropologists." By World War I, according to Robert Lowie, the general public was beginning to use the word "culture" in the new, nonelitist way.[45] Yet it was an uphill struggle, and many of Boas's students took on the task of redefining the concept, even though, according to Mead, some sociologists were using it at the turn of the twentieth century. Yet even Mead contended that as late as 1925, when she went to Samoa, most social science was written as though "culture" in terms of individual societies was unimportant in human behavior, and that practice allowed social scientists to use data collected in the United States as though it was universal. Even in 1928, when she published *Coming of Age in Samoa,* she asserted, the new definition of culture still wasn't in place.[46] Not until the 1930s did it take firm hold, when the economic deprivation of the Depression brought everyone down to a common level and made folk art and rural culture seem as important as the production of elite artists.[47]

Boas's egalitarian stance attracted graduate students; many of his first Ph.D. students came from either the German-Jewish or the Eastern European Jewish communities in New York City. A number born in Europe had immigrated to the United States with their families as boys: Robert Lowie came from Vienna, Alexander Goldenweiser from

Kiev, Paul Radin from Lodz, Edward Sapir from Pomerania. They were from different social classes and income levels: Alfred Kroeber's father was a wealthy importer, Lowie's a small businessman, Radin's a reform rabbi, Goldenweiser's a radical intellectual, Sapir's an impoverished cantor. Connected by networks of community and ethnicity, however, they became close. Radin and Lowie had been friends since childhood, and Goldenweiser joined their circle when he met them as undergraduates at City College. Kroeber wasn't Jewish, but like Boas he came from the German-Jewish community in New York, which was closely knit and intermarried. (Kroeber was German, as was Boas's wife.) Infused with the democratic values of the revolution of 1848, that community was politically liberal and ethnically assimilationist.[48]

At universities in the United States in this era, such Jewish backgrounds were unusual for graduate students and professors, most of whom came from Anglo elites. Yet by 1910 Columbia College had many Jewish students. That happened because its students were drawn from the outstanding graduates of the New York City public high schools and, given the large Jewish immigration to New York and the tradition of learning among Jews, by 1910 many of those graduates were Jewish. Clark Wissler was an Anglo student of Boas's from the Midwest who took over his curatorship at the Museum of Natural History when he resigned; he called Boas's Jewish students "queer foreigners." Leslie White, another Midwesterner who studied with Boas for a time, claimed that German-speaking Jews so dominated the department that he felt like an outsider. White left Columbia to finish his degree at the University of Chicago.[49]

Paul Radin described these students of Boas as having transferred to anthropology from other disciplines because of the innovative nature of the new field as Boas defined it. (Kroeber had been in literature, Sapir in German, Lowie in biology, Wissler in psychology, and he in history.) They were "rebels" and "dissenters" who saw anthropology as offering "unlimited scope for new vistas."[50] Mead described them as enthusiasts excited by Boas's vision of mounting "a giant rescue operation to preserve the vanishing fragments of primitive cultures and languages."[51] Most of them began by studying the Plains Indians, under Boas's campaign to provide grammars for languages and ethnographies for cultures that were disappearing. A founding generation of academic anthropologists, they completed their studies a decade ahead of Benedict and Mead, who were their students and then their professional friends and antagonists.

By the outbreak of World War I, however, the constituency of graduate students in anthropology at Columbia had shifted. Male enrollment dropped off, as young men enlisted in the army, while the war undermined the unity in the German-Jewish community, which split along pro-German and pro-Allied lines. The Columbia administration offended liberal Jews by introducing discriminatory tests as requirements for admission to the college, while Boas's dispute with Nicholas Murray Butler over the war resulted in a reduction of the anthropology department's funds and faculty lines. By 1919 only two graduate students were in residence, and one was Gladys Reichard. Boas and Elsie Clews Parsons decided that women could replace the missing men. Boas's male students could be difficult, often exhibiting, in Mead's words, "stiff-necked opposition" and "disgruntled yielding."[52] On the other hand, he enjoyed teaching the undergraduates at Barnard, who were intelligent—and respectful.

Parsons appealed to the students in Boas's class at Barnard and in her class at the New School to become anthropologists: Benedict responded to that appeal. Ruth Bunzel and Esther Schiff, both graduates of Barnard, in turn served as Boas's secretary, and each then persuaded him to admit her to the Ph.D. program. As Jews who grew up in the prewar German-Jewish community, both responded to Boas. He warmed to them, and, treating him like a favorite grandfather, they broke through his reserve. They taught him how to smoke cigarettes— a major symbol of youthful rebellion in the 1920s. The assertive Esther Schiff called him "Papa Franz," and the name stuck. Benedict and Mead, more distant from him at this point than the other women, began using it a few years later.[53]

Boas neither wrote about gender nor participated in women's rights activities. His wife was the daughter of a "Forty-Eighter" who was Abraham Jacobi's best friend, but she stayed at home and raised their children. On the other hand, Boas was close to Mary Putnam Jacobi, Jacobi's wife, the eminent physician and women's rights activist who supported equality for women in the professions; one assumes that she pressured him to treat his women students fairly. Grateful to the women who had rescued his graduate program, Boas enlisted them in the campaign to shift control of anthropology from the museums to the universities. In 1925 he engineered the election of Bunzel, Benedict, and Reichard to the council of the American Anthropological Association.[54]

Like many women anthropologists in the discipline's early years,

Schiff and Bunzel both did their fieldwork among the matrilineal
Pueblo Indians, whose women-centered institutions appealed to
them—and among whom Boas thought women would be safe. Schiff
did general ethnology, while Bunzel focused on the potters of Zuñi. By
becoming skilled in the women's craft of pottery, Bunzel pioneered a
new fieldwork approach. Schiff and Bunzel maintained amicable relations with their Columbia colleagues. The reserved Bunzel kept out of
disagreements; Schiff's assertiveness might have caused conflicts, but
she married in 1923 and left the graduate program, to reenter it in the
late 1930s after her husband died. Still feisty, she then publicly differed
with Benedict over her portrayal of the Zuñi in *Patterns of Culture* as
placid and Apollonian, and Benedict incorporated her perspective in
later work.[55]

How DID THE MALE anthropologists trained by Boas react to the
women who suddenly appeared in their midst? None of those men had
feminist credentials the equal of Boas's, but they seemed to accept the
women. After all, women had long been ethnologists. In the late nineteenth century Alice Fletcher and Matilda Coxe Stevenson had been
pioneers in the field: Fletcher had studied the Omaha Indians and
Stevenson the Zuñi. Even before World War I the men had welcomed
Elsie Clews Parsons to their ranks. They realized that because tribal
societies often prohibited Western men from studying their women,
women anthropologists were needed to investigate women's roles.[56]

Mead wrote that Boas's male students extended their liberal views
on race and their sense of minority status as Jews to include women,
who, she maintained, were welcomed more readily into anthropology
than into any other academic field. Yet that welcome, in her view,
wasn't "unequivocal"; these men were prey to "uncertainties" and
"incompatible leanings."[57] In this era of fears of "feminization" and of
the growth of nativism and racism, they also may have internalized the
widespread anti-Jewish stereotypes, experiencing the Jewish "self-
loathing" that scholars have identified as a reaction to charges of
effeminacy especially directed against intellectuals and ethnic men.[58]
Thus in his autobiography Robert Lowie wrote of being a "marginal
man." In his high school on the Lower East Side of New York, he
reported, the major interest of the other boys was in the heavyweight
champion of the world, while he was interested in his schoolwork.[59]
He was a sissy in their eyes.

The negative reactions of the male Boasians to the women in anthropology were subtle. None of these men were openly misogynist; all were sensitive to the women's rights movement, highly visible in New York before World War I, with suffragists and labor union women marching in huge parades. These men were sympathetic to the aspirations of their wives: Sapir, Kroeber, and Lowie all married professional women. They encouraged Benedict and Mead, participated in seminars with them, and engaged in conversations with them—until Mead had a disastrous affair with Sapir just before she left for Samoa in the late summer of 1925. After that, his animus against her played a role in turning them against her; Sapir, Goldenweiser, Radin, Kroeber, and Lowie were very close.

Each of them had issues with women. Take Alexander Goldenweiser, for example. With his flair for the dramatic, he was liked by everyone. He spent hours counseling Benedict in the course she took with him at the New School. He studied the Iroquois tribes, renowned for their matrifocal traditions. In his *Early Civilization* (1922), he praised women's creativity in tribal cultures, while noting that "androcentric" mores oppressed them even in those cultures.[60] Yet he was a womanizer who was disgraced professionally over his extramarital affair with an Iroquois woman. Benedict found love letters from women to him "hidden" in a desk drawer in the anthropology department seminar room.[61] After being denied tenure at Columbia, Goldenweiser had difficulty finding a permanent job. Although he praised Mead's conclusions about the free sexuality on Samoa when many other male anthropologists criticized her, in 1927 he wrote that women were inferior to men in rationality and thus couldn't become real intellectuals.[62] Two years later he drew from Freud's negative judgments about women to describe them as "an enigma, a menace as well as a joy." By 1936 he referred to women as "peculiar creature[s] with a distracting and at times repulsive periodicity in [their] life cycles . . . and a fascinating but always excessive and always disturbing influence on men via sex."[63]

Like Goldenweiser, Paul Radin had a difficult career. In letters to one another the male anthropologists who had known him since childhood called him a "trickster" and a "scamp."[64] In the early 1920s he was fired from his job at the Bureau of Indian Ethnology in Washington, D.C., because of suspicions that he had embezzled bureau funds, although eventually he did impressive work. In 1926, when he taught on a temporary basis at Columbia, he drew graduate students away from Benedict.[65] In his 1933 history of ethnology, he called Mead's work "superficial and largely subjective" and contended that Benedict "dogmatically includes and excludes in an unjustifiable and arbitrary manner."[66]

Alfred Kroeber, formal and controlled, was called Kroeber, not Alfred. His prodigious scholarly output rivaled that of Boas; his wife called him as "Daemonic" as his mentor.[67] He underwent analysis; Mead described him as having a "continuous gentle solicitude for the psychologically vulnerable"; he helped Benedict with her fieldwork among the Serrano.[68] He also developed a highly rational theory that a cultural "superorganic" determined human history, a "majestic order pervading civilization," which he tested by studying the cycles of fashions in women's dress, reducing women's bodies to statistics.[69] He appreciated independent women and had a number of female graduate students, but he disliked women who had loud voices or who "lionized" him. Benedict found his criticism of the work of others usually calculated not to offend; like her he was deaf in one ear. Yet she distrusted his attitude toward professional women and found him insulting when he came to Columbia for a semester in 1932 as a visiting professor and paid no attention to her work.[70]

As for Robert Lowie, he coauthored an article on women with the feminist scientist Leta Hollingworth in which they included her attack on the scientific proof for male superiority along with his rebuttal of the feminist argument that matriarchal societies preceded patriarchal ones.[71] In a letter to his sister, he explained that he met Leta at a dinner party and they debated the differences between the genders. She persuaded him that there wasn't a "quantitative difference" between men and women, although he still thought that there was a "qualitative" one—in terms of genitalia and reproduction. He couldn't decide whether or not he accepted feminism.[72]

Lowie chided Benedict for underplaying women's participation in the vision quest in her work on the subject, but he wrote Radin in 1920 that he looked forward to getting together to discuss eucalyptus trees, luscious figs—and female perversity.[73] He wore three-piece suits and timed his lectures to the minute, but he romanced women and proposed to several. He confessed to his sister, however, that only six-foot-tall, powerfully built women attracted him sexually: he called this his "complex."[74] Both Kroeber and he preferred studying the masculine cultures of the Plains Indians to that of the matrifocal Pueblos, which were too feminine for their taste. To Kroeber, the latter "do not evince the manly, upstanding incisiveness of the Indians of the Plains, their directness in personal intercourse, the interesting play of personality."[75] According to Sabine Lang, the martial ideal of masculinity of the Plains Indians, generally taller and more muscular than the Pueblos, fascinated the male anthropologists.[76]

Edward Sapir described himself as a "dainty man" because he liked to write poetry, while he was also a "hungry man" who craved the "crassness of life."[77] In an article in the *New Republic* in 1916, he made fun of woman suffrage, joking that it would extend the unfortunate power women had over men in the home into the public sphere. Yet it also frightened him: when he thought about women voting, "there will not down a feeling of alarm, an incipient panicky state of mind."[78] His poetry contains references to women who are sirens luring men to their doom. Sapir shared Benedict's dislike of the imperious Elsie Clews Parsons, expressing that dislike in masculine terms in a letter to Leslie White. "You might solve her difficulties by having intercourse with her," he advised White. "Her interest in science is some sort of neurotic mechanism."[79]

Still, the male Boasians probably considered themselves sympathetic to women, and, in fact, they often were. At the meeting of the British Association for the Advancement of Science in Toronto in 1924, a meeting that Sapir organized, the American anthropologists present became fascinated by Carl Jung's new concept of "introvert" and "extravert" as categories to classify human nature. Playfully applying the categories to themselves, most wanted to be classified as introverts, since Jung placed intuitive and sensitive intellectuals in that category. It didn't seem to bother them that he also identified it with women. None of them wanted to be classified among his extraverts, individuals who mostly lived in the external world and lacked self-awareness.

RUTH BENEDICT'S RESPONSE to the men in anthropology was subtle, in keeping with her aloof public personality and her masklike demeanor. That subtlety was evident from the outset of her career in anthropology, when she paid no attention to Stanley's objections to her entering a discipline classified as a science. Stanley identified with his work; he didn't want competition from Ruth. Unable to stop her, he retreated even more, extending their vow of "silence" about their private lives to avoiding her colleagues and students. During the one

ALAMEDA FREE LIBRARY

occasion when she entertained some of them at their home in Bedford Hills, he stayed in his darkroom, developing photographs.[80]

Benedict either deferred to her male colleagues in anthropology or subtly mastered them by absorbing their work into her scholarship in ways they didn't realize. Kind and sympathetic, she tried not to anger anyone. Except for Elsie Clews Parsons, she had good relations with the Columbia anthropologists. She kept in contact with Stanley Benedict and Edward Sapir after her close relationship with each ended; she was friendly with all of Margaret Mead's husbands. Even when the male anthropologists around Boas turned against Mead, they rarely criticized Benedict as harshly. With her shyness and her weak hearing, she could appear frail, a woman needing male protection. Mead described her as "fragile, appealing to the chivalry and solicitude of those with whom she works."[81] There was also her haunting beauty and her flickering "Mona Lisa" smile, and these features gave her a certain sexual allure. Sometimes she seemed mysterious, even witch-like, and that, plus her height and her athletic body, could give men pause. Many of the male anthropologists couldn't figure her out: in the 1930s, before choosing her as a model of self-realization, Abraham Maslow called her "the Benedictine enigma."[82]

In Benedict's early years in anthropology many of the male anthropologists fell under her spell. Goldenweiser spent many hours at the New School counseling her; Lowie supervised her dissertation; Kroeber helped her with her interviews on her first field trip. Sapir didn't always treat her well, but he supported her intellectually during her first years in the discipline. After reading her article on the vision quest, he was so impressed that he wrote her that she was the one to produce the theory that Boas hadn't provided.[83]

Like these men, Benedict was an intellectual. She enjoyed the abstractness of theory, and she had read and absorbed the major thinkers of the age: Nietzsche, Santayana, Dewey. Robert Lowie included her, along with Radin, Sapir, and Goldenweiser, as the "super-intelligentsia" of anthropology.[84] Lowie's grouping had partly to do with his annoyance at the four of them (Benedict, Radin, Sapir, and Goldenweiser) for poking fun at his empiricism, and he never entirely lived down having used a line from a Gilbert and Sullivan operetta in a formal work of anthropology. Yet the grouping also indicated that the men in anthropology accepted Benedict, with her rational theorizing, more fully than they did other Columbia women in anthropology.

In reaction to the "masculinization" of the social sciences, most women in them entered "feminized" subfields like social work. Benedict took a daring path: she abandoned the profession of social work to enter an academic field dominated by men. And unlike most women in anthropology, who did fieldwork and wrote ethnographies, she took up theory. Her boldness is striking. With the exception of Mead, no other woman of her generation of anthropologists attempted to enter the intellectual inner sanctum. Nor did many other women academics or intellectuals in other fields. One can count the other eminent women theorists in the United States between the 1920s and the 1960s on the fingers of one hand: Hannah Arendt and Karen Horney, both German émigrés who taught at the New School; perhaps Jessie Barnard in sociology and Mary Beard in history, both married to male academics; perhaps Elsie Clews Parsons, if one classifies her empirical approach as modernist in intent.[85]

Moreover, Benedict centered her early scholarship on men. Both her dissertation and the article on the vision quest focus on men. Indeed, the vision quest was mostly a male experience, especially among the Plains Indians. What stands out in her writing on the subject is the masochistic cruelties Plains Indian males inflicted on themselves, either to produce the vision that would define their lives or as part of ceremonies such as mourning for the dead or worshipping the sun. Thus Blackfoot males cut off finger joints; Dakota and Cheyenne males cut off pieces of skin; Cheyenne males allowed themselves to be attached to poles by wooden pins driven through their flesh; Crow males sacrificed finger joints, cut off pieces of skin, and practiced "all the variants of the sun dance torture." Benedict connected that male violence to the waging of war: among the Plains Indians adulthood meant warfare, she wrote, and their "reward" for their self-torture was "enhanced prowess in deeds of warfare."[86]

In analyzing the vision quest she could do the kind of diffusionist study of contiguous cultures that was still popular among anthropologists. She could also explore the subject of religion and her own Christian beliefs in the context of her horror over the senseless deaths of millions of young men in World War I. For the self-torture of the Plains Indians bore a resemblance both to the male agonies in World War I and to the torture visited on Jesus Christ at his crucifixion—a suffering young man at the center of a religion. Suffering and salvation: those were central themes of her poetry and her life. How to "ascend to the high ground" without the guidance of evangelical religion; how to deal with her demons; how to "burn with a gemlike flame" without burning up—those were major issues in her life. She had long identified with Christ in the guise of her father; he stood at the center of her imaginary world. Theseus in the labyrinth trying to escape the Minotaur: that was a more frightening, although similar, image of a young man facing destruction.

Yet her early conclusions with regard to the vision quest are startling: she found that in some tribes the experience was more standardized than mystical, more an expected ritual than an epiphany. Thus she could distance herself further from the religion of her childhood, with its emphasis on sin and guilt and its prohibitions on sexuality. And the vision quest confirmed what she had learned from James Frazer's *Golden Bough* about the widespread worship and sacrifice of young men in world religions. Frazer's book, an important text for intellectuals and poets of Benedict's generation, was the kind of universalized diffusionist effort that Boas didn't like. It was a study of the myths of the young vegetation gods—Attis, Adonis, Dionysus—who in ancient Mediterranean societies were sacrificed in the late winter so that in the spring a new young god could impregnate the earth and symbolically ensure that crops would grow. The existence of this universal myth reduced Christ to the descendant of these earlier young gods and made even more horrible the deaths of young men during World War I.

Ruth Benedict's anger against Stanley and against male aggression was a theme in both "The Bo-Cu Plant" and "Mary Wollstonecraft." Her early work on the vision quest among the Plains Indians also reflected her concern about male power, for that power could kill young men as well as turn women into pawns controlled by men. Her most forceful statement linking aggressive males to war was her article "The Uses of Cannibalism," a brief Swiftian satire that she wrote in the mid-1920s and never published. In modern times, she wrote, both patriotic allegiance and the craving for violence have been unsuccessfully met by "oaths, blood-and-thunder, and vows to undertake the death of industrious households," which have resulted only in "the death, in great numbers and with distressing tortures, of young men in sound health and vigor." In contrast, she pointed out sarcastically, some tribal societies dealt with their needs for violence and group superiority through a ritualized cannibalism in which hardly anyone was actually killed.[87] The headhunters of the Malay Archipelago ate prisoners they took in war, but they carefully negotiated their wars with their opponents, agreeing on a time when both sides "joined forces with the fierceness of males in breeding season." After one side killed a warrior from the opposing side, the war was over, and the victors feasted on the body of their victim. To satisfy a society's patriotic fervor and its craving for violence, wrote Benedict, "nothing could be more harmless" than consuming "one useless body per year."

Cannibalism as a metaphor for human cruelty recurs elsewhere in her work. It is there in the cannibalism of the Kwakiutl, a centerpiece of *Patterns of Culture*. It is there in her only published writing on the Serrano, "A Brief Sketch of Serrano Culture," which appeared in the *American Anthropologist* in 1924. In its concluding passages, Serrano braves dress and skin a deer they have slain in a deer hunt. They use every part of the animal. "The bones were pounded in the mortars while fresh, and eaten in a sort of paste." In this passage the Serrano don't drink their life from a cup of clay; now they pound the animal they have killed to a pulp and eat every bit of it. Such imagery exemplifies her use of monsters and beasts in her anthropological writing and her poetry to personify the dark side of Dionysus: her monsters and beasts include the shaman of the Shasta Indians of Northern California with blood oozing out of her mouth; the flying witches of Dobu in Melanesia; the unicorn; Frankenstein; Orion; the Minotaur; Medusa— most, but not all, symbolic extensions of the devil of the "Bo-Cu Plant" and the Juggernaut of "Mary Wollstonecraft."[88]

Benedict's emotionalism in her journals and writings was sometimes extravagant, despite her attempts to control it through disciplined writing and an ironic point of view. Yet she could be calculating in promoting herself. By studying the Plains Indians Benedict challenged the male anthropologists at Columbia. Many of these men had begun their careers by doing fieldwork among those tribes as part of Boas's grand scheme to record the details of their original cultures and to create grammars and writing for them before Westernization took over. Sapir, Radin, Lowie, Kroeber—they had all participated in Boas's initiative. More than that, by doing a library study of the entire vision quest experience rather than an ethnography of one tribe, Benedict symbolically absorbed these male scholars, reducing them to footnotes in her text.

Her dissertation reflected the despair she felt after World War I. Sounding like Robert Lowie with his "shreds and patches," she reflected both Boas's empiricism and the modernist emphasis on diversity—the breaking down of evolutionary wholeness—when she wrote in her conclusion that "man builds up his culture out of disparate elements, combining and recombining them," and that it is a "superstition" that "the result is an organism functionally related." The religions of the Plains Indians were characterized by heterogeneity. Some tribes had no concept of a guardian spirit, while others turned the visions of the vision quest into commercial transactions, buying and selling them. Some reserved the experience for grown men. Yet her metaphor of the cup implied cultural wholeness; when involved in doing fieldwork she sensed the common elements of a culture, and that sense impelled her to find an "integrating principle." Even in her dissertation she glimpsed a "social patterning" in operation in individual societies.

Benedict was earnest and idealistic, yet there was calculation in the way she positioned herself. In her journals and letters, she rarely revealed her calculating side, but it is evident in a letter she wrote to Mead in 1932, when Mead was doing fieldwork in New Guinea and was depressed about her future. In the letter, Benedict counselled Mead on how to conduct her career. "I'm all for scheming for advantage in the game," she wrote. Yet "one has to be very wary of showing the scheming." The best path to take is to affect an "exaggerated show of indifference," for "they'll come around the faster." Then she took a different direction. In anyone's life, she mused, there are only a few occasions on which aggressively pushing one's interests can get one anywhere—perhaps eight days in a life of eighty years. Otherwise, the best procedure is to work hard and stay in the background, although those eight days are very important, and "one needs to be ready to take advantage of them."[89] Thus in her public demeanor Benedict seemed cool and unruffled, a skilled professional, a friend to everyone, with the devils inside her apparently under control, and her ambition, no less powerful than that of Mead, a concealed force.

BENEDICT BOTH DISLIKED masculine power and was drawn to it, even as she attempted to reconcile the male and female sides of herself. Her name, Benedict, may have been an ironic redefining of herself as male, but the pseudonym that she used for her poetry, "Anne Singleton," combined genders. "Anne" rhymes with "Stan"; "Singleton" can be read as "single tone," as a combination of male and female into one note. This musical reference underscored the musicality of the lyric poetry that she wrote, a form that dated back to the poetry written by Sappho as verse lyrics to be sung to the accompaniment of a lyre.

Elizabeth Stassinos has speculated that Benedict derived the name

"Singleton" from Joseph Conrad's character "Old Singleton" in *The Nigger of the "Narcissus."* No direct evidence supports this hypothesis, but it is plausible. Conrad's novel is about a group of sailors on a ship reacting to an African-American sailor among them; Singleton is the oldest able seaman, a "learned and savage patriarch," with a powerful chest and large biceps, "tattooed like a cannibal chief." The ship sails over the seas in a world devoid of women; the sailors are "the everlasting children of the mysterious sea," with its "unconcerned immensity." Conrad's male world of seamen resembles Benedict's male world of surveyors, imperialists, and the devil of "The Bo-Cu Plant." And Singleton seems an appropriately complex masculine self for Benedict, since Conrad's character has a female side that is revealed as he reads Edward Bulwer-Lytton's *Pelham*, a novel influential in establishing in literature the character of the dandy—the effeminized man of fashion who also appeared in real life.[90] Thus Benedict as Singleton was masculine, although with a soft, feminine side.

THROUGHOUT THE 1920S, while she wrote her anthropology, Benedict also wrote poetry. She published her poems in the many poetry journals that appeared in the postwar period. In 1912 Harriet Monroe of Chicago had launched a poetry vogue when she founded *Poetry*, the first of many small poetry magazines edited by women to appear. The "demon saleswoman" for women's poetry, the patrician Amy Lowell, advanced its cause with her vibrant public readings of her poetry, the startling masculinity of her large body and her cigars, and her championing of women poets. They were the vanguard of a female surge of creativity in the arts, as Gertrude Stein, H.D., Marianne Moore, and others emerged from the long tradition of women writing poetry—and reinvented it. Like the women explorers who invaded another male space and whose memoirs Mead read with gusto, they challenged men. They defied male modernists like Eliot and Pound, who were often antiwoman in their verse, by writing poetry in women's traditional lyric style, yet with an intellectualism and emotionalism unmatched by men.[91] Their popularity is evident as poet Edna St. Vincent Millay became a model for the flapper, the independent New Woman of the 1920s.

Adopting a male approach to poetry was liberating. Poets like Amy Lowell, Gertrude Stein, and Louise Bogan, the latter a close friend of Benedict's and Mead's, went so far as to take on a masculine persona in their poetry. They wanted to remove themselves from the image of the sentimental woman poet that had dominated the nineteenth century—in what was called the "nightingale" tradition—and that continued to resonate in the poetry of Edna St. Vincent Millay. "In the room the women come and go / Talking of Michelangelo": T. S. Eliot's famous lines trivializing intellectual women had little to do with them. Influenced by Symbolists like Yeats and Pound and by seventeenth-century metaphysical poets like Donne who wrote about reason and emotion, love and death, suffering and salvation in the same breath, they outdid even Eliot in their use of these themes. For they identified with emotionalism—that was decidedly female territory—but they tried to control it. "They absorbed the male modernists and then used them to elaborate female themes of love and madness." They were "anti-modern modernists."[92]

Unlike other female poets of her time, Benedict never used the first-person singular in her poetry, and she shifted between male and female voices. Androgyny was endemic to the Western poetic imagination. It was an inheritance from Plato made pressing as poets dealt with the tradition since the Greeks of inspiration as female—and actual writing as male (the master/muse tradition). Yet in Benedict's poetry men are often trapped: Theseus is trapped in the labyrinth; Orion is confined to the heavens; Christ suffers and is crucified. Sometimes a female exists who can release them, as Ariadne rescues Theseus. Differing from other women poets of her age, Benedict didn't focus on myths of female bonding: the story of Demeter and Persephone, the mother trying to find the daughter, doesn't appear in her poetry.[93] And in contrast to Louise Bogan, who identified with her male side to the extent that some scholars think she didn't like women, Benedict strove for balance.

Her most powerful poem with this motif is "Unicorns at Sunrise," which she wrote in 1924 and published in *Poetry* in 1930. The unicorn is the legendary beast with one horn in the center of his forehead. Only a virgin—the purest form of femininity—can tame him. In the mystical tradition the unicorn is a symbol for gender crossing or for the androgynous soul; in Western iconography he is associated with wisdom, because the horn grows out of the forehead, the position of the mystic's "third eye" and an entry point for the rational brain. In the Christian tradition the unicorn is the savior who raised a "horn of salvation" for man's sins. The virgin who snares him is Mary, his mother, whose virtue he can't resist.[94]

"Unicorns at Sunrise" reveals an unrecognized involvement of Benedict's during these years with a mystical sect called the Order of the Golden Dawn, an offshoot of Theosophy by way of the Rosicrucians. Both Yeats and Pound belonged to the sect, whose doctrines were based on alchemy and the tarot, kabala and Christianity, and whose ritual drew from the Egyptian Book of the Dead. In that ritual the unicorn was a symbol for the soul, and astrological signs (based on the stars) were used as divinatory objects. Christ's cross was also important, as a phallic symbol of the power of the male, as was the rose, a genital symbol of the beauty of the female. These symbols combined in the androgynous being, the unicorn, which was at the heart of the religion.[95]

Such mystical, antimaterialist sects flourished in the early-twentieth-century era of secular modernism and capitalist expansion, and their members took a vow of secrecy. Symbolist poets, like Yeats and Pound, believing that a world of invisible symbols existed beyond the real world, were attracted to these sects. Yet Benedict's experience may simply have involved reading about them, not participating in their mystical order. Mead identified Yeats's essays as important reading for Benedict and her. In his essays Yeats writes about his "daimon," the female alter ego through which he shaped himself, his bright and dark other who was his mask of redemption, not just of concealment.[96]

Benedict's "Unicorns at Sunrise" is a response to Yeats's play *The Unicorn from the Stars*, about a visionary young Irishman who dreams of leading an army of unicorns to war against modern materialism in order to return humankind to the glory of ancient Celtic times, when "men warred one to another, man to man . . . and they grew hard and strong in body." In her poem Benedict reduces Yeats's global setting to a forest and a farm. She reconfigures his focus on the male power of the unicorns to reintroduce the virgin as no less a warrior than the great beast. In her poem the unicorn is overpowered, not by the virgin's innocence, but by the force of her desire. Benedict's "unicorn" is a symbol for the soul, as he is in Yeats's play and in the symbolism of the Order of the Golden Dawn, but she rejects the astrological symbols that are important in Yeats's play, as well as in his poetry and his religion. In her universe, unicorns are "native of celestial ways unroofed / Of zodiac."[97]

Benedict's unicorns are male and very sexual. "After a night of long loneliness and lack" they come "light-hoofed with gladness." In lines that sound sexually menacing, they paw "the leafy-hidden track" of the forest with "forefeet that are slim and velvet-black." Yet in "Unicorns at Sunrise," in contrast to the original myth of the unicorn and the virgin, the virgin isn't passive. In the second verse of the poem she symbolically mounts the phallus (the horn) to become the unicorn. In the last verse she rejects the domesticity of "ripened corn" and "fire on the hearth" to range freely as a being beyond gender.

Thus Benedict tried to energize herself to leave Stanley, to challenge the male anthropologists, to cope with the elusive Margaret Mead, to tame the beast inside her, and to bring the male side of herself to the fore. Like Benedict's pseudonym Anne Singleton, the unicorn becomes a "single horn," unpledged to any truth, to any one position, soaring free in her/his own identity. That horn has many meanings. It is the "horn of plenty" symbolizing prosperity. As a musical horn it can send its piercing notes soaring above the soldiers on the battlefield to sound a reveille or above the symphony orchestra to voice a solo. Or it is the symbol for the phallus and thus for sexuality. In the farm area near Norwich where Benedict was raised, the wedding night included a charivari, the old ritual in which members of the community made noise under the windows of the bridal chamber until the newly married pair came out to give them food or money. That ceremony was called "horning."[98] Like most of her poems, "Unicorns at Sunrise" has many meanings.

> Some night after long loneliness and lack
> At dawning down the light they'll come light-hoofed
> With gladness, pawing the leafy-hidden track
> With forefeet that are slim and velvet-black
> And native of celestial ways unroofed
> Of zodiac.
>
> Run then, no instant staying, up the hill,
> Hot with desire of their curved horn,
> And leap to him, the foremost, no man born
> Has mounted to good purpose, and no skill
> Made less than unicorn.
>
> Throw slack the reins, and keep no memory
> Of foolish dreams we dreamed of ripened corn
> In barns, and red fire on the hearth.

Be free
As unicorns, that are but fantasy
Unpledged to any truth, a single horn
Against reality.

In 1935, after Benedict read Mead's *Sex and Temperament in Three Primitive Societies*, with its argument that "masculine" and "feminine" are categories that don't correspond to male and female, she wrote Mead that the book had inspired her to take another look at herself. "The whole question of sex and sex differences has been a passion with me throughout my life," she asserted. "I have raged at times at the virago and the pin-headed female." Finally, referring to herself in the context of Mead's book, she wrote, "I turned myself into an androgyne."[99]

In *A Room of One's Own* (1929), Virginia Woolf presented her famous brief for androgyny. "The normal and comfortable state of being," she wrote, "is when the two live in harmony together, spiritually cooperating. If one is a man, still the woman part of the brain must have effect; and a woman must have intercourse with a man in her. Coleridge perhaps meant this when he said that a great mind is androgynous." In referring to Coleridge's statement, Woolf drew from the long tradition of androgyny in Western literature. Benedict and Mead knew that tradition well from Michelangelo and Shakespeare, Blake and Shelley, and Yeats and the mystical tradition he followed. It was there in feminists like Margaret Fuller and in sexologists like Havelock Ellis and Edward Carpenter, who couldn't move beyond the male-female binary of their age, and in Magnus Hirschfeld and Sigmund Freud, who could.[100] To find a way to reconcile her masculine and feminine sides, to deal with the aggressive masculinity that she saw as a threat to society and with the rational masculinity that she saw as its salvation, to use the feminine as embodied in Ariadne or Beatrice to find the masculine, or to move beyond the entire binary construction, to become androgynous in Woolf's sense of the term—that was a major project of Ruth Benedict's life and of her scholarship.

CHAPTER 8

Free Love and Samoa

WHEN MARGARET MEAD and Ruth Benedict met at Barnard in 1922, the sexual rebellion of the decade was in full swing. The flapper, devoted to smoking and speakeasies, petting parties and dances like the two-step and the tango, had translated the prewar feminist call for personal transformation into the realm of pleasure. As modern as her short dress, she might be a career woman or an adventurer, like Margaret Mead going to Samoa. Yet in her popular representations she wasn't much of a social activist. The press in the 1920s, sounding like today's media, demonized the prewar feminists as physically unattractive and as antimale, as "the old school of fighting feminists who wore flat heels and had very little feminine charm." Confusing several generations of women's rights thinking, psychologist Lorine Pruette wrote that "the flapper looks on feminism as out-of-date, that anti-man stuff."[1]

Still, by seizing male prerogatives like drinking and smoking, previously limited among women to prostitutes and "fast" girls, mostly urban and working class, the flapper had expanded women's rights into the private sphere of men. With her masculine bobbed hair and bound breasts, she hinted that women's defiance might go further. Yet she didn't resemble the "mannish woman" of the sexologists; her prototype was the young boy of the homosexual ideal. With her youth and small size, she calmed fears of female masculinization.[2]

Mead drew from the image of the flapper as a sex radical when in an unpublished essay in 1974 she depicted herself as a sex crusader in the 1920s. Feminists like her mother, she contended, worked to close saloons, end prostitution, and achieve votes for women. A second group demanded birth control. A third investigated the sex practices of other countries by reading "handbooks on erotic behavior from India" that showed how a woman could have hours of pleasure from a lover "who had learned to postpone orgasm and ejaculation."[3] By Indian sex handbooks she meant the Kama Sutra; the male technique was *coitus reservatus*; she probably based these sex reformers on herself. She ended her discussion there, on a heterosexual note, appropriate to the era she was writing about—an era sexually free and yet attempting to enforce heterosexual monogamy.

For a move was under way to domesticate the flapper's dangerous boy/girl sexuality through heterosexual marriage. Experts on adolescence and on education excoriated schoolgirl crushes because they might produce lesbians. Marriage manuals in the Victorian era had condemned foreplay—when they mentioned it at all—but such manuals now often recommended it. The new wisdom was that married women needed to be satisfied in the sex act and that intercourse and the missionary position might not be enough, although men should remain in control, with mutual orgasm the goal. The new dispensation rejected Victorian sexual repression—and its homoeroticism—to encourage what has been called "compulsory heterosexuality."[4]

"The era of wonderful nonsense," "the great spree," "the Jazz Age"—no other decade in the history of the United States has spawned so many attempts as the 1920s to capture its essence in a phrase. Ruth Benedict used a standard one in referring to it as "the roaring twenties."[5] She thereby emphasized its flamboyance and downplayed its conservatism. Yet by the 1920s many prewar New York rebels either had died or, disillusioned by the war and the "red scare" of 1919, had left the city. Emma Goldman was deported for her anarchist views; Mabel Dodge Luhan moved to Taos; Inez Milholland suddenly died from acute pernicious anemia. Heterodoxy declined in membership. Ernest Hemingway and F. Scott Fitzgerald left the United States for Paris, where lesbian expatriates like Gertrude Stein and Natalie Barney already lived. Floyd Dell became conservative and moved to the suburbs; new Greenwich Villagers like Edmund Wilson eschewed politics for cultural criticism and re-created bohemia around personal fulfillment as their goal.[6] The prohibition amendment was passed, as were laws severely restricting immigration from Eastern Europe and the Mediterranean region; the Ku Klux Klan flourished.

Yet the reform impulse didn't disappear. In her radical phase at Barnard in the early 1920s, Mead found causes to join. Despite conservative trends in the academic disciplines, progressive idealism survived at universities like Columbia. In 1922, Benedict's report in the anthropology department seminar to which she invited Mead was on John Dewey's *Human Nature and Conduct*. In that book Dewey referred to "two schools of social thought about reform." The first, dominant before the war, focused on modifying social institutions; the second, dominant after it, focused on modifying individual attitudes. Dewey wanted the two approaches combined, and he praised anthropologists for their input. "The reason for the present great development of scientific interest in primitive human nature," he wrote, "is the interest in progress and reform."[7]

"The ultimate objective remains an inward affair, a matter of attitude," wrote Benedict. "My generation," wrote Mead, "was more concerned with individuals than with social movements," with "the potentialities of the human spirit."[8] Women's organizations like the League of Women Voters existed, but neither Benedict nor Mead joined them. Both were critical of separate women's groups that didn't include men. Mead contended that "radical" feminists had created a "new tyranny" by not recognizing women who remained in the home and by focusing on the special interests of women, not joining with the labor movement in a common cause.[9]

Benedict and Mead defined themselves as scientists, scholars, teachers, and writers who operated through persuasion, not activism. Drawing on John Dewey, they advocated social cooperation, individual regeneration, and progressive education, by which Mead meant what we call "socialization"—the molding of the child by the family and society as much as by the school. They saw themselves as part of a group of younger intellectuals who embraced the relativity of cultures and looked to the formation of a national culture in the United States that would combine races and ethnicities into a mix called "cultural pluralism." Horace Kallen, a favorite social philosopher of theirs, called for a democracy of nationalities, based on "cooperative harmonies."[10] Such ideas ratified their study of non–Anglo-European cultures and led them to embrace concepts of grassroots democracy that would emerge full force in American social thought during the Depression era of the 1930s, as Mead slowly abandoned the radicalism of her college years and Benedict turned more toward the left.

On May Day 1925, Mead and other Ash Can Cats placed a basket of flowers outside Edna St. Vincent Millay's door in Greenwich Village. It was a tribute to the poet, who was leaving New York City and the demands of fame and a bohemian lifestyle to live in rural upstate New York. That 1925 tribute to Millay resonates with other May Day experiences of Mead's: the baskets of flowers at the women's colleges to celebrate romantic friendships; the birthday cake with red candles at Barnard to honor the Bolshevik Revolution. This time Mead symbolically took from Millay a flame for her generation. For she was going to Samoa that summer; three years later, with the publication of *Coming of Age in Samoa*, she would become a legend in her own right, herself a symbol of the flapper, adventurous and free.

GIVEN THE SEXUAL REBELLION of the 1920s, free-love ideas flourished. In 1929 Beatrice Forbes-Robertson Hale wrote that "never in any age or race has there been such a storm of cure-all notions and counter-attacks to conventional custom and morality as is now breasting in America and Western Europe."[11] In her free-love coalition Hale included sex educators, birth control advocates, and popular writers like Englishmen Havelock Ellis and Bertrand Russell—and their wives, Edith Ellis and Dora Russell, who also advocated a freer sexuality in lectures and in print. Many free-love advocates, expanding on Freudian ideas, contended that individuals needed to satisfy their sex drive to avoid "complexes." Others, influenced by Ellen Key and Havelock Ellis, followed neo-Romantic doctrines to assert that sexuality could invigorate individuals and lead to a perfect society. With the divorce rate skyrocketing to one marriage in seven and, in some cities, to one in two, even centrists like Judge Ben Lindsey of Denver proposed trial marriage and free divorce as a way to prevent "varietism" in relationships—by which he meant free love. Lindsey's "companionate marriage," limited to young people before they had children and including free birth control and easy divorce, gained widespread support; his term "companionate marriage" defined the ideal of marriage as a partnership.[12]

Greenwich Village radical journalists V. F. Calverton and Samuel Schmalhausen edited a number of popular compilations of articles on new trends in American culture; Mead contributed to several of them. In his own writings, Calverton combined Freud with Marx to call for a new psychosociology. Schmalhausen went further. He called the "sex revolution" the "most recent and profound phase of the scientific revolution," and he asserted that "love may yet save the world." He contended that because sex relations with the same person inevitably become boring, sex practice should extend to "playful experimental behavior that approaches by perilous degrees to abnormality and perversion." Renowned psychologist William Alanson White praised Schmalhausen for his "humanizing psychology."[13]

In the 1920s sexual experimentation was widespread among the avant-garde and the young. Mead noted that "kissing parties" were common in her adolescence before World War I; historian Paula Fass contended that by the 1920s group petting parties often provided "the first initiations into erotic play." In her study of Greenwich Village in the 1920s, Caroline Ware noted that free-love practices, originating in the Village, spread throughout the city: "petting parties" were held even in Brooklyn. In *Patterns of Culture*, Benedict included the new sexuality in the reforms she proposed, as she advocated "divorce, secularization, and the ... petting party."[14] And bisexuality was in vogue in sophisticated circles, a product of the sexual experimentation of the age and the popularity of Freud, who proposed that humans were born "polymorphous perverse." In Harlem as well as in Greenwich Village individuals crossed gender lines to experiment with new sexual behavior.[15]

In his pre–World War I radical phase, Floyd Dell had proclaimed that sexual experimentation was typically American. The United States, he wrote, was the home of "the Oneida Community, of the [Victoria] Woodhull and [Tennessee] Claflin 'free-love' movement, ... of a hundred other obscure but pervasive sexual cults."[16] Indeed, the sexual practices at Oneida, based on the Kama Sutra and including the aim of ensuring female orgasm, were the centerpiece of the popular sex manual written by W. F. Robie, *The Art of Love*. Mead was a fan of the manual, which includes information about genital manipulation and lubrication, positions in intercourse, and oral sex. Disclaiming any intent to promote sex outside of marriage, Robie stated that he provided such information to strengthen marriage, since he thought that ignorance about sex lay behind what he identified as the widespread interest in free love. He attacked both the free-love movement and homosexuality, contending that men who practiced free love became effeminate, while he excoriated "Amazonian bonds or lesbian plague spots."[17]

In 1931, reviewing a number of recent sex manuals in the *Birth Control Review*, Mead praised Robie's work as direct and inclusive, although she recommended that because it might embarrass inexperienced lovers, they should try a less comprehensive manual first.

Nonetheless, the young people of this generation, she maintained, have developed "a habit of rebellion" against the "smug sentimentalities" of the "romantico-religious phraseology" of the sex manual writers of the late nineteenth century. Edmund Wilson, for one, read Robie's manual to women to seduce them. Mead stated that she and her friends read Robie and Havelock Ellis; she sent Robie's *The Art of Love*—and Ellis's work with the same title—to a female friend of hers in Australia who was interested in free love.[18]

Ellis's manual is as comprehensive as Robie's. He covers the sex practices at Oneida and those of the Kama Sutra; he notes the importance of the clitoris to female sexual satisfaction as well as women's ability to have multiple orgasms. He extols mutual orgasm, while criticizing men for their insensitivity to women's need for genital stimulation and women for insensitivity to men's problems with sexual performance, including impotence and premature ejaculation. He describes a woman in the sex act as a musical instrument—a comparison that, he states, he derived from Honoré de Balzac's *The Physiology of Marriage*. He quotes Balzac's comparison of the husband who is unskilled in performing what came to be called foreplay to an orangutan trying to play a violin. He outlines his free-love ideology, in which he forbids jealousy, sees friendship as erotic, and advocates variety in sexual partners. He quotes from Edward Carpenter's *Love's Coming of Age* on the need for spirituality in relationships and, conversely, on the importance of sexual love to realizing spirituality. Praising ancient fertility ceremonies, he suggests occasional group sex "to release the natural energies pent up by civilization." In 1953 Mead described Ellis's work as aesthetic and ethical—and not pornographic.[19]

When Ruth Fulton married Stanley Benedict in 1914, they agreed to the principle of divorce on demand. In her paper for Elsie Clews Parsons in the New School class in 1919, Ruth Benedict called for sexual freedom in marriage. When Margaret Mead married Luther Cressman in 1923, they agreed to divorce on demand, to Margaret's keeping her maiden name, and, going further than Ruth and Stanley, to the elimination of jealousy in their relationship. Under that part of their agreement, Margaret and Luther could have affairs with impunity.

By then Mead had formulated her free-love position. It had a manipulative side, as when in *Coming of Age in Samoa* she described sexual relations in Samoa mostly in terms of technique and in her one reference to a Western text in that book praised the behavior of the protagonist of *The Affairs of Anatol.*[20] That was the book that had shocked her when she was sixteen with its male protagonist seducing women. On the other hand, her free-love views could be gentle and egalitarian, in line with the ideas of Ellis and Carpenter. She called those views an ethical position, almost a religion. In *Coming of Age in Samoa,* she referred to "the young advocate of free love who possesses a full quiver of ideals and sanctions for her conduct."[21]

Mead discussed her free-love views in a letter that she wrote to her sister Elizabeth from Samoa in the fall of 1925. Elizabeth had written her for advice after her first physical experience with a boy at a "moonlight party." Mead counseled her in language drawn from Havelock Ellis to regard her body as an "instrument of joy" that could thrill to the touch of any "deft hands." But she also advised Elizabeth to be certain that her sense of physical pleasure wasn't momentary but was connected to affection between her partner and herself and to her aesthetic sensitivity that thrilled at seeing a work of art or hearing an opera. It should also be part of the rest of her life and not episodic— and it could be experienced with either a man or a woman. "Don't you have crushes on girls?" Mead asked her sister. Echoing the tenets of the Victorian system of gender socialization, under which girls' affection for girls and for boys could be interchangeable, she continued, "You can just as easily have crushes on boys." The worst behavior, she maintained, was that of men who went from "one wanton to another," with no loving attitude toward any of them.[22]

In Mead's free-love system, sex was a force that produced aesthetic and spiritual empowerment. In his autobiography, Luther Cressman described it as the joyous source of creativity that made life worth living. Beauty in literature, art, architecture, and music came from it; it permeated nature and all human intimacy. Margaret had, indeed, persuaded Luther to abandon whatever conservative views he had once held; she seems to have persuaded him to adopt free love. Eliminating jealousy was central to the free-love ethic. "It would be an insult to both me and my husband," Mead stated, "to expect marital fidelity on the part of either of us."[23] Jealousy had destroyed free love among the prewar Greenwich Village radicals like Max Eastman and Floyd Dell, since most of them couldn't handle their partners' being involved with someone else.[24] Yet if jealousy didn't exist, everyone could do what they wanted and no one would get hurt. And if sex was free-flowing, then everyone was a potential partner for everyone else.

That was Mead's ideal. Exactly when she put it into practice over the course of her life is difficult to determine. She made a commitment to Benedict to reject other female lovers, and except for her involvement with Marie Eichelberger, she may have kept to her pledge for a number of years. She fell in love with Reo Fortune, who wanted fidelity, and she agreed to that for a time. Finally, there was Gregory Bateson, already a believer in free love when she met him, who offered her a flexible arrangement. It wasn't easy for Margaret. She didn't want to hurt anyone; the pain of Marie Bloomfield's suicide went deep. Thus in a crisis she acted according to a number of scenarios, while exercising her creative imagination to justify her behavior and keep everyone happy. Her appetite for life and love was huge, but she had apprehensions about both. And her schemes could backfire, leaving her the loser. That's what happened with Gregory Bateson, the great love of her life that she lost after thirteen years of marriage.

Edward Sapir called her a "moonbeam" and claimed that she was in love with love.[25] Indeed, falling in love invigorated her: she hardly needed sleep; her food tasted better; her creativity increased. But she was afraid of hurting others or of being exposed. She had a tendency to tell people what they wanted to hear. She lived for the moment and liked being married, with the security of commitment and the possibility of the ideal love celebrated by Ellen Key and free-love advocates. Margaret was sweet and intense, optimistic and brilliant, controlling and demanding. "Mercurial" and "temperamental," as a friend described her, she had a "Cleopatra" side that drew others to her like moths to a flame.[26] As she grew older, there was also the allure of her fame.

IN SEPTEMBER 1923, Margaret Mead married Luther Cressman in her Episcopal church in Buckingham, Pennsylvania, near her family's farm. Waves of nausea swept over her the morning of the ceremony, but she went through with it anyway. Ruth Benedict wasn't present; she was still in New Hampshire with Stanley at their cabin on a lake. Margaret and Luther spent a disastrous weeklong honeymoon in a cottage on Cape Cod. Claiming that she needed privacy to finish a book report for a seminar, Margaret slept in a separate bedroom. Bewildered by her behavior, Luther walked on the beach alone. In *Blackberry Winter* Mead hinted that she had been frigid on that honeymoon. Using Havelock Ellis's musical metaphor, she wrote that Luther was proficient as a performer but she wasn't a good enough musical instrument to respond.[27]

Once they returned to New York and their regular lives, the situation improved. Luther began studying for a Ph.D. in sociology at Columbia, taking courses with William Fielding Ogburn and Franz Boas, while serving part-time as the minister of a church in Brooklyn. Margaret worked on her master's degree in psychology and her Ph.D. in anthropology and edited Ogburn's statistical journal. She didn't, however, help Luther with his church: she had given up her ambition to be a minister's wife years before. Still, she liked the role of newlywed wife, receiving wedding gifts, decorating their tiny apartment, giving what passed as formal dinner parties, cooking on a two-burner stove. Luther remembered that as a couple they were close to Ruth Benedict.[28] That may seem surprising, but Ruth always cultivated Margaret's husbands, whether out of esteem or kindness, or to be close to Margaret.

Luther and Margaret never quarreled. The malleable Luther seemed willing to put up with anything, including Marie Eichelberger's constant presence and Margaret's friends' using their apartment for romantic trysts—while some of them dismissed him as an intellectual lightweight. Margaret often shared that opinion. "I don't see how you and Léonie live," Margaret remembered him saying. "The rate at which things are going on in your heads all the time, it just tires me to think about it."[29] For his part, Luther found Margaret's moods quixotic. Like all emancipated young people in the 1920s, he remembered, she talked openly about sex, but she often went through the motions of sex with him without really enjoying it. Many years later, in *Male and Female* (1949), Mead counseled women to fake orgasms to keep their husbands happy; there's no indication in her papers when—or whether—she followed that advice in her own life. Their marriage kept deteriorating, Luther confessed. He told Ruth of his sorrow that he couldn't give Margaret "ecstasy."[30]

Yet Margaret needed Luther as her patient father when she became a confused child, challenged by a weak physique and the dramas she kept creating. Her neuritis kept recurring; then her leg was broken when a taxi hit her as she chased her hat "on a dark, windy night, out into the middle of Broadway." She telephoned Ruth Benedict from the hospital emergency room, and Ruth exclaimed: "You miserable child. What have you done to yourself now?"[31] For several months Margaret hobbled around on crutches, with her leg in a cast. Luther seems always to have been there for her; he became something of a confidant to her in her affairs with Edward Sapir and Reo Fortune.[32] He was so secure in his masculinity, Margaret asserted, that helping her with the housework didn't bother him. In later years, drawing on Ben Lindsey's "companionate marriage," she advocated trial marriages for students and called her marriage to Luther her student marriage—a description he didn't like.

Did Luther know about Margaret's affairs with women? In his autobiography he doesn't mention them, although he hinted in an interview with Jane Howard that he knew something. He described Marie Eichelberger as following Margaret around "like a pet dog," and he related an incident that occurred when he and Marie were alone in the apartment and Marie asked him to show her his penis because she had never seen one. He did so; she showed him her breasts. She went home and developed a stomachache. Benedict later characterized Marie to Margaret as terrified of heterosexual sex.[33]

As for Luther, he may not have been as innocent as he seems; after all, he embraced Margaret's free-love views, and when Margaret went to Samoa he went to England to study birth control, which was connected to the free-love movement there. Women found him attractive, and two of Mead's women friends fell in love with him. Mead described one as an "intense neurotic" who slept on the couch in their apartment for a time and who, falling in love first with her and then with Luther, persuaded him that he was a Don Juan. The second friend was Eda Lou Walton, a poet who had studied anthropology at Berkeley, taught literature at New York University, edited one of the day's small poetry journals, and was close to both Benedict and Mead. When Margaret decided to divorce Luther she tried to pair him with Eda Lou, to make certain that he was taken care of, although he didn't respond to that scheme. On the other hand, Margaret criticized Luther for having "an abnormal vicarious satisfaction" in her relationships;[34] his acting as her confidant may not have been without guile.

DURING THEIR MARRIAGE Margaret was so often absent that Luther joked about having to make appointments to see her. As in college, she crafted a life of her own, one still filled with "intense personal relationships." After graduating from Barnard, most of the Ash Can Cats remained in New York, and she saw them a lot. She found them jobs and lovers; she counseled them about their lives. Every year in December, to celebrate Léonie's, Pelham's, and her birthdays that month, the three of them had dinner at the Greenwich Village restaurant where in college they had laid a candle on the table and lit it on both ends, and they repeated that ritual each year as part of their birthday celebration.[35]

Margaret also became close to a number of young women poets whom she met through Léonie Adams, and Ruth did too. The group included Eda Lou Walton and Louise Bogan, probably their most gifted member. (In 1954 she and Léonie Adams shared the prestigious Bollingen Prize in poetry.) All wrote in the lyrical, antimodern modernist style of women poets of this era; most had grown up outside New York and moved to Manhattan, as Benedict and Mead had. They found one another through publishing in poetry journals and speaking at poetry readings, held throughout New York City in a time when poetry was very popular. They held poetry evenings and parties at which they drank bootleg liquor and played rhyming games. They shopped for clothes and went to the movies together. Always the organizer, Margaret persuaded William Fielding Ogburn to hire Louise Bogan and Léonie Adams to help her edit his statistical journal. Like most poets, they had a hard time making ends meet.[36]

Edmund Wilson was friends with—and had affairs with—Edna St. Vincent Millay, a friend of Bogan's, and then with Léonie Adams. He wasn't much of a poet himself, but he was an important critic, and he liked the poetic style of the female poets of the day. He wanted to marry Millay, but she turned him down; he later married writer Mary McCarthy—in what turned out to be a disastrous union. Short and rotund, he nonetheless attracted intellectual women, whom he knew how to flatter. He had an appealing feminine sensitivity—as well as a destructive, lady-killer side. Although he knew Benedict and Mead, he didn't mention them in his literary criticism or in his voluminous diaries. Given his vicious handling of Adams—detailing her sexual behavior in a diary that was later published—they may have been lucky that he overlooked them. Sensitive to his treatment of Adams, Mead called him a "decadent little egoist."[37]

Ruth and Margaret became closer. They went to Boas's graduate seminars together. They had dinner together and went to the theater, although those evenings were few, since Ruth had to sit in a front row in order to hear and Margaret, an impoverished graduate student, couldn't often afford the tickets for those seats, unless Ruth paid. Margaret introduced Ruth to the members of the Ash Can Cats; Ruth knew those who had taken the introductory anthropology course with Margaret. "We are all Boasites," Hannah Kahn ("David") had proclaimed in 1923.[38] Ruth joined the poetry group and became close to Marie Eichelberger, who promptly included Ruth in her circle of adoration. Both Ruth and Margaret complained about Marie's intense hero worship and her acute bouts of depression, but they could not resist her willingness to take care of practical matters for them, her deep appreciation of everything they did, and her happiness in their presence. She was another chronic depressive attracted to Mead's intensity. "I get whatever pleasure I can from other people," Marie wrote Margaret.[39]

As the relationship between Ruth and Margaret deepened, Margaret recalled, "we spent hours telling each other stories about people the other had never met, wondering and speculating why they had done or felt or thought what they seemed to have." They discussed their lives, talked anthropology, poetry, philosophy, and "the minutiae of real life"—the details of people's personalities and motivations—which both of them loved to analyze. Ruth wrote in a poem that Margaret "tossed back the ball of jest and judgment on the latest play" with "lazy ease," toyed "in approved modern way with the newest art," and exploded a "conceit of so-and-so's philosophy."[40]

Ruth also had a life of her own, one involving family members and friends from Vassar and Columbia. She saw Natalie Raymond, the stepdaughter of a wealthy businessman in Pasadena, whom she had met on a visit to her sister and her mother, who remained living there. Ruth characterized Natalie as a "gay soul."[41] Sixteen years younger than Ruth, Nat turned up in New York with a roommate and no money; she had a history of both lesbian and heterosexual affairs. In 1931 she would become Ruth's partner. Ruth kept Nat separate from Margaret, but she shared her friendship with Edward Sapir with her, showing Margaret his letters and talking about him with enthusiasm. "Her vividly relayed conversations and letters from Sapir," Mead later wrote, "became part of my thinking before I came to know him."[42] Trusting Margaret, Ruth didn't seem to realize the potential for trouble in what she was doing. Sapir was two years older than Ruth and seventeen years older than Margaret; nonetheless, Ruth generated a sensual current in Margaret that was directed toward him.

By the fall of 1924, a year after Margaret's marriage, Ruth was writing poetry that pleaded for a stronger commitment from her. In "This Gabriel," she reproached Margaret for idolizing her as a "favorite teacher" and not regarding her as an equal.[43] She wanted Margaret to be "a companion in harness," not just an acolyte. The "Gabriel" of the

title refers to the hero of Longfellow's *Evangeline*, the poem she had
rewritten in her own words her senior year in high school, and to the
archangel Gabriel, God's chief deputy and messenger, a figure of revelation, wisdom, and mercy, central to Judaism, Christianity, and Islam.
Benedict begins "This Gabriel" by calling her chronic depression her
"pitiful permanence." She contrasts her "gray / And dusty" journey
through life with that of an optimist like Mead, whose path is "upwind-
ing through the stars." Then she shifts mood. She writes of "common
scars" won on a "simple tree." The reference is to Christ, a repeated
figure in her poetry, and to humanity winning "infinity" through
Christ's sacrifice on the cross.[44]

Yet the reference to "common scars" seems to include Margaret
as well as herself, as does the Christ figure, "himself no less
infinity / Than they." It is as though some person or event had
wounded each of them—or that all humans are scarred by the difficulties of living. Gabriel wants more than just praise and the loneliness of
"walking the stars," out in space, at an "even pace," shaped to a "crystal citadel." The reference is to the white, crystalline world of Benedict's daydream:

> He wrought a pitiful permanence
> From jagged moments, and dismay
> And tears more purposeless than pain.
> He smiled, knowing the gray
>
> And dusty journey for the same
> Man saw upwinding through the stars;
> Himself no less infinity
> Than they. He liked their common scars
>
> The better for their being won
> as his upon a simple tree,
> Wounding a transience and a flesh
> Innocent of divinity.
>
> What comfort had he had in praise
> That makes of him this Gabriel
> Walking the stars, his even pace
> Shaped to a crystal citadel?[45]

By the end of 1924, two years after they met, Benedict and Mead had become lovers, as Ruth persuaded Margaret to abandon her "foolish one-sided preference"—for a heterosexual relationship with Luther—and brought her into a "great glowing affirmation of reciprocity."[46] In other words, Ruth persuaded her to try a bisexual approach again, as she had in college. She offered Mead more: freedom to follow the "pattern" of her personality, to do what she wanted in free-love fashion with no jealousy on Ruth's part. When Margaret graduated from Barnard Ruth gave her a "no strings attached" fellowship; now she offered the same in their emotional relationship. "There aren't any obligations on your part," she wrote to Margaret.[47] Yet it's doubtful that Ruth yet realized exactly what that "pattern" of Margaret's might involve, how easily she fell in love, especially with men.

Such a self-denying relationship on the part of Benedict was in accord with her sense of herself. She was thirty-seven, approaching midlife, in love with a younger woman. She wanted an Ariadne to lead her out of her emotional labyrinth, a daughter she could mother, and a partner who could help her master Elsie Clews Parsons and the men in anthropology. Marguerite Arnold advised Ruth that she ought to undergo analysis, for the controlled and distant self she displayed in public was simply too disconnected from her passionate private self. Marguerite worried that she would break down under the strain of trying to keep herself under control.[48] But Ruth was ambivalent about Freud and still determined to work out her psychological issues herself. Literature, philosophy, and anthropology were her guides. She would control emotion through reason: Apollo would unite with Dionysus; she would combine her masculine and feminine selves and discipline her devils. Schooled by nineteenth-century neo-Romanticism, she wanted to achieve a true love that would last. Attuned to the free-love movement, she wanted to root out jealousy, the sense of ownership of another, from her makeup. To be free she had to allow Margaret to be free. That was the bargain she offered, and Margaret stretched it to the limit.

Ruth ought to have seen that Margaret had learned manipulation and sexual control from her father and that she had ambivalent feelings about her mother, whom Ruth in some ways resembled. Like Emily Mead, Ruth had a lovely smile, but she could be emotionally withdrawn and cold; she was, like Emily, an intellectual with an interest in reform. Margaret preserved into adulthood her childhood drive to find an older mentor—and a mother preferable to Emily—but it was debatable how long she would remain in a dependent position in any relationship. Margaret sometimes used double-edged metaphors in her letters and poems to Ruth, beautiful images that have an underlying sting.[49] In her poem "Absolute Benison" she characterized their relationship in terms of the larkspur and the rose. The rose, of course, has thorns; the larkspur, associated with death and mourning, is poisonous, named for its resemblance to the claw of a bird. Thus the burials of the larkspur offer no "benison," no blessing. Then Margaret revises the larkspur image into the song of the lark, a joyous cascade, but one ambiguous for their relationship, since the first lark song sleeps in the darkened garden "where all eternal replicas are kept."

> *Those who delighted feed on difference*
> *Measure the larkspur higher than the rose,*
> *Can find no benison in burials,*
> *The only absolute that summer knows.*

> *But those who weary of this variance . . .*
> *Turn with nostalgia to that darkened garden*
> *Where all eternal replicas are kept,*

> *And the first rose and the first lark song*
> *Since the first springtime have slept.*[50]

   How did Benedict characterize Mead? She was her daughter and protégée in anthropology, her partner, lover, and best friend. She was also her blithe spirit, who could lift her moods and show her how to be happy. In a draft of *An Anthropologist at Work*, Mead wrote that Benedict believed that when she was feeling intense and happy she attracted others, but when she became depressed she thought she was so unattractive that nobody could possibly want her.[51] Ruth described her feeling for Margaret in a lovely, lyrical statement, in which for once she presented her depressions as a simple matter, not a calamity: "When I'm happy your love makes me sing tira-lira, and when I'm blue it holds a liveable world before my eyes."[52]

AT THE SAME TIME that Ruth was pressuring Margaret for a deeper commitment, Margaret met Edward Sapir at the convention of the

British Association for the Advancement of Science in Toronto in September 1924. Sapir organized the meeting; anthropologists from New York City attended it. Ruth wasn't there; she was in New Mexico doing fieldwork. But Margaret was indomitable: she made a play for Sapir. Giving a paper on Polynesia, the subject of her doctoral dissertation, she must have been a sensation, with her small body and her sharp, critical mind.[53]

Talkative and flirtatious, Margaret caught Sapir's attention; his wife had recently died, and he was looking for a new wife—and a mother for his children. "Talking to him was magnificent," she remembered. "He'd say half a sentence and I'd say half a sentence and he'd say half a sentence and things just went up in fireworks that were delightful." For his part, Sapir called Mead an "astonishingly acute thinker," who created new ideas "at breakneck speed."[54] Margaret later confessed to Ruth that she knew exactly what she was doing in attracting Sapir. She was unhappy with Luther. Sapir reminded her of her father; he represented a "symbolic" extension of Ruth into heterosexuality.[55] The situation had oedipal overtones, since Edward and Ruth were close and both were much older than she—a symbolic father and a mother to her. It also indicated that Margaret was identifying with Ruth to the point that she would seduce a man Ruth may have desired for herself. Yet Margaret's free-love beliefs justified her behavior, for they held that love for one individual should extend to everyone that individual loved. Following that principle, Margaret was obliged to become close to Sapir, who was Ruth's close friend. Edward and Margaret didn't become lovers until the next spring, however, a few months before she left for Samoa.

The convention in Toronto was a milestone for Margaret, both professionally and personally. The meeting was abuzz with the presidential address that the eminent anthropologist C. G. Seligman of the University of London had given to the Royal Anthropological Institute of Great Britain and Ireland the year before, in which he praised the typologies of introvert and extravert which psychologist Carl Jung had devised to categorize individuals and societies. Seligman suggested that they be applied to tribal societies. By 1923 evolutionary anthropology was in retreat, and diffusionism, still popular, seemed to many not to be going anywhere. Indeed, some of the English anthropologists were taking it in a universalizing direction that Boas didn't like—toward viewing all advanced civilizations as arising in Egypt. Boas praised the sophistication of African civilizations like ancient Egypt, but he wasn't an Afrocentrist. The Boasians were looking for a new universal scheme for a science of society. The fascination with typologies—a form of classification—was everywhere: reviewing a book that year proposing comradeship, assertion, and submission as universal typologies, Benedict referred to "the recent [large] output of fundamental classifications of human types"; earlier that year Sapir had proposed the categories of "genuine" and "spurious" as a way of ranking societies.[56]

Western thinkers had long used dualistic typologies to categorize societies and the forces behind change: Hegel had his synthesis and antithesis; Nietzsche his Apollonian and Dionysian, and William James his tough-minded and tender-minded—and Jung claimed all of them as predecessors. He derived his types from his psychiatric patients and from the day's two main classifications of mental illness: hysteria (manic-depressive syndrome), the basis of his extraversion, and dementia praecox (schizophrenia), the basis of his introversion. Moreover he derived four emotional qualities from the Gnostic philosophers—thinking, feeling, intuition, and sensation—to propose that his two drives could combine with these four qualities to create eight additional categories. Given the frequent identification of "savages" with the mentally ill of Western societies, anthropologists were interested in mental illness, and Jung didn't tread on their territory the way Freud did in *Totem and Taboo*—in his theory, relating to prehistory and based partly on kinship studies in Australia, that the incest taboo originated in a band of brothers seizing power from their father.[57] Jung roamed over history, concluding that the East, with its mystical religions, was introverted, while the West, expansive and imperialist, was extraverted. These ideas seemed fresh and new in the 1920s: the words "extravert" and "introvert" entered the language and were widely used, as they still are today.[58]

The New York anthropologists at the convention had fun applying Jung's categories to themselves; Sapir would use them to catalogue societies for a number of years. Mead had studied them in her course with Ogburn at Barnard; with severe neuritis in her right arm that semester making it difficult for her to write, she did her term paper as a series of drawings that ended with a schizophrenic man falling down a flight of stairs. Jung's typologies percolated in her thinking until, in the early 1930s, she formulated a type theory of her own, partly drawing on them, with the help of Reo Fortune and Gregory Bateson.

In *Psychological Types* Jung also asserted that mental normality and abnormality exist along a continuum, not across a divide, and he implied that abnormality could dominate cultures as well as individuals. Those ideas anticipated Benedict's conclusions in *Patterns of Culture*, as did Jung's use of Nietzsche's dualism between Dionysus and Apollo as a precursor to his system. She contended, however, that Jung hadn't influenced her that much; she didn't like fitting individuals and cultures under a small number of categories. For many years she contended that the classifications she used in *Patterns of Culture* couldn't necessarily be applied to societies other than the ones she had focused on in the book.[59]

Jung's theories raised the issue of gender. Although in *Psychological Types* he commented only briefly on his categories as gendered, elsewhere in his work he maintained that males possessed a female "anima" and females a male "animus"—in what seems a variation on contemporary notions of inversion. Most present-day feminists take Jung as misogynist, on the grounds that he usually rated the animus superior to the anima, but he had feminist followers in New York. Chief among them was Beatrice Hinkle, a Greenwich Village analyst and writer, who used Jung's types to conclude that men and women varied more by type of personality than by gender. A member of Heterodoxy, Hinkle began her career at Cornell Medical College, where Stanley Benedict worked; Ruth recommended Hinkle to Sapir as an analyst for his wife. Hinkle's partner, Constance Long, a physician and psychologist, made a brief for bisexuality, asserting that everyone is both heterosexual and homosexual and that "we should seek to make the best of both worlds."[60] Her advice sounds like what Benedict and Mead were doing. It's tempting to speculate that Hinkle and Long influenced them, although neither ever cited these feminist Jungians in their letters or their writings.

AT THE 1924 CONVENTION in Toronto, as Mead listened to the British anthropologists talking about the societies they studied as "their" societies, she suddenly realized that she wanted to have "her" society. She didn't want to study one of the Pueblo tribes, like Boas's other women graduate students. She wanted to become like the intrepid women explorers who went to new places and whose travel accounts she read. Exploration was in the air. "That was the year," Mead wrote, "that Roy Chapman Andrews brought back dinosaur eggs from the Gobi Desert [to the Museum of Natural History], and everything ancient stirred the public imagination. People were talking about prehistoric American mound buildings; the British excavations in Athens; the lively dispute over King Tutankhamen's tomb in Egypt."[61]

Mead decided to go to the South Seas; the societies she had studied for her dissertation were located there. Franz Boas insisted on Samoa and recommended the subject of adolescent girls to her. He worried about sending a young woman alone to a tribal culture, and he especially worried about Margaret, whom he found "high strung and emotional."[62] Samoa, a protectorate of the United States, had colonial residents and many tourists. Because of the emergence of the flapper, the subject of adolescent sexuality was in the air, and Boas wanted someone to disprove the evolutionary theory of G. Stanley Hall, his antagonist at Clark University, that the emotionalism of adolescence was an inevitable evolutionary stage. Given Margaret's small size, he thought that the Samoans—tall and large-boned—would assume that she was an adolescent and would open up to her, and that's exactly what happened.[63] Boas's daughter Franziska had been a classmate of Margaret's at Barnard: he probably had some inkling of the behavior of the young women there. In his written instructions to Margaret, he asked her to find out if Samoan girls had crushes on each other.[64]

Leaving the United States for a time would give Margaret a break from the problem of what to do with Ruth, Luther, and Edward—each wanting commitment from her. Yet it took courage for a woman in her twenties to go alone to Samoa, and Margaret didn't like to go anywhere alone. She asked another female anthropology student to go with her, but that individual refused; predictably, Margaret didn't ask Luther to accompany her. In the months before going to Samoa she seemed so distressed and her arm hurt so much that Ruth took her to see a neurologist. Margaret possessed great bravado, but she seemed close to a breakdown again. In interviews with the *Philadelphia Public Ledger* before she left and a Honolulu paper on the way, however, she stated that she was going to Samoa to understand the behavior of the flapper and to determine the "proper way" to handle such young women in schools and juvenile courts.[65] Now she sounded like the mature Mead, a calm, competent expert, able to handle any situation.

Boas wasn't the only male mentor who urged Samoa on Mead. So did William Fielding Ogburn, whose journal she was editing, and Clark Wissler, head of the anthropology division of the Museum of Natural History. Wissler had ties to the Bernice P. Bishop Museum in Honolulu, which was funding studies of Pacific Island societies: Mead received funding from that museum to write a general ethnography of Samoan society. Wissler and Ogburn were both members of the National Research Council's Committee on Research in Problems of Sex; the NRC funded Mead's Samoa research on adolescence. They pressed Mead to investigate sexual behavior, for Samoa was a place of pleasure in the popular imagination, where previous studies had found both sexual repression and freedom. Such a study, they thought, would have a significant impact on sexual attitudes in the United States.[66] Wissler was considering hiring Mead as a curator; he wanted her to bring renown to the anthropology division.[67] It was a tall order for a twenty-three-year-old woman who had never been outside the United States, but she took it seriously.

Edward Sapir, not Margaret, told Ruth Benedict about his affair with her protégée.[68] Shocked and hurt, Ruth realized that Sapir was focusing the emotion he had repressed during his wife's illness on Margaret, who was fascinated by his passion. Ruth desired Margaret for herself, but she also worried that the strong-willed Sapir would turn Margaret into a wife and mother and divert her from the brilliant career that Ruth anticipated for her. Ruth sprang into action. She convinced Boas to let Margaret go to the South Seas; she became a confidante to both Edward and Margaret. Sapir wrote her long letters about his feelings for Margaret, and Margaret wrote her ones in which she alternately agreed to give up Sapir and then backed down. Sapir wasn't aware of the depth of Benedict and Mead's involvement; Margaret later wrote Ruth that he was jealous of Léonie Adams, not of Ruth.[69]

In a repentant moment, Margaret agreed to Ruth's plan that she cool Sapir's ardor by engaging in nervous attacks and fainting spells to convince him that she was extremely neurotic; Margaret called the scheme "unequaled in the annals of Italian poisoning diplomats."[70] However, it didn't work, for the melodrama she created captivated Edward even more. Ruth then persuaded Margaret to tell him about her free-love views to discourage him, but he developed a Pygmalion impulse to reform the errant Margaret. He decided that she was suffering from a "prostitution complex" that resulted from her girlhood conviction that she was unattractive and that drove her to have promiscuous intercourse with men to prove her desirability. Alternatively, he concluded that she had a compulsion to make others happy by sacrificing herself, in a sort of religious prostitution. More simply, he realized that Margaret had an abnormal fear of hurting anyone.[71]

Still, she baffled him. He wrote Ruth: "The more she loves Luther, the more she loves me?" That belief, a free-love tenet, made no sense to him. For a moment he distrusted Margaret. "It's all words, arrangements, escapes, duplicity, and unconscious demands for dominance." That interpretation of her behavior was probably correct, but Sapir also appealed to Margaret's masochistic side, the desire to be dominated as well as to dominate. When he announced that he intended to reshape her, to "hew right and left, as a sculptor flakes off his marble bits with courage and coolness," that intention didn't cool her ardor. He wrote to Ruth that Margaret possessed "the erotic impulse" so strongly that she needed to have a child to bring it under control.[72]

Sapir's attitude toward Benedict changed that summer of 1925 when he complained to her about Margaret's free-love views—and she supported Margaret. Suspecting that Ruth wasn't as repressed as he had thought, he now chided her for exhibiting "something cruel, Ruth, in your love for psychic irregularities." Beneath her mask he now saw passion and anger, and he cautioned her that she might break down: "Do you not feel that you extract your anger from a mutely resisting Nature who will have her terrible revenge?"[73] He wanted her to remain a controlled, rational person on whom he could depend. Her change confused him, since he thought she was devoted to Stanley, while Margaret was obviously disenchanted with Luther.

As for Margaret, she went on trying to keep everyone happy. In the weeks before leaving for Samoa she spent a weeklong second honeymoon with Luther on the Rhode Island coast. He called it "intense."[74] On their way there, they spent several days with Ruth and Stanley at their cabin in New Hampshire, as though they were just two married couples on holiday together. It was one of only two occasions on which Margaret met Stanley. It turned out that Ruth had told him that Sapir was in love with Margaret, not with her, and that had relieved his anxiety, for he had been insanely jealous of Sapir.[75] Seeing Margaret with Luther also must have put to rest any suspicions he may have had about Ruth and her, at least for a time. After returning from New Hampshire and Rhode Island, Margaret spent an intense weekend with Sapir at her family's farm, keeping him happy, too.

Meantime, she and Ruth decided to go to the Grand Canyon for a day to discuss the situation. Ruth planned to go to New Mexico in early August to do fieldwork among the Zuñi; Margaret had to go to San Francisco to catch the boat for Samoa. They could detour to Arizona, and no one would know. Visiting the Grand Canyon was one of Margaret's dramatic gestures. That deep gulf cut into the land by a river bears a resemblance to the ravine on her family's farm in her childhood where she had taken "best friends" to pledge eternal friendship; its natural setting recalls Benedict's "delectable mountains" of her daydream.

For her part, Ruth made the train ride to Arizona equally dramatic. As they crossed the country, she had Margaret read the letters Sapir had written to her and she delivered what she thought would be the deathblow to the affair: Edward, she told Margaret, suffered from an obsessive jealousy so severe that he hadn't been able to bear his wife's talking on the phone to his male friends in anthropology, like Paul Radin or Alexander Goldenweiser, or sitting next to them at dinner. "The warping," she told Margaret, "goes deep." Nestled in Ruth's arms on the train, Margaret sobbed over the letters.[76]

Once at the Grand Canyon, they found a deserted place on the rim and settled under a rock formation partway down. They stayed there that day, watching the cloud formations overhead, looking into the vast natural formation, with its striated rock in muted hues of copper, red, and white and its columns upthrusting from the canyon floor. Once again Ruth persuaded Margaret to give Sapir up.[77] The story among their close friends was that they became lovers there, although Margaret's letters to Ruth suggest an earlier date. Yet the tale of consummation in the Grand Canyon gave to their relationship an epic quality—grounding it in the ravine of Mead's childhood and Benedict's fantasy world now connected to a spectacular natural setting. It was a memory to treasure in the years ahead, when memories became very important to their relationship.

Several days later, in a letter to her grandmother, Margaret used genital imagery of internal and external, of rivers and pinnacles, in describing their differing impressions of the canyon. "She [Ruth] was impressed by the effort of the river to hide a torturing need for secrecy which had made it dig its way, century by century, deeper into the face of the earth. And the part I loved the best was the endless possibilities of the miles of pinnacled clay, red and white and fantastic, ever changing their aspect under a new shadowing cloud."[78] For once Mead depicted herself as masculine in a relationship, as "miles of pinnacled clay," with a "new shadowing cloud" showing endless possibilities. Benedict, however, was on some level afraid of their affair. After the saga with Sapir, she focused on the river, a female symbol, and its "torturing need for secrecy." She seemed to want to hide even from herself, to find emotional distance from the situation with Margaret and Edward.

Once in Zuñi, Benedict cheered up. After all, Margaret had committed herself, and that gave Ruth increased energy. She wrote to Margaret about the landscape in confident terms, about how she had gone up under the sacred mesa "along stunning trails where the great wall towers above you always in new magnificence." Now she wasn't a suffering Christ. She didn't have a "torturing need for secrecy." For a moment she visualized herself in grandiose terms, as God the Father creating a magnificent urban landscape. "When I'm God I'm going to build my city there," she declared.[79]

Yet Ruth might have waited to visualize herself so grandly, for once on Samoa, Margaret did exactly what she had promised Ruth she wouldn't: she continued writing passionate letters of commitment and disavowal to Sapir. Predictably, though, he met another woman, and in January 1926, four months after she left New York, he gave Margaret an ultimatum: either she committed herself to him or he would marry the other woman. She still couldn't make up her mind, so he did what he threatened; writing her a letter rejecting her, he married his new love. Their affair was over. Heartbroken, Margaret burned his letters in a bonfire on the beach.

As with much of Mead's behavior during these years, there are two narratives with regard to Samoa. The first involves the competent Mead, focused entirely on her fieldwork. The second involves a Mead who could hardly cope, who lacked confidence in herself, and who obsessed over her relationship with Sapir. Yet once that issue was settled, her mood improved considerably—for the resolution of the affair coincided with the adolescent girls opening up to her about their sexual behavior. And, no matter her emotional state, Mead always worked very hard.

Mead spent eight months in Samoa, from September 1925 to the end of May 1926. She spent much of the fall on the main island of Tutuila, learning the language and doing interviews. During that time she spent ten days in a local village, where she was chosen a *taupou*, the virgin who represented the honor of the village on ceremonial occasions. In early November she moved to Ta'u, a distant, less Westernized island, where the culture was closer to its traditional form; as a Boasian, she wanted to document Samoa's "ethnographic present." Neither the history of the islands nor the impact of Westernization was part of her project. Still, prompted by her wide-ranging intellect and her desire to be comprehensive, she included some material on those aspects in appendixes in *Coming of Age in Samoa*. That approach also characterized her later work on New Guinea, in which in her main argument she downplayed history and the impact of Westernization and then included them in subsidiary statements.

On the island of Ta'u she was also away from her status as a *taupou* and thus better able to interview ordinary people. Moreover, the Christianity professed by most Samoans had less influence on the girls on the distant island, and only a few Anglo-Europeans lived there; she would be able to approach the girls more easily. Once on Ta'u, she rented a room in the home of the officer who ran the naval dispensary on the island; her room was a large half-screened porch on the back of the house.

It's impossible to assess Mead's work in Samoa without addressing the much publicized attacks on her findings by the New Zealand anthropologist Derek Freeman. In his first critique, *Margaret Mead and Samoa* (1983), Freeman rejected her conclusions that the Samoans weren't violent and that their unmarried young people were sexually free. In the fieldwork that he did for the book, Freeman found considerable violence and a rigid sexual code under which, he contended, adolescent promiscuity couldn't have existed. Freeman, however, did his research several decades after Mead—and on a different part of the Samoan island chain.

In a second book, *The Fateful Hoaxing of Margaret Mead* (1999), Freeman contended that Mead couldn't have interviewed the Samoan adolescents she claimed to have interviewed because she spent her time on ceremonial visits as a *taupou* and did interviews for her general ethnography of Samoa for the Bishop Museum. He charged that she obtained her data on the adolescent girls from a Samoan man she had an affair with and from two girls she knew from the main island who, drawing on Samoa's joking tradition, had fooled her by telling her what she wanted to hear, never expecting that she would believe their stories.[80]

Was Mead's research flawed? Freeman contended that she didn't know how to do fieldwork, because Boas hadn't trained her in it. Yet she had studied social science methodology at Barnard and at Columbia's Teachers College with some of the nation's leading experts. She had read case histories at Hull House when she visited it with her aunt Fanny as a child, and she had helped her mother do her fieldwork among the Hammonton Italians. Rather than being incompetent in fieldwork methods, Mead was more sophisticated in social science approaches than most anthropologists of her day. When it came to constructing a research plan, she turned to those approaches, since neither Benedict nor Boas gave her much advice about how to proceed, despite her requests in letters to them to tell her what to do. But Boas had devised his own approach in his initial fieldwork among the Eskimos, and he expected his students to do the same, while Benedict seemed to trust Mead to be able to do it on her own.

Moreover, as Mead herself pointed out, her findings about free sexuality made up only a small part of her conclusions about Samoa in *Coming of Age in Samoa*, for that sexual behavior was largely confined to adolescents between the ages of eighteen and twenty-one. Children went nearly naked, but they didn't engage in sexual experimentation, although it was inevitable that they knew about sex, given the communal nature of the Samoan household and houses consisting of one large room in which family and kin members lived. Boys and girls before the age of eighteen were separated, with girls kept busy doing child rearing and household labor. Married adults might have affairs and divorce was easy, although Mead was aware that if a husband caught another man having sex with his wife he could demand a demeaning show of deference from his rival. Yet of the 297 pages in *Coming of Age in Samoa*, Mead pointed out, only 68 dealt with sex.[81]

Her main focus in the book, Mead contended, was not on sex but on the process by which children became adults—a process that we call "socialization" and she called "education." She celebrated the Samoan family structure, which was communal and extended, for she thought that it diffused the kind of tension that was endemic to the Western nuclear family and that it produced healthier adults. In fact, if children didn't like the family to which they had been born, they could be adopted into another one. Mead did conclude, as Boas suspected, that adolescence wasn't a troubled period in Samoa and that there was a smooth transition from childhood to adulthood, but she also reported on the rigid structure of Samoan society, under which behavior was restricted by class and governed by a precise code of conduct.[82]

In her fieldwork on Samoa Mead used several approaches. She did an ethnography of Manu'a, the administrative district of Samoa that included Ta'u and two small nearby islands, for which she interviewed informants and observed ceremonies and daily life, focusing on kinship. She wrote that fieldwork up as the ethnography of Samoa for the Bishop Museum. That work was a useful background to her study of adolescent sexuality. For that study she went further, cataloguing the inhabitants of her three villages on Ta'u by age, sex, relationship, occupation, marital status, kinship, and number of children. She thus established an introductory procedure that she followed in her later fieldwork. She also interviewed thirty adolescent girls, to determine their attitudes and behavior. Some may have told her what she wanted to hear, as Freeman contended, although it seems doubtful that all thirty lied to her, especially since she chose them from families of differing rank to make certain that she had a varied sample and she interviewed them individually. Mead was shrewd: there's no reason to suspect that she didn't know that Samoa had a joking tradition and that she didn't take that cultural practice into account in doing her interviews.[83]

Mead could have checked what the adolescent girls told her. There were three small villages on Ta'u on a strip of land between the beach and the surrounding hills, with another village located at a distance. It was a small territory, and Mead wasn't shy. In *Coming of Age in Samoa* she stated that the young children in the villages spied on the couples engaged in sex; she contended that such activity took place in the open, under the palm trees that ringed the villages. She could have spied on those couples herself. Indeed, she wrote Benedict that she had "taken chances" to get her sex material. She wrote Ash Can Cat Leah Josephson Hanna on January 29 that she had been out late the night before, "scrutinizing" the lovers by moonlight.[84]

Moreover, serving as a *taupou* wasn't a liability; it gave her a special access to the culture. Besides, she was a *taupou* for a village on the main island, not for Ta'u. During her stay in Samoa the people were drawn to her. Anthropologists had studied them before but never one like this: a tiny young woman who looked like an adolescent, with her riveting eyes and dynamic manner. They called her "Makelita," and the adolescent girls accepted her as one of them. One might conclude that she charmed the Samoans as much as she did individuals elsewhere.

Margaret wrote to Eda Lou Walton that she had considered having an affair with a handsome young Samoan man who understood the pleasures of casual romance, but she remembered her position as a representative of the National Research Council, and she didn't.[85] In late January she wrote to Benedict that one night she had been alone in her room with a young man who was the village's most experienced man "in matters of the heart," and he had told her about the "amours" of his friends "with complete candor."[86] Even if she had been intimate with these two men, however, the experiences would have enhanced her knowledge of Samoan sex practices. Freeman contended that Mead spent so much time being a *taupou* that she couldn't have interviewed her thirty informants thoroughly, but he seems unaware of her intense working habits. A navy chaplain who occupied another room of the house where she lived remembered her as often there—and as working from early morning until well into the night. By the middle of December she wrote Benedict that she had almost finished cataloguing the inhabitants of the three villages on Ta'u.[87]

Freeman contended that living in the home of a Westerner rather than in a Samoan home hindered Mead's research. In fact, given the rigid etiquette of Samoan society, the adolescent girls couldn't have spoken freely to her in their homes, which in any event didn't offer much privacy. Besides, they liked Mead's space, where they escaped Samoan formality. School wasn't in session when Mead was in Ta'u, and they were bored. As early as the end of November, soon after her arrival, she complained to Boas that she had to lock the door to keep them out; by January she complained that she couldn't get rid of them. They woke her up at dawn and came around all day, eager to talk. At night, joined by the boys, they danced on her porch, doing their traditional dances, dressed in native garb, wearing flowers, shell necklaces, and bracelets of leaves for the occasion, with coconut oil on their bodies. Their dances were individualized, with the girls' movements "langorous" and "suggestive" and the boys' movements athletic and punctuated with rhythmic slapping of their bodies. Dancing was very important to Samoan culture, according to Mead; everyone could then be free from the society's rigid etiquette code.[88]

Still, she wrote Franz Boas in the middle of December that she hadn't gathered anything very interesting or tangible yet about adolescent sexual behavior but she wasn't going to alter her material to make a showier report to the National Research Council. Her negativism prompted Boas to reply that she should be patient; his experience of fieldwork was that informants often didn't open up until just before the investigator was leaving, as over time they became more attached to the individual examining their culture.[89]

Freeman charged that Mead overlooked the violence of Samoan culture, especially the practice in which young males sought to prove their masculinity by raping girls asleep at night in their homes, using manual penetration as their technique and trusting that under the darkness of night they could pass as the girls' lovers. Mead admitted that he might have a point. In an afterword to the 1969 edition of *Social*

Organization of Manu'a, her ethnography of the three islands, she asserted that she and Freeman had reached different conclusions probably because the perspective of the girls who were her subjects differed from that of Freeman's adult males. Yet in *Coming of Age in Samoa* she noted attempts at rape on the part of young males who surreptitiously entered the girls' homes at night, when families were asleep; but she discounted those young men as rejected suitors whom the girls easily resisted. Still, she was puzzled that some of the "most charming and good-looking youths of the village" became *moetotolos,* or night crawlers; surely they could attract sexual partners on their own without resorting to violence.[90] She wondered, however, if a severe hurricane that occurred in early January might have disoriented the village so much that the young men stopped for a time using the girls "as pawns in male rivalries."[91]

During that hurricane Mead rose to the occasion. She didn't panic when she was shut up with the other Anglo-Europeans on the island in a partially drained water tank to survive the fierce storm, which destroyed the houses of the villages. In fact, shortly before it occurred she protected a Samoan girl from the drunken advances of one of the Anglo officials on the island. After it ended, she took over cooking meals for a time. These actions may have helped her gain the confidence of her informants. And she wrote to Benedict that after the hurricane ended the adults in her villages were preoccupied with rebuilding their houses.[92] Their preoccupation may partly explain why the girls were so open with her, since the adults weren't overseeing them as strictly as usual.

At the end of January Mead wrote Benedict that her room was always full of adolescents. "I never get any time alone," she complained. She borrowed an empty house and under the cover of giving "examinations," she interviewed the girls one by one.[93] On February 15 she wrote Boas outlining the information about personal matters such as menstruation that the girls she was interviewing had given her. She had found out that the young people were promiscuous; she had only to interview the girls about the details; she apologized for having written a "blue" letter the month before. The girls "pressure me from morning to night," Mead wrote Boas.[94] By the end of March she wrote to Benedict that she was sick of talking "sex, sex, sex" with her adolescent girls all day long. But Ogburn and Wissler had wanted that information so much that she persisted until she got a lot. "I've got lots of nice significant facts," she wrote. Indeed, she worried that she didn't have enough information for the ethnography for the Bishop Museum, not for the analysis of adolescent sex.[95] And contrary to Freeman's contention that she hid this project from Boas, she was open about it in her letters to him.

DESPITE THE WORK Mead accomplished during the fall and winter—learning the language, becoming a *taupou*, surveying her villages in Manu'a—in her letters to Ruth she continually confessed a lack of confidence in herself. She wondered over and over why she had come. She felt insecure and incapable, with her "inferiority complex" in control; she was certain that she was going to fail.[96] She came down with the usual neuritis in her arm, and she developed an eye infection. The heat and humidity were awful and the bugs unbearable. "I'm just going to give up and get a job taking change in a subway," she wrote Benedict in December.

She kept writing to Sapir during the fall and winter, and she told Ruth about doing so; in a dramatic moment she described her interchanges with Sapir to Ruth as "a dance of death." She cried all the time. "You can't get people's secrets from them if you are on the verge of breaking into tears," she wrote Ruth. In fact, much of the contents of her letters to Ruth from Samoa—even after the end of the affair with Sapir—are about her relationships in the United States. When Léonie Adams wrote Margaret in December that she was hurting Luther deeply and Luther wrote her about how much he cared for her friend who had slept on their couch, she started worrying about him. "You know," she wrote Ruth, "I've always used my relationship with Luther to keep the world from rocking." If she didn't have the habit of "systematic work," she wrote Benedict, she wouldn't have gotten much done.[97]

Ruth's encouragement and love buoyed up Margaret's spirits and kept her working. In her letters Margaret was extravagant in praising Ruth. She fantasized about their lovemaking, felt "ecstasy" when she thought of Ruth's beauty, dreamed of kissing her eyes and lips, of running her hands through her hair. "Knowing you, Ruth, has been the same blessed peace-giving effect as knowing there is a god." Ruth's love, she wrote, brings a "divine carelessness to my step." "There are times," she wrote, "when it is intolerable to remember the sound of your voice or the feel of your hair. Tonight is one of them, one of the times I come to your room no matter how late the hour or how inopportune the time." She wrote of dreaming that they could teach classes in anthropology together and do research in Samoa together. She had learned the Samoan language: she could do ethnography, while Ruth took down native legends through an interpreter. Don't you hamper yourself as an anthropologist, she asked, by repeatedly going to the Southwest?[98]

Ruth wrote Margaret in a similar vein, about love and longing, about the pain of separation and the joy when they would be together again. They planned that Margaret would finish in Samoa by the summer and then meet Luther in Europe and spend a month with him. They would then meet in Europe, spend a month together, and go to the International Congress of Americanists in Rome in September. Ruth fantasized in her letters about their meeting, how Margaret would cry when they met, how they would renew their love. To Margaret's dream of teaching together, she replied: "Let's have our department of anthropology and if all the men flunk, let them. We could show them the possibilities they're blind to." She referred to Stanley as the "bread" of love and to Margaret as the "wine."[99]

In her letters to Margaret, Ruth was calm and understanding. I decided to trust you a long time ago, she wrote. You have the right to do anything you want with your life. She didn't want to show Margaret her devils, didn't want to act like a "depressed idiot" or a "raging five-year-old" in front of her. She understood that Margaret loved a number of people, and she struggled with her feelings of jealousy and hurt. Margaret's lovers—Luther, Marie, Ruth herself—were a "close fraternity," she wrote. "We must all wait until you tell us what the course will be." She respected Margaret's having to spend a month with Luther in Europe; he was her heterosexual partner, and that side of her needed to be fulfilled. "He mustn't have his time cut down."[100]

Yet there is worry in Ruth's letters. Margaret seemed unable to give up Sapir, and that was troubling. Then she failed to tell Ruth that she knew about his other woman before Ruth did. Her constant self-pity was dismaying; making herself into a martyr transferred the blame for her behavior to others. In December she wrote that she was hurting everyone, but she simply couldn't decide between Edward, Luther, and Ruth. Edward might be right, she wrote Ruth, in concluding that there was something wrong with her. "I haven't done anything dreadful yet," she wrote, "but that doesn't mean that I won't soon." She described her emotions as "kaleidoscopic."[101] Such sentiments weren't reassuring to Ruth. "My constant struggle," Ruth replied to Margaret, "is to take your hurt lightly."[102] In January Edward gave up Margaret for the other woman, and even though Margaret burned his letters she seemed relieved to be finished with him in her letters to Ruth. Now she could go back to Luther and Ruth.

In her letters Ruth detailed involvements of her own. Being open about such involvements was part of free-love practice, but Ruth produced a lot. She described a date she had with Natalie Raymond. She told Margaret about going to a conference in New Haven and staying with Lydia Simpson, who had soft fair hair and dark brown eyes, "the pupils all a piece with the iris." She enthused over the great improvement in her relationship with Stanley after he realized that she and Edward Sapir weren't involved. "It's very precious to have your husband give you all the love he has," she wrote Margaret.[103] She also told her about Leone Newton's new love interest, how the two of them were taking a class of hers and "were all over each other," as though to stiffen Margaret's resolve in having given up Leone.

Ruth was right to be worried. For the last letters Margaret wrote to her from Samoa before leaving in May suggest that the immediacy of their involvement was waning for her, now that she hadn't seen Ruth for so long and didn't so badly need her support, since she had succeeded in doing her research. She wrote about her relief at leaving the home of the navy doctor, for he dominated his wife and had developed an aversion to Margaret because he thought his wife was attracted to her. Something of a racist, he became so annoyed at the many Samoan girls constantly on Margaret's porch that he declared his house off-limits to them. Luckily, she had gotten plenty of material by then. And she felt triumphant in the end that she had finished ahead of schedule. She was proud of herself for learning the language; she thought that she had acquired a "curious strength" that year. She called it a "muscular nerve."[104]

Everything seemed in order for Margaret and Ruth to resume their love involvement, except for the fantasy Margaret had about Ruth that began with one of her beautiful images about their love—and ended with a barb. When she was a child, she wrote Ruth, she imagined what it would be like to see God. "I always felt as if a door would just swing open and shut and that would be all the Beatific vision one could stand. I get the same feeling now when I try to imagine what it would be like to be in your arms again, and I can't think about it for more than a second, with almost a feeling of relief when the doors swing shut, for I feel as if I couldn't stand a longer glimpse."[105]

To be called a divinity, with the word's implications of perfection—and of distance—must have been both gratifying and alarming. Margaret's inability to visualize being in Ruth's arms "for more than a second" seems to indicate a hesitation about their relationship. That hesitation might have been the product of the passage of the months they spent apart dulling Margaret's memories of their time together. Yet the reference to her relief from the intensity of Ruth as a beatific vision when the doors swing shut, cutting off the vision, could also have indicated a hesitation about homosexuality. That hesitation would form the backdrop to her falling in love with yet another man, the young anthropologist Reo Fortune, when she met him on the boat from Australia to Europe, on the second leg of her voyage home from Samoa.

WHAT DID MEAD FIND out about adolescent sexuality on Samoa? She wrote to Benedict that she had learned a lot, but in her letters she wasn't explicit about her findings. The Samoan sex practices replicated "many modern points of view," she wrote, although there were significant differences "from our pattern." She didn't describe the differences in her letters, however, and her field notes located in the Library of Congress collection are, as she described them to Benedict, "cryptic and illegible and brief."[106] The major report of what she found is contained in the published *Coming of Age in Samoa*; the typescript manuscript for the book in the Library of Congress doesn't differ from what's in print.

In *Coming of Age in Samoa*, Mead reported that the transition to adulthood in Samoa was smooth, as Boas had suspected; the practice of free sexuality, she reported, facilitated the transition and led to contented marriages. It did so, in Mead's depiction, partly because it was organized in terms of heterosexuality, just as in the United States. There were differences between the two countries; girls and women working together in Samoa engaged in sex play as a "pleasant and natural diversion," as did adolescent males who were close friends. Nor did the Samoans stigmatize homosexuality as an identity. Yet they accepted it, in her view, because heterosexual sex included "homosexual" practices. "The more varied practices [than in the United States]" standard in heterosexual sexual relations on Samoa "preserve any individual from being penalized for special conditioning."[107]

Still, her description of the one "pervert" she saw on the islands wasn't complimentary. The girls on Samoa regarded the effeminate

Sasi as "an amusing freak," while the men he tried to seduce looked on him "with mingled annoyance and contempt." (She defined "perversion" as being "incapable of normal heterosexual response.") She noted that three of the girls she analyzed as "deviants" were "mixed types" who didn't demonstrate "genuine perversion."[108]

According to Mead, same-sex relations on Samoa were minor and occasional. Her answer to Boas's question about "crushes" was that the girls didn't have them, except for those who attended the single-sex Christian boarding school. She attributed this lack of homosexual desire to the fact that the Samoans employed all the "secondary variations" in engaging in heterosexual sex. She applauded the Samoan definition of sex as play, with technique crucial. "Familiarity with sex," she wrote, "and the recognition of a need of a technique to deal with sex as an art, have produced a scheme in which there are no neurotic pictures, no frigidity, no impotence . . . and the capacity for intercourse only once in a night is counted as senility." (The term "sex as an art" comes from Havelock Ellis.)

Moreover, the acceptance of a wide range of sexual practices as normal ensured that there was always a "satisfactory sex adjustment" in marriage. "The effects of chance childhood perversions, the fixation of attention on unusual erogenous zones with consequent transfer of sensitivity from the more normal centers . . . all the accidents of emotional development which in a civilisation, recognising only one narrow form of sex activity, result in unsatisfactory marriages, casual homosexuality and prostitution, are here rendered harmless."[109] Thus she proposed that full sexual expression in heterosexual relations could produce a major social reformation, including ending the prostitution that reformers in the United States had decried for several decades.

She went further in focusing on heterosexuality. In Mead's Samoa, men are the sexual initiators. They have knowledge of techniques that the women regard "with a sort of fatalism as if all men had a set of slightly magical, wholly irresistible, tricks up their sleeves"—although Mead notes that older women sometimes initiated the boys into sex, as older men did the younger girls. Still, "amatory lore is passed down from one man to another. . . . The girls learn from the boys," Mead asserted, and a man who didn't satisfy a woman was ridiculed. In *Coming of Age in Samoa*, Mead didn't explain what she meant by "amatory lore" and "slightly magical, wholly irresistible tricks."[110] Writing ten years later about Samoan sex techniques, she was clearer. "The Samoans recognize and practice a wide variety of foreplay techniques but have standardized only one position of intercourse, face to face."[111] In a letter to sex researcher Robert Dickinson in 1929, she wrote that the time spent on coitus was brief and that the girls gained satisfaction mostly through manual stimulation. She also asked him for his medical opinion on her conclusion that "introducing so-called perverse behavior into heterosexual relations" improved them.[112]

Mead included detailed charts at the end of *Coming of Age in Samoa* giving figures for menstruation, masturbation, and homosexual and heterosexual experiences for the thirty girls she interviewed. Those figures indicate that masturbation was nearly universal, while seventeen of the girls had had homosexual experiences and twelve heterosexual experiences. Her analysis of these interviews, however, indicated that the homosexual experiences were casual, a prelude to heterosexual sexuality and marriage.

The details in Mead's charts, in addition to her closeness to the girls and the care she took in interviewing them, indicate that they told her a lot about their sexual behavior. As was typical of her, the melodrama in her letters to Ruth Benedict in the fall and winter only increased her ability to work. And her involvement with Ruth kept her going, for Ruth believed in her genius and her ability to do the research she intended to do. In the end, however, she put her innovative research design together herself: neither Boas nor Benedict told her how to do it. Indeed, in judging *Coming of Age in Samoa* one needs to keep separate the information she collected in her interviews from the conclusions she drew from it. For she wrote the book in New York after she had returned from Samoa and had met Reo Fortune, when she was trying to persuade him to marry her and he was resisting partly because of her relationship with Ruth. Demonstrating that homosexual practices improved heterosexual sex could reassure him. Moreover, it also was in line with her utopian free-love views, under which free love, she believed, could produce major social reform.

MARGARET'S FALLING IN LOVE with Reo Fortune greatly complicated her relationship with Ruth. Most immediately, Ruth had to deal with the disruption of the plans that she and Margaret had made for Europe. Stanley had failed her as well. She spent the month of June with him in the British Isles to celebrate their wedding anniversary, and that trip turned into a disaster when he was irritable the whole time. He had probably fallen for the other woman; in an undated diary fragment, Benedict identified 1926 as the year that occurred. While Margaret traveled around France and England that summer, first with Luther and then with Reo, Ruth roamed alone—to Berlin, Chartres, the South of France. As for Luther, he reported in his autobiography that his time with Margaret was difficult, for Louise Rosenblatt, who was in Europe to study there for a year, traveled with them. And Margaret seemed preoccupied with Reo, even though she wrote in *Blackberry Winter* that in Carcassone she chose Luther over him. When they reached Paris, Luther seemed almost relieved to deliver her to Reo and to return to the United States. Yet like many of Mead's lovers he had hedged his bets: when in London he had met the woman he would marry after he and Margaret divorced.[113]

In the middle of Ruth's travels, she spent a week in Paris with Margaret, Reo, and a homosexual friend of Reo's named Max Bickerton, who lived in Japan. Ruth had to listen to Margaret's explanation that she had never expected to meet someone young and vibrant like Reo, that she had been unable to stop herself from falling in love with him, and that she had become so obsessed with her own problems that she couldn't stop herself from hurting Ruth. After that week, Ruth wrote Margaret cold, distant letters from the various hotels in which she stayed. In those letters, Ruth seems in control of her emotions, although an entry in her journal, written at Nice, indicates suicidal despair: "Passion is a turn-coat, but death will endure. Life must be always demeaning itself, but death comes with dignity." Finally, seething over what seemed Margaret's endless excuses for staying with Reo, she wrote a letter ordering her to appear at the convention in Rome.[114]

A telling document in Mead's papers is a one-page memorandum dated 1957 and titled "Notes by MM on What Really Happened." The document is about the summer of 1926. It portrays a jealous Ruth, plagued by her devils, angry with Stanley for spoiling their trip and determined to leave him—or to break up with Margaret. According to the document, Margaret went off with Reo after the week in Paris because Ruth ordered her to do so in a fit of rage. In this version of what happened, Mead describes her travels with Reo as a "battling platonic nightmare": he was so angry about her relationship with Ruth that he was impotent. A letter from Reo to Gregory Bateson in 1935 confirms that description: Reo states that in the summer of 1926 he was possessive and sadistic toward Margaret because of his anger over her relationship with Ruth.[115]

Ruth and Margaret played out their passions in their furious quarrel over Michelangelo's Sibyls in the Sistine Chapel. Ruth's jealousy was the issue, as well as Margaret's betrayal. Ruth had managed to handle Margaret's relationships with Luther, Edward Sapir, and Marie Eichelberger, but this affair with Reo was the last straw. She threatened to end their relationship. Faced with the immediacy of hurting Ruth, Margaret probably retreated and expressed undying love. In a note written the day after the quarrel, Ruth backed down. Assuming responsibility for it, she apologized for her behavior. She traced the quarrel to her hatred of her devils. When they were loose, she wrote, "I feel as unclean as a leper, and I don't act very well. I then want you to escape from them—and I do what I can to make you go." But she loved Margaret so much that she didn't have the strength to face losing her.[116]

Whatever damage the quarrel caused to their relationship, the note repaired it, at least for the time being. They decided to return to their husbands in New York, while continuing their relationship. Any future for Margaret and Reo remained undecided: he went to England to take up his fellowship at Cambridge. Leaving Rome, Margaret and Ruth went to Marseilles to take a ship for the United States. But there was a further development in their relationship, for Margaret had a new intellectual confidence derived from her success on Samoa and her conversations with Reo, who was versed in psychology and knew a good deal of anthropology.

On the ship to the United States, Mead and Benedict began an intense discussion about anthropology that, according to Mead, lasted "for years." Mead made a stand: she asserted, following Jung, that the way to connect culture and human behavior and thus to establish an intellectual direction for the field of anthropology was to find a theory that established a systematic relationship between universal characteristics of humans and their representations in specific cultures. Benedict disagreed. She thought that no theory was necessarily any better than any other and that cultures had little coherence.[117] That was her position in the fall of 1926, a position that reflected both the stance she had taken in her dissertation and her gloom in Europe over Mead's behavior. Yet a year later she changed her mind, inspired by a new impetus from her fieldwork among the Pueblo Indians and a new turn in her relationship with Mead.

CHAPTER 9

Bread and Wine

Creating a Friendship, 1926–1931

"PEOPLE I AM IN LOVE WITH are wine," Margaret Mead once asserted. They are "exciting, wonderful, lovely." Yet they are neither "necessary" nor "exclusive." For "you drink one good wine with one dish and another good wine with another."[1] That description of her love affairs reflected the "Don Juan" philosophy that would shock Edward Sapir into calling her a "bored adventurer." It was, however, only one mode of Mead's loving. She could be generous and caring, in line with the free-love views that she had expressed in her letter to her sister Elizabeth from Samoa. She inspired friends, lovers, and husbands to construct richer books, better careers, more effective lives. She wrote that her friends had an "incorrigible" tendency to see her as a mother, because she treated adults the way her grandmother had treated her parents, as children needing encouragement and discipline.[2]

Yet Mead could also be a child, playful and fun, but sometimes insecure, needing reassurance. That's how she often was at the start of a relationship, before her propensity to assert control, to become argumentative, even to throw tantrums appeared. Ruth Benedict sometimes excused that behavior as part of Margaret's "baby" side. "I mean you laugh like a baby and you cry like a baby," Margaret remembered her saying, "and you make faces like a baby. You just express your emotions like a baby."[3] Mead often stated that her real age, the age she felt inside, was between ten and eleven. Sapir had captured that side of her in his poem "Ariel," when he described her as rising through the clouds with "little wise feet." "I walked with a light step, the step of an eleven-year-old," Mead explained. "I had no apparent cares in the world, no weight on my shoulders burdening me down."[4] Actually, she often had a lot on her mind—professional and personal worries, concerns about friends and family—but she didn't show it. "One of the reasons they [the men in anthropology] dislike you," Benedict said, "is the way you walk."[5] That walk was jaunty, with head held high.

Mead's friendship with Benedict was special. Employing a religious metaphor, Mead asserted that "certain individuals, the 'gifted ones,' could be stained-glass windows into heaven, through which a light is shone, which I would otherwise never see."[6] In addition, Ruth and Margaret often symbolized their connection through the metaphor of bread and wine from the Christian rite of Communion—or through the cup of clay from Ruth's story about the Serrano Indian chief. As a chalice holding the Communion wine, the cup represented the ecstasy of the search for unity with God and the sacred marriage between Christ and his believers that brought them to the divine as they partook of his body and blood.

The cup of Communion symbolized the spiritual bond between Benedict and Mead. We merge into one, Margaret wrote Ruth, in science as in love. As we depend on "one mind and then the other," she continued, we become united.[7] Stanley was the bread of love, but Margaret was the wine. Both these women, it should be remembered, were grounded in mystical Christianity: Ruth with her childhood evangelical Baptist faith; Margaret with her High Church Episcopalianism. Their use of the symbols of Christianity to express their love drew from their traditionalism brought into the modern era: Victorian lovers often described their love in religious terms—as sacred, holy, hallowed, as partaking of the divine, as infused by the spirituality of the personas of the Trinity become one.[8] According to Susan McCabe, poet Amy Lowell used "the transubstantiation of the bread and wine into the body and blood of Christ" and their consumption by the communicants as an image of lesbian sex: that, too, may have been Ruth's intent.[9]

Ruth also saw herself as a suffering Christ. That is a theme in her poetry written for Margaret, as Margaret merged with her and withdrew, learned from her and loved her, rejected her and returned. Disciplining her Dionysian emotions through writing poetry and anthropology, drawing upon the Apollonian part of herself, Ruth achieved a measure of self-control. Through suffering she found salvation: it was a Christian theme secularized in Nietzsche and expressed in her college essay on Euripides' *The Trojan Women.*

In a poem titled "Eucharist" that she dedicated to Mead and that Mead used as the frontispiece to *An Anthropologist at Work,* Benedict expressed this theme of suffering and salvation. (The word "Eucharist" refers to the rite of Communion, especially the wafer that over time replaced the bread in many churches). The poem draws on Plato's myth of the cave, in which the humans in the cave see only the shadows of themselves or of one another thrown by the light of a fire; they resist the truth. The "light" in Benedict's poem is female, and in the end light's body is consumed only by those who, "storm-driven down the dark," have been shipwrecked but have survived, for whom suffering has brought wisdom. They are the ones who see the truth; the others see only illusion.

> *Light the more given is the more denied.*
> *Though you go seeking by the naked seas,*
> *Each cliff etched visible and all the waves*
> *Pluming themselves with sunlight, of this pride*
> *Light makes her sophistries.*
>
> *You are not like to find her, being fed*
> *Always with that she shines on. Only those*
> *Storm-driven down the dark, see light arise,*
> *Her body broken for their rainbow bread*
> *At late and shipwrecked close.*[10]

There were limitations to Margaret's affection for Ruth. No friendship is perfect. Jealousy, boredom, selfishness—those emotions lurk at the edges of any relationship. The fifteen-year difference in their ages bothered Margaret. When Reo met Ruth in Paris in the summer of 1926, he was shocked by how much older than Margaret she looked. Yet Margaret sometimes saw the age difference between them as a disadvantage to her, not to Ruth. She realized that Ruth was more versed in philosophy and literature than she and a better poet: "She's read fifteen years of books that I haven't read. She's experienced fifteen years more of life, and sooner or later she is going to run out of being interested in me." In the early years of their relationship, Margaret feared that she might say something wrong, that she wouldn't sustain the brilliance she thought Ruth expected of her. She remembered an occasion when she and Ruth were talking about Edna St. Vincent Millay's poetry and she said that Millay's "Renascence" was her best poem and Ruth disagreed. Margaret was embarrassed because she got that opinion from Eleanor Phillips, her Ash Can Cat antagonist who was a know-it-all, and simply repeated it. She felt like a fool.[11]

Margaret sometimes thought of their relationship in terms of the Bible story of the sisters Mary and Martha, disciples of Christ. The story is a parable extolling spirituality above worldly pursuits, as Christ rebukes Martha for attending to domestic concerns while Mary listens to his teaching. Margaret thought of herself as a Martha who took care of others emotionally and who seemed so tough that she was "someone whom no one ever protects, whom it is safe to hate." Ruth, by contrast, was a Mary. She was fragile, "appealing to the chivalry and solicitude of those with whom she works."[12] Like so many others, Mead was drawn to Benedict's fragility, but that quality of hers could be frustrating. For it hid her strength and her subtle control, how she managed to achieve what she wanted by being so nice.

There was animosity toward Margaret on the part of the male anthropologists, and sometimes Margaret suspected that Ruth was partly responsible for their dislike. She thought that Ruth felt contempt for men like Sapir and Lowie and they sensed her disdain. Margaret wondered: "Was there something in Ruth Benedict's voice, some deep competitive feminist note?"[13] Perhaps that "feminist note" annoyed the men, leading them to attack Mead, Benedict's young, tough protégée. Ruth, after all, had masterminded the scheme of Margaret telling Sapir about her free-love views—and he became very angry with her because of those views.

Yet Margaret and Ruth's commitment to each other went deep. Each read and criticized the other's work. Ruth took care of Margaret's publications, her professional mail, and her finances when she went overseas. She sent her articles and books to read; she helped Marie Eichelberger with Margaret's personal needs. Ruth took pride in the accomplishments of this woman who was like a daughter to her. One of the greatest satisfactions of Ruth's life, her sister, Margery, wrote to Margaret after Ruth died, was bringing Margaret into anthropology and then watching her "carry the torch into fields where she could never go."[14] Given her hearing problems and her slowness in learning languages, Ruth knew that she wouldn't be a good fieldwork partner for the speedy Margaret, who could catch nuances from conversations that Ruth would strain to hear.

Ruth and Margaret told each other secrets about their lives that they shared with almost no one else. Margaret revealed her "dead baby" dreams; Ruth told Margaret about her fantasy world of her father and the Sibyls and her henhouse dream. Despite their conflicted personalities and the vogue for psychoanalysis in the 1920s, neither underwent formal analysis; they explored their inner selves with each other. Benedict referred to their conversations as "psychoanalysis." "There isn't a better term to christen it with," she wrote.[15] Their relationship—conflicted and compelling, intellectual and emotional—involved a process akin to the transference of analysis, as each understood herself through the other. Margaret was Ariadne to Ruth's Theseus, Beatrice to her Dante, Maud Gonne to her Yeats, all of them aspects of the feminine to guide the masculine to a richer sense of self. And Margaret used Ruth in a similar manner to understand herself. Frances Herskovits, the wife of anthropologist Melville Herskovits and a close friend of both of them, told Margaret in 1928 that she mimicked Ruth in her behavior.[16] That's not surprising: Margaret was still young, still exploring who she was.

Using a Freudian term, each referred to her "obsessional self." The phrase denoted Ruth's devils and Margaret's fixation with pleasing everyone, her fear that disaster might strike if she didn't keep her close friends happy. The term also referred to the homosexual part of their original bisexuality that hadn't disappeared as they matured, as Freud thought it should. "Your obsessional self," Ruth wrote Margaret, "is always looking for a creature from the upper realms at whose feet you can lay an offering." But, Ruth continued, she wanted an equal "denizen" and Margaret was the only "denizen" for her. The word "denizen" means inhabitant, in the sense of an alien admitted to a new country. Once Ruth decided for homosexuality, she wrote Margaret that she felt as though she were living with her in the "delectable mountains" of Ruth's fantasy world.[17]

Were they lesbian? In the scores of letters they wrote to each other from the early 1920s to the mid-1940s, neither used the term "lesbian" to refer to herself or to the other, although Margaret referred to other women they knew as lesbian. In 1934 Margaret wrote to Gregory Bateson that she suspected that her sister Priscilla suspected that she was lesbian, but she wasn't.[18] "Mixed type" was the term that she used. She didn't adopt the term "bisexuality," with its connotation at that point of a "third sex" in which, in the case of women, a masculine persona predominated in their psychological selves. In the fall of 1928, soon after she married Reo Fortune, Margaret wrote Ruth that she was trying to achieve a "perfect balance" between her "two loves"—her heterosexual love for Reo and her homosexual love for Ruth—but she was having difficulty doing so. Two years before, she wrote, when she was still married to Luther and she left Ruth's room near Columbia in the evenings after spending time with Ruth to go home to him, she kept seeing Reo's face; now, married to Reo and in Manus with him, she kept seeing Ruth's face. Yet despite the shifts in her desires, she assured Ruth that she didn't have any inclination toward a "single allegiance."[19]

Still, Mead wanted to consider herself a true woman. In 1929 she wrote to Benedict that she wouldn't stay in a marriage because of social expectations; in other words, after her experience with Luther she was determined to desire and love the man to whom she was married. In 1947 in a letter to Benedict she asserted that she couldn't conceive of her life as not oriented to a man. "No number of women or children," she stated, "really mean the same thing to me." Yet in the next line of the letter she called her need to be married one of her "blocks"—one assumes by "blocks" she meant barriers to deciding for lesbianism, as Benedict had. Later in her life, after Benedict had died and she and Gregory had divorced and Rhoda Métraux was her partner, Mead changed her opinion once again, stating that the best sexual arrangement over the life span was homosexuality during adolescence, heterosexuality in the middle years of life, and homosexuality in old age.[20] Thus a woman could have a family during her fertile years and be assured of companionship and love during the rest.

A case can be made that Margaret married Luther as a cover for her lesbian involvements in college and after, but she was passionate about Reo when she married him and she remained in love with Gregory Bateson even after their divorce. She liked being married; she had been brought up to believe in it. But she was sensitive to her parents' problems in marriage and how their staying together hadn't really solved the problems. To the avant-garde, unconventional Mead, divorce was a legitimate option, although to maintain professional respectability it was important to end a marriage without scandal. Mead's keeping her maiden name helped her in maintaining her image as an independent career woman. She quietly obtained her divorces in Mexico, and the press never criticized her for them.

By the mid-1930s Ruth had become a lesbian, and Margaret didn't like it; she wanted Ruth to remain both homosexual and heterosexual, a "mixed type." In reply to Ruth's statement that Margaret lived with her as her "denizen" in her "delectable mountains," Margaret replied that she didn't live there except in Ruth's eyes and that she had been important to Ruth only in the "journeying thither," in helping her to realize the strength of her homosexual inclinations. In that sense only she had been "a proper denizen."[21] Ruth's decision threatened their relationship—and her sense of her own identity. "I don't want to be a man," Margaret declared emphatically. Referring to Ruth's desire to have been born in ancient Egypt, she stated: "I don't want to be born in some other period." Even today, she wrote in a draft chapter of her autobiography, "the thought of possibly having one of those obscure masculinizing diseases fills me with more horror than any other imagined malign fate."[22] It looks like "the same old point," Margaret wrote to Ruth after leaving her for Reo. Drawing on Ruth's favorite Bible story of Ruth and Naomi, Margaret asserted: "I can say whither thou goest I will go, but I can't say thy god will be my god."[23] Margaret wanted to be a woman and, despite her deep bond with Ruth, she kept falling in love with men.

WHEN BENEDICT AND MEAD returned to New York from Rome in 1926, they resumed their regular lives. Margaret lived with Luther, and Ruth lived with Stanley in Bedford Hills on the weekends and in her room in New York during the week. With Gladys Reichard on leave, Benedict took over teaching the introductory course at Barnard that year, and Mead was her assistant, teaching discussion sections at the Museum of Natural History, in a reprise of the course in which they had met four years before. Benedict returned to collecting folktales and editing the *Journal of American Folk-Lore;* Mead took up her curatorial duties at the museum and worked on finishing her dissertation, her ethnography of Samoa, and her "Adolescent Girl in Conflict," which became *Coming of Age in Samoa.*[24]

In spite of Reo's bad behavior in Europe, Margaret remained fascinated by him. Whatever she had promised Ruth in Rome about giving him up, it was only a matter of time until she contacted him. She loved his youth—so different from Benedict and Sapir—as well as his exuberance, his foreign exoticism, and his good looks. He was a year younger than she; she called him "the boy." A provincial from New Zealand, he had never "seen a first-class play or an original painting or heard a live presentation of a first-class orchestra."[25] Yet he loved learning, and he was steeped in poetry, Freud, and anthropology; he had been raised in the Episcopal Church. He may have been untutored in high art, but he had intellectual nerve: when she met him on the boat he was writing a book on dreaming, modeled after Freud's *Interpretation of Dreams*, in which he was analyzing his own dreams. He had a puckish sense of humor, a mischievous smile, and a mind that veered off in all directions, before suddenly coming to a brilliant point. And, like Margaret, he wrote poetry.[26]

The son of an Episcopal missionary who had left the priesthood to become a farmer, Reo had been raised in a family struggling to get by. He had gone to school on scholarships; when Mead met him he was en route to Cambridge to study there on a scholarship he had won. He had flirted with the Communist Party, and he was passionate about the need to end control of native cultures by Western missionaries and governments.[27] Appropriate to his father's religious vocation, his name, Reo, was the Maori word for "the word." "It was like meeting a stranger from another planet," Mead wrote, "but a stranger with whom I had a great deal in common." His brother Barter described him as an innocent lost in Mead's sophisticated world.[28]

Margaret overlooked Reo's inability to make small talk, his competitiveness, his awkward manner, and his rages: some of her friends thought him mentally unstable. Gregory Bateson thought that he had genius but that "the paths to it are rough and crooked." His mind had a "curious zigzag violent progression."[29] Given the eidetic visions that she and Ruth Benedict had, that tendency of his may not have seemed alarming to Margaret until later, when it became a reason for ending their marriage.

Above all, she was drawn to his virile masculinity. He was tall and athletic, with rugged good looks, and a love of the outdoors. Skilled at mountain climbing, he would be a superb partner in remote places, although his virility could have a downside. "He came from a culture where boys were physically disciplined and men struck women," wrote Margaret. He told her stories that were "possibly not true, but terrifying." One was about "his Irish grandfather who was said to have locked his grandmother in the kitchen with a stallion, and the words 'I hope he damn well stamps you to death.' "[30] In the culture of Cambridge University, where, according to Gregory Bateson, masculinity had been "restrained into a delicate feyness," Reo was like a bull in a china shop. He could be kind and caring, shy and withdrawn, but he liked to dominate women, and that appealed to Margaret's "feminine" side. "So now you have your caveman," Marie Eichelberger remarked, "and likemindedness all at once."[31] Thin, over six feet tall, he resembled her father in body type—as Gregory Bateson did.

He wasn't entirely retrograde when it came to sexual attitudes: his homosexual friend Max Bickerton had been with him in Paris; his sister had been fired from her job as a nurse because of an involvement with a woman. On the boat going to meet Reo in New Zealand in the fall of 1928, Margaret met an Australian anthropologist whom she described as a "mixed type" and who seemed taken with Reo. "I suppose I should begin to wonder about Ray," she mused, "although I swear he'd never know what it was about."[32] When he first met Margaret, Reo had been dismayed that she was married and upset by her relationship with Ruth, but he tried to come to terms both with Ruth and with Margaret's free-love views—or as much as she shared with him.

Once he reached Cambridge University and the anthropologists there, he centered his interest on New Guinea, a fieldwork location for British anthropologists ever since A. C. Haddon and a group of colleagues from Cambridge in 1898 had inaugurated modern English anthropology by studying the tribes of the Torres Straits off the coast of Australia. Like many English graduate students in anthropology, Reo found his way to the graduate seminar that Bronislaw Malinowski taught at the London School of Economics, open to graduate students at other institutions in the region. Reo then contacted A. R. Radcliffe-Brown, who had been trained at Cambridge and was teaching at the University of Sydney and who had money from the Rockefeller Foundation for studies of Melanesia.

By the 1920s Malinowski and Radcliffe-Brown were the innovators in British anthropology. Both used a "functionalist" approach based on studying the interrelationships among social institutions in a given society. Radcliffe-Brown liked neither the concept of culture nor a focus on individuals; identified with the study of kinship and heavily influenced by Emile Durkheim, he was a "comparative sociologist" in the Enlightenment tradition of focusing on systems, rules, order, and stability. Malinowski, more sympathetic to studying "culture" and individuals, was often credited with having invented the "participant-observer" approach in anthropology when he was stranded on the Trobriand Islands during World War I and spent considerable time with the tribal society there. Anthropologist Anna Grimshaw calls him a romantic at heart.[33]

The American anthropologists had mixed feelings about Radcliffe-Brown and Malinowski. Margaret Caffrey maintains that most Boasians found their functionalism obvious and out-of-date, the product of an antievolutionism they had only recently taken up, although the Americans had espoused it for over a decade.[34] They also found Radcliffe-Brown, who wore fashionable clothes and a pince-nez, haughty and dictatorial. He was born plain "Brown" to a lower-middle-class family, and he had invented his aristocratic last name. Malinowski, Polish by birth and upbringing, was ebullient and down-to-earth, but he was a womanizer and a prima donna.[35]

Yet each man in his own way was an adventurer: Malinowski's first book, *Argonauts of the Western Pacific*, published in 1922, is the story of bold Trobriand Islands traders sailing in canoes through dangerous waters, like the buccaneering explorers of the West, to participate in the *Kula* exchange of goods in the islands of the region, as they brave an island presumably populated by not only naked Circes who might swim out to greet them but also ubiquitous and invisible dangerous flying witches. In contrast, Radcliffe-Brown's first—and only—book, *The Andaman Islanders*, also published in 1922, is cautious. A ethnographic catalogue of ritual on the Andaman Islands between Burma and Sumatra, the book stresses the power of society over individuals and downplays ecstasy to focus on order in describing collective activities like dancing.[36] Yet traditionalist Cambridge wouldn't hire the flamboyant Radcliffe-Brown and so he roamed, teaching in turn in South Africa and Australia and then at the University of Chicago, trumping other anthropologists by forming a tight connection with the Rockefeller Foundation. For his part, Malinowski stayed at the London School of Economics until he secured an appointment at Yale in the late 1930s.

Both Malinowski and Radcliffe-Brown were potential allies for Mead, who was fearful of Sapir's reactions to the end of their affair and his closeness to other male Boasians. Malinowski wrote a testimonial for the cover of *Coming of Age in Samoa*, since the free-love behavior that Mead found on Samoa paralleled the sexual freedom he had found among the Trobrianders. But Reo Fortune kept her away from Malinowski, for he feared his ability at seduction and her potential readiness to respond. And Fortune and Malinowski had a love-hate relationship, since the Dobuans that Fortune studied were located near Malinowski's Trobrianders, and that juxtaposition between their fieldwork sites produced both closeness and conflict between these two volatile, ambitious men. Once Mead found out that Malinowski had accepted Sapir's condemnation of her, she mostly stayed away from him.

Radcliffe-Brown was a different matter. He liked Margaret's work, and she liked his. Once she and Reo married in New Zealand, they went to Sydney and she met him. Shrewd about people, Margaret saw through him. She found him arrogant, as she had expected, but with considerable charm. (Reo had earlier described him in a letter to her as playing seventeenth-century French songs on the piano in the evening while spinning tales of kinship relations in Australia as though he were playing intricate games of chess.)[37] Margaret realized that he was insecure; he needed, Margaret thought, "constant assurance of his omnipotence, or is it potency?"[38]

Flattery came easily to Margaret, and she was always on the lookout for new mentors and new theoretical approaches. She incorporated Radcliffe-Brown's ideas so fully in some of her writings that he came to regard her as his student. He regularly assigned her ethnography of kinship in Manus in his graduate classes.[39] She wrote that work, published as *Kinship in the Admiralty Islands* (1934), after a student of Malinowski's accused her of knowing nothing about the subject in a review of *Growing Up in New Guinea*, her study of Manus child rearing. It was part of her ongoing project to prove to her detractors that she knew what she was doing. She would hardly have overlooked the matter of kinship relations, basic to any ethnographic investigation and an important part of the preliminary census that she took of every society that she studied.

EVEN THOUGH REO had been difficult in Europe, Margaret wrote to him after she returned to New York, taking the blame for their conflicts. "If I have hurt you," she asserted, "I'd walk back over the stony road we've traveled with bare feet if I might repair the hurt." No matter what she had said to Luther and Ruth, she told Reo that she wanted to marry him. As always, she fantasized about the future: Reo could teach at Yale and finish his Ph.D. there, while she worked at the

Sibyl of Delphi.
Art Resource

Guido Reni, *Aurora Leading the Dawn*. A reproduction of this painting
hung on Mead's bedroom wall when she was a child.

Art Resource

El Greco, *Fray Hortensio Felix Paravicino*.
This is how Benedict visualized her dead father.
Museum of Fine Arts, Boston

Museum of Natural History. They could live halfway between New Haven and New York during the week and use Ruth's room in New York on the weekends, when she was in Bedford with Stanley. (Was that wishful thinking on Margaret's part?) Or Reo could finish his Ph.D. at Cambridge, and she would move there and be Mrs. Fortune and "that awful animal, a lady scientist." Reo could make the decisions about their careers; she would give up her Samoan research to follow him to Melanesia. "I'll make any sacrifice necessary," she assured him. Reo later accused her of making promises she never intended to keep.[40]

Luther found her just as dramatic and capricious as before she left for Samoa. The pain in her arm returned; she developed eyestrain. "What's this about Margaret thinking that life is strange?" Louise Bogan asked Benedict in the spring of 1927. "Léonie says that she had a dreadful blue fit a while back." Luther wrote to a woman he had met in London and would marry as soon as he and Margaret were divorced that Margaret was deeply in love with Reo and that he was abusing her.[41] Since Margaret and Reo were an ocean apart, the comment seems odd, although Luther may have been referring to the summer before, when even Reo admitted that he had been hard on Margaret.

Margaret's indecision over yet another man troubled Ruth. She had reservations about Reo. For she thought that he, like Sapir, had a possessiveness that would hamper Margaret's career, and she didn't think he would make a good father. In her own marriage, she had to deal with Stanley's falling in love with another woman and ending their sexual relations. She put up a brave front about it to Margaret, but it wasn't easy for her. Sometimes anger and depression took her over; in later letters she apologized to Margaret for acting like a five-year-old. Or she became cold and withdrawn, retreating into what Margaret called her "ivory tower" mode. Margaret accused Ruth of having "a woman's need for dependence on personal relations with a man's desire to have them on very special terms."[42] In other words, Ruth wanted an exclusive relationship with Margaret.

Benedict and Mead wrote many poems to each other between 1926 and 1928, and those poems constitute another conversation between them about their relationship. Take, for example, Benedict's poem "Dedication," which she both dedicated to Mead and chose as the dedication to a volume of her poetry that she put together for publication—and then abandoned when a publisher turned it down. The poem is about bees gathering honey in the summer from the white flowers on hawthorn bushes. By winter those flowers will turn into berries, called haws. "Dedication" begins with a description of the warmth of the summer sun and the fragrant odor of the white flowers. Yet the petals of the flowers fall to the ground and the weather turns dark, as the act of bees gathering the pollen becomes akin to rape. The poem finishes with vaginal images of a secret liquid in the roots of the plants, located deep in the earth, as though that is a place of deep passion and peace.

> *Haws when they blossom in the front of summer,*
> *Snow-breasted to the sun, and odorous*
> *Of wind-dissolved honey, flaunt their bodies,*
> *Secret and quick, to eyes incurious.*
>
> *Their fertile golden dust the wind shall scatter,*
> *Surfeited bees maul yet one feast the more,*
> *And all their dainty-stepping petals flutter*
> *At last and publicly to grassy floor.*
>
> *Still through their roots runs the most secret liquor*
> *No wind shall tamper, no hurrying bee shall sip;*
> *Let the haws blossom, let their petals scatter,*
> *In covert earth wine gathers to their lip.*[43]

One thinks of the situation in anthropology, with fissures beneath loyalty among individuals and groups, or of Benedict's and Mead's private lives, with conflicted marriages and love relationships. In the feast of the bees, in their feeding frenzy, all secrets might be exposed. Yet no matter the tensions in their lives, Margaret and Ruth had each other. That was Ruth's deepest desire.

Margaret's "From the Marshes" can be read as a response to "Dedication." In the poem Margaret rejects Ruth's desire for oneness—and her vaginal imagery—to suggest that she prefers a more varied sexuality.

> *You whose tree of life is rooted*
> *In a spare and chosen upland . . .*
> *You do ill to love a sapling,*
> *Rooted in a yielding marshland*
> *With little leaves so quick to answer*

> *Breezes you would never notice;*
> *And pale roots so swift to follow*
> *Small deceptive snow-fed rivers,*
> *Roots so thin and frail and witless*
> *That a burrowing mole could turn them*
> *Blind as he to straighter courses.*[44]

Many of the poems Margaret wrote in these years express gratitude and love to Ruth. Margaret wrote "Green Sanctuary" after they returned from Rome. It expresses a deep sense of union. It also hints at a woman-centered sexuality, as "sweet-tongued leaves" above the narrator's bed fold her in a "singing peace."

> *Your love is a green room in spring*
> *Where quiet councilling breezes blow. . . .*
> *With sweet-tongued leaves above my bed*
> *You fold me in a singing peace.*

Referring to "Green Sanctuary," Margaret wrote to Ruth: "What a picnic psychoanalysts would make of that poem." To Freudians, she asserted, the poem would reveal Ruth as a mother image, with the poem expressing "perfect womb symbolism." Implying that she agreed with that interpretation, Margaret commented that she hadn't liked her mother very much and that Ruth now filled that role in her life.[45]

Margaret's ambivalence toward Ruth is apparent in "Abnegation," dated November 1926, two months after they returned from Europe:

> *O sweet impassioned artist, turn away*
> *Blunt not your fervour on this brittle clay.*

The ambivalence becomes rejection in Margaret's "Our Lady of Egypt," written the same month:

> *Your touch can bring*
> *No semblance of the old fire back,*
> *O lady journeying into Egypt.*[46]

By the following spring, Margaret wrote "The Gift." In this poem she thanks Ruth for helping her sharpen her intellect and understand her sexuality. No longer will Margaret be envious of "the melodies that fall from human lips" while she can only give "straight, formal kisses"—the implication is that she learned about a range of sexual expression from Ruth. Through Ruth, Margaret has also overcome her fears of her academic elders: no longer is she "an anxious child / Awed by articulate elders." Moreover, because of Ruth, she no longer fears her desire for both sexes, the "two swift hands" of love. Yet Ruth has also freed her to follow "untraveled ways" as well as "traveled" ones. In line with her free-love beliefs, she concludes that other relationships would enhance the one between Ruth and her. She writes poetically that she will press "all encountered beauty" upon Ruth's "lips of loveliness."

> *For you have given me speech!*
> *No more I'll sit, an anxious child*
> *Awed by articulate elders,*
> *Dumb in envy of the melodies*
> *That fall from human lips, while mine*
> *Can only give straight, formal kisses. . . .*

> *No more I'll fear that love*
> *Will strangle in his two swift hands*
> *A speechless heart. . . .*

> *All traveled and untraveled ways*
> *Are for me now.*
> *For all encountered beauty I may press*
> *Upon your lips of loveliness.*[47]

In the summer of 1927 Margaret went to Germany to see the Pacific Islands collections in the museums there and to spend time with Reo, on his way to Australia and then to Melanesia. She wanted to test their love—and their sexual compatibility. All went well; once she returned to New York she wrote him that she was happy that the birth control they used had worked and she hadn't become pregnant, since she wasn't ready to have a child. They may have visited Magnus Hirschfeld's sex clinic in Berlin; Margaret asked William Fielding Ogburn for the address before she left.[48] Once she returned, she separated from Luther and filed for divorce in Mexico on the grounds of desertion. New York State accepted Mexican divorces, Margaret wrote Reo, and they were issued after a brief appearance before a judge, with a petition signed by both parties in hand.[49] She went to Mexico the next spring for a few days to receive the final decree.

Given Stanley's rejection of her and Margaret's continuing involvement with Reo, Ruth had to do something. She had to find a way to deal with Margaret's ease at falling in love, with "the consequences of your [Margaret's] warmth and capacity of human relationships." She had to stop "the old dead pessimism about our relationship"; that mood got them nowhere. The devils, she wrote, "were very hard masters," and she had to control them.[50]

That summer, with Margaret in Germany, she took her life in hand. She went to the Southwest again to study the Pueblo tribes, and this time she came up with the configuration concept that became the basis of *Patterns of Culture.* While she was studying the Pima Indians, a tribal society immediately to the southwest of the Zuñi, her perceptions fell into place: she had the experience of sudden intuition common to creative discovery, as she realized with "a sense of revelation" that Pima culture resembled that of the Indians of the Plains and that it was different from the culture of the Zuñi and the other Pueblo Indians—even though, according to the principle of diffusion, the Pima and the Zuñi cultures, which were geographically close, ought to have been similar.[51]

The insight came to her during a Pima ritual she was attending when she realized that the peyote the participants took as part of the ritual produced a sense of ecstasy. The Zuñi, in contrast, took the drug in very small quantities and experienced no such state. Other contrasts fell into place. She realized that the Plains Indians, with their vision quests and their self-torture, resembled the Pima, as did the Serrano and other California tribes. She decided that the Pueblos were measured and Apollonian and that the other tribes were Dionysian. With this perception in hand, she concluded that cultures, like individuals, were organized according to types, what she called "configurations" and then "patterns." No longer was she cynical about the possibility of finding a universalizing theory as she had been the summer before in Europe; she had found one by herself, in the American Southwest.[52] Now she could put her research together and make a major professional statement.

In late August she was able to write Margaret that she felt Margaret had "denied everything in the world but Ray." Because of that involvement, perhaps their love "could be shifted to a more casual footing."[53] She was striking a new note in their relationship, one involving a less passionate commitment, one that she had threatened to enforce in Rome the summer before. That note would become dominant during the next year.

ONCE MARGARET RETURNED to New York from her summer trip to Germany and left Luther in the fall of 1927, she moved in with Ash Can Cats Pelham, David, Léonie, and Louise—and predictably developed a case of anxiety. "It was a rocky winter," she later wrote.[54] Her parents were upset about her pending divorce; Reo was in Melanesia; Léonie was chasing the aloof Louise Bogan and coping with Edmund Wilson. Pelham was recovering from a disastrous affair with an anthropology curator at the Museum of Natural History. Then there was Luther. Feeling guilt over leaving him, Margaret agreed to keep the existence of his girlfriend in London a secret, causing some of her friends to treat her as "inhuman, trifling with his [Luther's] affections, exploiting him."[55] By then he had probably given up Eda Lou Walton and Margaret's other friend; Margaret later told Ruth that he had decided that he couldn't handle multiple relationships.[56]

The issue of her sexual orientation also was troubling. How could she go off with Reo if she was homosexual? She had to make a decision. The dead baby dreams of her college years continued, and they weren't easily shrugged off. She dreamed about murdered babies, whose death she had caused, about babies killed by others, and about babies who were abandoned and then lost. What was the meaning of those dreams? Perhaps repressed grief over the death of her baby sister, Katherine, caused them. Perhaps the dead babies represented her younger sisters, Elizabeth and Priscilla, whom she feared she hadn't protected from their father's manipulations. She later speculated that the dead babies represented herself, that something in her had been destroyed in childhood.[57]

Reo had been writing a book on dreams when they met on the boat from Australia to Europe. By the mid-1920s dream analysis was in vogue among psychologists and the general public. Freud's study on dreaming was a best-seller; there was even a popular parlor game based on analyzing dreams. Psychologists contended that sexual orientation could be determined from dreams: homosexuals had homosexual dreams; heterosexuals had heterosexual dreams.[58] Aboard the ship with Reo in 1926, Margaret dreamed many dreams for his project: in *The Mind in Sleep*, his book on dreaming published in 1927, Reo included anonymously one that Margaret dreamed about a woman who wouldn't have sex with her lover, while she failed to appear at an Episcopal Mass to swing the censer because she was trying to close a door that wouldn't stay shut.[59] That dream seemed to indicate hesitation about heterosexuality, since the homosexual "door" wouldn't stay shut, as the dreamer refused to have sex with her lover. It was the opposite of the vision Margaret had had on Samoa about Ruth being a divinity—a vision that seemed to indicate a hesitation about homosexuality.

Margaret decided to write a book about dreaming. It was a psychological project, not an anthropological one. For her data, she collected accounts of dreams and daydreams from her friends, including Léonie, Louise, and David; she also put together a questionnaire soliciting information and had friends fill it out. In answering the questionnaire, Ruth included a detailed description of her fantasy world with her father and the Sibyls as well as of her henhouse daydream. She also included descriptions of two recent night dreams—as well as analyses of them. The first dream, titled "The Remodeled Farm House," is a variation on her henhouse daydream. She is in her grandfather's farmhouse, and it is decrepit and disordered. She decides that she must remodel it. In the second dream, which she titled "The Chosen Twin," she is in a tower with Franz Boas's twin grandsons: the first grandson is named Robert and the second X. Both boys jump into a pool of water hundreds of feet below: X survives, but Robert is killed.[60]

Ruth interpreted the dream about her grandfather's farmhouse as meaning that she had "rebuilt her life according to the most uncongenial pattern." In other words, in marrying Stanley she embraced heterosexuality, but that orientation wasn't working for her. In the second dream she identified with "Robert" because Robert was the name her parents had intended to give her had she been a boy. She thought that the fall into the water symbolized her baptism at the age of eleven, when she was spiritually reborn. She continued: "I presume I identified with a self I might have been."[61] That self was male; in her dream Benedict wanted to undergo a rebirth to that self.

The dream-research file contains Margaret's accounts—and some analyses—of many dreams of her own, some in fragments and a few written as letters to Reo. She dreamed that her book was titled "Sue's Sin." She dreamed that Reo was a hermaphrodite, that she had syphilis, and that on the way to Rome she put an ice cube on her clitoris. She dreamed about being in Rome with Ruth, and that Gladys Reichard, a rival in anthropology at Columbia, accused her of not having worked hard enough in Samoa and then beat her with a stick, while Ruth, wearing a glass skirt, tried to defend her and was cut by the glass. In Rome, Margaret wrote, she had first realized how fragile Ruth was. She dreamed that when Reo first met Ruth in Paris he was "struck dumb" by the difference in age between Ruth and her. She dreamed that Edward Sapir's new wife was homosexual and that he was impotent. She dreamed that her father "with all the American muscle" made love to her in a woodshed: "enormous sensation on my part but no orgasm." She commented that her mother would be surprised by that behavior but that "Ruth wouldn't be."

In analyzing her dreams, Mead focused on her sexual orientation— a subject the Ash Can Cats discussed at a party they held during the dream-research project. Deb Kaplan claimed that Margaret had recently changed her sexual identity: she had switched from heterosexuality to homosexuality. The others asserted that she had always been partly homosexual. Deb attacked homosexuality as abnormal; Margaret contended that the only valid argument against it was that it reduced the number of births. Yet given her relationship with Reo, Margaret felt guilty about her homosexual inclinations. "The dead baby," she wrote, "is a heterosexual attitude neglected and starved, and finally dead and rotting, but hidden away from everyone." One of her dreams was about securing a new passport to Reo's heterosexual world. "The whole business," she wrote, "is an expression of a suppressed fear that after all I am primarily a homosexual person." So great was her confusion that she crossed out "homosexual" and wrote "heterosexual" above it.

Margaret never published her dream research as a book. It obviously became too personal for her to do so. Yet her analyses of her dreams suggest that in marrying Reo she had to fully embrace her heterosexual side. Her conclusions in *Coming of Age in Samoa* imply that she was on the way to that decision when she wrote the book. Thus she maintained that the Samoans tolerated homosexuality because heterosexual sex among them included "homosexual" foreplay, while it was the men who were versed in sex technique. In making this argument, she reported her findings on Samoa faithfully, but those findings also served to reassure Reo about his potency, that he shouldn't feel threatened by her homosexual experiences because they would enhance their sexual relations—just as "homosexual sex" in general, when translated into foreplay, could revolutionize the conduct of sex in the United States, ending infidelity and prostitution. The conclusion may seem overblown, but free-love advocates believed that free sexuality could produce substantial individual and social reform.

Margaret had her own issues with the male phallus; they would emerge center stage in her life when Reo, Gregory Bateson, and she were together in New Guinea in 1933. Yet Reo could be passionate and caring, and Margaret always found him sexually appealing. And she hadn't read W. F. Robie and Havelock Ellis as an academic exercise. She was sophisticated about sexual technique and physical response.

But Margaret was still ambivalent about heterosexuality. During the spring of 1928, she wrote a story expressing her ambivalence. The story, "Underground," is about a stenographer named Minnie—whose name resembles "Millie" in her college story "Lassitude." Minnie rides the subway in New York to and from work, and as the crowded car speeds through the underground tunnels, an anonymous man gropes her. She both lusts after him and fears him. The story includes a policeman who turns out to be an archangel who refuses to stop her from going into the hell of desire and dread that the subway represents—with its tunnels a metaphor, like Ruth's labyrinth in her journal entry, for the internal self. On some level Margaret wanted Ruth, the archangel Gabriel in Ruth's 1924 poem to her, to stop her from marrying Reo, to protect her from phallic desire.[62]

And she didn't want to hurt anyone, especially Ruth. As she made the decision for Reo, she had a series of troubling eidetic visions. In the first one Ruth was a priestess, wearing a silver robe, with a silver helmet on her head, standing on a pyramid made of black opals, hundreds of feet high—before she lay down on a bier. Then Ruth was a marble statue in a garden, until Margaret broke off a chip of her thigh and destroyed her perfection. Then the two of them were figures in a tapestry, and Margaret cut herself out of the tapestry with a huge pair of scissors and destroyed it. Then Margaret saw herself as Saint Sebastian, pierced by arrows and covered with tiny triangular wounds—and Ruth passed by and didn't stop.[63] Saint Sebastian, a Roman soldier, was shot with arrows for helping Christians escape from a Roman prison; his martyrdom was a favorite subject in Western art.

Margaret thought of herself as feminine and as a potential mother: to her, that self-image implied heterosexuality and marriage. She was ready to try marriage with a different sort of man. She hadn't liked the assertive masculinity of her father, but Luther Cressman's passivity hadn't satisfied her either. Reo Fortune was a masculine man with a

sensitive side. Mead later stated that she had hesitated to marry Fortune because, agreeing with Benedict, she didn't think he would make
a good father, but a gynecologist told her that she had a tipped uterus
and couldn't carry a baby to term, and so she assumed that Reo and she
wouldn't have any children. That cleared the way for her to marry him
and to regard the books they produced as their babies. Letters she
wrote to him when she was still in love with him, however, contradict
her statement that she hadn't wanted children with him. Loving Reo,
she could put aside her doubts about him as a father. When she listened to Ruth, the doubts returned.

So Margaret went to New Zealand in the fall of 1928 to marry Reo.
In doing so, she could forget those "triangular" wounds of her fantasized Saint Sebastian. She had gotten away from the triangle between
herself, Ruth, and Reo, without losing either of them. And she was able
to write to Franz Boas that he could now send her anywhere in the
world that he would send a man to do fieldwork, because she no longer
needed protection as a woman alone.[64] Besides, she could do a more
complete ethnography with a husband as her partner than by herself—
or with another woman—for he could study the men of the tribe while
she studied the women.

MARGARET'S DECISION FOR REO rather than Ruth was also influenced by the increased hostility to homosexuality in American culture
by the late 1920s. In the article on bisexuality that she wrote for *Redbook* in 1974, Mead stated that for a brief time in the early 1920s alternative sexual identities were tolerated, but by the end of the decade the
drive to repress homosexuality was dominant and the orientation
became stigmatized "as a kind of disease."[65] Freudians were abandoning Freud's ambiguity about homosexuality to view it as a dangerous
perversion, "latent" from the original bisexuality, ready to take over.
They were turning into dogma Freud's speculation that homosexuality
might be a factor in neurosis and contending that to achieve individual
and community mental health, it had to be eliminated. In 1929, with
the onset of the Depression, municipal authorities in New York and
other cities launched campaigns against "fairies" on city streets and
"pansies" in nightclubs. In the early 1930s the film industry put into
place a code interdicting the open portrayal of sexuality, including
homosexuality, in films.[66]

From her early years Margaret had a fear of being exposed, and by the late 1920s the possibility of exposure was real. Wanda Neff's novel, based on the behavior of Mead and her friends at Barnard, was about to be published. There was no telling what Edward Sapir might say or do. There were rumors that Margaret was homosexual. In the spring of 1926 the secretary in the anthropology department at Columbia asked Ruth if Margaret was a lesbian because of the excitement Léonie and Pelham had exhibited one day in the office over Margaret's return from Samoa.[67]

Once Mead finished *Coming of Age in Samoa*, she decided to study early childhood behavior. It was a safe topic—and one appropriate to an age in which child rearing and education were major concerns. She wanted to counter the belief that "primitive" people thought in the same categories as the mentally ill and as children in "civilized" societies and thus were lower on the evolutionary scale than adults in the West. Given her conclusions in *Coming of Age in Samoa*, it was probably better to stay away from the subject of sex. She didn't want her private behavior to become a subject of scandal—or of blackmail.[68]

In her review of Floyd Dell's extraordinary *Love in the Machine Age*, Mead only mildly protested Dell's assertions—the result of his psychoanalysis—that a vast increase in the number of homosexuals in modern societies threatened to destroy Western civilization and that the proponents of free love, who in his opinion were gaining a mass following, displayed an "infantile homosexuality" that was anal-erotic and sadistic.[69] Retreating from her undergraduate radicalism, Louise Rosenblatt wrote a dissertation on the English Aestheticist writers in which she avoided discussing their variant sexuality and concluded that their erotic defiance of mainstream Victorianism was a matter of their "half humorous" style. She buried the Oscar Wilde trial in a few sentences in a footnote.[70]

In the late 1920s some popular novels had homosexual and bisexual themes, and Benedict and Mead read a number of them. That reading included Robert Herrick's *The End of Desire* (1932); David Garnett's *Go She Must!* (1927); Rosamond Lehmann's *Dusty Answer* (1927); Virginia Woolf's *Orlando* (1928); and Marcel Proust's *Cities of the Plain* (1927).[71] None of these novels had problems with the censors: a reviewer in the *New York Times* called Proust's explicitly homosexual *Cities of the Plain* "literary" and its treatment of homosexuality "delicate." When Neff's *We Sing Diana* was finally published in 1928, the critics noted its homosexual theme but found the novel boring and made no attempt to link it to Mead.[72]

As for Lehmann's *Dusty Answer*, Mead later recommended it to her daughter to help her understand her bisexual orientation. The novel is set in the English countryside and at Cambridge University after World War I, and in it sexuality is a force flowing through nature and humans that can't be denied. Its female protagonist has romances and sexual relations with most of the novel's central male and female characters one by one, in fields and forests. The novel draws from the free-love milieu of post–World War I England that Gregory Bateson knew well from his early adulthood.

A number of novels with homosexual and bisexual themes escaped censorship in the 1920s, but the censors successfully prosecuted Édouard Bourdet's play *The Captive*, a hit in major European cities that played to packed houses on Broadway in the fall of 1926 and the spring of 1927. The play is about a young Parisian woman who can't stop herself from leaving her husband to go off with her older lesbian lover—who herself is married. Theater historians consider it among the most famous dramatic productions to appear on the New York stage in its day, mostly because of the furor it caused as the first to present homosexuality openly on Broadway. That excitement was heightened because Mae West's dramatic satire *Sex*, about prostitution, was playing on Broadway at the same time, while West had also opened a spoof of *The Captive*, called *The Drag*, in Patterson, New Jersey. In *The Drag*, a young man becomes engaged to hide his homosexuality—just as the young woman in *The Captive* marries to cure herself of her attraction to the older woman.[73]

Benedict and Mead saw *The Captive* when they were in Paris in the summer of 1926, and they saw it again that winter in New York. Mead remembered lesbians in New York wearing violets in its honor, since the older lesbian in the play sent violets to her younger female lover.[74] The police closed both *The Captive* and *Sex*, and Mae West was unable to find a Broadway theater for *The Drag*. As a result of the open homosexuality in *The Captive* and *The Drag* the New York State legislature amended the state's obscenity statute to include plays depicting "sex perversion."

Radclyffe Hall's famed novel *The Well of Loneliness*, about a lesbian who feels like a man trapped in a woman's body, appeared the next year. Published in England in July 1928, and an immediate best-seller, it was banned in that country, but the response was different in the United States. When it was published in December of that year, its sales soared; the attempt to ban it failed when the courts ruled that the depiction of same-sex love in the novel was realistic, not perverse. As long as a lesbian was portrayed as inverted and "mannish" in a work of literature, thus conforming to the medical and popular stereotype, the portrayal was acceptable.[75]

The problem with *The Captive* may have been that, in contrast to *The Well of Loneliness*, it depicted lesbians not as masculine women unattractive to men but as women who could attract both women and men, since the women in the play who have the affair with each other are both married. With the younger woman leaving her husband to go off with the older woman, the play might be interpreted as suggesting that women must separate themselves from men to be truly free. On the other hand, in the play the husband of the older woman describes the younger woman as a "captive" in a "phantom and shadow" world of lesbians, who act like vampires, taking women over in the guise of liberating them. The play is set in Paris, a fabled place of deviant sexuality; the older character in *The Captive* seems drawn from the Parisian lesbian, a new stereotype of homosexual women that represented them as elegant and sophisticated women of the world, not mannish inverts. She was a character in novels like *Dusty Answer*, in which the protagonist loses the woman she loves to this new sort of Parisian lesbian. Based on the lesbians in the circle in Paris around American expatriate Natalie Barney, she would complicate even more Mead's perception of homosexuality as both liberating and confining.

The attacks on *The Captive* and *The Well of Loneliness* must have troubled Benedict and Mead, especially in light of the age difference between them and Benedict's position as Mead's teacher, a relationship often demonized in popular literature about lesbians. Mead had long feared exposure. By 1935, in an article she wrote for the journal *Forum*, a public interest magazine, she alluded to that fear—and she linked it to the issue of sexual identity. "A person without full sex membership" she wrote, "is worse off than a man without a country." In many professional fields, Mead implied, successful women faced being identified as mannish and thus homosexual. That possibility was a "handicap" that generated a "paralyzing fear." "Every woman who enters a field where in proportion as she is successful she will be voted unwomanly," Mead concluded, "works under a handicap, a handicap of paralyzing fear."[76] Thus the spirit of the times, as well as her own inclinations at that point, impelled Mead to choose Reo Fortune as her primary life partner.

Once Margaret returned from Germany in the fall of 1927, Ruth painfully concluded that she was probably going to lose her to Reo. As early as September of that year, Margaret wrote to Reo that Ruth had accepted their involvement and was "totally without pain."[77] That statement may have been an exaggeration, but Ruth did feel that she had to change her attitude toward Margaret, to be even less possessive than before. They talked that year about the ability of anyone to change. Margaret believed that individuals could learn from experience and reshape themselves, but Ruth thought that everyone was constructed according to a fixed "pattern" that didn't change. Over the course of a lifetime, "you just wind yourself tighter and tighter like a cocoon," she stated.[78]

After Margaret's involvements with Edward and Reo, Ruth was fearful that Margaret would repeat her pattern of commitment and retreat over and over, hurting her too often. It was better to decrease the intensity of their relationship, as she had suggested in Rome the summer before. Besides, Margaret might still have children, and that was a sticking point. Later, when Ruth and Natalie Raymond became partners, they considering adopting a child, but Margaret and Ruth rejected that possibility.[79] They still responded to the biological argument about fulfillment through having a child; that reasoning suggested that Margaret should marry and have a child with a husband.

Once she had decided to limit their involvement, Ruth's feeling about herself and their relationship improved. She knew that Margaret had a need for "passionate explorations." "The economy of your life I see as a managing of excess wealth," she wrote her. Ruth had tried for years to root out jealousy in herself, but she hadn't succeeded. "My problem has been," she wrote, "to kill back that part of my affection that thought in terms of 'we' and 'us.' " Sex produced a sense of possession; jealousy was inevitable. It would be better to forge an intellectual and spiritual bond, with sex secondary. "How little the lovemaking solved in our feeling for each other," Ruth concluded.[80] They had been lovers for nearly three years, and the newness had worn off. Margaret realized that they hadn't often enough regarded sex as play. "We'd always lapse into that sudden deathly seriousness."[81]

Ruth needed stability and trust with Margaret. She wanted to put a "tabu on power." To make her love always "unhampering," Ruth had to end her jealousy.[82] So at some point before Margaret left New York to marry Reo in September 1928, they made a "bargain." They pledged undying devotion to each other—with no strings attached, and with no expectation of sex. It might happen between them; it might not. Indeed, Ruth interdicted it when Margaret returned to New York from Manus with Reo; she didn't want to compete with him for Margaret's affections.[83]

That bargain drew from the neo-Romanticism of their youth and their free-love commitment to spirituality as well as from the romantic female friendships of the Victorian system of gender socialization of their childhoods, in which the emotion of togetherness could be more important than physical intimacy, as in the Biblical story of Ruth and Naomi, or in Ruth's retelling of Evangeline's love for the Shawnee woman as a sense of spiritual oneness. Margaret and Ruth's love existed beyond time and space, in a secret place of the heart. "Our love is an untrammeled home, where we both come with confidence," Ruth wrote, and Margaret replied: "The center of my life is a beautiful walled place; the central core of my being has been closed around your perfection." They existed in a "perfect circle where all questions are answered and all is made clear." "I'm not of the punch-clock school," wrote Ruth. "Eternity is in the winking of an eye, and we've countless eternities." Margaret replied: "I love you and other people." But, she continued, the others exist "only in time and space."[84]

Benedict wrote a poem about it titled "Visitation":

> *You did not cross my threshold: the soft dust*
> *Lies thickly in the path you never took. . . .*
> *I turned from watching your swift form to make*
> *A chamber for the thought of you,*
> *A room from which I took all meagre and unshapely things,*
> *Leaving only four white walls as foil for*
> *Your remembered beauty.*
> *You did not come into my house and yet*
> *You'll have a room within it all your days.*[85]

During the summer of 1928, they lived together for two months before Margaret went to New Zealand to marry Reo; they took over the apartment that Margaret had shared with a number of Ash Can Cats the previous year. Aside from a period during World War II, when they both were employed in Washington, D.C., it was the only time they lived together. They both worked hard that summer, as Ruth taught summer school at Columbia and Margaret put her collections at the museum in order and finished her publication projects, as she always did before she went to the field. They fell into bed exhausted at night and got up early in the mornings, devoting Sundays to each other. Benedict read Marcel Proust's *Swann's Way*, the first volume of *Remembrance of Things Past*, the great modern novel of memory and of homosexuality, as by the final volumes of the multivolume work most of its main characters turn out to have been homosexual—or bisexual—all along. In *Swann's Way*, the taste of the madeleine cakes that the narrator eats with his mother takes him back to the enchanted time of childhood. When Margaret was doing fieldwork in Bali in 1938 with Gregory Bateson, and Ruth stopped writing letters for a time, Margaret feared that Ruth was rejecting her. She read *Swann's Way* to remember the ecstasy of the summer they spent together.[86]

That summer was about experiencing the fullness of their relationship, about creating a rich resource of memories to draw on as time went by. It was about confirming the romantic tradition that lovers don't have to see each other to remain intertwined, that the best kind of love is other-directed and not narcissistic, that it can occur across time and space, without jealousy. It was about reinventing Margaret's dream world of *The Brushwood Boy* and *Peter Ibbetson* in their adult lives and finding a way to maintain their friendship in the face of the personal and professional pressures on them that might destroy it.

BENEDICT'S ABILITY TO CHANGE their relationship was related to her new intellectual confidence. While Mead did her dream research during the winter of 1927 and the spring of 1928, Benedict worked out her theory of cultural configurations and wrote her first paper on it, "Psychological Types in the Cultures of the Southwest." As always when Mead was in New York, they met frequently. This time they analyzed individual cultures to see if they fit into Benedict's theory that a dominant pattern defines each culture, creating a group of abnormal individuals who don't fit in. Mead was writing her ethnography of Manu'a, and she crafted a concluding chapter in that study using Benedict's idea of configurations, choosing the rigidity of Samoan social behavior under their system of "etiquette" as the defining "pattern" of the society.[87] She and Benedict discussed deviancy a lot that year, as each puzzled over her sexual orientation and Benedict decided to include homosexuality in her paper as an abnormality shaped by society. Mead always contended that they had created the configuration theory together, but she credited Benedict with the decision to take up the subject of "deviancy."[88]

Whatever the strains in their intimate relationship, their intellectual partnership remained strong. Mead didn't dispute Benedict's ideas as sharply as she did those of others. "I stopped arguing over interpretations with you because I adore you," Mead wrote Benedict.[89] That doesn't mean that they didn't disagree. Mead hardly wanted to become Benedict's double; Benedict wanted an intellectual partner, not a clone. Their disagreements would appear in Mead's *Sex and Temperament in Three Primitive Societies*, in many ways a response to Benedict's *Patterns of Culture*.

In the fall of 1928, once Mead left New York to meet Reo Fortune in New Zealand, Benedict gave a paper on the configuration concept at the International Congress of Americanists, held that year in New York. She wrote Mead that she was the hit of the convention. She felt that she had triumphed over Elsie Clews Parsons. An empiricist and diffusionist, Parsons didn't like Benedict's configurationist perspective; in fact, she was floored when Benedict applied the terms "Dionysian" and "Apollonian" to American Indian cultures. "Elsie was speechless," Benedict wrote to Mead, "and rose to make all sorts of pointless addenda when she recovered her breath."[90] Benedict had seized the moment and captured the immediate future.

Ironically, although Ruth had taken the position in her conversations with Margaret that no one ever changes, she herself changed that year. That is apparent in a poem she wrote in the spring of 1928 called "And His Eyes Were Opened." It documents another conversion on her part: this time to rejecting the religion of her childhood—a rejection that reflected her new optimism, her abandoning her view of herself as a suffering Christ. In Ruth's poem about eyes being opened, the light that suddenly falls causes the "mask" to be withdrawn and the "scars" to be viewed as "lovely" in the "sunshine of day." Now Christianity is an "insubstantial fable." Christ is a historical figure who died and wasn't resurrected. No one shifted a stone, as the Bible story had it, to allow him to leave his grave. Now Benedict is "newly minted." She can take off her "mask" and feel joy.[91]

> *Suddenly from the sky, lacquered with light,*
> *Light fell, a mask withdrawn, and the gold stars*
> *Stood fixed in austere heaven. It was not night,*
> *For still the jewel of the water lay*

Thick-flawed with glitter, its more lovely scars,
And sunshine splintered on the grass all day. . . . .

Secure in sight that held its level way
To tangible barriers, he left to us
The insubstantial fables, that some day
No stone being shifted, suddenly will bare
The world new-minted, the sky luminous
With stars at noonday, timeless on the air.

The successive titles she gave to her book of poetry, which she never published, indicate her growing maturity. At first she called it "The Winter of the Blood," a title that seems to refer to the relationship between Mary Wollstonecraft and Fanny Blood as well as to her conflicted relationships with Margaret and Stanley. It also seems a reference to her aging: in 1927 she was forty years old. Then she retitled the volume "November Burning," a title indicating that, once again, she was on the Pateresque path of finding a resolution to her life through "burning with a gemlike flame." She didn't abandon her sensitivity to suffering and death: in ancient times European folk burned fires in late November to ward off the "death" of winter.[92] Her final title, "Ripeness Is All," is taken from the line in Shakespeare's *King Lear* in which Edgar tells the aged Gloucester, despairing of his fate, that "ripeness is all"—in other words, that he should accept the nihilism of death, or appreciate the wisdom that aging can bring, or learn to enjoy the fullness of the moment. It was the kind of rich metaphor, drawn from nature, that Benedict esteemed. On the other hand, she told Margaret that she was considering "Point Counter Point" as the title of the volume.[93] That seems an ironic commentary on their disagreements and their poems filled with conflict and doubt.

At the end of their summer together, Margaret, just before she sailed to meet Reo in New Zealand, fell in love with yet another man, an art connoisseur named Morris Crawford, associated with Columbia University. She went to lunch with him; he tried to seduce her. He seemed a double of her—intellectual, constantly talking and laughing, with an intense energy. She couldn't resist him, she wrote Ruth; she had never met anyone like him; it was like looking in a mirror. They had "a common delight and enthusiasm for existence, for activity, for people, for ordering the universe, for running a three-ring circus."

He proposed fantastic schemes: a famous dress designer would dress her, and she would write a popular treatise on dress. They would live in New Bedford, Massachusetts, with whaling vessels nearby; he would paint and she would write. They wouldn't have any casual relationships because "in such an absorbing game, there wouldn't be time for them." They would visit a "crazy" couple who always tried to seduce their guests and who practiced "a highly rarefied form of the spectator perversion." She would analyze everybody and "explain everything"; he would produce odd types to "dance for her." She would write a book about it all.[94] Indeed, among her letters to Ruth after she left New York to marry Reo is a page of notes for a chapter in "The Ultimate Book on Individuality." It would focus on some sexual abnormality like exhibitionism or spectatorship and then illustrate it in the behavior of individuals "in a graded scale of complexity." After all, she wrote, everyone has the same drives. "Finally," she speculated, "you would have samples where sophistication, education, wealth were all bent in an elaborate and complex pattern to the satisfaction of exactly the same basic need as when it was found in the simplest physiological terms."[95]

There's no telling whether Morris meant what he said. Once Margaret was with Reo, Morris faded from her mind. Before that happened, however, she predictably felt herself in turmoil and she predictably turned to Ruth for advice. "I'd felt so safe, so settled, so 'conservative,'" she wrote. But now she felt hopelessly at sea, as though she had done something wrong. "Ray should fill my field of attention and exclude other men as you do other women. I don't have to be afraid of meeting the loveliest woman God ever made. I'm sealed and bound to you." She felt guilty about leaving Ruth. "One human being has no right to more than our love gives me, and this snatching about the universe at extra bits is all doomed."[96]

Yet Margaret's fling with Morris didn't bother Ruth; she didn't even care if Margaret had sex with him. "I'm not troubled by Crawford," she wrote Margaret. "If it were otherwise, you wouldn't have your passionate explorations. You would have to be subdued, and I love you so wholly for what you are." In fact, Ruth stated that for Morris's sake she was sorry he hadn't gotten the sex that he wanted. When Margaret continued to express guilt, Ruth admonished her. She might be her mother confessor, but she wasn't her judge. "Your letter tonight asks to be forgiven and what does that mean? The whole picture of me as someone who punishes and forgives is too fantastic for me to get."[97]

Margaret pried herself away from Morris and left on the boat to Australia—on which she met a young violinist interested in "primitive music." Trains and boats, liminal places away from regular life, moving across land and oceans, going to faraway locales—these places and adventures energized Margaret. Shipboard communities had captain's tables, dancing, games, masquerade balls, decks on which to promenade, with life stories shared to the swaying of the ship, the smell of the sea, the sight of a universe of water stretching in all directions. It was a perfect setting for romance, as Margaret met new people in these intense, anonymous environments. She often had a shipboard romance; this time the young violinist suddenly asked her to marry him at the end of the trip.[98] She was bemused: it wasn't much of a romance, but once again she had worked her magic.

RUTH WAS ALSO able to distance herself from Margaret because she had decided to look for other sexual partners. She didn't want to be "a masochist," wearing "hair shirts."[99] She saw a lot of Margery Loeb, another friend of Margaret's from her Barnard class. Margery was bubbly and youthful, although very neurotic, according to Margaret.[100] Between 1928 and 1931, her name appears more often in Benedict's datebook than anyone else's. Lydia Simpson from New Haven also reappeared, the woman with the soft fair hair and dark brown eyes, "the pupils all a piece with the iris." There was also "the bushman," Wendell Bush, a Columbia professor over eighty years of age, whom Ruth called her "octogenarian lover"; he took her to expensive restaurants and gave her extravagant presents—and made no sexual demands. He gave her the "logos and the trinity" of deep devotion and asked for nothing in return, Ruth wrote Margaret. Abandoning fidelity for a varied sexuality was difficult for Ruth; she had to draw on all the Dionysianism in herself to do it. She had to become like Margaret.

The poetry of Robinson Jeffers helped her. In 1928, in a book review she wrote for the *New York Herald Tribune* under her pseudonym Anne Singleton, she praised Jeffers's epic poem *Cawdor*.[101] Many critics found his poetry a regression to Gothic horror—with its bleak, tempestuous seascapes located on the Northern California coast; characters involved in incest, murder, and deviant sexuality; and plots drawn from Greek tragedy. Still wrestling with issues that her culture defined as perverse, Benedict found him inspiring. He deals with new themes, she wrote: "with love that mocks its object, with passion for understanding that breaks the mind and degrades the soul, with humanity caught in a net of desire 'all matted in one mesh.' " Ruth wrote to Margaret that Jeffers was "non-masculine" in his sensitivity to suffering and the demonic drives in humans. Margaret wrote back that if Ruth ever met Jeffers she might fear him "more than anyone else you might come to know."[102]

In her review of Jeffers's poetry, Benedict echoed Nietzsche in writing that Jeffers had found "the idea back of the fable of Oedipus: he that transgresses the laws of nature shall know of her secrets." In her journal she expressed her enthusiasm for him in a passage that reflected his Nietzschean virtuosity. "There is only one problem in life," she wrote, "that fire upon our flesh shall burn as a knife that cuts to the bone, and joy strip us like a naked blade. . . . Some by incest have broken the crust and travelled to this earth-core of aliveness; some have made pain the bedfellow of their imagination and licked blood from the welts they have laid upon the flesh of their most beloved."[103] Such extravagant language—and the resolve behind it—seemed necessary for Ruth to take a new direction, to consider lovers other than Stanley and Margaret. Did it draw on actual experiences in her life? Or was it a cry from her soul, the product of an eidetic vision she hadn't yet disciplined into poetry?

Ruth's most important involvement now was with a man named Thomas Mount. Initially the lover of a friend of hers, he entered her life when he came along with her friend for dinner. Ruth was flattered when he told her that she was the first female genius he had met who actually looked like one. Younger than Ruth, Tom had the adolescent gaiety that she liked: she called him a charming, ambitionless boy.[104] He had already been married twice, and he had left his job as an advertising executive to travel and write "the great American novel."

Ruth fell in love with Tom; their relationship was passionate. It gave her the nerve finally to separate from Stanley; she spent the nights immediately before and after that separation with Tom, discussing "important plans," as she put it in her date book. Whatever those plans were, they didn't change Ruth's life; Tom left Ruth some months later to marry a young woman who could have a child, and he sailed off with her to Europe to write his novel. When he returned, he wanted to resume the affair with Ruth. She was then involved with Natalie Raymond, but the attraction between her and Tom was still strong and the only way she could keep him at bay was by telling him that she was committed to another man. He didn't know about her homosexual inclinations, Ruth wrote Margaret, for she had never told him about them. And he knew her too well to believe her if she told him that she had become celibate.[105]

Did Ruth think of this relationship in terms of marriage? Did she give up for a time her search to understand her woman-loving side and her psychological journey to find an undiscovered country? Involvements on the part of older women of accomplishment with younger men—and younger women—aren't unusual; youth can be drawn to the wisdom and experience of age as much as age is drawn to the freshness of youth.[106] In some ways, Tom was like Margaret Mead.

In an unpublished journal fragment, Ruth analyzed the affair in literary terms, turning to a work of fiction to understand her experience, as she and Margaret often did. In this instance Ruth chose Ivan Turgenev's *A Month in the Country*, a play about a doomed love affair between a well-to-do, older married woman living a privileged life in the country and the young man who is the tutor of her ward. The play suggests that such relationships bridging age and class don't work. The older woman, however, can't stop herself from becoming involved: her sex drive is too demanding. "I've only got one excuse," she states, "it was all beyond my power." The same, it might be concluded, was true for Ruth with her young and feckless male lover.[107]

AFTER MARGARET MARRIED Reo in New Zealand, they went to Sydney, Australia, to spend several months with A. R. Radcliffe-Brown. Then they went to Manus to do eight months of fieldwork. They received a copy of the just published *Coming of Age in Samoa* while on Manus, and also a copy of an article Edward Sapir published damning Mead and the book—without mentioning her or it by name. Despite his marriage, Sapir smoldered with anger at Mead for her behavior toward him. Once *Coming of Age* appeared, he couldn't restrain himself, for the book upheld modern views about sex that he detested.

Sapir's 1928 article was published in the scholarly *American Journal of Psychiatry*; the next year he published nearly the same piece in H. L. Mencken's popular *American Mercury*: he seemed driven to reach a wide audience. Referring only to a young woman, he called her a "bored adventurer," "a hetaera," and a "prostitute" so jaded that she was sexually frigid. He attacked her for failing to realize the importance of jealousy in a committed relationship, for a "true lover" in his view couldn't stand any hint of infidelity. He accused her of having misinterpreted her data, charging that her belief in the "enrichment of personality" through "multiple experience" prevented her from viewing "organismal responses skeptically." He asserted that all "primitive" societies had rigid taboos on sex and that none permitted sexual license.[108] Luckily for Mead, Sapir wrote in an elliptical style, making it difficult to figure out the identity of the young woman he attacked. The articles didn't have much impact on her reputation outside academic circles. But they were disastrous for Mead there, since anyone who knew her work would realize whom Sapir was attacking.

Sapir's vendetta against Mead began before she published *Coming of Age*, and it continued for years. In 1925, when she was in Samoa, Sapir moved from Ottawa to a position in the anthropology department of the University of Chicago. The next spring, after Sapir and Mead had broken up, Bronislaw Malinowski stayed with him on a tour of anthropology departments in the United States. Sapir roundly criticized Mead, and Malinowski repeated Sapir's criticisms to the male anthropologists wherever he went. In 1929 Sapir wrote to Benedict, still cordial with him, that Mead was a "loathesome bitch," a "malodorous symbol" of everything he hated in American culture. Sapir told his version of the affair to his male friends in anthropology. In 1932 Mead wrote to Benedict that Sapir was trying to do them in because of wounded vanity, while Kroeber would do anything to please Sapir, and Malinowski was jealous of her in-depth research methods.[109] Over the years Mead and Benedict were convinced that Sapir's animus spread throughout the profession, motivating negative reviews of Mead's work in professional journals. As late as 1937, Mead complained to Benedict that she wasn't being consulted in the profession because of the old canard spread by Sapir and Malinowski.[110]

Yet Mead wasn't defeated. In 1932 she responded to Sapir's attacks in an article on jealousy that she wrote for one of Calverton and Schmalhausen's compilation of articles on cultural trends. In response to Sapir's contention that jealousy is the proof of real love, she argued that it revealed only self-doubt and an inferiority complex on the part of the individual exhibiting it. Without mentioning him by name, she maintained that it was characteristic of men who were short, had weak sexual endowments, or were old.[111] Thus she launched the ultimate attack: she questioned Sapir's masculinity. It may not have been the wisest approach, given the loyalty of the men in anthropology to Sapir and his own dislike of her. But within a few years Mead would become charitable in writing about men, once she met Gregory Bateson and a number of male psychologists and sociologists who would champion her cause.

MARGARET AND REO spent eight months among the Manus; they came back to New York City in the fall of 1929. When Margaret returned, Ruth was involved with Tom Mount, Lydia Simpson, and Margery Loeb, and Margaret didn't like it. She wanted to continue their sexual relationship, but Ruth refused: so long as Margaret was married to Reo, she didn't want to compete with him for Margaret's affections. Margaret wrote in *An Anthropologist at Work* that Ruth "kept us all in separate rooms and moved from one to another with no one following to take notes."[112] Ruth had turned the tables on Margaret; and, too, they had reestablished their relationship on a different plane, one without sexual manipulation. They remained devoted to each other, held together by the spiritual and intellectual bond they had crafted. They spent time together whenever they could. Ruth was now ready to accept whatever Margaret did without recrimination, to cheer her on in doing fieldwork or in attracting yet another lover. She had finally moved beyond jealousy, to a place where by giving Margaret freedom she found freedom for herself.

And Margaret deeply appreciated that Ruth accepted her behavior and allowed her to roam. Because of this, their love could be eternal and spiritually ecstatic. In a moment of deep commitment to Ruth, she wrote her that their relationship affected every part of her life. Everything from the passing street scene to her most complex interactions with others was deepened by their love, and every experience she had by herself intensified her feelings for Ruth. "You will never know what a priceless gift you've given me," she wrote to Ruth, "in giving me a perfect love no least inch of which I need ever repay." It was a tribute to Ruth's generosity and to the deep love they shared, no matter their commitments to others. In a moment of poetic passion, realizing her own debt to Ruth, Margaret described her anthropology as a flower for Ruth's hair.[113]

PART V

Intellect and Emotions

CHAPTER 10

"Two Strings to His Bow"

Ruth Benedict and Patterns of Culture

T HE RELATIONSHIP BETWEEN Ruth Benedict and Margaret
Mead might be viewed as a conversation, one carried on in
poems and letters, through phone calls and personal encounters, with its initial intellectual culmination in two books, Benedict's
Patterns of Culture (1934) and Mead's *Sex and Temperament in Three
Primitive Societies* (1935). Published a year apart, the books reached a
large audience among academics and the general public. Foundational
for the field of anthropology, they were reform texts for the 1930s.
They were controversial, especially among anthropologists, but the
criticism furthered their authors' reputations. Even some of the books'
harshest critics in anthropology assigned them as reading in their
classes. They remain stimulating reading today.[1]

Each author focuses on three societies: Benedict on the Zuñi of
New Mexico, the Dobuans of Melanesia, and the Kwakiutl of Vancou-
ver Island, British Columbia; Mead on three New Guinea societies,
the Arapesh, the Mundugumor, and the Tchambuli. In each book one
society is peaceful (the Zuñi for Benedict; the Arapesh for Mead) and
the other two are more violent (the Dobuans and the Kwakiutl for
Benedict; the Mundugumor and the Tchambuli for Mead). Both
authors identify the dominant "pattern" in their societies, while they
also identify social deviants, to prove that the sort of individuals
regarded as abnormal in one society might be regarded as normal in
another. Both suggest that an entire society can be organized around

an "abnormal" pattern, and both criticize the society of the United States.

In *Patterns of Culture* Benedict concluded that men control most societies and that women are oppressed in most of them. Before Mead wrote *Sex and Temperament*, she used a similar "patriarchal" analysis in her work. In her studies of the Manus (1930) and the women of an Omaha community in Nebraska (1932), she depicts women as subordinate to men. The Manus women are pawns in a system of exchanges accompanying marriage; the Omaha women are so enmeshed in their traditional culture that they don't take advantage of their legal rights under the laws of the United States. In both societies group rape is glorified by men.[2] In her article on jealousy (1931), Mead asserted that "throughout history women have been the *insecure* sex. Their status, their freedom of action, their very economic existence, their right over their own children, has been dependent upon their preservation of their personal relations with men." In 1935, in an article on women in tribal societies, she identified a "widespread and biologically defined political disability of women."[3]

There is a point-counterpoint to the writing of Benedict and Mead during these years, as Mead both honored her mentor and disagreed with her. Benedict didn't criticize Mead's work in print, and Mead mentioned *Patterns of Culture* in *Sex and Temperament* only to praise it. Yet in that book she took apart the concepts of gender and homosexuality, which Benedict mostly left standing in her 1934 work, while she challenged Benedict's dismissal of heredity in the formation of personality and her brief for homosexuality as a superior identity. Indeed, Mead held out for the importance of inherited characteristics, while she made a case for "bisexuality."

In *Patterns of Culture* Benedict followed the modernist project of assembling reality around abstract patterns, although she stressed that the psychological terms she applied to her societies—Dionysian, Apollonian, paranoid, megalomaniac—might not fit any other society than the ones to which she applied those terms. "It would be absurd," she wrote, "to cut every culture down to the Procrustean bed of some catchword characterization."[4] Her "modernism" wasn't simple: it always encompassed on some level the emphasis on variety of her doctoral dissertation, the breaking down of absolutes. Moreover, she argued that Western categories for mental disturbances, like schizophrenia and manic-depressive disorder, probably didn't hold for non-Western societies: she thereby challenged their validity even for the

United States.[5] She implied a similar possibility with regard to gender, pointing the way to Mead's revisions in this area.[6]

In breaking down the concepts of gender and sexuality in *Sex and Temperament,* Mead might in fact be classified among literary analyst and queer theorist Joseph Boone's "queer modernists"—writers in the 1920s and 1930s whom Boone identifies as viewing sexual identity as multifaceted and as anticipating the "queer" analysis of today.[7] Yet Mead, committed to marriage and motherhood, backed off. She eliminated "feminine" and "masculine" as markers of identity, but she didn't abandon "male" and "female" because she viewed reproduction as crucial to humanity and she didn't know of any society without those categories. She proposed a radical definition of human identity based on personality traits rather than on sex roles—and a conservative definition of it based on anatomy and reproduction. Moreover, although she defined gender as fluid, Mead looked for temperamental classifications that could be applied cross-culturally to individuals and societies, to create a universal scientific grid.

Finally, the subject of race was never far from Benedict's and Mead's thinking. They lived in a city with a multiethnic population, studied cultures with dark-skinned populations, and were students of Franz Boas, the greatest academic antiracist of the age. By 1933 Hitler ruled Germany, the Nazis burned Boas's books, and academic refugees from Hitler's Germany appeared in New York City—including Karen Horney and Erich Fromm, who became friends with Benedict and Mead. The New School, ignoring the anti-Semitism of most American universities, raised the funds to launch the University in Exile, with refugees as its faculty.[8]

This historical context, as well as the theoretical similarities and differences between Benedict and Mead, must be kept in mind in reading the next four chapters, in which I will analyze their intellectual stances in the areas of gender, sex, and race, with my focus on *Patterns of Culture* and *Sex and Temperament.* I will also continue to narrate the story of their lives.

WHY DID BENEDICT write *Patterns of Culture?* One can trace its genesis to her early years as an anthropologist, when her work on the vision quest so impressed Edward Sapir that he predicted she would write the book on theory that Franz Boas hadn't produced. Sapir hoped that the book he envisioned might reach a popular audience as well as a professional one. He worried, however, that it couldn't be done; he thought that "dyed-in-the-wool anthropologists" knew too many facts and were too proud of their "erudite negativism" to write a book that would appeal to the public. He concluded that "a semi-literary outsider" needed to do it for them."[9] With her poetic gift, however, Benedict might be the insider who could produce the needed theory and present it clearly.

Sapir actually meant to write the work himself, but he never did. He had a title for it, "The Psychology of Culture," and he proposed to H. L. Mencken that he would write a series of articles on the psychology of six tribal societies for the *American Mercury*, but Mencken turned him down.[10] In the 1920s he studied the American Indian Athabaskan languages, especially Navajo, and he wrote articles defending the nuclear family and attacking the new sexual freedom—and Margaret Mead. Together with psychiatrist Harry Stack Sullivan, a close friend, he successfully promoted a "personality-and-culture" interdisciplinary concentration, raising Rockefeller money to support it. (Benedict and Mead later took over its leadership.) Moving to Yale University in 1931, he established the first working seminar in the new concentration, recruiting students from a number of overseas cultures to study their own cultures, while he was instrumental in establishing the Institute for Human Relations there.[11] His seminar was a forerunner to the project on contemporary cultures that Benedict and Mead established at Columbia after World War II.

Sapir was critical of the theoretical direction that Benedict was taking. He disliked her use of "Apollonian" and "Dionysian" to apply to Native American cultures, as well as her focus on abnormality and on cultural configurations, although in an article on religion in 1928 he noted the constraint of the Pueblo Indians in their rituals and the "collective ecstasy" of the Plains Indians in theirs.[12] Without mentioning Benedict by name, he accused her of making cultures seem bizarre when they weren't, of focusing on the concept of culture rather than the individual as a way of hiding her own self, and of failing to realize that cultures were mainly collections of individuals who interpreted cultural patterns in "endlessly different ways." The last statement reflected Sullivan's dynamic "self psychology," which posited that the individual personality is constantly being reconstructed through interactions with other individuals and the broader society.[13]

Benedict rejected Sapir's criticism. Citing him by name, she wrote in 1932 that "cultures may be built solidly and harmoniously upon fantasies, fear-constructs, or inferiority complexes."[14] That same year, after listening to a speech he gave, she complained to Mead that he was slighting the power of societies to shape their members, and she expressed dislike of his use of his personal feelings about football to illustrate individual reactions to social institutions. The vast majority of the members of any culture, she contended, are "shaped to the fashion of that culture."[15]

Her disagreements with Sapir, however, formed only part of Benedict's motivation for writing *Patterns of Culture*. Indeed, Alfred Kroeber played a role, when he was a visiting professor at Columbia during the spring semester in 1932. Benedict wrote to Mead that the two of them gossiped "amiably" and "quite a lot." Yet he infuriated her when she thought that he treated her work as unimportant and then, in his course "Personality and Culture," analyzed "half a dozen cultures for whether Superman could have been bred in them." Predictably, according to Benedict, he "gave the laurels to the Plains [Indians.]"[16]

According to Mead, Benedict became so upset with Kroeber that she impulsively plunged into writing *Patterns of Culture*.[17] Benedict was sensitive to male slights: in her introduction to her 1935 collection of Zuñi mythology, she drew from Alfred Adler's theory of a universal inferiority complex producing a "masculinity complex" to assert that powerful women in American society aroused a "masculine protest" in men. That protest was rare among the men in Zuñi, she contended, even though their matrilineal, matrifocal society gave women considerable authority. It was, however, "so common an element in our civilization." In 1937 she wrote to her student Ruth Landes that "this business of masculine protest being reinforced by being in the same field is terrible."[18]

In her early work on the vision quest, Benedict subtly challenged the men in anthropology by drawing from their work on individual Native American tribes to construct a broad interpretation of Indian religion. She did something similar in *Patterns of Culture*, as she used Reo Fortune's work on the Dobuans and Boas's on the Kwakiutl. Fortune had taken Margaret Mead away from her; now she absorbed his research. He hesitated to let her use his Dobu material, but she had approved his Ph.D. work at Columbia and had gotten him research grants and he could hardly refuse. Besides, including him with Boas and herself in a book intended for a wide readership could make his reputation—and Fortune was ambitious. Benedict wrote to him—in New Guinea with Margaret Mead—that she intended to highlight his "sensational material" and that strategy would make people remember his work.[19]

With regard to Boas, Benedict had become as close to him as Elsie Clews Parsons had ever been. In many ways they were like a father and a daughter. By the mid-1930s he was in his seventies and in declining health; she ran the department at Columbia for him. By the late 1930s she had assumed his position as a spokesperson on race. Mead wrote that Benedict became a "second self" to Boas; Kroeber, for one, agreed.[20] In describing the Kwakiutl in *Patterns of Culture* as "megalo-maniac," Benedict by implication placed Boas in that category, for his drive to create a new anthropology in the United States and to extend its agenda throughout the world suggested a driving ambition. Boas wrote a laudatory introduction to *Patterns of Culture*, but he eventually criticized Benedict for downplaying the gentle family life of the Kwa-kiutl. Indeed, Boas prided himself on his gentleness at home. Benedict did mention the Kwakiutl's supportive family life, but she did so in the middle of a paragraph, where it is easily overlooked.[21]

By using Boas's research on the Kwakiutl in a book designed for a general readership, she was paying tribute to him, keeping her distance from her male peers in the field, and using his reputation to justify her work. Benedict criticized the other male Boasians in her letters to Mead, but she had only words of praise for Boas. During the period that she wrote *Patterns of Culture*, she kept quiet about what she was doing. The anthropologists in New York were all "riding some patented horse" of their own, she wrote Mead, interested only in their own point of view. She was deliberately not consulting them about the book she was writing, telling them vaguely that she was writing an arti-cle, not something full length.[22] She didn't want to subject herself to their criticism; she already knew that Sapir and Kroeber didn't like her theories. In reviewing *Patterns of Culture* Kroeber, like Sapir, criticized her for failing to take normality into account.[23] He didn't think that societies were as abnormal as she made them out to be.

Benedict's work wasn't antimale, nor was Benedict herself; she dis-liked overbearing male behavior, but she defined herself in terms of a male/female division in which her masculine side was strong. More-over, in her writing she cited male philosophers like Nietzsche and Santayana while overlooking feminist authors like Charlotte Perkins Gilman and Ellen Key, despite her enthusiasm for them before World War I. She may have wanted to establish a male genealogy to ensure her acceptance as a theorist in a male intellectual world; she may have rejected these feminist writers because their evolutionary progressivism seemed wrongheaded to her after the devastation of World War I and her espousal of Boas's antievolutionism.[24] Still, she carried her emphasis on male progenitors to an extreme in her presidential address to the American Anthropological Association in 1947. In that address she called for a new humanistic direction in anthropology of the sort she had learned in college. Yet she didn't mention Laura Wylie or Gertrude Buck, the literary critics who had taught her at Vassar. Rather, she cited works on Shakespeare written primarily by men.[25]

Her attacks on aggressive masculinity in her work suggest that she appreciated a gentle male style. On the walls of her office at Columbia hung portraits of Franz Boas and an aging Blackfoot chief.[26] These were men of wisdom and authority. They were also men softened by the process of aging, which can have a cross-gendering effect, with women becoming more assertive and men more serene.[27] Benedict liked Boas for his grandeur and rationality and his sweetness as "Papa Franz." She liked the Blackfoot Indians for combining spirituality with practicality and for living in the real world, not one of visions. Their vision quest was rational more than metaphysical: it was expressed in bundles of branches that were bought and sold. In the summer of 1939 she went with a group of students to Montana to study the Blackfoot. It was only the second field trip she had taken since 1927, when she studied the Pima and came up with the configuration concept.

She wrote to Mead describing the Blackfoot as "my Blackfoot, with such zest in the here and now and [who] work off their great energy with the simplest and most obvious symbolism." Also, their leaders identified themselves with their people to the point of seeing everyone's well-being as part of their own. Among the Blackfoot, caring for the old and the hungry was not a charity but an obligation, for they believed that a denial of rights to one individual threatened the rights of all. Her stand with regard to the Blackfoot sounds akin to the ideas of FDR's New Deal; it would influence her in the reform program she drew up during World War II. She also noted the Blackfoot institution of the *taka*, a lifetime friendship between two men, in which they slept together the first night after a hunt without considering themselves homosexual.[28] Both Benedict and Mead remained interested in "deviancy" and how it functioned in prestate societies. They also wanted to understand their relationship—and themselves.

BENEDICT'S PERSONAL CIRCUMSTANCES, too, motivated her to write *Patterns of Culture*. By the mid-1930s her life was relatively stable. She had a regular job at Columbia; she was winning professional honors. In 1932 the journal *Science* named her as one of five leading anthropologists in the United States; in 1933 *American Men of Science* starred her name as one of 1,250 outstanding scientists among the 22,000 scientists listed. She joined Boas, Parsons, Sapir, Lowie, Kroeber—and Stanley Benedict—in this high ranking. She was further listed as one of three outstanding women in science in the United States.[29]

Whatever Kroeber thought of her work, many of her peers judged it outstanding. Her articles and book reviews appeared in popular intellectual journals; she regularly reviewed books for the *New York Herald Tribune*. She was editor of the *Journal of American Folk-Lore*. She had been a member of the executive board of the American Anthropological Association and president of the American Ethnological Society; she chaired the Committee on Anthropology and Psychology of the National Research Council. She was a fellow of the American Association for the Advancement of Science and of the New York Academy of Sciences. Yet in the ten years after receiving her Ph.D., she had published only five major articles, in addition to her collections of Zuñi mythology and of Cochiti folktales. It was time to stake out a position. From New Guinea, Mead cheered her on. "People have been so used to thinking that you wouldn't challenge their high and mighty," she wrote to Benedict. By writing her book on theory, she would be "taking them by the postern gate."[30]

Moreover, Benedict had solved many personal issues, including the riddle of her sexual identity. Tom Mount's leaving her for a younger woman had been the last straw. She now decided to give up on men. After a particularly annoying conversation with Sapir, whom she saw from time to time, she wrote to Mead that she was "just giving thanks to God that there was no man living whose whims and egotisms I had to take seriously." Even when Stanley and Tom talked about women, they often sounded like Otto Weininger, a turn-of-the-century philosopher who contended that all humans were born bisexual—and then damned women as inferior to men.[31] Mead wasn't certain that she agreed with Benedict on the subject of men. "You have very high standards for men," she wrote Benedict, "much higher than you have for women."[32]

Ruth now formed a monogamous partnership with Natalie Raymond; her experiment in free love hadn't worked out. Tom Mount rejected her; Lydia Simpson was difficult; Margery Loeb attempted suicide when Ruth wasn't attentive.[33] She was tempted to become celibate, but she rejected that impulse. "When touch seems such a sweet and natural human delight," she wrote in a journal fragment, "I resent rooting it out. . . . If the flesh is superb and functioning healthily," she continued, "better delight in it." She regretted giving up variety in sexual relationships—she mourned "the murdered pleasures of the senses." Yet "some human drive of the senses" made her monogamous. She was really happy only with "the kind of human intercourse that can only come out of much more complicated arrangements than spending a night together."[34]

Ruth had been friends with Natalie in New York; she met her again in the summer of 1931, on a visit to her sister and mother in Pasadena. Nat had lost weight and was "shapely—beautiful and arresting." Ruth often commented on the beauty of women in her letters to Margaret but never on the appearance of men. Although Nat was living with a man, she had a history of lesbian relationships. The next fall, she moved in with Ruth in New York, and Stanley pulled strings to get her into the graduate program in biochemistry at Cornell Medical College.[35] Nat was younger by sixteen years and Ruth worried about the age difference, but they were happy. She wrote in her journal: "Loving Nat and taking such delight in her I have the happiest condition for living that I've ever known."[36] It was what she had wanted with Margaret Mead and hadn't been able to achieve.

In her journal she described her sexual orientation in terms of the masculine-feminine division that had long influenced her self-image. She had found the way to balance that division. Thus she had her healing vision of the bisexual, masculinized Egyptian sphinx—her answer to the riddle about the nature of life and of humans that the Greek sphinx posed. In a journal fragment she compared the Apollo Belvedere, a masculinized representation of the bisexual god, with Horus, the sky god of Egypt who, when represented as human, had a geometrically stylized body. "The comparison of the Apollo Belvedere with any old Egyptian Horus," she wrote, "is all the proof one needs of the superiority of perversion over any normalcy no matter how cultivated."[37] Benedict used the term "perversion" ironically; the Apollo Belvedere is large and muscular—with a pronounced penis.

In a letter to Margaret in 1938, Ruth wrote that she was rarely depressed anymore. "I don't have the devils anymore," she wrote, "it's hard to put into words how completely they've gone." She felt as though she were living permanently in her "delectable mountains." She had found the serenity she hadn't been able to reach through Pater's emotional ecstasy—or through practicing free love. She had finally been able to turn from Dionysus to Apollo, from emotion to reason, and the shift was working. "It's like a little piece of eternal life," she wrote Mead.[38] It was because of the serenity she projected to others that Abraham Maslow, a student of hers in the 1930s, chose her as a model in his theory of self-actualization, which proposed that everyone has the potential to achieve a transcendent self. Maslow thought that Benedict had achieved that self.

Yet Nat turned out to be another lover of Benedict's who had difficulty with commitment. "She is in many ways a child who'll never grow up," Benedict wrote Mead. Finding other lovers, both men and women, Nat cut off sex with Ruth and rationalized the rejection by claiming that she had never had much of a sex drive. Ruth wasn't convinced. She wondered if Nat was someone for whom heterosexual relations were "the most thoroughly congenial ones." On the other hand, "her whole history is against that." Ruth speculated further, drawing from the conservative biology that had influenced her when she married Stanley: "It might be that she is only at ease in sex if children were the ultimate implication." Yet Ruth wrote Margaret that she didn't miss the sex with Nat.[39] Even though she continued to live with Nat through the 1930s, she turned to other women.[40]

In the early 1930s, with her vision of the Egyptian sphinx Ruth had an epiphany that enabled her to craft a better sense of self: taking on a lesbian identity was important in that transformation. She had gone through a long process of centering herself, of finding the "true" self that her friend Karen Horney came to believe should be life's goal, as did other neo-Freudians, such as Abraham Maslow. Horney proposed, as did others, that beneath the anxiety endemic to Western civilization lay the "true" self, peaceful, resourceful, caring.[41] Horney attempted to find that self in her own life through "self-analysis," a procedure about which she wrote a book; Benedict had engaged in "joint analysis" with Mead to do so.

Concepts of a "true self" and "centering" are fundamental to Buddhism and Sufism—mystical religions of the East. Like other neo-Freudians, Horney eventually studied Zen Buddhist techniques. Poetry and anthropology were Benedict's methods; she had rejected Yeats's Order of the Golden Dawn and its mystical view of reality long before. She had some interest in Eastern techniques: she devoted a chapter of *The Chrysanthemum and the Sword* to Japanese self-discipline, writing favorably about Zen Buddhist meditation and retreat from the world.[42] Focusing on self-actualization, Abraham Maslow contributed to the development of the existential-humanistic psychology of the early 1960s called the Third Force; he traced its origins partly to Benedict's ideas about Apollonian and Dionysian drives. He eventually described his "self-actualized" individual as an "Apollonian mystic."[43]

Giving expression to her masculine side and becoming lesbian in identity also motivated Benedict to write *Patterns of Culture* after years of hesitation. Writing that book took courage, as she focused her intellectual work on her personal issues as a woman, a homosexual, and an individual troubled by emotional instability. Her friends teased her for being unable to tell research from therapy in writing it.[44] Yet that merging of self and scholarship, of intellectualism and identity, produced the originality of *Patterns of Culture*. Moreover, her boldness encouraged Mead to follow her in addressing the tabooed subject of homosexuality. With her fear of being found out, Mead might not have had the nerve to do it on her own.

Yet Benedict's focus on culture allowed her to avoid exposing her own self. Sapir wasn't far off when he charged that in studying the patterns of culture Benedict was hiding from herself. Her concept of "patterns" was a brilliant insight in an age of dictatorship, when individual liberty was being eliminated in a number of Western societies. Yet she concealed herself behind that concept; the book contains nothing about female homosexuality. Nonetheless, because of Benedict's passion for her subject, which united the personal with the political, she was able to write the kind of book that Sapir had contended was impossible for a "dyed-in-the-wool" anthropologist to write, one that could capture the imagination of the public and of anthropologists as well.

Did she permanently end her depressions? That's hard to say. She enjoyed her successes, and *Patterns of Culture* eventually turned out to be a triumph, despite the criticisms of anthropologists like Sapir and Kroeber. Finding the Blackfoot, becoming more political by the late 1930s, and entering the public arena during World War II were satisfying. By the mid-1930s Ruth made peace with her sister and her mother, just as Margaret came to terms with her father in that period—and with her mother later. Bertrice Fulton, fulfilled by caring for her grandchildren and working with the YWCA, was even able to end her mourning for her husband. She lived to the age of ninety-five, dying in 1953, five years after Ruth. Ruth often visited Bertrice and Margery in Pasadena. Community leaders there, Margery and her minister husband were involved in the efforts for racial integration in Pasadena and Los Angeles in the 1950s and 1960s.[45]

Yet Benedict was troubled by her difficulties with Natalie Raymond, as she was by her ongoing problems with the men at Columbia. The last journal fragment of Benedict's that Mead published in *An Anthropologist at Work* was dated 1934; in it Benedict once again expressed deep discontent. She praised the virtues of a monastic life. Perhaps someday, she mused, a culture will arise that fosters a detached spiritual life and yet encourages adventure, with a "prodigal security." "It would be so amply foundationed upon verities that are not the sport of time and chance that incidents of faithlessness, of failure, of death, would not touch its being."[46] A year later, in 1935, she wrote her bleak "The Story of My Life," in which she plunged into the dark side of her family and her self. That same year she focused on irrationality in *Patterns of Culture*.

"BENEDICT WAS MESSIANIC, like the rest of us," wrote Abraham Maslow.[47] His reference was to the reform sentiment in the 1930s among intellectuals reacting to the breakdown of the economy in the United States and to the rise of fascism in Europe. Maslow's comment might also be taken as a reference to the style and purpose of Benedict's *Patterns of Culture*, a work that is ironic and passionate, pragmatic and poetic, scientific and feminist—and critical of the aggressive masculinity and materialism of American culture.

Patterns of Culture is a reform work on a number of levels. Benedict made a brief in it for cultural relativism as a way of combating racism and of exposing the Eurocentric bias of Western social science, in which conclusions based on research done on European and American subjects were assumed to be universal. She also contended, as did Mead, that anthropology was the most reliable of the social sciences, because tribal societies, with their small, homogeneous populations, were excellent laboratories for studying social behavior. In them "it is possible to estimate the inter-relationships of traits . . . in a way which is impossible in the cross-currents of our complex civilization."[48]

Because of their small size and homogeneity, tribal societies weren't oriented toward reform: Benedict agreed with Mead that the best hope for change lay in a society like the United States, with its critical thought and its heterogeneous population of varying ethnicities. But some features of tribal societies were superior to those of the United States—like the Samoan extended families and the commitment of the Blackfoot to social welfare. Like Mead, Benedict believed in the superiority of the Western scientific tradition. She criticized the "romantic primitivism" popular in the United States in the 1920s as well as the mysticism of societies like those of Melanesia. "A talent for observation," she wrote, was wasted in Melanesian tribes on "the negligible borders of the magico-religious field." To fully utilize that talent for observation, societies needed a "scientific methodology."[49]

Moreover, Benedict had a reforming interdisciplinary perspective—one that she shared with Mead. Throughout the 1920s Boasian anthropologists were leaders of an interdisciplinary movement challenging the discipline-bound, inward-looking focus of the social sciences, caught up in the conservative turn in academic scholarship toward quantification and monographic scholarship in that decade. Reacting against these trends, critics like Van Wyck Brooks and Lewis Mumford repudiated the university to become public intellectuals. Benedict and Mead also entered the public arena of thought, but they remained in the academy. Meanwhile, reform-minded sociologists and psychologists, such as their friends Robert Lynd, John Dollard, and Erik Erikson, turned to anthropology for a broad approach. Among the last of the social sciences to emerge as an academic discipline, anthropology retained a sense of dynamic newness and universality when other disciplines were entering the specialist phase. Nor did it lose its strong ties to the humanities, despite its scientific orientation. Like Franz Boas, the leaders of anthropology he trained were both determined and reform-minded.[50] Their culture-and-personality concentration was a major interdisciplinary endeavor.

In *Patterns of Culture*, Benedict borrowed from other disciplines. Her view of societies as integrated entities drew from sociologist Emile Durkheim, who defined societies as organic wholes; from historians Wilhelm Dilthey and Oswald Spengler, who interpreted historical periods and cultures as driven by dominant themes; and from the Gestalt school of psychology, which held that the whole is greater than the sum of its parts—a theory based on experiments on sight and sound, bearing the imprimatur of a "hard science." By the early 1930s many of the major Gestalt theorists had emigrated from Germany to the United States.[51] In her presidential address to the American

Anthropological Association, Benedict noted the influence on her of her college reading in philosophy and literary criticism—after all, her terms "Apollonian" and "Dionysian" came from Nietzsche's *Birth of Tragedy.*

By the early 1930s the concept of "patterns" was everywhere: in Sapir's linguistic theories; in Benedict's belief that no one can change the "pattern" of his or her personality. Poets discussed "patterns"; Amy Lowell wrote a poem called "Patterns" about World War I having destroyed Victorian certainties. Above all, Benedict's theory of "patterns" governing societies grew out of the modernist project that reconstructed reality as geometric abstractions from its constituent parts—as Picasso was doing in art, Frank Lloyd Wright in architecture, and modernist poets with language.

In 1927, seven years before *Patterns of Culture* appeared, Alexander Goldenweiser noted that the cultural-pattern concept was emerging throughout the social sciences and that it was related to the concepts of form and system in the plastic arts, music, and abstract disciplines such as mathematics and logic. "Unless we are badly misguided," he wrote, "a concept of the general type of pattern or Gestalt may yet come to mark an epochal advance in our conceptual explorations." Mead asserted that anthropologists had been using the word "pattern" for some time to denote either specific groups or universals like religion that characterize all human societies. Benedict's genius lay in connecting it to individual cultures.[52]

As an interdisciplinary scholar, Benedict borrowed mostly from psychology. Yet she wasn't a Freudian. She might be grouped loosely with Karen Horney and Erich Fromm as a neo-Freudian; that's how Mead characterized herself by the mid-1930s.[53] The only psychologist Benedict cited in her footnotes to *Patterns of Culture* was Gardner Murphy, a psychologist at Columbia who was a friend of hers. By using the literary terms "Apollonian" and "Dionysian" she implicitly critiqued the scientism of the social sciences; the terms "paranoia" and "megalomania" predated Freud. If anything, her use of psychology was "eclectic"—a term Murphy used in his study of contemporary trends in psychology to characterize many psychologists of the day.[54]

As an eclectic, Benedict drew from Adler and Jung, while using Freud selectively. For example, she borrowed Freud's idea of "wish fulfillment" (from *The Interpretation of Dreams*) to explain the content of folktales. Yet she didn't like his theories of individual development—the libido, the Oedipus complex, and his categorizations for infant development based on oral, anal, and genital zones. She expressed that dislike in her 1938 review of Horney's *Neurotic Personality of Our Time*. Freud's theory of civilization as growing out of the conflicts within a "primal horde" and his post–World War I social psychology focused on the irrationality of modern society may have influenced her: in *Patterns of Culture* she seems to have plunged into Freud's tumultous "unconscious."[55]

As a reformer, Benedict remained devoted to John Dewey, especially to his emphases on education and on social engineering through the leadership of experts in the social sciences. She rejected the Marxist theory that the economic system determines culture, maintaining that creative acts on the part of impersonal forces were the deciding factor. The process, she contended, was akin to creating poetry; it was aesthetic, not materialist. It responded to a variety of impulses—social, psychological, economic, artistic, individual. It had a historical component, for cultures usually developed over time. She wrote in 1929: "Man evolves always elaborate traditional ways of doing things, great superstructures of the most varying designs, and without very striking correlations with the underpinnings on which they must each and all eventually rest."[56] The socialism that Mead espoused as an undergraduate didn't attract Benedict; if anything, she converted Mead to a Deweyian point of view, beginning with the anthropology department seminar in 1922. By the later 1930s, however, Benedict followed Dewey into embracing a modified state socialism and supporting the New Deal and its more radical programs for housing and welfare.

Following Dewey in his *Human Nature and Conduct*, Benedict cautioned that attempts to bring social change into being must take custom into account. In "The Science of Custom," published in 1929, she sounds downright conservative. "We all know that culture changes," she wrote. "We hope, a little, that whereas change has hitherto been blind, at the mercy of unconscious patternings, it will be possible gradually, insofar as we become genuinely culture-conscious, that it shall be guided by intelligence."[57] In *Patterns of Culture*, written at the height of the Depression, her position was more to the left, and she alluded to generational conflict as a force for change. "No society," she wrote, "has yet attempted a self-conscious direction of the process by which its new normalities are created in the next generation. Dewey has pointed out how possible and yet how drastic such social engineering would be." Yet she flirted with evolutionary thinking when she wrote, "minor changes of today, divorce, secularization, and the prevalence of the petting party, could be taken up and become traditional, with the same richness of content of older patterns for older generations."[58] By 1940, in her book on race, she had moved further to the left.

PATTERNS OF CULTURE begins with a defense of anthropology as a science: doing fieldwork is akin to doing experiments in laboratories, and the results can serve as the basis of a science of society. The book, however, draws from Benedict's poetic side. Indeed, she couldn't prevent herself from thinking and writing poetically. According to Abraham Maslow, words came to her intuitively, as they do to a poet. She struggled with words that came to her mind that she dared not say in public as a scientist, words "that could be said over a martini, but not in print."[59] She felt that in her professional writing she had to be detached and rational. "She had the disciplined mind of a scientist," wrote her student Victor Barnouw, "but she sometimes spoke in the Delphic language of poetry."[60] In 1941, she used "hourglass" and "siphon" to categorize cultures in a lecture she gave to a class at Columbia. On hearing these terms, her student Sidney Mintz thought of Keats.[61]

Yet she was influenced by the new direction in science taken by Albert Einstein and Max Planck that disputed the Newtonian view of the universe as ordered and that saw scientists as guided by intuition as well as reason—what Einstein called a "cosmic religiosity." Both Benedict and Mead studied a culture until they felt as though they were part of it; then they constructed a narrative. Benedict's student Dorothy Lee wrote that this approach at first baffled their students, who were accustomed to the older methodology in which "the observer and the observed" were kept separate throughout the process of interviewing, observing, and writing. When they understood the new technique, they liked it. Lee thought that Benedict was like Albert Einstein because she used both rationality and intuition in doing her work.[62] Benedict might be seen as possessing what Evelyn Fox Keller, in pointing to the importance of intuition to scientific advance, called "a feeling for the organism."[63]

A number of literary writers influenced Benedict in crafting *Patterns of Culture*. The first was Virginia Woolf, whose work she often read. In January 1932, as she contemplated writing her book on theory, she wrote Mead that she had read Woolf's *The Waves*, published the year before. She liked how Woolf used six individuals in the novel to portray a culture, although she disliked their sameness and the lack of any "violent temperaments" among them. George Santayana and Robinson Jeffers also influenced her in writing the book. Santayana had been a favorite of hers since college. Her use of three societies in *Patterns of Culture* mirrored his use of three philosophers—the Greek philosopher Lucretius, the medieval poet Dante, and the Romantic poet Goethe—in *Three Philosophical Poets*, in which he views them not as individual agents but as reflections of the societies in which they lived. Citing Georg Hegel's dialectic, he describes their diversity as ultimately combining into "a unity of a higher kind." He writes: "Each is typical of an age. Taken together they sum up all of European philosophy."[64] One might propose that in *Patterns of Culture* the Apollonian Zuñi, the paranoid Dobuans, and the megalomaniac Kwakiutl sum up the whole of American culture.[65]

In *Three Philosophical Poets* Santayana made a brief for poetry as philosophy. He contended that the insight of poets who have a "practised and passionate imagination" can afford true understanding.[66] Santayana's "practised and passionate imagination" resembles Einstein's "cosmic imagination"; such stands gave Benedict the courage to use her poetic intuition in doing her scientific work. Moreover, the unity of the trinity, reflected in Santayana's book, appealed to Benedict; she had used that design in her proposed biographical study of Mary Wollstonecraft, Margaret Fuller, and Olive Schreiner. Such triangles have been symbols for the trinity of the nuclear family, of Christianity, of cosmic birth, of women's bodies.[67]

Robinson Jeffers also influenced Benedict in writing *Patterns of Culture*, as she responded to his focus on human perversity in his modern retellings of the ancient Greek tragedies. In 1931 Benedict and Mead's friend Edmund Wilson, a bellwether of cultural trends, published his influential *Axel's Castle*. Responding to the Depression, he called for poets and novelists to abandon Symbolism and return to realism. The individualism of Symbolism, he contended, had played itself out in a decadent sexuality that had become ridiculous in characters like the neurotic nobleman in Joris-Karl Huysmans's novel *À rebours*, who retreats from the world to cultivate bizarre sensations.[68] Yet Benedict followed Jeffers, not Wilson. Jeffers was a poet of decadence, a quintessential antimodern modernist, but Benedict wasn't far behind him. He inspired her to take the themes of her poetry and of her psyche—the horror, the despair, the monsters—into her study of culture. She had already done that in "The Bo-Cu Plant" and "The Uses of Cannibalism"—both unpublished.

Jeffers wrote epic poetry. Ever since Homer, that was a masculine genre. None of the women poets of the 1920s took up the epic; their forms were the lyric, the sonnet, and the ballad. Over the ages of Western literary expression almost no woman had written in the epic form. In some of the wisest advice Edward Sapir ever gave Benedict about her poetry, he suggested that the poetic forms she was using were constraining her. "You need to try a long-breathed form, say imaginative narration, in blank verse," he told her. "You may need an absolutely clean field for the development of your rich imagery."[69] She took his advice, but not in the genre of poetry. *Patterns of Culture* is an epic, sweeping in scope. It is Apollonian in its measured cadences and Dionysian in its plunge into horror—but it is masculine in its epic range. It's a jeremiad against American culture on the part of a Biblical prophet; a lamentation over the sins of a beloved civilization in the voice of a Puritan divine. Benedict was forty-seven when she wrote *Patterns of Culture*. She was a woman at the midpoint of her life, entering menopause, at the height of her powers.

There's a sense of irony in the book, and irony is a modernist mode. Yet there was a tragedy at the core of Benedict, and she let her anger loose in *Patterns of Culture*, a work of catharsis as much as imagination, a Cassandra's "marriage song of her shame" as much as a scientific and satirical treatise intended to rouse a sentiment for reform: she was as much an antimodernist as a modernist. In his famous analysis of her work, anthropologist Clifford Geertz defined her as engaging in a process of "self-nativising," as juxtaposing "the all-too-familiar and the wildly exotic in such a way that they change places."[70] Yet Geertz's apt term for her creative process doesn't encompass the full extent to which her sense of the contemporary historical period and her feminism were involved in her approach.

Like most of the great masculine epics, *Patterns of Culture* has a journey motif. Benedict chose the one that had always fascinated her: the hero's descent to hell before his ascent to heaven, as in Dionysus going to Hades to rescue his mother, Dante descending through the seven levels of hell before ascending through purgatory and then to heaven, John Bunyan's pilgrim mired in the "Slough of Despond" before reaching the "delectable mountains." All were metaphors for the internal self, for the Dionysian depths of emotionality and the Apollonian heaven of rationality and peace.

Benedict begins her tale with the land of the Zuñi, a peaceful place, and then descends to the hell of the Dobuans and the Kwakiutl. The land of the Dobuans, with neither ritual nor religion, is a dead environment, like those swampy hells of fire and muck that Dante descends to.[71] Even husbands and wives don't trust each other, for anyone may use deadly charms against anyone else at a moment's notice. Every village is organized in a circle around an ancestral cemetery. Sorcerers are ubiquitous, dispensing amulets for protection and destruction, while everyone dreams about terrible flying witches.

The Kwakiutl are just as bad. They hold potlatches, great feasts at which the wealthiest individuals in the community give away everything they have accumulated during the previous year to their rivals. At those feasts frenzied people bite flesh out of each other's arms, while a young man kills someone, eats part of the corpse, and then vomits out the flesh. Shamans bite their tongues until the blood flows down their cheeks. That behavior mirrors their cosmology, in which their chief god is a cannibal who employs a female slave to supply him with corpses, while his guard, a raven, eats their eyes. His slave, a bird with a long, sharp beak, fractures their skulls and sucks out the brains.

From the hell of these cultures, Benedict returns to a middle ground, a serene place where she engages in a rational argument about the need to understand abnormality, to further individuality, and to adopt Deweyian social planning. And where is her heaven? It may exist among the Zuñi. In her interpretation, the Zuñi are dedicated to self-control and serenity, with an aversion to competition and violence and only a "slight emphasis" on personal possessions. Women have a high position in the society, since they own the family property and descent and kinship are traced through them. Yet Benedict didn't like Zuñi conformity, the way the culture stifled individual expression in the interest of the group. In this regard, she preferred the Plains Indians, who might indulge in violence, but whose vision quest—an individual experience—fostered individuality. She criticized their warlike tendencies, but she also described their warfare as mostly a matter of "counting coup," in which they scored points by stealing horses or battle garb, or touching an adversary's body or horse, with almost no injuries or deaths.

Her most positive description of any group in *Patterns of Culture* is of the men-women among the Plains Indians. Drawing on Elsie Clews Parsons's work on the Zuñi berdaches, she recognized that they were often ridiculed in Zuñi. But she thought that their situation was different among the Plains, where their role was more fully developed than in any other Native American culture area. Although the attitude toward them was sometimes "touched with malaise in the face of a recognized incongruity," they were for the most part regarded as superior, because they could support a household by the male activity of hunting as well as by the female activities of beadwork and curing animal skins. And because of the man-woman's physical strength and his desire to succeed in his new female role, he excelled in these occupations. Any social scorn was directed against his male partner, who usually didn't contribute much to the household. In any event, the berdache's household "was already a model for all households through the sole efforts of the berdache." For the man-woman had "two strings to his bow," wrote Benedict, and "no one in the culture was richer."[72]

Benedict's passages on the Plains berdaches can also be read as a critique of Kroeber's celebration of the masculinity of the Plains Indians in his lectures at Columbia in 1932. The institution of the berdache made the male anthropologists uncomfortable, and they avoided it, often assuming that effete males took on the role to avoid becoming warriors and that they were ridiculed for doing so.[73] Yet that wasn't their only position on the subject. In 1937, in an article reviewing the literature on the men-women in American Indian tribes, Kroeber praised the Indians for institutionalizing a role for homosexuals. The antihomosexual attitudes of the American mainstream, he contended, created conflict and tension for everyone. Evaluating the treatment of homosexuals in the United States and among the Native Americans, he asserted that "it cannot be concluded that the difference between the Indian and ourselves is greater enlightenment on our part."[74]

PATTERNS OF CULTURE drew from Benedict's calculating side as well as her aesthetic and intellectual ones. That pragmatic side is evident in the fact that she gave up writing poetry as she turned to writing the book. During the Depression, male critics derided women's lyric poetry. Like Edmund Wilson in his criticism of the Symbolists, they called for a new, tough realism, suggesting that only men could produce it. In 1930 a reviewer in the *Yale Review* attacked Louise Bogan's poetry, which was similar to Benedict's. "We have fallen in verse upon finicky and constricted times," he wrote. "Dour and cryptic little poets are making notes for each other on the immediate status of their personal disillusions and disgusts."[75] It was a strident attack on the female poets' lyrical style and their themes of despair and death. Benedict couldn't avoid that criticism. She saw how difficult it was for her friends Léonie Adams and Louise Bogan to lead lives as poets. Both drank too much; both were hospitalized for emotional instability. Each married a literary critic, and neither woman's husband treated her well. For Léonie it was Edmund Wilson all over again. Bogan became a recluse, and Benedict didn't see her anymore.[76]

Anyway, Benedict wanted to prove to Edward Sapir that she could write his popular book. And she wanted to replicate Mead's fame. Just as Mead had done during the publication process for *Coming of Age in Samoa*, she took care with the title, the design on the cover, the choice of type, and the promotion of the book. As Mead often did, Benedict wrote the book for a general audience. She had taken that approach with "The Bo-Cu Plant" and "Mary Wollstonecraft," but it hadn't worked. Now she had the formula: extraordinary societies, striking intellectual conclusions, social relevance. Both she and Benedict, Mead later wrote, were fighting a battle for truth and they fought that battle with "the whole battery at our command, with the most fantastic and startling examples that we could muster."[77] It would be hard to conceive of more fantastic or startling societies than the ones Benedict described in *Patterns of Culture*.

Although writing was difficult for Benedict, she wrote this book more easily than she had ever thought possible. "Aren't you astonished," she wrote Reo Fortune in August 1932, several months after she had started it, "that I should really get some 40,000 words [c. 200 pages] already together for a book?"[78] And when Mead wrote to her from Tchambuli, contending that her first chapters were too academic and that no one wanted to hear about German philosophers like Spengler, whose theories about historical change she discussed, Benedict paid little attention. Tom Mount and David (Hannah Kahn) had read the book, she replied to Mead, and they were general readers who liked it.[79]

By this point she had largely solved the issues of religion and reason and of emotion and self-realization that had long troubled her. She could write about the horrors of the religion of the Kwakiutl because she had resolved them for herself. In a series of entries she wrote for the *Encyclopaedia of the Social Sciences* on religion, magic, and myth, Benedict took a stand in favor of a rational skepticism and a social-psychological point of view. Thus she maintained that myth and folklore were no more than wish fulfillment, and magic was mechanistic. It involved a philosophy, not a mysterious connection between animate objects and a spirit world. Even the Zuñi snake dance, with priests handling the dread rattlesnake, winding it around their bodies and putting its head into their mouths, wasn't dangerous, since they removed the poison from the snake's poison sac before they danced with it. Benedict now viewed magic as dangerous in a new way, for it could lead to "fear neuroses" such as those that troubled Freud's "obsessional neurotics."[80]

When Benedict completed these articles, not much was left of her earlier espousal of Pater and Yeats and the search for secular ecstasy through symbols that might lead to a sense of unity with an all-encompassing universe. "Scientific advance," she wrote, "is always furthered by giving up pantheism." God was no more than the trickster figure of American Indian religions—or he was a "doddering old woman."[81] These articles in the *Encyclopaedia of the Social Sciences* suggest that reason had come to predominate in Benedict's life. She had become the rational male that becoming homosexual implied to her.

One might conclude that the monsters in *Patterns of Culture*—among them the cannibal gods of Kwakiutl, the flying witches of Dobu, and the young men of the Plains tribes engaging in self-torture—served as devices to criticize cultural behavior. And one might also see them as designed to attract readers. Benedict wrote *Patterns of Culture* in the early 1930s, at the height of the public fascination with monsters in the movies. *Dracula, Frankenstein,* and Rouben Mamoulian's *Dr. Jekyll and Mr. Hyde* were released in 1931; *The Mummy* in 1932, *King Kong* in 1933. The Depression cut movie attendance in half, but sixty million Americans still attended the movies each week. The monsters in Benedict's *Patterns of Culture* had a considerable audience from which to draw.[82]

Moreover, *Patterns of Culture* addressed the issues of race and gender raised by *King Kong*, the most successful of the many movies about explorers and tribal societies made during this era. Kong is a symbol of unbridled male lust, an evolutionary throwback. As such, he both represents extreme masculinity (the gorilla) and projects notions of violent sexuality onto black men. Benedict's project in *Patterns of Culture* was to defuse those notions, first through a reasoned argument against racism, and second, by showing a range of reactions among the men of different races she focuses on. Thus the men of Zuñi are as Apollonian as the women; in many of the Plains Indian cultures warfare is a game in which men "count coup."

And her monsters are complex. First, they aren't all men of color: a number of them are white—and American. Second, they aren't all men: there are females among them. Third, they reflect the monstrous form the modern state can take, paranoid and megalomaniac, with its repressions enforced through modern weapons of terror. Benedict had witnessed that terror during World War I; she didn't want to see it again. She mentions neither Hitler's Germany nor Mussolini's Italy in *Patterns of Culture*, but they stand as paranoid and megalomaniac states behind the small tribal societies that were her subjects.

Finally, those monsters might be read in terms of the "monstrous" attitudes of American society toward homosexuals in the 1930s. As often occurs during periods of social crisis, homophobia increased in tandem with an idealization of aggressive masculinity and an eroding position for women, who were accused of taking jobs away from men and demoted in many professions.[83] With regard to homosexuals, local statutes widened the sodomy laws, which criminalized behavior, to include vague definitions of "perverse" sexual identity. Police raided gay bars and arrested individuals for alleged homosexual offenses; in New York City vigilante groups organized campaigns against "perverts." Blackmail was common. By 1936 shock therapy and prefrontal lobotomies were being used to "cure" homosexuals. Several years later, in response to a number of serial murders sensationalized by the newspapers, a national "sex crime panic" broke out. Its premise was that homosexual men responsible for the killings roamed the country, looking for children to molest and kill.[84] In the American imagination, homosexual men had become monsters.

IN 1959, eleven years after Benedict's death, literary critic Richard Chase, who had studied with her as a graduate student at Columbia, reviewed *Patterns of Culture* for the Columbia University journal *Forum*. In his review he attacked Benedict for wanting "a too bland social order, in which masculine aggression is still." What concerned Chase more than anything else was her criticism of male leaders in the United States, including "family men," "officers of the law," and "business men."[85] In fact, she characterizes them in harsh terms as arrogant egoists, reprehensible as any man among the Dobuans out to kill his neighbor or among the Kwakiutl holding an extravagant, destructive potlatch. She states that members of these prestige groups in the United States are as psychopathic as any criminal. She compares them to the Puritan leaders of New England in the seventeenth century, whom she describes as psychoneurotics who put women to death as witches.[86]

In his review, Chase criticizes her for "toppling important male images, one by one." In so doing, he writes, she displays "only a foolish feminism, not an independent mind." Was Benedict a feminist—in terms of her day or of our own? Women are oppressed in Benedict's narrative: under capitalism, she writes, men often regard their wives as objects of display that they possess.[87] She notes that in matrilineal societies men invariably hold the positions of power, while in every culture the "adult prerogatives of men are more far-reaching" than those of women. Yet women in her narrative have authority: they aren't just victims. The matriarchs of Zuñi have power in the family and in kin groups. There are also the flying witches of Dobu, the female shamans of the Shasta tribe of Northern California, and the matrilineal inheritance patterns in Dobu, as in Zuñi. Yet the position of women isn't Benedict's major concern. Rather, as Chase implies, her focus is on men. Men in her tribal societies are aggressors; aside from the Zuñi priests, her dominant males aren't gentle. The "abnormals" in her societies possess the characteristic of gentleness. The individual who is "disoriented" among the Dobuans is the friendly individual who does not seek "to overthrow his fellows or to punish them." She doesn't discuss any abnormal individuals among the Kwakiutl, but we can assume that, as among the Dobuans, they are the gentle men without much drive to accumulate property.

In contemporary America, her main "abnormals" are the hobos, unemployed men who journeyed around the country in railroad boxcars, with little hope during the Depression of finding work. She realized that they could become "potentially vicious," but that resulted from the "asocial situation" into which they were forced. She admires them. The opposite of her "psychopathic" male patriarchs who controlled the society, they were a stream of men continually enlarged by those to whom "the accumulation of property is not a sufficient motivation." Benedict doesn't cite any source on the hobos, but a large literature existed on them, going back to the turn of the century, when Josiah Flynt did a study on homosexuality among hobos that Havelock Ellis reprinted in *Sexual Inversion*. Benedict only hints at the homosexuality in this group, noting that some of them, with an "artistic temperament," became "members of expatriated groups of petty artists."[88]

While praising difference in *Patterns of Culture* and pointing to gentle men as a cultural ideal, Benedict didn't develop a full-blown theory of patriarchal control. She had hinted at that possibility in "Mary Wollstonecraft" when she termed male control of society a "Juggernaut." Yet by 1929, in her article "The Science of Custom," she used the word "Juggernaut" to criticize institutions in general, not men in particular. In *Patterns of Culture*, a diffuse and nongendered force produces her cultural patterns. It is a "dominant drive"; it emerges as some quality comes to the fore on what Benedict calls the "arc of personality," her metaphor drawn from the arc of the rainbow to denote the variety of human and social qualities. An arc is basic to science: in geometry, it is an unbroken part of a curve or circle; in electricity, the bridge between two conductors; in astronomy, the course of a heavenly body.[89]

The predominating quality on Benedict's "arc of personality" for each society might be economic, religious, demographic, or individual. She described the process as akin to the emergence of artistic styles in Western civilization, with Gothic architecture her major example. That style of architecture began in "what was hardly more than a preference for altitude and lift." After that, some unconscious "canon of taste" drove it along.[90]

In the final analysis, Benedict's concept of patterns isn't gendered, and her feminism in the book is subtle, although real. Yet even though she was a cultural determinist, she never abandoned her belief that men and women are different by nature; she never completely gave up the masculine/feminine binary. She held that position in writing "Mary Wollstonecraft"; her Plains Indian man-woman in *Patterns of Culture* combines the genders but keeps them distinct by having "two strings in his bow." She returned to it in a speech she gave in the mid-1930s at a banquet celebrating sculptor Malvina Hoffman for her sculptures for the Field Museum in Chicago of more than one hundred men and women from Africa, Asia, Europe, the Pacific Islands, and North America. The major female sculptor in the United States in that era, Hoffman did the sculptures to document racial types for posterity.[91]

It's hard to evaluate Hoffman's sculptures, given her reliance on a concept of racial types that is considered racist today. Benedict criticized calling them "racial types," for that designation in her opinion honored a "bastard science."[92] They were, she contended, excellent depictions of people from differing cultures, nothing more. Having stated that reservation, she singled out two sculptures for praise. The first, of a Pueblo woman, Benedict described as earthy and serene. "She has never had and will never have a moment of emotional abandon, yet she has the calm of the earth in her eyes and in her firm undistorted mouth." After years of coping with her own emotionality, Benedict appreciated self-control and peace.

The second figure she praised was, surprisingly, Hoffman's Masai warrior. "Tall as his six-foot spear," he was a "column of human strength and power." "You know that the Masai are bred to warlike exploit," she continued, "and that he is sure in every muscle of his body of the honor his tribesmen accord to the able warrior in the prime of life." Yet Benedict didn't end her speech with him; instead, she turned to Hoffman's sculpture of a Zuñi man. The Zuñi are not warlike, she stated. They will defend themselves against aggressors, but once any military action is ended, their most able warriors become priests who guard the villages to ensure peace. "It is no accident," she concluded, that "Zuñi women have faces that show no lines of anxiety." For it was warriors turned into priests, soldiers turned into gentle men, who were the heroes of the Zuñi social order, in Benedict's estimation.

PATTERNS OF CULTURE provoked a storm of criticism. Attacks on Benedict's research base came first. Some critics contended that Reo Fortune's research on the Dobuans was flawed. He spent only six months there; he studied only forty individuals in three villages; no one had retested his results. Others contended that Benedict had overstated the violence in the Kwakiutl culture, which was in reality mostly a matter of performance, put on for show. Esther Goldfrank charged that Benedict's depiction of the Zuñi as noncompetitive was wrong.

Benedict answered Goldfrank through an article on the Zuñi that her student Irving Goldman wrote for *Competition and Cooperation Among Primitive Peoples* (1937), a collection of papers that Mead edited; the papers were written by colleagues and graduate students at Columbia and based on discussions at a seminar held in 1935. The seminar, funded by the Social Science Research Council, addressed issues of cooperation and competition in a world of economic depression and national aggression; it was the first study funded by an academic foundation to investigate traits in "primitive" cultures as a possible basis for change in Western societies. Mead wrote the essay on the Samoans, but Benedict shaped Goldman's essay from behind the scenes.[93]

Goldman begins by restating Benedict's conclusions on the Zuñi: the society is cooperative, nonmaterialistic, and egalitarian with regard to gender roles. Yet he also describes Zuñi society as filled with contention. Husbands and wives engage in constant disputes. There is resentment against wealthy individuals. Members of the religious societies dislike their priests. Catholics and Protestants disagree, and there are pro-white and antiwhite factions. Animosities and grudges are common; the Zuñi defame each other at the slightest pretext. Beneath their surface affability lies hostility and "continuous malicious scandal-mongering." Much of the difficulty, Goldman suggests, results from contact with the United States government and the white settlers. The resentments and personal dislikes also result from the use of shame as the chief social sanction in Zuñi society. Because shame is based on public criticism of personal behavior, individuals internalize it to engage in continual criticism of one another.[94]

"Shame" and "guilt" were popular analytic categories among scholars in the 1930s, as individuals often blamed their economic problems during the Depression on themselves, while the influence of Freud suggested looking for hidden motives beneath surface realities. "Shame" and "guilt" appear throughout the essays in Mead's volume, since the seminar participants decided that everyone writing an essay for the book should apply them to the society studied. That Goldman, overseen by Benedict, found "shame" so readily in the culture of the Zuñi indicates her willingness to incorporate her critics' point of view.

Like any new intellectual paradigm, Benedict's about the force of "patterns" in cultures stimulated other scholars to go beyond it. Sapir faulted her for overlooking the role of the individual in the social order, and his criticism resonated across the academic disciplines. It validated the life-history method, and when psychoanalysts became involved, the impulse turned into a full-scale effort to psychoanalyze cultures. The most important outgrowth of that effort was the culture-and-personality seminar at Columbia under Ralph Linton and Abram Kardiner in the late 1930s.

In fact, John Dollard's life-history approach influenced Benedict and Mead in doing their anthropology, not just in writing their 1935 memoirs. In 1936 Benedict secured a grant from the National Research Council to put together a manual for fieldworkers entitled "Handbook of Psychological Leads for Ethnological Field Workers." The completed manual focused on studying culture in terms of the individual, using Freudian and configurationist approaches to conclude that the superego is built up through a process of identification with the parents and that individuals who live in the same culture will exhibit common personality characteristics. It lists questions to ask individuals in collecting their life histories. The questions relate to child-rearing techniques, attitudes toward parents, sexual practices, life cycle choices, and participation in social institutions and cultural forms.[95]

According to Katherine Pandora, *Patterns of Culture* was a focal point for a new discourse in the behavioral sciences in the 1930s centered on the relativity of cultures. Psychologists Gordon Allport and Gardner and Lois Murphy, friends of Benedict and Mead's, led the new movement, which continued in the interdisciplinary mode of the 1920s.[96] Benedict's work played a role in converting Karen Horney from a Freudian using Freud's childhood zones and the oedipal relationship to a neo-Freudian who traced neurosis to cultural impacts. Others used Benedict's theories of social pathology to analyze modern dictatorships. Still others turned their attention to the issue of how individuals were socialized to conform to their culture's patterns; in *Escape from Freedom* Erich Fromm used the concepts of sadism and masochism to analyze the appeal of the contemporary dictators. In *Naven* (1936), Gregory Bateson noted that *Patterns of Culture* had influenced his thinking "very profoundly" as he devised a structure of dynamic social interaction between forces blocking change and those promoting change, expressed in "cumulative interaction between individuals."[97] Trained as a biologist, Bateson had an abstract yet organic way of thinking in terms of systems and interconnections and a penchant for redefinition and renaming.

Yet even before Bateson in *Naven* published his revision of Benedict's work—which Mead helped him write and which Benedict criticized in draft—Mead had registered her disagreement with *Patterns of Culture* in *Sex and Temperament*. It was part of the intellectual conversation between Benedict and Mead, loving and supportive, but with independence of judgment on both sides.

CHAPTER 11

The "Squares" on the Sepik

Sex and Temperament, *Part 1*

URING THEIR MARRIAGE, Margaret Mead and Reo Fortune often had difficulty getting along, but they reconciled their differences for a time in the village of Peri on Manus, where they went in the late fall of 1928. In Peri, Margaret studied child rearing and Reo the religion. Doing fieldwork there wasn't easy, since the houses were built on poles in a bay—and Margaret couldn't swim. Yet the villagers watched out for her, and as on Samoa she did more than she had planned: to understand child rearing she had to study adults as well as children. Margaret worked all the time and at first was critical of Reo for spending much of the day reading and smoking and then rousing himself to observe a ceremony, until she realized that his observations were brilliant. Once she devised a term for his procedure—she called it "event analysis"—she felt all right about him.[1] She didn't like Manus society, with its materialism, Puritanism, and sexual double standard, but its parallels to the United States in these matters fascinated her. She revisited it five times between 1950 and 1971, as its people adapted to Westernization.[2]

In the fall of 1929 she and Reo returned to New York, and their relations deteriorated. He felt his masculinity threatened by her sudden fame from *Coming of Age in Samoa*, and he didn't like sharing her with her many friends. Studying at Columbia to finish his Ph.D., he suspected that Ruth Benedict and Margaret were involved in a lesbian circle there.[3] That probably wasn't true; there isn't much evidence that Ruth's intimacy with the women at Columbia at this point went beyond affection, and as long as Margaret was married to Reo, Ruth refused to have sex with her.[4] By the summer of 1930, hardly a year after Margaret and Reo had come to New York, they were back in the field—this time in Nebraska to study a community of Omaha Native Americans, with Margaret focusing on the women and Reo on the men's vision quest.

During that summer Margaret became fascinated by a young Omaha man who was becoming a berdache. His behavior was so ambiguous that she couldn't tell if he was male or female. Tribal members were calling him "her"; he was turning from doing men's work to doing women's work. In tribal dances, dressed as a man, he began dancing among the men, and then, putting on jewelry, he danced among the women. Reo's homosexual friend Max Bickerton came to visit from Japan, and he thought that the young man's walk was exactly like that of the male prostitutes in Japan. Margaret thought that he didn't walk the way women walked; his movements in walking seemed to come from some fantasy of his about how women moved. The tribe's prostitute refused to have sex with him; tribal members made fun of him. When he was a young boy, she was told, several women had examined his genitalia and predicted that he would become a man-woman.[5]

She had observed homosexual individuals in the societies she had previously studied: in Samoa she had noticed a young male "pervert" and several adolescent "mixed type" females; on Manus she saw casual homosexual behavior among the boys and among a few adult homosexuals of both sexes, although she thought that a taboo against any behavior but heterosexual intercourse was mostly observed.[6] Yet she had never before seen someone in the process of crossing the sexual divide. Was her Omaha young man a "congenital invert," someone with an innate drive toward homosexuality? He might be a transvestite, someone who cross-dressed and could be heterosexual: contemporary anthropologists usually catalogued the Indian men-women as such—when they didn't view them as "passive" homosexuals (men who took the passive role in intercourse). He might be a transsexual (hermaphrodite) with indeterminate genitalia: the women may have been looking for that when they examined him as a boy.[7]

He also raised the issue of the relative influence of biology and culture in shaping sexual identity. Mead accepted Benedict's cultural determinism, but she wasn't so certain that culture was paramount when it came to gender: she felt intuitively that heredity was important, as in the differences between herself and her siblings. She also puzzled over the contrasts between Ruth and herself when Ruth said that she couldn't imagine her (Margaret) as a man—and then said that she would make a better father than mother. Wasn't she entirely feminine? By 1930 Ruth had separated from Stanley and was involved with Tom Mount, but she was considering the choice of being exclusively lesbian. Margaret wanted her to remain a mixed type. She needed to study sexual identity again, as she had in her dream-research project, this time in greater depth and with more scholarly rigor.

It was very hot in Nebraska that summer; Margaret and Reo didn't have time to learn the language; they worried that their Americanized informants weren't telling them the truth. They began bickering again. In the fall they went back to New York City, not the best place for them as a couple, with Margaret surrounded by friends and the demands of fame and the possessive Reo feeling left out. Yet they worked hard. Reo completed his monograph on the Dobuans and also his Ph.D., writing up his Manus research for his dissertation. Margaret wrote her works on the Manus and the Omaha and brought her collections at the museum up-to-date. But Margaret was determined to go back to the field; despite their conflicts in Nebraska, she and Reo did better there than in New York. They considered studying the Navajo, but Franz Boas vetoed that idea because Gladys Reichard was already in the Navajo territory.[8] They decided to return to New Guinea.

In later writings, Mead described this second round of New Guinea research as though she knew what she was going to do from the start. Drafts of *Blackberry Winter* and the text of *Sex and Temperament*, however, reveal some confusion.[9] She knew that she wanted to study the sex roles of men as well as of women. She thought that she had to study cultures that separated masculine from feminine, although at this point she thought that most societies operated in terms of that binary, as she stated in *Sex and Temperament:* "I shared the general belief of our society that there was a natural sex-temperament which could at the most only be distorted or diverted from normal expression." She had considered even mixed types, she wrote, to be composed of men with feminine temperaments and women with masculine ones.[10] To do a proper study, she thought that she should take heredity into account, although neither she nor Reo knew any biology.[11] Then she decided that before addressing biological issues she should determine how sex differences functioned culturally; that's what William Fielding Ogburn had stressed in his class at Barnard—to look for cultural explanations before biological ones.

From today's perspective, Mead's acceptance of an absolute distinction between masculine and feminine seems overdrawn, especially given the work of contemporary psychologists like Beatrice Hinkle and the existence of the bisexual chic of the 1920s. Yet belief in the "mannish lesbian" was strong: Radclyffe Hall's *Well of Loneliness* had fixed the figure in the popular imagination; Freud had asserted that in homosexual women "bodily and mental traits belonging to the opposite sex are apt to coincide."[12] The major analysis of homosexuality by an anthropologist was Edward Westermarck's *Origin and Development of the Moral Ideas.* After summarizing the ethnographic accounts of homosexuality worldwide, Westermarck concluded that "all shades of variation" existed between "inversion" and "normal sexuality" but that most homosexuals were "inverts."[13] The eminent Harvard psychologist William McDougall wrote that although the precise correlation between inversion and same-sex love was uncertain, it did exist. In *The Dominant Sex,* a popular feminist work of the 1920s, Mathilde and Mathias Vaerting contended that in societies that women controlled—like the Amazon ones—women became masculine in behavior. Recent analysts of the masculine/feminine binary in the 1930s conclude that sexologists and psychologists remained convinced of its existence.[14] In *Patterns of Culture* Benedict used the word "homosexual" interchangeably with "invert."[15]

When Margaret and Reo left New York for New Guinea this second time, they were bound for the main island and for the Sepik River, its chief waterway. Numerous villages were located on its banks and tributaries within a hundred-mile radius, with differing languages and cultures. There were, however, some similarities, such as ceremonial houses for special men's activities, in which the men made masks and ritual flutes and welcomed the mythical Tamberan beast, a symbol of male power that they fantasized came to their villages and from which women hid, fearing it although they never saw it. In such societies, gender roles seemed clear-cut. And German anthropologists had found "congenital" inverts in New Guinea, as well as tribes in which they reported that the young men lived in the men's houses and practiced homosexuality before they married.[16]

It was daring to go to the Sepik, since the colonial authorities had only recently ended head-hunting in the region. Caroline Tennant Kelly, an Australian friend of Reo's who became close to Margaret, depicted her on the Sepik as an adventurer challenging men: "How dare you, Margaret, take away the one remaining river where the men can boast of their deeds with headhunters and the like and hold drawing rooms spellbound and then you go tripping up and down as if it was Sydney harbor."[17] Yet that experience on the Sepik enabled Mead to make a conceptual breakthrough about gender and sexuality—and about her own identity. Also crucial was her chance meeting with Gregory Bateson, a young English anthropologist trained at Cambridge whom Reo had known there. He was already on the Sepik, studying a tribe with magnificent triangular men's houses—one in which the men carved masks with long phallic noses and participated in a ritual in which men dressed like women and women like men.

AT FIRST EVERYTHING in New Guinea went wrong. When Reo and Margaret reached the coast, Margaret sprained her ankle. Then the native bearers that Reo had bullied into carrying their goods—and Margaret—across the mountains to the interior deserted them on the side of a mountain, among a small, scattered tribe. Reo and Margaret decided to stay and study that tribe, whom they called the Arapesh, after the native word for "human being." They remained for eight months, and Margaret grew to like the Arapesh a lot. She found them gentle and maternal, with a focus on growing things—yams, young wives, and babies. Reo often went off with the men to the coast on trading missions, and the women came and sat with her, singing softly "in the chilly evening." They treated her as kin and expected her to protect them from sorcerers. Living with them, she became "as soft and responsive as the people themselves."[18]

The Arapesh defined sex as a gentle force, with both men and women passive in behavior. In contrast to Western societies, she concluded, men weren't identified as "spontaneously sexual"; the ideal male was the opposite of the Western ideal—which Mead defined as violent and domineering under an athletic body and a handsome face. And the Arapesh women were so passive in the sex act that most reported that they didn't have orgasms when Mead described the physical response to them: their experience of sex involved a "diffused warmth and ease."[19] In terms of Mead's research intentions, however, the Arapesh didn't define gender in terms of a masculine/feminine binary; thus they didn't fit into her research design. She had to find another tribe.

Leaving the Arapesh, she and Reo crossed the mountains and came to the Sepik River and to a tribe they decided to study called the Mundugumor, today called the Biwat. In this tribe, as among the Arapesh, the men and women behaved in a similar manner, but they were aggressive and narcissistic, not maternal and gentle. They had an active sex life, but they didn't like raising children. They had a "rope" system of kinship that pitted fathers against sons and mothers against daughters. They practiced infanticide and incest; Margaret saw dead newborn infants floating in the river, and she saw fathers sleeping with daughters in large rush-plaited, covered baskets, designed for protection against the Sepik's fierce mosquitos.[20] After three months with the Mundugumor, Margaret had to leave.

In *Blackberry Winter* and its drafts Mead portrayed Fortune as difficult during the year they spent in these two tribal societies. Among the Arapesh he sometimes became so frustrated by their passivity, she wrote, that he threatened them physically and she would have to intervene between them and his "lifted hand."[21] He went to the coast with trading parties of Arapesh men. Left alone on the mountain, cold and damp, she learned in a letter from Ruth Benedict that the American anthropologists had turned down a huge grant from the Rockefeller Foundation to study tribal societies worldwide because Radcliffe-Brown was slated to head the project. Margaret became seriously depressed. Would tribal societies be documented before they disappeared? Would her life continue to be a round of coping with Reo and studying tribal societies?

She had what seems like a midlife crisis, just as Ruth did in these years, although Margaret was only thirty-one. Then she lifted her depression by deciding that she had achieved so much that she didn't have to be responsible to anyone or anything—her parents, Boas, or anthropology (one assumes she also included Reo and Ruth). She could now do what she wanted. It was a declaration of independence that she would refer to frequently in the years ahead; its effect in the next year or so seems to have been to justify her involvement with Gregory Bateson—and to make her more independent in dealing with Ruth.

In *Blackberry Winter* Margaret depicted Reo's behavior as continuing to be hostile when they reached the Mundugumor. He identified with the aggressive natives, made a mistake in determining their kinship relations, and didn't treat her well. Hostile behavior on Reo's part undoubtedly occurred, but he had his own reasons for it: Margaret had more money than he; she had taken over their research agenda. She refused to let him accept a position at the University of Sydney he was offered, and she persuaded him that her version of the Arapesh as gentle and maternal was the correct one, even though the men in the trading parties told him about gender conflicts and violent behavior in their society.[22] It's no wonder that this proud, ambitious man, who liked submission in women, became sullen and difficult—or that Margaret wrote to Ruth soon after they left the Mundugumor complaining again about a bleak future, doing endless fieldwork with Reo and being criticized by the male Boasians. She wanted to continue "scheming or planning or intriguing for fame." In her reply Ruth counseled her to bide her time and wait for the "eight days in a life of eighty years" in which "aggressively pushing one's interests could get one somewhere."[23]

Yet Margaret's letters to Ruth also contain a different narrative, one in which her marriage improved once she and Reo returned to the field. Away from New York, Reo felt more self-confident, more like a successful anthropologist than a hanger-on to the famous Mead. Noting her satisfaction with him, Margaret wrote to Ruth that she had turned thirty and Reo was approaching that age and that they both had grown up.[24] In this version of their relationship, they both dislike the Mundugumor. They leave because they can't get any more information about the original culture, which is what they were trying to uncover. As Boasians they were looking for the "ethnographic present," but as was the case with many of these Sepik societies, colonial intervention had undermined the culture and demoralized its people, making knowledge of rituals and traditional behaviors hard to retrieve.

In letters to Ruth, Margaret is excited about Reo's plans to write a book on the Mundugumor focusing on incest as the organizing principle of the society. She and Reo decide to have a baby, based on a shared negative reaction to the antimaternal attitude of the Mundugumor, not just on Margaret's independent impulse—which is how she would describe the decision in *Blackberry Winter*. In response to the news of the decision for conception, Ruth wrote: "I laughed at your true anthropologists' way of arriving at the momentous decision: by way of a cultural trait."[25] During the next months Margaret must have become pregnant, for she had a miscarriage the next April.

Thus far, male and female behavior didn't differ in the two societies she had observed. And in contrast to other anthropologists earlier in New Guinea, she hadn't seen any homosexuals, although she noticed that the passive Arapesh males were prey to homosexual seduction and rape when they came in contact with a male member of another tribe.[26] Nor did she observe the homosexual behavior among the Arapesh boys that she had seen among the Samoan and Manus boys, even though they engaged in much "giggling and puppyishness."[27] She didn't record any observations of lesbian behavior among the Arapesh and the Mundugumor; one assumes that she didn't see any such behavior. These observations with regard to homosexuality would later become important in her conclusions about sexuality in New Guinea.

Margaret still thought that she had to study a society with differing sex roles. So she and Reo had to find another Sepik society. They contacted Gregory Bateson, although they hesitated to encroach on his territory. He was willing to help them, since he couldn't understand the Iatmul, the tribe he was studying, and Mead and Fortune were senior anthropologists with books to their credit, while he had published very little. They might be able to help him. He would lead them to the Tchambuli (now called the Chambri), a small tribe resembling the larger and more powerful Iatmul, who were situated on adjacent territory. Meantime, Christmas was approaching. Mead and Fortune decided to go to a celebration at Ambunti, the local government station on the river. Hitching a ride on a government launch, they stopped by Gregory's village to pick him up.

Margaret wasn't expecting much from Gregory; the rumor on the Sepik was that he was disorganized and had Englishwomen with him, and Margaret hadn't liked the one article he had published on the Iatmul.[28] Yet her apprehensions vanished the minute she met him. When she and Reo entered his house to greet him, his first words to her were that she looked tired. Then he offered her a chair. She was swept away. She wrote to Benedict that when she met Gregory her marriage tumbled down around her like a "house of cards."[29] Who was Gregory Bateson? Why did he have this effect on her?

IN THE FIRST PLACE, Gregory came from a distinguished family of freethinkers and women's rights advocates, one connected to the intellectual aristocracy of England, members of the group of families including Darwins and Huxleys who had been Quakers and businessmen in the early nineteenth century and who by late century held positions of authority at Oxford and Cambridge and in the government bureaucracy.[30] His father, William Bateson, was a famous geneticist associated with Cambridge University who had, in fact, coined the word "genetics." Gregory was named after Gregor Mendel, who discovered variety in genetic inheritance. Gregory's mother, Beatrice Durham, had been a renowned beauty and one of seven sisters known for their independence. None of the other sisters married; Gregory called his aunt Edith Durham, the Balkan explorer, a "crazy old witch" who tyrannized them.[31] Gregory attended Charterhouse, an elite public school, and then Cambridge University.

Where Reo was unsophisticated, with a rough masculinity, Gregory could act like an aristocrat. He was tall (six feet five inches in height) and thin, but he was gentle, without apparent aggressiveness and with lots of British charm. He was sensitive to people's moods; Margaret called his personality "as sweet as the kingdom of heaven."[32] That sensitivity could translate into sexual magnetism; women fell in love with him after a conversation. In letters he wrote to Margaret after she returned to the United States and he was in England, he described several such episodes in detail. For his part, Gregory seems to have been drawn to women who were unhappily married.

Moreover, he held free-love views. He had adopted them at Cambridge when he came under the influence of Noel Teulon Porter, who ran a local hostelry called the Half Moon. The wayward son of a Manchester industrialist, Porter spent much of his youth working as a gamekeeper and wagon driver on gentlemen's estates, while he studied biology and sexology on his own. He took up sexology, he stated in his autobiography, when a lesbian couple who were farm workers seduced him for a threesome. With a rough-hewn brilliance, an irresistible manner, and extraordinary nerve, Porter persuaded Cambridge professors to accept him as something of an equal, while he participated in birth control organizations in London and became friends with Margaret Sanger, Havelock Ellis, and Edward Carpenter. According to Porter, he read the proofs for Carpenter's *Love's Coming of Age* and cut out a lot of material that would shock middle-class readers.[33]

Wearing sandals and corduroy breeches, with a pronounced limp from a childhood accident—or brawl—Porter looked like a combination roughneck and Biblical prophet. His gift for conversation and his knowledge about sex attracted Cambridge undergraduates to him for information about birth control and counseling about sexuality. Anthropologists like Bronislaw Malinowski frequented the Half Moon; Porter could talk a good intellectual line. He called for combining sexology, anthropology, biology, and botany into a discipline he called "ecology."

What went on at the Half Moon besides tea and sympathy remains obscure. The pub was off-limits to the women students at Newnham and Girton Colleges, and Porter describes himself in his autobiography as the leading expert on female homosexuality in Europe—without explaining what that meant. Calling himself heterosexual in a lecture he gave on homosexuality, he remarked that everyone has spells of homosexuality.[34] He stated that he knew the eminent German sexologist Magnus Hirschfeld, whom he didn't like, and Hirschfeld's lover Peter, whom he did. He claimed that passive homosexuals like Peter often converted active lesbians to heterosexuality. Bateson described Porter to Mead as charming and poised, and as so passive in their relationship that Bateson had to be the "excitable" one. He also described Porter as detesting all aggressive men—who disliked him in return.[35]

Bateson hinted in letters to Mead that he and Porter had been lovers; he wrote to Benedict that his relationship with Porter was remarkably similar to hers with Mead.[36] In a letter to "Johnny" in 1930, Gregory referred to "Johnny," "Steve," and himself as a "trinity" at the Half Moon. "Finally," he continued, "fruit, much beautiful fruit has been received."[37] Although "fruit" was slang for homosexuals by 1930, Johnny and Steve were females. Steve was probably Elizabeth Stevenson, whom Gregory had met through a friend at Cambridge and who was known as Steve. Johnny was Joan Bee, a young ward of Porter's; Porter stated that Margaret Sanger wrote to him that she had never seen anyone attract so many individuals of all kinds as Johnny and that she had never expected that a man and a woman could have a relationship like the one he had with Johnny. What that relationship involved isn't revealed. Porter didn't marry Johnny, although he later married a woman called "Muss," whom Gregory described to Margaret as fey.[38]

Gregory seems to have been one of the undergraduates who went to Porter for counseling. For he fell into troubling depressions; there had been problems in his childhood family. His father, large and overbearing, had unconsummated affairs with students from Newnham and Girton. His parents ignored Gregory, while doting on his two older brothers. At the age of fourteen he reached his full height, and he vowed to repress his feelings, for he feared that, given his size, if he became angry with anyone he might kill them. Then his two older brothers died tragically: his eldest brother was killed as a soldier in World War I; his second brother committed suicide under the statue of Eros in Picadilly Circus, because of unrequited love. After that, Gregory's mother smothered him with attention.[39]

Moreover, there were problems at Charterhouse. It had a system of fagging, under which younger boys acted as servants to older ones. Fagging, as the term implies, could also involve active/passive homosexuality, with older boys initiating younger ones. Geoffrey Gorer, an English writer, mostly homosexual, who was later a close friend of Margaret Mead's, attended Charterhouse about the same time as Gregory Bateson. In an unpublished, fictionalized autobiography, he suggested that his sexual orientation was related to the fagging at the school. Gregory distanced himself from the system, writing that the boys at the school were divided into the intellectuals and the athletes, who oversaw the fags. One assumes he was an intellectual. How the two groups interacted he didn't say.[40]

Gregory was still grieving over his family tragedies when he entered Cambridge. He began studying biology there, but he transferred to anthropology after he met A. C. Haddon by accident on a train and learned that Haddon had also originally studied biology and then had switched to anthropology when he went to the islands of the Torres Straits to study their biology and found the natives more interesting— and their culture in danger of disappearing under the impact of Westernization. Haddon suggested to him that he could study one of the tribes on the Sepik River that used phallic masks and had large men's ceremonial houses.[41] That sort of adventure intrigued Gregory. Yet, lacking a sure sense of self, he found Noel Porter and became "a lame duck in Noel's collection."[42]

Gregory was intellectually gifted, but he had problems with motivation. He was so disorganized that he sometimes wore mismatched socks and clothes with holes: Reo called him "aggressively untidy," and so did Noel Porter.[43] Margaret was organized and fast, with a gift for motivating others. Gregory was dazzled by her mind and her intensity, and he was attracted, like so many others, to her neediness, her small size, and her sweetness. The two held similar free-love beliefs. It isn't surprising that they fell in love.

Reo didn't give Margaret up easily. He didn't practice free love; Margaret probably hadn't told him fully about her beliefs, which she had mostly put on hold when she married him.[44] And Reo and Gregory were attracted to each other; during their time among the Tchambuli, they played endless games of chess. "Thank god for chess," Margaret

wrote Ruth.[45] Gregory was a cosmopolitan Cambridge graduate and
Reo a provincial from New Zealand whom his brother described as
lost in Mead's sophisticated world.[46] That naivete of Reo's needs to be
kept in mind in examining what happened in Tchambuli—as well as his
jealousy of Gregory because the anthropologists at Cambridge had
sent Gregory to study a magnificent tribe on the Sepik and Reo had to
go off to Australia to find Radcliffe-Brown and the tiny Dobu tribe.[47]
There is also the fact that Gregory, two years younger than Margaret,
regarded her as more experienced than he in anthropology—and in the
ways of the world.

AFTER MARGARET AND REO picked Gregory up at his camp on the
Sepik, they continued on to Ambunti. The expected Christmas celebration, however, turned into a melee. Seventeen men were there, and
they spent three days, on and off, drinking and fighting. Margaret and
Gregory had to restrain Reo from joining in the fighting: he was furious with a recruiter for the colonial copra plantations in New Guinea
who was there and who was known for his especially harsh treatment
of the adolescent males he signed up for the work. In between, they
discussed anthropology and played bridge. Several days later they
climbed a mountain to investigate a tribe for Margaret and Reo possibly to study. On the way back down they were hot and sweaty, and
Gregory suggested that they bathe nude in a stream. Reo was shocked,
but Margaret wasn't: nudity was part of free-love practice. Shortly
thereafter, Margaret and Gregory formally fell in love when they sat
across a table talking for fifteen minutes and established a spiritual
connection. They called that experience the "episode of the second
goats."[48]

Margaret's Tchambuli, like Gregory's Iatmul, had large men's
houses and a rich ceremonial life—and differing gender roles. The setting was gorgeous: the society was located beside a lake that was
gleaming ebony in color (there was dark vegetable matter in it). Purple
lotuses and large pink and white water lilies floated in the lake, and
white osprey and blue heron fed from it. The mountains where the
Arapesh lived formed a distant backdrop; the Arapesh, Mundugumor,
and Tchambuli societies were only a hundred miles distant from each
other. Yet there were problems in Tchambuli. Malaria was rife on the
Sepik, and Margaret, Reo, and Gregory all came down with it. The illness can be controlled with quinine, but its high fever can cause hallu-

cinations. Moreover, neither the attraction between Margaret and Gregory nor Reo's suspicions of it would go away. And Margaret wasn't the only woman in Gregory's life. Two other women had been present during his time on the Sepik. The first was Elizabeth Brown, known as Bett. The second was Elizabeth Stevenson Cubhold, known as Steve, of Gregory's Half Moon days.

Bett was an anthropology student whom Gregory had met at Malinowski's graduate seminar at the London School of Economics. In 1929 she left her husband to run off to New Guinea with Gregory; three years later she left him to marry a riverboat captain who took cargo and passengers up and down the Sepik. She explained to Gregory that her sailor was masculine and adventurous, a gypsy, like herself, and she doubted that Gregory would ever give Steve up.[49] As for Steve, she was like Bett an adventurer. Young and seductive, she had a toughness that is apparent in her letters. Gregory described her as an "odd sort of soft fey, with a brickiness in it"; she was feminine, with a masculine directness. A friend of Gregory's asserted: "I have never heard of a life too tough for her."[50]

Once she learned about Steve, Margaret decided to intervene, not only because of her feelings about Gregory but also because Steve's dramatics kept him from working. In her letters to Ruth, Margaret constructed a number of Steves: she was a Leone Newton "in capacity for sex and violence"; then she was a combination of Leone and Margaret's sister Elizabeth, a gentle artist. Finally, she was a child who had never grown up and who needed mothering. "All of her experiences of sex have been fiascos and a lot of work needs to be done to straighten her out," Margaret wrote.[51] By this point, Steve sounds like Ruth's childish Natalie Raymond. In years ahead Margaret cast her as a Parisian fey, deft and elegant—like the older lesbian in Bourdet's *The Captive*, whom neither men nor women can resist.

Steve, who eventually returned to England, remained in Margaret's and Gregory's lives for years. She represented youth and irresponsibility to Gregory, and he couldn't entirely give her up. She wrote plays that weren't produced and stories that weren't published, married and divorced with panache, had both male and female lovers. Her letters, whether to Gregory or to Margaret, are tough, sly, and filled with tales of interesting complications and schemes, such as becoming a stewardess on a ship so that she could cross the Atlantic to see Margaret whenever she wanted.[52] On Margaret's part, her sympathy toward Steve in her letters to Ruth from New Guinea, the way she took Steve over, had much to do with her need to convince Ruth that she was a Martha who wasn't capricious, that she was a mature adult who could handle the situation. Ruth's letters to Margaret during this period mainly concern Natalie Raymond: Mead's drama on the Sepik didn't upset her.

Either Bett or Steve may have been at Ambunti during the Christmas celebration. In a letter to her family and friends, Margaret describes, but does not name, a woman who was there, "an almost ambiguous female with a rattrap mouth, mascara eyes, and a wholly suspicious and deadly restraint of manner." She had hitched a ride to Ambunti. Lone women didn't wander down the Sepik—given its crocodiles, male adventurers, and native people who had only recently given up head-hunting. In *Blackberry Winter* Margaret described the still anonymous woman differently, as having "just been released from prison for having killed her baby."[53] Letters to Gregory from Bett and Steve suggest that one of the women had an abortion the summer before. He and Steve had broken up that fall, but they always got back together, and it would have been just like her to show up in Ambunti. And Bett was still fond of Gregory. At some point she was with them in Tchambuli: in *Sex and Temperament*, Mead thanks "Mr. and Mrs. MacKenzie of the *Lady Betty*" for bringing supplies to them when they were there. Mrs. MacKenzie was Bett.[54]

THE THIRD ACT in Mead's drama on the Sepik, the time with Reo and Gregory in Tchambuli after the months with the Arapesh and the Mundugumor and the interlude in Ambunti, began soon after Margaret and Reo had settled in Tchambuli and Gregory began coming to their camp for company. To pass the time, they played rhyming games and bridge; Gregory and Reo played chess. They discussed themselves and their work, and that discussion became a kind of game. Ruth Benedict had sent Margaret a draft of *Patterns of Culture*, and it became central to their discussions. They decided that Benedict hadn't adequately explained the origin of deviants, nor why they would be different in differing cultures. Her rejection of biology didn't convince them. According to Margaret, Gregory thought like a biologist, "moving easily from one science to another, making analogies, now from physics, now from geology."[55] Gregory and Margaret confessed that they felt themselves deviants in their cultures; they were also certain that most societies contained many more deviants than the small number for which Benedict allowed, given her belief in the power of social control.[56]

Focusing on Ruth's "arc of personality" and on Margaret's interest in gender, they located their own personalities on an arc, with masculinity (M) and femininity (F) at either end.[57] They discussed one another in depth, sharing the stories of their lives, their friendships, their understanding of their own personalities. They concluded that Margaret and Gregory were sensitive and maternal and that Reo was masculine and possessive. Given Margaret's later reputation for aggressive behavior, the willingness of these men to accept her version of herself as feminine and caring indicates the strength of her sweet, dependent side. Yet if "feminine" and "masculine" were binary categories dividing females and males, Margaret and Gregory should be different, not similar. They roamed over history to check the standard division and quickly realized that it didn't work with figures like Jesus Christ, who was both masculine and feminine.[58] As Margaret wrote Ruth toward the end of their stay in Tchambuli, they were combining fieldwork with "applied biography."[59]

Then they placed the societies they were studying in New Guinea on the arc, and in those societies, they realized, the standard division also didn't work. Both sexes were feminine among the Arapesh and masculine among the Mundugumor, while in Tchambuli the women were masculine and the men feminine. Among Gregory's Iatmul the opposite was the case: the women were feminine and the men masculine.

Margaret had already identified herself with the gentle Arapesh— and Reo with the harsh Mundugumor. She now realized that the solution to the puzzle of gender had been there during all her time in New Guinea. It was simple: not all societies function according to the standard masculine/feminine division of the West; her basic assumption had been wrong. If that was the case, then categories different from "masculine" and "feminine" had to apply: males and females must be constructed by qualities like aggression or gentleness that cross over gender and then are shaped by societies into specific roles. "I came to New Guinea to find sex differences," she wrote Ruth, "but I found temperamental differences, innate, individual, irrespective of sex."[60] She had taken William Ogburn's advice to find cultural explanations for behavior before biological ones to an extreme: under Gregory's influence, she had constructed a theory of genetic influence from cultural information.

Yet they didn't stop with individual identity; they wanted to construct a system that could also explain the societies they were studying. Both Mead and Bateson were scientists, influenced by the basic drive of Western science toward classification. But Benedict's classifications in *Patterns of Culture* were too vague and simple for them; they wanted to devise a more complex and more precise grid than her categories that applied to only a few cultures; they wanted one that could be applied to all societies. While Mead was still among the Mundugumor, Benedict wrote her that "you write about the numbers of classifications you might get by going through the cultures of the world and how helpless we are without stable classifications the psychologists ought to have provided us with." Benedict disagreed. She replied that she reacted to Mead's position just as she did to a novelist using Freudian categories to describe his characters. Doing that simply resulted in his not looking at "the real person he is describing."[61]

But Mead wouldn't be deterred from her universalizing project. Now Gregory remembered that Gregor Mendel had reported his genetic experiments in multiples of four; Margaret recalled that Jung's theory of psychological types contained four modes of emotional behavior.[62] Reading cultures in terms of Benedict's notion of cultures as "personality writ large," they roamed widely, constructing a fourfold division based on the four societies they were studying and other tribal cultures they knew, like the Samoans and the Maori in Reo's New Zealand. At the same time they decided that there were a limited number of temperamental types—manifested in both individuals and societies—each with its own set of inherited behavioral traits.[63] The trick now was to identify the traits.

They had started with M and F; needing four types they came up with two more: "Turk" and "fey." The first denoted a powerful manager; the second someone gentle, removed from reality, sometimes theatrical. They based these categories on the ballet impresario Sergey Diaghilev, of the Ballets Russes, famed for his aggressive domination of his company, and his renowned protégé—and reputed lover—Vaslav Nijinsky, who combined athletic, masculine leaps with sensual and feminized movements to become a major matinee idol. Nijinsky was the Rudolf Nureyev of his day, and Gregory identified with him. Gregory also found the Nijinsky-Diaghilev combination useful in understanding the Iatmul, who seemed to him both effeminate and highly masculine—and sometimes theatrical.[64]

They derived the word "fey" from the Scottish word for fairy.

"Fairy" and "fey" were contemporary terms for homosexuals, but in their system "feys" weren't necessarily homosexual. Nijinsky, for example, married and had children, although Margaret later seemed jubilant in reporting to Gregory in a letter that the newspapers had declared him a homosexual, his wife a mannish lesbian, and their marriage a cover.[65] Diaghilev and Nijinsky were Russians, not Turks, but the Turks, with their harems, boy prostitutes, and conquests in the Near East, were a symbol of phallic potency to the West. In one of her circular letters to her family and close friends, Mead described the polygamous households of the Mundugumor society as efficient labor pools different from the Middle Eastern "harems," which satisfied a "Turklike lust."[66]

As they discussed these matters in the close quarters of the mosquito hut, it was inevitable that Gregory and Margaret's attraction to each other would cause problems, given Reo's capacity for jealousy and the fact that they were carrying on a love affair—even if it was sexually innocent—under his very eyes. When Gregory was with the Iatmul, whose villages were several hours away, he and Margaret corresponded through notes they sent via native couriers. In one note Gregory told Margaret that he considered the "episode of the second goats" to be the consummation of their relationship and that they didn't need to have sex after that.[67] Margaret seems to have taken that decision in stride, for in a note to Gregory she suggested that they meet in dreams, in a version of her ritual with her high school sweetheart. "Do you know the formula from *Peter Ibbetson?*" she asked him. "If you cross your hands behind your head and never stop dreaming of where you want to be, when you go to sleep you'll be there." Following that formula, she told him, she had long, novelistic dreams about the two of them.[68]

Then Reo intercepted the note from Gregory to Margaret about the "episode of the second goats." He was furious. Margaret calmed Reo down by having Gregory read Reo's *Sorcerers of Dobu* and praise him for it, while she had Reo read the notes Gregory had written to her and told him that she was following the principle that as love partners they should extend their bond to all their intimate friends—and those friends now included Gregory. She reported to Gregory that at first the idea confused Reo, for it suggested "a possible experience so alien to him, he'd never have dreamt it possible." Once he understood it, however, he liked it. He proceeded to write a letter to Luther Cressmen expressing love for Luther's relationship with Margaret.[69] If

Luther received the letter he must have been baffled, since after Margaret and he divorced they didn't communicate.

Yet she herself was confused. Their living situation was awful, with no privacy, not even a lock on the bathroom door. There was malaria, mosquitos, bugs. The mosquito hut was tiny—eight by eight feet square—with two men each over six feet tall crowding into it. Reo was furious if she and Gregory were alone together. And Margaret didn't give up on Reo. When Gregory was away with the Iatmul, they had wonderful conversations. By March she wrote Ruth that she was annoyed with herself. "My feeling for him [Gregory] has been composed of a 14-year-old's delight with a large amount of childish play in it." She analyzed herself in familiar terms: "I've little power to confine my love to one person or to stave off making him miserable." She also asserted that she had a strong maternal feeling for Gregory and a tendency "to weave my excitement about him into a religious-romantic picture of the stained glass window variety." In this version of her relationship with Gregory, she described him as akin to Ruth's Tom Mount.[70]

She used Ruth's personality as a medium for understanding the situation. She saw Reo as an introvert similar to Ruth. His every sensation had a violent, eidetic quality. Ruth wasn't quite that way, but her pain had compelled Margaret to stay with her and Reo's pain was having the same effect. And Gregory could become cold, just like Ruth. He sometimes retreated into an "ivory tower" more inaccessible than hers. They called these retreats his "Bengali fits"—a name that seems to refer to Rabindranath Tagore, the mystical Bengali poet, a favorite of both of theirs. And like Ruth, Gregory could fly off the handle, suddenly becoming domineering.[71] But he was also distressed by their situation in Tchambuli, for he was attracted to Reo—and Reo to him—and he felt guilty about breaking up Margaret's marriage. And so Margaret wavered between the two of them, pregnant with Reo's child and guilty about leaving her marriage.

Some combination of Margaret's and Gregory's guilt and Reo's anger prompted them to work out a theory of sexuality as well as of temperament. They decided that marriages between M (masculine) and F (feminine) were the best sort because they were based on the magnetism of difference, while those between Fs wouldn't work because they were too much like relationships between brothers and sisters. Applying these definitions to themselves, Margaret and Gregory gave up their romance—since they both were F—and she and Reo reconciled, since Reo was M. Margaret wrote to Ruth that she and Reo were happier than they had ever been. "It doesn't mean we are less different," she wrote, "but now we can symbolize that difference completely, where before it was a source of heat and separation—as well as of excitement."[72] She still felt sexually drawn to Reo and still hoped that they could make their marriage work. She also could now spend time alone with Gregory, since Reo wasn't suspicious of them any longer.

In March, Margaret wrote her "Summary Statement of the Problem of Personality and Culture," outlining their thoughts about gender. The document is difficult to describe, for it's somewhat incoherent, as though she was on a high—perhaps from malaria, or from the intensity of their interactions, away from regular society. F and M, caring maternal and possessive paternal, are the categories for all human beings, according to the document, and each category contains an equal number of males and females. "Turks" and "feys" result from crossing Ms and Fs. The document speculates about correlations of the types with medical conditions, results of twin studies, cultural taboos, psychoanalytic categories like "anal" and "oral," human characteristics like left-handedness, and the smell of vaginal secretions and semen producing affinities between individuals. As usual, Mead's comprehensive intellect was at work.

"Male" and "female" as reproductive categories are realities in every society, the document asserts, as are differing physiological attributes: height, facial features, and body frame. The document notes that these physiological attributes can be grouped into regularities called "constitutional types." Noting the Boasian belief that race passes through family lines, not nations, the document suggests that gender, like race, is rooted in the biology of reproduction, and that it can be expressed through varying combinations.

The "Summary Statement" also contains speculation about behavior in the sex act. Because F individuals are "polymorphous perverse," they don't have much specific sex. "Specific sex," according to the document, means that both partners are active in the sex act, with both having an orgasm: the woman's can be clitoral, not vaginal. Although "specific sex" isn't a necessity for F individuals, if they intend to marry they must reproduce on a smaller scale the natural magnetism between M and F.

At some point after Margaret wrote the "Summary Statement," they abandoned M and F to move to the four directions of the compass, North, South, East, and West, and to the attributes identified with them: the quietist East, with its contemplative religions; the innovative and expansive West; the cold, phallic, and domineering North; the South hot, filled with all kinds of sexualities.[73] Their categories M and F now became North and South. They retained Turk and fey, but they didn't use East and West much at this point. They identified Margaret and Gregory as Southern and Reo as Northern. Speculating about parents, friends, siblings, and former lovers, they catalogued Steve and Ruth Benedict as Northern and Marie Eichelberger and Edward Sapir as Turks. That was Reo's idea, according to Margaret, because he was jealous of them. They called their system the "squares" or the "zones"; Margaret called their categories "soul rakings."[74]

The theory of the "squares" was conceived in the hothouse atmosphere of a mosquito hut next to a lake black as ebony, with the air in the hut charged with sexual electricity. The theory itself always remained something of a game. It was akin to the chess and bridge that they played. Chess is played on squares; bridge partners are North, South, East, and West. But neither their scheme nor the way they devised it should be dismissed as foolish. Playing games to arrive at innovative scientific theories has been characteristic of Western scientists since the beginning of the twentieth century. Games of chance led to probability theory, and John von Neumann recast economics in terms of poker and chess. Nobel laureate John Nash, the schizophrenic mathematician portrayed in the movie *A Beautiful Mind*, played games and invented new ones as a prelude to his scientific discoveries.[75]

To accommodate everyone they knew, they mixed up their categories. An individual could be Northwest or Southeast, or even temporarily take on the characteristics of a different square. One could, for example, "go fey." They devised subcategories: to characterize Margaret's energy and drive and her drama they devised the term "exhibitor"; for Gregory's passivity they came up with "inhibitor." They analyzed their categories in terms of "sadism" and "masochism"; Margaret contended that she became domineering only when she faced someone who was masochistic. In October, back in New York, she identified Léonie and Ruth as "tetraploids"—people in whose souls the entire human tragedy is played out—although she soon dropped this category. Gregory later wrote Reo that Margaret's ideas could sometimes seem like "wild geese flying in the wind."[76]

By the time they left Tchambuli, they had devised a complex

scheme for both individuals and cultures, one that went beyond Bene-dict's theory of overriding "patterns" and dissenting "deviants." In 1941 Mead described their scheme to a journal editor, when she and Bateson still intended to write a book about it, before they became estranged. "It does seem possible," she explained, "to identify a series of temperaments which express themselves differently in different cul-tural settings but which seem to retain a systematic relationship to each other and a systematic relationship to the dominant emphasis of the culture." Every culture, she continued, has a differing impact on temperament, which it stylizes in terms of gestures and movements, although it can't change the original physical types.[77] Thus human appearance is rooted in biology but shaped by culture. Still, it's possi-ble to construct a general theory of their interrelationships that includes all cultures and all physical types. Unfortunately, Mead never completely worked out the theory. When she and Bateson separated in the late 1940s, she largely gave it up as a scholarly project.

THROUGH PLAYING THE GAME of personality, Margaret reached a radical conclusion: human nature is composed of emotional qualities, like aggression or caring, that don't necessarily coincide with mascu-line and feminine. Moreover, if masculine and feminine don't exist, then inversion—and homosexuality as an orientation—doesn't exist, except in the case of "congenital inverts." She hadn't seen anyone with a homosexual orientation among either the Arapesh or the Mundugu-mor, while the Tchambuli and the Iatmul interdicted it so successfully that no one took it up, although there was homosexual symbolism in ceremonies and in everyday life—which indicated, she later decided, that it once had existed but didn't any longer.[78] In March 1933, Margaret wrote a letter to Ruth challenging Ruth's new homosexual orientation. The letter expressed Margaret's new conviction that an individual's sexual response is geared to her or his partner and to the situation.

> The kind of feeling which you classified as "homosexual" and "heterosexual" is really sex adopted to like or understood tem-peraments versus sex adopted to a relationship of strangeness and difference. I believe every person of ordinary sex endow-ment has a capacity of diffuse "homosexual" sex expression and specific climax—according to the temperamental situation. To

call men who prefer the diffuse experience "feminine" or women who feel only the specific "masculine" or both "mixed types" is a lot of obfuscation—or nonsense.

Margaret insisted to Ruth that Ruth wasn't homosexual. In fact, she wasn't even a "mixed type." "You're a perfectly good woman," Margaret wrote, "who prefers different temperamental types and responds differently to them."[79]

Ruth didn't reply to Margaret's pronouncement; by that point she was involved in her drama with Nat and annoyed with Margaret for criticizing *Patterns of Culture* as too academic. When Margaret, concerned about Ruth's silence, asked her if something was wrong between them, she put Margaret off, replying that everything was fine, only that relationships went through different stages. As usual, she only praised Margaret: "Excitement is your proper element, and I hadn't guessed it would be waiting for you at the headwaters of the Sepik. With you, an exciting relationship doubles your zest for work."[80]

DURING THOSE INTENSE conversations in Tchambuli, Margaret, Reo, and Gregory were studying an eroticized culture—that's how Margaret described the Tchambuli in *Blackberry Winter* and *Sex and Temperament*. There were frequent ceremonies and dancing, with the noise of drums, flutes, and gongs in the air. There was a reversal of sex roles. The women produced the goods for trading, working in large, cooperative groups, and they were "solid, preoccupied, powerful," with "shaven unadorned heads." The men arranged their hair in delicate curls and wore bird-of-paradise headdresses and elaborate penis sheaths. They walked with mincing steps. Sensitive to hurts, they easily burst into rages.

According to Mead, the women in Tchambuli were more sexual than the men; they took the lead in intercourse. Often sexually unsatisfied by the men, they used smooth stones for "auto-erotic activity." In dancing, both men and women decorated themselves with flowers and feathers, oiled their bodies, and masked their faces. The women were "explosively" sensual. At every celebration a group of women engaged in "rough" homosexual play, but the feminized men didn't engage in homosexual sex. Gregory Bateson told Mead and Fortune about Naven, the central ritual of the Iatmul, which involved a transvestitism in which the men dressed in rags as dirty old women, expressing hostility to the women, while the women dressed in male finery, expressing envy of the men.[81]

Tchambuli society was polygamous, and men might beat their wives, but the women were powerful—and the men feared them. In the top of every men's house, concealed from view, was the wooden figure of a woman with an enormous vulva, painted scarlet. Origin myths suggested that women had once controlled the society, owning the men's ceremonial houses and culture in general. On the outside of every men's house (Tchambuli had fifteen) was a large all-seeing eye, painted in red and white.

In this setting, on Easter weekend in April 1933, Margaret, Reo, and Gregory took the final step into a kind of madness—what Mead later called a folie à trois. Were they all suffering from hallucinations brought on by malaria? Did Margaret have an eidetic vision? She invented a tribal society from the squares, with separate languages for North and South and secret societies. As they played out their mania, each of them put on a color that represented his or her square. She seemed to name those colors in *Sex and Temperament*, identifying the gentle Arapesh with yellow, the fierce Mundugumor with deep red, the Tchambuli female with deep orange, and the Tchambuli male with pale green. Reo identified himself with the "apostles"; everyone else was an angel, a devil, or a Turk.[82]

Were Bett and her husband there? Were the Tchambuli people involved? Margaret was friendly with the women of the village, who came to her house with their children every afternoon for medical treatment—and to be entertained, for she and Reo were a "continuous circus" for them.[83] Indeed, the Tchambuli people always expected them to give up their strange ways and adopt native customs and dress. Were the observer and the observed now reversed, with the Tchambuli people enjoying the antics of the anthropologists rather than the other way around?

Margaret announced that she was going to submit the "Summary Statement" to a scientific journal. Afraid that she had gone mad, Reo hid the paper. At this point, everything exploded. Whether because of the paper or a temporary dementia, Reo hit Margaret, knocking her to the ground. She proceeded to miscarry, and she blamed the miscarriage on him. It must have been dreadful for her, given her dreams about dead babies and the dead babies she had seen in Mundugumor floating in the river. Now it was happening to her. She later described the fetus as a dead baby; they probably had to bury it. She identified with the child, and she turned on Reo. Becoming hysterical, she called him a murderer and a "cut-throat northern destroyer." She suddenly wanted to live protected in a walled garden, to be "a marsupial in Gregory's body." Denying that Northerners had a gentle side, she changed the meaning of that square, now defining Northerners as arrogant and violent, almost as bad as Turks. Reo was no longer her ideal husband; individuals on the same square now made the best marriages.[84] She seemed ready to abandon Reo for Gregory.

In that horrible scene after the miscarriage, Margaret frightened Reo: "Your neurosis was projected with accusations of sadism in such a way as to make you seem more devil than human," he later wrote her. He turned on Gregory, accusing him of causing the miscarriage by romancing Margaret, calling him a cannibal who had eaten their baby. Tempers were flying, and so were physical threats. Reo had a gun; Gregory hid it. That was enough. They decided to break camp and go to Sydney.[85]

THE STORY MARGARET TOLD Ruth in her letters was somewhat different. It omitted the folie à trois, the miscarriage, and the nasty scene. In Margaret's version for Ruth, Reo came down with malarial fever, and a scorpion bit her. They both had to go to bed, while Gregory sensibly went for a boat to take them back to Sydney. She now described her happiness with Gregory as the same as hers and Ruth's, with the same balance of activity and passivity and the same complete understanding.[86] The implication was that Margaret now had her love life under control; above all, she wanted Ruth to regard her as a grown-up, not as a child. She didn't lie to Ruth; she simply didn't tell her the whole narrative of what had happened at this point.

And she hardly wanted to be reminded of the deaths in her life—her sister Katherine, Marie Bloomfield, her own baby. The horror of the miscarriage, her attempts to block it from her mind, are sufficient to explain the frenzy of her actions during the next months. And she had created another triangle, with herself at the apex. Two individuals again wanted her, passed their energy through her, created multiple sites of desire among the three of them—and others. Once again, with her femininity and her mental brilliance in force, Margaret had masterminded another dramatic, and shifting, situation. Once again, she was living her life as though she were the heroine of a novel, with her genius as an actress, a producer, and an anthropologist in evidence. Participating in such dramas, however, only seemed to increase Margaret's creativity and her ability to work.

Once in Sydney, she moved in with Carrie Kelly. Reo and Gregory found rooms elsewhere; as in Tchambuli, the two of them played a lot of chess. Furious with Margaret, Reo took up with a woman named Mira, known in Sydney's bohemia for seducing men and getting money from them. Steve later boasted that if only Reo had stayed longer in Sydney, she could have snagged him. Reo later found a woman named Muriel, whom Timothy Kelly, Carrie's husband, described as a "blowsy barmaid type." Margaret wavered between Reo and Gregory, and she also became involved with Steve—as friend, lover, fictive mother, or all three.

In a diary that Steve kept at the time she revealed that Margaret seduced her and that she fell in love with Margaret, who was her first female lover. Their lovemaking, Steve asserted, had transformed her. Since adolescence she had dreamed of women; men had meant nothing to her, although she had struggled for years to overcome those feelings through having many affairs with men and then marrying Neville Cubhold. Yet Steve didn't become completely lesbian after her experience with Margaret; she later had male as well as female lovers, including sometime relationships with both Margaret and Gregory.

Where Carrie Kelly may have fit in these intertwinings in Sydney remains obscure. Several years previously, she had taken up anthropology after organizing little theaters in Sydney. Her husband, Timothy, was the owner and editor of a combination physical fitness, true confession, and birth control magazine. Carrie had originally been a friend of Reo's but, encouraged in her career ambitions by Margaret and sharing her taste for intrigue, she switched her allegiance to Margaret and became a fervent convert to the "squares." She defined herself as a Southerner—her code word for sexually free.[87] After Margaret returned to New York, she sent Carrie her favorite sex manuals by W. F. Robie and Havelock Ellis.

In an emotional encounter with Margaret, Reo again became furious. Later he wrote her that in Sydney she had indulged in "a neurotic mess of sado-masochistic terminology and queer and often unclean behavior." In other words, she had engaged in some free-love activity. Reo no longer liked the theory of the "squares"; he now decided that Margaret had invented it to end their marriage. "Deal with people as people," he wrote to her, "you can make people beastly or the reverse by what you think they are."[88] As for Gregory, he also may have had other involvements. If the dramatic Carrie Kelly can be believed, they included Muriel as well as Steve.[89]

In letters to Ruth, Margaret provided a different version of the events in Sydney, one in which Steve, Mira, and she were friends and she was in control, with her manager side, her Martha, dominant. She arranged for places for everyone to live and made certain they were fed. Gregory calmed Reo down. Remaining attracted to each other, they continued to play chess. Then Margaret wrote Ruth a frantic letter cautioning her not to read the letter Gregory had written until she got to New York and could explain it. Again, Margaret's two versions of what happened aren't necessarily contradictory. She was probably frequently in tears, while she managed the practical arrangements. Her moods could turn quickly from love to anger, from childish dependency to mature control. And there was her mental brilliance, her endless energy, her spinning of webs of explanation, her ability to talk her way out of most situations.[90]

Benedict remained loyal to Mead. Her first response to the situation in Sydney was to write to Margaret that it had all the makings of a farce. Then, suddenly worried, she counseled her friend to be careful, for she might destroy her professional reputation. She urged her not to go off with Gregory but to come back to New York with Reo "more or less." At the very least, Margaret needed to give the appearance of being a deserted wife. Be certain, Ruth wrote, that you don't feel too guilty about Reo: "you know your genius is to feel responsible." She worried that the anthropologists in Sydney might find out what had happened and spread scandalous gossip. "You'll be shocked by my Mrs. Grundy comments. It has nothing to do with my feelings for you, only with the long years scandal follows one professionally."[91]

By late August Margaret couldn't handle the situation, and she left alone for New York by boat. Once she left Sydney, she wrote love letters to both Reo and Gregory. She told Gregory that the voyage was therapeutic—she was bursting into tears only occasionally—but she still felt incompetent, and she badly needed him. At the same time she told Reo that she still loved him and that she would switch from anthropology to psychology to end any competition between them, if that would save their marriage. Meantime, she had a fling on the boat with a professor from New Zealand whom she called a Northerner. Both Carrie and Gregory chided her for becoming involved with an individual so similar to Reo, but she replied that she had needed someone to talk to.[92]

In November, Gregory and Reo separately left Sydney for England; Gregory had a research fellowship at Cambridge, and Reo had one at the London School of Economics. If Reo had returned to New York, Margaret might have gone back to him, for in his physical presence she had difficulty resisting him. But he was angry with her and determined to find a job before he saw her, and so he stayed away. In fact, she didn't see him again for years. And once in New York she decided that she didn't want Reo back; his letters to her were filled with recriminations and repudiation of the "squares," while Gregory wrote loving letters, expanding on the scheme, which Margaret was selling to her family and close friends. Her father, for one, had fun calling her a Northerner, despite her protests.[93]

Once Margaret returned to New York and told Ruth everything, Ruth was distressed by her behavior and baffled by the theory of the "squares." Margaret didn't like Ruth's reaction. In letters to Gregory she defined her in the negative terms she now used for Northerners. She wrote Gregory that Reo had been right. Ruth was too old for her; she had never been anything more than a mother to her. Gregory, not Ruth, was her twin. Then Ruth backed down and accepted the "squares" and, with their friendship restored, Margaret fell into the old groove—although she now was more willing to disagree with Ruth. She admitted to Gregory that Ruth might have been difficult because she was bewildered by "my various simultaneous and contradictory attitudes."[94] She also told Gregory that she had been angry with Ruth because, once again, she refused to have sex with her. Yet Margaret still delighted in Ruth. "Although all love making and so all physical integration depending on responsiveness is out," she wrote, she could still "weave my feeling for her into this spring as I have, more vividly, into so many other springs."[95] Again happy with Ruth, Margaret decided that she and Gregory needed to expand their use of the "squares." They were using Northern and Southern too much. She now defined Ruth as a Westerner, as a pioneer.[96]

Gregory and Margaret weren't faithful to each other in any conventional sense: freedom in relationships was part of their bargain. In letters to Margaret, Gregory described his involvements, including several weekends spent with Steve in England—they were unconsummated, according to him. "A net without a keeper," he wrote Margaret, "is like a fish without a tail." He assured her that he wouldn't have sex with men; she had cured him of that. As for other women, they would have to accept Margaret's priority in his affections if they wanted to have sex with him.[97]

Margaret assured him that a brief involvement on his part with someone else didn't bother her. For her part, she mostly told him about flirtations—except for her relationship with Yale social psychologist John Dollard. She described him as "a fiery eyed Southerner raised a Catholic who had been psychoanalyzed." She implied, however, that her relationship with the married Dollard wasn't sexual and that it kept her faithful to Gregory. "John's unfailing affection and inaccessibility have done a lot to keep me steady," she wrote, "and you've had a more complicated row to hoe where there was no one who regarded you as inaccessible."[98]

However, she didn't tell Gregory about her weekends in the White Mountains with Jeannette Mirsky and Mirsky's lover, William Whitman. Jeannette, another member of Margaret's class at Barnard, who had written a popular book on arctic explorers, was now a graduate student in anthropology at Columbia studying with Benedict—as was Whitman. In the spring of 1934 Margaret sublet her apartment and moved in for several months with Jeannette, whom she described to Gregory as an extraverted Southerner. Jeannette's husband was abroad; Bill Whitman was a Southerner who reminded Margaret of Gregory. In a letter to Carrie Kelly, Margaret described a weekend they spent in the White Mountains. "It's in the Southern square," she wrote. A two-girls-and-a-man weekend, it can only be successful if everyone is in that square. She is a cat's-paw, she tells Carrie, but she is being well treated.[99] (A cat's-paw is someone who is hunted, as in a children's game.)

In good free-love fashion, Margaret now brought her intimate friends together. She had Ruth correspond with Gregory, and she wrote Noel Porter. Ruth helped Margaret keep Reo in the dark about what she was doing: writing Gregory almost daily, working on a divorce, and attempting to find Reo a job and a new wife—just as she had tried to pair Luther Cressman with Eda Lou Walton when she divorced him. Ever since Marie Bloomfield's death Margaret had feared hurting anyone. Yet she wanted her way. So she covered all angles, always on an emotional brink, but never falling over. "I had continual minor breakdowns," she wrote to Gregory, "and that's why I never had a major one."[100]

Margaret recruited her close friends as confederates. Carrie Kelly was her link to Reo. "Try to keep Reo's halo on," she wrote to Carrie. "I have a job, a family who are secure whom I love, hundreds of friends, a publisher for my work, a secure and walled-in life. Reo has no job, more enemies than friends, no one to back him up." Yet what she wanted done could be confusing. "Your letter was a little difficult to comprehend, as usual," Ash Can Cat Leah Josephson Hanna wrote to her. "I couldn't get quite straight what was public and what private so I compromised by saying practically nothing except that I'd had a letter which was incomprehensible—which everybody seemed quite willing to believe, my love."[101]

Margaret tried hard to find Reo a job: she felt responsible for him. Besides, Reo had to sign their divorce papers, even in Mexico. She didn't have much success on the employment front, for during the Depression jobs in anthropology were hard to find and Reo had a reputation for being difficult. Ruth finally got him a research grant from Columbia University—partly financed by Margaret—so that he could return to New Guinea and study another tribe in the central highlands. The Kamano he chose turned out to be even more ferocious than his Dobu, and the colonial authorities, fearing for his safety, made him leave before he finished his fieldwork. Ironically, he sensed that female bonding around menarche and childbirth was central to the culture, but the men wouldn't let him interview the women and so he couldn't find out if that speculation was correct: he needed a female anthropologist along to do those interviews.[102]

Accepting Margaret's assertions that she was giving up men to devote herself entirely to anthropology, Reo signed the divorce papers in 1935. After that, his career went downhill. He didn't produce an ethnography of the Kamano—or of the Mundugumor or the Arapesh—aside from an article on the latter. He married a woman to whom he had been engaged before he met Margaret; he taught for a time in China and then wound up on a modest fellowship at Cambridge University. Some people thought that Margaret destroyed him; others that his mental instability took over. Ann McClean contends that he was too much of a gentleman to publish much work critical of his ex-wife and that stymied his career. Whichever version is accurate, he wrote Margaret accusatory letters about her behavior on the Sepik River for many years after they divorced.

BY 1935 RUTH and Margaret had put their relationship back together in accordance with their bargain that gave them both freedom. Ruth was living with Natalie Raymond; Margaret lived with various friends before she found her own apartment. They saw each other for lunches and dinners; occasionally they spent the night together. They worked together in the spring of 1934 and the fall of 1935 on the cooperation-and-competition seminar at Columbia; they wrote their life histories for John Dollard. Ruth taught at Columbia, supervised graduate students in the field, ran the department for Franz Boas, edited the *Journal of American Folk-Lore*. Margaret taught an extension course at Columbia; worked on her collection at the Museum of Natural History; wrote books and articles; went to conferences, including ones in Hanover, New Hampshire, in the summers of 1934 and 1935. In the summer of 1935, Ruth and Margaret vacationed in New England together. But Ruth mostly spent summers at the farm in Norwich, which she had inherited from her aunt Myra, and Margaret didn't visit her there. Protective of their professional and public reputations, they kept the depth of their involvement a secret.[103]

In 1935, Mead, and especially Benedict, became close to Karen Horney, who had moved to New York the year before. John Dollard had done a training analysis with her; he introduced them. Benedict attended Horney's lectures at the New School in 1935; Horney switched her perspective that year from a Freudian feminist analysis to a neo-Freudian cultural one. Benedict's cultural determinism ratified her change. Erich Fromm also came to New York; he and Horney were intimate, and the four of them spent evenings together. They often played the game of analyzing cultures that Benedict and Mead seemed never to tire of. Benedict and Mead would describe a culture; Horney and Fromm would analyze it.[104]

From the fall of 1933, when Mead returned to New York from Sydney, to the spring of 1936, when she went to Singapore to marry Gregory Bateson, she worked hard to shore up her professional reputation, writing several impressive articles. Mead drew a distinction between her ethnographies, her scholarly articles, and her popular works. She wrote popular works to educate and persuade, part of her commitment to education and reform. She wrote ethnographies and scholarly articles as contributions to her profession. To see her at her scholarly best, one needs to read this work.

In 1931, for example, she wrote a searching article on her fieldwork methodology in which she answered the attacks of Sapir and the other male Boasians. She detailed her use of social science techniques, unfamiliar to most of them, while pointing out that they overlooked women's lives, which she focused on. She described the initial survey she used for understanding societies, the one cataloguing the people by age, kin, family grouping, and status that she had devised in Samoa. Beyond that, she tailored her research design in complex ways to the problems she was studying. Interested in father-son relationships in Manus, for example, she studied a number of groupings: sons and fathers, foster sons and fathers, children born to men at different points in their economic careers, siblings reared by different adults, children raised by widows, and those raised in homes in which mothers were dominant. Attacking her critics, she chided Malinowski, with whom she was often compared, for arguing on the basis of casual observation of Trobriand Islanders that delayed weaning was good for babies. He hadn't interviewed mothers or children, or set up control groups to provide checks and balances.[105]

A second article that she published in a psychology journal outlined the configurationist approach that she and Benedict used and made a plea to psychologists to pay attention to "primitive" cultures in their work. She wrote a searching review of Géza Róheim's *Riddle of the Sphinx*, demonstrating a complex understanding of Freud. She wrote a foreword and afterword to *Cooperation and Competition Among Primitive Peoples*, the volume of seminar papers on the subject that she edited.[106] She began writing an ethnography of the Arapesh, which eventually ran to several volumes.

She continued to find mentors and close male friends. John Dollard was one: he helped her understand Freudian theory and introduced her to his life-history approach; he was an associate of Sapir's on his Yale culture-and-personality project. Howard Scott was another: he was the founder of a movement called Technocracy and a former lover of Eleanor Steele. He argued that Marxism and the concept of class were irrelevant to the future that techology would bring, one based on machines and the sharing of information and in which nation-states would join together in a world federation. For a brief time in the mid-1930s Scott was all the rage, until he was exposed for having fabricated career credentials and denounced as a fraud. But that didn't deter Margaret, who was convinced of his genius and attracted to his forceful masculinity: he was, she stated, a "man of the frontier." Under his influence she gave up whatever Marxist ideas she still preserved from her college years; his theories underlay a number of her ideas after World War II.[107]

Above all, there was the English writer Geoffrey Gorer—a friend, not a mentor—whom she met at the end of 1935 when he came to New York on a tour to promote his book *Africa Dances* and to whom she remained close for the rest of her life. Impressed by his knowledge and his eagerness to learn sophisticated fieldwork methods, she and Benedict gave him a crash course in them. Because of their difficulties with the male Boasians, they welcomed new confederates. Gorer remained in the United States to help Benedict produce her "Handbook of Psychological Leads for Ethnological Field Workers"; he became a research associate in Sapir's research project at Yale. His feminine masculinity, sophistication, upper-class wit, and British charm were irresistible to Mead, as were his town house in London, his country house in Sussex, and his contacts in England's literary and homosexual circles—he was, for example, close to W. H. Auden.[108] Benedict liked him, but not romantically: she left that up to Mead.

Possessing an eclectic mind and a deft pen, Gorer had written popular studies of the Marquis de Sade and of Balinese culture and would publish one on American burlesque, as well as a scholarly study of the Lepchas of the Himalayas based on the fieldwork techniques Benedict and Mead had taught him. He wanted to become the preeminent foreign observer of the United States for the twentieth century, like Alexis de Tocqueville for the nineteenth; he joined Benedict and Mead in their project on contemporary cultures after World War II. Like Mead, he was a popularizer, and he defended her against all attacks. When Bateson left her, her friends thought that she would marry him, but that seems unlikely.[109] In the many letters that they wrote to each other over the years, there aren't any love letters, only a guarded exchange when Margaret was on Bali in which she contended that love relationships enhanced one's ability to work, while Geoffrey maintained that true artists needed emotional detachment to be productive.

Soon after she married Gregory, Geoffrey wrote her that because she and he (Geoffrey) were both Southerners according to the theory of the squares, their feelings for each other could only be like those of a brother and a sister: Margaret doesn't seem to have told him that she had decided that Southerners made the best marital partners. When John Dollard hired Gorer as a research associate on the Yale project, Mead warned him that Gorer was opinionated, even fanatical. In a letter to Bateson, she described him as a "Southern excitor"—cataloguing him under the theory of the "squares" exactly as she catalogued herself. Yet unlike her, she reported to Bateson, he had no indecision about his sexual orientation.[110]

AFTER MARGARET RETURNED to New York from Sydney and Gregory went back to Cambridge, it wasn't certain that they would wind up together. In the late summer of 1934 they spent a secret two-week vacation together in Ireland, and in the spring of 1935 Gregory lectured at Columbia and at the University of Chicago. But they didn't marry until the spring of 1936, a year after Margaret's divorce from Reo.

In returning to England Gregory went back to Noel Porter and to the pleasures of a bachelor life at Cambridge University. Noel tried to convince Gregory that his relationship with Margaret wouldn't last. As with all his female lovers, Noel contended, Gregory would eventually identify Margaret with his domineering mother, whom he unconsciously wanted to possess—and to destroy. Margaret worked hard to persuade Gregory that Noel was wrong and that she was, in fact, gentle and dependent. That interpretation wasn't wrong; it was simply one-sided. "I am not going to be made into a Turk mother," Margaret wrote to Gregory, "and I am not going to see you as a sweet Fey child." When the aging Noel Porter decided to sell the Half Moon and retire to the country, she indulged Gregory's fantasy that they would buy it and run it.[111]

Margaret had much to give Gregory: energy, intellect, drama, discipline, a skill at psychological analysis. Even if she wasn't always accurate, she wove a compelling tale. She did eventually serve as a mother figure to him, but for a number of years her controlling side didn't emerge—or Gregory, like Reo, chose not to see it. In their early years together she projected emotional need, even insecurity. As she had with Reo, she told Gregory that she would do whatever he wanted, that she felt incompetent and always searched for mentors. And Margaret realized that Gregory was confused about his masculinity—and her dependence made him feel strong. There were his virile father's unconsummated affairs and his brothers' tragic deaths; he had a lot of anger inside. He fell into his "Bengali fits"; upon occasion he could rage like the rest of them.

Charles Doughty's *Arabia Deserta* fascinated Gregory; he claimed that he had learned how to do fieldwork from it. Doughty was the first European to visit the desert tribes of Arabia, and his book is an account of his travels—alone, dressed in native clothing, wandering from tribe to tribe. The story he tells is one of triumph over adversity, as he toughens his body and spirit to become like the bedouin Arabs, nomads following herds of camels. Doughty saw them as Semites, noble men who included the Hebrew patriarchs. Gregory valued Doughty's description of the Arab: "He is living up to the eyes in a cloaca, but his forehead reaches to the sky." "Cloaca" means a sewer; the reference is to the Turks' occupation of Arabia. In Doughty's book, the Turks are venal and corrupt. The Arabs are noble "primitives," models of masculinity for Victorian men.[112]

For years Gregory dreamed of a watercolor by William Blake, *Satan Exulting Over Eve*, that hung on a wall of his childhood home. In the painting Eve swoons on the ground with a partially eaten apple in her hand. The naked devil hovers stretched out above her, and a serpent is coiled around her. In the painting, the serpent is a part of Satan's body, for, being an angel, Satan has no genitals of his own. Did Gregory think of himself as a devil with women, as an ambiguous male who was both powerless and all-powerful? That would be a hard position for anyone to occupy.[113]

During their correspondence over the three years before they married in 1936, Margaret's love for Gregory deepened. Their relationship, however, was as much about spirituality and touch as about phallic sexuality. Both of them regarded that fifteen minutes in New Guinea, their "episode of the second goats," as the consummation of their relationship. Margaret wrote to Ruth even before she left Tchambuli that she had decided that "specific sex" was suited to people who couldn't communicate with each other and that it wasn't necessary between people who understood each other. "It's only where there is no urgency of passion," she wrote, "that one can capture that rootless lily in the sky delight."[114] Thus the strong sex she had with Reo didn't matter in her relationship with Gregory.

Margaret wrote to Gregory that with him she had truly been feminine for the first time in her intimate relationships. With Luther she had been the stronger partner, and with Reo the sexual magnetism between them had confused everything. Under their first definition of the "squares," she explained, when they had defined Gregory and her as feminine (F) and Reo and Steve as masculine (M), she would have described her relationship to Gregory as homosexual and her relationship to Steve as heterosexual. (She sounds as though she had been reading Magnus Hirschfeld—or listening to Noel Porter.) By this statement she meant that Steve, as a Northerner, was dominant in sex, while both Gregory and she were passive. She now thought, however, that true heterosexual relationships didn't work when differences in temperament—Northern and Southern—were involved. Thus she could only be feminine—and truly heterosexual—with a feminine man, someone passive in sex. "Do you think that is a possible explanation, Darling, of why I picture myself so contentedly, curled up in your arms, hidden away in any house you chose, wearing your name like a warm hood to protect me from winter winds?"[115]

This analysis seems based on "active" sex as involving penetration by the male, with "passive" sex no less pleasurable. Yet she later told Gregory's analyst that she had been spontaneously sexual when she met Gregory. Over the years, however, she'd had to mute her spontaneity because he didn't like it. She told her own therapist that she interpreted "cherishing" from males as potency and that she was "receptive and permissive up to the phallic stage," which she saw as destructive. After it passed, she was then receptive to a genital stage. She told Erik Erikson, the Freudian analyst who was her friend, that when she married Gregory, his mind and personality had such an appeal to her that she was willing "to accept the price that went with his undeveloped sexuality." She continued: "I can assess the price I have paid in eleven years of inexpressiveness and count it fully worth it."[116]

After she returned from Sydney to New York in 1933, however, she seems to have had different expectations. In an article she wrote for Ira S. Wile's *The Sex Life of the Unmarried Adult* that year, she once again described the practice of sexuality in Samoa with enthusiasm. In Samoa sex is play, she wrote, a skill at which one becomes adept. It is permitted in all hetero- and homosexual expression, with "any sort of artistic addition." (The phrase "artistic addition" draws from Havelock Ellis.) Samoans, she continued, don't connect sex to monogamy. "Jealousy, special devotion, an excess of feeling are bad form."[117] She seemed enthusiastic about her relationship with Gregory, enthusiastic about free love. By the summer of 1934, a year after returning from New Guinea, she would begin writing her report from that research—a report that would become *Sex and Temperament in Three Primitive Societies.*

CHAPTER 12

From the Hanover Conference to the Witches of Bali

Sex and Temperament, *Part 2*

I N THE SUMMER OF 1934, as Margaret Mead began writing *Sex and Temperament*, she participated in an interdisciplinary seminar at the Hanover Inn in New Hampshire to design a high school curriculum on human behavior. The first such conference she attended, it had a major impact on her. It was there that she met sociologists Robert Lynd and John Dollard. She also became friends with Lawrence Frank, the organizer of the conference and a funding administrator for the Rockefeller Foundation. Frank was a scholar in his own right and a reformer who followed the ideas of John Dewey and was interested in Freudian and sociological approaches to childhood. He had a near religious zeal for interdisciplinary enterprise, a skill at bringing scholars together, and a fondness for the give-and-take of conferences. He used Rockefeller money to set up child-study centers, and he funded projects to bring psychiatrists and anthropologists together in what was called the culture-and-personality school—projects like Sapir's seminar at Yale composed of foreign scholars studying their own cultures. According to Mead, Frank put the field of the behavioral sciences together "almost singlehandedly."[1]

Frank brought Mead into his inner circle; he became a mentor to her in the networking of conferences and in interdisciplinary enterprise. She regarded him as akin to Julian Gardy, her friend in high school, as a confederate in planning action. Erik Erikson found Frank the most maternal man he had ever met, but Mead called him a Turk,[2] for he was a brilliant administrator who brought people together and inspired them to do significant work.

What interests me especially about the Hanover Conference is a packet of background materials for it on the subject of homosexuality, prepared by Lura Beam, a well-known sex researcher. The packet contains excerpts from books, articles, and novels. The authors include W. Béran Wolfe, a prominent U.S. follower of Alfred Adler, and Wilhelm Stekel, one of Freud's early associates. The packet also includes excerpts from Proust's *Remembrance of Things Past* and from Sapir's articles attacking Mead (apparently Beam didn't know that the articles were directed against her).[3] The excerpts are homophobic, from Wolfe's statement that homosexuality lies in the "borderland" between neurosis and crime, to Sapir's attack on the "naturalness of homosexuality," to Proust's description of an aging nobleman with a taste for being whipped and for having sex with young men. Stekel is the most extreme. In *Bi-sexual Love* he followed Freud in arguing that everyone is born bisexual and that the homosexual part of the self remains latent after the transition to heterosexuality. This condition didn't trouble Freud, but Stekel thought it could cause major personal and social harm. In his view, homosexuality had to be eliminated.

Mead's letters don't mention this material, although her position on sexual orientation in *Sex and Temperament* implicitly criticizes it. In a letter to Gregory Bateson, however, she referred to a typescript paper in the packet of background materials that summarized investigations by biologists into gender. The paper, written by Earl Engle, an endocrinologist at Columbia University Medical School, reviews recent hormonal research on gender, including the "well-known" finding that males secrete female hormones and females male hormones and that the stallion, the most masculine of animals, secretes more female hormones in his urine than a pregnant woman does in hers. This finding contradicted the belief that males have only male hormones and females only female ones. Moreover, the paper summarizes research from constitutional-type theorists who correlated body build with variables like mental illness and disease. It related to the statement about constitutional types that Mead made in her "Summary Statement on the Problem of Personality and Culture." Such theories were popular partly because, although the manner in which genes and hormones functioned was unclear, body features such as height and size were obvious manifestations of them. Such features might be used to figure out the influence of heredity on personality.

Mead began writing *Sex and Temperament* during the Hanover Conference; she finished it that winter. In December she wrote Gregory Bateson about a recent conversation of hers with Earl Engle in which he suggested even more more radical conclusions about gender. Because chromosomes, glands, and embryological development determine the sex of humans in multiple ways, Engle had decided that biologists could no longer precisely state what constituted a man or a woman.[4] Engle's statement reinforced the conclusions that Mead, Bateson, and Reo Fortune had come to on the Sepik River about the relative nature of "masculine" and "feminine" and that Mead was making a central theme in her book. In the end, however, she didn't include the new information that Engle gave her; in fact, she didn't include evidence from hormonal research at all.

MEAD HAD QUALMS about writing *Sex and Temperament* without Reo Fortune's input, and she was concerned about his threats to expose her research on the Arapesh as wrong, although she was confident about her findings. Their disagreement may have been a case of two researchers studying the same society and coming up with differing conclusions. Yet she also needed his help with the Mundugumor and the Tchambuli, for she had spent only four months studying the former and three studying the latter. In the end, she devoted a lot of the book to the Arapesh, whom she had studied for eight months, and she covered the Tchambuli and the Mundugumor more briefly. She justified the brief coverage by explaining in the book's preface that Reo had been responsible for the ethnographic work on these two societies— but she didn't mention that he refused to share it with her.[5] And she wrote a subtext into her Arapesh chapters that drew from Reo's depiction of that society as violent and that might be seen as undermining her conclusion that the society was maternal and cooperative. The approach, however, was consistent with her writing on Samoa and the other New Guinea societies, in which she noted many threads in the culture, while choosing one as dominant, following the configurationist approach.

In Reo's absence, she turned to Gregory, since he knew the Iatmul and the Tchambuli better than she. His input influenced the book. "If the squares weren't a contribution," she wrote to Gregory, "I'd feel pretty sad about the Tchambuli work; I certainly did little."[6] That self-criticism, however, went too far: she had done her standard survey, observed rituals, and recorded field notes. John Dollard, whom she thanks in the introduction to *Sex and Temperament*, probably helped her with the Freudian themes in the book.

In the first instance, *Sex and Temperament* implicitly criticizes Benedict's *Patterns of Culture*, while mentioning that work only briefly—and positively. Benedict had dismissed the impact of heredity on personal identity, while she had idealized her Plains berdache. She had proposed that cultures could be "deviant" and their "deviants" normal in other societies, but she hadn't analyzed her category of deviancy. She hadn't especially analyzed gender in her three prestate societies, except for the Zuñi, although her criticism of the category of "abnormality" pointed the way to attacking all existing categorizations with regard to deviancy and gender. In *Sex and Temperament* Mead opened up Benedict's conclusions in these areas.[7] With regard to gender, Mead hovered on the edge of the "queer modernism" that Joseph Boone has identified as existing in the 1920s and 1930s, but, remaining devoted to "male" and "female," she didn't take the plunge into abandoning the idea of gender.

Mead's *Sex and Temperament* isn't always easy to understand. To begin with, she didn't use the word "gender" in it. Nor did she use that word in her *Male and Female* (1949); even by the late 1940s it hadn't acquired its present-day meaning. That didn't happen until feminists in the 1970s adopted the distinction between sex as biology and gender as culture from medical clinicians working with transsexuals in the 1950s; these clinicians had introduced the distinction—and the word "gender"—in assigning a gender to transsexual children. In 1931, on the way to New Guinea, Mead met a "lady reporter" in Sydney who used the term "gender consciousness."[8] The term intrigued her, for it seemed a good way to describe what she planned to do in New Guinea—to focus on the sex roles of men as well as of women. Yet she didn't adopt the term. Instead of "gender," she used the word "sex"—to refer to both the social and the biological constructions of the self. Where we use the word "gender" to mean the social self as differentiated from the sexual self, Mead used the terms "sex role" or "sex personality." Those terms, less precise than "gender," were rooted in biology.[9]

The words "sex" and "temperament" in the title of Mead's book are important in understanding it. She didn't use the word "personality," as she had in her title to the "Summary Statement on the Problem of Personality and Culture," which she wrote in Tchambuli. "Temperament," an old term, dates to the ancient Greeks and is related to words like "temperature," meaning the heat of the body, and to the belief that human dispositions are determined by four humors, hot, cold, moist, and dry, corresponding to fire, air, water, and earth. Psychologist Abraham Roback contended that by the 1930s the words "personality," "temperament," and "character" had acquired so many meanings that it was hard to distinguish one from the others.[10] Mead later stated that by "temperament" she meant "innate individual endowments" or "genetic makeup."[11]

In writing *Sex and Temperament* Mead had to satisfy Ruth Benedict and Gregory Bateson, since they were the primary critics of the manuscript. And she had to consider Reo Fortune's response. She couldn't use the theory of the "squares" explicitly, since when she returned to New York she realized that, with its feys and Turks, its Northerners and Southerners, it might be considered bizarre—or racist. In January 1933, her first month in Tchambuli, Hitler became chancellor of Germany. Given dictatorial powers by parliament, he suspended free speech; that spring, he purged all leftists from his party. If they had known about his rise to power when they were in Tchambuli, Mead wrote, they might never have pursued their theories about temperament. But they were isolated from the outside world; their only knowledge about Hitler came from an article written by journalist Dorothy Thompson that had been sent to them and that dismissed him as inconsequential.[12] As soon as Mead got back to New York, however, she realized how dangerous he was. He preached a doctrine of "Nordic supremacy": his Nordics, from Northern climes, might be confused with her Northerners. It was best to keep the "squares" out of her book.

Keeping faith with Benedict, Mead used her configurationist approach to argue that individuals are primarily shaped by culture, although she reformulated Benedict's "arc of personality" by placing individual temperament foremost. Despite using "temperament" in the title of the book, however, she mentioned only birth order, being a twin, and being born in a caul (with part of the fetal membrane attached to the infant's head) as possible biological influences in personality formation, and she only alluded to constitutional types. She omitted two parts of the reasoning that she, Bateson, and Fortune had used at Tchambuli to prove that masculinity and femininity are socially constructed: the argument from their own personalities, which might be dismissed as unscientific, and the theory of the "squares." She didn't refer to Earl Engle's paper on hormonal research or to her conversation with him. She thanked him in her introduction to *Sex and Temperament* for his input, although that input isn't apparent in what she wrote.

Instead, in discussing temperament she began by supporting Benedict's cultural determinism, her conclusion that biologists hadn't proved that temperament was transmitted through "basal metabolism" or the "ductless glands."[13] "We are forced to conclude," Mead wrote, "that human nature is almost unbelievably malleable." Then she backed off. "If human nature were completely homogeneous material . . . deviant individuals wouldn't so often appear." Accommodating Benedict's ideas, she concluded: "Let us assume that there are definite temperamental differences between human beings which if not entirely hereditary at least are established on a hereditary base soon after birth. Further than this we cannot go at present."[14] What she meant by "temperamental differences . . . established on a hereditary basis soon after birth" isn't clear; she may have been referring to the theory advanced by psychologist Gordon Allport of Harvard that personality emerged in the newborn infant only after the "original stream of activity meets the environment, acting upon it and being acted upon."[15]

To redraw Benedict's "arc of personality" in terms of individual impulses, Mead used an aesthetic argument. She wrote: "It is as if we had represented the Arapesh personality by a soft yellow, the Mundugumor by a deep red, while the Tchambuli female personality was deep orange, and that of the Tchambuli male, pale green." Yet if we peer more closely, she continued, we see, just as in the spectrum of the rainbow, "in each case the delicate, just discernible outlines of the whole spectrum." This spectrum is the range of individual differences in temperament. From this range each culture selects its dominant personality type and then enforces that type on its members as they grow up.[16] Mead didn't make clear how "rainbows" and "colors" are related to the biology of human beings.

Mead's use of biology in *Sex and Temperament* is puzzling, and so is her approach to homosexuality. In the first place, her conclusion that there wasn't any homosexuality in the societies she studied seems overdrawn, especially in light of the cross-gender behavior among the Tchambuli and in the Iatmul's Naven ceremony and their frequent wordplay about anal intercourse. She later proposed that in small tribal groups the absence of homosexuality should be regarded with caution, as "cultural loss in the absence of any individuals to fill the role may be rapid," although knowledge of the role could continue to exist in language and rituals; she even suggested that societies conquered by the colonial powers might interdict homosexual behavior and identities or hide them because they realized that Westerners disapproved of the orientation.[17] Yet in *Sex and Temperament* she praised societies in which homosexuality didn't exist; in doing so she seems hostile to it. She described the Arapesh, among whom she didn't see any homosexuals, as without any "psychosexual maladjustment"—by which she meant homosexuality.

Her attitude toward homosexuality, however, like her attitude toward biology, wasn't simple. For she didn't dislike all homosexuals, only the active male who was aggressive in behavior. Moreover, she also disliked dominant heterosexual males. After her experiences with her father and with Edward Sapir and Reo Fortune, she didn't like aggressive men. Thus she praised the Arapesh males for their gentle, passive behavior and for their belief that men aren't "spontaneously sexual."

Her dislike of aggressive men is also apparent in her discussion of the men-women of the Plains Indians. Opposing Benedict's conclusion that these individuals were celebrated, Mead contended that they were ridiculed and scorned, for they didn't dress or act in accordance with their society's required aggressive masculinity. Indeed, she argued that the "frantic" insistence on such masculinity—the warrior ideal—drove gentle males into the berdache role.[18] With regard to the young man she had observed becoming a berdache in the Omaha community in 1930, Mead now contended that he was a congenital invert, perhaps a transsexual, whom the women had directed into the berdache role because they remembered how it functioned before the U.S. conquest, when the original society was intact.[19]

Mead didn't like the masculine aggressiveness of the Plains Indians. And she didn't like that of the Mundugumor—or of a group of young males in Tchambuli, whom she described as "violent, possessive, and actively sexed, intolerant of any control." She called them "viriloid" and, using Benedict's distinctions, identified them as the central deviants in Tchambuli society. Mead didn't like domineering males. In her friend-of-the-court brief for Walter Spies on Bali in 1939, she wrote that the active homosexual male often begins as heterosexual, but his drive for power is so strong that dominating over women no longer satisfies him, so he turns to boys and passive males. Passive male homosexuals, on the other hand, turn to their role because they identify with their mothers or spend time in single-sex institutions where homosexual activity among the males is standard.

"Society," she wrote in the Spies brief, "cannot exist where there is too much aggression among the males." And in a short memorial to Spies, she wrote that his "continuing light involvement" with Balinese youth was part of his repudiating the "dominance and submission, authority and dependence, which he associated with European culture."[20] She didn't mention the intense masculinity displayed by Hitler and infused throughout the Nazi system, although it's probable that she was aware of it—and of the rumors of homosexual behavior among Hitler's male elite.[21]

In describing the "viriloid" Tchambuli youth, Mead called them "actively sexed," and she described the Mundugumor as "positively sexed."[22] In her discussion of sex in the "Summary Statement on the Problem of Personality and Culture" she suggested that by "actively sexed" males she meant those who primarily adopted the missionary position. Yet in *Sex and Temperament* her attitude toward that sort of sex was negative, since she identified it with aggression. Moreover, although she seemed surprised when the Arapesh women told her that they didn't have orgasms, she neither criticized nor pitied them. Instead, she theorized that because the Arapesh used the kiss as a feature of sex they had a full genital development, even though oral sex was tabooed.[23] (She didn't reconcile the contradiction, although she noted that kissing was often lacking in tribal cultures.) But she liked the feeling of warm satisfaction they said they derived from intercourse, while she emphasized the gentle behavior of Arapesh men in sex, noting that the culture didn't possess the Western belief that men are "spontaneously sexual."[24]

In *Patterns of Culture* Benedict maintained that any deviant behavior on the part of homosexuals resulted from the way society treated them. Mead didn't disagree with the point about social control, but she challenged Benedict's implicit acceptance of homosexuality as an identity when she used "homosexual" and "invert" as interchangeable and her belief that, because of the power of social conditioning, there weren't many "abnormals" in any society. Implicitly rebutting Wilhelm Stekel's contention in the excerpts from his work included in the Hanover Conference packet that "latent homosexuality" was a major problem for American society, Mead turned his argument on its head. She contended that "latent homosexuality" wasn't the issue; the problem was that individuals suffered because society forced them to repress their homosexual side. In a nearly Swiftian reversal of reality reminiscent of Benedict, she defined almost everyone in American society as bisexual, highly neurotic—and deviant.[25]

According to Mead, everyone in the United States underwent a draconian socialization in childhood to stereotypical gender roles. "Ways of sitting or relaxing, ideas of sportsmanship and fair play, patterns of expressing emotions, and a multitude of other points"—all were imposed on children to make them identify themselves as masculine or feminine, and to drive them crazy. "Every time the point of sex-conformity is made, every time the child's sex is invoked as the reason why it should prefer trousers to petticoats, there is planted in the child's mind the fear it may not really belong to its own sex at all."[26]

With regard to adults, the definition of homosexuality as a dangerous perversion prevented individuals from satisfying their homosexual side and forced some who did so to become completely homosexual. The woman who became "mannish" might not choose to "cross over sex lines" unless society defined her mildly masculine behavior as inappropriate for her sex. And such women often tragically considered themselves unsuited for childbearing. As for men, who were, she thought, raised to be domineering, they often turned to submissive men as sex partners in single-sex groups. As a result, their anxiety about their masculinity increased, since a true man was supposed to desire only women. Or, confronting a dominant woman, they might doubt their masculinity. And men who conformed most closely to the dominant role for males were "the most suspicious and hostile toward deviating women." Moreover, those individuals who didn't follow the norm confused those who did. In everyone, "a seed of doubt, of anxiety, is planted" about their gender and sexual identity.

Drawing rigid sex lines between masculine and feminine also produced the Oedipus complex. Without the distinction in gender roles, children wouldn't view their parents as separate kinds of beings, nor identify with one over the other. Nor would they, as a result of identifying with the same-sex parent, turn to homosexuality.[27]

Yet in Mead's cultural scheme, homosexuals are more maladjusted than heterosexuals: the problem stemmed from their giving up the drive to procreate. No matter that adoption was an option in her day and that Ruth Benedict and Natalie Raymond had considered it, biological reproduction was what counted to Mead. In a society like the Arapesh, which drew no distinction between "masculine" and "feminine" as personality constructions but maintained one between men and women as reproductive beings, there was much less "psycho-sexual" maladjustment than elsewhere. That was because "one basic aspect of a child's position in the universe is left unchallenged: the genuineness of its membership in its own sex." The counterproductive division between masculine and feminine was gone, while the security of reproductive membership remained. The child "can continue to watch the mating behavior of its elders and pattern its hopes and expectations on that." "Once a woman has borne a child," she wrote in *Male and Female*, "her full sex membership is assured."[28]

Since the beginning of the twentieth century biologists have viewed sexual reproduction as the most significant event in the biological world.[29] Associating with Gregory Bateson and Earl Engle, Mead brought that belief, as well as her own desire for a child, into the concluding sections of *Sex and Temperament*. When she married Reo Fortune, she hadn't worried much about her presumed inability to have children; her books could be her children. Over time that attitude of hers changed. She had spent years helping native women to give birth, watching their pain and pleasure. They had accepted her as kin, while she had studied their children and identified with them; they had confirmed her sense of the unity of humans and nature and of reproduction and birth as elemental parts of human life. Her revulsion against the antimaternal attitude of the Mundugumor also was crucial to her conclusions about male and female, as was the intense feeling the Arapesh had for their children.

Yet she hinted at her fears of the homosexual drive she felt in herself when she wrote that if men and women lost their reproductive identity, they lost their "psycho-sexual" security. Drawing from her disagreement with Benedict over Benedict's search for a "new country" when Mead denied that she was a "denizen" there, she used metaphors of citizenship in *Sex and Temperament* to describe the security of feeling part of a reproductive group. She referred to the "inalienable right" of being male or female; she criticized women who identified themselves as men for engaging in an act of "sex-disenfranchisement." In her article in *Forum* in 1935, she wrote: "A person without full sex membership is worse off than a man without a country."[30]

In societies like the Arapesh that didn't have a masculine/feminine division in gender roles, she maintained, there weren't any "homosexuals." She didn't mean that homosexual behavior couldn't occur; it was homosexuality as an identity that didn't exist. From *Coming of Age in Samoa* on, she had praised "homosexual" behavior; it was the active/passive distinction—whether for homosexuals or heterosexuals—that she disliked. She couldn't publicly state her belief that bisexuality was the healthiest form of sexual identity, but she alluded to the possibility in *Sex and Temperament*. By 1961 she stated that she had always disliked the word "homosexual" because of the confusion in its meaning between behavior and identity.[31] She didn't, however, suggest an alternative term.

In proposing that gender was multifaceted and sexuality a diffuse drive, Mead came close to becoming a "queer modernist"—but she pulled back. She believed in marriage; she wanted to have a child. On one level she was hostile to the "homosexuality" (the "maleness") in herself and in Gregory Bateson. She didn't want to lose him to Noel Porter and the Half Moon or to the male "fey" culture of Cambridge University. And she still thought of herself as feminine: that self-identity created a problem for her in her belief that cultures determined the "sex roles" of women and men, that gender varied by individual cultures. She eliminated "feminine" and "masculine" from her definition of gender, but she reintroduced both categories as positive toward the end of *Sex and Temperament*. In the last pages of the book, she referred positively to "essential femininity" and "essential masculinity." Drawing on her love of dressing in feminine styles, she wrote: "Just as a festive occasion is the gayer and more charming if the two sexes are dressed differently, so it is in less material matters."[32]

Moreover, she found it impossible to discard entirely the cultural imperatives that men should be strong and masculine. As much as she liked the gentle Arapesh males, for example, she criticized that culture for going too far in scripting the male role as maternal, for, she maintained, some "assertive" elements of masculinity were necessary to ensure social progress. She issued an additional caution about the Arapesh: "Too vivid an appreciation of the rewards of receptivity are incompatible with adult male roles and may even lead to inversion."[33] In other words, if men and women were defined as too similar and if cultures defined sexual behavior too much in terms of "receptivity" and not enough in terms of phallic control and orgasmic climax, men might reorient themselves to their feminine side and become homosexual.

Drawing from her Deweyian philosophy, she asserted that "a sacrifice of distinctions in sex-personality may mean a sacrifice of complexity." In other words, she believed that the ethnic and regional diversity of the United States produced its vitality. Drawing on her propensity to bring all sides of a debate together, to create webs of connections, she extended that principle of diversity to sexual identity. In a society without sex distinctions, she concluded, individuals maladjusted in terms of their "psycho-sexual role" would no longer exist. Yet with them would disappear "the knowledge that there is more than one set of possible values." Mead's reform politics rested on the value of complexity over simplicity; she believed that the hope for the future lay in the many groups and ethnicities of a democratic society like the United States.[34] That principle of complexity could extend to sexual orientation, to viewing it as functioning best for society if a variety of sexualities were in operation. In the end she was sympathetic to Benedict's lesbian orientation, her existing as a denizen in a new country.

IN *SEX AND TEMPERAMENT* Mead disagreed with Benedict about the nature of the berdache and of homosexuality, and in her concluding chapters she also disagreed with her mentor about the position of men in American society. Although she disliked aggressive men, her analysis of the Tchambuli led her to see their behavior as stemming from insecurity. She described the adult men in Tchambuli, who acted like women, as the most neurotic men she had ever seen. The sexes were out of balance there, and that was a problem. With their rampant sexuality, their "shaven, unadorned heads," and their "solid, preoccupied, and powerful" behavior, the Tchambuli women had taken over the masculine role. She called the homosexual sex she saw them engaging in "rough play," even though she usually identified sex between women as gentle and caring. She later wrote that women were "cherishing" when they engaged in sex with each other, while men engaging in sex with other men practiced "emotional asymmetry."[35] Above all, the Tchambuli women had taken over the masculine role of economic provider.

In this second line of reasoning about men in *Sex and Temperament*, she viewed them as more insecure than domineering. In *Patterns of Culture* Benedict had noted that all societies consider men's occupations more important than women's. Mead agreed with this estimation, but she turned it on its head, concluding that men's occupations are considered superior because men's egos are fragile. In *Male and Female*, written a decade later, she carried the male-insecurity thesis further, contending that men envied women's anatomy and their childbearing role so much that they suffered more from "womb envy" than women did from Freud's "penis envy."[36]

Her relationship with Gregory Bateson and the other men in her life influenced her in taking this position on men. She was concerned about Bateson's sense of incomplete masculinity—and in real life she used her femininity to bolster his masculine self. In *Coming of Age in Samoa* she had viewed "homosexual sex" as operating to improve "heterosexual sex," and that perspective helped Reo Fortune tolerate—as much as he could—her relationship with Benedict. Similarly, in *Sex and Temperament* she wove her love for a man and her desire to reassure him into a work of scholarship.

On one level, *Sex and Temperament* was a tribute to Benedict, as Mead used Benedict's configurationist theory rather than Radcliffe-Brown's functionalism or Clark Wissler's acculturation approach that she had used in studying the Omaha. (That approach involved analyzing the current state of a society—including the impacts of Westernization—rather than the "ethnographic present.") *Sex and Temperament* was also a tribute to Bateson, whose expertise on the Tchambuli was crucial to the book. I don't mean to suggest that Mead reported her findings for these societies inaccurately, although she responded to a number of individuals in writing the book. While completing it, she confessed to Bateson that she was perhaps depending too much on others "to pick up the pieces and tie up the loose ends."[37] Moreover, her concluding chapters, which relate her findings in her three tribal societies directly to the situation in the United States, drew from a number of agendas—scholarly, political, personal. And those agendas may have influenced her ranking of dominant and deviant behaviors in the societies in the main part of the book.

It wasn't hard to see that both her father and Reo Fortune were insecure underneath their masculine bluster. Moreover, when she was a child her grandmother had maintained that girls were faster to develop than boys; from her earliest years she had been sturdier and more capable than her brother. While she was writing *Sex and Temperament* she became involved with John Dollard, another sensitive man who had difficulty with her powerful personality. She was forming professional and personal friendships with men who could protect her against the assaults of the male anthropologists, and she wanted to honor those men, mostly sociologists and psychiatrists, like Lawrence Frank, Erik Erikson, and Erich Fromm. She recognized their insecurities; she wanted to support them.[38] And despite her diatribes against the male anthropologists in her letters to Benedict, she wasn't entirely comfortable attacking them openly. She preferred to mend fences and to demonstrate her humanity.

The situation for men in the United States in the 1930s reinforced Mead's sense of male sensitivity and insecurity. Studies of men out of work during the Depression showed that those men blamed their predicament on themselves more than on the economic system. The ideal of aggressive masculinity resurfaced in the 1930s, motivated by "a crisis in masculinity" among men, who often felt impotent in the face of unemployment. Edmund Wilson and other literary critics called for a new masculine realism; it appeared, for example, in the "tough guy" heroes of hard-boiled detective fiction written by Dashiell Hammett and Raymond Chandler and in the gangster and the cowboy in films. Comic strip superheroes like Dick Tracy and Superman were created, and Superman's secret identity in the regular world was the bumbling Clark Kent. Dagwood Bumstead, of Blondie-and-Dagwood fame, was initially meant to satirize the upper-class homosexual type, before he became an ineffectual man who relied on his domineering wife. He was, as Mead put it in *Sex and Temperament*, a "hen-pecked" husband, or, as she put it in *Male and Female*, a Caspar Milquetoast type.[39]

In her article in *Forum* in 1935, Mead sympathized with professional women who, she maintained, might be classified as "homosexual" if they stepped out of line. In her article on "primitive" women published that same year, she identified women in general as oppressed in almost every society. Yet in *Sex and Temperament* she saw it differently. Now it was the women who were powerful, while their position as "economic providers" threatened the men. One wonders if on some level she extended that thesis to herself. Did she see both Gregory Bateson and Reo Fortune as threatened by her employment at the Museum of Natural History and her income from her books when they had difficulty finding work?

BEGINNING BY CRITICIZING male power in the early 1930s, Mead swung full circle to argue that men were the victims of female power. This was "postfeminism" with a vengeance—or it was Mead covering every position, bringing all sides together and not worrying about contradictions. Still, in *Sex and Temperament* she wasn't charitable to the feminist movement, which she implied was partly responsible for the problems of men. The United States, she wrote, "has bred a generation of women who model their lives on the pattern of their school-teachers and their aggressive, directive mothers. Their brothers stumble about in a vain attempt to preserve the myth of male dominance in a society in which girls have come to consider dominance their natural right."[40] She called the women's rights leaders of her mother's generation "violent feminists."

Mead didn't cite any feminist theorists in *Sex and Temperament*, except for Emily Putnam, whom she criticized for not including more about men in *The Lady*. She also mentioned Mathilde and Mathias Vaerting's *The Dominant Sex*. She liked that book better than Putnam's, since the Vaertings included men in their analysis, although she was critical of their haphazard use of anthropology. Absent from Mead's book are the major theorists of early feminism: Olive Schreiner, Charlotte Perkins Gilman, Ellen Key, Elsie Clews Parsons.

Yet Mead's feminism—or lack of it—can't be seen apart from her mother, who was still a leader of reform organizations in Pennsylvania in the 1930s. It's doubtful that Mead derived her criticisms of powerful women entirely from Emily Fogg Mead: both Gregory Bateson and Geoffrey Gorer had formidable mothers, and Elsie Clews Parsons was still a bête noir in anthropology for Mead and Benedict. Yet Mead doesn't seem to have come to terms with those childhood years in which Emily immersed herself in her women's rights and reform activities and left caring for the children to her mother-in-law—and to Margaret. In a series of letters to her mother from Bali in 1938, Margaret criticized Emily's feminism. She drew from themes in popular and feminist writing as early as the 1920s about the antimale nature of the turn-of-the-century women's rights movement, in which Emily had been a leader. "The evil of the prohibition movement," Margaret wrote, "was that they defined men as the problem. A lot of the anti-war movement was based on the idea of men liking war, liking getting away from wives and families, getting drunk, whoring and raging about. [But] men should keep men in order. . . . Men who see women as moral mentors are permanently crippled emotionally."[41] Was she referring to her mother's attempts to control her father's behavior? In drafts of *Blackberry Winter* written in the early 1970s, she came to a different conclusion about that behavior, viewing her father as welcoming her mother's morality as a means of self-control.

In 1938, however, she extended her criticism of powerful women to the women in the contemporary women's movement, making them sound like the descendants of her antimale women's rights advocates at the turn of the century. "The professional feminist thinks very often she is friendly to men, but actually she is friendly to the things in men which she wants to be herself." She didn't identify what she meant by "things in men"; one assumes that she meant some version of force and power. Anyway, she continued, what men need is "the feeling that women are different from themselves, and that women are friendly to just those aspects of masculinity which are peculiarly masculine and which women have not got."[42] In other words, she seems to recommend that women operate according to some version of the masculine/feminine binary that she had criticized in *Sex and Temperament* only three years before.

Geoffrey Gorer called Mead a "third-generation feminist," and that designation elucidates her feminist position. Gorer spelled out what he meant in an unpublished biographical statement about Mead that seems derived from conversations with her. The first generations of feminists, he contended, had to prove to a doubting world that they could function in male professions as ably as the men. Her mother and grandmother had succeeded in doing that. Because of their success, Margaret didn't have to prove herself in the same way. She could espouse a different kind of feminism, one based on celebrating women's difference from men, while not criticizing the men. As a woman she could do things that men couldn't do: she could use her feminine intuition and skills to carve out new intellectual and career territory. Thus in her fieldwork she studied domesticity and child rearing—and she proved to the academic world the importance of these women's concerns.[43]

How she reconciled this celebratory notion of women's separate sphere of interest with her writings on women as oppressed and her attack on them as improperly domineering in *Sex and Temperament* and other works isn't entirely clear. Yet those contradictions in her thinking may also have stemmed from her chronological position in the middle decades of the twentieth century, bringing together strains of analysis that had been separated in her mother's generation, when feminists who celebrated motherhood split off from women's rights advocates who demanded equality and sometimes sounded antimale. Mead stood in the middle, reflecting the influence of two positions in the early twentieth century—and her own experience of being married and having a career.[44]

Mead often criticized the feminist movement and refused to apply the term to herself. Yet as Gorer's "third-generation feminist" she had absorbed her mother's ideas as a child, and she sometimes echoed those concepts in her work. She proposed radical notions about gender identity and about child rearing, and she always advocated communal living. On occasion she sounded like the women's rights advocates of the 1900s and the feminists of the 1960s in excoriating men for oppressing women. At other times—as in the concluding chapters of *Sex and Temperament*—she was sympathetic to men and indicted feminists for being antimale, while she celebrated domesticity and child rearing and took a separatist position, maintaining that women should use their special skills to create a better world. She held those ideas together with the force of her personality and the complex mode of a work like *Sex and Temperament*.

These themes help to explain the contradictions in *Sex and Temperament*, especially its rejection of "masculine" and "feminine" while retaining "male" and "female." That contradiction, which is even stronger in *Male and Female*, has long puzzled critics. Given Mead's celebration of child rearing, Betty Friedan in *The Feminine Mystique* identified her as the architect of the back-to-the-home movement of the 1950s. The feminists of the 1970s, however, focused on her argument that sex roles were social constructs to claim her as their forerunner. In answer to the charge of contradicting herself, she wrote in her ebullient fashion in 1950 that "we not only can have it both ways, but many more than both ways." She also asserted broadly, again without clarifying what she meant: "The biological bases of development as human beings . . . can be seen as potentialities by no means fully tapped by our human imagination."[45]

It's unusual to identify Mead as a biological visionary, but in many ways she was. Even well-known biologist Helen Fisher, in her introduction to the most recent edition of *Sex and Temperament*, describes Mead's "new ways of seeing" as involving her stand for the social construction of gender. Mead was never a precise utopian: she realized the potential of science and technology to create a perfected future, but she feared their destructive power and realized the pitfalls of prediction, so she rarely tied down those claims to specific prophecies. In this instance, however, her utopianism involved the theories of constitutional types—theories in which physical appearance was a strong component.

Her most persuasive statement reconciling her adherence to procreation with her attack on the categories of femininity and masculinity occurs in *Male and Female*, written when Hitler was no longer in power. In this statement, focused on constitutional types, she provides a taste of how radical her stance drawn from biology could be. For she proposed reversing centuries of Western adherence to hierarchical ideals of masculine and feminine beauty based on light over dark, youth over age, and height and muscularity in men and smallness and delicacy in women. Those standards are at the heart of patriarchical oppression, as enduring as the oppressions of race and class, to which they are intimately related. In Mead's utopian scheme the basis for classifying male and female appearance would be radically different. Small men would be classified with small women, fat men with fat women, and domineering men with domineering women. The major distinction between male and female left standing would be pregnancy and childbearing. In this new arrangement, "masculine" and "feminine" would take on new meanings. The statement went:

> The fiery, initiating woman would be classified only with fiery, initiating men of her own type. . . . When the meek little Caspar Milquetoast was placed side by side not with a prize-fighter, but with the meekest female version of himself, he might be seen to be much more masculine than she. The plump man with soft breast-tissue, double chin, protruding buttocks, whom one has only to put in a bonnet to make him like a woman, when put beside the equally plump woman will [have a masculinity] still indubitable when contrasted with the female of his own kind. . . . And the slender male and female dancers, hipless and breastless, will seem not a feminine male and a boyish female, but male and female of a special type.[46]

MEAD'S *SEX AND TEMPERAMENT* both celebrated and critiqued Benedict's *Patterns of Culture*. As much as she depended on Benedict in writing this book, Mead was separating herself from the woman who was her fictive mother. Students go beyond professors; daughters reject mothers. Benedict realized this in *Patterns of Culture* when she pointed to generational rebellion as a force behind social change. She had launched Mead's career, and Mead had done exactly what she wanted. She had become famous; she had helped Benedict understand her identity; she had inspired her to write *Patterns of Culture*. Without Mead, Benedict could never have achieved her brilliant career. She would never stop loving Mead, reading her work—and pursuing her own career.

Benedict's letters to Mead during these years contain only encouragement and praise. To expose their disagreements, one has to examine their published work. In letters to Benedict, Mead was critical of *Patterns of Culture*, but Benedict's only written response to *Sex and Temperament* was to praise it ambiguously for having shown her that over the course of her life she had turned herself into an "androgyne"; in other words, Mead had validated her combination of masculine and feminine. Reviewing *Sex and Temperament* in the *New York Herald Tribune*, Benedict praised Mead for her many insights—while making no reference to any input from her. By 1935, when *Sex and Temperament* was published, Benedict was working with Mead on *Cooperation and Competition Among Primitive Peoples* and overseeing her student Irving Goldman in writing a criticism of her analysis of Zuñi culture. Benedict could take criticism; she understood the dialectical nature of scholarly discourse and scientific advance.

Moreover, Benedict drew from Mead in defining the basis of homosexuality in an article, "Sex in Primitive Society," that she wrote in 1939. In that article she maintained that the berdache role came into existence primarily in Native American societies that drew a sharp distinction between male and female roles. That was the case with the Dakota, she now asserted, in which the berdaches took the passive role in sex with men. Among the nearby Ojibwa, however, there weren't any berdaches because this society didn't differentiate gender roles. A woman, for example, could go on the warpath or become a shaman: she didn't need to become a woman-man to do so. In *Sex and Temperament*, Benedict wrote, Margaret Mead had shown the importance of the belief in a division between male and female to the existence of homosexuality, which was mostly a matter of social conditioning.[47]

Once Mead began writing about gender, Benedict ceded the subject to her; her brief analysis of male and female in her article in 1939 is unusual for her during those years. And Mead began to use Benedict's configurationist model less. Other individuals with differing approaches now became important to her, including Erik Erikson, a Freudian trained in Europe and analyzed by Anna Freud, who specialized in early childhood development and had studied anthropology with Alfred Kroeber at Berkeley. At this point in his career Erikson was emphasizing a variation on Freud's theories of early personality development, his oral, anal, and phallic stages.

Mead applied those stages in some of her work, including that on the Balinese. And she listened even more closely to Gregory Bateson, trained in biology, with his analytic, organic mind that saw subtle connections, shifting realities, and nuanced structures behind social and cultural forms. As long as they were married, he was an intellectual partner and guide for her, as important as Benedict had ever been. Mead always found mentors to follow; Bateson now became preeminent among them. Through him, she asserted, "I have finally realized my complete dream of having someone to follow."[48]

IN THE SPRING OF 1936 Margaret Mead married Gregory Bateson in Singapore, on their way to Bali, where they would remain until 1938. They had discussed the possibility of studying the Balinese while they were still in Tchambuli and constructing the "squares." Under its rubrics, Bali represented a type of cultural personality that neither Mead nor Bateson had studied: one entirely "fey." From a film she had seen on the Balinese, Mead remembered that their men and women had a similar body type: they were small and wiry; the women had small breasts and the men fatty nipples that resembled breasts. The Balinese also had a distant, removed personality, one that Mead and Bateson later described as "vacant" or marked by "awayness."

The Balinese were theatrical, continually putting on artistic productions—dance, theater, and puppet shows—while also producing art and artifacts. Trance was common among them, from spontaneous trances of ordinary people to those of seers and of actors in plays. Trances could be calm or agitated: Mead was to see young men in trance walking on coals and biting off the heads of chickens. It added up to what seemed to Mead and Bateson a "schizophrenic" pattern, in line with current definitions of that mental condition as involving hearing voices and being removed from personal and social interaction.

Given Gregory's "Bengali fits," Margaret's and Ruth's eidetic visions, and Reo's moods, Gregory and Margaret had become interested in that mental condition. Ever since the evolutionists of the late nineteenth century had equated "primitive" peoples with the mentally ill, some anthropologists had been interested in concepts of mental abnormality. Jung's theories about culture were based on his psychiatric patients; the mentally ill were of major interest to Benedict in *Patterns of Culture*.[49] The challenge with the Balinese was to determine how temperamental categories operated in a society in which "being fey" predominated—and physical types were similar across gender. Moreover, evidence from Balinese culture might substantiate Ruth's contention that what was considered abnormal in one culture was normal in another—and that the definitions of mental illness based on Western experience might have to be revised in light of their expressions in a non-Western culture.

Once Gregory returned to Cambridge from Sydney in 1932, he persuaded the administrators of a mental asylum near Cambridge to let him interview their schizophrenic patients. But he found those patients "too far gone" in their illness for him to get much information from them. He wrote Margaret in 1934 that they should instead study "incipent schizophrenics." Yet he cautioned her: "If we are to do the lunatics we should certainly work with a definite time limit and with a steady established life as a base. I have come to realize how near lunacy all this playing with the squares is."[50]

Meanwhile, another friend of Mead's from her undergraduate years at Barnard, a wealthy New York writer named Jane Belo, also stimulated her interest in Bali. Belo had been studying Balinese ritual for some time. She and her husband, composer Colin McPhee, who studied its music, had a house on Bali, and they spent time there. Then a proposal from the new dementia praecox committee—"dementia praecox" was the older term for schizophrenia—offered funding to scholars to study the condition. In addition to all this, Geoffrey Gorer had written a travel book about Bali, which he had visited.

Going to Bali seemed ideal: Margaret and Gregory could remove themselves from criticism of their marriage. Bali had a reputation then, as now, for its beauty. They had a significant theoretical question to explore. Bali wasn't a "primitive" society; they could live in some comfort there. Hundreds of thousands of people lived on the island; its society was different from those they had studied in New Guinea. It had a caste system derived from India by way of Java centuries before. Elites practiced the Hindu religion, while the ordinary people had a traditional religion and culture based on ancient folk beliefs and practices. Wanting to focus on ordinary people, Margaret and Gregory spent much of their time on Bali studying the population of an impoverished mountain village, while also setting up stations in an old palace in the district headquarters and in a priestly household in a nearby city.

There was also a community of European expatriates on Bali. Like Belo and McPhee, many were drawn to Bali because of its art, music, and dance. They included Katherine Mershon, a dancer, and the German artist Walter Spies, a sophisticated painter and connoisseur of Balinese art who encouraged native painters and worked to preserve the traditional culture of the island. This community welcomed Mead and Bateson. Mershon and Belo assisted them in their research; Spies found them a house in which to live and ceremonies to observe. The situation was different from New Guinea, where the colonial administrators were often racists with little respect for the native people. The group of Europeans and Americans on Bali celebrated the native culture.[51]

During her time on Bali, Mead became fed up with the criticisms of her work as journalistic. Why was it, she wrote John Dollard, that psychoanalysts and social workers celebrated her work, while anthropologists carped at her? Still, she was determined to prove herself to them. While Bateson took photographs, she observed daily life in a determined manner. She wrote Dollard that she intended to demonstrate to everyone's satisfaction that she didn't just pick incidents out in the life of a people and study them to the exclusion of everything else. To show the depth of her research she was keeping a record of literally everything that happened in the village.[52]

Yet she didn't entirely reject the criticism of her work. In her introduction to *Balinese Character* (1942), a collection of over 750 of the photographs that Bateson took on Bali, with accompanying text, Mead seemed to agree with her critics when she defined her previous fieldwork methodology as having "serious limitations." The problem, she stated, was that she couldn't adequately convey to her readers what her informants had told her in their native language because she wrote in English, while because she hadn't been raised in their culture she couldn't thoroughly understand their thought processes. She called her previous work, with its inevitable imprecision, close to "fiction."[53] In 1941 she suggested to Benedict that they hold a conference on the need for anthropologists to disclose in their ethnographies their personal situation with regard to the people they were studying: their age, class, status, gender, and personal prejudices. To make certain that hidden features of their personalities were disclosed, Mead suggested that they take Rorschach and other personality tests and include the results in the ethnographies they wrote.[54]

Her use of the word "character" in the title of her book on Bali with Gregory Bateson may also indicate that she viewed ethnographies as problematic, for "character" can mean the characters in a play or a novel, operating in a fictional world. Mead used the term "plot" for a new technique—which she drew from Freud via Erikson—of finding key moments in childhood and then correlating them to episodes of the central rituals of a culture; in *Male and Female* she described the societies that she had studied as like the "old novels"—such as those by Dickens—that had long casts of characters in them. Yet in an article in which she discussed the relationship between the words "personality," "character," and "temperament," she placed them in a hierarchy—and added the word "constitution" to indicate the importance of body type. "Personality," the overriding word, could be broken down into temperament, the inherited predisposition; constitution, the body configuration; and character, how the individual takes on social patterning.[55] According to Abraham Roback, neo-Freudians used the word "character" to identify the ego and the superego as opposed to the libido.[56]

To document Bali, Bateson and Mead took photographs. That was a way of getting around the dependence on "words," a dependence that might lead her astray; with numerous photographs supporting her, no one could contend that she hadn't seen what she said she saw.[57] In the end they took thousands of photographs—25,000 altogether. Bateson took the photographs; Mead did the note-taking. Soon after they arrived the film he had brought with him ran out, so he ordered film from the United States in hundred-foot rolls, which he cut to the right size himself. He developed his negatives each night after they finished the day's work. They photographed sequences of events in religious ceremonies and plays, and they especially photographed interactions between parents and children, particularly women breastfeeding their babies. They also made films. They became supreme observers, using cameras to record cultures, inaugurating the field of visual anthropology.

In her introduction to *Balinese Character*, Mead wrote a brief description of Balinese society. As she expected, she didn't find males and females differing that much in physiology or in possessing the same calm, remote manner. Yet the major figures in dramatic productions were a ferocious witch and a gentle dragon, and the productions culminated in a fight between their followers, with those of the dragon going into trance and symbolically killing themselves with their swords. The witch wore a ferocious mask, with animal tusks; she had long, menacing fingernails and a high, eerie laugh. Mead described the witch in an article on Bali she included in *Childhood in Contemporary*

Cultures, a book she edited with Martha Wolfenstein, as wearing "the accentuated symbols of both sexes, with long protruding tongue, pendulous breasts, covered with repulsive hair."[58]

Employing a Freudian perspective, Mead interpreted those figures as representing the mother and the father in Balinese culture. She concluded that mothers, through a process of subtle rejection of their children, beginning with breast-feeding, generated a repressed anger that exploded symbolically in the figure of the witch. In contrast, the dragon represented the gentle Balinese father, who soothed his children and played with them. Yet the culture seemed fixated on the male sex organ. Mothers played with their son's penises when they were babies, and boys played openly with their own. Cockfighting was a central social event. Every man owned a cock and spent hours grooming and playing with it, ruffling its feathers and putting pepper on its anus to make it a more aggressive fighter. And dramatic productions were filled with obscenities about anal sex.[59]

Yet Mead didn't find much active/passive homosexuality on Bali. As in Samoa, she observed casual homosexual play among the young boys. As among the Arapesh, she observed little adult homosexuality. Since the sexes were so similar, men could just as well have sex with women as with men. Because of the male passivity, however, young men easily became partners for outsiders who approached them—again like the Arapesh. There weren't any Balinese laws against homosexuality, and no one could conceptualize sex relations without the male penis. She observed several female homosexuals, but the "initiator" among them used an artificial male phallus. She later concluded, however, that the Balinese may have realized that Westerners were hostile to same-sex relationships and they ended homosexuality for this reason—while traces of it still remained in their plays.[60]

Mead didn't like Balinese culture. She didn't like the people's lack of initiative and their high energy level that seemed to go only into art and drama. She found the Balinese frustrating to work with. They didn't respond to her; Bateson called them "gazelles." She could vamp a New Guinea culture in twenty minutes by cuddling a baby, she asserted, but nothing she did seemed to work with the Balinese—except to pay them for interviews and for putting on plays and ceremonies. The people in their mountain village regarded them at first as Brahmin aristocrats or as Western tourists, only there to gawk.[61] She finally reached them through her doctoring, for she had Western medicines that were effective in treating fevers and sores.

The Balinese irritated Mead because of her American drive and energy and her desire to see the world transformed. In a letter to Benedict, she characterized them as "anal feys," using Freud's term for his stage of infant development focused on retention. "They have charm, but no warmth," she wrote. "They work tirelessly, but they have no sense of enterprise. They are like clocks wound up when young for life," and "they dissipate all strain in artistic expression." "Feys could never be culture planners," she wrote to Geoffrey Gorer, who liked Balinese culture for its calmness, its aesthetic view of life, and its lack of a drive toward domination. Gorer wrote to Benedict that he thought Margaret was nostalgic on Bali for "American Rugged Individualism." By this phrase, he hastened to add, he didn't mean any "will to power," but rather the American emphasis on individuality.[62] Fascism was advancing in Europe, and Mead was living in an outpost of a colonial power. Attention to social change was imperative.

In contrast to the "primitive" societies she had studied, whose small size and homogeneity made them relatively easy to analyze, Bali was too complex to understand quickly, Mead decided. She kept encountering elements of the culture that she couldn't assimilate into her understanding. She finally called them "survivals" from an earlier period of time.[63] Whether she continued to view the Balinese as "incipient schizophrenics" remains moot; she didn't write about that issue. In 1952, however, she stated that schizophrenics were simply one variation of the human race with their own special potential and that Balinese society should be praised for having translated that potential into a distinctive culture.[64]

Yet Mead's portrait of manipulating mothers and gentle fathers on Bali fed into the growing criticism of mothers in the United States. Indeed, by the 1930s some Freudians were asserting that "overbearing" mothers were destroying sons. Mead joined the critics of mothers for the first time in an article in 1936. Lawrence Frank, John Dollard, and Erik Erikson all subscribed to the belief; Gregory Bateson would expand it into his theory of the major cause of schizophrenia proceeding from overbearing mothers. Recent scholars studying the "mother-blaming thesis" find its genesis among middle-class social workers, both male and female, in the 1920s. Undergoing the process of professionalization, the argument goes, they separated themselves from their working-class clients by adopting a critical attitude toward the mothers who came to see them. Mead interacted with that group through Lawrence Frank and especially through Caroline Zachry, a friend of theirs who ran a major child-development clinic in New York City, and who subscribed to the "mother-blaming" thesis. She included it in her findings from a large project on adolescents that she ran in New York City, a project that Mead participated in.[65]

GREGORY AND MARGARET seemed happy on Bali, but there were underlying problems. They worked round the clock, with Gregory taking photographs and Margaret writing down observations all day long before they fell, exhausted, into bed. The last thing they did at night was wash their faces in the water he had used in developing the day's photographs. One wonders how much Gregory liked taking on Margaret's work habits. He had wanted her to motivate him, but did he really want to work at her feverish pace?

There was also a problem with Jane Belo, who assisted Margaret with her work. Jane wasn't an easy person to deal with; Mary Catherine Bateson would describe her as "extraordinarily delicate in her perceptions" and "beautiful and a little withdrawn." She later became seriously schizophrenic, and she spent years in mental hospitals or drugged with Thorazine.[66] Colin McPhee, her husband during her time on Bali, was mostly homosexual; as long as she was married to him she looked for male lovers, and men responded to her beauty. Margaret described Jane to Carrie Kelly as having, like Steve, "learned her manners from Parisian fairies." They have, Carrie responded, "an uncanny knack of making one feel protective and male."[67] And there was Gregory, with his history of involvements with unhappily married women and his free-love beliefs. He and Jane had a brief affair.

Before that happened, Jane had a furious quarrel with Margaret over the way Margaret treated her. In a sense, Jane had apprenticed herself to Margaret—but she was neither a neophyte in studying Bali nor an official student of hers. After several months on Bali, Jane decided that Margaret was bullying her, and she told her off. To work out their difficulties they wrote letters to each other, and those letters are an important source revealing Margaret's sense of herself. Her letters focus on how Jane has failed to understand her and has hurt her. In her close relationships with others, she maintains, she always lets them take the lead. Sometimes she "danced to their tune" so hard that they forgot the original terms of the relationship; in this case Jane had agreed that Margaret was to be the boss, and now Jane was demanding a lot of authority. "I don't like playing the dominant role with anyone,"

Margaret wrote, "I like people to be equal or superior to me." If anything, "I consider my weakness to others to be a defect." She didn't like to show her vulnerability, she stated, but she confessed: "I seem to have so little control over the quivers in my voice." "I do cry easily," she finished, "much more easily than you think."[68]

Jane replied that Margaret was wrong. The real problem was Margaret's jealousy of her femininity. Every time Margaret saw her in a new dress, or a bed-jacket, or even smiling at a group of Balinese, Margaret acted aggressively toward her. Margaret didn't seem to realize that her mental and administrative abilities were so substantial that she didn't need to use her femininity to get ahead—but Jane, much less gifted than she, did. Whenever the two of them were together with Gregory and Jane flirted with him, Margaret became especially domineering. She tried to attract Gregory away from Jane through her verbal brilliance, like a male bird showing off his plumage to a female to attract her sexually. And, Jane continued, Margaret's approach worked. For Jane never saw anything but a look of adoration for her in Gregory's eyes. She finished by assuring Margaret that she would never have an affair with a friend's husband.

Like many individuals in such a situation, she didn't entirely mean what she said—at least the part about not seducing a friend's husband. She and Gregory had the affair, and Margaret, whose free-love beliefs didn't permit jealousy, remained friends with her. Once back in the United States, Jane divorced Colin McPhee and married Columbia professor Frank Tannenbaum, a radical who studied Mexico and Latin America. They were close to Gregory and Margaret; Margaret remained close to Jane's ex-husband Colin McPhee.

Jane and Margaret's letters to each other weren't the end to this matter, for Margaret wrote other close friends about her problem with Jane. It seemed to surprise her, to reveal something about herself that she couldn't understand—or didn't want to accept. In a letter to Geoffrey Gorer she wrote that she knew she sometimes talked in an excited manner, which made others feel she was being aggressive. But Jane had complained so much about her delivery that she had slowed it down to the point that she felt as if she was speaking in slow motion. Yet Jane still accused her of speaking too fast and of being aggressive.[69] She reported to Ruth that she was baffled that Jane seemed to think of her as a man; Ruth didn't respond to that statement. The issue of Margaret's aggression wasn't resolved: she got into a similar debate with John Dollard, who didn't like it when she attacked his ideas. With the advent of World War II, scholars were studying aggression; it's not surprising that the issue appeared in Margaret's personal life. In fact, Dollard wrote a major analysis of that emotional drive. He himself was argumentative, while sensitive to criticism and slights. The squabbling between him and Margaret became too much for him; their friendship ended when they quarreled over the United States' entry into World War II.[70]

MARGARET AND GREGORY finished their work on Bali in 1938. Then they went to New Guinea to restudy the Iatmul; they stayed there eight months, until war appeared imminent. The Walter Spies incident brought them back to Bali briefly, when the Dutch government suddenly arrested all suspected European homosexuals who had come to their territories in the Far East, presumably to have sex with the passive young men there. Even Jane Belo was arrested because of a compromising photograph. Gregory went to the police to plead her case; his defense got her off. Spies was also arrested, and Mead wrote her friend-of-the-court brief to help him. Yet as much as she liked Spies, Mead wasn't convinced that all the homosexuals who had come to the Dutch territories were as nonexploitative of the young men there as he. She wrote to Ruth that she sometimes sympathized with the Dutch, who were attacking promiscuity, not "dignified personal relationships." "Why men can't manage inversion except in terms of promiscuity and prostitution," she asserted, "is difficult to understand."[71]

The "active males" that she had criticized in *Sex and Temperament* were troubling her again. And they would continue to do so. In 1961 she went so far as to contend that the homosexual rape of young men was so extensive that it needed to be regulated by a social mechanism as powerful as the incest taboo.[72] Had Mead on some level internalized the homophobia of American culture? Did her statement relate to the youthful experience at school or elsewhere of one of the men in her life? Her strongest stand in the 1961 article was for bisexuality, and that's not surprising, given her position in *Sex and Temperament*. Now she was willing to use the evidence from genes and hormones. Recent endocrine research, she contended, had proved that bisexuality was the basic drive of many animal species and of humans. If same-sex behavior was "natural," then individuals who considered themselves to be incapable of a homosexual response had failed to develop their full potential. She proposed—as Freud had years before—that the real issue to investigate might be heterosexuality and not homosexuality. And she pointed to the wide range of homosexuality in human cultures—from the berdaches of the Plains Indians to the Marindanims of New Guinea, a tribal society whose members believed that everyone was homosexual by nature and that heterosexuality was difficult to achieve.[73] By 1962, writing about the 1950s, she criticized heterosexual men for their "phallic athleticism."[74]

The outbreak of World War II ended anthropological work overseas for the duration of the conflict, and it changed the direction of Mead's career. She and Bateson had devised a huge project to study Bali. They intended to bring sociologists, psychologists, and anthropologists to the country, teach them about Balinese society at a conference, and then assign each to a village, along with an interpreter and a bilingual secretary, for detailed work. The result would be a definitive study of the island. She and Bateson had even taken a three-year lease on a Balinese palace to serve as the center for the project. When World War II broke out, they abandoned their plans.

But the grand impulse behind it would reappear in Mead's thinking, as she returned in 1939 to a United States threatened by a world war and shifted her focus from prestate societies to national and international issues. Moreover, she was pregnant, and she looked forward to the birth of her child and to being together again with Ruth Benedict.

CHAPTER 13

Race, Gender, and Sexuality

IN THE CENTER OF the Columbia University campus, amid its huge neo-Baroque and neo-Renaissance buildings, stands a statue of the goddess Columbia, a version of the Roman Athena, the goddess of wisdom and war. Dating from the 1890s, when the buildings on the present campus were constructed, the goddess Columbia is seated in a chair—or on a throne—with a book on her lap, a scepter in one hand, and a crown on her head. Her arms are raised as though to bless the university. She is a Sibyl of knowledge and authority, the goddess as alma mater, the mother of us all. The statue isn't far from the graduate anthropology department; during their years at Columbia, Benedict and Mead must have passed by it many times.[1]

The entrance to the American Museum of Natural History, where Benedict first taught Mead and Mead spent more than fifty years as a curator, has a different sculptural motif, one constructed in the late 1920s. It celebrates Theodore Roosevelt as an imperialist, a big game hunter, and a very masculine man. Outside the museum is a statue of Roosevelt, mounted on a large horse between an African and a Native American man. The figures, each dressed as a naked "savage" in a loincloth, stand on either side of Teddy and the horse; Roosevelt leads them to "civilization." Inside the foyer, Teddy's life is depicted in frescos with captions like "Only those are fit to live who do not fear to die" and "Aggressive fighting for the right is the noblest sport the world affords." Words like "truth" and "justice" are there: no male leader in American history could attain heroic stature without honoring such values. When Mead was a curator, the atrium also contained sculptures of Africans killing lions, with a room off to one side filled with stuffed elephants. They were tributes to Roosevelt as a hunter and to the museum's explorers who killed big game to be stuffed and displayed at the museum. In the tribute to Roosevelt, women aren't in sight. If anything, it honors the men who ran the museum during the first decade of Mead's employment there, who conceived the memorial and raised the funds to build it—and a number of whom were racists dedicated to Anglo-European supremacy.[2]

These monuments at Columbia and at the museum stand as silent witnesses to the importance of race and gender in the nation's memory and its traditions of intellect and learning. How were Benedict and Mead treated as women at those two institutions? What were their views on race? Did they see a connection between race and gender? In *Sex and Temperament in Three Primitive Societies* and *Male and Female*, Margaret Mead wrote the major treatises on gender for her era, while in *Race: Science and Politics*, published in 1940, Ruth Benedict did the same for race. Indeed, after *Patterns of Culture* Benedict largely gave up writing about women, while Mead took up the subject. Similarly, Mead at first left the subject of racial justice to her friend, taking it up with the coming of World War II. Her earlier stance on the matter raises the issues of her employment at the Museum of Natural History and of the meaning of the theory of the "squares" in terms of the question of race. That theory remained important in her private life for many years, but she didn't refer to it directly in her published writings, except briefly in *Blackberry Winter*.

DESPITE THE CENTRAL POSITION of the statue of the goddess Columbia at Columbia University, women faculty at the institution weren't treated well. They were relegated to Barnard, Teachers College, and the General Studies Program. The graduate faculty included few women professors; Ruth Benedict didn't become an associate professor until 1937 or a full professor until 1948, shortly before she died. Even when she served as de facto chair of the department for Franz Boas in the 1930s, she couldn't enter the male faculty dining room, from which women were barred; the graduate Faculty of Political Science, which included anthropology, functioned, according to Robert Lynd, as "a very exclusive gentlemen's club."[3] As Boas's retirement approached, Edward Sapir and Alfred Kroeber in turn were offered the senior position, which they turned down. Benedict wasn't seriously considered to replace Boas.

The choice of Ralph Linton from the University of Wisconsin when Boas retired in 1937 was acceptable to her at first. He was a jovial man and a compelling teacher. He had praised her concept of "patterns" in print, although he was more a sociologist than she, interested more in social status and role than in culture. In *The Study of Man* (1936) he substituted the notion of esprit de corps for her "patterns" and based it on the male bonding in football teams and armies.[4] She might have guessed then that they would conflict.

Indeed, Linton identified with male "feats of daring." He never forgot his Mayan bearer during a college vacation he spent in the Guatemalan backcountry, when a poisonous snake bit the bearer on his hand and the man cut the hand off with a machete to stop the poison from spreading. To join the American Expeditionary Forces during World War I, Linton added several years to his age; as a member of the Rainbow Brigade, he fought in four of the five major battles of the war. After the war ended, he showed up for the Columbia graduate program in anthropology dressed in his uniform, and the pacifist Boas criticized him so roughly for wearing it that he withdrew from Columbia and went to Harvard instead. Linton couldn't handle Benedict's reserved manner—the way she smiled vaguely and wouldn't debate him. He thought she was haughty and dismissive—and jealous of him for getting the Columbia job.[5]

Margaret Mead was on Bali during these years; in her letters to Mead, Benedict complained a lot about Linton. In 1938 she wrote: "it's perfectly possible that I may have to wallop Linton hard in public someday. He is a swine."[6] As for Linton, he became "near psychotic" in his dislike of Benedict. He charged her with improperly financing the research of her Ph.D. students when she supported them from her own funds; he accused her of being a communist. According to Robert Suggs, a graduate student at Columbia, Linton wrote (under a pseudonym) detective stories in which a female anthropologist tries to kill a male one.[7] Remembering Linton as a colleague at Yale in the early 1950s, after Benedict's death, Sidney Mintz recollected that he claimed he had killed her through witchcraft. "He produced for me, in a small leather pouch," Mintz remembered, "the Tanala material he said he had used to kill her."[8]

After he came to Columbia, Linton became friendly with psychoanalyst Abram Kardiner, a popular instructor at the New York Psychoanalytic Institute who had studied with Boas years before and had been analyzed by Freud. Influenced by the cultural approach to

analyzing personality, Kardiner broke with the psychoanalytic ortho-
doxy to reject Freud's infant zones of development and the Oedipus
complex as rooted in biology. At Linton's suggestion, he moved the
culture-and-personality seminar he was conducting at the institute
to Columbia. His seminar involved his psychoanalyzing ethnographies done by the Columbia anthropologists, including Benedict's on
the Zuñi, to establish guidelines for ones the seminar would commission, although only one investigator—to Alor, one of the islands of
Indonesia—was ever dispatched. John Dollard came from Yale to
attend the seminar; Erich Fromm and Abraham Maslow showed up
from time to time; even Sapir came once or twice.[9] Harry Stack Sullivan appeared and told Benedict that he had broken with Sapir and was
looking for new allies in the field of anthropology.[10] Some years later
she would teach courses for him at his Washington School of Psychiatry, in Washington, D.C.

The caustic Kardiner was as domineering as Linton, and he didn't
have much respect for Benedict's work. That is apparent in his chapter
on her in his history of major figures in anthropology, in which he criticizes her for engaging in "exaggeration and omission" in reducing cultures to dominant and deviant patterns, while he pictures the "tough,
scowling face of Boas" looking over Benedict's shoulder in firm disagreement with her approach, as her attention strays "from science to
poetry." In an oral interview toward the end of his life Kardiner praised
her physical beauty—while describing her as not intelligent and her
work as not substantial.[11]

Benedict's homosexual orientation, however, may have repelled
Linton and Kardiner, both highly masculine men. She was living with
Natalie Raymond; she defended homosexuality in her work. By the
mid-1930s Wilhelm Stekel led the Freudians in charging that homosexuality was dangerous to the nation's mental health; by 1945 Kardiner became a crusader against same-sex love. In analyzing him,
Freud had traced his personality issues to his "latent homosexuality."
In his book *Sex and Morality*, published in 1954, Kardiner was adamant
that homosexuality had to be eliminated to ensure national stability.[12]

Benedict attracted women as graduate students. Some of them, like
Ruth Underhill and Ruth Landes, were older, and they entered
anthropology after having established themselves in other careers, as
Benedict had. Underhill had been a social worker in New York City;
Landes had worked for black causes in Harlem.[13] Ash Can Cat Hannah
Kahn ("David") often worked as Benedict's secretary; Jeannette Mirsky

was her advisee. All Benedict's students—male and female—admired her for her deep sensitivity to them and to the cultures they studied. They were her children, whether they were female or male. She listened to their personal problems, corresponded with them when they were in the field, and found them fellowships. She even gave them money from her own funds, as she had years before in her "no strings attached" fellowship to Mead. By the late 1930s, she was well off financially; Stanley died in 1936 and left most of his large estate to her. Ruth Landes described how Benedict's graduate students felt about her: "You invoke something like religious enthusiasm among those of us who draw breath from great personal qualities rather than from the pursuit of ambition."[14] Her women students called her "Ruthi."

Reo Fortune charged that there was a lesbian circle in the department, although there isn't much evidence to support his suspicions. In 1936 Mead and Benedict's friend and associate in anthropology Ruth Bunzel suddenly declared her love for Benedict, and they became involved. Benedict had been alienated from Natalie Raymond for some years, but she wasn't deeply committed to the affair with Bunzel; she wrote Mead that she didn't think Bunzel was really homosexual, only fed up with men, whom she attracted but always frightened off. Bunzel taught in General Studies, the extension division of Columbia; she wanted to be closer to the center of the department, which Benedict was chairing. But she turned out to be difficult for Benedict to handle; in 1938 Benedict wrote to Mead that Bunzel disliked the distance that she maintained between them so much that she felt as though she were sitting on a volcano.[15] Benedict and Bunzel remained together on and off for the next year or so, although no documentation about the affair exists aside from Benedict's references to it in several letters she wrote Mead. Eventually both of them found other female partners.

Benedict influenced the gender composition of the graduate student body in anthropology: during the years she was in the department, Columbia had more women graduate students in anthropology than any other program in the nation (almost none of the programs had any women faculty). Writing on the subject of women in anthropology in 1940, Benedict echoed Mead in maintaining that the discipline needed women so that women's activities in tribal societies would be studied. She pointed out that teaching jobs in anthropology in colleges and universities were reserved for men, although she also noted that few of the women's colleges offered courses in anthropology. She helped women at Columbia: she found a lectureship for Mead in the

General Studies Program, and she tried to find Ruth Bunzel a position in the graduate department. She was successful in hiring Gene Weltfish, a Ph.D. student of hers who studied Indian crafts. When Weltfish's position came under question because of her leftist activities, Benedict stormed into a meeting of administrators to protest.[16] As editor of the *Journal of American Folk-Lore*, she was important to women's increased visibility in the folklore society in the 1930s.[17]

After Linton came to the department, Benedict continued as administrative chair for a time. She put together programs to study the indigenous cultures of Latin America and of the Blackfoot tribes, and another program, "The Culture and Personality of the North American Indians," involving twenty tribes. She and Geoffrey Gorer devised the "Handbook of Psychological Leads for Ethnological Field Workers," based on Dollard's life-history method. She dispatched graduate students to a number of Latin American and U.S. Indian areas included in her broad plans, but she never edited the volume of papers they wrote from their fieldwork that she had intended to edit to sum up this research; ultimately Linton took over the project. She did little fieldwork herself in these years, aside from overseeing students studying the Mescalero Apache in 1930 and the Blackfoot in 1939.

In 1938 Marie Eichelberger wrote to Mead that the demands of administration, teaching, and research were overwhelming Benedict. Marie worried that Ruth was depressed; she wore the same blue suit almost every day—and this time, unlike when Margaret first met her, it wasn't a feminist gesture. She didn't go out much in the evenings.[18] Marie, whose hero worship of both Benedict and Mead hadn't diminished and who continued to take care of Mead's personal needs when she was in the field, worried about everyone. Troubled by Marie's letters and by Ruth's failure to write very often, Margaret asked Ruth about her emotional state. She knew that Ruth had started taking hormones for menopausal symptoms the previous year; Ruth had complained that she no longer seemed to have any sex drive.[19] Ruth answered that she wasn't depressed: she was feeling contemplative. She wrote Margaret about having found the country for which she had long searched and about feeling as though she was living in her fantasy world with her father and her beautiful people.

Once Benedict published *Patterns of Culture*, her position as a public intellectual seemed secure, although her problems in the anthropology department didn't go away, especially with Linton there. Displaying her resilience, however, she responded to a difficult situation by taking her career in imaginative directions—by writing *Race*, working for the federal government during World War II, and turning to the study of contemporary cultures once the war ended.

AFTER *PATTERNS OF CULTURE* was published, Benedict didn't write much about gender. With the publication of Mead's *Sex and Temperament*, she left that topic to Mead. In 1938 Mead wrote her that she was thinking of writing a book about sex differences, and she asked Benedict for her opinion on the subject. Benedict replied that she had no ideas about it—either from personal experience or from her knowledge as a scholar. "I'm certain that they're there but I don't have anything to say."[20] Given her years of writing on the subject, her answer is surprising; it seems like an attempt to avoid the question rather than to provide any information. Her two major books after *Patterns of Culture* were *Race*, published in 1940, and *The Chrysanthemum and the Sword*, published in 1946. Both books focus on historical and structural features; they don't investigate gender roles in any depth.

In private letters Benedict continued to maintain that the genders were different, not similar. In two letters she wrote in 1943 she linked the position of women to that of blacks. That year a Dr. Oliver Cope of Vassar College pointed out to her in a letter that she had written extensively about racism but that she hadn't addressed the issue of "sex prejudice." Benedict replied that she was "shocked" to realize that he was correct. She tried to articulate a position, although her stance was contradictory. Maintaining that in every culture men and women were always "dipped in the same dyeing vat," she noted that she had written a brief article several months before in which she coupled race and sex to argue that just as the differences between the races shouldn't be eliminated, it was "false" to "minimize certain differences between the sexes."[21] She didn't say what those differences were.

She clarified her position somewhat in her reaction to several draft chapters of a book on sex differences by Amram Scheinfeld that a friend sent her to read and criticize. In a letter to him, she wrote that she didn't disagree with his conclusion that men and women are different, but she didn't like his use of a "false biologism." She was aware that women, as he pointed out, voted for male candidates in elections, just like men. But he was wrong in contending that an innate feminine nature, rooted in dependency, led women to imitate their husbands in voting. Rather, in a culture based on hierarchy, women internalized mainstream attitudes about gender to become as antiwoman as men. The same principle applied to other issues. Women weren't "innately" pacifist, as he had argued; blacks were also pacifist. Both groups were sensitive to the violence of war because they were victims of oppression. Benedict continued to believe in the power of culture over individuals, but in this statement about the sensitivity of blacks and women to the violence of war cultural control wasn't absolute and the oppressed didn't entirely accept their oppression.[22]

Benedict didn't participate in women's organizations during these years; she remained as critical of them as she had been before World War I. In 1940 novelist Pearl Buck wrote her a letter expressing alarm that a growing fascist mood in the nation was coming to bear on women as scapegoats for causing the Depression. Buck asked Benedict what she intended to do. Benedict replied that she disagreed with Buck's premise; in her opinion women's position had improved since the early 1930s. What bothered her wasn't the treatment of women but rather women who took action apart from men. She expressed that stance again in a speech in 1941 in which she maintained that separate women's organizations had been needed to achieve woman suffrage, but that on most issues women were most effective when they worked together with men.[23]

On the other hand, Benedict didn't avoid the issue of race. Her close association with Boas and her concern about the rise of Hitler to power in Germany were factors in this. But she had long been sensitive to the issue: her natal family supported abolitionism; in college she had reacted to the criticism lodged against Vassar students who had lunch with Booker T. Washington by writing an antiracist paper on race in Shakespeare's plays. Living with Italian, Swiss, and German families during her tour of Europe after college sensitized her to ethnic issues; she had served immigrant communities as a social worker and studied racialized societies as an anthropologist.[24]

The graduate students at Columbia also played a role in her decision to take up the issue of race. The dispute between Benedict and Linton polarized them, but they reunited around a radicalism that appeared in the Depression era, especially in cities like New York and on urban college campuses like Columbia. "It is most pleasant," wrote one of them, "at last to feel that being a liberal or a radical automatically injects one into the 'in' group."[25] Moreover, a new cadre of Jewish students, many with undergraduate degrees from City College, came to study with Boas. As with his Jewish students early in the century, he attracted this new group because of his stand against racism, in this case against Hitler's anti-Semitism. Indeed, Boas's works were among the first books that the Nazis publicly burned.[26]

Neither Boas nor the radical students converted Benedict to socialism or communism, but she became more activist and leftist by the late 1930s. As a member of various committees of the Progressive Education Association, located at Columbia's Teachers College, she participated in drawing up antiracist programs for elementary and secondary schools. Along with friends of hers on the faculty there, she participated in founding the Society for the Psychological Study of Social Issues.[27] She joined groups of intellectuals working for the republican cause during the Spanish Civil War; she circulated petitions and helped organize rallies. Organizations to which she belonged were suspected of communism, and the FBI kept a file on her. Given her homosexuality, Benedict was sensitive to discrimination, and she was very close to Boas, almost his "second self." Her liberalism, her stand against racism, her relationship to Boas and the graduate students, her controversy with Linton, her ceding the subject of gender to Mead— these factors motivated her by 1939 to undertake her major work on race.

BENEDICT'S APPROACH TO RACE must be seen in terms of Boas's having redefined the idea of culture to mean the product of a society in general rather than as that of "civilization" or elites. By thus democratizing and relativizing the culture concept, he allowed anthropologists to investigate cultures from a color-blind, nonracist perspective. As George Stocking has written, "Boas' problem as a critic of racial thought was to define the 'genius' of a people in other terms than racial heredity."[28] His solution was to eliminate race as a significant variable.

Given the virulent racism of the day, adding a theory of race to ethnological approaches could have turned all of anthropology into a debate over evolutionary racist thinking. Addressing the issue of including race as a category of analysis in doing ethnography, Alexander Goldenweiser implied the same stance as Boas. "From the standpoint of the cultural anthropologist," he wrote, "the presence of race is an encumbrance. In his concrete studies, he practically always disregards it." He concluded that there wasn't a problem in this approach, since it was obvious "to even the casual observer" that the cultural divisions of mankind were much more complex than the racial divisions and that "within each race all sorts of cultures are to be found, not only qualitatively different ones, but also different in degree of advancement."[29] Benedict began *Patterns of Culture* with a rousing attack on racism, but in the rest of the book she didn't mention the subject. "Bodily form, or race," she wrote, "is separable from culture, and can for our purposes be laid to one side except at certain points where for some reason it becomes relevant."[30]

Many of Boas's students wrote articles or books attacking racism or added a section about the relativity of cultures to their general works on anthropology. In the nineteenth century, physical anthropologists had devised the schemes of racial classification by head size and brain capacity in the first place; they established anthropologists as experts on race. Boas steered graduate students like Zora Neale Hurston to the subject of race. He persuaded Melville Herskovits to study the children of mixed marriages—in order to disprove the belief that they mostly inherited the "bad traits" of their parents. Herskovits later wrote books maintaining that cultural practices of the African groups from which the slaves were taken remained strong among blacks in the United States both during slavery and after emancipation.[31]

Benedict regularly wrote reviews for the Sunday book review section of the *New York Herald Tribune*, and she often reviewed books on race. The articles she wrote in the 1920s and 1930s sometimes open with an attack on racism, as does *Patterns of Culture*. During this period she waited for Boas to undertake the popular book on race that he had long talked of writing, until it became apparent as he approached his eighties that he wasn't going to do it. Given Hitler's strident racism, Benedict felt impelled to write the book. Otto Klineberg, a Boas student who specialized in disproving the "scientific" proofs of black inferiority, noted that the racists were often better writers than the antiracists. "Truth," he wrote, "is not necessarily on the side of the most articulate."[32] *Patterns of Culture* had demonstrated Benedict's ability to do popular writing; she needed to do it again. Besides, when Jews wrote about race they might be dismissed as engaged in special pleading, but Benedict was an "Old American" who could claim an unbiased position in the contemporary racist United States. Boas oversaw her book, especially the sections on physical anthropology, an area in which Benedict wasn't an expert.

When they wrote about race, Boas's students repeated one another's arguments, and Benedict repeated those arguments too. Thus she noted that matters like eye color, hair color, size of the nose,

Mead, four years old, with her mother,
Emily Fogg Mead, 1905.
Courtesy of the Institute for Intercultural Studies, New York City

Mead at sixteen, 1917.
Courtesy of the Institute for Intercultural Studies, New York City.

Blackberry Winter. Elizabeth Mead Steig's watercolor of the Holicong Farm, 1935.
Courtesy of the Institute for Intercultural Studies, New York City

Mead and Luther Cressman, Doylestown, 1918.
Courtesy of the Institute for Intercultural Studies, New York City

Mead and Katharine Rothenberger,
King and Queen of the Pageant,
DePauw University, 1920.
*Courtesy of the Institute for
Intercultural Studies, New York City*

Three Ash Can Cats: Léonie Adams, Eleanor Pelham Kortheuer, and Margaret Mead, Barnard College.
Courtesy of the Institute for Intercultural Studies, New York City

Mead on the eve of departure for Samoa, 1925.
Courtesy of the Institute for Intercultural Studies, New York City

Mead in Samoan dress, with her friend Fa'amotu.
Courtesy of the Institute for Intercultural Studies, New York City

Mead on Manus, with Ponkiau,
Bopau, and Tchokal.
*Courtesy of the Institute for
Intercultural Studies, New York City*

Mead with Reo Fortune in Peri
Village, Manus.
*Courtesy of the Institute for
Intercultural Studies, New York City*

Anthropologists from New Guinea: Gregory Bateson, Mead, and Reo Fortune, arriving in Sydney from Tchambuli in 1932.
Courtesy of the Institute for Intercultural Studies, New York City

Mead with Gregory Bateson.
Courtesy of the Institute for Intercultural Studies, New York City

The Ash Can Cats, 1930s.
Courtesy of the Institute for Intercultural Studies,
New York City

and blood type don't correlate by race. In terms of skin color, the variations within groups are greater than the variations between groups. She pointed out, as had other Boasians, that genetic inheritance among humans isn't the same as among animals; humans living in isolation don't develop into species. Besides, the laws of Mendelian inheritance prove that variety, not sameness, is the rule in genetic descent. And because humans, unlike most animals, have migrated over vast areas of land, "racially pure" genetic stocks don't exist. Historically, there had been movements and intermarriages of people from Asia to Europe and the American continent, and of other groups into South Africa and Polynesia. Even the Arabs, she pointed out, took wives from the native populations in countries they conquered. She alluded to the same behavior on the part of European males in imperial armies and the civil service living in foreign lands, especially before white women arrived. It was also a fundamental principle of Boas that race was a matter of family lines, not inheritance through nations or races, and Benedict reiterated this.

Benedict's work on race, like her other writing, has distinctive features. Given her usual structuralism, her most interesting departure—from the viewpoint of a historian—is her discussion of the history of racism. In the first instance she traced it to the rise of nationalism. The Roman empire was based on the idea of a united civilization, and provincials of whatever ethnic group could become citizens and even administrators in it. Christ preached a doctrine of equality and the "brotherhood of man." The notion of union existed until the "juggernaut" of nationalism appeared in the thirteenth century, producing an "international anarchy" that had continued to the present. In the sixteenth century, the economic drive of imperialism, particularly the desire for land and a cheap labor force, had emerged with the exploitation of the New World, and it had produced racism, as differing economic groups encountered one another in frontier regions. In the eighteenth century the word "race" had shown its flexibility as it expanded to include the idea of class; in the clash between nobles and commoners in France in that century the nobles defined their antagonists as a different race.[33]

Although Benedict excoriated "racism" in *Race*, she didn't abandon the concept of race itself. Given her usual emphasis on cultural factors, her retaining the concept is surprising, for it provided an opening for biological explanations to return. She wrote that the concept of race still might be useful for scientists looking for "a hereditary glandular condition" or a "metabolic peculiarity" that might be associated with a particular race. At points in *Race* she realized the problem with using the word "race," with its connotation of biological and evolutionary hierarchy. She then used the word "ethnicity" instead. Contemporaries of hers—Magnus Hirschfeld, for example—abandoned the word "race." Hirschfeld, like others, substituted the word "ethnicity." In his major work on race, *We Europeans*, biologist Julian Huxley, later a friend of Mead's, used the word "type"—a word Benedict had used in her college paper on race in Shakespeare's plays. Benedict's student Ashley Montagu suggested using the word "caste."[34]

Following Franz Boas, Benedict accepted the division of humans into three racial groups: Caucasian, Negroid, and Mongoloid—white, black, and yellow; none of the Boasians gave up racial classifications entirely. She continued to characterize European "Caucasians" as composed of Nordics, Alpines, and Mediterraneans—classifications originally devised by the racists. She recommended the cephalic index as a useful instrument in some situations to determine "racial" membership. She herself confused "race" with "nation," even though she cautioned against making that mistake, because the intermingling of populations over time had produced national populations that were mixed by racial type. Yet she reported that Boas had dropped the Caucasian category of race and reduced his classifications to two: Negroid and Mongoloid. He made this change because the people of the Ainu tribe, located on a remote Japanese island, had European features that he decided had originated in a mutation and had spread through migration and conquest from Asia to Eastern Europe to form the basis of the Caucasian race. Thus "Caucasians" weren't an independent racial strain; they were actually "Mongoloids."[35]

Despite the liberalism of Benedict's approach to race, gender as a category of analysis is absent from *Race*, just as it is absent from the work of all the Boasians on the subject. Benedict's "races" and "racists" are largely disembodied entities, although she did note that racist theorists after Darwin focused more on power and force as positive racial traits than had previous theorists, thus implying that aggressive masculinity was connected to imperialism. Benedict viewed "racism" as akin to the Puritan belief in the Elect—the select group God had chosen to be saved—as an ideology under which a ruling group claimed a superior status for itself without any basis for the claim. She didn't go so far as to hold Puritanism responsible for racism, but she wrote that by the late nineteenth century the Elect had become "the hunting pack."[36]

Still, the implication of Benedict's "Bo-Cu Plant"—written some twenty-five years previously—that male imperialism involved the rape of women as well as of nature and the "racial other"—doesn't appear in *Race*. In her college paper on Euripides' *Trojan War* Benedict realized the horror of forced concubinage for women, but in *Race* she described the race mixing decreed by Alexander the Great and by the Roman emperors as well as the Arabs placing native women in their polygamous marriages as they spread across the Middle East as "marriage," without examining whether or not the women so placed had any choice in determining their fate. She mentioned, but didn't analyze, the forced race mixing under American slavery and European colonialism. Nor did she carry over from her early work like "The Uses of Cannibalism" her stress on the victimization of young men in warfare or her sense of differing masculinities to break up the racist group into its components by age, status, and gender.

In *Patterns of Culture*, with her attack on male patriarchs in the United States, Benedict came close to articulating a theory of patriarchal control as the organizing principle of human societies, but she drew back from it. In her letter to Amram Scheinfeld she stated that women and blacks were comparable in terms of being oppressed and that both identified with their oppressors and enforced majority values on themselves, while both resisted their oppression in such matters as embracing pacifism. In an age when the populations of many countries seemed to follow authoritarian leaders blindly, that thesis was attractive to Benedict, a major proponent in the 1930s of cultural determinism.

In opposition to Melville Herskovits, who maintained that American blacks had retained many elements of African culture, Benedict contended that the forced migration to the Americas and the centuries of oppression under slavery had destroyed their knowledge of their original culture and they largely accepted their oppression in the South.[37] From that position she adopted a civil rights stance and an egalitarian economic agenda as the means of gaining equality for them. Although she was never a Marxist, she now realized the importance of economics and class in social analysis. Thus she argued that racism emerged partly out of class distinctions. She also speculated that the culture of poor whites in the South had heavily influenced black culture there, especially with regard to religion and music. Her argument from economics has merit, but she would have done better to adopt Herskovits's argument about the retention of elements of African culture, given what scholars now accept as the roots of African-American cultural expression in African precedents. Blacks, she argued, had been turned into a disadvantaged class; the solution to their problems lay in economic "social engineering" as well as in programs of civil rights and education. And that agenda had to be extended to disadvantaged whites as well, for their racist attitudes were mostly a product of their poverty.[38] Finally, in contending that only the state had the power to bring such reforms into being, she supported the radical thrust of FDR's New Deal.

Benedict realized that discrimination against minorities had existed before the rise of the nation-state; she noted the persecutions of the Jews by the Christian Inquisition and the long history of anti-Semitism in Europe. Yet she didn't mention the persecution of women as witches in premodern Europe or that of homosexuals, even under Hitler's regime. She probably considered that raising such issues could be regarded as special pleading, a wrongheaded approach in a book focused on race and written by a woman. Unless she was careful, her book could be dismissed as feminist propaganda.

Benedict was aware of possible parallels between race and gender: in her letter to Amram Scheinfeld she maintained that minorities internalize their oppression and then oppress themselves. That is a sophisticated position, one that feminist and postmodernist thinkers have articulated only recently. In her published work, however, she didn't dwell on the point. In *Race*, for example, she expressed a greater interest in the psychology of the oppressors than in the situation of the oppressed; she focused more on "racism" than on "race." Her letter to Scheinfeld also indicates that she realized that women could internalize their own oppression to become as racist and as antiwoman as men. By the late 1930s, as she wrote in her letter to Pearl Buck, she didn't view the oppression of women as a major social problem; it's clear in *Race*, however, that she considered the oppression of blacks to be such an issue.

WHAT ABOUT MARGARET Mead? Did she link the issue of race to that of gender? And what was her situation at the American Museum of Natural History? In terms of gender discrimination, the museum was similar to Columbia. The administration was organized according to a gender hierarchy, under which the central administrators and most of the curators were men. In 1928 there were only two women among the fifty-three curators in the museum's natural history divisions and only one woman (Mead) among the six curators in the anthropology division. The outreach divisions of education and public health contained a larger number of women, as might be expected in those feminized professions: among seventeen employees in those divisions, seven were women. Numerous women worked in the museum as secretaries and clerks. For a time, Mead's friends Pelham Kortheuer and Margery Loeb both held such jobs—which Margaret found for them.[39]

No evidence exists that Mead ever directly challenged the male hierarchy at the museum, but it's doubtful that such efforts on her part would have produced any change—except for a request for her resignation. Like Benedict, Mead had problems being promoted: she spent most of her career at the museum as an associate curator. In any case, she was often away. During the first thirteen years of the job she was often absent on field trips. During World War II she worked for the federal government; when she returned to the museum after the war, she maintained a rigorous schedule of lecturing and attending conferences around the nation and sometimes abroad.

Yet her presence at the museum, given the numbers of male administrators, was significant. By the 1930s she had become an explorer as famous as any of the museum's male explorers; her achievements contributed to upgrading the anthropology division in the museum, just as Clark Wissler had hoped when he hired her. Paleontologist Henry Fairfield Osborn became president of the museum in 1908, and he didn't retire until 1935. In his first years there he was contemptuous of the anthropology division, for he thought ethnologists were bogus scientists who collected gossip from their informants, and the museum's dispute with Boas hadn't helped to change those views. When he retired, however, he regarded anthropology as one of the two main fields at the museum.[40] The publicity Mead brought to the museum must have helped to change his opinion.

Mead kept her distance from the administrators. When she began at the museum, she took over a storeroom at the top of one of the towers of the huge building to serve as her office, and she kept that office until her death. To reach it one had to climb a stairway and then proceed through passages lined with old file cases and papers stacked against the walls. The office was private and secretive; it was reminiscent of the room farthest away from the rest of the family that Margaret took for herself in each of her childhood homes. She could come and go as she pleased; she was far from the male administrators. Administrators at the museum whom Jane Howard interviewed found Mead dynamic and confrontational, although they didn't specify what issues concerned her. According to Howard, Mead's principal friends at the museum were the wives of the curators who were explorers. They went along with their husbands on their expeditions, and they often became well-known explorers in their own right. In 1926 they formed an organization, the Society of Women Geographers, to which Mead belonged; by 1929 it had forty-one members in the United States and forty-six abroad.[41]

Mead must have known about the racism of the museum administrators, with Henry Fairfield Osborn its director and Madison Grant on its board of directors. In *Race*, Benedict identified the two of them as the leaders of early-twentieth-century racism in the United States. Grant, a lawyer and naturalist, had written the major racist treatise of the day, *The Passing of the Great Race*, with an introduction by Osborn. Osborn was known for his many fossil finds and for his evolutionary Darwinism. Clark Wissler, Mead's boss, complained—after Osborn retired—that he had turned the museum into "an illustrated appendix to the *Origin of Species*."[42] Grant and Osborn were leaders of the nation's major eugenics societies, located in New York; in 1921 Osborn had the museum host the Second International Congress of Eugenics. At that meeting Osborn publicly attacked Boas's work. Boas replied in an article in the *American Mercury* in which he cited Mead's findings in her master's essay about the culture-bound nature of the IQ tests.[43]

Despite his later disavowal of Darwinism, Clark Wissler expressed racist sentiments in his *Man and Culture*, published in 1923. In the 1900s, as a graduate student at Columbia, he had called Boas's Jewish students "queer foreigners"; when Boas resigned from the museum in 1905, he took over his curatorship. In a cautious statement in his 1923 book, crafted not to offend, Wissler suggested that "indirect" evidence seemed to suggest that Euro-Americans might outperform other groups on intelligence tests and in cultural achievements.[44] Wissler was a conciliator by temperament, and he tried to maintain comity among the various factions in the museum—and with the Columbia anthropologists—although after he took over Boas's position at the museum relations between Boas and the museum were strained.

Wissler was quiet and unassuming: Mead remembered almost none of her conversations with him during the many years she served under him. "I never met anyone," she stated, "who felt he knew him." In a letter to Gregory Bateson, she categorized him as fey, according to their doctrine of the "squares."[45] Robert Lowie, who had been Wissler's student and then a curator on his staff for twelve years, thought that he sometimes went too far in being conciliatory: in a letter to his sister, Lowie accused Wissler of a "timorous truckling" to the "Osborn gang."[46]

Despite his racist eugenics, Osborn also tried to keep peace among the factions at the museum—and with Boas at Columbia, who displayed an uncharacteristic political subtlety in keeping a line of communication open to the museum. Osborn left his curators alone, so long as they did their work; he permitted Boas's students access to the museum in teaching and doing research. His autobiography is silent about his eugenics beliefs.[47] Yet none of the liberal anthropologists were completely egalitarian on the issue of race: Boas himself thought that racial divisions existed. Robert Lowie replied to a letter from Osborn chastising him for writing a negative review of Wissler's 1923 book by stating that he thought a good case could be made for racial difference, but Wissler hadn't made it.[48]

Wissler approved Mead's projects. He gave her grants to replace her salary when she was in the field; he let her come and go as she pleased. So long as she bought artifacts in the field for the museum and maintained her collections when she came back, no questions were asked. In fact, her position as an "Old American," with an ancestry going back to the original colonists, must have been attractive to the museum administrators in the first place, contributing to their willingness to hire her. Nothing, probably, was said openly, either about their stance or hers, although when she told Wissler that she wanted to go to Manus to test the racist assumption that the mental development of tribal people was akin to that of children in modern societies, he suggested that she should continue working on sex. Yet she did that research with impunity, and it continued in the Boasian antiracist mode of dealing with racial societies without focusing on race.

In 1931 Mead got up the nerve to ask Wissler why she hadn't been given a raise in the five years she had worked at the museum. He replied that he didn't know what Osborn thought of her work, and he feared that if Osborn actually read what she wrote, he might make trouble for her. Once Boas and Osborn retired, he told her, he was certain that relations between the museum and the Columbia anthropology department would improve, and that would enhance her position at the museum.[49] It's no wonder that she felt her childhood fear of authority return when Osborn's assistant suddenly called her into his office one day. It's also not surprising that she was cautious about the issue of race.

Before World War II, Mead didn't write on race in the same way that Benedict did. She wrote her master's essay attacking the racial bias in the IQ tests, and in her work on Manus she disproved the theory that tribal peoples remained at the evolutionary level of "civilized" children, although she published that study in a British professional journal, not one in the United States. All of her work, written to prove cultural relativity, can be seen as an attack on evolutionary, racist thinking. Yet she didn't make the same impassioned pleas in her early work that Benedict did against racism. Nor did she deliver the same hard-hitting attacks in book reviews against the racist eugenicists. It is as though by the mid-1930s Benedict and Mead divided the issues of gender and race between them, with Benedict focusing on race and Mead on gender. When W. E. B. Du Bois wrote Mead in 1935 asking her to contribute to the *Encyclopedia of Negro History*, she turned him down, replying that she wasn't an authority on the Negro question—except with regard to the people of Melanesia, who probably had a Negroid strain in their makeup.[50]

That same year Annie Nathan Meyer, founder of Barnard College and an activist on behalf of racial equality for Jews and blacks, wrote Mead asking for her help in removing Madison Grant from his position on the board of the American Museum of Natural History. She sent Mead an article she had written about Grant in which she detailed his racist views and questioned why he was a member of the board of a museum supported by taxpayers' money. According to Lenora Foerstel and Angela Gilliam, Mead responded with a brief, handwritten note in which she stated that "all of us here [at the Museum] are only too cognizant of the point you mention." She took no other action. It wasn't until the 1940s that public criticism of the museum for the racist attitudes of its administrators began; in 1940 Mead began focusing on race.[51]

This is not to suggest that Mead was racist. She constructed her ethnographies—of Samoa, the Omaha, the four Melanesian societies she studied—to prove the relativity of cultures, and they countered the racial nonsense about evolutionary hierarchy that the museum's leaders were spreading. After 1921 the membership of Osborn and Grant's eugenics society declined, and by the late 1920s the antiracist arguments of the Boasians seemed to be having an impact. At that point the rise of Hitler to power in Germany and the spread of his racist doctrines couldn't have been predicted.[52] For nearly sixteen years—from 1923 to 1939—Mead saw her fieldwork in messianic terms, as a mission to record "priceless" information that otherwise would be lost. To her, as to Boas, Benedict, and the other Boasians, that task was as important as their crusade against racism. Had World War II not intervened and had she remained married to Gregory Bateson, she might have gone back to focusing on fieldwork when the war ended. She did restudy the Manus five times.

Mead's private letters contain what might be construed as racist statements, although such statements are infrequent and they don't exist in her public writings. Most occur in the context of her Samoan research, when she first encountered a large group of people of color overseas and also reflected on why it was that Europeans found the Samoans, who were tall and brown-skinned, so handsome. Her first comment, which she made soon after she arrived, was that the natives were "gorgeous, too muscular to be pretty and most magnificent." On further reflection, she thought that their beauty might have something to do with their possibly Caucasian origins; some contemporary commentators had advanced that thesis. She noted that half-blooded Samoans were more attractive than full-blooded ones, because "they are lighter, their hair is less bushy, and their features are more delicate." With regard to the adolescents she studied on the island of Ta'u she wrote that Leialofa, who had white blood, was the prettiest child in the three villages there.[53]

As time went by, however, her perception of skin color on Samoa changed, as she became disgusted with the status-conscious Anglo colonial administrators and residents and penetrated deeper into the native culture. After eight months on Samoa she wrote to her sister Elizabeth that when she saw tiny brown children running over the white sand on the beach they were so beautiful that she could well believe that the original humans had been brown. She considered having an affair with a Samoan man, and she became so fed up with the racism of the naval doctor in whose house she lived on Ta'u that she wrote Eda Lou Walton that she would have been happy to spend her time with the Samoans and never see a white person again.[54]

In *Fair Sex, Savage Dreams,* Jean Walton analyzes a number of incidents in Mead's life to suggest that her record on race is flawed. Yet each one she uses can be interpreted differently. Take the incident involving Mead and Reo Fortune and the masquerade ball on the ship from Australia to Europe in 1926. Looking for costumes for the ball, they accepted the offer of the chief steward to lend them outfits worn by the lascar (East Indian) crew members. To look more authentic, they blackened their faces. They didn't realize that the steward was playing a joke on them. As they went in their costumes to the captain's table, the steward took them aside to tell them that they had committed an offense in going to the captain's table dressed as "filthy black lascars" who did the dirtiest work on the ship. They must apologize to the captain. They did so, and Margaret, seething inside, explained that blackface in the United States was an accepted masking role that wasn't considered racially offensive at a masquerade.[55]

Walton accuses Mead of insensitivity to blackface as a racist performance. Yet Mead's blackening her face can be seen as a gesture against the whites on the ship and an expression of solidarity with the "black" Samoans she had just left. The minstrel tradition stereotyped blacks, but it also overturned gender and class. It played with "the process of identity change that turned poor into rich and immigrants into Americans." Its wide cast of characters contained the confidence man, an American trickster. By the early twentieth century male transvestites were among its most popular performers.[56] By wearing trousers to the ball, Mead was cross-dressing, and that may have been the most shocking part of her masquerade costume, for even in 1926 trousers were forbidden attire for respectable women.

Walton also identifies as racist Mead's description of how white men visiting her on the Sepik River looked like "paper dolls" in the context of the black people she was studying but after she spent time with the whites, the natives receded into the background. In fact, her reaction can be interpreted as a rich description of what it is like to be immersed in a nonwhite foreign culture and then the "shock" one experiences on first encountering the pasty faces of white people. In terms of richness of color, white faces aren't attractive. "When I came back from New Guinea," Mead told James Baldwin, "white babies looked like whales. And I don't much like the way white people look in the tropics, because they get so sunburned and worn."[57]

Walton doesn't seem aware that Mead disliked the masculine colonial administrators, with their aggressive, hard-drinking ways and their contemptuous treatment of the natives. She didn't like the plantations the white settlers had established, where they often mistreated the young New Guinea men they hired as contract laborers.[58] She didn't welcome visits from most of those administrators, interrupting her concentration. In this reaction, gender and race operated together. As a woman vis-à-vis these men, she was in a position like that of the natives they oversaw. She had to play up to them and stay in their good graces in order to be permitted to do fieldwork. When Fortune and she were on Manus he confronted the colonial administrators about their racism, but they paid no attention to him. In a moment of discouragement in Mundugumor, she wrote to Benedict that she and Reo stayed in the field "by various underhanded methods, by playing a little politics, if not a lot."[59]

A case can be made that even Mead, schooled in racial egalitarianism by her mother and grandmother and closely associated with Franz Boas, couldn't escape the racism of her society, but that case needs to be made with care. Take, for example, her use of the word "pickaninny." In one of the bulletins she sent to her family and friends from Mundugumor, she referred to the dead babies she saw in the river as "pickaninnies." When she decided to include that bulletin in her *Letters from the Field*, she wrote to her editor asking her to remove the word from the text, and the editor substituted the word "infant."[60] Moreover, Otto Klineberg remembered that when she was a guest speaker at a Quaker institute he organized, she used the word "pickaninny" to refer to New Guinea children. She suddenly realized her gaffe and was deeply embarrassed by what she had said, especially since the audience was half black; tears slowly ran down her cheeks.[61]

In her analysis of Mead's work, Louise Newman accuses her of ethnocentrism and charges that she believed in the superiority of the West. Yet Newman overlooks Mead's preferences for institutions and behaviors in the societies she studied over their counterparts in the West, as well as her many criticisms of Western values and practices. She doesn't seem aware of Mead's scathing criticism of the policy of the United States government toward the Native Americans in *Changing Culture of an Indian Tribe*, of her celebration of childbearing and child rearing in the cultures she studied and the communalism of the family in Samoa as superior to the nuclear family of the West, or of her criticism of aggressive masculinity and American materialism, of her brief for breaking down sex roles. Newman pays no attention to Mead's argument that ethnic diversity is a major strength of U.S. society, or to the fact that her thinking about Westernization was influenced by the belief that the internalization of modernization on the part of tribal societies was inevitable.

I don't find Mead's work, as Newman does, "riddled" with her taking advantage of Western power relations to do her fieldwork or with titillating Western fears that it was dangerous for a white woman to be alone with "primitives." Mead's several public references to studying cultures in New Guinea only recently removed from cannibalism didn't constitute a major theme in her self-presentation. That presentation stressed that as a woman she had the advantage of being able to study women's activities in tribal cultures, for those activities were usually off-limits to male anthropologists.[62]

Mead was an effective practitioner of what Malinowski called "the ethnographer's magic"—the ability to read oneself into another culture, to become part of it. How deeply she penetrated the cultures she studied is debatable; even she came to see that as an issue when in 1973 she described her work as close to fiction. She came to realize the difficulties inherent in studying cultures with a different language and different thought processes from her own. Whether the tribal peoples she chose to study wanted her there is another matter. Many premodern societies have an ethic of hospitality. She was backed by the colonial administrators. She brought with her, as she often pointed out, medicines and a rudimentary skill at doctoring to treat illnesses the native healers couldn't cure. Among the Tchambuli she and Reo Fortune provided "entertainment" to the natives.

Moreover, she disliked the use of the word "primitive," with its connotation of inferiority to Western societies, as a description of tribal peoples. She tried to eliminate that connotation by defining "primitive" as meaning cultures without a written language. She suggested that the term "homogeneous" replace "primitive" to describe tribal cultures; that term was based on her conclusion that these societies, generally small, with strong family and kinship ties, were more unified—and unidimensional—than those in the West.[63]

Boas and his students often paid their informants, but Mead didn't turn her fieldwork into a commercial transaction—except among people like the Balinese, who demanded money for doing interviews or putting on ceremonies. And the native people gave back in kind what they received. Reo and she wound up studying the Arapesh in 1931 because Reo bullied a group of males into carrying their large amount of gear over the mountains, and those men paid him back by stranding them among the Arapesh. Anthropologists in general hadn't done well when they tried to influence government policies. In the late nineteenth century, for example, Alice Fletcher had lobbied for the disastrous U.S. policy of imposing private ownership of property and the nuclear family on the Native American tribes. Lola Romanucci-Ross, who worked with Mead in her 1951 restudy of Manus, stated that Mead felt a moral responsibility not to tamper with the societies she studied, although she could be aggressive in getting administrators to intervene in matters of hygiene and nutrition—and Romanucci-Ross found Mead aggressive in personal interactions with her.[64]

By the 1930s Mead belonged to several organizations devoted to Indian rights, while she was on the board of several liberal Jewish organizations. By the 1940s she became a leader in the movement for applied anthropology, and she worked for civil rights legislation. She attended conferences, gave speeches, and spoke on the radio on the subject. For many years she was on the board of the Hampton Institute, a black college in Virginia. One can cite innumerable personal and public instances in which she took a stand against racism—from apologizing to Melville Herskovits for not realizing that her landlord had a "whites-only" policy when she sublet her and Luther's apartment to him in 1925 when she went to Samoa, to an incident her classmate Louise Schlichting remembered, in which Mead, speaking before a group in New Hampshire, began by saying: "If I had known this was going to be such a lily-white audience I would not have come."[65]

In *A Rap on Race*, her dialogue with James Baldwin, Mead found herself in the awkward position of arguing for racial amalgamation while Baldwin argued for racial separation as part of his support for the Black Power position of the 1970s. In that dialogue Mead was uncomfortable drawing a comparison between women and blacks. When she did so, she was drawn into supporting what she called the "women's lib" position that "women had internalized their own oppression"— that they had, as she put it, accepted a male version of who they were. She retreated from that position as quickly as Benedict had; in debating Baldwin, a well-known novelist and radical, Mead didn't want to get too close to Benedict's argument that blacks, like women, had internalized their own oppression to the point that the original black culture was destroyed and they mostly took their cues from the culture of Southern poor whites. Baldwin would have ridiculed her if she had taken that position.

The dialogue with James Baldwin resulted from a conversation she had with a young black man who was an editor at *Redbook* about her experiences of race in New Guinea. To more graphically illustrate to him how horribly the native young men who were recruited to work on the colonial plantations were treated, she characterized their experience as similar to that of blacks in the South. When she first went to the South in 1942, she told him, she was horrified by its rigid segregation between blacks and whites and the superior attitude of the whites. She felt as though she had gone back to New Guinea. She thought that John Dollard was right when he identified the position of blacks in the South as akin not to a social class but rather to a caste, for the whites considered them almost a different species. Given this editor's perception of her sensitivity to the issue of race, he conceived the idea of the conversation between her and Baldwin.[66]

In speaking with Baldwin, she enunciated a complex vision of race similar to her radical revisioning of gender. To illustrate that vision, she referred to a picture she had seen in a magazine published in Hawaii. The picture had Asian, African, Caucasian, and Polynesian faces around the edges, but toward its center, the faces became less definite. The central face was so racially mixed that it couldn't be placed in any racial group. "But," she concluded, "you couldn't have the face at the center without the faces at the edges." That image combined her liberal support for racial amalgamation with James Baldwin's separatist position. It could also be viewed as analogous to the radical view about sex and gender she had enunciated in *Sex and Temperament*, in which masculine and feminine stood at the edges of her point of view, to support a more unified person at the center.

WAS MEAD'S SCHEME OF the "squares" racist? Examining it from the perspective of race sheds light on the connection between race and gender in Mead's and Benedict's thought in general. In her professional writing, Mead rarely referred to the doctrine of the "squares." When she was back in New York from New Guinea, she realized that she couldn't, since it could be taken as racist, especially with the rise of Hitler to power in Germany. "The Nazi period," she later wrote, "was a deterrent to research on race differences and even proved a deterrent to research on constitutional differences and national character in which race wasn't mentioned. The belief was that research on any kind of difference that might be innate was liable to be misused."[67]

Yet Mead remained fascinated with the classifications she, Gregory Bateson, and Reo Fortune had worked out under the "squares." She persuaded her family and friends to use them privately. She sometimes used them playfully and sometimes seriously. She even devised a test based on the reactions of individuals to a series of incidents she crafted through which personality types according to the "squares" could be determined. Her letters to Bateson in 1934 and 1935 are filled with her attempts to put such a test together, as she consulted psychologists and other professionals she met at conferences and at talks she gave, without always revealing what she was working on. She finally chose several situations for her subjects to analyze and then decided what points on the "squares" were indicated by each analysis. Her notes on her "squares" test in her papers at the Library of Congress indicate that she gave the test to Geoffrey Gorer, Abraham Maslow, Katharine Rothenberger, Eleanor Pelham Kortheuer, and Eleanor Phillips—but not to Ruth Benedict.[68]

Mead liked to lead a life that was exciting and multifaceted, but she also liked to put it in order. She liked to have a husband, a best friend, a safe space in a tower away from the male administrators at the Museum of Natural History—and from the conventional world that might find her out. She liked eccentricity and variety, but she also wanted to be in control. She appreciated colors and patterns in her clothes, but she wore a corset and white gloves. Knowing and using the "squares" became a mark of closeness to Mead. It was a way of defining her inner circle of friends through a code they shared. Benedict, however, never fully accepted the scheme. Although she eventually searched for a way to rank cultures, she never liked typing human beings.

Reo Fortune repudiated the "squares" soon after they left Tchambuli; in later years he wrote letters to Mead charging that it was racist. She never answered him, but Gregory Bateson did. He admitted that in developing the "squares" they engaged in "bad" science when they attributed negative qualities to various societies, like the Turks. Yet in doing so, he contended, they referred only to unfortunate qualities produced by the influence of Europeans and not to indigeneous characteristics of the native society.[69] The argument was ingenious, if not entirely convincing. There were, however, other ways of countering the racist charge.

At the time many scholars were drawn to categorizing human nature and cultures; the "squares" drew from that impulse. As early as 1924, Benedict referred to "the recent [large] output of fundamental classifications of human types." That year the anthropologists at the

Toronto conference of the British Association for the Advancement of Science that Edward Sapir organized became fascinated by Jung's typologies for classifying individuals and societies. In 1932 Gardner Murphy wrote that "to sort and classify personalities, to group and bundle them according to their several characteristics, has gotten to be a favorite practice." The discovery of glands and hormones produced classifications of individuals based on endocrine functioning; in 1934 Mead wrote Gregory Bateson expressing interest in a new study of types by Gordon Allport based on the vocabulary of human gestures and the length of the stride. She also recommended W. A. Willemse's *Constitution-Types in Delinquency* to Bateson. That book noted that biotypologies were being invented all over Europe; even E. R. Jaensch in Marburg had devised a typology from his studies of individuals who saw eidetic images.[70]

By the 1930s, according to historian Elazar Barkan, classifying individuals and "races" according to differential cranial capacities and mental abilities had proven largely inaccurate, thus undermining racist arguments, although scientists preserved a "space" in which they could reassert variations on these theories when they developed more sophisticated approaches. Barkan overlooks, however, the schools of classification based on constitutional type, or body build. As Earl Engle noted in his paper on the biological causes of homosexuality written for the Hanover Conference in 1934, doctors and psychologists, not just physical anthropologists, developed the constitutional-type approach. Most physical anthropologists concerned themselves with the skull or the skeleton, the hard framework of the body that doesn't decay after death. They focused on the search for skeletal remains of ancient humans to plot out the migrations of prehistoric peoples and the development of the evolutionary scheme.[71] Some, however, became interested in classifying humans according to body build: in the mid-1920s even Boas launched a project comparing the pelvic dimensions of Italians and Jews; Emily Fogg Mead did measurements for him among the Italians in Hammonton.

In his Hanover Conference paper, Engle reported on some of the constitutional-type schools. According to him, the interest in constitutional types had begun with doctors studying diseases, who tried to determine, for example, if thin people were more susceptible to tuberculosis than fat people. In 1951, J. M. Tanner sketched the genealogy of a sizable group of contemporary constitutional-type theorists, tracing them back to an Italian school and a French school, both dating to the 1890s. Tanner grouped the schools together under the rubric "differential anthropology." According to him, some of its adherents took measurements—an approach called anthroposcopy—and others used observation, often of photographs—an approach called anthropometry.[72] Some researchers in the field justified their studies by maintaining that it was impossible to determine how hormones and genes operated; measures such as height, weight, and body mass were the most visible bodily results of their functioning.

The most important constitutional-type theorist in the 1920s and 1930s was Ernst Kretschmer of Marburg, Germany. A psychiatrist for a mental institution, Kretschmer studied detailed photographs of the unclothed bodies of 260 psychotic male patients to conclude that types of body builds correlated with types of psychoses. Manic-depressive disorder correlated with individuals with stocky bodies; he called them "pyknic." The schizophrenics in his photographs were long and lanky or tall and muscular; he called the first "asthenic" and the second "athletic." He extended these definitions to the general population. Kretschmer did no cross-cultural comparisons, and he didn't include women, for he contended that their bodies varied too much to be classified. That problem, however, didn't stop him from classifying humans on the basis of his sample of men. That had been characteristic of this "science" since the ancient Greeks, when Hippocrates identified types by observing body builds.[73]

Although some theorists of constitutional types contended that their definitions corresponded to major racial types, others rejected that contention. In the pre–World War II debate over race, racial hierarchies had been sufficiently discredited that many theorists of constitutional types in this era hesitated to include race; in his work on genius, for example, Kretschmer contended that the quality appeared most often in frontier regions, where constitutional types and races intermingled. In investigating genius, however, Kretschmer didn't include women: he thought women of genius were really men in female bodies.[74] Once Hitler came to power, the hesitation about identifying race with constitutional type disappeared; it was easy to equate Hitler's Nordics with Kretschmer's athletes and to argue for Nordic superiority—even if Kretschmer's athletes had originally been schizophrenic.

Margaret Mead and Gregory Bateson's fascination with constitutional-type theories probably had something to do with their own difference in body build, with Margaret tiny and Gregory huge—a difference also characteristic of Mead's tall father and short mother. The tall, athletic men of the Plains Indians intrigued the male anthropologists; even Ruth Benedict reported that the Hopi people of Arizona were small, while the nearby Mohave people were large.[75] Physical appearance has an obvious influence on self-confidence. Alfred Adler analyzed that psychological factor, focusing on the insecurity of short men; Mead picked up the point in her article "Jealousy" in 1931. Even Edward Sapir included Kretschmer's theories about constitutional types as well as Adler's about the psychological insecurity of short men in an entry on "Personality" that he wrote for the 1934 *Encyclopedia of the Social Sciences.*[76]

At least the believers in the typologies of body build renounced the realm of the brain and the skull that had produced the cranial-capacity studies, including the cephalic index and the mental testing that Mead, like other analysts, rejected because it was culture-bound. Kretschmer, for one, had shifted from the head to the body for his typologies because the skull was immobile—and it couldn't be seen with the naked eye, while the body obviously could. And he concluded, using a circular argument characteristic of most theorists constructing typologies, that "the similarity of types reached by various authors in various parts of the world proves their correctness."[77] In other words, when researchers elsewhere used his types to analyze groups of people and found similar types in those groups, their findings proved that his original calculations were correct.

Such typologies, however, could be malleable instruments, if the principle that most people fell between categories was applied. Gregory Bateson was so taken with Kretschmer's scheme that he praised it in *Naven*. Yet he noted that Kretschmer cautioned that his classifications should be viewed as on a continuum, not on different scales, with most individuals falling somewhere in between. Many constitutional-type theorists made that disclaimer, before forgetting it and discussing their data in terms of polarities. Bateson, however, believed Kretschmer, as he stated in a footnote in *Naven*. "Although the external world is perhaps not built upon a dualistic basis," he wrote, "dualisms and dichotomies provide a convenient technique for describing it, and this technique is so standardized in our culture that there is little hope of avoiding it." Yet he continued by stating that he agreed with Kretschmer that "we should expect to classify individuals on a scale varying between the extremes."[78]

Mead's "Summary Statement on the Problem of Personality and

Culture," which she wrote while she was in Tchambuli, is one of the few instances in her writing in which she indicated that the analysis of race influenced her analysis of gender. In fact, in one sentence in that document Mead suggests that her theory of gender was based on the Boasian theory of racial variability. That was the notion that the variability between individuals in any racial group is greater than the difference across racial lines: in his writing about race, Kroeber called it the principle of "overlapping." For according to the laws of Mendelian inheritance, even very small incidences of intermarriage would produce large varieties in populations over time.[79]

Mead had spent years working in places where racial types were both intermixed and separate. When she traveled to her societies in the South Pacific she went through Hawaii, and she often stopped and visited friends there. By the 1920s Hawaii was becoming as ethnically mixed as it is today. In his work on race, Ashley Montagu explained that the original Polynesian people had been a maritime group from which the Maori, the Samoans, and the Hawaiians were descended, with much intermixing along the way; the people of New Guinea, on the other hand, had remained relatively isolated until the nineteenth century—the word "Melanesia" is derived from the Greek word for "black."[80] That doesn't mean that the people there were all of one type: in an article on racial variation in Melanesia, Mead wrote about people with light brown skin, such as the Trobrianders, and people whose skins were blue-black, like those who lived in the Northern Solomons. With regard to hair, she described people in the Admiralty Islands as having wavy hair, while the hair of the Fijians was very kinky. Men six feet tall were common along the Sepik, while there were people as small as pygmies elsewhere in New Guinea.[81] "Even among the most inbred and isolated groups, very marked differences in physique and apparent temperament will be found," she wrote. And individuals of the same constitutional type could be standardized by different cultures into exhibiting different personalities. Thus Arapesh males might be feminine in personality but their physique was as masculine as that of the Mundugumor or the Tchambuli.[82]

Yet while acknowledging variation, Mead had to argue for sameness; otherwise her notion of a limited number of temperamental types expressed through constitutional types would break down. What she came up with was a sliding scale: the Samoans might be tall and large-boned and the Balinese small and slight, but there was a range of similar constitutional-type variations within those physiological limits. As cultures standardized personalities, they would, in essence, work with the same range of temperamental qualities, but the physiological ranges might differ.

Mead had no difficulty identifying herself with the Arapesh and Fortune with the Maori and the Mundugumor, for masculine and feminine cut across racial divisions, as did reproduction. To a large degree, race was irrelevant to their conversations on gender. Yet in an undated fragment of a note in her papers, located among her New Guinea materials, with the word "Tchambuli" scrawled on it, Mead speculated that race, like gender, could also be mapped out using the doctrine of the "squares" to make it disappear. One assumes she meant that variables like hair and eye color, body build, and facial physiognomy could be regarded in such a way that racial categories would become as irrelevant as masculine and feminine. However, she didn't explain what she meant by the statement.[83]

Like Benedict, Mead enunciated attitudes toward gender that prefigured more recent ideas on the subject, just as both of them sometimes expressed views about the similarities between the categories of race and gender that sound like the ideas of recent theorists. Yet their expressions of such attitudes were episodic, neither regularized nor worked into any broader theory. For the most part they kept race and gender separate.

That separation, however, was characteristic of most of the liberal thinkers on gender and race in this era, in which it seemed that women were achieving their goals but African-Americans weren't. Benedict and Mead considered women's advancement to have been so successful that they no longer saw the need for a women's rights movement. As for blacks, they were prevented from voting in the South and subjected to discrimination in all areas of the country. Congress wouldn't pass an antilynching amendment. By the 1950s women were returning to their traditional role in the home, while the civil rights movement demanded equality for blacks in the public arena. These opposing movements suggested a difference between gender and race, not a similarity: black males belonged in the public sphere; white women in the private sphere. Mead and Benedict didn't address the question of where black women belonged.

There hadn't always been a split between the women's movement and the movement for racial equality. In the early nineteenth century, women's rights advocates had compared the inferior position of women in law and society to the position of the enslaved blacks in the South. At that point a case could be made that both were severely oppressed. Nineteenth-century biologists and anatomists had used cranial measurements of women similar to those they used for ethnicities and races to prove that women, like other minorities, were inferior to men. They went so far as to argue that women, like the "lower races," had narrow heads and protruding jaws. "Recapitulation" theory posited that white children existed on the evolutionary scale in the same position as "primitive" adults—and so did adult white women.[84] By the 1920s the cranial and evolutionary indices had been discredited with regard to women, particularly by the work of Leta Hollingworth, but they still existed for blacks in measurements like the IQ tests. And with the ratification of the woman suffrage amendment in 1920, the improvement in the position of women seemed substantial, while blacks were falling behind.

Not until the 1960s did the militant women's movement again compare the position of women with that of blacks, although in *American Dilemma* (1944), his famed study of blacks in the United States, Gunnar Myrdal pointed to the similar difficulties women and blacks had in being elected to public office, in gaining salaries equal to white men, and in being subject to white male paternalism.[85] With only limited theory about the connections between race and gender readily available to them, Benedict and Mead realized that there were analogies between the two subjects, but they didn't focus on them. Devoted to the priority of the civil rights movement, attempting to hold the line against racism, Benedict didn't focus on gender, while both of them adopted a philosophy that saw women as equal in rights with men, although separate in talents and potentials. There was a path to success for women who wanted careers: it was a path they had followed.

In fact, upon occasion both Benedict and Mead viewed women as privileged—and even as oppressors of male sons. And they didn't take the step of applying the categories of "male" and "female" to the category of race: black women as a separate group aren't present in their analyses of either race or gender. Indeed, according to historian Ruth Feldstein, academic discourse in general during the era blamed black mothers as well as white mothers for men's problems, while black women, unlike white women, were sexualized in that discourse; such positions can be found in the writings, for example, of John Dollard as well as of Abram Kardiner. On the other hand, communist publications regularly used the terms "triple burden" and "triple oppression" to characterize the status of black women, who were exploited by race, class, and gender.[86]

Yet such sophisticated thought linking gender and race by and large wouldn't appear until the feminist movement of the 1960s, and especially not until black women raised their separate oppression as an issue in the 1970s. And Mead was constrained in her writings on race by working at the American Museum of Natural History during a phase when major administrators were racist, while Benedict was freer to join the Boasians in attacking racism directly. Mead might have done so through extending her gendered theory of the "squares" to race, but it was the very racism of the period that held her back. Making public the theory of the "squares" in the context of Hitler's rise to power in Germany would probably have exposed her to severe criticism and even ridicule.

By the 1940s, however, World War II had begun, and Benedict and Mead joined the crusade on the part of social scientists to save the world for democracy. Given the emotional and egalitarian mood within the United States created by the war, Mead no less than Benedict became empowered to attack racism and to include racial equality as a major part of her humanitarian program.

PART VI

World War II
and Beyond

CHAPTER 14

Ripeness Is All

T HE OUTBREAK OF WORLD WAR II was a clarion call to
Ruth Benedict and Margaret Mead to extend their scholarship into activism. Benedict's sister, Margery Freeman, wrote
that the war brought Ruth out of her ivory tower and made her realize
that politicians, psychologists, and ordinary citizens needed her
anthropology more than ever before.[1] Benedict herself didn't immediately come to that conclusion. In September 1939, when Hitler
invaded Poland, she was on vacation in San Francisco. "Right now,"
she wrote Mead, "I'm sunk." It seemed as though World War I was
being repeated, with Germany again invading another country. The
earlier war had caused Benedict to question all her values, deeply distressing her. "It seems like the same trap all over again, and you know
how I hate that feeling."[2]

Visiting friends in Berkeley, she met Ruth Valentine, a friend of
Natalie Raymond's from Pasadena, and they drove back to Southern
California together along the coastal route, stopping in Big Sur—
Robinson Jeffers country. In that stark seascape, with tall cliffs, pound-
ing surf, and forested land nearby, she had time to think, and she felt
better. She realized that this wasn't the same as World War I, that this
time the moral issues, with Hitler in power in Germany, were much
more clear-cut. She was ready to help out. She had a sabbatical that
year, and she decided to spend it in Pasadena, writing her book on race.
Once back in that city, she moved in with Valentine, a school psychologist in Los Angeles who had a house near Margery's. She finally gave
up Nat and Ruth Bunzel; Valentine became her partner.

Mead's support of U.S. intervention was immediate, despite the existence of strong antiwar sentiment in the nation. She was married to an Englishman whose country was directly threatened; she had decided that American isolationism after World War I had contributed to the rise of Hitler. She returned to the United States from Bali in the spring of 1939. "I came home to a world on the brink of war," she wrote, "convinced that the next task was to apply what we knew, as best we could, to the problems of our own society."[3] That fall, while Ruth remained in Pasadena, Margaret was in New York, working at the Museum of Natural History, lecturing and writing articles, teaching at Vassar College and commuting to Poughkeepsie by train, waiting for the birth of her child and for Gregory's return from England, where he had impulsively gone to help out. In December Mary Catherine Bateson was born; Gregory missed her birth by several weeks. Ruth, in Pasadena, wasn't at the birth either. She was recovering from a bout of pleurisy—and perhaps she didn't want to be away from Ruth Valentine. She crocheted a pair of booties for the baby, using an old family pattern. She hadn't done such handiwork, she wrote Margaret, for a good fifteen years.[4]

In 1939, with the death of Sapir and the waning prestige of Kardiner's culture-and-personality seminar at Columbia, due in part to his break with Linton and the onset of the war, Benedict and Mead became the dominant figures in the culture-and-personality school. By the spring of 1940 both were involved with the new field of national character studies they devised, with the assistance of Gregory Bateson and especially of Geoffrey Gorer. Within three years both were in Washington, working for the war effort. In 1942 Mead became secretary of the Committee on Food Habits of the National Research Council's Division of Anthropology and Psychology; in 1943 Benedict became an analyst of overseas cultures for the Office of War Information (OWI). Their careers had indeed taken a new turn.

ONCE MEAD AND BATESON returned to the United States from Bali, Larry Frank recruited them for the Committee for National Morale, a group of academics formed to address the issues of patriotism at home and propaganda abroad—or psychological warfare, as the latter was being called. How to motivate Americans, after a decade of economic depression, to support the war effort and to accept the personal sacrifices that might be required was a major issue, as was the need to generate data about the populations of enemy and occupied nations for intelligence operations. Needing trained experts quickly, the government looked to psychologists and other academics. Mead wrote that the psychological front was as important as the military and economic ones, and it was especially the case because of Hitler's skillful manipulation of mass attitudes. "Social psychology, tried out on a naive experimental scale in the last war, and since rationalized by the Axis powers," she asserted, "is the most significant addition to political life."[5]

The Committee for National Morale was one of many such groups formed by scholars, as academics forgot divisions between specialists and generalists, conservatives and radicals, and pooled their expertise to save the world from, as Mead put it, "the darkest tyranny that ever threatened it." By 1942, with the United States at war after the Japanese attack on Pearl Harbor in December 1941, twenty-two research seminars had been formed to further the war effort. They crisscrossed the social and behavioral sciences, advising the government on everything from "Hitler's personality to popular attitudes in the United States toward wardens at air-raid shelters."[6] Interdisciplinary organizations such as the National Research Council and the Social Science Research Council established special committees to aid the war effort. (The NRC had been founded during World War I to link academics with the federal government; the SSRC dated from 1924.)

From the beginning of their involvement in the war effort Benedict and Mead saw themselves as using their anthropological expertise to analyze the cultures of contemporary nations—as a necessary preliminary step to developing effective policies toward them. Benedict had been interested for some time in applying the anthropological techniques of interviews and participant observation to doing such studies, for she thought that these techniques would produce better results than those of historians and political scientists, which were based on examining documents and archival sources. It wasn't difficult for them to refocus their work on the contemporary period, since they had always linked their studies of tribal societies to contemporary issues. A number of their academic friends pointed the way, especially Robert Lynd, in his famed study of Muncie, Indiana, written with Helen Lynd, and John Dollard, in his *Caste and Class in a Southern Town*.[7] And in the 1930s, with the economic crisis shaping the consciousness of scholars, the kind of acculturation study that Mead did in 1930 of the women in an Omaha community, focused on the impact of modernization, was becoming increasingly popular, while anthropologists turned to studying folk cultures in the United States and found jobs with the folklore project of the New Deal's Works Progress Administration (WPA). At the same time, applied anthropology emerged as a new direction in the field, and Mead and Benedict were leaders in it.

In October 1939 Mead wrote to Benedict that she was confident she could devise a plan to survey public attitudes through sampling newspapers and conducting interviews.[8] Within a year, working with Bateson, Gorer, and Benedict, she produced a method for analyzing national character. They called it "culture at a distance." (Bateson jokingly called it "culture cracking.") Because the war made interviewing individuals in their native lands impossible, they decided to interview foreign nationals living in the United States, especially well-educated professionals, who could serve as analysts of their native cultures in their own right. Dollard's life-history strategy and the insights of psychologists like Erik Erikson supported their belief that individual development and national character were closely connected and that child rearing both reflected and shaped culture. They could use the questions that Benedict and Gorer had assembled in 1936 in their "Handbook of Psychological Leads for Ethnological Field Workers" and apply them to contemporary cultures. The difficult part was to check their results by region, class, and other groupings that might produce variations on central themes. It was no longer sufficient to use the intuitive approach that Benedict had used in *Patterns of Culture*; many anthropologists and social scientists had modified that approach.[9]

They didn't stop with interviews. They had studied ceremonies and rituals in pre-state cultures; Benedict had compiled and compared mythologies and been the editor of the *Journal of American Folk-Lore* until 1940. Thus they analyzed newspapers, films, and other cultural products to understand the societies being investigated.

Gregory Bateson studied German propaganda films to understand Hitler's appeal; Benedict wrote a brief analysis of governing councils in China, in which gentry and peasants jointly made decisions, to see if contemporary Western societies might profit from them. They addressed the cautions that Mead raised in her introduction to the book she and Bateson did on Bali about language barriers inevitably producing "fictions" by using nationals from the countries under observation as interviewers. To ensure that their results had scientific credibility, they employed testing techniques, especially the popular Rorschach test, in which individuals give their reactions to a series of black blobs to reveal their true personality. They took the tests themselves and administered them to their research associates and to the individuals they studied. In 1943 they established the Institute for Intercultural Studies, through which to coordinate their studies of contemporary cultures.

That same year academics in organizations like the Committee for National Morale began taking positions with war agencies established by the federal government and with civilian agencies concerned with the war effort. Many served as consultants from their home institutions. John Dollard, for example, stayed at Yale, but he did psychological consulting for the Department of the Army. Erik Erikson worked on special projects for the Committee for National Morale and then for Benedict at the OWI. Ralph Linton taught for the U.S. Navy in the School of Military Government and Administration established at Columbia University. Rhoda Métraux, a Ph.D. in anthropology from Yale, worked first as an assistant for Mead at the Committee on Food Habits and then as an assistant for Bateson at the Office of Strategic Services (OSS), when he went to work there in 1943.

Meanwhile, the federal government had established the Office of War Information to gather data and provide position papers for government agencies. The OSS—the forerunner of the CIA—was also established to conduct intelligence work. Leonard Doob, a psychologist affiliated with the Yale Institute of Human Relations, headed the OWI, and Henry Murray, a psychologist from Harvard who was a friend of Benedict's and Mead's, headed the OSS Psychological Division. Academics staffed both agencies.

Benedict was responsible for the job Mead took with the Committee on Food Habits. In 1938, M. L. Wilson, an enterprising undersecretary at the Department of Agriculture and an admirer of *Patterns of Culture*, asked Benedict to give a speech to his department. In her speech Benedict made a plea to take the cultural milieu into account in studying food production and distribution. She also spoke positively of "siphon economies," in which wealth was widely distributed, and negatively of "funnel economies," in which wealth accumulated in the hands of a few. Tribal societies with funnel economies, she contended, had high rates of violence and mental illness; siphon economies had satisfied and prosperous populations.[10] Her scheme implied support for the continuation and extension of New Deal policies.

The speech, with an audience of more than a thousand federal employees, was well received. Benedict and Wilson corresponded, and he asked her about the scholarship on food distribution and consumption, prompting her to do research on the subject. When Wilson was appointed coordinator of the federal nutrition program, he found a place for her on the Committee on Food Habits, founded in 1941 at his request. When the Committee on Food Habits decided to hire a paid executive secretary to run a Washington office, Benedict suggested Mead, who was offered the post. She learned of her appointment on December 7, 1941, the day the Japanese bombed Pearl Harbor.

Once she took the Committee on Food Habits position, Margaret commuted to Washington from New York, and Marie Eichelberger and a nanny helped Gregory care for the two-year-old Mary Catherine during the week. In the summer of 1942, Gregory, Mary Catherine, and Margaret moved into the bottom floor of Larry Frank's brownstone in Greenwich Village, with Larry and his family on the upper floors. They established a semicommunal household, in which Frank's wife, Mary, helped to look after Mary Catherine along with her own children. They spent their summers with the Frank family and other academic friends in the New Hampshire community of Cloverly, where the Franks had a summer house. Ruth Benedict occasionally visited there. The living arrangements worked well, and Margaret rented a small house in Washington, D.C., to live in during the week, returning to New York on the weekends. She had achieved the communitarian living she had long praised. She had also found a way to combine motherhood and a career in a manner that suited her.

Benedict began working for the government two years later, in the fall of 1943, as an analyst of overseas cultures for the OWI—a position that came to her through Geoffrey Gorer. OWI officials were so impressed with a memorandum he wrote about the Japanese for the Committee for National Morale recommending that the emperor be allowed to remain on the throne even after the war that they offered him a position analyzing foreign cultures.[11] When he decided to return to England, Gorer recommended Benedict for his position, and she was offered it. Franz Boas had died in 1942; she still had problems with Ralph Linton. The opportunity to do research away from the demands of teaching and administration appealed to her, as did being at the center of national operations during the war—and close to Mead again. In 1942 she wrote a pamphlet on race with Gene Weltfish that the War Department published and widely distributed; it raised a furor when a Southern congressman discovered a statement in it that Northern blacks had scored higher than Southern whites on the IQ tests of soldiers during World War I. That negative publicity didn't stop her appointment. In the exciting Washington environment, academics in government formed lunchtime study groups in government cafeterias and evening study groups in people's homes. In 1944 she became a lecturer at the Washington School of Psychiatry, under the aegis of Harry Stack Sullivan.

When Benedict came to Washington, she moved into Mead's house. Ruth Valentine was often there with her, but that was fine with Mead; she herself was often gone, lecturing around the country or spending time with Gregory and their daughter in New York. Mead had accepted Benedict's decision to have a lesbian partner long before, just as Benedict accepted her decision to marry Gregory Bateson. They had reached an intellectual and personal accommodation years before based on freedom for both of them that continued the vitality of their friendship whether they were together or apart. In 1944 Margaret wrote to Gregory that it was very "placid and pleasant" to live with Ruth. "It's really extraordinary," she continued, "how easily I pick up the relationship when we have seen so little of each other for so long." She didn't know what brand of cigarettes Ruth smoked any longer, or whether she still took sugar in her coffee, "but in all important matters it was the same."[12]

WHEN MEAD BECAME the administrator for the Committee on Food Habits, what was called "foodways" hadn't received much attention from anthropologists. Nor had Mead given the issue of what people eat much attention in print, aside from reporting that in New Guinea the food was awful, while in Bali it was excellent. She had, however, included an analysis of food habits and rituals among the Arapesh in the detailed ethnography she wrote of that society: she was aware of the actual and symbolic importance of food to human populations.[13] In 1941 the issues of food production, distribution, and nutrition had emerged as particularly important, given the deprivation of the Depression as well as estimates that up to one-third of the U.S. population was malnourished. And there was the matter of feeding a nation at war. These matters weren't simple problems, since they involved issues of rationing and of how to persuade people to eat more healthful food.[14]

Moreover, high-level federal jobs for women were hard to find, and

Mead's administrative credentials weren't substantial, since during much of her tenure at the Museum of Natural History she had been away on field trips. Aside from the American Anthropological Association, she belonged to few professional organizations; she hadn't voted in federal elections since 1924. Those factors influenced her to take the Committee on Food Habits job, in which she anticipated having the flexibility to do what she wanted that she might not find in a government agency.[15]

No matter her lack of experience, Mead's administrative skills were in evidence from the outset. With a limited budget, she had to be innovative. Realizing the importance of survey research as a tool for information and persuasion, she and Rhoda Métraux worked out an inexpensive method of sampling public opinion by having volunteers from anthropology departments, mostly students, conduct interviews around the country.[16] Applying a cultural perspective, she viewed food issues as connected to the customs and habits of regional and ethnic populations; she had another assistant analyze the diets of various European groups in the United States to determine the nutritional value of these diets and the receptivity of the populations who consumed them to changing their eating habits. She generated projects at a number of universities, including one at the University of Iowa on food consumption and dietary habits in general, and others at the University of Chicago on food habits among black and white sharecropper families in southern Illinois and among Indians and Mexican-Americans in the Southwest.

With Eleanor Roosevelt as her model, she toured the country observing what people were doing and saying about food. She promoted a "block plan" of neighborhood organization to the Office of Civilian Defense as a way of bringing people together and disseminating information: these informal groups became central to the general home-front effort during the war. Going beyond the matter of food, she set up a coordinating agency in her office to transmit information from anthropologists to the government, and she participated in planning an office located at the Smithsonian Institution to transmit information to the government from experts in all the social sciences.

She was, as usual, on leave of absence from the Museum of Natural History. As she had done there, she used her position in Washington as a base from which to undertake other activities. She expanded her lecturing and writing, putting together a way of life that, as she described it, "was to continue through the war and in a sense ever since, working from one platform to another, using my writing and lecturing abilities as ways to get from one place to another."[17] In the summer of 1940 she participated in discussions at Larry Frank's summer home about doing a documentary film on women's contributions to community life for the Congress of American Women, a network group of prominent women; she was being drawn into work on behalf of women.[18] During that summer she and Gregory put their photographs from Bali in order and chose the ones to include in *Balinese Character*. During the summer of 1943 the OWI sent her on a lecture tour of England; from that experience she wrote her book *And Keep Your Powder Dry*, a study of the American character that she was proud of having written in twenty-one days.

In contrast to Mead, Benedict approached her position at the OWI as a scholar, not an administrator-activist. She did studies of Denmark, Thailand, and Rumania, in particular. Her study of Denmark was commissioned to provide background information for setting up an underground movement there; the one on Thailand was designed to offer guidelines for planning a campaign of psychological warfare— since Thailand was an ally of Japan—and then for occupation and reconstruction of the country once the war ended. Benedict's assistants helped her by interviewing foreign nationals and analyzing cultural materials; she commissioned studies from scholars such as Erik Erikson. Her study of Japan was the most famous one she did at the OWI—and the only one she expanded into a popular book. She was asked to do it in 1944, as the Americans launched a major offensive against Japan and the hope was that the war might be ending. She didn't think that either the American people or federal bureaucrats knew much about Japan; she wanted the U.S. occupation of the country and the reconstruction of its society to be a success.

The Chrysanthemum and the Sword is considered the premier work of the national-character-studies approach developed by Benedict and Mead. It was a best-seller in the United States, and even in Japan it has sold more than two million copies. It showed once again that Benedict could soar above other analysts, writing with a measured intensity, elucidating Japanese culture in terms of a series of dualisms—the primary one being the chrysanthemum of beauty and order, a flower beloved by the Japanese, and the martial sword of the samurai, representing death as well as discipline. Focusing on shame and guilt as the basic categories of Japanese psychology, she used a modified configurationist approach, paying attention to the sophisticated sociological models that Ralph Linton and Gregory Bateson, among others, had developed. She found the central element of the culture in a devotion to hierarchies of caste, class, gender, and age, a pattern realized by a series of exchanges of duty and devotion within the hierarchy.

One recent analyst, following a strain of Japanese criticism of Benedict's book, contends that a class structure as well as ideas of guilt and of democracy existed in Japan; it wasn't the totalizing culture that he thinks Benedict described. Once again her configurationist approach, no matter how subtly applied, may have caused a problem in her analysis, with its focus on dominant and deviant strains. And her "culture at a distance" approach, which in the case of *The Chrysanthemum and the Sword* involved interviewing Japanese nationals in the United States, was always open to question. Indeed, Benedict never visited Japan; she relied on her interviews and on materials like movies and novels.[19]

Yet Benedict avoided emphasizing any primitive irrationality or neurosis in the Japanese character, even though that viewpoint predominated in American writing on Japan at the time, including the article by Geoffrey Gorer.[20] Benedict stressed the austerity and self-discipline in the culture, especially in the Japanese devotion to yoga. Still, in her presentation the Japanese weren't Puritans: she identified an ethic of pleasure that was evident, for example, in the Japanese bathing ritual. Disagreeing with the standard conclusion that the swings from gentleness to brutality they evidenced in the conduct of the war revealed "a neurotic people wracked with insecurity," Benedict wrote that the Japanese were able to change from one behavior to another "without psychic cost."[21]

Benedict didn't cast blame on the Japanese. She wanted the Americans to understand them in the context of the difficulty in introducing democracy to their hierarchical system, in which "proper station" took precedence over everything else. As in *Race*, history is a major factor in her analysis of Japan—and so is child rearing, a subject the scholars of national character considered crucial, given their neo-Freudian emphasis. In a footnote to *The Chrysanthemum and the Sword*, Benedict noted, but didn't comment on, Geoffrey Gorer's assertion that the authoritarianism in the Japanese character was produced by a rigid toilet training introduced in the first year of life. In what seems an answer to Gorer, she emphasized the culture's late weaning practices, with the breast accessible to the baby on demand—a practice that, she implied, might create a gentle, flexible character.

Sex and gender, however, aren't of overriding concern in this book.

In his brief analysis of Japan, Gorer had interpreted the dichotomies of Japanese culture as gendered, with the female "dark" and "passive" and the male "light" and "active"; he contended that these distinctions stemmed from the subservience of the Japanese boy to elder males and his aggressive stance toward older women.[22] Benedict didn't refer to these arguments of Gorer's, and she didn't analyze her dualisms as gendered. She did, however, view Japanese women as oppressed under a sexual double standard, with the geisha an established companion for married men. But she observed that women were powerful in running the household, raising children, and functioning as mothers-in-law, with power over sons and daughters-in-law. It was an analysis of women as powerful and powerless that had often appeared in her writing—going back to the written statements she had made in her course at the New School with Elsie Clew Parsons about the Anglo women living near the Zuñi Indians as subservient to their husbands, and yet independent as schoolteachers and domineering as wives.

Moreover, because of the Japanese devotion to the male-dominated family, Benedict contended, they had no concept of "being a homosexual"—in other words, of having a homosexual identity. They were shocked when they heard that some adult men in the United States played the passive role in sex, for they considered that position degrading to male dignity. One wonders how Benedict might have categorized the Japanese homosexuals that Reo Fortune's homosexual friend Max Bickerton had described in 1930 as walking like the berdache-in-the-making among the Omaha in Nebraska, whom Mead was closely observing, when he visited Reo and Margaret there. Perhaps they were "male geishas," a group that Benedict mentioned in *The Chrysanthemum and the Sword* but didn't analyze.[23]

Benedict didn't include any analysis of gender in the other national character studies that she did for the OWI—except in her brief study of Thailand. In that piece she concluded that although men seemed in charge in Thailand, women had significant indirect power through granting and withholding favors to them. "Success for the man," she wrote, "depends on skilled maneuvering." Yet she dismissed women more easily than she had previously done in writings like *Patterns of Culture*, in which she had noted their oppression in male-dominated societies. In her introduction to Rebecca Reyhder's *Zulu Woman*, a book that analyzes the life of one of the Zulu king's many wives, she overlooked the king's brutal behavior toward his wives, behavior that Reyhder stressed. By focusing on the king as trapped by the need to keep the Zulu tribes loyal and to deal with the incursions of whites, Benedict implicitly exonerated him for his repressive treatment of his wives.[24]

Despite her sympathy to the plight of the oppressed, in *The Chrysanthemum and the Sword* Benedict discussed neither the U.S. internment of Japanese nationals and Japanese-American citizens during the war nor the atom bombs the United States dropped on Hiroshima and Nagasaki in 1945. Mead justified Benedict's omitting the issue of the bomb by maintaining that when Benedict wrote the book neither the Americans nor the Japanese were factoring Hiroshima into their thinking about the postwar reconstruction of Japan—and that was the issue for Benedict.[25] Yet when Mead heard about the dropping of the bomb, she tore up the manuscript of a book she had written on postwar internationalism because she decided that the bomb, posing a threat to the existence of humanity, had reshaped history.[26] Given Mead's strong reaction, Benedict's overlooking the bomb in *The Chrysanthemum and the Sword* is puzzling.

Hilary Lapsley makes the case that Benedict left Hiroshima out of the book because she didn't want to alienate the Pasadena group that included Natalie Raymond and Ruth Valentine as well as their friend Ruth Tolman, a psychologist who was married to physicist Edward Tolman, who taught at the California Institute of Technology near Pasadena and had been involved in developing the bomb.[27] Valentine was in Washington with Benedict, and both Tolmans were also there, in government positions. According to Lapsley, J. Robert Oppenheimer, "the Father of the Atomic Bomb," had also been a professor at Caltech, and he had been involved with Natalie Raymond. The argument is plausible, although in writing a book that was partly a brief to engender American goodwill toward the Japanese, Benedict may not have wanted to stir up a moral debate over the bomb. Indeed, her book influenced General Douglas MacArthur's policies considerably during the Allied occupation and reconstruction of the government.[28]

In 1946, when John Hersey's bellwether book *Hiroshima* began to stir up that debate, Benedict wrote one of the first reviews of the book, in which she referred to "the nightmare magnitude of the [bomb's] destructive power." Yet in the immediate postwar era, according to Paul Boyer, many writers avoided referring to the bomb, while the American people, terrified by it, made scientists like Oppenheimer into cultural heroes. That attitude slowly shifted, but Oppenheimer's security hearings for disloyalty didn't occur until 1954.[29] There wasn't any overt reason that Benedict needed to protect him, although something private and undocumented may have been involved.[30]

TWO ISSUES WERE paramount to Benedict and Mead during World War II: how to win the war and how to motivate the American people, after a decade of economic depression, to make the sacrifices that the war required. In addition, they were concerned with how to make a just peace and a new world order and how to ensure that the heightened tensions of war wouldn't increase racism and anticommunism in the United States. They were also concerned with how to prevent the social scientists in the government from becoming servants of state power, as academics did work that was "classified" and not open to public scrutiny. Benedict and Mead both did such work, although exactly what that involved remains unclear. Mead stated that she taught groups of Americans posted to the Far East about the cultures they would encounter. Some of Benedict's work planning underground movements was classified.[31] Yet because of her activism in the late 1930s on behalf of organizations suspected of communist sympathies, Benedict didn't receive a top security clearance, while Mead took care not to join any organization that she thought might come under suspicion.

Benedict and Mead took their "messianism" of the 1920s and the 1930s and their Deweyian program of individualism, democracy, and social engineering to the national and world stages. They worried that authoritarian tendencies in the United States, in the form of anticommunism and the expansion of the federal government during the war, might destroy democracy at home and abroad, and they looked to local communities and small groups as the key to counteracting this by generating morale and defending the just society. Mead wrote that the United States needed to have a "democratic psychology" in planning propaganda, one coming from the citizenry and not from those in power. People all over the country, in her view, should exercise leadership, informed by the expertise of trained social scientists.[32] Mead worried about the destruction of traditional institutions upholding democracy. The government must support the productive middle class, she wrote in 1942, for without support that group could easily fall into the reactionary mind-set that had led to the rise of Hitler in Germany.[33]

In *And Keep Your Powder Dry*, Mead called for individual Americans to band together in their "towns," "blocks," "union locals," and "ships," to pool their resources behind the national effort.[34] In her position with the Committee on Food Habits she worked with the Office of Civilian Defense to establish neighborhood councils. She appreciated smallness and face-to-face encounters. She had liked studying small tribal societies in which she could learn everyone's name; she liked university seminars and small conferences. The latter became a passion with her; attending numerous meetings every year, she came to view them, probably overoptimistically, as part of a trend in Europe and the United States to take decision making away from the state and to return it to "small groups, committees, councils and other small local, but formal, gatherings."[35] Mead's most famous state-ment with regard to her emphasis on small groups was: "Never doubt that a small group of thoughtful committed citizens can change the world."

From the beginning of the "morale movement," with the formation of the Committee for National Morale, Mead wrote, the groups involved realized that morale had to come from the "grass roots." She was also convinced that what she called the "third generation" needed to generate it. She liked metaphors relating to "trios": according to Geoffrey Gorer, she was a third-generation feminist; she blended three generations in her family. In applying "third generation" to eth-nicity, she domesticated the radical sentiments of her college years. She now regarded the United States as a melting pot and concluded that ethnic groups had blended with the "Old American" descendants into a unified American population in the "third generation." She was aware that ethnicity was still a force in the United States and that African-Americans were subject to virulent racism, but in her patriotic rhetoric of World War II, designed to inspire Americans to engage in a crusade against what she saw as a powerful threat to democracy, she stressed sameness, not difference.[36] She had supported "cultural plu-ralism" in the 1920s and she didn't give up on that idea as a way to shape the society and polity of the United States, but she had also adopted the integration favored by liberals in the 1940s and 1950s—as her dialogue with James Baldwin in the 1960s made clear.

Benedict articulated sentiments similar to Mead's, although as usual she was less enthusiastic about contemporary United States institu-tions. In studying both the tribal council of the Blackfoot Indians and the local councils in China, she concluded that the West could learn a good deal from them about democratic decision making through consensus, particularly in local organizations composed of all citizens. Aside from her positive descriptions of the gender egalitarianism of the Zuñi and the individualism of the Plains Indians, she had downplayed her admiration for pre-state societies, attempting to avoid charges of romanticizing them. But Hitler was being called "primitive," and that label could lead to a version of the old evolutionary distinction between "primitive" and "civilized" societies, with tribal societies at the bottom once again. Benedict used the positive features she identified in tribal societies to support her reform views; reviewing Erich Fromm's *Escape from Freedom*, she challenged Fromm's assertion that the concept of freedom didn't exist in primitive societies.[37]

Her admiration for local councils and for consensus was also an outgrowth of the typologies she developed for ranking societies. After years of asserting that she didn't like cataloguing societies and hadn't done so in *Patterns of Culture*, she drew up her own typologies. She and Mead had long maintained that tribal societies were laboratories where data could be gathered in order to reach scientific conclusions about what institutions and behaviors worked best. "From the first," Mead wrote, "our interest was in how to respect the values of each civilization while finding values cross-culturally that were ultimate."[38] Benedict tried to do that. Now in her fifties, she wanted to make a culminating statement based on her years spent studying "primitive" societies and to find a scientific way to determine the "good society"—one that truly promoted individual and social well-being.

Benedict tried unsuccessfully to rank tribal societies by geography, climate, size, racial type, and gender—using matrilineal and patrilineal descent as her dividing principle for gender. She rejected gender as her determining factor when she realized that some societies she disliked, such as the Dobuans, had a matrilineal descent pattern, while other societies that she liked, such as the Arapesh, were patrilineal. She then came up with the concepts of "synergy," "siphon," and "hourglass" (she later changed "hourglass" to "funnel"), and those neutral terms seemed to her to work. She derived "synergy," her unifying term, from medicine, where it meant a combined action of chemicals and cells to produce a beneficial result. In line with the vogue for analyzing human nature in terms of "frustration" and "aggression," she focused on the promotion of nonaggression, rather than happiness, as her measure of a society's worth.

Abraham Maslow called Benedict's typologies "the most viable, post-Marxian theory of the good society."[39] Maslow, of course, was a great admirer of hers. She also devised a ranking by economic structure, one that she derived from Ruth Bunzel, in which "funnel societies" channeled wealth into the hands of a few men who had little concern for anyone else, while "siphon societies" constantly spread wealth throughout the community.[40]

In an article in the *Atlantic Monthly* in 1942, she contrasted her favorite Blackfoot Indians with the Chuckchee of Siberia. She doesn't use her terms "synergy," "siphon," and "funnel" in this piece, although they inform it. The Chuckchee resemble the Dobuans and the Kwakiutl of *Patterns of Culture*; in her description they seem monstrous. Living in prosperity from hunting the abundant reindeer herds they follow, free of any political structure, they are nonetheless murderous, tortured by horrible gods, deeply competitive, and filled with dread. The Blackfoot, on the other hand, are optimistic and free from violence. They operate according to an ethic of care: leaders identify with followers, the wealthy make certain that everyone is provided for, and leadership positions are open to talented individuals. True freedom, Benedict asserted, means not only individual independence but also taking on responsibility for others.[41]

In wartime, she noted, cooperation thrives in the United States. The impulse was evident in the formation of local councils and in the willingness of the people to accept rationing during World War II. That spirit, she contended, must be carried over to the peace. She called this mutuality a necessary part of "civil liberties." No man can be free, she asserted, unless all men are free; she worried that the democracy of the United States would falter because its system of government was based on reconciling special interests at the expense of the individual and its economy benefited the few over the many. The United States ran the risk of becoming a "funnel" rather than a "siphon" society. She preferred what she called a "joint stock" economic model based on the widespread participation of individuals in the nation's wealth to an unregulated "capitalist" one controlled by the rich. It was an extension of her position in *Race*, where she identified social class and economic insecurity as primary causes of racism and called for a program of support for the financially disadvantaged to end their discontent directed against African-Americans.

Cohesive societies committed to individualism and democratic consensus building in small groups—these were the linchpins of Benedict's and Mead's social philosophy in those years. Such a program had precedents in classic American institutions like the New England town meetings and the voluntary associations for a variety of purposes that commentators since Alexis de Tocqueville in the 1830s had viewed as characteristic of American democracy. Their agenda drew from the republican ideology long central to an American creed dating back to Thomas Jefferson that valued independent producers and then the small town—a populist creed especially enunciated in the 1890s and again in the 1930s, when the capitalist system seemed to have broken down.[42] And small groups and mutuality were comforting in an era of frightening military aggression, totalitarian states, and a growing internal anticommunism that expanded the existence of communist subversion out of all proportion to reality. At the same time, both Benedict and Mead supported the founding of the United Nations, as a way to bring interdependence on a world scale and to end the nationalism that by Benedict's analysis was the ultimate source of racism—and of Hitler's rise.

Both women studied national character in this era to promote cultural relativism and internationalism and to end viewing nations and ethnicities in terms of race. That tendency would for the most part disappear during World War II and its aftermath, as "race" retreated to a term meaning skin color. But the old meaning in terms of ethnicity and nations could reappear at any point—or another word might be coined or redefined—to reintroduce new hierarchical distinctions. Mead wrote that in the studies of contemporary cultures that she, Benedict, and their associates were doing, national character had nothing to do with race. To the contrary, she asserted that they were interested in the institutions and forces that shaped individuals as they matured. Upbringing, not race, she declared, produced the differences between national groups.[43]

Beyond that, their national-character studies favored social reform and a new internationalism. In contrast, "our nations are set up on a segmented plan, each with its own interests," wrote Benedict critically, "so that nations fight."[44] Mead made the same point more grandly. Combining the ideas of the eminent John Dewey with those of the somewhat shady Howard Scott, building on a vision of an end to world discrimination that both she and Benedict derived from Franz Boas, Mead's imagination soared to embrace individualism, technology, and the concept of "patterns" that Benedict had made famous. "If we wish to build a world in which all use all men's diverse gifts," Mead wrote, "we must go to school to other cultures. We must find models and patterns which, orchestrated together on a world scale, will make a world as different from the old as the machine world was from the craft industries of the middle ages."[45] Thus Mead and Benedict embarked on their grandest scheme of ethnographic fieldwork in the study of comparative cultures, and this time Benedict took the lead.

BETWEEN 1938 AND 1940, as they reacted to the widening war and put together their plan to study the characters of a number of nations, Benedict and Mead coped with an unexpected personal crisis. It began when their close friends Jeannette Mirsky and Hannah Kahn—nicknamed "David" by the Ash Can Cats—became involved in a romantic triangle, as Jenny's husband, Arthur Barsky, fell in love with David when Jenny was in Guatemala doing fieldwork. David had been a stalwart of the Ash Can Cats from its beginnings; Jenny was a student of Benedict's and a member of Mead's Barnard class with whom Mead had lived during the spring of 1934, when Arthur Barsky was in Europe.

The problem was that Jenny wouldn't give Arthur a divorce, and under the stringent divorce laws of the day, there would be no divorce without Jenny's consent—unless Arthur proved that she had committed adultery. She had been involved with anthropology graduate student William Whitman for some time, but Arthur didn't seem to know about it. To complicate matters further, Whitman was married—and he waffled on whether or not he would divorce his wife and marry Jenny. Arthur Barsky was a successful plastic surgeon, Jenny a graduate student without much money. She was furious with him for taking up with one of her friends and terrified of being alone. Then Whitman was killed in a freak accident, and Jenny was doubly bereaved. None of the individuals involved in this triangle acted responsibly. Charges and countercharges flew; they seemed to relish dramatic confrontations and retreats into angry sulks.[46]

Margaret and Ruth's letters to each other from 1938 through 1940 are filled with discussions of the Jenny-David-Arthur problem, as though they were sublimating other worries through this drama or mourning its damage to the Ash Can Cats and the potential loss of Jenny to anthropology, for Mead considered her a protégée. Despite their fame, Benedict and Mead always remained loyal to Mead's friends from her days at Barnard—the Ash Can Cats, Marie Eichelberger, Margery Loeb, Jane Belo, Jeannette Mirsky. Similarly, Benedict had found lovers in the circle composed of Natalie Raymond,

Ruth Valentine, and Ruth Tolman. And the Jenny-David-Arthur triangle was reminiscent of other triangles Benedict and Mead had been involved in: the one with Edward Sapir before Margaret went to Samoa; Margaret's involvement with Luther Cressman, Reo Fortune, and Ruth before she went to New Guinea with Reo. They had resolved those triangles, but they had experienced pain in doing so; they identified with the individuals involved in this one.

Another issue was that Ruth was close to David and Margaret to Jenny. David had helped Ruth with her editing and proofreading and had taken courses with her at Columbia. "Of all the Ash Can Cats," Ruth wrote to Margaret in 1930, "it's David I'd call on if stranded."[47] As for Margaret, Marie Eichelberger asserted that she assumed Margaret would take Jenny's point of view because she had always been so fond of her. Meanwhile, Ruth was annoyed with Jenny because the fieldwork she did in Guatemala wasn't first-rate and also because she refused to give Arthur a divorce. "I do criticize Jeannette," Ruth wrote Margaret, "because no one can sink lower than to hold onto a husband who wants to end a marriage."[48]

The situation blew up in the summer of 1939. Ruth was in Montana on her field trip to the Blackfoot when Arthur Barsky came to see her and asked her point-blank if she would testify that Jenny had had a lover. Faced with direct confrontation, angry with Jenny, Ruth agreed. When Jenny found out, she contacted Margaret, informing her that she would tell the newspapers that Ruth was a lesbian if she followed through on her promise to Arthur. Margaret telephoned Ruth, chastising her so severely that Ruth took to her bed, deeply depressed. Why was Margaret so angry? Was she afraid that Jenny might expose her as well? After all, there were those months that Margaret had lived with her. Margaret soon backed down, informing Ruth that even if she tried to testify at the divorce hearing, the judge would probably regard her testimony as hearsay, and disallow it.[49] Having gone through two divorces, Margaret knew the legal side of divorce. In the end, after she returned to the United States from New Guinea, Margaret took over resolving the situation.

Margaret's telephone call angered Ruth: Margaret wrote Gregory Bateson that she thought that Ruth stayed in Pasadena that year because she wanted be away from the Jenny-Arthur-David problem.[50] Indeed, Margaret had chastised her over the phone for not putting Arthur off by obfuscating the situation, as she would have done. Ruth didn't agree. She could withhold information, she wrote Margaret, but she couldn't refuse to give it when asked directly. Ruth rarely displayed annoyance at Margaret in her letters, but this time she did. "No doubt this is a Turk-culture case," she wrote to her in March 1940. "I thought all fall and spring you were impatient with my ethics because they aren't the Law of the Land."[51] In other words, she hadn't done what Margaret wanted. Now she informed her that she had told Arthur only that she would testify in a settlement out of court about the alimony, not in a regular divorce court. The real problem, she had found out, was that Natalie Raymond had already given Arthur an affidavit about her knowledge of the affair, and Nat, who had worked in Arthur's office, knew a lot.[52] To have agreed to testify, Nat must have been very angry with Ruth for leaving her for Ruth Valentine, who had been a friend of hers.

The divorce went through, and Arthur and David married. As might have been expected, Benedict and Mead cut off relations with them—and with Jenny. They fade out of their lives, and only that phone call of Mead's to Benedict remains. Was she asserting control over Benedict, the child turned into the parent? After all the times that Benedict had cautioned Mead about the danger of her personal behavior compromising her career, the tables were turned.

There was also the matter of Margaret's marriage to Gregory. In her letters to Ruth, Margaret didn't mention any problems in that relationship; indeed, it seemed to be working. He was a dutiful husband and father. Devoted to their joint research and to Margaret and Ruth's national-character studies, he participated in their enterprises and did his own work; he played a major role in raising Mary Catherine after Margaret moved to Washington. Yet strains emerged full-blown when in 1943 Gregory joined the OSS and went to the Far East as a "psychological expert" to plan and execute "psychological warfare" against the enemy. It sounds as though he was off on a masculine adventure as a spy in the Far East. He didn't return until the war was over.

During those years Gregory became involved with other women. Margaret wrote to Carrie Kelly that whenever she and Gregory were separated for any length of time, a "Steve" appeared, and it took her a good deal of effort to sort out those situations. How long she was able to convince Gregory that she was totally feminine isn't clear; at some point he began to dislike her controlling side, even though her energy fueled him into performing in high gear—as it had also prodded Reo Fortune toward achievement. A fellow anthropologist captured the difference between them when he described Margaret as walking down a long corridor at the Museum of Natural History, two steps ahead of Gregory, furiously talking and gesturing with her hands, taking two steps to his one. Gregory walked behind her, quietly nodding agreement. She was like "a principle of pure energy," Gregory said. "I couldn't keep up, and she couldn't stop."[53]

Yet initially they had defined themselves through each other: like Ruth, Gregory became an alter ego for Margaret. Margaret defined Ruth as Northern, then "tetraploid," and then Western—while Gregory was always Southern, just like her. Yet she knew that Ruth and Gregory were similar in their gentleness and their intellectuality. That's part of the reason why Margaret's sense of connection with Gregory was as strong as the one she had with Ruth. In 1947 Margaret wrote Carrie Kelly that her work had come to depend on his theoretical formulations.[54] But in the end her Daemonic energy, her controlling ways, and the speed with which her mind worked overwhelmed him; he couldn't deal with her ability at instant and complete recall and how she could obfuscate every situation by ever more intricate explanations, turning what initially seemed like clear-cut issues into complex dilemmas.

During her years with Gregory, Margaret wrote Carrie, the part of him that wanted to be a great scientist and that identified with her had battled the other part that wanted to leave her and to have a romantic adventure and "be himself." Thus, as she put it, there were recurrent "Steves." It had been hard, she wrote Carrie, always to represent the "sober course" and "to have almost anyone with a beautiful face or pretty voice represent all the romance and excitement in life."[55] Yet in retrospect she thought all the difficulty had been worth it; she never lost her sense of deep communion with Gregory. None of it was easy. Sometimes she tried the completed-circle strategy of their free-love beliefs and attempted to create triangular relationships, as she had with Steve. Sometimes she let Gregory go off on his own, as with Jane Belo. She still saw Ruth; she saw Geoffrey Gorer. Gregory had an affair with Rhoda Métraux; when it ended Rhoda became Margaret's partner for the rest of her life.

In 1949, a year before they divorced, Gregory angrily wrote Margaret rejecting not only their marriage but also applied anthropology, "culture cracking," and bisexuality. "Tiresias," he wrote, "is the eternal observer—bisexual and deathless and unforgetting." Tiresias was the Greek soothsayer whom Zeus struck blind because, after having been a man and then a woman, he declared that women have more pleasure in sexual relations than men. The implication was that Gregory wanted to pursue his masculine self wholeheartedly; he didn't want any more ambiguous sexuality in his life. Two years later, responding to his hostility, Mead expressed her continuing love for him and her anguish over their divorce: "I suppose it is better to be trapped by love than by hostility, but certainly the tightness of the trap doesn't look very different when the irons press into the flesh."[56] Fleeing Margaret again, Gregory moved to Northern California, married and divorced and married again, had several children, and ended his career teaching at the new campus of the University of California at Santa Cruz.

Yet Margaret wasn't "faithful" to Gregory in any traditional sense of the term. There were other individuals in her intimate life, both male and female, new friends and old acquaintances. In New Guinea in 1938, when they went there to restudy the Iatmul after their several years in Bali, she had a brief liaison with the official government anthropologist for New Guinea, E. P. Chinnery, whom they called "Chin." She had met him ten years previously, when she first went to New Guinea with Reo Fortune; at that point she described him to Benedict as sweet and easygoing, with a shrewish wife and four daughters. She often interacted with him during her years in New Guinea. His résumé in her papers indicates that he had undergraduate and graduate degrees from Cambridge University and that he had published many papers on New Guinea society. The biographer would pay little attention to him— except for a note that Mead wrote to him in 1938 telling him that she had come down with a mild venereal infection. "You can take it," she wrote, "as a specially delicate compliment."[57]

Mead remained dedicated to her free-love beliefs and to the bisexuality that she had recommended in *Sex and Temperament* and which she continued to practice. She remained as attractive to others as always, able to seduce with her sensitivity, her brilliant mind, her magnetic eyes, her fame. Sex for her remained central to human interactions, so long as a spirituality involving respect and affection accompanied any physical connection. Free love remained to her "an ethical system," "almost a religion."

ONCE THE WAR ENDED Mead returned to the American Museum of Natural History. She lectured locally and nationally, ran the Institute for Intercultural Studies, oversaw her collection at the museum and did some teaching at Columbia, attended conferences and seminars, raised her child. Gregory Bateson returned from the Far East in 1945; a year later he moved out of their home; by 1949 he had moved to California. They divorced in 1950. Benedict returned to her position at Columbia, but it remained contested terrain. When Ralph Linton went to Yale in 1946, her situation improved: she was promoted to full professor in 1948, just before her death. Yet Linton was replaced by Julian Steward, and although Benedict and Steward were cordial to each other, he represented a new direction in anthropology, one that combined materialism, evolutionism, and ecology to focus on areas of culture like agriculture and the economy. In the new emphasis on broad themes and not individual cultures there was something of Kroeber's "superorganic."[58]

Steward had been trained at Michigan by Leslie White, originally a student of Boas in the 1910s who had left Columbia for Chicago because he felt ill at ease among the German-speaking Jews at Columbia. At Chicago, Edward Sapir became his mentor; White developed a new, more progressive evolutionary model of development. A polemicist of considerable ability, White saw himself as the "dragon-slayer" of Boasian cultural determinism.[59] Thus Benedict and Mead's past continued to haunt them, as White's student, Julian Steward, came to Columbia. Meanwhile, numbers of male war veterans entered the department at Columbia as graduate students, and they gravitated to Steward, finding Benedict's approach too "poetic" for their taste. Columbia's program was large, and Benedict continued to attract graduate students, but the new division in the department wasn't easy on her. According to Mead, the Boasian cultural emphasis had been almost completely eliminated.[60]

Benedict was energized by her war service and the success of *The Chrysanthemum and the Sword*, and she viewed herself as the successor to Boas. She continued to work for world peace—and the cultural point of view in anthropology. She fulfilled that vision by establishing her project at Columbia in studying contemporary cultures worldwide and raising the funds for it. The money came to her when the Office of Naval Research decided to fund studies to achieve world peace. *The Chrysanthemum and the Sword* impressed them; they trusted Benedict to deliver what she promised. Her grant was large: it totaled $100,000.

Mead helped Benedict administer the project, known as Research in Contemporary Cultures. Its participants included Gregory Bateson, Geoffrey Gorer, Erik Erikson, Ruth Valentine, and Rhoda Métraux— all close friends or lovers. Larry Frank was there on the sidelines, but

John Dollard wasn't involved: he and Mead were no longer friends. The remainder of the participants came from fourteen disciplines and sixteen nationalities, and they included undergraduates and amateurs, many of the latter volunteers. In the end, the grant from the United States Navy proved insufficient to support the project's 120 participants working on seven cultures over a period of four years. Benedict obtained a grant from the Rand Corporation to support a study of the Soviet Union; with her inheritance from Stanley a financial cushion, she poured her salary and stipends from lecturing and writing into the project, which eventually expended a quarter of a million dollars in funds.[61]

Using Benedict and Mead's "culture at a distance" approach, the participants in the project interviewed nationals from the nations being studied who were living in the United States. They analyzed newspapers, journals, movies, and novels. Putting into practice their ideas about the value of democracy and consensus, Benedict and Mead made their operation nonhierarchical. They split up the work by groups for each nation being studied, and they assigned each participant to at least two groups—in one of which he or she took on a leadership role and in the other the role of a critic. The project participants met biweekly to discuss their progress.

The project ran into problems from the start. Some of them stemmed from Geoffrey Gorer, with his tendency to take extreme stands and his occasional contempt for college professors—as when he titled his work on burlesque *Hot Strip Tease*, as though thumbing his nose at academic respectability.[62] The major publication from the project, *The Study of Culture at a Distance*, praised Gorer for having done more than any other anthropologist to develop the study of national character.[63] Yet in his work on "Great Russia"—by which he meant the culture of Russia apart from the rest of the USSR—Gorer came up with the hypothesis that the practice of swaddling babies had produced the authoritarian Russian character. If one accepted the importance of pre-oedipal influence on personality formation and then interviewed Russian émigrées who talked about swaddling, as Gorer did, that thesis might be the result. But Gorer contended that he had derived it from a chance remark that Mead had made.[64] The public reaction was predictable: critics who were already accusing Benedict and Mead of "messianism" in their claims for studying world culture and bringing world peace now laughed at Mead. They called the swaddling hypothesis "diaperology."

Writing in *Commentary* in 1950, Robert Endleman traced what he saw as extravagances in their national-character approach to Gorer, but he also criticized Mead and Benedict for failing to take into account systems of social organization, group differentiation, hierarchical structures, history, and politics. They had in actuality tried to cover these areas, and Mead wrote a number of articles on their methodology explaining this. They could, however, always be charged with not having included enough, with having covered only a part of a culture and not its entirety, no matter how many variables they included. In fact, Endleman thought that political organizations such as nation-states were simply too complex to hold to a single worldview; he called the entire project "politically naive."[65]

Loyal to her close friends, Mead defended Gorer's thesis about swaddling in an article she wrote for the *American Anthropologist*. In her typical fashion, she placed swaddling in the context of myriad meanings through which it became a complex puzzle that Gorer had brilliantly constructed for others to solve. She reduced swaddling to a hypothesis useful in testing broader issues such as the parent-child relationship; she denied that it was the sole explanation for the Russians' authoritarian adult character; and she chided those who had assumed that Gorer meant to apply it to any other culture. It had to do only with Russia, and it was useful only insofar as the swaddling could be compared with similar practices in the rest of Eastern Europe and elsewhere.

Mead took on scholars who contended that the hypothesis couldn't be proved for earlier eras, maintaining that theory didn't have to be historicized. She replied to political scientists who didn't think that child-rearing methods revealed much about culture by restating the arguments for their importance from John Dollard onward. She wondered if the attack on the theory didn't have to do with an American aversion to the limitation of movement imposed by swaddling, given the "major commitment" of Americans to freedom of movement—evident in the movement to the frontier.[66]

She didn't mention that swaddling was enforced by mothers, who wrapped the babies. This was a postwar era of "mother blaming," when men again needed to assert their authority against women who had left the home for work. Historians of the social sciences and of academic culture in general haven't investigated their subjects in the years from the 1920s through the 1950s in terms of "masculinization" and "feminization." However, those might be important categories to apply to these decades, especially given the strains of a resurgent aggressive masculinity that historians are finding in the anticommunist agitation of that time and in culture more generally.[67]

By 1950, the year of her divorce from Bateson, Mead was particularly annoyed by the attacks on the project. In a letter to Gorer, she focused on his book *The American Character*. She criticized him for the slimness of his writing, for not documenting anything sufficiently, and for his extreme Freudian positions. "I spend all my days on the firing line," she wrote, "taking the whole rap of anger, criticism, contempt." She accused him of going too far with psychoanalytic theory.[68] In this book he took "mother blaming" to an extreme by attacking mothers as responsible for nearly every problem of American society, including infantilizing their sons. Mead had her own set of issues with mothers, but she had never taken the thesis that far. And Mead questioned Gorer's interpretation of authoritarianism in Japan as produced by too-early toilet training and of that in Russia as produced by swaddling. These assertions also went too far.

Gorer and Mead patched up their disagreement, and they remained friends, although he dropped out of the Columbia project and returned to England. But she had Rhoda Métraux and a host of other supporters around the country, both old and new friends. As was her way, she was already making peace with Leslie White and Julian Steward and their evolutionary approach. In 1947 she reviewed *Touchstone for Ethics*, by T. H. Huxley and Julian Huxley, writing that she liked their definition of evolution as a process generating "greater variety, more complex organization, higher levels of awareness, and increasingly conscious mental activity."[69] Within a few years she incorporated evolutionary concepts in her work, as she moved toward a greater emphasis on biology and ethnology, demonstrating the eclecticism that had always characterized her work and that allowed her to take up new positions and blend them with old ones. She brought even Benedict into the evolutionary circle, as she characterized Benedict's patterns determining cultures as shifting, not as fixed entities, enabling a society to be open to new forms of behavior. It was certainly a dynamic interpretation of what Benedict had meant.[70]

Gorer wasn't the only problem for the Columbia project. There was the difficulty in using psychologists who were professional therapists as interviewers: they wanted to solve the problems of the individuals they interviewed. There was the problem of acculturation to American culture on the part of informants, an accommodation that might taint their reaction to the culture from which they came. Were informants who had assimilated—or even partly assimilated—to American culture capable of giving objective information about their original culture? There was a space shortage at Columbia University, and the researchers had to conduct their large operation in various locations in the city, creating alienation among the various groups—and an administrative nightmare. There was the problem with continuing to use nationals in the United States from the countries they were investigating when the war had ended and they could send interviewers to those countries to question natives who had never left. The Jewish members of the project protested so vehemently against including Jews as members of Eastern European nationalities that Mead and Benedict split off a separate task force on Eastern European Jews.

Mead chaired the general meeting held in May 1948, the last meeting before the plenary group dispersed for the summer. She complained that they still didn't have a frame of reference; indeed, there wasn't a single abstract principle they had come up with that everyone in the room agreed upon. Still, she was enthusiastic about the future. The Russian, Chinese, and Jewish groups were going strong, and groups on Syria and Spain were starting their research. The group on France was going to conclude its deliberations in the fall, and the Czech group had sent interviewers abroad.[71] As she usually did, Mead finished on a positive note.

IN THE LATE 1940S Mead wrote articles about women for a variety of popular publications; her positions in these articles, as always, were many and varied. For example, she argued that the women's movement and technology had freed women from their biological role of childbearing and child rearing, but women had used their freedom to create an irresponsible "matriarchy." Women must redesign themselves and the world in terms of their biological role. Mead applauded the success of women in professional careers but she worried about unmarried women without children, and she chided women for devaluing women who were homemakers. She attacked Mary Beard's celebration of women in *Woman as Force in History* as outdated; she criticized Alfred Kinsey's renowned studies of sexuality in men and women as mechanistic, dealing with sex only as performance, not in terms of pleasure and personal connection. For her part, she preferred Havelock Ellis.[72] She called for inventions and institutions to take the drudgery out of

the home, the "semi-voluntary slavery to housework." Her innova-
tions included emergency centers to care for children who were ill.[73]
Standing in the midst of the stream of the twentieth century, one thing
Mead didn't see coming was women's return to the home.[74]

As Mead's marriage to Gregory Bateson fell apart during these
years, she went to Benedict for solace and help. In the summer of 1947
she taught the seminar in American Studies in Salzburg, Germany. She
had expected Gregory to go with her, but at the last moment he backed
out. Deeply depressed, she wrote Benedict from aboard the ship en
route to Europe that she was lifting her spirits by daydreaming about
marrying Geoffrey Gorer; by reminding herself that she had to go
back to what Gregory called "culture cracking"; and by remembering
that Gregory had never been involved in the project as much as Geoffrey. She wrote that she was also thinking about the book on males and
females, which she hoped to finish by the end of the summer. She
thanked Ruth for her constant help—reading her manuscripts, taking
care of practical matters while she was away, intervening with Gregory
on her behalf. "You were born a Martha," she asserted, "and a Martha
you will remain."[75]

The book that she referred to was *Male and Female*, which she
began writing in 1947 and finished the next year.[76] She published it in
1949. It was her culminating statement on gender; she never took up
the subject again in such depth. She reiterated her view from *Sex and
Temperament* that homosexuality and heterosexuality were cultural creations from temperamental predispositions that were better left fluid.
She was still uncertain about the influence of genes and hormones on
humans—although in later years she would come to believe that they
had a decisive impact. In this post-Hitler era she was more open with
regard to constitutional types—and how they might revolutionize gender arrangements.

She remained as broadly inclusive—or as contradictory—as she had
been in *Sex and Temperament*. She stated, for example, that if sex differences were quantified between the sexes, most of them would disappear. Moreover, she noted that children continuously reinterpret their
gender as their bodies develop, thus calling the notion of a fixed sexual
identity into question. Biological regularities related to reproduction
exist, however, and they must be taken into account. Thus as she had in
Sex and Temperament she referred to "essential womanhood," while she
emphasized that women's intuitive and nurturing nature provides
them with special ways of thinking and feeling. She didn't suggest that

achieving women should return to the home; she wanted the importance of women's mothering to be acknowledged and she wanted achieving women to take their maternal abilities into their work.

Above all, she viewed roles and relationships as difficult for men, and here her new interest in what has come to be called sociobiology came into play. "My early exposure to theories from the behavior of rats," she wrote, "prepared me to be responsive to such studies and to welcome the wealth of material on ethnology."[77] She probably was referring to studies that she learned about in her college courses in psychology. That material from the study of animal and primate species was extensive by the post–World War II period. It convinced her that men weren't monogamous by nature and that they had to be socialized to be good fathers and family members. Moreover, her years of observing pre-state societies, she contended, had taught her that women's reproductive biology—their assurance of motherhood—made them more secure than men. She called for a "men's rights movement" that would address the issue of the difficulties of being a man in the competitive United States. Throughout their lives men had to compete with women—with their sisters in their childhood families, with more mature and higher-achieving girls in school, with women in their professions. She thought that this competition was a mistake; in fact, she posited that a subtle demand for the same character structure for the sexes—for women to become more like men—was spreading, and she didn't like that at all.

Yet Mead didn't advocate a return to tradition. She wanted the adoption of a balance in which the sexes would be viewed as reciprocal but their special abilities taken into account. On the one hand, she argued that "we cannot flout the recognized biological needs of our mammalian nature. We are made to continue the human race."[78] On the other hand, she asserted that when an occupation was limited to one sex, it lost "a rich differentiated quality." To prove her point, she cited the lack of men as teachers in primary and secondary schools and the lack of women as college professors and as researchers in the sciences oriented toward human behavior; with their sensitivity to others, women were especially suited for these sciences. She thought that involving fathers in child rearing was crucial to ensuring healthy families.

In *Male and Female* she took many different stands, covering a variety of issues. As a Freudian, she stressed the pre-oedipal period as especially significant to human development, and, foreshadowing the later theories of Nancy Chodorow, she maintained that girls had an easier time growing up than boys because they could retain their identification with the mother and didn't have to switch their identification to the male gender of the father, as boys did. She criticized modern society for decreasing the period of sexual latency by allowing dating behavior at earlier ages and creating a situation in which competition for dating partners mirrored the competitiveness of the society in general and placed too much pressure on immature young people.

However, she didn't include her visionary ideas, expressed in articles she wrote during this period, that housework should be eliminated by technology, that families should be communal, and that there should be special community centers for children who were ill. Thus the conservative positions in *Male and Female*, rather than the progressive ones in the articles, stood as expressing the totality of her views. With considerable justification, Betty Friedan could contend that Mead was the architect of the back-to-the-home movement of the 1950s.

There's no indication of Benedict's response to this book, although she probably read it. Indeed, she had long believed that women were both powerful and powerless under patriarchal arrangements and that men and women were different by nature. She probably didn't disagree with Mead's point of view. One can visualize her, bemused by Mead's flow of words, smiling her "Mona Lisa" smile and standing to one side, silently urging her friend on.

DURING THE SUMMER of 1948, Benedict went to Europe. She hadn't been there since the disastrous summer of 1926; she hadn't been outside the United States since then, except for a trip to Guatemala with Natalie Raymond in 1938. After the enthusiastic reception of *The Chrysanthemum and the Sword* and the excitement generated by the research project she had created at Columbia, she felt good about herself. She had moved beyond her despair over the summer in Europe in 1926, when Mead had gone off with Reo Fortune and had left her alone, wandering from city to city. For a number of years she had been interviewing individuals from European cultures in the United States; she wanted to experience what those cultures were actually like on their own territory.

Yet she wasn't in good health. She had suffered from high blood pressure and dizzy spells for some time; when she had arranged to take a government-sponsored visit to Europe in 1945, to inaugurate a program of studies of German communities, the army doctor who examined her wouldn't let her go. But she didn't curtail, or even slow down, her activities. She seems to have intended to die, like Franz Boas, still active and trying to change the world. She had never feared death; she had always embraced it as a form of peace. So she went on teaching, lecturing, writing, and engaging in a full range of professional activities. As far as can be determined she kept on smoking, a habit she and her friends had picked up in the 1920s; her beloved Franz Boas had died at a luncheon at Columbia University after lighting up a cigarette and saying, "I have a new theory of race."

In December 1947, she dealt with the exhilaration and the difficulties of her tenure as president of the American Anthropological Association, as the action of the governing council changing the term of the president in the organization's constitution cut her time in office down to six months. Refusing to run for another term as president, she protested silently against her treatment. Historian Margaret Rossiter calls Benedict's refusal "as strong a statement of dissatisfaction with any professional organization as any woman took publicly in this period," which contained, according to Rossiter, a "minefield" of resentment against women in the scientific professions.[79] As her presidential address Benedict gave a defiant speech in which she defended her cultural approach and the worth of the humanities in providing models for analysis in the face of the evolutionary, "scientific" approach that was dominant at Columbia and was spreading throughout the field of anthropology.

Some of her friends thought that she hadn't aged well, that she looked old and tired. Others, however, had a different impression. Biologist G. E. Hutchinson sat next to her at a dinner after a committee meeting and observed, as many people had throughout her life, that she had an "unearthly beauty." He described her as looking like a Sibyl, "a mythical wisewoman, at once from the remote past and the distant future." When Erik Erikson saw her just before she sailed for Europe in the summer of 1948 he described her as looking "as much like a young girl, as she looked like a man, without being in the least juvenile or mannish."[80] Her sister, Margery, commented that she had overcome her depression and shyness to take on a public role that she would never have thought possible when she was young. She used to wish that she had never been born, Margery wrote, but now she wanted more hours in the day and more years ahead. She had long

avoided public appearances, but now she met with government committees, spoke at conferences, gave public speeches. She had despaired
of finding any meaning in life, but now her life was fulfilled.[81]

Benedict received an invitation to attend a UNESCO conference
in Czechoslovakia during the summer of 1948, and doctors didn't have
to pass on her health for her to go. Mead described Benedict's experience of that summer trip at the first meeting of the plenary session of
the Columbia project in the fall, which took place after Benedict had
died. Benedict, Mead reported, had enjoyed visiting associates of the
Columbia program who were in Europe, and the UNESCO conference was a great success. Benedict loved her experience of Europe. As
she visited Czechoslovakia, Poland, France, Belgium, and the Netherlands, all places she had studied through their cultural productions and
the nationals she had interviewed in the United States, she saw her
work on national character come alive. She especially liked the Poles;
she formed a picture of them that she hadn't had before. In the
Netherlands she went to a Van Gogh exhibit with Dutch people who
had collaborated with the Germans during the war and, with typical
restraint, simply "listened to what they didn't like about Van Gogh."
She returned to the United States "bubbling with enthusiasm." She
seemed in good health; she looked forward to teaching and to resum-
ing the contemporary cultures project.[82]

Her heart gave out on Monday, September 12, ten days after she
returned from Europe. Rushed to the hospital, she died the next Friday, from a coronary thrombosis. She was lucid and peaceful during
the week, ready to accept what happened. Mead was in the hospital
with her; and Ruth Valentine was there toward the end. Remaining in
Los Angeles that summer, she hadn't joined Benedict on the trip to
Europe. In Benedict's handbag on her death was a letter from her sister
Margery, received some days before, which revealed that Valentine had
become involved with Ruth Tolman—and that she had decided that
relationship wasn't working. She would definitely return to "the old
gal—the famous anthropologist."[83] When news of Benedict's hospital-
ization came, Valentine took the train from Los Angeles to New York
and was with her during her last hours.

Mead was distraught when Benedict died. She went for counseling
to Gotthard Booth, whom she saw during her time of troubles with
Gregory Bateson. At Ruth's memorial service, she read a tribute to her
friend, and she published another in the *American Anthropologist*,
describing her there as a transitional figure, using a metaphor both

familiar and distanced. "She was a figure of transition," Mead wrote, "binding the bright sureties of a past age, to which she was full heir, to the uncertainties which precede a new era in human thinking." Mead was looking to the future, not the past, to the new thinking that she, still in her forties, was engaging in—about mental health, biology and technology, the family, the new global perspective. Yet she remained true to her friend. She completed Benedict's projects: she carried on the Columbia program of cultural studies until funding ran out several years later; she took over the supervision of Benedict's graduate students.

She had loved Benedict beyond measure; she would miss her friend and lover, her sister, mother, and mentor. Now they would truly have to meet in dreams. Without Benedict, Mead would never have attained her brilliant career: Benedict gave her the inspiration to build upon her insights and to extend them, to go beyond her in her thinking while retaining her affection and support. A woman raised in the Victorian era, Benedict had confronted and embraced the modern era, while retaining the integrity of the past. "We shall not look upon her like again," Mead concluded.[84] Now it was time for Mead to go ahead, to forge a career that would continue for the next thirty years, until she died in 1978 at the age of seventy-seven, world renowned. She would, indeed, construct the brilliant career that Benedict had expected of her and, by achieving it, come full circle to fulfill the dreams of her friend.

Notes

ABBREVIATIONS

AA	American Anthropologist
AW	An Anthropologist at Work
BW	Blackberry Winter
CTK	Caroline "Carrie" Tennant Kelly
ES	Edward Sapir
GB	Gregory Bateson
GG	Geoffrey Gorer
MFF	Margery Fulton Freeman
MM	Margaret Mead
RFB	Ruth Fulton Benedict
RFF	Reo F. Fortune

ARCHIVAL AND INTERVIEW SOURCES, WITH ABBREVIATIONS

AC Amherst College. Archives and Special Collections, Amherst College Library. Louise Bogan Papers.

APS American Philosophical Society, Philadelphia. Typescript letters between Benedict and Mead; Franz Boas Papers; Elsie Clews Parsons Papers.

BC Barnard College Archives. Ms. material relating to Barnard College and Mead's career as a student there.

Cam-U Cambridge University, England, Special Collections and Manuscripts. Typescript autobiography of Noel Teulon Porter, "As I Seem to Remember."

CCHS Chenango County Historical Society, Norwich, New York. Mss. and newspaper clipping collection of Shattuck, Fulton families, pertaining to Ruth Benedict's childhood.

CM Carleton Mabee interviews with Mead family members and friends, in possession of Carleton Mabee, Gardiner, New York.

CU Columbia University. Rare Book and Manuscript Library, Butler Library, Jane Howard Papers; Jane Howard interviews with approximately two hundred of Mead's friends and associates, for her book *Margaret Mead: A Life.*

CU-Oral Oral History Project, Columbia University. Interviews with Mead and Benedict friends and associates Abram Kardiner, Otto Klineberg, Rhoda Métraux, and Louise Rosenblatt and with Lissa Parsons Kennedy, Elsie Clews Parsons's daughter.

JH Jean Houston oral interview with Mead, LC.

HU Harvard University, Elizabeth Bancroft Schlesinger Library. Inez Milholland Papers.

LC Library of Congress, Manuscript Division. Margaret Mead Papers and the South Pacific Ethnographic Archives; Gregory Bateson Papers.

NPL Norwich Public Library, Norwich, New York. Clippings files on Shattuck, Fulton families pertaining to Benedict.

NU Northwestern University, Charles Deering McCormick Library of Special Collections. Melville Herskovits Papers.

NYPL New York Public Library, Manuscripts and Archives Division. Erich Fromm Papers.

OC Occidental College, Eagle Rock, Los Angeles, California. Special Collections, Mary Norton Clapp Library. Margery Fulton Freeman Papers, containing MFF memoirs of family and RFB; RFB diary at ages 11–12.

PS Philip Sapir. Typescript letters between RFB and ES, in possession of Philip Sapir, Bethesda, Maryland.

RHS Rye Historical Society, Rye, New York. Elsie Clews Parsons Papers; file on ECP lecture course at the New School, 1919.

SU University of Sussex, England, Special Collections. Geoffrey Gorer Papers.

UC University of Chicago, Special Collections. William Fielding Ogburn Papers.

UCB University of California, Berkeley. Bancroft Library, Alfred L. Kroeber Papers; Robert H. Lowie Papers.

UCSC University of California, Santa Cruz, Special Collections. Gregory Bateson Papers.

VC Vassar College, Archives and Special Collections. Ruth Fulton Benedict Papers; classbooks, college yearbooks, literary magazines, etc., relating to college careers of Ruth Benedict and Bertrice Shattuck.

VU Victoria University, Wellington, New Zealand, Manuscripts and Special Collections. Reo Fortune Papers.

YU Yale University, Beinecke Library: Papers of Léonie Adams—William Troy, Eda Lou Walton, Edmund Wilson; Special Collections: Karen Horney Papers.

Acknowledgments

1. Lois W. Banner, "Margaret Mead, Men's Studies, and Women Scholars," *American Studies Association Newsletter,* spring 1988.

2. Jane Howard, *Margaret Mead: A Life* (New York: Simon & Schuster, 1984); Judith Schachter Modell, *Ruth Benedict: Patterns of a Life* (Philadelphia: University of Pennsylvania Press, 1983); Margaret M. Caffrey, *Ruth Benedict: Stranger in This Land*

(Austin: University of Texas Press, 1989); and Hilary Lapsley, *Margaret Mead and Ruth Benedict: The Kinship of Women* (Amherst: University of Massachusetts Press, 1999).

Prologue: Rome, 1926

1. Edward Sapir (ES) to Ruth Benedict (RFB), Oct. 26, 1926, in Ruth Benedict, *An Anthropologist at Work: Writings of Ruth Benedict*, ed. Margaret Mead (New York: Houghton Mifflin, 1959), p. 183 (hereafter cited as *AW*); Margaret Mead, *Blackberry Winter: My Earlier Years* (New York: William Morrow, 1972), p. 187 (hereafter cited as *BW*); and Margaret Mead (MM) to Ken Emory, Mar. 24, 1928, Jane Howard Papers, CU. On the conference as disorganized, see Gladys Reichard to Elsie Clews Parsons, Nov. 4, 1926, Elsie Clews Parsons Papers, APS.

2. John Bunyan, *Pilgrim's Progress from This World to That Which Is to Come*, ed. James Blanton Wharey (Oxford: Clarendon Press, 1960), p. 55; William Vaughan, *William Blake* (London: Tate Gallery, n.d.); Peter Ackroyd, *Blake: A Biography* (New York: Alfred A. Knopf, 1996); and Ruth Benedict, "Daydreams," Dream Research File, LC, Margaret Mead Papers, A-3. All subsequent references to LC are to this Mead archive unless otherwise specified.

3. *AW*, p. 84.

4. Margaret Mead, "Margaret Mead," in *A History of Psychology in Autobiography*, ed. Gardner Lindzey et al. (Englewood Cliffs, N.J.: Prentice-Hall, 1974), vol. 4, p. 309 (hereafter cited as Lindzey).

5. Julian Steward, review of *An Anthropologist at Work*, by Margaret Mead, *Science* 129 (1959): 382; Theodora Kroeber, *Alfred Kroeber: A Personal Configuration* (Berkeley: University of California Press, 1970), p. 263; Luther Sheeleigh Cressman, *A Golden Journey: Memoirs of an Archaeologist* (Salt Lake City: University of Utah Press, 1988), p. 128; and Jean Houston oral interview with Margaret Mead (hereafter cited as JH), p. 144. Jean Houston's searching oral interview with Mead, nearly five hundred pages long and entitled "The Mind of Margaret Mead," is in LC, Q-17 and Q-18.

6. Mary Catherine Bateson, *With a Daughter's Eye: A Memoir of Margaret Mead and Gregory Bateson* (1984; New York: Pocket Books, 1985), p. 18.

7. See Margaret Mead, *Ruth Benedict* (New York: Columbia University Press, 1974), p. 35; Ruth Benedict, obituary, "Franz Boas," *Science* 97 (Jan. 15, 1943): 60; Mead, "Balinese Character," in *Balinese Character: A Photographic Analysis*, by Gregory Bateson and Margaret Mead (New York: New York Academy of Sciences, 1942), pp. xi–xii; and Margaret Mead, *Letters from the Field, 1925–1975* (New York: Harper & Row, 1977), p. 2.

8. Robert S. Liebert, *Michelangelo: A Psychoanalytic Study of His Life and Images* (New Haven: Yale University Press, 1983), pp. 83 ff. On the Sistine Chapel and gender, I have relied on Loren Partridge, *Michelangelo: The Sistine Chapel Ceiling, Rome* (New York: George Braziller, 1996); Even Yoet, "The Heroine as Hero in Michelangelo's Art," in *The Sistine Chapel*, ed. William E. Wallace (New York: Garland, 1995), pp. 381–85; Creighton Gilbert, "The Proportion of Women," in *Michelangelo: On and Off the Sistine Ceiling* (New York: George Braziller, 1994), pp. 59–113; and Marina Warner, *From the Beast to the Blonde: On Fairy Tales and Their Tellers* (New York: Farrar,

Straus & Giroux, 1994), pp. 70–74. The first modern biographer to claim Michelangelo as homosexual was John Addington Symonds, in *The Life of Michelangelo Buonarroti*, 2 vols. (London: John C. Nimmo, 1893).

9. See M. C. Bateson, *With a Daughter's Eye*, p. 134; MM to RFB, Jan. 7, 1939, LC, B-1; MM to Marie Eichelberger, Feb. 5, 1939, LC, B-4. In using the term "masquerade," I note Joan Riviere's "Womanliness as Masquerade," *International Journal of Psycho-Analysis* 10 (April–July 1929): 303–13, which has become a classic in feminist thought. Following Riviere, one might posit that Benedict used femininity to mask her true self, although other interpretations, as I will suggest, also can apply. She defined herself, however, in accord with the masculine/feminine binary dominant in American culture—as did Mead. On the "mannish lesbian," see Margaret Gibson, "The Masculine Degenerate: American Doctors' Portrayals of the Lesbian Intellect, 1880–1949," *Journal of Women's History* 9 (winter 1998): 78–101.

10. On the Blackshirts in Rome, see Mead, *Anthropologists and What They Do* (New York: Franklin Watts, 1965), p. 116; JH, p. 306.

11. Margaret Mead, "final draft," typescript, June 1973, biography of Ruth Benedict for Columbia University, LC, I-235.

12. Sigmund Freud, *The Standard Edition of the Complete Psychological Works of Sigmund Freud*, ed. and trans. James Strachey (London: Hogarth Press, 1953–1974), vol. 15, p. 120.

13. Judith Halberstam, *Female Masculinity* (Durham, N.C.: Duke University Press, 1998), p. 21.

14. Beverly Burch, *Other Women: Lesbian/Bisexual Experience and Psychoanalytic Theory of Women* (New York: Columbia University Press, 1997). In " 'They Wonder to Which Sex I Belong': The Historical Roots of the Modern Lesbian Identity," *Feminist Studies* 18 (fall 1992): 469, Martha Vicinus paraphrases Eve Kosofsky Sedgwick to propose that sexual behavior is unpredictable, various, and affected by both same-sex and opposite-sex influences. See Sedgwick, *Epistemology of the Closet* (Berkeley: University of California Press, 1990), p. 85. On postmodern feminism, see Judith Butler, "Gender Trouble: Feminist Theory and Psychoanalytic Discourse," in *Feminism/Postmodernism*, ed. Linda J. Nicholson (New York: Routledge, 1990), pp. 324–40. See also Teresa de Lauretis, *The Practice of Love: Lesbian Sexuality and Perverse Desire* (Bloomington: Indiana University Press, 1994), p. xix.

15. I borrow Ruth Rosen's riveting phrase "the world split open" for the impact of "Second Wave" feminism to apply to the influence of feminism at the turn into the twentieth century. See Rosen, *The World Split Open: How the Modern Women's Movement Changed America* (New York: Viking, 2000).

16. For classic complaints about the feminization of American culture, see Henry James, *The Bostonians* (1886; New York, Dial, 1945), p. 283, spoken by Basil Ransom: "The whole generation is womanized . . . it's a feminine, a nervous, hysterical, chattering, canting age. . . ."; and George Santayana, "The Genteel Tradition in American Philosophy" (1911), in *Santayana on America: Essays, Notes, and Letters on American Life, Literature, and Philosophy*, ed. Richard Colton Lyon (New York: Harcourt, Brace & World, 1968), pp. 37–38. The literature on masculinization is large. See Kristin L. Hoganson, *Fighting for American Manhood: How Gender Politics Provoked the Spanish-American and Philippine-American Wars* (New Haven: Yale University Press, 1998);

Gail Bederman, *Manliness and Civilization: A Cultural History of Gender and Race in the United States, 1880–1917* (Chicago: University of Chicago Press, 1995); and Arnold Testi, "The Gender of Reform Politics: Theodore Roosevelt and the Culture of Masculinity," *Journal of American History* 82 (Mar. 1995): 1520–23. On the misogyny of the fin-de-siècle, see Elaine Showalter, *Sexual Anarchy: Gender and Culture at the Fin de Siècle* (New York: Viking, 1990); and Bram Dijkstra, *Idols of Perversity: Fantasies of Feminine Evil in Fin-de-Siècle Culture* (New York: Oxford University Press, 1986).

17. I am grateful to art historian Eunice Howe for pointing out to me the condition of the Sistine Chapel ceiling in 1926.

18. Abraham H. Maslow, *The Farther Reaches of Human Nature* (New York: Viking Press, 1971), pp. 41–42, and *Motivation and Personality* (New York: Harper & Bros., 1954), p. xiii.

19. The Spies brief is "Background Statement About Homosexuality," Walter Spies file, LC, N-30. The complexities in these matters of self-identity and disclosure are evident in the oral interview I did in August 1999 of ninety-year-old Lily Turner, a founder of off-Broadway theater in the 1920s and 1930s who lived for many years in Greenwich Village with anthropologist Ruth Bunzel, a friend of Benedict's and Mead's, and Bunzel's partner, Rosemary Zagorin. Turner told me that no one in her circle used the term "lesbian"; instead, like Benedict and Mead, they used "homosexual." She also told me that neither she, Bunzel, nor Zagorin was lesbian; they lived together because of the housing shortage after World War II. They didn't have children because after the horrors of World War I they didn't want to bring children into such a flawed world. She had a lesbian affair in Paris at the end of the 1920s, but she didn't like the way women made love, so she turned to men, although she was too independent to live with her male partner. He was the director of publicity at the American Museum of Natural History for many years; thus she knew Mead well. She remembered Mead as liking to discuss whom she was sexually attracted to and who was sexually attracted to her. Turner confirmed that Benedict and Bunzel had an affair in the late 1930s. See page 381. On Turner, see the *New York Times*, Jan. 21, 1996.

20. In " 'But We Would Never Talk About It': The Structure of Lesbian Discretion in South Dakota, 1928–1933," in *Unequal Sisters: A Multicultural Reader in U.S. Women's History*, ed. Vicki L. Ruiz and Ellen Carol DuBois, 3d ed. (New York: Routledge, 2000), pp. 409–25, Elizabeth Lapovsky Kennedy locates the reluctance of some women to call themselves "lesbian" in a "culture of discretion" keyed to their living in both a public heterosexual world and a private one of lesbian relationships in which the dichotomy of heterosexuality and homosexuality wasn't yet "hegemonic." The situation seems even more complicated with regard to Benedict and Mead. Mead may have used "bisexual" in private conversations. In a letter to Helen Lynd, June 18, 1938, she referred to "bisexual symbolism." LC, R-10, unidentified file.

1 / *Pioneering Women and Men*

1. The major genealogical source for Benedict's life is the entry "Ruth Benedict," in *Current Biography* (New York: H. W. Wilson, 1941). In her biography of Benedict, Margaret Caffrey has excellent genealogical information. For Mead, see Lindzey;

Fanny Fogg McMaster, *A Family History* (St. Joseph, Mich.: privately printed, 1964); Emily Fogg Mead, "Emily Fogg Mead," LC, S-2; and Margaret Mead, "Life History," LC, S-9.

2. Ruth Benedict, *Patterns of Culture* (Boston: Houghton Mifflin, 1934), p. 248.

3. Lindzey, p. 304.

4. Margaret Mead, "The Cultural Contributions of Cultural Anthropology to Our Knowledge of Psychobiological Development," in transcript, "Study Group on the Psychobiological Development of the Child," from a conference at the World Health Organization, Jan. 26–30, 1953, LC, F-79.

5. "Ruth Benedict," *Current Biography*. In the pre–World War I era, Benedict's female relatives in Norwich proudly belonged to the Daughters of the American Revolution, which in upstate New York then was focused on civic improvement. See Paula Baker, *The Moral Frameworks of Public Life: Gender, Politics, and the State in Rural New York, 1870–1930* (New York: Oxford University Press, 1991), pp. 149–50.

6. Howard interview with Roger Revelle, CU; Margaret Mead, "Revisions of the Long Quotes in the Angelica Gibbs Ms.," LC, Q-13. See also Winthrop Sargeant, "It's All Anthropology," *New Yorker*, Dec. 30, 1961, pp. 31–44; and Margaret Mead, "New Roles for Women," ms. speech, Erie College, 1948; "Her Strength Is Based on a Pioneer Past," *Life*, Dec. 24, 1956, "Changes in Women's Cherishing Role," *Saturday Evening Post*, ms. 1962, and "Christmas in Minnesota," *Redbook*, Dec. 1976. Clipping and ms. files, LC. Margaret Mead, *Male and Female: A Study of the Sexes in a Changing World* (New York: William Morrow, 1949), p. 31.

7. Lindzey, p. 304.

8. Mead, introduction to *The Golden Age of American Anthropology*, ed. Margaret Mead and Ruth Bunzel (New York: George Braziller, 1960), pp. 6–8. Margaret Mead, *And Keep Your Powder Dry: An Anthropologist Looks at America* (New York: William Morrow, 1942), pp. 35–56.

9. Benedict, *Patterns of Culture*, p. 276; *AW*, p. 147. See also Ruth Benedict, *Journal of American Folk-Lore* 43 (1930): 120–22, and *Race: Science and Politics* (1940; New York: Viking, 1959), pp. 99–100. On the anti-Puritanism of American intellectuals in the 1920s, see Warren I. Susman, *Culture as History: The Transformation of American Society in the Twentieth Century* (New York: Pantheon Books, 1984), pp. 34–49.

10. Margaret Mead, "Ruth Fulton Benedict, 1887–1948," *AA* 51 (1949): 457.

11. I have taken Benedict's words from poems published in *AW*; Mead's words come from unpublished poems in LC, Q-15.

12. Sargeant, "It's All Anthropology," p. 33; Margaret Mead, "What Home Means to Me," *Perfect Home*, Nov. 1955, clipping, LC, and "Revisions of the Long Quotes in the Angelica Gibbs Ms." See also interview with Martha Glardon, CU. According to Mary Catherine Bateson, Mead believed that buying artifacts for herself when she was collecting them for the museum constituted a conflict of interest; see *With a Daughter's Eye*, p. 71. In later years, Mead had a collection of Balinese sculptures and paintings that had belonged to Gregory Bateson. Interview with Wilton Dillon, CU.

13. M. C. Bateson, *With a Daughter's Eye*, p. 96.

14. Ruth Landes, "A Woman Anthropologist in Brazil," in *Women in the Field: Anthropological Experience*, ed. Peggy Golde (Chicago: Aldine, 1970), p. 120; "Ruth Benedict," *Current Biography*; Modell, *Ruth Benedict*, p. 164.

15. M. C. Bateson, *With a Daughter's Eye*, p. 103.

16. Justin D. Fulton, *Memoir of Timothy Gilbert* (Boston: Lee & Shepard, 1866), and *Woman as God Made Her: The True Woman* (Boston: Lee & Shepard, 1869).

17. William G. Rothstein, *American Physicians in the Nineteenth Century: From Sects to Science* (Baltimore: Johns Hopkins University Press, 1972), pp. 154–72, 230–46; and Martin Kaufman, *Homeopathy in America: The Rise and Fall of a Medical Heresy* (Baltimore: Johns Hopkins University Press, 1971).

18. Obituary, S. J. Fulton, *Chenango Union*, Dec. 10, 1896; and James H. Smith, *History of Chenango and Madison Counties, New York* (Syracuse: D. Mason, 1880), p. 425.

19. Newspaper clipping, no date, no citation, Benedict Family File, CCHS. On dairy farming in upstate New York, see Nancy Grey Osterud, *Bonds of Community: The Lives of Farm Women in Nineteenth-Century New York* (Ithaca: Cornell University Press, 1991), pp. 19–52.

20. Howard Tripp, comp., "The First Baptist Church of Norwich, New York, A History as Originally Written by Charles R. Johnson," typescript, 1961, records, First Baptist Church, Norwich, N.Y.

21. Obituary, John Samuel Shattuck, *Norwich Sun*, Oct. 14, 1913. On the percentages of young people attending college, see Patricia Albjerg Graham, "Expansion and Exclusion: A History of Women in American Higher Education," *Signs: Journal of Women in Culture and Society* 3 (summer 1978): 759–73.

22. On James Fogg's lack of ability as a businessman, see McMaster, *Family History*. On his desire to be a politician, see Mead, "Life History."

23. MFF, "The Mother of Ruth Fulton Benedict," OC.

24. Obituary, Mrs. S. J. Fulton, *Chenango Union*, June 10, 1897; "Obituary—Ella L. Fulton," *Norwich Sun*, Jan. 2, 1927; MFF, "Paternal Grandparents of Ruth Fulton Benedict," OC.

25. Mary Roberts Coolidge, in *Why Women Are So* (New York: Henry Holt, 1912), pp. 231–32, recalled hearing about widespread charges of hermaphroditism lodged against college women after Clarke's attack. Lee Chambers-Schiller, *Liberty: A Better Husband; Single Women in America, the Generation of 1780–1840* (New Haven: Yale University Press, 1984), pp. 43, 199–204, notes sexualized slang terms for college women.

26. Lynne Vallone, *Disciplines of Virtue: Girls' Culture in the Eighteenth and Nineteenth Centuries* (New Haven: Yale University Press, 1995), p. 118.

27. Graham, "Expansion and Exclusion."

28. Redding S. Sugg, *Motherteacher: The Feminization of American Education* (Charlottesville: University Press of Virginia, 1978), p. 106. See also Polly Welts Kaufmann, *Women Teachers on the Frontier* (New Haven: Yale University Press, 1984); Anne Firor Scott, "The Ever Widening Circle: The Diffusion of Feminist Values from the Troy Female Seminary, 1822–1872," *History of Education Quarterly* 19 (spring 1979): 3–25; and Kathryn Kish Sklar, *Catharine Beecher: A Study in American Domesticity* (New Haven: Yale University Press, 1973), pp. 168–83.

29. Ruth Bordin, *Alice Freeman Palmer: The Evolution of a New Woman* (Ann Arbor: University of Michigan Press, 1993), p. 191.

30. Steven M. Buechler, *The Transformation of the Woman Suffrage Movement: The Case of Illinois, 1850–1920* (New Brunswick: Rutgers University Press, 1986), p. 58.

31. CM, interview with Elizabeth Mead Steig.

32. Ms. records, Women's Baptist Missionary Society, First Baptist Church, Norwich, N.Y., handwritten minutes of meetings contained in ledger book.

33. Obituary, "Mrs. Emily Mead, a Sociologist," *New York Times*, Feb. 22, 1950.

34. The classic analysis of female bonding in the nineteenth century is Carroll Smith-Rosenberg, "The Female World of Love and Ritual: Relations Among Women in Nineteenth-Century America," *Signs: Journal of Women in Culture and Society* 1 (autumn 1975): 1–29. On the homoeroticism in these relationships, see Lillian Faderman, *Surpassing the Love of Men: Romantic Friendship and Love Between Women from the Renaissance to the Present* (New York: William Morrow, 1981), pp. 145–204. My research into adolescence and single-sex female schools supports much of Smith-Rosenberg's analysis, although the rush to emphasize heterosexual relationships has almost overwhelmed it. Cf. Karen Lystra, *Searching the Heart: Women, Men, and Romantic Love in Nineteenth-Century America* (New York: Oxford University Press, 1989); and Linda K. Kerber, "Separate Spheres, Female Worlds, Woman's Place: The Rhetoric of Women's History," *Journal of American History* 75 (June 1988): 9–39.

In *A Very Social Time: Crafting Community in Antebellum New England* (Berkeley: University of California Press, 2000), pp. 62–78, Karen V. Hansen finds attachments to both husbands and friends; in *In the New England Fashion: Reshaping Women's Lives in the Nineteenth Century* (Ithaca: Cornell University Press, 1999), pp. 66–92, Catherine E. Kelly contends that female romantic friendships didn't survive into adulthood, except for "an understated reciprocity." Neither author investigates community rituals or artifacts. See the discussion in chapter 4 of the present book. Mead's statement about Boston marriages is in the drafts of "Bisexuality," LC, I-245.

35. Deborah Gorham, *The Victorian Girl and the Feminine Ideal* (London: Croom Helm, 1982); and Laurie Buchanan, " 'Islands of Peace': Female Friendships in Victorian Literature," in *Communication and Women's Friendships: Parallels and Intersections in Literature and Life*, ed. Janet Doubler Ward and JoAnna Stephens Mink (Bowling Green, Ohio: Bowling Green State University Popular Press, 1993), pp. 77–96. See also Theodore L. Smith, "Types of Adolescent Affection," *Pedagogical Seminary* 11 (June 1904): 193.

36. Martha Vicinus, in "Distance and Desire: English Boarding-School Friendships," *The Lesbian Issue: Essays from Signs*, ed. Estelle B. Freedman et al. (Chicago: University of Chicago Press, 1985), p. 47, finds the terms "rave," "spoon," "pash" (for passion), "smash," "gonage" (for being gone on), and "flame" being used for romantic friendships at boarding schools in both England and the United States. An article on college girl slang in the Smith College student newspaper for 1894 reported that the word "crush" usually meant an attachment between a younger and an older student. If the object of the "crush" got tired of it, she resorted to "squelching," which could turn into a "d.s.," or "dead squelch." See the website fivecolleges.edu, writings, 1893–94, slang. Such words became connected to heterosexual desire by the 1890s. J. Redding Ware, in *Passing English of the Victorian Era: A Dictionary of Heterodox English, Slang, and Phrase* (New York: E. P. Dutton, 1909), asserts that by 1895 "crushed" was being used in place of "mashed" or "spoony" and that these words referred to male-female attraction.

On passionate relationships between young men, see E. Anthony Rotundo, *American Manhood: Transformations in Masculinity from the Revolution to the Modern Era* (New York: Basic Books, 1993), pp. 74–91.

37. Ann Braude, *Radical Spirits: Spiritualism and Women's Rights in Nineteenth-Century America* (Boston: Beacon Press, 1989); and Leigh Eric Schmidt, *Consumer Rites: The Buying and Selling of American Holidays* (Princeton: Princeton University Press, 1995), pp. 40–77.

38. Ralph Waldo Emerson, "Friendship," (1841), reprinted in *Essays: First Series* (Boston: Houghton Mifflin, 1864), pp. 191–217.

39. Rotundo, *American Manhood*, p. 83; Timothy J. Gilfoyle, *City of Eros: New York City, Prostitution, and the Commercialization of Sex, 1790–1920* (New York: W. W. Norton, 1992), p. 165. On Victorians and male-female intercourse, see Carroll Smith-Rosenberg, "The New Woman as Androgyne: Social Disorder and Gender Crisis, 1870–1936," in Smith-Rosenberg, *Disorderly Conduct: Visions of Gender in Victorian America* (New York: Alfred A. Knopf, 1985), pp. 245–96. For the argument that Victorian love was fully sexual, see Lystra, *Searching the Heart*, although Lystra overlooks the specifics of sexual performance. For the argument that middle-class Victorian sex practice was limited, see Steven Seidman, *Romantic Longings: Love in America, 1830–1930* (New York: Routledge, 1991), pp. 39–50, 209; Seidman, "The Power of Desire and the Pleasure of Danger: Victorian Sexuality Reconsidered," *Journal of Social History* 24 (fall 1990): 47–67; and Carol Z. Stearns and Peter N. Stearns, "Victorian Sexuality: Can Historians Do It Better?" *Journal of Social History* 18 (summer 1985): 626–34. For the connection between masturbation and homosexuality, see Vern Bullough and Martha Voigt, "Homosexuality and Its Confusion with the Secret Sin in Pre-Freudian America," *Journal of the History of Medicine and Allied Sciences* 28 (Apr. 1973): 143–55. See also Emma Walker, "Crushes Among Girls," *Ladies' Home Journal*, Jan. 1904, and "Your Daughters: What Are Her Friendships?" *Harper's Magazine*, 1913.

40. See E. G. Lancester, "The Psychology and Pedagogy of Adolescence," *Pedagogical Seminary* 5 (July 1898): 61–89. In "Why They Failed to Marry," *Harper's New Monthly Magazine* 156 (March 1928): 466, based on her study in the mid-1920s of the sex lives of 2,200 women, Katharine Bement Davis reported similar findings for women who had gone to college at the turn of the century. See also Davis, *Factors in the Sex Life of Twenty-two Hundred Women* (New York: Harper & Bros., 1929). In *College Girls: A Century in Fiction* (New Brunswick: Rutgers University Press, 1995), pp. 148–55, Shirley Marchalonis finds smashing a standard theme in the novels about women's colleges.

41. Helen Lefkowitz Horowitz, *Alma Mater: Design and Experience in the Women's Colleges from Their Nineteenth-Century Beginnings to the 1930s* (New York: Alfred A. Knopf, 1984), p. 41; Barbara Miller Solomon, *In the Company of Educated Women: A History of Women and Higher Education in America* (New Haven: Yale University Press, 1985), p. 89; Barbara Heslan Palmer, "Lace Bonnets and Academic Gowns: Faculty Development in Four Women's Colleges, 1875–1915" (Ph.D. diss., Boston College, 1980); Debra Herman, "College and After: The Vassar Experiment in Women's Education, 1861–1924" (Ph.D. diss., Stanford University, 1979); Mary W. Craig, "History," *Class Day Book*, Vassar College, 1885; Mary Augusta Jordan, "Spacious Days at Vassar," *The Fiftieth Anniversary of the Opening of Vassar College* (Poughkeepsie, N.Y.: Vassar College, 1916), p. 52; and Helen Wright, *Sweeper in the Sky: The Life of Maria Mitchell, First Woman Astronomer in America* (New York: Macmillan, 1949).

42. Letter to the *Yale Courant*, reprinted in the *Cornell Times*, Mar. 15, 1873; and

Alice Stone Blackwell to Kitty Barry Blackwell, Mar. 12, 1882, Blackwell Family Papers, LC. Cited in Nancy Sahli, "Smashing: Women's Relationships Before the Fall," *Chrysalis: A Magazine of Women's Culture* 8 (1978): 21–22. Jonathan Katz quotes more extensively from the letter in *Gay/Lesbian Almanac: A New Documentary* (New York: Harper & Row, 1983), pp. 178–79. See also Anne MacKay, comp. and ed., *Wolf Girls at Vassar: Lesbian and Gay Experiences, 1930–1990* (New York: St. Martin's Press, 1993). My research in the Vassar archives and elsewhere indicates that romantic friendships remained institutionalized in the student culture at least through 1909, when Ruth Fulton graduated.

43. Miriam Gurko, *Restless Spirit: The Life of Edna St. Vincent Millay* (New York: Thomas Y. Crowell, 1962), p. 54; and Agnes Rogers, *Vassar Women: An Informal Study* (Poughkeepsie, N.Y.: Vassar College, 1940), p. 85. I have constructed the social life and living arrangements at Bertrice Shattuck's Vassar from Horowitz, *Alma Mater;* Herman, "College and After"; and Craig, "History," *Class Day Book,* in ms. materials, class of 1885, VC.

44. MFF, "Mother of Ruth Freeman Fulton," OC.

45. Vassar College, *Class Day Book,* 1909; "Class History—A Debate," p. 6, pamphlet in Class Box, 1909, VC.

46. Emily Fogg Mead, "Story of My Life" and "A College Woman of Sixty," unpub. mss., LC, A-8. On Wellesley and women in this era, see Patricia Ann Palmieri, *In Adamless Eden: The Community of Women Faculty at Wellesley* (New Haven: Yale University Press, 1995).

47. E. F. Mead, "Story of My Life" and "A College Woman of Sixty."

48. Rosalind Rosenberg, *Beyond Separate Spheres: Intellectual Roots of Modern Feminism* (New Haven: Yale University Press, 1982), pp. 38–39.

49. William Leach, *True Love and Perfect Union: The Feminist Reform of Sex and Society* (New York: Basic Books, 1980), pp. 77–78. There is no study of gender interaction at coeducational colleges, aside from Helen Lefkowitz Horowitz, *Campus Life: Undergraduate Cultures from the End of the Eighteenth Century to the Present* (New York: Alfred A. Knopf, 1987), primarily on the 1920s. In *College Girls,* pp. 117–27, Marchalonis reports that in college novels set at coeducational schools the women students were mainly concerned with attracting male students and that the college men didn't treat them well at first. See also Alice Stone Blackwell's letter to Kitty Barry Blackwell; and Willystine Goodsell, *The Education of Women: Its Social Background and Its Problems* (New York: Macmillan, 1924).

50. The term "feminism," coined in France, was first used in the United States in 1910. "Woman's rights" was used for most of the nineteenth century, with "women's rights" replacing it in the 1890s. I follow the standard practice of using "women's rights" throughout this era, until feminism appeared in 1910 as a separable movement.

51. Olive Schreiner, *The Story of an African Farm* (1883; London: Library of Classics, n.d.), pp. 177, 186. On Schreiner, see Cherry Clayton, *Olive Schreiner* (New York: Twayne, 1997).

52. See Lois W. Banner, *Women in Modern America: A Brief History,* 3d ed. (New York: Harcourt Brace, 1995), pp. 36, 73–105.

2 / *Apollo and Dionysus: Ruth Benedict's Childhood*

1. See John Dollard, *Criteria for the Life History* (New Haven: Yale University Press, 1935). According to Mead, Dollard worked out his life-history approach when he, Mead, and Benedict were working together at a seminar at Columbia in 1935. "We all wrote life histories for it," Mead noted. Lindzey, p. 316.

2. A typescript version of Ruth Benedict's "The Story of My Life" is in the draft version of *AW*, LC, 1–90. It appears in *AW*, pp. 97–112. In addition, the autobiographical and family narratives for Benedict's childhood include: 1. Typescript statements about Benedict's relatives in Norwich and a memoir of Benedict's life, written by her sister, Margery Fulton Freeman, in the Margery Fulton Freeman (MFF) Papers at Occidental College (OC), and two long letters from Margery to Margaret Mead shortly after Benedict died. One letter, dated Sept. 14, 1948, is in LC; the second, dated Sept. 18, 1948, is in the Ruth Fulton Benedict Papers at Vassar College (VC). 2. Benedict's unpublished journal (diary) for 1897–1898, when she was ten and eleven years old, in OC. 3. Benedict's journal entries from college to about 1935 and her diary entries for 1925–1926. Most are in *AW*, with unpublished journal fragments at VC. (The handwritten version of the diary contains entries not in the published version.) 4. A statement of her daydreams, in Mead's Dream-Research File, LC, A-2. 5. Material in Norwich, N.Y., in newspaper articles, court records, and in Bertrice Shattuck's diary for 1876 and 1877, when she was sixteen and seventeen, in Norwich Public Library (NPL), the Chenango County Historical Society (CCHS), and the Chenango County Court House. Previous biographers of Benedict did not have access to the recently discovered Norwich material; to the Margery Fulton Freeman Papers, OC; or to the recently opened additions to the Margaret Mead Papers at LC. My account of Benedict's childhood draws from all of these sources.

3. For these descriptions, I draw on my own experience of Norwich; on Albert Phillips, "Annals of Norwich: Along the Chenango Canal," 1984; and on "Chenango County: A Look Back," n.d., pamphlets in CCHS. For the opera house, see *Chenango Union*, June 24, 1880.

4. For Benedict as sensuous and athletic, see *AW*, pp. 86, 110.

5. *AW*, pp. 111–12, "The Story of My Life."

6. For the texts of these poems see bartleby.com: Great Books Online, taken from *The Harvard Classics, English Poetry II: From Collins to Fitzgerald; English Poetry III: From Tennyson to Whitman.*

7. Ruth Benedict, "Day Dreams," Dream-Research File, LC.

8. Idem.; journal fragments, VC; RFB journal, Oct. 2, Oct. 4, 1897, OC.

9. *AW*, pp. 102–6, "The Story of My Life."

10. Ibid., p. 100.

11. Ibid., p. 107. On Ruth's mother's piety and church attendance, see Bertrice Shattuck's diary, CCHS, as well as Benedict's comments on her in "The Story of My Life," *AW*, p. 111. With regard to Benedict's reaction to her baptism, see her diary, July 24, 1898, OC.

12. MFF, "Fred S. Fulton, M.D.," OC.

13. Benedict, "Day Dreams."

14. Margaret Mead, "Out of the Things I Read," in *Moments of Personal Discovery*, ed. R. M. MacIver (New York: Institute for Religious and Social Studies, Jewish Theological Seminary of America, dist. by Harper & Bros., 1952), p. 37.

15. MFF, "Family Life of Ruth Fulton Benedict," p. 2; *AW*, p. 104, "The Story of My Life."

16. Mead, *Ruth Benedict*, p. 61. For the history of hormonal research, see Nelly Oudshoorn, *Beyond the Natural Body: An Archaeology of Sex Hormones* (New York: Routledge, 1994). For nineteenth-century medical views of cyclic vomiting, see L. Emmett Holt, *The Diseases of Infancy and Childhood* (New York: D. Appleton, 1898). Holt contended that it occurred more frequently in girls than in boys and most often in "neurotic families." John M. Keating, *Cyclopaedia of the Diseases of Children* (Philadelphia: J. B. Lippincott, 1890), vol. 3, p. 23: "The essential element in the production of recurrent vomiting is a state of nervous depression." David R. Fleisher and Marla Matar, in "Review: The Cyclic Vomiting Syndrome: A Report of Seventy-one Cases and Literature Review," *Journal of Pediatric Gastroenterology and Nutrition* 17 (1993): 361–69, conclude: "Only three large series of patients have been reported in the English literature during the past 60 years." This study also suggests a connection to emotional instability and migraine headaches. A review of the literature on cyclic vomiting in the *New York Times*, Nov. 24, 2001, links it to a neurologic malfunction or flawed stress-hormone activity.

A distinction must be drawn between cyclic vomiting and anorexia nervosa and bulimia, rare before adolescence. My thanks to Joan Brumberg of Cornell University for pointing this out to me and to Richard Stiehm, a pediatric physician at UCLA medical school, for directing me to relevant research.

17. Benedict refers to her imaginary friend in "The Story of My Life," *AW*, p. 100. The reference to family quarreling is in the unpublished statement in the Dream-Research File, LC. I have derived the birth dates of Benedict's aunts from the genealogy of her family, VC, 39.2.

18. Obituary, Hetty D. Shattuck, *Chenango Union*, Aug. 9, 1900.

19. MFF, "Mother of Ruth Fulton Benedict," OC.

20. Benedict, "Day Dreams."

21. Samuel Fulton advertised in the local newspapers as a specialist in the diseases of women and children. See *Chenango Union*, Jan. 2, 1879.

22. MFF, "Paternal Grandparents of Ruth Fulton Benedict." The descriptions of the Fultons, including the sarcastic portrayal of Ella Fulton as "noble" and "daunting," are in MFF memoirs, OC.

23. The wills are filed in the Surrogate Court Records, Chenango County Courthouse, Norwich, N.Y. Samuel's will was recorded Dec. 6, 1896; he died on Dec. 17. Harriet's will was recorded on July 6, 1896; she died on Jan. 18, 1897.

24. Obituary, John S. Shattuck, *Norwich Sun*, Oct. 13, 1913.

25. *AW*, p. 102, "The Story of My Life."

26. Idem.

27. See Randall Balmer, *Blessed Assurance: A History of Evangelicalism in America* (Boston: Beacon Press, 1999); George Marsden, *Fundamentalism and American Culture: The Shaping of Twentieth-Century Evangelicalism, 1870–1925* (New York: Oxford Uni-

versity Press, 1980), pp. 43–108; and Brooks Hays and John E. Steely, *The Baptist Way of Life* (Englewood Cliffs, N.J.: Prentice-Hall, 1963).

28. Margaret Mead, foreword to Ruth Benedict, *Race: Science and Politics*, rev. ed. (New York: Viking Press, 1959), p. xi.

29. Ruth describes her feelings about the baptism in her childhood diary.

30. *AW,* p. 84.

31. Ruth Benedict criticizes working mothers for coming home from work too tired to respond to their children in "Speech Before Seminar, Committee on the Study of Adolescents," typescript mss., Feb. 12, 1937, VC. Margery Fulton Freeman notes her belief that Bertrice didn't understand Ruth in MFF, "Family Life of Ruth Fulton Benedict," p. 3, OC.

32. The references to depression occur in 1877 on Feb. 1, Feb. 12, Apr. 1, Aug. 29, Oct. 8, and Dec. 4. During 1878 many of Bertrice's entries concern Fred Fulton. The entry about the nervous attack is on July 7, 1878.

33. *AW,* p. 98, "The Story of My Life."

34. See Frederick Fulton to Bertrice Shattuck, Sept. 15, 1877, May 28, 1878, VC, 39.16.

35. Bertrice Shattuck diary, Mar. 1878.

36. Samuel I. Fulton, "Frederick Fulton—A Memoir," newspaper clipping, records of the Chenango County Homeopathic Society, CCHS.

37. Sigmund Freud, "Mourning and Melancholia," in *Standard Edition,* vol. 14, pp. 239–58; John Bowlby, *Attachment and Loss* (New York: Basic Books, 1980), vol. II: "Separation," pp. 247–57. Irvin D. Yalom, *Existential Psychotherapy* (New York: Basic Books, 1980). In "Reuben Davis, Sylvia Plath and Other American Writers: The Perils of Emotional Struggle," in *An Emotional History of the United States,* ed. Peter N. Stearns and Jan Lewis (New York: New York University Press, 1998), pp. 431–59, Bertram Wyatt-Brown notes, as have many analysts, that creative artists often suffer from manic-depressive syndrome. He traces it to their frequently having a parent die in their childhood.

38. Houston interview with Mead, p. 342; Benedict, "Speech Before Seminar, Committee on the Study of Adolescents."

39. The story of Cato's suicide and that of a neighborhood girl is in a journal fragment, VC. See also Henry Romilly Fedden, *Suicide: A Social and Historical Study* (London: Peter Davies, 1938). Birth-order studies usually identify the firstborn as especially independent. For a differing view, see Frank J. Sulloway, *Born to Rebel: Birth Order, Family Dynamics, and Creative Lives* (New York: Pantheon Books, 1996).

40. W. H. Hudson, *A Crystal Age* (London: T. F. Unwin, 1887), p. 248. Benedict discusses Hudson's influence on her fantasy world in her analysis of her daydreams in the Dream-Research File. Hudson was a neo-Romantic naturalist and mystic whose novels were very popular in the late nineteenth century. See Amy D. Ronner, *W. H. Hudson: The Man, the Novelist, the Naturalist* (New York: AMS Press, 1986).

41. Leon Surette, *The Birth of Modernism: Ezra Pound, T. S. Eliot, W. B. Yeats, and the Occult* (Buffalo, N.Y.: McGill–Queen's University Press, 1993), p. 178.

42. Ruth Benedict, review of *The Neurotic Personality of Our Time,* by Karen Horney, *Journal of Abnormal and Social Psychology* 22 (1938): 133–35.

43. *AW,* p. 98, "The Story of My Life."

44. Friedrich Nietzsche, *The Birth of Tragedy and The Genealogy of Morals*, trans. Francis Golffing (Garden City, N.Y.: Anchor Books, 1956), p. 129; Kay Redfield Jamison, *Touched with Fire: Manic-Depressive Illness and the Artistic Temperament* (New York: Free Press, 1993), pp. 97; 104. (Manic-depressive syndrome is now called bipolar disorder.) See also Joel Schmidt, *Larousse Greek and Roman Mythology*, ed. Seth Benardete (New York: McGraw-Hill, 1980), pp. 32–33, 84–85; and Anthony Storr, *The Dynamics of Creation* (New York: Atheneum, 1972).

45. Nietzsche, *Birth of Tragedy*, p. 61; Benedict, *Patterns of Culture*, p. 79.

46. *AW*, p. 86; journal fragment, VC.

47. *AW*, p. 85. The term "eidetic" was coined in the early 1920s for especially vivid mental images that are not hallucinations. Some researchers concluded that such images were memories of actual happenings; some contended that children and artists regularly had them. Schools of perceptual investigation grew up around them, especially at the University of Marburg in Germany. After World War II, they were discredited because their major proponent backed Hitler's theories about race. Mead applauded their reappearance in the 1960s, because she maintained that both she and Benedict had eidetic visions. JH, pp. 106–7. See also Gardner Murphy and Friedrich Jensen, *Approaches to Personality: Some Contemporary Conceptions Used in Psychology and Psychiatry* (New York: Coward-McCann, 1933), p. 33.

48. The first description of the dream is in *AW*, p. 85. The second, more explicit, is in the Dream-Research File, LC.

49. *AW*, p. 87.

50. In analyzing Benedict's poetry, I have drawn on Lee Upton's study of the poetry of Louise Bogan, Benedict's close friend, in *Obsession and Release: Rereading the Poetry of Louise Bogan* (Lewisburg, Pa.: Bucknell University Press, 1996). Upton contends that Bogan explored her psyche and her childhood in her poetry. Like Benedict, Bogan had a difficult childhood; she had vague memories of her mother abusing her and of her father being involved. With regard to the lyric poetry they both wrote, Bogan stated that "if it is at all authentic, it is based on some emotion—or some actual occasion, some real confrontation." Bogan to Sister M. Angela, Aug. 20, 1966, in Louise Bogan, *What the Woman Lived: Selected Letters of Louise Bogan, 1920–1970*, ed. Ruth Limner (New York: Harcourt, Brace, 1973), p. 368.

51. Richard Dellamora, *Masculine Desire: The Sexual Politics of Victorian Aestheticism* (Chapel Hill: University of North Carolina Press, 1990), p. 65; Karla Jay, *The Amazon and the Page: Natalie Clifford Barney and Renée Vivien* (Bloomington: University of Indiana Press, 1988), pp. 83–85; Oscar Wilde, *De Profundis*, in *Collected Works of Oscar Wilde*, ed. Robert Ross (1908; London: Routledge, 1993); and Surrette, *Birth of Modernism*, p. 178. Like many modernists, Benedict was influenced by James Fraser's *Golden Bough*, which centered on the myth of the dying and reviving young male vegetation god in ancient religions. See John B. Vickery, *The Literary Impact of "The Golden Bough"* (Princeton: Princeton University Press, 1973).

52. See Janet Liebman Jacobs, *Victimized Daughters: Incest and the Development of the Female Self* (New York: Routledge, 1994); Judith Lewis Herman, *Trauma and Recovery: The Aftermath of Violence—From Domestic Abuse to Political Terror* (New York: Basic Books, 1992); and Judith Lewis Herman, *Father-Daughter Incest* (Cambridge, Mass.: Harvard University Press, 1981).

53. Marcia Westkott, *The Feminist Legacy of Karen Horney* (New Haven: Yale University Press, 1986), p. 190.

54. Ruth Benedict, "The Science of Custom: The Bearing of Anthropology on Contemporary Thought," *Century Magazine* 117 (April 1929): 641–49, and *Patterns of Culture*, p. 32. Margaret Mead, "Incest," in *International Encyclopedia of the Social Sciences*, ed. David L. Sills, 17 vols. (New York: Macmillan, 1968), VII, 115–22. Mead and Reo Fortune found what seemed to be brother-sister and father-daughter incest in the tribal societies they studied in New Guinea.

55. Ruth Benedict, "Continuities and Discontinuities in Cultural Conditioning," *Psychiatry* 1 (1938): 161–67.

56. *AW*, p. 109, "The Story of My Life."

57. Justin D. Fulton, "Woman as Temptor" in *The True Woman; Woman as God Made Her* (Boston: Lee and Shepard, 1869).

58. On Pillsbury Academy, see Larry Dean Pettegrew, *The History of Pillsbury Baptist Bible College* (Owatonna, Minn.: Pillsbury Press, 1981).

59. RFB journal fragment, VC.

60. *AW*, p. 84.

61. Exodus 2:22.

62. Margaret Mead, "Temperamental Differences and Sexual Dimorphism," *American Journal of Psychoanalysis* 37 (1977): 180, and "End Linkage: A Tool for Cross-Cultural Analysis," in *About Bateson: Essays on Gregory Bateson*, ed. John Brockman (New York: Dutton, 1977), p. 176.

63. *AW*, p. 106, "The Story of My Life."

64. Idem. See also Manfred Lurker, *The Gods and Symbols of Ancient Egypt: An Illustrated Dictionary*, rev. ed. (London: Thames & Hudson, 1980), pp. 33–34, 107.

65. *AW*, p. 495.

66. *AW*, p. 103, "The Story of My Life."

3 / *"The Young-Eyed Cherubim": Margaret Mead's Childhood*

1. Mead's positive version of her childhood can also be found in two brief biographies of Mead, written in 1943 and 1964, both based on interviews with her. See Edna Yost, "Margaret Mead," in *American Women of Science* (Philadelphia: Frederick A. Stokes, 1943); and Allyn Moss, *Margaret Mead: Shaping of a New World* (Chicago: Encyclopaedia Britannica Press, 1963). See also MM to Beryl Epstein, Oct. 20, 1977, LC, I-308. Both these accounts contain information that isn't in the other autobiographical sources. Mead's memoir written for Dollard downplays her bisexuality, possibly because Mead was involved with Dollard when she wrote it. It is contained in LC, S-9.

2. Houston interview with Mead, p. 333.

3. Mead, "Out of the Things I Read," p. 37. By the 1970s, given feminist criticism of Freud, Mead became more critical of his theories. See Margaret Mead, "On Freud's View of Female Psychology," in *Women & Analysis: Dialogues on Psychoanalytic Views of Femininity*, ed. Jean Strouse (New York: Grossman, 1974), pp. 95–106.

4. *BW* draft, called "Chap. 1" and dated Jan. 22, 1971, p. 14. The *BW* drafts are in LC, I-204 to 209.

5. In Lindzey, Mead describes these features of her upbringing as providing her with skills essential to fieldwork; she also notes them in less detail in *Blackberry Winter* and its drafts.

6. Lillian G. Genn, "The New Morality: A Talk with Margaret Mead," *Modern Maturity* 13 (Aug./Sept. 1970): 22, LC, I-189. In less ebullient descriptions, she narrowed the decades to two. Cf. *BW*, p. 85.

7. Lindzey, p. 302.

8. Margaret Mead, *The Changing Culture of an Indian Tribe* (New York: Columbia University Press, 1932), p. iii.

9. Emily Fogg Mead, "The Italians on the Land: A Study in Immigration," *Bulletin of the Bureau of Labor* 70 (May 1907): 473–533.

10. Moss, *Margaret Mead*, p. 28; Lindzey, p. 299; *BW* drafts, "Background of Books," p. 7; "Adolescence," p. 6.

11. Mead, *Male and Female*, p. 456.

12. Moss, *Margaret Mead*, p. 23; Houston interview with Mead, p. 55.

13. Lindzey, p. 296.

14. Yost, "Margaret Mead," p. 218.

15. Emily Fogg Mead, "The Place of Advertising in Modern Business," *Journal of Political Economy* (March 1901): 218–42.

16. Lindzey, p. 307.

17. For attacks on Mead, see Paul Radin, *The Method and Theory of Ethnology: An Essay in Criticism* (1933; New York: Basic Books, 1966); Robert H. Lowie, *The History of Ethnological Theory* (New York: Farrar & Rinehart, 1937), p. 275; and Lindzey, p. 317. The major attack was launched by Edward Sapir in 1928. See chapter 9 of the present book. For Derek Freeman's attacks, see Freeman, *Margaret Mead and Samoa: The Making and Unmaking of an Anthropological Myth* (Cambridge, Mass.: Harvard University Press, 1983) and *The Fateful Hoaxing of Margaret Mead: A Historical Analysis of Her Samoan Research* (Boulder, Colo.: Westview Press, 1990).

18. Lindzey, p. 301; JH, pp. 82, 147.

19. Mead used the term "blackberry winter" as early as 1952 in a paper she gave at the convention of the Modern Language Association in which she mourned the replacement of the oral tradition of folk cultures by modern means of communication. See Margaret Mead, "Cultural Bases for Understanding Literature," in *Anthropology, a Human Science: Selected Papers, 1939–1960* (Princeton, N.J.: Van Nostrand, 1964), p. 225. This wasn't the first time an author used the term in a title. Robert Frost titled a short story "Blackberry Winter."

20. *BW*, p. 1.

21. Ibid., pp. 10–11.

22. JH, p. 45; *BW* draft, "My Father and Academia," p. 3.

23. *BW*, p. 43.

24. Ibid., pp. 41–42. The word "Melanesia" includes New Guinea and the many islands off its coasts.

25. William Leach, *Land of Desire: Merchants, Power, and the Rise of a New American Culture* (New York: Pantheon Books, 1993), pp. 15, 160, quoting from Edward Sherwood Mead, *Corporation Finance*, 6th ed. (1910; New York: D. Appleton, 1931), pp. 361–62.

26. *BW* draft, "Father and Academia," p. 3.

27. Patricia Grinager, *Uncommon Lives: My Lifelong Friendship with Margaret Mead* (Lanham, Md.: Rowman & Littlefield, 1999), p. 51.

28. *BW*, p. 44.

29. JH, p. 51.

30. Ibid., p. 50.

31. Margaret Mead, "Notes for GCB [Gotthard Booth]," Feb. 10, 1941, LC, R-10.

32. JH, pp. 50, 173.

33. Ibid., p. 50.

34. Ibid., p. 46; Mead, "Life History," pp. 1–3.

35. See Lillian Jane Rickert Ziemer, "Memories of a Loyal Secretary," *Pennsylvania Gazette*, Oct. 1975. Clipping, LC, I-256.

36. Interviews with Leo Rosten and Ken Heyman, CU.

37. This episode is described by Eleanor Pelham Kortheuer in her joint interview, along with Deborah Kaplan Mandelbaum, CU. In Karen Summerfield, "New Paltz Author Studies Margaret Mead: A Scientist in Public Life," *SUNY Research* 84 (Jan./Feb. 1984), LC, Q-13, Carleton Mabee reports friends of Mead's referring to her "tough drill sargeant's voice." In chapters on Margaret Mead and her sisters in *Sisters: Love and Rivalry in the Family and Beyond* (New York: Morrow, 1979), p. 282, Elizabeth Fishel makes a similar comment. Fishel interviewed Margaret and Elizabeth for the book.

38. *BW*, p. 29.

39. MM to RFB, fragment, undated, unidentified file, LC, Q-13.

40. Interview with Lenora Foerstel, CU.

41. Mead, "Life History," p. 3; *BW*, pp. 31–32.

42. E. F. Mead, "Story of My Life."

43. For Emily's comments about her lack of emotions and her attitude toward sex, see E. F. Mead, "A College Woman of Sixty." In her interview with Carleton Mabee, Elizabeth claimed that her mother didn't use birth control.

44. JH, p. 79.

45. Margaret Mead and James Baldwin, *A Rap on Race* (Philadelphia: Lippincott, 1971), p. 26.

46. Mead, "Life History," p. 2.

47. CM, interview with Elizabeth Mead Steig.

48. *BW*, p. 49; Mead, "Life History," p. 3.

49. *BW*, pp. 49, 65.

50. *BW* draft, "Books as Background," p. 3; JH, pp. 33–40.

51. *BW*, p. 1; BW draft, "Books as Background," p. 1.

52. Grinager, *Uncommon Lives*, p. 96.

53. JH, p. 341.

54. Mead discusses searching for a twin after her sister's death in a number of sources; the details I cite, which expand her account in *BW*, come from a draft of an article on equity and brotherhood, rejected by *Redbook*, LC; outline, "Lives of a Healer," by Carmen de Barraza, edited by Margaret Mead, LC, I-295; and *BW* draft, "Having a Baby," p. 2.

55. Mead, "Life History."

56. *BW* draft, "The Pattern My Family Made for Me," p. 5.

57. Lindzey, p. 305.

58. Instructor's comment on stories, Oct. 1920, and class notes, exercises, and other writings, LC, A-14.

59. Interview with Léonie Adams, CU; *BW* draft, "Life Span," p. 3.

60. JH, p. 334.

61. In analyzing Mead's early fiction, I have used three ms. stories in LC, Q-19: "The Blind Woman," n.d.; "The Young-Eyed Cherubim," n.d.; and "Lassitude," June 24, 1924. See also JH, p. 334.

62. *Merchant of Venice* 5.1.60–62:

> There's not the smallest orb which thou behold'st
> But in his motion like an angel sings,
> Still in quiring to the young-eyed cherubins. . . .

63. *BW*, p. 86; Lindzey, p. 298.

64. JH, p. 142.

65. *BW* draft, "Marriage and Graduate School," p. 4.

66. *BW* draft, "Schooling," p. 2.

67. *BW* draft, "Life Span," p. 4.

68. *BW* draft, "Energy," p. 6.

69. *BW* draft, "Having a Baby," p. 2; Lindzey, p. 302.

70. Art historian Eunice Howe informed me of Reni's popularity. On the Venus de Milo as a model of beauty, see Lois W. Banner, *American Beauty* (New York: Alfred A. Knopf, 1983), pp. 110, 138.

71. Margaret Mead, "Medical History of Involvement of the Intestinal System, May, 1978," unpub. ms., LC, Q-32.

72. Her discussions of her eidetic visions, the description of Houston leading her through one, and her statement dating the onset of the dead baby dreams to her college years are in JH, pp. 221–22.

73. Ibid., p. 210.

74. MM to RFB, Jan. 30, 1926, LC, S-3.

75. JH, p. 339.

76. Cressman, *Golden Journey*, p. 192; letter fragment, dated day after Christmas, 1926, Dream-Research File, LC.

77. JH, pp. 505–6.

78. The first description of the room is in Lindzey, p. 301; the second is in *BW*, p. 18.

79. JH, p. 30.

80. Grinager, *Uncommon Lives*, p. 178; Lindzey, p. 301; *BW*, p. 18; JH, p. 362.

81. *BW* draft, "Siblings and Playmates," p. 2.

82. JH, p. 30.

83. *AW*, pp. 88–89.

84. *BW*, pp. 144–45.

4 / *"Smashing": Female Romantic Friendships*

1. *BW* drafts, "Love and Friendship," p. 1, "Adolescence," p. 11.

2. *BW,* p. 81; JH, p. 421.

3. See Marylynne Diggs, "Romantic Friends or a 'Different Race of Creatures': The Representation of Lesbian Pathology in Nineteenth-Century America," *Feminist Studies* 21 (summer 1995): 317–40. The homoerotic narrative of Mead's childhood in the drafts of *Blackberry Winter* is absent from the published version, which features her friendships with boys in high school and her engagement to Luther Cressman, and introduces Miss Lucia mostly to focus on Mead's sorrow when Lucia broke her engagement, thus ending a heterosexual connection. On female romantic friendships, see chapter 1 of the present book.

4. *BW* draft, "Brothers and Sisters," p. 1.

5. John H. Gagnon and William Simon, *Sexual Conduct: The Social Sources of Human Sexuality* (Chicago: Aldine, 1973). Smith-Rosenberg, in "Female World of Love and Ritual," identifies mother-daughter bonding as the source of female friendships. On sisters as the source, see Carol Lasser, " 'Let Us Be Sisters Forever': The Sororal Model of Nineteenth-Century Female Friendship," *Signs: Journal of Women in Culture and Society* 14 (autumn 1988): 158–91. In *The Bonds of Womanhood: 'Woman's Sphere' in New England, 1780–1835* (New Haven: Yale University Press, 1977), pp. 168–82, Nancy F. Cott locates their origin in girls' peer groups.

On reading and self-creation, see Helen Lefkowitz Horowitz, " 'Nous Autres': Reading, Passion, and the Creation of M. Carey Thomas," *Journal of American History* 79 (June 1992): 68–95. An in-depth study of the popular representations of women's friendships in novels, paintings, and poetry remains to be written. For some material, see Linda W. Rosenzweig, *Another Self: Middle-Class American Women and Their Friends in the Twentieth Century* (New York: New York University Press, 1999).

6. *BW* draft, "Love and Friendship," p. 4; Lindzey, p. 308; Mead, "Life History," p. 9.

7. *BW* draft, "Adolescence," p. 11.

8. Idem.

9. Idem.

10. Annie Fellows Johnston, *The Little Colonel at Boarding-School* (Boston: L. C. Page, 1903). The Little Colonel series also includes: *The Little Colonel,* 1896; *The Little Colonel's House Party,* 1900; *The Little Colonel's Holidays,* 1901; *The Little Colonel's Hero,* 1902; *The Little Colonel's Christmas Vacation,* 1905; *The Little Colonel: Maid of Honor,* 1906; *Mary Ware: The Little Colonel's Chum,* 1908; *The Little Colonel Stories,* 1909. All were written by Annie Fellows Johnston and published in Boston by L. C. Page.

11. See Edward Carpenter, ed., *Ioläus: An Anthology of Friendship,* 2d ed. (London: Swan Sonnenschein, 1906), p. 3.

12. See Louis Arundel, *The Motorboat Boys Down the Coast: Or, Through Storm and Stress in Florida* (Chicago: M. A. Donoghue, 1913).

13. See *St. Nicholas Magazine,* May–Sept. 1899, "Quicksilver Sue," and Feb.–April, 1900, "The Colburn Prize."

14. JH, p. 64.

15. The undated notes to Margaret from Marjorie are in the DePauw University file, LC, Q-17. Internal evidence in the notes indicates that they were written when Mead was in high school.

16. On Ruth Carver, see MM to Alice, July 12, 1915; and Ruth to MM, Aug. 8, 1921, LC, C-2, unidentified file. See also Ruth to MM, LC, B-12, undated, unidentified, general correspondence file. Ruth went to Radcliffe College, came back to Buckingham, and decided to marry her boyfriend. That decision depressed her, until she remembered that Luther Cressman was an ordained minister and that, if he performed her wedding ceremony, she would retain a special bond with Margaret.

17. Annette Federico, *Idol of Suburbia: Marie Corelli and Late-Victorian Literary Culture* (Charlottesville: University Press of Virginia, 2000); Rita Felski, *The Gender of Modernity* (Cambridge, Mass.: Harvard University Press, 1995); Richard L. Kowalczyk, "In Vanished Summertime: Marie Corelli and Popular Culture," *Journal of Popular Culture* 7 (1974): 850–63; and Marie Corelli, *Ardath: The Story of a Dead Self* (1889; New York: Rand McNally, n.d.), p. 499.

18. BW draft, "Love and Friendship," p. 7; and Charlotte Mary Yonge, *The Dove in the Eagle's Nest* (New York: A. L. Burt, 1866). See Barbara Dennis, *Charlotte Yonge, 1823–1901, Novelist of the Oxford Movement: A Literature of Victorian Culture and Society* (Lewiston, Me.: Edwin Mellen Press, 1992).

19. *BW* draft, "Love and Friendship," p. 8.

20. Ibid., pp. 5, 13.

21. Ibid., p. 11; Mead, *Male and Female*, pp. 284–86.

22. Margaret Mead, "Transcript of Appearance Before Gilbert Advertising Seminar, 1969," LC, I-176.

23. *BW* draft, "Love and Friendship," p. 9.

24. Ibid., pp. 6–9. Rudyard Kipling, *The Brushwood Boy* (1899; New York: Doubleday, Page, 1907); George Du Maurier, *Peter Ibbetson* (1891; New York: Limited Editions, 1963).

25. See Denis de Rougemont, *Love in the Western World*, trans. Montgomery Belgion (1940; New York: Pantheon, 1949); Richard Wightman Fox, *Trials of Intimacy: Love and Loss in the Beecher-Tilton Scandal* (Chicago: University of Chicago Press, 1999), p. 83; and Emerson, "Friendship," p. 193. See also Seidman, *Romantic Longings;* Lystra, *Searching the Heart;* and Charles R. Forker, *Skull Beneath the Skin: The Achievement of John Webster* (Carbondale: Southern Illinois University Press, 1986), pp. 235–52.

26. *BW* draft, "Love and Friendship," p. 9; JH, pp. 215, 230.

27. These passages in Ellis remained constant from the first publication of *Sexual Inversion* in 1895 to the last edition during his lifetime, in 1936. See Havelock Ellis, "Sexual Inversion in Women," in *Alienist and Neurologist* 16 (April 1895): 142. Ellis derived his data on homosexuality from his lesbian wife and her friends.

28. Margaret Mead, *Coming of Age in Samoa* (New York: William Morrow, 1928), p. 165, and *Sex and Temperament in Three Primitive Societies* (New York: William Morrow, 1935), p. 300.

29. *BW* draft, "Real High School," p. 7.

30. Mead, "Life Story," pp. 8–9; JH, pp. 49–50.

31. BW draft, "Love and Friendship," p. 21.

32. Idem.

33. RFB diary, OC.

34. Sir Walter Scott, *Lady of the Lake*, in *Collected Works of Sir Walter Scott* (New York: Greystone Press, n.d.), pp. 345–405; and Louisa May Alcott, *Eight Cousins: Or, The Aunt-Hill* (1875; Boston: Little, Brown, 1894), p. 166.

35. Ruth 1:16–17. Ruth underscored the point about female bonding when she stated in her memoir that she preferred the story of Ruth to that of Ramona, the heroine of the popular novel *Ramona*, by Helen Hunt Jackson, about the tragic love between the mixed-race Ramona and a Native American man. In *Ramona* the mother figure, unrelentingly racist, rejects Ramona; in the Book of Ruth the mother figure Naomi remains close to Ruth. On the importance of the story of Ruth to nineteenth-century women, see Hugo Black, *Friendship* (Chicago: Fleming H. Revell, 1898), frontispiece. On Ruth as a hero for lesbians, see Claude J. Summers, ed., *The Gay and Lesbian Literary Heritage: A Reader's Companion to the Writers and Their Works, from Antiquity to the Present* (New York: Henry Holt, 1995), p. 97.

36. I have derived the attendance figures from Mabel Dodge Luhan, *Intimate Memories* (1936; New York: Kraus Reprints, 1971), vol. 1, pp. 223–29.

37. AW, p. 109.

38. Lois Palkin Rudnick, *Mabel Dodge Luhan: New Woman, New Worlds* (Albuquerque: University of New Mexico Press, 1984), pp. ix, 212–13; and Mabel Dodge Luhan, *Intimate Memories*, pp. 223–29.

39. Luhan, *Intimate Memories*, pp. 212–21.

40. *AW*, p. 109.

41. Ruth's rewriting of *Evangeline* is contained in the draft of *AW*, LC, I-90.

42. Henry Wadsworth Longfellow, *Evangeline: A Tale of Acadie* (1848; Boston: Houghton Mifflin, 1896). On the popularity of reading Longfellow in high schools and for the setting of *Evangeline*, I have relied on John Mack Faragher, "A Great and Noble Scheme: The Expulsion of the Acadians, 1755," unpub. paper, University of Southern California, Nov. 1, 1999. Margaret Mead also read Longfellow in high school. "Young people graduating from high school in 1918 had plenty of Longfellow in their ears." Mead, "Out of the Things I Read," p. 39.

43. The Shawnee woman in *Evangeline* is Indian and thus not to be trusted to act respectably, according to Victorian conventions. See Lillian Faderman, "Female Same-Sex Relationships in Novels by Henry Wadsworth Longfellow, Oliver Wendell Holmes, and Henry James," *New England Quarterly* 51 (Sept. 1978): 316.

44. "Retrospectively Selected to Keep," mimeo. ms., *AW* draft, LC, I-90.

45. In writing about Ruth Fulton's Vassar, I have used Herman, "College and After"; Horowitz, *Alma Mater*; Palmer, "Lace Bonnets and Academic Gowns"; Solomon, *In the Company of Educated Women*; Lynn D. Gordon, *Gender and Higher Education in the Progressive Era* (New Haven: Yale University Press, 1990); Mary Caroline Crawford, *The College Girl of America* (Boston: L. C. Page, 1905); and especially the autobiography of Henry Noble MacCracken, *The Hickory Limb* (New York: Charles Scribner's Sons, 1950). MacCracken became Vassar's president in 1915.

46. On Wylie and Buck, see Elisabeth Woodbridge Morris, ed., *Miss Wylie of Vas-*

sar (New Haven: Yale University Press, 1934); and Gertrude Buck, *Toward a Feminist Rhetoric: The Writing of Gertrude Buck*, ed. JoAnn Campbell (Pittsburgh: University of Pittsburgh Press, 1996). On Salmon, see Louise Fargo Brown, *Apostle of Democracy: The Life of Lucy Maynard Salmon* (New York: Harper & Bros., 1943). On Washburn, see Margaret Floy Washburn, "Some Recollections," in *A History of Psychology in Auto-biography*, ed. Charles Murchison (Worcester, Mass.: Clark University Press, c. 1930–c. 1939), vol. 2, pp. 335–58.

47. On Wylie and Buck's criticism, see Campbell, *Toward a Feminist Rhetoric*; Laura Johnson Wylie, *Social Studies in English Literature* (1916; New York: B. Blum, 1971), and *Studies in the Evolution of English Criticism* (Boston: Ginn, 1894); and Joan Shelley Rubin, *Constance Rourke and American Culture* (Chapel Hill.: University of North Carolina Press, 1980). Rubin contends that Wylie and Buck influenced Rourke, a student of theirs two years ahead of Ruth Fulton.

48. Laura Johnson Wylie, introduction to George Eliot, *Adam Bede*, ed. by Wylie (New York: Charles Scribner's Sons, 1917); Robert B. Westbrook, *John Dewey and American Democracy* (Ithaca: Cornell University Press, 1991), p. 39; and Jane Addams, *Twenty Years at Hull House* (1910; New York: New American Library/Signet, 1961), pp. 90–257.

49. Dorothy Lee, "Ruth Fulton Benedict, 1887–1948," *Journal of American Folk-Lore* 62 (Oct.–Dec. 1949): 345. On Louise M. Rosenblatt and the reader-response school, see John Clifford, "Introduction: Reading Rosenblatt," in *The Experience of Reading: Louise Rosenblatt and Reader-Response Theory*, ed. John Clifford (Portsmouth, N.H.: Boynton/Cook, 1990), p. 1. Rosenblatt acknowledged Benedict's influence on her in *Literature as Exploration* (New York: D. Appleton-Century, 1938). Katherine Pandora, in *Rebels Within the Ranks: Psychologists' Critique of Scientific Authority and Democratic Realities in New Deal America* (Cambridge: Cambridge University Press, 1997), p. 161, notes the influence of Wylie and Buck on Benedict, psychologist Lois Barclay Murphy, and sociologists Constance Rourke and Caroline Ware. She identi-fies them, along with Lucy Salmon and economics professor Herbert Mills, as "the Vassar School of Social Critique."

50. Ruth Benedict's published essays in the *Vassar Miscellany* are: "The High Seri-ousness of Chaucer," Oct. 1907; "*The Trojan Women* of Euripedes," Nov. 1907; "Charles Lamb: An Appreciation," Jan. 1908; "Walt Whitman," Mar. 1908; "*Lena Rivers*, by Mary J. Holmes," May 1908; "The Fool in *King Lear*," Nov. 1908; "Litera-ture and Democracy," March 1909; and "The Racial Traits of Shakespeare's Heroes," June 1909. Mead published another of Benedict's college essays, "The Sense of Sym-bolism," in *AW*, pp. 113–17.

51. Benedict, "*The Trojan Women* of Euripedes," pp. 56–57.

52. The lines are from Walt Whitman, "Crossing Brooklyn Ferry," in *Leaves of Grass* (1855; Philadelphia: David McKay, 1900), p. 186. I have quoted from Benedict's essay and retained her line breaks, which are different from those in the standard edi-tion.

53. See Walter Pater, *Marius the Epicurean: His Sensations and Ideas* (1885; New York: Macmillan, 1910), vol. 1, p. 97.

54. *AW*, p. 116.

55. On mysticism and the Symbolists, see W. B. Yeats, *Essays* (New York: Macmil-

lan, 1924); and Arthur Symons, *The Symbolist Movement in Literature* (1899; New York: Haskell House, 1971), pp. 327–28. Richard Candida Smith, *Mallarmé's Children: Symbolism and the Renewal of Experience* (Berkeley: University of California Press, 1999), overlooks their mysticism and focuses on their modernism.

56. On Santayana, I have relied on Robert Dawidoff, *The Genteel Tradition and the Sacred Rage: High Culture vs. Democracy in Adams, James, and Santayana* (Chapel Hill: University of North Carolina Press, 1992); and Henry Samuel Levinson, *Santayana, Pragmatism, and the Spiritual Life* (Chapel Hill: University of North Carolina Press, 1992). I have also read George Santayana, *Interpretations of Poetry and Religion* (1900; New York: Harper & Bros., 1957); *The Life of Reason* (1905–1906; Amherst, N.Y.: Prometheus Books, 1998); and *Three Philosophical Poets: Lucretius, Dante, and Goethe* (1910; Cambridge, Mass.: Harvard University Press, 1927).

On Nietzsche I have used Kelly Oliver and Marilyn Pearsall, eds., *Feminist Interpretations of Friedrich Nietzsche* (University Park: Pennsylvania State University Press, 1998); and Kathleen Marie Higgins, *Nietzsche's Zarathustra* (Philadelphia: Temple University Press, 1988). I have also read Friedrich Nietzsche, *The Birth of Tragedy* and *Thus Spake Zarathustra*, trans. Thomas Common (New York: Macmillan, n.d.).

57. Nietzsche, *Thus Spake Zarathustra*, p. 61. On Benedict's sending this book to Mead to read on Samoa, see *AW*, p. 548. Eve Kosofsky Sedgwick finds a homosexual subtext in Nietzsche's writings, in which he drew from the writers of the late-nineteenth-century Platonic revival to valorize the strong male body, while attacking male effeminacy. See Sedgwick, *Epistemology of the Closet*, p. 134.

58. Frank M. Turner, *The Greek Heritage in Victorian Britain* (New Haven: Yale University Press, 1981), pp. 369–414; *AW*, pp. 134–35; and Walter Pater, *The Renaissance: Studies in Art and Poetry* (1877; London: Macmillan, 1925), pp. 233–39. Dennis Donoghue, in *Walter Pater: Lover of Strange Souls* (New York: Alfred A. Knopf, 1995), p. 112, contends that Pater meant the phrase to refer to Plato's *Symposium* and thus to homosexuality. According to Edmund Wilson, echoing many commentators, Pater's conclusion expressed "the ideal of a whole generation." Edmund Wilson, *Axel's Castle: A Study in the Imaginative Literature of 1870–1930* (New York: Charles Scribner's Sons, 1931), p. 33.

59. *AW*, p. 135.

60. Alexander Roob, *The Hermetic Museum: Alchemy & Mysticism* (New York: Taschen, 1997), p. 11.

61. Santayana, *Life of Reason*, pp. 155–56.

62. Margaret Mead, "Cultural Determinants of Sexual Behavior," in *Sex and Internal Secretions*, ed. William C. Young, 3d ed. (Baltimore: Williams & Wilkins, 1961), vol. 2, p. 1455.

63. Margaret H. Welch, "Life at Vassar College," *Harper's Bazaar*, Dec. 8, 1900, 2009–17.

64. L. Gordon, *Gender and Higher Education*, pp. 144–45, notes the wedding ceremony; see also Crawford, *College Girl of America*, pp. 60–62, and Karin Huebner, "The Student Culture of Athletics and Smashing: Smith College, 1890–1905" (M.A. thesis, University of Southern California, 2003).

65. Julia Augusta Schwartz, *Vassar Studies* (New York: G. P. Putnam's Sons, 1899), pp. 258–59. On the Daisy Chain and its invention, see Sherrie A. Inness, *Intimate Com-*

munities: Representation and Social Transformation in Women's College Fiction, 1895–1910 (Bowling Green, Ohio: Bowling Green State University Popular Press, 1995), p. 62, and MacCracken, *Hickory Limb*, p. 23. The class song for Margery and Ruth's graduation referred directly to smashing.

> *The flowers that came for Hall Play,*
> *tra la la*
> *Have nothing to do with her fame,*
> *tra la la*
> *'Tis only her crushes' devotion,*
> *they say.*

See Class Box, class of 1909, VC.

66. I quote these descriptions from the *Vassarion,* 1909. On the Renaissance usage of "salad" meaning youth, see Shakespeare's *Antony and Cleopatra,* in which Cleopatra contrasts her mature passion for Mark Antony to the innocence of her "salad days." *The Tragedy of Antony and Cleopatra* 1.5, 85–86.

67. James M. Saslow, *Ganymede in the Renaissance: Homosexuality in Art and Society* (New Haven: Yale University Press, 1986).

68. *As You Like It* 1.2.238.

69. The cast for *As You Like It* is listed in the *Vassarion.* On the coaching in male movements, see A. Rogers, *Vassar Women,* p. 85.

70. The draft of a letter to "My Dear Miss Keys," [Sept. 1910], is in RFB, unpub. journal, VC. In *We Sing Diana* (Boston: Houghton Mifflin, 1928), p. 54, Wanda Fraiken Neff identifies the meaning of the salutation.

71. Neff, *We Sing Diana,* pp. 54, 62–63.

72. Louise Rosenblatt oral interview, CU-Oral.

73. See Harriot Stanton Blatch and Alma Lutz, *Challenging Years: The Autobiography of Harriot Stanton Blatch* (New York: G. P. Putnam's Sons, 1940), p. 108. On Margery and Ruth at the suffrage meeting, see MFF, answers to "100th Anniversary Questionnaire," Nov. 1956, Vassar College Alumnae Office. Margery listed their major experiences at Vassar as the suffrage meeting in the graveyard, a visit by Booker T. Washington in their senior year, and late-night conversations about smoking.

74. Charlotte Perkins Gilman, *Women and Economics* (1898; New York: Harper & Row, 1966), p. 28.

75. Benedict, "Racial Types in Shakespeare's Plays," *Vassar Miscellany,* 1909, pp. 48–86.

76. *BW* draft, "Adolescence," p. 6; and Margaret Mead, "Comments on the *Redbook* Report on Female Sexuality, Apr. 17, 1978," p. 9, LC, I-258. See Arthur Schnitzler, *Anatol: A Sequence of Dialogues by Arthur Schnitzler; Paraphrased for the English Stage by Granville Barker* (New York: Mitchell Kennerley, 1911).

77. Margaret Mead, "And Some Are Bisexuals," *Redbook,* May 31, 1971, p. 5; and Edward Sapir, "The Discipline of Sex," *American Mercury* 16 (1929): 413–20, and "Observations on the Sex Problem in America," *American Journal of Psychiatry* 8 (1928): 519–34.

78. Helen Lefkowitz Horowitz, *The Power and Passion of M. Carey Thomas* (New

York: Alfred A. Knopf, 1994), pp. 166–67; Sharon O'Brien, *Willa Cather: The Emerging Voice* (New York: Oxford University Press, 1987), pp. 135–36; and Théophile Gautier, *Mademoiselle de Maupin*, trans. Paul Selver (London: Hamish Hamilton, 1948).

79. In discussing the sexologists, I focus on R. von Krafft-Ebing, *Psychopathia Sexualis* (New York: Medical Arts Agency, 1906), a translation of the 12th German edition; and on Havelock Ellis, "Sexual Inversion in Men," "Sexual Inversion in Women," and "The Nature of Sexual Inversion," in *Studies in the Psychology of Sex* (New York: Random House, 1936), vol. 2, pp. 271–384. I have also used the 1902 edition of this work, which differs from the 1916 one. I have also read Sigmund Freud, *Three Essays on the Theory of Sexuality* (originally published in 1905), translated and newly edited by James Strachey (New York: Basic Books, 1962); Edward Carpenter, *Intermediate Sex: A Study of Some Transitional Types of Men and Women* (London: Allen & Unwin, 1908); and Magnus Hirschfeld, *The Homosexuality of Men and Women*, trans. Michael A. Lombardi-Nash (1913; New York: Prometheus Books, 2000). I focus on Krafft-Ebing, Ellis, Freud, Hirschfeld, and Carpenter as the most important sexologists of this era.

On them, I have also read Joanne Meyerowitz, *How Sex Changed: A History of Transsexuality in the United States* (Cambridge, Mass.: Harvard University Press, 2002); Steven Angelides, *A History of Bisexuality* (Chicago: University of Chicago Press, 2001); Lisa Duggan, *Sapphic Slashers: Sex, Violence, and American Modernity* (Durham, N.C.: Duke University Press, 2000); Jennifer Terry, *An American Obsession: Science, Medicine, and Homosexuality in Modern Society* (Chicago: University of Chicago Press, 1999); Margery Garber, *Vice Versa: Bisexuality and the Eroticism of Everyday Life* (New York: Simon & Schuster, 1995); George Chauncey, *Gay New York: Gender, Urban Culture, and the Making of the Gay Male World, 1890–1940* (New York: Basic Books, 1994), and "From Sexual Inversion to Homosexuality: The Changing Medical Conceptualization of Female 'Deviance,'" in *Passion and Power: Sexuality in History*, ed. Kathy Peiss and Christina Simmons (Philadelphia: Temple University Press, 1989), pp. 87–117; and Lillian Faderman, *Surpassing the Love of Men: Romantic Friendship and Love Between Women from the Renaissance to the Present* (New York: William Morrow, 1981), and *Odd Girls and Twilight Lovers: A History of Lesbian Life in Twentieth-Century America* (New York: Columbia University Press, 1991). The most recent biography of Ellis is Phyllis Grosskurth, *Havelock Ellis: A Biography* (New York: Alfred A. Knopf, 1980).

80. Hirschfeld, *Homosexuality of Men and Women*, pp. 249, 338. On Hirschfeld, see also James D. Steakley, "*Per scientiam ad justitiam:* Magnus Hirschfeld and the Sexual Politics of Innate Homosexuality," in *Science and Homosexualities*, ed. Vernon A. Rosario (New York: Routledge, 1997), pp. 133–54.

81. See Karl Heinrich Ulrichs, *The Riddle of "Man-Manly" Love: The Pioneering Work on Male Homosexuality*, 2 vols., trans. Michael A. Lombardi-Nash (Buffalo: Prometheus Books, 1994); and Freud, *Three Essays*, p. 8. Ulrichs derived his ideas partly from *Mademoiselle de Maupin*.

82. Carpenter, *Intermediate Sex*, p. 66. Many sexologists realized that homosexual men could be virile, but they couldn't conceptualize homosexual women as feminine.

83. Havelock Ellis, "Sexual Inversion in Women," in *Studies in the Psychology of Sex*, vol. 2, p. 258; and Hirschfeld, *Homosexuality of Men and Women*, p. 54. Ellis con-

tended that the women attracted to homosexual women were those who couldn't attract men and that homosexual women sometimes dressed and acted like ordinary women in order to conceal their inversion. "Sexual Inversion in Women," p. 222.

84. According to the *Oxford English Dictionary*, "gender" was an old term that sometimes meant simply genus, or type. In languages where it can refer to neutral nouns as well as masculine and feminine ones, some languages have as many as twenty such classifications. See *Webster's Encyclopedic Unabridged Dictionary of the English Language* (New York: Gramercy Books, 1994). The OED traces the first use of "gender" to mean the social self to "second wave" feminists in the 1970s, although Meyerowitz, in *How Sex Changed*, finds doctors who treated transsexuals in the 1960s using it in the present-day meaning. On the endocrinologists, see Oudshoorn, *Beyond the Natural Body*, and Thomas Laqueur, *Making Sex: Body and Gender from the Greeks to Freud* (Cambridge, Mass.: Harvard University Press, 1990).

85. Mead, "And Some Are Bisexuals," LC, I-245.

86. Hirschfeld, *Homosexuality of Men and Women*, p. 46.

5 / "Mary Wollstonecraft": Ruth Benedict and Early Twentieth-Century Feminism

1. Essay by Benedict on her experiences in Switzerland, *Norwich Sun*, May 1910.

2. *AW*, p. 519. The quotations from Benedict's journal in this chapter come from the published version in *AW*; most can also be found in the journal fragments in VC. On Wollstonecraft's importance to feminists in the 1910s, see Beatrice Forbes Robertson-Hale, *What Women Want: An Interpretation of the Feminist Movement* (New York: Frederic A. Stokes, 1914), p. 30.

3. *AW*, p. 519.

4. Ibid., p. 119.

5. Ibid., pp. 119, 121, 123.

6. Richard Handler, "Ruth Benedict and the Modernist Sensibility," in *Modernist Anthropology: From Fieldwork to Text*, ed. Marc Manganaro (Princeton, N.J.: Princeton University Press, 1990), pp. 163–82, views Benedict as representative of the modernist obsession with self-expression and self-realization.

7. On Ruth Fulton's missionary society, see Stanley Benedict to RFB, March 27, 1913, LC, S-14; on suffrage and women's rights activities in Los Angeles, see Gayle Gullett, *Becoming Citizens: The Emergence and Development of the California Women's Movement, 1880–1911* (Urbana: University of Illinois Press, 2000). Los Angeles had the largest women's club in the nation.

8. *AW*, p. 126.

9. Ibid., pp. 119, 122.

10. Stanley Benedict to RFB, Feb. 12, 1913, LC, S-14.

11. *AW*, p. 120.

12. Idem.

13. Ibid., p. 141.

14. Ibid., p. 123.

15. Ibid., pp. 126, 130.

16. Ibid., p. 131.

17. See Laura L. Behling, *The Masculine Woman in America, 1890–1935* (Urbana: University of Illinois Press, 2001); Fran Grace, *Carry A. Nation: Retelling the Life* (Bloomington: Indiana University Press, 2001); Martha Banta, *Imaging American Women: Idea and Ideals in Cultural History* (New York: Columbia University Press, 1987), pp. 92–139; Abby Wettan Kleinbaum, *The War Against the Amazons* (New York: New Press, 1983); and Smith-Rosenberg, "The New Woman as Androgyne," p. 271. On the possibility that the sexologists' descriptions of homosexual women's dress influenced the actual dress of lesbians, see Lisa Duggan, "The Trials of Alice Mitchell: Sensationalism, Sexology and the Lesbian Subject in Turn-of-the-Century America," *Signs: Journal of Women in Culture and Society* 18 (summer 1993): 791–814.

18. Havelock Ellis, *Sexual Inversion*, p. 262.

19. *AW,* pp. 129–30.

20. MFF, "Family Life of Ruth Fulton Benedict," p. 6.

21. Esther S. Goldfrank, *Notes on an Undirected Life: As One Anthropologist Tells It* (Flushing, N.Y.: Queens College Press, 1978), p. 222; *Much Ado About Nothing,* ed. A. R. Humphreys (London: Methuen, 1981), p. 93; and *AW,* pp. xvi, xix.

22. On the new feminism of 1910, see Nancy F. Cott, *The Grounding of Modern Feminism* (New Haven: Yale University Press, 1987), pp. 3–50; and Kate E. Wittenstein, "The Heterodoxy Club and American Feminism, 1912–1930" (Ph.D. diss., Boston University, 1989). On the European situation, Katherine Anthony, *Feminism in Scandinavia and Germany* (New York: Henry Holt, 1915), remains interesting. There is no study of the international free-love movement.

23. For Key's writings, see Ellen Karolina Sofia Key, *The Century of the Child* (New York: G. P. Putnam's Sons, 1909); *The Morality of Woman, and Other Essays,* trans. Mamah Bouton Borthwick (Chicago: Ralph Fletcher Seymour, 1911); *Love and Marriage,* trans. Arthur G. Chater (New York: G. P. Putnam's Sons, 1911); *The Woman Movement,* trans. Mamah Bouton Borthwick (New York: G. P. Putnam's Sons, 1912); *Rahel Varnhagen: A Portrait,* trans. Arthur G. Chater (New York: G. P. Putnam's Sons, 1913); and *The Renaissance of Motherhood,* trans. Anna E. B. Fries (New York: G. P. Putnam's Sons, 1914). In viewing Key as both radical and conservative, I have drawn on Floyd Dell, *Women as World Builders: Studies in Modern Feminism* (Chicago: Forbes, 1913), pp. 76–89. See also William English Carson, *The Marriage Revolt: A Study of Marriage and Divorce* (New York: Hearst's International Library, 1915).

24. Key, *Love and Marriage,* p. 33, *Morality of Woman,* pp. 16–17, *Renaissance of Motherhood,* p. 105, and *Rahel Varnhagen,* p. 108. Like many turn-of-the-century evolutionists, Key seems to have believed in the inheritance of acquired characteristics, a doctrine that maintained that children would inherit the perfection their parents developed in their personalities, thus vastly speeding up the reform process.

25. Key, *Morality of Women,* p. 12, and *Renaissance of Motherhood,* p. 37.

26. Key, *Love and Marriage,* pp. 51, 90, and *Woman Movement,* pp. 73, 79, 126–27. Louise Sofia Hamilton Nystrom, *Ellen Key: Her Life and Her Work,* trans. A. E. B. Fries (New York: G. P. Putnam's Sons, 1913), pp. 47, 99. According to Nystrom, Key engaged in "spiritual banquets" with two women friends in Stockholm; she derived her ideas about a transcendent heterosexual love from her parents' marriage.

27. Key, *Love and Marriage,* pp. 78–79, and *Woman Movement,* pp. 59, 75–78.

28. On men's studies theory, see Harry Brod and Michael Kaufman, eds., *Theorizing Masculinities* (Thousand Oaks, Calif.: Sage, 1994).

29. Key, *Woman Movement*, p. 16, and *Love and Marriage*, p. 77.

30. Benedict discusses the importance of Key's *Rahel Varnhagen* to her "Mary Wollstonecraft" in a fragment, Mary Wollstonecraft file, VC, 32.

31. Key, *Rahel Varnhagen*, p. 303.

32. Charlotte Wolff, *Magnus Hirschfeld: A Portrait of a Pioneer in Sexology* (London: Quartet Books, 1986), p. 191.

33. Warren I. Susman, "Personality and the Making of Twentieth-Century Culture," in Susman, *Culture as History*, pp. 271–85; A. A. Roback, *The Psychology of Character* (London: Routledge & Kegan Paul, 1952); and Gordon W. Allport, *Personality: A Psychological Interpretation* (New York: Henry Holt, 1937), pp. 24–101. Richard Wightman Fox, "The Culture of Liberal Progressivism, 1875–1925," *Journal of Interdisciplinary History* 23 (winter 1993): 639–60, deals with the continuing theological importance of the word "personality" as well as with its multifaceted meanings.

34. Havelock Ellis, *The Art of Love* and *Psychology of Sex in Relation to Society*, in *Studies in the Psychology of Sex*, vol. 4, p. 218. Edward Carpenter, *Love's Coming of Age* (1896; Chicago: Charles H. Kerr, 1908).

35. See Sheila Rowbotham and Jeffrey Weeks, *Socialism and the New Life: The Personal and Sexual Politics of Edward Carpenter and Havelock Ellis* (London: Pluto Press, 1977); and Emile Delavenay, *D. H. Lawrence and Edward Carpenter: A Study in Edwardian Transition* (New York: Taplinger, 1971). See also Jo-Ann Wallace, "The Case of Edith Ellis," in *Modernist Sexualities*, ed. Hugh Stevens and Caroline Howlett (Manchester, U.K.: Manchester University Press, 2000), pp. 13–40.

36. Carpenter, *Love's Coming of Age*, p. 121.

37. *AW*, p. 132.

38. Ruth Benedict, "South Wind," unpub. poem, VC, 48.26.

39. For biographical information on Stanley Benedict, see Elmer Verner McCollum, "Biographical Memoir of Stanley Rossiter Benedict, 1884–1936," in National Academy of Sciences, *Biographical Memoirs*, vol. 27 (Washington, D.C.: National Academy of Sciences, 1952), pp. 157–77.

40. *AW*, p. 143; journal fragment, VC, 36.1.

41. *AW*, p. 343.

42. MM to RFB, May 9, 1929, LC, S-3; journal fragments, VC, 36.1.

43. MFF, "Family Life of Ruth Fulton Benedict," p. 6.

44. On pre–World War I feminism and bohemianism in New York City, see Christine Stansell, *American Moderns: Bohemian New York and the Creation of a New Century* (New York: Metropolitan Books, 2000); Sandra Adickes, *To Be Young Was Very Heaven: Women in New York Before the First World War* (New York: St. Martin's Press, 1997); and Leslie Fishbein, *Rebels in Bohemia: The Radicals of "The Masses," 1911–1917* (Chapel Hill: University of North Carolina Press, 1982). For the feminist position, see Cott, *Grounding of Modern Feminism*, and Wittenstein, "Heterodoxy Club."

45. Ruth criticized the feminist meetings in draft, "Mary Wollstonecraft," VC. Wittenstein, "Heterodoxy Club," p. 26, notes the "consciousness-raising" aspect of the meetings.

46. Shari Benstock, *Women of the Left Bank: Paris, 1900–1940* (Austin: University

of Texas Press, 1986), p. 72. On World War I, see John Keegan, *The First World War* (London: Hutchinson, 1998).

47. The typescript draft of "The Bo-Cu Plant" is in the draft copy of *AW*, LC, I-90. Mead suggested that Stanley Benedict may have provided the plot for the story, although themes relating to Ruth Benedict's life and her stances on gender are contained in it. See Lois W. Banner, " 'The Bo-Cu Plant': Ruth Benedict and Gender," in *Reading Benedict/Reading Mead*, ed. Banner and Dolores Janiewski (Johns Hopkins University Press, forthcoming).

48. On the female demons in art and literature, see Bram Dijkstra, *Idols of Perversity: Fantasies of Feminine Evil in Fin-de-Siècle Culture*. For a more balanced view, see Elaine Showalter, *Sexual Anarchy: Gender and Culture at the Fin-de-Siècle*. For the reversal by feminist writers, see Nina Auerbach, *Woman and the Demon: The Life of a Victorian Myth* (Cambridge, Mass.: Harvard University Press, 1982). According to Richard Dellamora, *Masculine Desire*, the female demons were symbols of rebellion and gender crossing to writers like Swinburne and Pater.

49. *AW*, p. 142.

50. Benedict, typescript fragment, unpub. undated ms. file, VC, 55.

51. *AW*, p. 194.

52. Ibid., pp. 5–6. On Brooke, see John Lehmann, *Rupert Brooke: His Life and His Legend* (London: Weidenfeld & Nicolson, 1980). For his popularity in the United States, see Margaret C. Anderson, *My Thirty Years' War: An Autobiography* (New York: Covici, Friede, 1930), pp. 53–55.

53. B. Forbes-Robertson Hale, *What Women Want*, pp. 242, 85. See also Rheta Louise Childe Dorr, *A Woman of Fifty* (New York: Funk & Wagnalls, 1924), pp. 280, 314; Lorine Livingston Pruette, "The Evolution of Disenchantment," in *These Modern Women: Autobiographical Essays from the Twenties*, ed. Elaine Showalter (Old Westbury, N.Y.: Feminist Press, 1978), pp. 72–73; Linda K. Schott, "Women Against War: Pacifism, Feminism, and Social Justice in the United States, 1915–1941" (Ph.D. diss., Stanford University, 1985); William L. O'Neill, *Everyone Was Brave: The Rise and Fall of Feminism in America* (Chicago: Quadrangle Books, 1969); and Ellen Carol Dubois, *Harriot Stanton Blatch and the Winning of Women Suffrage* (New Haven: Yale University Press, 1997), p. 212.

54. *AW*, p. 146; and fragments, draft introduction, "Adventures in Womanhood," Mary Wollstonecraft file, VC, 56.7.

55. *AW*, p. 494; and William Godwin, *Memoirs of the Author of "A Vindication of the Rights of Woman"* (1797; New York: Woodstock Books, 1990). See also Eleanor Flexner, *Mary Wollstonecraft: A Biography* (New York: Coward, McCann & Geoghegan, 1972).

56. *AW*, p. 495; and Carol H. Posten, "Mary Wollstonecraft and 'The Body Politic,' " in *Feminist Interpretations of Mary Wollstonecraft*, ed. Maria J. Falco (University Park: Pennsylvania State University Press, 1996), pp. 85–104. In her recent biography of Wollstonecraft, Janet M. Todd downplays the violence on the part of Wollstonecraft's father and her sister's husband. See Todd, *Mary Wollstonecraft: A Revolutionary Life* (London: Weidenfeld & Nicolson, 2000).

57. *AW*, pp. 493, 501. The word "Juggernaut" refers to a huge idol dragged through the city of Benares, India. Devotees supposedly threw themselves under its

wheels. A standard reference in the missionary rhetoric of Benedict's childhood, it supposedly proved the superiority of Christianity over the brutality of heathenism. See Lois W. Banner, "The Protestant Crusade: Religious Missions, Benevolence, and Reform in the United States, 1790–1840" (Ph.D. diss. Columbia Univ., 1970), p. 322.

58. *AW,* pp. 496, 506, 515, 518.

59. *AW,* p. 497. Godwin, *Memoirs,* pp. 19, 467; and Mary Wollstonecraft, *A Vindication of the Rights of Woman, with Strictures on Political and Moral Subjects* (1792; New York: Source Book Press, 1971), p. 156.

60. Margaret Fuller, *Woman in the Nineteenth Century* (1845; Chapel Hill: University of North Carolina Press, 1980), pp. 51, 63, 75. See also Mary E. Wood, " 'With a Ready Eye': Margaret Fuller and Lesbianism in Nineteenth-Century American Literature," *American Literature* 65 (March 1993): 1–18.

61. *AW,* p. 142.

62. Idem.

63. Ruth Fulton Benedict, answers to "Questionnaire for Biographical-Address Register," Dec. 13, 1929, Alumnae Office, VC.

64. See Elsie Clews Parsons, *Fear and Conventionality* (New York: G. P. Putnam's Sons, 1914), *Social Freedom: A Study of the Conflicts Between Social Classifications and Personality* (New York: G. P. Putnam's Sons, 1915), and *Social Rule: A Study of the Will to Power* (New York: G. P. Putnam's Sons, 1916). For Parsons's life, see Desley Deacon, *Elsie Clews Parsons: Inventing Modern Life* (Chicago: University of Chicago Press, 1997). My interpretation of Parsons differs from that of Deacon, who in her impressive and laudatory biography, views Parsons as a leader of modernism. My research has uncovered other sides of Parsons, as well as manifestations of modernism into which Parsons doesn't fit. On the New School, see Peter Rutkoff and William B. Scott, *New School: A History of the New School for Social Research* (New York: Free Press, 1986).

65. In describing Parsons's course, I have used the file on it, titled "Women and the Social Order," in the Elsie Clews Parsons Papers, Rye Historical Society, Rye, N.Y. The material in this file is undated, mostly written by hand, and unorganized.

66. Recent writers on institutionalized homosexuality among the Native Americans reject the term "berdache," since it derived from Arabic and meant a boy prostitute. Each American tribe had its own name for those who took on such a role: e.g., the Navajo called them *nadle.* Benedict and Mead used the term "berdache," and I follow them in doing so, but I also use woman-man, man-woman, the terminology suggested by Sabine Lang, in her definitive *Men as Women, Women as Men, Changing Gender in Native Cultures,* trans. John L. Vantine (Austin: University of Texas Press, 1998). Lang places the preferred gender of the crossover category first, although Benedict and Mead do the opposite, referring to the berdache as man-woman. Walter L. Williams, *The Spirit and the Flesh: Sexual Diversity in American Indian Culture* (Boston: Beacon, 1986), analyzes those societies in which berdaches were spiritual leaders.

67. *AW,* p. 149. Mead read the initials of Benedict's "expert" on masturbation as "H. D."; in the handwritten text in the Vassar collection, I read them as "H. E.," which makes them an obvious reference to Havelock Ellis.

68. Benedict, "Anthropology and the Abnormal," *Journal of General Psychology* 10 (1934): 59–82. RFB to Dr. Weiss, May 2, 1933, VC, 2.8.

69. Gladys Reichard, "Elsie Clews Parsons," *Journal of American Folk-Lore* 56

(Apr.–June, 1943): 45–46; A. L. Kroeber, "Elsie Clews Parsons," *AA* 45 (1943): 253–55.

70. See *AW,* p. 8.

71. Ruth Benedict, in "Alexander Goldenweiser: Three Tributes," *Modern Quarterly* (summer 1940): 31–34.

72. Elsie Clews Parsons, "The Zuni La'mana," *AA* 18 (1916): 521–28.

73. Parsons, *Social Freedom,* pp. 27–28, and "Crime and Perversion," *Medical Review of Reviews* 22 (1916): 191–92.

74. Elsie Clews Parsons, "The Aversion to Anomalies," *Journal of Philosophy, Psychology, and Scientific Methods* 12 (April 15, 1915): 213, and "Sex," in *Civilization in the United States: An Inquiry by Thirty Americans,* ed. Harold E. Stearns (New York: Harcourt, Brace, 1922), pp. 309–19. On masturbation leading to homosexuality, see Havelock Ellis, "Perversion in Children," in *The New Generation: The Intimate Problems of Modern Parents and Children,* ed. V. F. Calverton and Samuel Schmalhausen (New York: Macauley, 1930), pp. 523–53.

75. Robert Herrick, *The End of Desire* (New York: Farrar & Rinehart, 1932), pp. 7–23, 127, 242–43, 248.

76. Robert Herrick, *Chimes* (New York: Macmillan, 1926), p. 109. Both Esther Goldfrank and Parsons's daughter, Lissa, thought that Parsons preferred men to women. See Goldfrank, *Notes on an Undirected Life,* p. 41, and Lissa Parsons Kennedy oral interview, CU-Oral.

77. MM to RFB, Nov. 3, 1932, LC, S-3.

78. *AW,* p. 342.

6 / *DePauw University, Barnard College, and the Making of Margaret Mead*

1. *BW* draft, "Real High School," p. 7.

2. *BW* draft, "Schooling or Adolescence," p. 10, title on individual page of draft chapter, "Adolescence." Margaret Mead, *Anthropologists and What They Do,* p. 157.

3. *BW,* pp. 89–90.

4. Ibid., p. 95.

5. MM to Emily Fogg Mead, Feb. 20, 1920, LC, A-11. I describe the clothing from the pictures in Mead's DePauw yearbook, *The Mirage,* 1920, LC, A-14.

6. Katharine Rothenberger, "Remembering Margaret Mead," Fort Wayne *Journal Gazette,* Dec. 5, 1978, clipping, Jane Howard papers, CU. On the sororities, see Edith Rickert, "The Fraternity Idea Among College Women," *Century Magazine* 85 (Nov. 1912): 97–106, and "Exclusiveness Among College Women," *Century Magazine* 85 (Dec. 1912): 227–35. Rickert, a Renaissance scholar at Vassar, notes the importance of dress to sorority women, as well as the hierarchies that governed their behavior.

7. MM to Emily Fogg Mead, Sept. 21, Oct. 12, 1919, LC, A-11.

8. MM to Emily Fogg Mead, Jan. 13, 1920, LC, A-11.

9. MM to Gregory Bateson (GB), Jan. 7, 1935, LC, R-2.

10. The note from Katharine to Margaret is unsigned, but it is in Katharine's handwriting, in the DePauw University file, LC, Q-7.

11. Katharine Rothenberger to MM, Feb. 25, Apr. 8, 1922, LC, C-1.

12. Edward Mead to MM, Oct. 13, 1919, n.d., 1919; Apr. 16, Apr. 30, 1920, LC, A-4; Martha Ramsey Mead to MM, Sept. 21, 1919, LC, A-17.

13. Emily Fogg Mead to MM, n.d. 1919, LC, A-11.

14. MM to Priscilla Mead, Nov. 22, 1919, LC, Q-7.

15. MM to Emily Fogg Mead, Nov. 2, 1919, LC, Q-2; MM to Martha Ramsey Mead, Nov. 19, 1919; March 1, 1920, LC, A-17.

16. *BW,* p. 96.

17. MM to Emily Fogg Mead, Nov. 12, 1919, LC, A-11.

18. *BW,* p. 105; MM to Emily Fogg Mead, Feb. 28, 1920, LC, A-11.

19. Interviews with Ken Heyman, Frances Cooke MacGregor, Frances Howard, Florette Henry, CU.

20. Gregory Bateson as quoted in JH, pp. 163–64.

21. RFB to MM, Dec. 10, 1933, R-1.

22. Judith Thurman (quoting Plutarch), "The Queen Himself," *The New Yorker,* May 7, 2001, 75.

23. Vincent Sheean, *The Indigo Bunting: A Memoir of Edna St. Vincent Millay* (1951; New York: Schocken Books, 1973), p. 36.

24. Lindzey, p. 309; *BW* draft, "College," p. 7.

25. T. George Harris, "A Conversation with Margaret Mead," *Psychology Today* 4 (July 1970): 58–64.

26. MM to Martha Ramsey Mead, Nov. 8, 1920, LC, A-17.

27. On Barnard, I have used Horowitz, *Alma Mater,* pp. 134–42, 247–61; Rosenberg, *Beyond Separate Spheres;* Alice Duer Miller and Susan Myers, *Barnard College: The First Fifty Years* (New York: Columbia University Press, 1939); Marian Churchill White, *A History of Barnard College* (New York: Columbia University Press, 1954); and Rosalind Rosenberg, "Changing the Subject: Women and the Invention of Gender at Columbia," unpub. ms., 2002. Emily Putnam, *The Lady: Studies of Certain Significant Phases of Her History* (1910; Chicago: University of Chicago Press, 1970); and Mead, *Sex and Temperament in Three Primitive Societies,* p. ix.

28. Virginia Crocheron Gildersleeve, *Many a Good Crusade: Memoirs* (New York: Macmillan, 1954); and *Barnard Bulletin,* May 4, 1923. On speakers, students, and social welfare, see the *Barnard Bulletin* from Sept. 1922 to June 1923, when Mead was its editor.

29. Interview with Deborah Kaplan Mandelbaum, CU.

30. MM to Emily Fogg Mead, Sept. 30, 1920, LC, Q-2.

31. MM to Martha Ramsey Mead, Feb. 6, 1921, LC, A-17.

32. In describing the Ash Can Cats, I have relied especially on *BW* and its drafts; Jane Howard's interviews; CM interviews with Eleanor Pelham Kortheuer and Karsten Stapelfeldt; Mead, "Life History"; and Louise Rosenblatt oral interview, CU-Oral.

33. *BW* draft, "Barnard," p. 6; Mead, "Life History," p. 10.

34. Interview with Deborah Kaplan Mandelbaum, CU. Constance Rourke, *American Humour: A Study of the National Character* (New York: Harcourt Brace, 1931), pp. 1–49.

35. Mead, *Ruth Benedict,* p. 3.

36. *BW,* p. 112.

37. Scholars have assumed that Minor Latham took the group's name from the Ashcan school of painters, although other derivations are possible. Margaret carried a kitten, the class mascot, in the fair during her first fall at Barnard; she wrote a column called "Cat's Corner" for the *Bulletin.* She also wrote a vignette for her writing class about the garbage cans under her apartment window, which Latham may have read. See Class Notes and College Papers, LC, A-14, A-15.

38. *BW* draft, "College Barnard," p. 6. Edna St. Vincent Millay, *A Few Figs from Thistles: Poems and Sonnets* (1922; New York: Harper & Bros., 1928), pp. 1–2.

39. Interviews with Léonie Adams, Deborah Kaplan Mandelbaum, and Luther Cressman, CU.

40. Louise Rosenblatt oral interview, CU-Oral.

41. *BW,* p. 115.

42. *BW,* p. 118.

43. Marie Eichelberger to MM, March 5, 1938, LC, B-4.

44. References to an "affair" between Léonie and Louise are in letters from Léonie to MM in undated file, general correspondence, LC, Q-13, and in letters from RFB to MM in the S file, LC. Pelham's husband, Karsten Stapelfeldt, asserted that Pelham expressed disgust whenever anyone mentioned that Benedict had seduced Mead (Karsten Stapelfeldt to CM, June 17, 1986, possession of Carleton Mabee). Margaret called Deb "as biological as a roan stallion"; in Mead's presence, Deb called homosexuality a perversion. Discussion, Dream of Feb. 11, Dream-Research File, LC.

45. Interview with Deborah Mandelbaum and Pelham Kortheuer, CU.

46. Chauncey, *Gay New York,* passim; and Liberator Ball flyer, Jan. 5, 1922, LC, C-1, general correspondence.

47. Mead, "Bisexuality."

48. MM to Emily Fogg Mead, March 7, Apr. 6, 1921, LC, Q-2.

49. Interview with Luther Cressman, CU.

50. Luther Cressman to MM, Sept. 22, Dec. 25, Dec. 27, 1921; Oct. 23, Dec. 3, 1922, LC, A-2.

51. Howard interview with Nancy Miller, CU; *Mortarboard,* 1923, p. 73.

52. Charlotte Lennox, *Euphemia* (Dublin: P. Wogan, P. Byrne, 1790.)

53. John Lyly, *Gallathea,* in *The Plays of John Lyly,* ed. Carter A. Daniel (London: Associated Universities Press, 1988), pp. 110–46.

54. Notices for the two plays are in the *New York Times,* Nov. 2, 1922. The letters and notes from Lee/Peter to MM ("Euphemia") are in LC, mostly in B-9, Q-11, Q-13, undated file, with a few in C-1 and also in R. For the most part they are undated, signed "Peter" or "Lee," and identifiable through Leone's handwriting.

55. The column is reprinted in Margaret Mead and Rhoda Métraux, *Aspects of the Present* (New York: Morrow, 1980), pp. 269–75, as "Bisexuality: A New Awareness."

56. Horowitz, *Alma Mater,* pp. 253–54.

57. Leone Newton (Lee) to MM, March 24, 1923, LC, Q-11.

58. *Mortarboard,* 1923, p. 73; interview with Karsten Stapelfeldt, CU; Howard, *Margaret Mead,* p. 175.

59. Lee to MM, March 24, 1923, LC, B-9.

60. Unpub. poetry file, LC, Q-15. With the exception of Pelham and Eleanor Steele, the Ash Can Cats had dark hair; in her picture in the yearbook Leone has blond hair.

61. RFB to MM, Dec. 19, 1925, LC, S-4.

62. Lee to MM, n.d., LC, R-6; MM to GB, Nov. 9, 1933, LC, R-1.

63. Mead wrote to Léonie Adams that Deb Kaplan reintroduced her to Leone Newton in 1930. MM to Léonie Adams, March 1, 1930, Adams-Troy Papers, YU.

64. For Margaret's major at graduation and the courses she took, see transcript, Margaret Mead, Barnard College, June 30, 1923. See also Patricia A. Francis, " 'Something to Think With': Mead, Psychology, and the Road to Samoa," unpub. paper, Association for Social Anthropology in Oceania, Feb. 16, 2001.

65. My argument about the social sciences, professionalization, and masculinization draws from James H. Capshaw, *Psychologists on the March: Science, Practice, and Professional Identity in America, 1929–1969* (Cambridge: Cambridge University Press, 1999); Helene Silverberg, ed., *Gender and American Social Science: The Formative Years* (Princeton, N.J.: Princeton University Press, 1998); Mark C. Smith, *Social Science in the Crucible: The American Debate over Objectivity and Purpose, 1918–1941* (Durham, N.C.: Duke University Press, 1994); Stephen J. Cross, "Designs for Living: Lawrence K. Frank and the Progressive Legacy in American Social Thought" (Ph.D. diss., Johns Hopkins Univ., 1994); Dorothy Ross, *The Origins of American Social Science* (Cambridge: Cambridge University Press, 1991); and Robert C. Bannister, *Sociology and Scientism: The American Quest for Objectivity, 1890–1940* (Chapel Hill: University of North Carolina Press, 1987).

66. Harold Stearns, "The Intellectual Life," in *Civilization in the United States*, pp. 135–50; and Kim Townsend, *Manhood at Harvard: William James and Others* (New York: W. W. Norton, 1996).

67. R. Gordon Hoxie et al., *History of the Faculty of Political Science at Columbia University* (New York: Columbia University Press, 1955), pp. 78–100. On the development of experimental psychology, especially at Columbia, see Edwin G. Boring, *A History of Experimental Psychology*, 2d ed. (Englewood Cliffs, N.J.: Prentice-Hall, 1950).

68. Louise Rosenblatt oral interview, CU-Oral. See H. L. (Harry Levi) Hollingworth, *Abnormal Psychology: Its Concepts and Theories* (London: Methuen, 1931).

69. William Fielding Ogburn, *Social Change with Respect to Culture and Original Nature* (1922; New York: Viking Press, 1933). No biography of Ogburn has been written; Bannister, *Sociology and Scientism*, contains information. See also Barbara Laslett, "Gender in/and Social Science History," *Social Science History* 16 (summer 1992): 177–95.

70. Cressman, *Golden Journey*, p. 110; and Margaret Mead, "Retrospects and Prospects," in *Anthropology and Human Behavior*, ed. Thomas Gladwin and William C. Sturtevant (Washington, D.C.: Anthropological Society of Washington, 1962), p. 121.

71. William Fielding Ogburn, Journal, March 24, 1944, William Fielding Ogburn Papers, UC; Bannister, *Sociology and Scientism*, p. 174; William Fielding Ogburn and Alexander Goldenweiser, eds., *The Social Sciences and Their Interrelations* (Boston: Houghton Mifflin, 1927), p. 9; and Robert W. Wallace, "The Institutionalization of a New Discipline: The Case of Sociology at Columbia University, 1891–1931" (Ph.D. diss., Columbia University, 1989), pp. 329–30.

72. H. L. Hollingworth, *Leta Stetter Hollingworth: A Biography* (Lincoln: University of Nebraska Press, 1943), p. 116.

73. Leta S. Hollingworth, *The Psychology of the Adolescent* (New York: D. Appleton, 1928), pp. 116–21, 130–36. In his preface to this book, Harry Hollingworth states that it was drawn from her class lectures and was the day's standard text on adolescence. Ogburn, *Social Change*, p. 327.

74. Mead, class notes, exercises, and other writings, LC, A-14, A-15.

75. Margaret Mead, "The City Dionysia," in ibid., Jan. 25, 1922.

76. Howard interview with Eleanor Pelham Kortheuer and Deborah Kaplan Mandelbaum, CU; CM interview with Karsten Stapelfeldt. See also Nona Balakin, "A talk with Dr. Latham," *Barnard Alumnae Magazine* (April 1953): 42 ff.

77. The letter is in the undated, unidentified file, LC, C-1.

78. "Leonard Bloomfield," *Dictionary of American Biography*, supplement 4 (New York: Charles Scribner's Sons, 1974), pp. 89–90.

79. *BW* draft, "Barnard," p. 16; MM to Martha Ramsey Mead, Feb. 6, 1923, LC, A-14. On Marie Eichelberger making herself indispensable to Mead, see Marie Eichelberger to MM, Aug. 22, 1923, LC, B-4.

80. Alice [Thwing] to MM, Jan. 21, 1923, LC, C-2, unidentified file.

81. The handwriting analysis is in LC, Q-35. Mead later asserted that she had the analysis done to assess the use of graphology in fieldwork. MM to Caroline Tennant Kelly (CTK), July 14, 1948, LC, R-8.

82. Mead, "Life History"; interview with Nancy Willey, CU.

83. Details of the deathbed scene are in the *New York Times*, Feb. 8 and 9, 1923.

84. Louise Rosenblatt contended that she—not Mead—found the body; both she and the *New York Times* identified the Barbellion book as beside it. Louise Rosenblatt interview, CU-Oral. See also Leonard Bloomfield to Marie Eichelberger, Apr. 21, 1923, LC, Q-11.

85. W. N. P. Barbellion, *The Journal of a Disappointed Man* (New York: G. H. Doran, 1919). See also Richmond H. Hillyar, *W. N. P. Barbellion* (London: Leonard Parsons, 1926).

86. M. Mead, "Notes for GCB," Nov. 6, 1947, LC, R-3.

87. MM to Martha Ramsey Mead, Oct. 15, 1922, LC, A-14.

88. MM to RFB, Sept. 6, 1938, R-7.

89. *BW*, p. 122; Mead, *Ruth Benedict*, p. 458; JH, p. 154.

90. MM to Martha Ramsey Mead, Oct. 15, 1922, LC, A-14.

91. Margaret Mead, "Notes After Reading *An Anthropologist at Work* Through," typed ms., file on biography of Benedict for Columbia Unversity, LC, I-235 (hereafter "After Reading *AW* Through").

92. *AW*, p. 4.

93. Idem.

94. JH, p. 154.

95. *AW*, p. 65.

7 / *"Unicorns at Sunrise": Anthropology, Poetry, Gender, and Ruth Benedict*

1. MM to Martha Ramsey Mead, Mar. 11, 1923, LC, A-14.

2. Margaret Mead, *Margaret Mead: Some Personal Views*, ed. Rhoda Métraux (New York: Walker, 1979), p. 287.

3. Ruth Benedict as quoted in *BW*, p. 122.

4. MM to Martha Ramsey Mead, Mar. 11, 1923, LC, A-14; *AW*, pp. 38–39. In *Patterns of Culture*, p. 19, Benedict recorded a variation on this story in which the chief told her about eating the plants of the desert and knowing their medicinal qualities— not about the hunt and the kill.

5. Mead, "After Reading *AW* Through."

6. Mead, *Some Personal Views*, p. 287. See Barbara G. Walker, *The Woman's Dictionary of Symbols and Sacred Objects* (San Francisco: Harper & Row, 1988), pp. 132–34; and Norris J. Lacey, ed., *The Arthurian Encyclopedia* (New York: Peter Bedrick Books, 1987), pp. 257–60.

7. Lindzey, p. 310.

8. Margaret Mead, "Group Intelligence Tests and Linguistic Disability Among Italian Children," *School and Society* 25 (April 16, 1927): 465–68.

9. Mead, "Out of the Things I Read," p. 44, and "A Certain Steadfastness," ms. draft article, *Redbook*, Jan. 1978, LC. See also Katherine Pease Routledge (Mrs. Scoresby Routledge), *The Mystery of Easter Island: The Story of an Expedition* (London: Hazell, Watson, & Viney, 1919).

10. Mead, "Speech of Acceptance" (National Achievement Award), *The Eleusis of Chi Omega* 42 (Sept. 1940): 397.

11. Mead, "A Certain Steadfastness"; MM to RFB, 1923, LC, S-3.

12. *AW*, p. 67.

13. RFB to MM, June 13, 1937, LC, S-5.

14. *AW*, p. 56, poem titled "New Year."

15. MFF, "Family Life of Ruth Fulton Benedict," p. 8. In a journal fragment, VC, Benedict dated Stanley's sexual rejection of her to 1926, when he fell in love with another woman.

16. JH, p. 427; and Regna Darnell, *Edward Sapir: Linguist, Anthropologist, Humanist* (Berkeley: University of California Press, 1990), p. 173.

17. On Sapir's voice and manner, see Robert McMillan interview with Stanley Newman, in McMillan, "The Study of Anthropology, 1931–37, at Columbia University and the University of Chicago" (Ph.D. diss., York University, 1986), pp. 93–94. On his wit, see Ruth Bunzel, "Edward Sapir," in Mead and Bunzel, *Golden Age of American Anthropology*, p. 439. On his intellect, see JH, p. 426; Alexander Goldenweiser, "Recent Trends in American Anthropology," *AA* 43 (1941): 158; and Alfred L. Kroeber, "Reflections on Edward Sapir, Scholar and Man," in *Edward Sapir: Appraisals of His Life and Work*, ed. Konrad Koerner (Amsterdam: John Benjamins, 1984), p. 131.

18. ES to RFB, April 8, 1924, PS; ES to RFB, Aug. 11, 1925, LC, S-15.

19. McMillan, "Study of Anthropology," p. 92, interview with Ruth Bunzel.

20. *AW*, pp. 57, 64.

21. *BW* draft, "Marriage and Graduate School," p. 14.

22. Goldfrank, *Notes on an Undirected Life*, p. 37.

23. *AW*, pp. 56–57, 62–63.

24. Marie Eichelberger to MM, Dec. 22, 1965, LC, B-4. Marguerite Arnold published a few poems. See "Clinic," "Divided," and "Joy," in *Poetry: A Magazine of Verse* (July 1925): 194–95.

25. *AW*, p. 67.

26. Ibid., p. 68.

27. RFB to MM, Sept. 10, 1928, LC, S-4.

28. RFB to MM, Aug. 1, 1925, LC, R-7.

29. Goldfrank, *Notes on an Undirected Life*, p. 21.

30. Mead, *Ruth Benedict*, p. 29. On Reichard, see Eleanor Leacock, "Gladys Amanda Reichard," in *Women Anthropologists: A Biographical Dictionary*, ed. Ute Gacs et al. (New York: Greenwood Press, 1988), pp. 303–9; and "Gladys A. Reichard—A Tribute," Barnard College memorial booklet, 1955, especially the statement by Frederica de Laguna that Reichard was shy and brusque.

31. MM to Geoffrey Gorer (GG), Jan. 17, 1939, SU.

32. Summerfield, "New Paltz Author"; JH, p. 358.

33. Lewis Mumford, *My Works and Days: A Personal Chronicle* (New York: Harcourt Brace Jovanovich, 1979), p. 80. The literature on Boas is voluminous. I have used, in particular, Douglas Cole, *Franz Boas: The Early Years, 1858–1906* (Seattle: University of Washington Press, 1999); Regna Darnell, *And Along Came Boas: Continuity and Revolution in American Anthropology* (Amsterdam: John Benjamins, 1998); George W. Stocking Jr., ed., *Volksgeist as Method and Ethic: Essays on Boasian Ethnography and the German Anthropological Tradition* (Madison: University of Wisconsin Press, 1996); Walter Rochs Goldschmidt, ed., *The Anthropology of Franz Boas: Essays on the Centennial of His Birth*, Memoirs of the American Anthropological Association, no. 89 (Washington, D.C.: American Anthropological Association, 1959); Robert H. Lowie, *Biographical Memoir of Franz Boas, 1858–1942* (Washington, D.C.: National Academy of Sciences, 1959); Alfred L. Kroeber et al., *Franz Boas: 1858–1942*, Memoirs of the American Anthropological Association, no. 61 (Washington, D.C.: American Anthropological Association, 1943); and Franz Boas, *Race, Language, and Culture* (New York: Macmillan, 1940), and *The Shaping of American Anthropology: A Franz Boas Reader*, ed. George W. Stocking Jr. (New York: Basic Books, 1947).

34. Alfred L. Kroeber, "Franz Boas: The Man," in *Franz Boas*, p. 23.

35. Rhoda Truax, *The Doctors Jacobi* (Boston: Little, Brown, 1952). See also Regina Markell Morantz-Sanchez, *Sympathy and Science: Women Physicians in American Medicine* (New York: Oxford University Press, 1985), pp. 190–202. On the masculinism of the polar explorers, see Lisa Bloom, *Gender on Ice: American Ideologies of Polar Expeditions* (Minneapolis: University of Minnesota Press, 1993).

36. In the most recent biography of Boas, Douglas Cole doesn't include anti-Semitism as a factor in Boas's difficult early career, which he attributes to bad luck, Boas's intransigence, and difficult administrators at the institutions that employed Boas, including the Field Museum in Chicago and Clark University. In *Freudian*

Fraud: The Malignant Effect of Freud's Theory on American Thought and Culture (New York: HarperCollins, 1992), pp. 40–55, E. Fuller Torrey has found anti-Semitism with regard to Boas in documents at the Museum of Natural History.

37. I have calculated these figures from Regna Diebold Darnell, "The Development of American Anthropology, 1879–1920: From the Bureau of Ethnology to Franz Boas" (Ph.D. diss., University of Pennsylvania, 1969), pp. 468–72. See also Adelin Linton and Charles Wagley, *Ralph Linton* (New York: Columbia, 1971), p. 2.

38. Franz Boas, "The Growth of Indian Mythologies," in *Race, Language, and Culture*, pp. 425–36; and Mead, *Ruth Benedict*, p. 21.

39. Mead, "Apprenticeship Under Boas," in Goldschmidt, *Anthropology of Franz Boas*, pp. 29–30.

40. *Letters of Edward Sapir to Robert H. Lowie*, privately published by Mrs. Luella Cole Lowie, 1965, and presented to the Peabody Museum Library, now Tozzer Library of Harvard University, Aug. 29, 1918; Feb. 21, 1921; and *AW*, p. 74.

41. Clyde Kluckhohn, "The Influence of Psychiatry on Anthropology in America During the Past One Hundred Years," in *Personal Character and Cultural Milieu*, ed. Douglas Haring, 3d rev. ed. (Syracuse: Syracuse University Press, 1956), p. 48.

42. Robert H. Lowie, *Primitive Society* (1920; New York: Liveright, 1947), p. ix. In the introduction to the 1947 edition, Lowie disavowed the phrase, explaining that he had used it because of the breakdown in Western values caused by World War I. For other writings of these anthropologists, see Alfred L. Kroeber, "The Superorganic," *AA* 19 (1917): 163–213; Paul Radin, *The Autobiography of a Winnebago Indian* (Berkeley: University of California Press, 1920); and Edward Sapir, *Selected Writings of Edward Sapir in Language, Culture, and Personality*, ed. David G. Mendelbaum (1949, Berkeley: University of California Press, 1963). On Clark Wissler, Mead's boss at the Museum of Natural History for many years, see Stanley A. Freed and Ruth S. Freed, "Clark Wissler and the Development of Anthropology in the United States," *AA* 85 (1983): 800–25.

43. Mead, "Apprenticeship Under Boas," p. 29.

44. Franz Boas to Emily Fogg Mead, July 30, 1925, Franz Boas Papers, APS.

45. Robert H. Lowie, *Culture and Ethnology* (New York: Douglas C. McCurtie, 1917), p. 5.

46. Mead, preface to the 1973 edition of *Coming of Age in Samoa* (New York: William Morrow, 1973), n.p.; and "Chi Omega Acceptance Speech," p. 399.

47. Mark C. Smith, "Knowledge for What: Social Science and the Debate Over Its Role in 1930s America" (Ph.D. diss., University of Texas, 1980), p. 17; Warren I. Susman, "The Thirties," in *The Development of an American Culture*, ed. Stanley Coben and Lorman Ratner (Englewood Cliffs, N.J.: Prentice-Hall, 1970), pp. 183–84. See also Carl N. Degler, *In Search of Human Nature: The Decline and Revival of Darwinism in American Social Thought* (New York: Oxford University Press, 1991), pp. 59–104.

48. On the background of these men, see in particular Leslie White, "The Social Organization of Ethnological Theory," *Rice University Studies* 52 (fall 1966): 1–66. On the German-Jewish community in New York City, see descriptions of it by Alfred Kroeber and Rhoda Métraux, who grew up in it. Alfred L. Kroeber, "The Making of the Man," in *Carl Alsberg, Scientist at Large*, ed. Joseph S. Davis (Stanford: Stanford

University Press, 1948), pp. 3–22; and Métraux, "Life History," LC, R-16. See also Elazar Barkan, *The Retreat of Scientific Racism: Changing Concepts of Race in Britain and the United States Between the World Wars* (New York: Cambridge University Press, 1992), pp. 90–95. In *A Time for Gathering: The Second Migration, 1820–1880* (Baltimore: Johns Hopkins University Press, 1992), pp. 220–26, Hasia R. Diner downplays the German-Jewish community's impacts on the larger Jewish society. Indeed, not all Boas's Jewish students came from it. For a view of the ironies in the work of Boas and his Jewish students confronting the "compounding power" of modernity, see Karen King, "Surviving Modernity: Jewishness, Fieldwork, and the Roots of American Anthropology in the Twentieth Century" (Ph.D. diss., Univ. of Texas, Austin, 2000). This work was not available to me in researching and writing this book.

49. Rosenberg, "Changing the Subject"; Suzanne Klingenstein, *Jews in the American Academy, 1900–1940: The Dynamics of Intellectual Assimilation* (New Haven: Yale University Press, 1991), pp. 1–8, 102, 607; Robert F. Murphy, "Anthropology at Columbia: A Reminiscence," *Dialectical Anthropology* 16 (1991): 65–75; Harold S. Wechsler, *The Qualified Student: A History of Selective College Admission in America* (New York: John Wiley & Sons, 1977), pp. 133–60; Robert H. Lowie, "Boas Once More," *AA* 58 (1956): 160; and Alfred L. Kroeber, "Pliny Earle Goddard," *AA* 31 (1929). With the exception of Sapir, none of the Boasian anthropologists has been the subject of a scholarly biography. See Darnell, *Edward Sapir.* For overviews of the lives of some of them, see Robert F. Murphy, *Robert H. Lowie* (New York: Columbia University Press, 1972); Julian H. Steward, *Alfred Kroeber* (New York: Columbia University Press, 1973); and Stanley Diamond, "Paul Radin," in *Totems and Teachers: Perspectives on the History of Anthropology,* ed. Sydel Silverman (New York: Columbia University Press, 1981), pp. 67–97. Their obituaries in *AA* are also useful.

50. Radin, *Method and Theory of Ethnology,* p. 97.

51. Mead, "Apprenticeship Under Boas," p. 30.

52. *AW,* p. 346.

53. A. L. Kroeber, "Franz Boas," pp. 23–24; Goldfrank, *An Undiscovered Life,* p. 18. Mead remembered that the graduate students in anthropology in 1922 included Benedict, Isabel Carter, Melville Herskovits, Irving Hallowell, and a man whose sister married Alexander Goldenweiser. See George Eaton Simpson, *Melville J. Herskovits* (New York: Columbia University Press, 1973), p. 2. See also Elsie Clews Parsons, "Read in Franz Boas Class at Barnard," APS, and Deacon, *Elsie Clews Parsons,* pp. 97–110.

54. See the listing of the council members in *AA,* 1925, vol. 27.

55. I describe Bunzel and Goldfrank from reading their work, from others' comments about them, and from my viewing of their video interviews in the "Daughters of the Desert" project at the Wenner-Gren foundation offices in New York City in the summer of 1999. Jennifer Fox did the interviews in 1985.

56. Lowie, *History of Ethnological Theory,* p. 134. See also Nancy J. Parezo, "Anthropology: The Welcoming Science," in *Hidden Scholars: Women Anthropologists and the Native American Southwest,* ed. Nancy J. Parezo (Albuquerque: University of New Mexico Press, 1983), pp. 3–37.

57. Mead, introduction to Mead and Bunzel, *Golden Age of Anthropology,* pp. 5–6.

58. Michael Rogin, *Blackface, White Noise: Jewish Immigrants in the Hollywood Melting Pot* (Berkeley: University of California Press, 1996), pp. 68–69. On Jewish "self-

loathing" and the history of effeminacy in this era, see Rogin, *Blackface;* and Sander Gilman, *The Jew's Body* (New York: Routledge, 1991), pp. 81–82. See also David D. Gilmore, *Misogyny: The Male Malady* (Philadelphia: University of Pennsylvania Press, 2001); and Alan Sinfield, *The Wilde Century: Effeminacy, Oscar Wilde, and the Queer Moment* (New York: Columbia University Press, 1994). Sinfield traces the connection between effeminacy and homosexuality, commonly made in the United States in the twentieth century, to the Wilde trial in 1895. See also Richard Hofstadter, *Anti-Intellectualism in American Life* (New York: Alfred A. Knopf, 1963).

59. Robert H. Lowie, *Robert H. Lowie, Ethnologist: A Personal Record* (Berkeley: University of California Press, 1959), p. 83.

60. *AW,* p. 179; Alexander A. Goldenweiser, *Early Civilization: An Introduction to Anthropology* (New York: Alfred A. Knopf, 1922). Goldenweiser derived the term "androcentric" from Charlotte Perkins Gilman, *The Man-Made World; Or, Our Androcentric Culture* (New York: Charlton, 1911); Mead, in her introduction to Mead and Bunzel, *Golden Age of Anthropology,* p. 8, identified his 1922 work as the first textbook in anthropology published in the United States.

61. Mead, "After Reading *AW* Through." Lowie and Goldenweiser were close; Lowie discussed Goldenweiser's chronic infidelity in his letters to his sister. See Robert H. Lowie Papers, UCB. On Goldenweiser's affair with an Iroquois woman, see William Cowan et al., *New Perspectives in Language, Culture, and Personality: Proceedings of the Edward Sapir Centenary Conference* (Amsterdam: John Benjamins, 1986), p. 229, and Deacon, *Elsie Clews Parsons,* p. 432.

62. Alexander Goldenweiser, "Sex and Primitive Society," in *Sex in Civilization,* ed. V. F. Calverton and S. D. Schmalhausen (Garden City, N.Y.: Garden City Publishing, 1929), pp. 52–66, and "Men and Women as Creators," in *Our Changing Morality: A Symposium,* ed. Freda Kirchwey (New York: Albert and Charles Boni, 1924), pp. 129–43, reprinted in Goldenweiser, *History, Psychology, and Culture* (London: K. Paul, Trench, Trubner, 1933).

63. Goldenweiser, "Sex and Primitive Society," p. 53. Alexander Goldenweiser, *Anthropology: An Introduction to Primitive Culture* (1936; New York: F. S. Crofts, 1946), p. 142.

64. See *Letters of Edward Sapir to Robert H. Lowie,* passim.

65. Mead, *Ruth Benedict,* p. 25.

66. Radin, *Method and Theory,* pp. 177–80. In a letter to Benedict, Radin criticized her for not taking history into account in her dissertation. See Paul Radin to RFB, Dec. 24, 1924, VC. On one occasion he expressed the opinion that women shouldn't be in the professions at all. Mrs. Henry Cowell to MM, Feb. 23, 1973, Jane Howard Papers, CU.

67. T. Kroeber, *Alfred Kroeber,* p. 264.

68. Mead, "After Reading *AW* Through."

69. A. L. Kroeber, "The Superorganic"; Alfred L. Kroeber, "On the Principle of Order in Civilization as Exemplified by Changes of Fashion," AA 21 (1919): 235–63.

70. See T. Kroeber, *Alfred Kroeber,* p. 264; RFB to MM, Nov. 6, 1928, LC, S-5. For comments linking his distanced behavior to masculinism in anthropology, see Kluckhohn, "Influence of Psychiatry," pp. 490–91. See also Eric Wolfe, "Kroeber," in Silverman, *Totems and Teachers,* p. 37.

71. Robert H. Lowie, with Leta S. Hollingworth, "Science and Feminism," *Scientific Monthly* 5 (1919): 277–84.

72. Robert Lowie to Risa Lowie, March 1, 1918, Robert H. Lowie Papers, UCB.

73. Robert H. Lowie, "Religion," in *The Making of Man: An Outline of Anthropology*, ed. V. F. Calverton (1924; New York: Modern Library, 1931), pp. 744–57; Lowie to Paul Radin, Oct. 2, 1920, Lowie Papers, UCB.

74. Robert Lowie to Risa Lowie, March 1, 1918, Robert H. Lowie Papers, UCB.

75. Alfred L. Kroeber, "Heredity, Environment, and Civilization: Factors Controlling Human Behavior as Illustrated by the Natives of the Southwestern United States," *Scientific American Supplement* 86 (Oct. 5, 1918): 211–12.

76. Lang, *Men as Women*, p. 31.

77. See Richard Handler, "The Dainty and the Hungry Man: Literature and Anthropology in the Work of Edward Sapir," *History of Anthropology* 1 (1983): 208–31.

78. Edward Sapir, "The Woman's Man," *New Republic*, Sept. 16, 1916, p. 167.

79. Toni Flores, "The Poetry of Edward Sapir," *Dialectical Anthropology* 11 (1968): 159; and Deacon, *Elsie Clews Parsons*, p. 260, quoting from E. Sapir to L. White, March 15, 1928, Leslie White Papers, University of Michigan.

80. *AW*, p. 343.

81. *BW* draft, "Marriage and Graduate School," p. 9. See also T. George Harris, "About Ruth Benedict and Her Lost Manuscript," *Psychology Today* 4 (June 1970): 51–52.

82. Abraham Maslow to RFB, Dec. 30, 1939; March 6, 1940, VC, 32.3.

83. ES to RFB, June 25, 1911; *AW*, pp. 49–53; ES to RFB, Aug. 7, 1923, PS.

84. Lowie, *Robert H. Lowie*, p. 135.

85. In *Cultural Margins: Women Intellectuals, Modernism, and Difference: Transatlantic Culture, 1919–1945* (Cambridge: Cambridge University Press, 1997), Alice Gambrell democraticizes the term "intellectual" to include artists like Frida Kahlo and poets like H.D., overlooking its historical connection to a rational, "male" model. For that meaning, see Thomas Bender, "The Emergence of the New York Intellectuals," in Bender, *Intellect and Public Life: Essays on the Social History of Academic Intellectuals in the United States* (Baltimore: Johns Hopkins University Press, 1993), pp. 80–88.

86. Benedict, *Patterns of Culture*, pp. 266–67.

87. Mead included Benedict's "The Uses of Cannibalism" in *AW*, pp. 44–48.

88. Mead reprinted excerpts from Benedict's "A Brief Sketch of Serrano Culture," in *AW*, pp. 213–21. In my identification of Benedict's "monsters," I have been aided by Elizabeth Diann Stassinos, "Ruthlessly: Ruth Benedict's Pseudonyms and the Art of Science Writ Large" (Ph.D. diss., Univ. of Virginia, 1994).

89. RFB to MM, Feb. 10, 1933, LC, S-5.

90. Stassinos, "Ruthlessly," p. 176; Joseph Conrad, *The Nigger of the "Narcissus"* (1897; New York: W. W. Norton, 1979), pp. 3, 9, 15.

91. Jayne E. Maret, *Women Editing Modernism: "Little" Magazines & Literary History* (Lexington: University Press of Kentucky, 1995); William Drake, *The First Wave: Women Poets in America, 1915–1945* (New York: Macmillan, 1987); and Louise Bogan, *Achievement in American Poetry* (Chicago: Gateway Editions, dist. by Henry Regnery, 1951), p. 53. On the sexism of the modernists, see Drake, *First Wave*; and Sandra M.

Gilbert and Susan Gubar, *No Man's Land: The Place of the Woman Writer in the Twentieth Century* (New Haven: Yale University Press, 1994).

92. Gloria Bowles, *Louise Bogan's Aesthetic of Limitation* (Bloomington: Indiana University Press, 1987), pp. 20–23. On the sentimentalism of Millay, see Elizabeth Frank, "A Doll's Heart: The Girl in the Poetry of Edna St. Vincent Millay and Louise Bogan," in *Critical Essays on Louise Bogan*, ed. Martha Collins (Boston: G. K. Hall, 1984), pp. 128–49. In her insightful " 'A Queer Lot' and the Lesbian Talent: Amy Lowell, Gertrude Stein, and H.D.," in *Challenging Boundaries: Literary Periodization in the United States*, ed. Joyce W. Warren and Margaret Dickie (Athens: University of Georgia Press, 2000), pp. 62–90, Susan McCabe uses the term "modernist antimodernism" to characterize these three poets. Benedict drew from their "lesbian" tradition, but much of her poetry doesn't include lesbian themes. See also Marilyn Farwell, "Toward a Definition of the Lesbian Literary Imagination," *Signs* 14 (autumn 1998): 100–18; Susan Stanford Friedman, *Penelope's Web: Gender, Modernity, H.D.'s Fiction* (Cambridge: Cambridge University Press, 1990); and Gilian Hanscombe and Virginia L. Smyers, *Writing for Their Lives: The Modernist Women, 1910–1940* (London: Women's Press, 1987).

93. Susan Gubar, "Mother, Maiden, and the Marriage of Death: Women Writers and Ancient Myth," *Women's Studies* 6 (1979): 301–15.

94. Timothy Materer, *Modernist Alchemy: Poetry and the Occult* (Ithaca: Cornell University Press, 1995), p. 53; Hans Biedermann, *Dictionary of Symbolism: Cultural Icons and the Meanings Behind Them*, trans. James Hulbert (New York: Facts on File, 1992), p. 360; and Marina Warner, *Alone of All Her Sex: The Myth and the Cult of the Virgin Mary* (New York: Alfred A. Knopf, 1976), p. 201.

95. See Terence Brown, *The Life of W. B. Yeats: A Critical Biography* (Oxford, U.K.: Blackwell, 1999). Materer, *Modernist Alchemy*, contends that the French symbolists initiated the occult movement, but because they took a vow of secrecy, little is known about their involvement. See also Kathleen Raine, *Yeats, the Tarot and the Golden Dawn* (Dublin: Dolmen Press, 1972); and Virginia Moore, *The Unicorn: William Butler Yeats' Search for Reality* (New York: Macmillan, 1954). Christian Rosenkreutz supposedly founded the Rosicrucians, a secret sect, in the fifteenth century. Theosophy was founded in 1875 by Madame Helena Blavatsky, a Russian aristocrat living in the United States who was down on her luck.

96. *BW* draft, "Marriage and Graduate School," p. 19. W. B. Yeats, *Essays* (New York: Macmillan, 1924). On Yeats's theory of masks and masking, see Janis Tedesco Haswell, *Pressed Against Divinity: W. B. Yeats's Feminine Masks* (DeKalb: Northern Illinois University Press, 1997).

97. *AW*, pp. 481–82. See also W. B. Yeats, "The Unicorn from the Stars" (1908), in *The Variorum Edition of the Plays of W. B. Yeats*, ed. Russell K. Alspach (New York: Macmillan, 1966), pp. 648–711.

98. See Osterud, *Bonds of Community*, pp. 109–13.

99. RFB to MM, Feb. 14, 1936, LC, S-5.

100. Virginia Woolf, *A Room of One's Own* (New York: Harcourt, Brace, 1929), p. 102. Both Mead and Benedict regularly read Woolf. See MM to RFB, Jan. 28, 1929, LC, S-3; MM to Eleanor Pelham Kortheuer, July 10, 1947, LC, R-10. On the tradition of androgyny in Western literature, see Warren Stevenson, *Romanticism and the*

Androgynous Sublime (Madison, N.J.: Fairleigh Dickinson University Press, 1996), and especially Diane Hoeveler, *Romantic Androgyny: The Women Within* (University Park: Pennsylvania State University Press, 1990). Hoeveler views the tradition in terms of a splitting between male and female.

8 / Free Love and Samoa

1. Dorothy Dunbar Bromley, "Feminist—New Style," *Harper's* 45 (Oct. 1927): 552–60; Lorine Pruette, "The Flapper," in Calverton and Schmalhausen, *New Generation*, p. 587. On the cultural rebellion of the 1920s, I have used Rachel Standish, "What Is Modish Is Doomed: Fashion and American Feminism from the 1910s to the Early 1930s" (Ph.D. diss., University of Southern California, 2000); Ann Douglas, *Terrible Honesty: Mongrel Manhattan in the 1920s* (New York: Farrar, Straus & Giroux, 1995); Rick Beard and Leslie Cohen Berlowitz, eds., *Greenwich Village: Culture and Counterculture* (New Brunswick, N.J.: published for the Museum of the City of New York by Rutgers University Press, 1993); Christina Clare Simmons, " 'Marriage in the Modern Manner': Sexual Radicalism and Reform in America, 1914–1941" (Ph.D. diss., Brown University, 1982); Paula S. Fass, *The Damned and the Beautiful: American Youth in the 1920s* (New York: Oxford University Press, 1977); Malcolm Cowley, *Exile's Return: A Literary Odyssey of the 1920s* (1934; New York: Viking, 1956); Frederick Lewis Allen, *Only Yesterday: An Informal History of the Nineteen-Twenties* (New York: Harper & Bros., 1931); and Floyd Dell, *Love in Greenwich Village* (New York: G. H. Doran, 1926).

2. Phyllis Blanchard, "Sex in the Adolescent Girl," in Calverton and Schmalhausen, *Sex in Civilization*, pp. 548–49. See also Laura Doan, "Passing Fashions: Female Masculinities in the 1920s," *Feminist Studies* 24 (fall 1998): 663–700; Erin G. Carlston, " 'A Finer Differentiation': Female Homosexuality and the American Medical Community, 1926–1940," in Rosario, *Science and Homosexualities*, p. 178; Martha Vicinus, "The Adolescent Boy: Fin de Siècle Femme Fatale?," *Journal of the History of Sexuality* 5 (summer 1994): 90–114. Margaret Mead, review of *The Evolution of Modern Marriage*, by F. Muller-Lyer, *Birth Control Review* 14 (Dec. 1930); Samuel D. Schmalhausen, "The Sexual Revolution," in Calverton and Schmalhausen, *Sex in Civilization*, pp. 349–436; Miriam Allen de Ford, "The Feminist's Future," *New Republic* 46 (Sept. 19, 1928); Ralph Werther [pseud.], *The Female-Impersonators* (1922; New York: Arno Press, 1975), pp. 153, 201. Psychoanalysts noted the homosexual resonance of the flapper look. See André Tridon, *Psychoanalysis and Love* (Garden City: Garden City Publishing, 1922), p. 184; and Wilhelm Stekel, *Bi-sexual Love*, trans. James S. Van Testaar (1922; New York: Emerson Books, 1950). p. 63.

3. Margaret Mead, draft ms., "Comments on the *Redbook* Report on Female Sexuality," pp. 12–13.

4. The criticism of schoolgirl crushes can be found in a number of discourses. For psychologists' criticism, see Phyllis Blanchard and Carolyn Manasses, *New Girls for Old* (1930; New York: Macauley, 1937), pp. 60, 96–111; for educators', see Willystine Goodsell, *The Education of Women*; for psychoanalysts', see Tridon, *Psychoanalysis and Love*, pp. 179, 187. Blanchard, trained by G. Stanley Hall, headed the Philadelphia Child Guidance Clinic; Goodsell taught at Columbia's Teachers College.

On Victorian sex manuals, see Seidman, *Romantic Longings*, p. 37. On old and new attitudes toward sex technique, see Peter Laipson, " 'Kiss Without Shame, for She Desires It': Sexual Foreplay in American Marital Advice Literature, 1900–1925," *Journal of Social History* 29 (March 1996): 508–19; Samuel D. Schmalhausen, *Why We Misbehave* (New York: Macauley, 1928), p. 30; and Iwan Bloch, *Anthropological Studies in the Strange Sexual Practices of All Races in All Ages*, trans. Keene Wallis (New York: Anthropological Press, 1933), p. 32. Abraham Brill, a noted Freudian analyst, stated that he had been raised to believe that fellatio "softened the brain." Sigmund Freud, *Leonardo da Vinci: A Study in Psychosexuality*, trans. A. A. Brill (New York: Vintage Books, 1947), p. 8. According to Mead, in her "Comments on the *Redbook* Report on Female Sexuality," p. 1, all unusual forms of sex were disapproved and often forbidden by law.

On "compulsory heterosexuality," see Adrienne Rich, "Compulsory Heterosexuality and Lesbian Existence," *Signs: Journal of Woman in Culture and Society* 5 (summer 1980): 630–60. As early as 1914 Sandor Ferenczi found what he called "compulsive heterosexuality" widespread. See Clara Thompson, "Changing Concepts of Homosexuality in Psychoanalysis," in *Women: The Variety and Meaning of Their Sexual Experience*, ed. A. M. Krich (New York: Dell, 1953), pp. 231–47. See also Rayna Rapp and Ellen Ross, "The Twenties' Backlash: Compulsory Heterosexuality, the Consumer Family and the Waning of Feminism," in *Class, Race, and Sex: The Dynamics of Control*, ed. Amy Swerdlow and Hanna Lessinger (Boston: G. K. Hall, 1983), pp. 93–107; and Christina Simmons, "Companionate Marriage and the Lesbian Threat," *Frontiers* 4 (1979): 54–59.

5. Ruth Benedict, "America Converts to Peace," unpub. typescript, VC.

6. June Sochen, in *The New Woman: Feminism in Greenwich Village, 1910–1920* (New York: Quadrangle Books, 1972), pp. 119–25, concludes that by 1920 most of the prewar Greenwich Village radical women had died or moved away. See also Cowley, *Exile's Return*; Daniel Aaron, "Disturbing the Peace: Radicals in Greenwich Village, 1920–1930," in Beard and Berlowitz, *Greenwich Village*, pp. 229–42; and Gorham Munson, *The Awakening Twenties: A Memoir-History of a Literary Period* (Baton Rouge: Louisiana State University Press, 1985).

7. John Dewey, *Human Nature and Conduct: An Introduction to Social Psychology* (New York: Henry Holt, 1922), p. 93.

8. Margaret Mead, preface to the 1975 edition of *Growing Up in New Guinea: A Comparative Study of Primitive Education* (1930; New York: Morrow, 1975). p. v.

9. Margaret Mead, "The Waste of Plutocracy," unpub. ms., 1924, LC, R-12.

10. MM to RFB, Aug. 30, 1924, *AW,* p. 285. (This letter discusses Randolph Bourne's *The History of a Literary Radical and Other Papers*, published in 1920.) My comments about Dewey and the intellectuals of the 1920s are based on Westbrook, *John Dewey*; Leonard Wilcox, *V. F. Calverton: Radical in the American Grain* (Philadelphia: Temple University Press, 1992); James T. Kloppenberg, *Uncertain Victory: Social Democracy and Progressivism in European and American Thought, 1870–1920* (New York: Oxford University Press, 1986); and especially Casey Nelson Blake, *Beloved Community: The Cultural Criticism of Randolph Bourne, Van Wyck Brooks, Waldo Frank, and Lewis Mumford* (Chapel Hill: University of North Carolina Press, 1990). Mead notes the influence of Horace Kallen on her in *And Keep Your Powder Dry*, p. 325. I quote Horace M. Kallen, *Culture and Democracy in the United States: Studies in the Group Psychology of the American Peoples* (New York: Boni & Liveright, 1924), pp. 11, 61, 121.

11. Beatrice Forbes-Robertson Hale, "Women in Transition," in Calverton and Schmalhausen, *Sex in Civilization*, p. 72.

12. Mrs. Havelock Ellis, *The New Horizon in Love and Life* (London: A. & C. Black, 1921), Havelock Ellis, *Little Essays on Love and Virtue* (New York: G. H. Doran, 1922); Margaret Sanger, *Woman and the New Race* (New York: Brentano, 1920), p. 117; and Ben B. Lindsey and Wainright Evans, *The Revolt of Modern Youth* (Garden City, N.Y.: Garden City Publishing, 1925). For divorce figures, see Lindsey and Evans, p. 211, and also Beatrice Hinkle, "Chaos of Modern Marriage," *Harper's New Monthly Magazine* 152 (Dec. 1925): 1–13.

13. Schmalhausen, *Why We Misbehave*, pp. 7, 39. White's comment is contained in his introduction to this work. Wilcox, *Calverton*, p. 69, identifies Calverton as a forerunner of Frankfurt-school philosophers like Herbert Marcuse, who combined Freud with Marx.

14. Fass, *The Damned and the Beautiful*, p. 266; Caroline F. Ware, *Greenwich Village, 1920–1930: A Comment on American Civilization in the Postwar Years* (Boston: Houghton Mifflin, 1935), p. 255; and Benedict, *Patterns of Culture*, p. 36. See also Dorr, *Woman of Fifty*, p. 448; Ernest Burgess, "Sociological Aspects of Sex Life," in *The Sex Life of the Unmarried Adult: An Inquiry into and an Interpretation of Current Sex Practices*, ed. Ira S. Wile (New York: Vanguard, 1934), pp. 116–54; Robert Staughton Lynd and Helen Merrell Lynd, *Middletown: A Study in American Culture* (New York: Harcourt, Brace, 1929), pp. 140–41; and William Cunningham, *Are Petting Parties Dangerous?* (Gerard, Kans.: Haldemann-Julius, 1928).

15. Faderman, *Odd Girls and Twilight Lovers*, pp. 62–92.

16. Dell, *Women as World Builders*, pp. 78–79.

17. W. F. Robie, *The Art of Love* (Boston: R. G. Badger, 1921), pp. 330–32. Mead's praise for Robie is contained in her review of Kenneth Ingram's *The Modern Attitude to the Sex Problem* and Helena Wright's *The Sex Factor in Marriage* in *Birth Control Review* 15 (April 1931): 120–21.

18. Mead, review cited in n. 17, above. Jeffrey Meyers, *Edmund Wilson: A Biography* (Boston: Houghton Mifflin, 1995), p. 65; JH, p. 426; CTK to MM, thanking her for sending the Ellis and Robie books, undated letter, 1930s, LC, B-9.

19. Havelock Ellis, *Art of Love* and *Sex in Relation to Society*, in *Studies in the Psychology of Sex*, vol. 4, pp. 218, 507–75; and Margaret Mead, "Sex and Censorship in Contemporary Society," in *New World Writing* (New York: Mentor, 1953), pp. 7–24.

20. Mead, *Coming of Age in Samoa*, p. 105.

21. Ibid., p. 172; JH, p. 428.

22. MM to Elizabeth Mead, Jan. 10, 1926, LC, Q-10.

23. Cressman, *Golden Journey*, p. 127. Sapir, "The Discipline of Sex," quotes Mead anonymously.

24. Fishbein, *Rebels in Bohemia*, p. 98.

25. ES to RFB, Aug. 11, 1925, LC, S-15.

26. Ethel [Goldsmith] to MM, [1935], LC R-9.

27. *BW* draft, "Marriage and Graduate School"; Cressman, *Golden Journey*, p. 98; *BW*, p. 126. In the introduction to the 1962 edition of *Male and Female*, Mead wrote: "In the 1920s an attempt to change the position of women was accompanied by an insistence on women's need for sexual climaxes comparable to men's, and the demand

that women respond to men became a burdensome demand on them to behave like musical instruments rather than full human beings."

28. Cressman, *Golden Journey*, p. 98.

29. JH, p. 279.

30. Interview with Luther Cressman, CU; RFB to MM, Jan. 28, 1926, LC, S-4.

31. See *BW* draft, "Energy," p. 12.

32. See Léonie Adams to RFB, Dec. 21, 1925, Léonie Adams–William Troy Papers, YU.

33. Reinterview with Luther Cressman, CU; RFB to MM, Nov. 17, 1928, LC, S-5.

34. Mead, "Life History," LC, S-9; MM to RFB, May 10, 1929, LC, S-5. In the 1930s Ethel (Goldsmith), Mead's friend who slept on her couch, wrote to her that if she didn't write she might send the newspapers "a full account of the unrequited homosexual love my strongly bi-sexual nature requires." Ethel to MM, LC, R-9, undated.

35. *BW* draft, "One to Many and Many to One"; JH, p. 217; CM, interview with Karsten Stapelfeldt.

36. Harriet Monroe, "Poetry Recitals in New York City," *Poetry* 28 (June 1926): 158. On Benedict and Mead's poetry circle, see Elizabeth Frank, *Louise Bogan: A Portrait* (New York: Alfred A. Knopf, 1985), pp. 87–89, which includes material from interviews with Mead. The only contemporary account of their readings is in a brief entry in Benedict's diary, Jan. 29, 1926, when Mead was on Samoa. Léonie Adams, Eda Lou Walton, Genevieve Taggard, and Edmund Wilson were present, in addition to Benedict, and Louise Bogan read. Benedict described Bogan, a tall brunette, as "a lovely figure—read with an accent of disdain, very becoming." *AW*, p. 77.

37. Rosalind Baker Wilson, *Near the Magician: A Memoir of My Father, Edmund Wilson* (New York: Grove Weidenfeld, 1989); and MM to RFB, 1929, LC, S-3. I have also relied on Meyers, *Edmund Wilson*, and Desley Deacon, "Me, Myself, and I: Mary McCarthy's Search for Her Self," unpub. paper, Organization of American Historians Convention, April 2001.

38. Hannah Kahn to MM, July 20, 1923, LC, C-1.

39. Marie Eichelberger to MM, Aug. 14, 1937, LC, R-7.

40. *AW*, p. 84; "Parlor Car—Santa Fe," RFB, unpub. poetry file, VC, 48.14.

41. RFB diary entry, Jan. 18, 1926, in handwritten version of diary, VC, 37.

42. *AW*, p. xvii.

43. *BW* draft, "Marriage and Graduate School," p. 19.

44. On the angel Gabriel, see Rosemary Guiley, *Encyclopedia of Angels* (New York: Facts on File, 1996), p. 69. The symbols in this poem are multifaceted, with the tree also referring to the classical god Dionysus, who, like Christ, was sacrificed in Near Eastern rituals.

45. *AW*, p. 486.

46. MM to RFB, Sept. 20, 1925, LC, S-3.

47. RFB to MM, Nov. 20, 1925, LC, S-4.

48. Marguerite [Arnold] to RFB, June 27, 1927, VC.

49. RFB to MM, Aug. 3, 1938, LC, S-5.

50. *AW*, p. 89. To decode the flower imagery in Benedict's and Mead's poetry, I have used F. F. Rockwell et al., eds. *10,000 Garden Questions: Answered by Fifteen*

Experts, rev. ed. (Garden City, N.Y.: Doubleday, 1952), and *Taylor's Encyclopedia of Gardening, Horticulture, and Garden Design* (Boston: Houghton Mifflin, 1936).

51. *AW* draft, p. 5, LC, I-90.

52. RFB to MM, Oct. 27, 1925, LC, S-4.

53. Mead was listed in the program as giving a paper on rank in Polynesia, but she remembered giving a paper on tattooing, a sexualized subject. See Mead, *Social Organization of Manu'a*, 2d ed. (Honolulu: Bishop Museum Press, 1969), p. xiv.

54. JH, pp. 426, 448; ES to RFB, Aug. 23, 1924, PS.

55. MM to RFB, Sept. 3, 1928, LC, S-3.

56. Ruth Benedict, "Toward a Social Psychology," *Nation* 119 (July 9, 1924): 50–51; and Edward Sapir, "Culture, Genuine and Spurious," *American Journal of Sociology* 29 (1924): 401–29.

57. On the interest of the anthropologists in schizophrenia and on the history of the condition in general, see S. P. Fullinwider, *Technicians of the Finite: The Rise and Decline of the Schizophrenic in American Thought, 1840–1960* (Westport, Conn.: Greenwood, 1982).

58. See C. G. Seligman, "Anthropology and Psychology: A Study of Some Points of Contact," *Journal of the Royal Anthropological Institute of Great Britain and Ireland* 54 (Jan.–June 1924): 13–46. C. G. Jung's book explaining his typologies was translated into English by H. Godwin Baynes and published in 1923 as *Psychological Types: Or, The Psychology of Individuation* (London: K. Paul, Trench, Trubner, 1923; New York: Pantheon Books, 1964). Frank McLynn, in *Carl Gustav Jung* (New York: St. Martin's Press, 1997), pp. 258–67, notes that the Freudians harshly criticized Jung's categories and he quickly abandoned them.

59. *AW*, pp. 248–61.

60. Constance Long, "A Psycho-Analytic Study of the Basis of Character," in *Proceedings of the International Conference of Women Physicians*, vol. 9: *Moral Codes and Personality* (New York: Women's Press, 1919), pp. 67–82. On Hinkle, see Beatrice Hinkle, "Arbitrary Use of the Terms 'Masculine' and 'Feminine,' " in idem, and *The Re-Creating of the Individual: A Study of Psychological Types and Their Relation to Psychoanalysis* (New York: Dodd, Mead, 1923). Phyllis Blanchard describes Hinkle as a major thinker on the nature of the sexes, in "The Sex Problem in the Light of Modern Psychology," in *Taboo and Genetics: A Study of the Biological, Sociological, and Psychological Foundation of the Family*, ed. M. M. Knight, Iva Lowther Peters, and Phyllis Blanchard (New York: Moffat, Yard, 1920), pp. 217–18, as does Alice Beal Parsons, in *Woman's Dilemma* (New York: Thomas Y. Crowell, 1926), pp. 72–74. See Alice Wittenstein, "The Feminist Uses of Psychoanalysis: Beatrice M. Hinkle and the Foreshadowing of Modern Feminism in the United States," *Journal of Women's History* 10 (summer 1998): 38–62. Nathan G. Hale, Jr., in *The Rise and Crisis of Psychoanalysis in the United States: Freud and the Americans, 1917–1985* (New York: Oxford University Press, 1995), pp. 68–69, identifies Hinkle as the psychiatrist for New York City intellectuals. For Ruth Benedict's advice to Edward Sapir about Hinkle, see ES to RFB, March 17, 1924, PS. Mead's therapist, Gotthard Booth, was a Jungian.

61. Mead, *Anthropologists and What They Do*, p. 115.

62. See *AW*, p. 288.

63. *BW* draft, "Felicities," p. 15.

64. Boas to MM, July 14, 1923, LC, B-2; *BW* draft, "Felicities," p. 15. In 1927 Mead wrote to Reo Fortune that when she told Boas she was divorcing Luther Cressman, he called her "pathological," with an "anti-sex complex." MM to RFF, Sept. 30, 1927, LC, R-4.

65. *Philadelphia Public Ledger,* Aug. 25, 1925; Honolulu, name of newspaper torn off, Sept. 28, 1925, Misc. Clipping File, LC, L-3, Henry Romeike Press Clipping Bureau, NYC.

66. MM to RFB, Mar. 20, 1926, LC, S-3; Terry, *An American Obsession,* p. 136; and Sophie Aberle and George W. Corner, *Twenty-five Years of Sex History: History of the National Research Council's Committee on Research on Problems of Sex, 1922–1947* (Philadelphia: W. B. Saunders, 1953).

67. Margaret Mead, introduction to *Margaret Mead: The Complete Bibliography, 1925–1975,* ed. Joan Gordan (The Hague: Mouton, 1976), p. 2.

68. JH, p. 427.

69. MM to RFB, Dec. 24, 1925, LC, S-3.

70. MM to RFB, July 16, 1925, LC, S-3.

71. ES to RFB, Aug. 11, Sept. 1, 1925, Sept. 1925, LC, S-15.

72. ES to RFB, Aug. 5, Aug. 18, Oct. 14, 1925, LC, S-15.

73. ES to RFB, Oct. 14, 1925.

74. Cressman, *Golden Journey,* p. 130.

75. RFB to MM, Nov. 5, 1925, LC, S-4.

76. RFB to MM, Sept. 2, 1925, LC, R-7.

77. MM to RFB, July 7, 15, [July], 1925, LC, S-3; RFB to MM, Sept. 2, 1925, LC, R-7.

78. MM to Martha Ramsey Mead, Aug. 3, 1925, LC, A-17.

79. RFB to MM, Aug. 24, 1925; *AW,* p. 291.

80. Freeman's use of sources is selective; he overlooks the large amount of data in the Mead Papers that disproves his argument. See Derek Freeman, *Margaret Mead and Samoa,* and *The Fateful Hoaxing of Margaret Mead.* Restudies of Mead's Samoan research support her conclusions. Women on Ta'u openly discussed sex techniques with Bonnie Nardi in 1984, and Nardi found many illegitimate children there. She didn't doubt Mead's findings about adolescent girls "in the slightest," although she doubted that their parents condoned their free sexuality. See Bonnie Nardi, "The Height of Her Powers: Margaret Mead's Samoa," *Feminist Studies* 10 (summer 1984): 323–37. Lowell Holmes found that the Samoan women wouldn't discuss sex with him because he was a man, suggesting that Freeman had the same difficulty. He also disputed Freeman's conclusion that the Samoans were violent. See Lowell Don Holmes, *Quest for the Real Samoa: The Mead/Freeman Controversy and Beyond* (South Hadley, Mass.: Bergin & Garvey, 1987). The most recent examination of the controversy, which supports Mead, is James Côté, ed., "The Mead-Freeman Controversy in Review," special edition of the *Journal of Youth and Adolescence* 29 (2000). See also Sharon Tiffany, "Imagining the South Seas: Thoughts on the Sexual Politics of Paradise in Samoa," *Pacific Studies* 24 (Sept.–Dec. 2001): 19–49, largely favorable to Mead.

81. Howard, *Margaret Mead,* p. 128.

82. Mead, *Coming of Age in Samoa,* p. 13.

83. MM to RFB, Dec. 15, 1925, LC, S-3. In a bulletin to family and friends, Mead called the Samoans "ready liars." March 7, 1926, LC, R-15.

84. Mead, *Coming of Age in Samoa*, pp. 135–36. Mead also noted the spying in *Male and Female*, p. 89; MM to RFB, March 4, 1925, LC, S-4; MM to Leah [Josephson Hanna], Jan. 29, 1926, LC, R-9.

85. MM to Eda Lou Walton, March 26, 1926, LC, R-4.

86. MM to RFB, Jan. 20, 1926, LC, S-3.

87. Interview with William Edel, CU; MM to RFB, Dec. 15, 1925, LC, S-3.

88. MM to Franz Boas, Nov. 29, 1925, APS; Mead, *Coming of Age in Samoa*, pp. 112–16.

89. MM to Franz Boas, Dec. 13, 1925; Franz Boas to MM, Jan. 4, 1926, APS.

90. Mead, *Coming of Age in Samoa*, p. 95.

91. Margaret Mead, "Conclusion 1969: Reflections on Later Theoretical Work on the Samoans," afterword to the 1969 edition of *Social Organization of Manu'a*.

92. MM to RFB, Jan. 12, 1926, LC, S-3.

93. MM to RFB, Jan. 20, 1926, LC, S-3.

94. MM to Franz Boas, Feb. 15, 1926, LC, N-1.

95. MM to RFB, March 29, 1926, LC, S-3; *BW* draft, "Samoa New Matter," p. 3; Mead, *Social Organization of Manu'a*, p. xiii.

96. MM to RFB, Dec., 1925, LC, S-3.

97. MM to RFB, Oct. 22, Dec. 7, 1925, LC, S-3.

98. MM to RFB, Sept. 5, Oct. 23, Oct. 30, 1925; Jan. 27, 1926, LC, S-3.

99. RFB to MM, Oct. 20, 1925; Jan. 27, 1926, LC, S-4.

100. RFB to MM, Sept. 20, Sept. 30, Nov. 10, Dec. 18, 1925, LC, S-4.

101. MM to RFB, Dec. 7, 1925, LC, S-3.

102. RFB to MM, Dec. 25, 1925, LC, S-4.

103. Idem.

104. MM to RFB, Apr. 11, Apr. 26, 1926, LC, S-3.

105. MM to RFB, May 6, 1926, LC, S-3.

106. MM to RFB, Jan. 4, March 4, 1926, LC, S-3.

107. Mead, *Coming of Age in Samoa*, pp. 70, 147, 151, 223.

108. MM to RFB, March 4, 1926, LC, S-3; Mead, *Coming of Age in Samoa*, p. 148.

109. Mead, *Coming of Age in Samoa*, pp. 149, 151, 223.

110. Ibid., pp. 149–50.

111. Mead, "Anthropology," in *Encyclopaedia Sexualis: A Comprehensive Encyclopaedia-Dictionary of the Sexual Sciences*, ed. Victor Robinson (New York: Dingwall-Rock, in collaboration with *Medical Review of Sciences*, 1936), p. 23.

112. MM to Robert Dickinson, Oct. 29, 1929, LC, C-2. There is no record of Dickinson's answer, although two years later he addressed the question critics of her research raised about how the Samoan young women had sex so freely without becoming pregnant, by contending that the coconut oil the young males slathered on their bodies was an effective spermicide. MM to RFB, summer 1931, LC, S-3.

113. For evidence of Stanley's irritation, see the diary that Ruth kept of the trip, VC. On Luther in Europe, see Cressman, *Golden Journey*, pp. 177–81, and *BW*, p. 162.

114. On Max Bickerton in Paris, see MM to Emily Fogg Mead, Aug. 22, 1926, LC, R-6. On Margaret's excuses, see MM to RFB, July 15, 1926, LC, S-3. On RFB's

suicidal despair, see *AW,* p. 153. On Ruth ordering Margaret to Rome, see RFB to MM, Sept. 3, 1926, LC, S-4.

115. The memorandum is in LC, S-11, miscellany file; RFF to GB, early December 1935, LC, S-1.

116. The note is in the undated, unsigned correspondence in the S Addition, LC.

117. Mead, *Ruth Benedict,* pp. 34–35.

9 / *Bread and Wine: Creating a Friendship, 1926–1931*

1. JH, p. 344.

2. Ibid., p. 31.

3. Ibid., p. 339.

4. *BW* draft, "Marriage and Graduate School," p. 6.

5. MM to RFB, March 29, 1938, LC, S-4.

6. *BW* draft, "Marriage and Graduate School," p. 19.

7. MM to RFB, Sept. 3, 1938, LC, S-4.

8. Lystra, *Searching the Heart,* pp. 240–47.

9. McCabe, "A Queer Lot," p. 72.

10. *AW,* p. 479.

11. JH, pp. 392–94; MM to RFB, June 29, 1932, LC, S-4.

12. *BW* draft, "Marriage and Graduate School," p. 19.

13. Ibid., p. 9.

14. MFF to MM, Sept. 18, 1948, VC, 117.2.

15. RFB to MM, Sept. 13, 1928, LC, S-5.

16. MM to RFB, May 27, June 9, 1928, LC, S-3.

17. RFB to MM, Aug. 3, 1938, LC, S-5.

18. MM to GB, June 22, 1934, LC, R-1.

19. MM to RFB, Nov. 7, 1928, LC, S-3.

20. MM to RFB, May 10, 1929, LC, R-3; MM to RFB, July 14, 1947, LC, R-7; interview with Don Amador, CU.

21. MM to RFB, Oct. 6, Oct. 14, 1938; July 14, 1947, LC, R-7.

22. *BW* draft, "Having a Baby," p. 1; JH, p. 323.

23. MM to RFB, Sept. 28, 1928, LC, S-3.

24. The final title of Mead's book, *Coming of Age in Samoa,* resonates with Edward Carpenter's *Love's Coming of Age,* the free-love text. Mead's publisher had input in shaping the book, as did George Dorsey, a popular writer and professional anthropologist who originally recommended her to William Morrow, her publisher. In *Anthropologists and What They Do,* p. 23, Mead stated that Dorsey suggested the title to her.

25. *BW* draft, "Meeting Reo," p. 3.

26. [Barter] Fortune résumé for Reo Fortune, VU; interviews with Ralph Bulmer, Peter Gathercole, CU.

27. MM to RFB, Nov. 2, Nov. 4, 1928, LC, S-3.

28. *BW,* p. 181; interview with Barter Fortune, CU.

29. Interview with Deborah Kaplan Mandelbaum, CU; GB to Ethel John Lungren, n.d., LC, S-1, miscellany file; GB to MM, Jan. 28, 1933, LC, R-2.

30. *BW* draft, "Sex and Temperament," p. 6; *BW*, p. 185.

31. GB to MM, Jan. 28, 1933, LC, R-2; MM to RFF, Aug. 13, 1927, LC, R-4.

32. GB to MM, Feb. 6, 1933, LC, R-2; MM to [RFB], Aug. 10, 1930, LC, Q-13, unidentified fragments in general correspondence; MM to RFB, July 18, 1930, LC, S-3.

33. On British anthropology I have used, in particular, Anna Grimshaw, *The Ethnographer's Eye: Ways of Seeing in Anthropology* (Cambridge: Cambridge University Press, 2001); George W. Stocking Jr., *After Tylor: British Social Anthropology, 1888–1951* (Madison: University of Wisconsin Press, 1995); Henrika Kuklik, *The Savage Within: The Social History of British Anthropology, 1885–1945* (Cambridge: Cambridge University Press, 1991); Nancy Lutkehaus, " 'She Was Very Cambridge': Camilla Wedgewood and the History of Women in British Social Anthropology," *American Ethnologist* 13 (1986): 776–98; George W. Stocking Jr., "Radcliffe-Brown and British Social Anthropology," in *Functionalism Historicized: Essays on British Social Anthropology,* ed. George W. Stocking Jr. (Madison: University of Wisconsin Press, 1984), pp. 131–85; Adam Kuper, *Anthropologists and Anthropology: The British School, 1922–1972* (New York: Pica Press, 1973); and Meyer Fortes, *Social Anthropology at Cambridge Since 1900* (London: Cambridge University Press, 1953).

34. Caffrey, *Ruth Benedict,* pp. 149–51.

35. For descriptions of Radcliffe-Brown, see Linton and Wagley, *Ralph Linton,* pp. 38–39; and Edmund R. Leach, "Glimpses of the Unmentionable in the History of British Social Anthropology," *Annual Reviews in Anthropology* 13 (1984): 21. On Malinowski, cf. Hortense Powdermaker, *Stranger and Friend: The Way of an Anthropologist* (New York: W. W. Norton, 1966), p. 35, and GB to MM, April 5, 1934, R-2.

36. Bronislaw Malinowski, *Argonauts of the Western Pacific* (1922; New York: E. P. Dutton, 1953); A. R. Radcliffe-Brown, *The Andaman Islanders* (1922; Glencoe, Ill.: Free Press, 1948).

37. RFB to MM, Sept. 19, 1927, LC, S-1.

38. *AW,* p. 311; MM to RFB, Oct. 13, 1928, LC, S-3.

39. Interview with Ian Hogbin, CU.

40. Letter fragment, MM to RFF, Feb. 28, 1927, Dream-Research File, LC; MM to RFF, Aug. 12, Aug. 27, 1927; Sept. 13, 1927, LC, R-4.

41. Louise Bogan, *What the Woman Lived: Selected Letters of Louise Bogan, 1920–1970,* ed. Ruth Limmer (New York: Harcourt Brace Jovanovich, 1973), p. 36; Luther Cressman to Dorothy Cecilia Loch, July 7, 1927, Jane Howard Papers, CU.

42. RFB to MM, June 18, 1927, LC, S-5; MM to RFB, July 23, 1931, LC, S-3.

43. *AW,* p. 473.

44. Nov. 9–11, 1926, Poems, Publications and Other Writings File, LC. Mead's unpublished poems and stories are in LC, Q-15, catalogued by year.

45. MM to RFB, Jan. 29, 1928, LC, S-3. "Green Sanctuary" is contained in a ms. compilation of Mead's poetry, dated 1927, titled "Song of Five Springs," and noted as for Ruth Benedict. LC, S-9.

46. See file for 1926, LC.

47. Poem dated Feb. 25, 1927, in folder for 1927, LC.

48. MM to William Fielding Ogburn, April 27, 1927, LC, Q-11.

49. MM to RFF, March 30, 1927, LC, S-1.

50. RFB to MM, Sept. 10, 1928, [Sept.] 1929, LC, S-4.

51. *AW,* pp. 201–12; Mead, *Ruth Benedict,* p. 35.

52. RFB to MM, Sept. 10, 1928, LC, S-5; Benedict, *Patterns of Culture,* pp. 78–79.

53. RFB to MM, Aug. 24, 1927, LC, S-5.

54. *BW* draft, "Meeting Reo," p. 13.

55. Idem. These matters are also discussed in MM to Léonie Adams, July 1, 1932, Léonie Adams–William Troy Papers, YU.

56. MM to RFB, June 6, 1928, LC, S-3.

57. Mead, "Notes for GCB," Feb. 10, 1941, LC, R-10.

58. Frederick J. Hoffman, *Freudianism and the Literary Mind* (Baton Rouge: Louisiana State University Press, 1957), p. 66; ES to RFB, Dec. 4, 1925, PS; A. A. Brill, *Psychoanalysis: Its Theories and Practical Application,* 3d ed. (Philadelphia: W. B. Saunders, 1922), p. 298; Hirschfeld, *Homosexuality in Men and Women,* p. 108.

59. Reo Fortune, *The Mind in Sleep* (London: K. Paul, Trench, Trubner, 1927).

60. I have reported Ruth's dream, as well as the rest of the information about the research on dreams, from the questionnaires and papers in the Dream Research File, LC. Much of this material is undated, unsigned, and in fragments.

61. The "X" she chose as the name of the twin may have referred to her female side, since as early as 1903 endocrinologists had identified the "female" chromosomes as "X." Knight et al., *Taboo and Genetics,* pp. 46–7, 67.

62. Mead, "Underground," LC, Q-15; *AW,* p. 3.

63. MM, Personal Notebooks, Apr. 20, 1928, LC, S-11. Mead stated that the priestess scene came from a scene in the Ziegfeld Follies, the sculpture scene from a Greek vase reproduction in Emily Putnam's *The Lady,* the tapestry scene from a label on a carbonate bottle that guaranteed that it would dislodge chewing gum, and Saint Sebastian from a poem she wrote called "Rose Tree of Assisi."

64. Mead, *Male and Female,* p. 5; *BW* draft, "Having a Baby," p. 4.

65. Mead, "Bisexuality," typescript, prepared for *Redbook,* May 31, 1974, p. 2, LC, I-245.

66. Wilhelm Stekel, *Bi-sexual Love;* G. V. Hamilton, "The Emotional Life of Modern Woman," in *Woman's Coming of Age,* ed. V. F. Calverton and Samuel Schmalhausen (New York: Horace Liveright, 1931), pp. 207–29; Carroll Smith-Rosenberg, "New Woman as Androgyne," in *Disorderly Conduct,* pp. 245–96; Chauncey, *Gay New York,* pp. 331–54; Faderman, *Odd Girls and Twilight Lovers,* pp. 93–117; Andrea Friedman, *Prurient Interests: Gender, Democracy, and Obscenity in New York City, 1909–1945* (New York: Columbia University Press, 2000); and John Loughery, *The Other Side of Silence: Men's Lives and Gay Identities; A Twentieth-Century History* (New York: Henry Holt, 1998), pp. 93–112. Friedman, "The Habitat of 'Sex-Crazed Perverts': Campaigns Against Burlesque in Depression-Era New York City," *Journal of the History of Sexuality* 7 (Dec. 1996): 203–39.

67. Addendum to "Dream of Dec. 16," Dream-Research File, LC.

68. *BW* draft, "Marriage and Graduate School," p. 16.

69. Floyd Dell, *Love in the Machine Age: A Psychological Study of the Transition from the Patriarchal Society* (New York: Farrar & Rinehart, 1930). Mead's review was in the *New York Evening Post,* April 5, 1930.

70. Louise M. Rosenblatt, *L'Idée de l'art pour l'art dans la littérature anglaise pendant la période victorienne* (Paris: H. Champion, 1931).

71. For MM and RFB's reading these novels, see MM to RFB, Jan. 28, 1929, and an undated letter, 1929, LC, S-3; MM to RFB, Nov. 3, 1932, LC, S-4.

72. On the reactions to Proust's *Cities of the Plain*, originally titled *Sodom and Gomorrah*, see Katz, *Gay/Lesbian Almanac*, pp. 440–41. On the reviews of *We Sing Diana*, see Edith H. Walton, "Post-War Novels—and Others," *Bookman* 67 (May 1928): 330; Alice Beale Parsons, "Not in Our Stars," *Nation* 126 (April 4, 1928), 384–85; and excerpts of other, similar reviews in *Book Review Digest, 1928* (New York: H. W. Wilson, 1929).

73. On *The Captive*, I have used Friedman, *Prurient Interests*; Leslie A. Taylor, "Veritable Hotbeds: Lesbian Scandals in the United States, 1926–1936" (Ph.D. diss., University of Iowa, 1998); Kaier Curtin, *"We Can Always Call Them Bulgarians": The Emergence of Lesbians and Gay Men on the American Stage* (Boston: Alyson, 1987); and Édouard Bourdet, *The Captive*, trans. Arthur Hornblow Jr. (New York: Brentano, 1926).

74. Mead, draft for "Bisexuality," LC.

75. On the reception of *The Well of Loneliness* in the United States, I have used Taylor, "Veritable Hotbeds."

76. Mead, "Sex and Achievement," *Forum* 94 (1935): 301–3.

77. MM to RFF, Sept. 13, 1927, LC, R-4.

78. MM to RFB, Jan. 4, 1926, LC, S-3; Margaret Mead, "Her Book, 1928," unpub. ms., LC, S-11.

79. RFB to MM, May 24, 1932, LC, S-5.

80. RFB to MM, Aug. 29, 1929, LC, S-5.

81. MM to RFB, June 12, 1928, LC, S-3.

82. MM to GB, Nov. 28, 1933, LC, R-1.

83. RFB to MM, July 26, 1929, LC, S-4.

84. RFB to MM, Sept. 1928; May 2, 1929, LC, S-5; MM to RFB, Sept. 4, 9, 21, 1928, LC, S-3.

85. Ruth Benedict's poem "Visitation" is in the special correspondence file, LC, S-4.

86. MM to RFB, Oct. 6, 1938, LC, B-2.

87. Benedict's article is reprinted in *AW*, pp. 248–61; Mead's conclusion is in *AW*, pp. 246–47.

88. *AW*, p. 202; Mead, *Male and Female*, p. 441.

89. MM to RFB, Dec. 27, 1928, LC, S-3.

90. *AW*, p. 308.

91. *AW*, pp. 187–88.

92. Sir James George Frazer, *The Golden Bough: A Study in Magic and Religion*, abridged ed. (New York: Macmillan, 1922), p. 633.

93. The various titles can be found in Benedict's papers. In letters to her, Sapir noted the titles "November Burning" and "Ripeness Is All." She suggested "Point Counter Point" in a letter to Mead. MM to RFB, May 4, 1929, LC, S-5.

94. Mead describes her relationship with Morris Crawford at length in a letter to Benedict. MM to RFB, Sept. 1, 1928, LC, S-3.

95. These notes, undated and unsigned, are in LC, S-3.

96. MM to RFB, Sept. 1, 1928, LC, S-3.

97. RFB to MM, Sept. 1928; July 10, 1930, LC, S-5.

98. MM to RFB, Sept. 28, 1928, LC, S-3.

99. RFB to MM, June 1, 1930, LC, S-4.

100. RFB to MM, Sept. 8, 1929, LC, S-4; MM to GB, Jan. 9, 1934, LC, R-1.

101. Bush and "logos" and "trinity" in RFB to MM, Sept. 28, 1928, LC, S-3. Anne Singleton, "A Major Poet," *New York Herald Tribune Books*, Dec. 23, 1928, reprinted in *Critical Essays on Robinson Jeffers*, ed. James Karman (Boston: G. K. Hall, 1990), pp. 73–75.

102. RFB to MM, Jan. 5, 1929, LC, S-5; MM to RFB, Feb. 21, 1929, LC, S-3. On Jeffers, see Robert Brophy, ed., *Robinson Jeffers: Dimensions of a Poet* (New York: Fordham University Press, 1995); James Karman, *Robinson Jeffers: Poet of California*, rev. ed. (Brownsville, Ore.: Story Line Press, 1995); and Robert Zaller, *The Cliffs of Solitude: A Reading of Robinson Jeffers* (Cambridge: Cambridge University Press, 1983).

103. *AW,* p. 154.

104. RFB to MM, March 26, May 4, 1929, LC, S-5.

105. RFB to MM, Nov. 24, 1932, LC, S-5.

106. See Lois W. Banner, *In Full Flower: Aging Women, Power, and Sexuality* (New York: Alfred A. Knopf, 1992).

107. Ivan Turgenev, *A Month in the Country: A Comedy in Five Acts*, trans. Isaiah Berlin (London: Hogarth Press, 1981), p. 99.

108. Sapir, "Observations on the Sex Problem"; "The Discipline of Sex." Sapir also published the latter article in *Child Study* (March 1930): 170–73; 187–88. According to Benedict, the article was also reprinted in a book on marriage that was edited by an assistant minister at her brother-in-law's church and issued by a religious press. RFB to MM, June 10, 1931, LC, S-5. In 1929 Sapir attacked Mead by name as incompetent in a review of *Anthropology and Modern Life*, by Franz Boas, *New Republic* 57 (1929): 279.

109. *BW* draft, "Meeting Reo," p. 4; JH, p. 429; ES to RFB, April 29, 1929, LC, S-15; MM to RFB, Dec. 2, 1932, LC, S-4. In 1930 Mead had Léonie Adams write to Edmund Wilson at the *New Republic*, asking him not to send her book on the Manus to Sapir to review, since "he has a bad case of prejudice in that quarter." Léonie Adams to Edmund Wilson, Oct. 5, 1930, Edmund Wilson Papers, YU.

110. MM to RFB, May 2, 1937, LC, S-4; RFB to MM, Apr. 27, 1936, LC, S-5.

111. Margaret Mead, "Jealousy: Primitive and Civilized," in Calverton and Schmalhausen, *Woman's Coming of Age,* p. 45.

112. *AW,* p. 3.

113. MM to RFB, May 14, 1932, LC, S-3; MM to RFB, Sept. 4, 1928, LC, S-3; RFB to MM, Aug. 3, 1938, LC, S-5.

10 / *"Two Strings to His Bow": Ruth Benedict and* Patterns of Culture

1. *Sex and Temperament in Three Primitive Societies* hereafter cited as *Sex and Temperament*. Mead's use of the term "primitive" in the title of this book is curious, given

her sensitivity to its pejorative connotations, her recommendation that "homogeneous" be substituted for it, and her counsel to Benedict not to use it in the title of *Patterns of Culture:* Benedict's first title was "Primitive Peoples: An Introduction to Cultural Types." *AW,* p. 322. The term "primitive," however, was familiar to the public. See Margaret Mead, review of *The Riddle of the Sphinx,* by Géza Róheim, *Character and Personality* 4 (Sept. 1935): 90. On the popularity of *Patterns of Culture,* see Alfred G. Smith, "The Dionysian Innovation," *AA* 66 (1964): 259.

2. Margaret Mead, *Growing Up in New Guinea: A Comparative Study in Education* (New York: William Morrow, 1930); *Changing Culture,* p. 150; and "Anthropology," in Robinson, *Encyclopaedia Sexualis,* p. 21.

3. Mead, "Jealousy: Primitive and Civilized," p. 46; and "Woman: Position in Society: Primitive," in *Encyclopaedia of the Social Sciences,* ed. R. A. Seligmann (New York: Macmillan, 1930–1935), vol. 15, pp. 439–42.

4. Benedict, *Patterns of Culture,* p. 242; AW, p. 324.

5. Ruth Benedict, "Anthropology and the Abnormal," *Journal of General Psychology* 10 (1934): 59–82, *AW,* p. 183.

6. Mead discussed the differences between them on this issue in "Temperamental Differences and Sexual Dimorphism," p. 179, in which she asserted that "Benedict believed in temperament (genetic makeup) to a degree, but she never had any theory of temperament."

7. Joseph Allen Boone, *Libidinal Currents: Sexuality and the Shaping of Modernism* (Chicago: University of Chicago Press, 1998), includes five writers (and four works they published) as "queer modernists": Bruce Nugent, "Smoke, Lilies, and Jade," 1926; Djuna Barnes, *Nightwood,* 1936; Charles Henri Ford and Parker Tyler, *The Young and Evil,* 1933; and Blair Niles, *Strange Brother,* 1931.

8. Rutkoff and Scott, *New School,* pp. 84–106. Horney was neither Jewish nor socialist; she left Germany because she didn't like its right-wing politics and because the Institute for Psychoanalysis in Chicago recruited her to its faculty. See also Lewis A. Coser, *Refugee Scholars in America: Their Impact and Their Experiences* (New Haven: Yale University Press, 1984), pp. 9–82.

9. ES to RFB, Aug. 7, 1923, PS.

10. ES to RFB, Aug. 23, 1924, PS.

11. On Sapir, I have especially used Darnell, *Edward Sapir,* pp. 223–358. On Sapir's general influence on the culture and personality school, see David F. Aberle, "Influence of Linguistics on Early Culture and Personality Theory," in *Essays in the Science of Culture; in Honor of Leslie A. White,* ed. Gertrude E. Dole and Robert L. Carneiro (New York: Thomas Y. Crowell, 1960), pp. 1–29; and Regna Darnell, "Personality and Culture: The Fate of the Sapirian Alternative," in *Malinowski, Rivers, Benedict, and Others: Essays on Culture and Personality,* ed. George W. Stocking Jr. (Madison: University of Wisconsin Press, 1986), pp. 156–83.

12. Edward Sapir, "The Meaning of Religion," *American Mercury* 15 (Sept. 1928): 76–77.

13. Edward Sapir's sharpest criticism of Benedict in these years was in "The Emergence of the Concept of Personality in a Study of Cultures," *Journal of Social Psychology* 5 (1933): 408–15. See also McMillan, "The Study of Anthropology." On Sullivan's "self psychology," see Philip Cushman, *Constructing the Self, Constructing*

America: A Cultural History of Psychotherapy (Boston, Mass.: Addison-Wesley, 1995), pp. 169–85.

14. Benedict, "Configurations of Culture in North America," *AA* 34 (1932): 1–27, reprinted in *AW,* p. 104. The remark directly criticized Edward Sapir's "Culture, Genuine and Spurious," *American Journal of Sociology* 29 (1924): 401–29, in which he used the presence or absence of cultural harmony to categorize societies. Before he met Sullivan in 1928 and solidified his focus on the individual, he used Jung's categories of introvert and extravert. See Otto Klineberg, "Historical Perspectives: Cross-Cultural Psychology Before 1960," in *Handbook of Cross-Cultural Psychology,* ed. Harry C. Triandis and William Wilson Lambert (Boston: Allyn & Bacon, 1980), vol. 1, pp. 36–37. See also "A Lecture by Dr. E. Sapir in Seminar on the Impact of Culture," [1931], LC, G-9.

15. On Benedict's reaction to Sapir's speech, see RFB to MM, Nov. 30, 1932, *AW,* p. 325; Benedict, "Anthropology and the Abnormal," *AW,* p. 278.

16. RFB to MM, April 2, 1932, LC, S-5.

17. Mead, *Ruth Benedict,* p. 38.

18. Benedict, *Zuñi Mythology* (New York: Columbia University Press, 1935), vol. 1, p. xxi; RFB to Ruth Landes, Jan. 26, 1937, VC, 31.3.

19. RFB to RFF, Aug. 2, 1932, *AW,* p. 321.

20. *AW,* p. 346; Alfred L. Kroeber, "Unpublished Reminiscences," quoted in Sally Fulk Moore, "Anthropology," in Hoxie et al., *History of the Faculty,* p. 157.

21. See Helene Codere, "The Amiable Side of Kwakiutl Life: The Potlach and the Play Potlach," *AA* 58 (April 1956): 334–51; and Benedict, *Patterns of Culture,* p. 241.

22. RFB to MM, July 20, 1932, *AW,* p. 319.

23. Alfred L. Kroeber, review of *Patterns of Culture, AA* 37 (1935): 690.

24. On the need for women writers to establish an authoritative genealogy, see Betsy Erkkila, *The Wicked Sisters: Women Poets, Literary History, and Discord* (New York: Oxford University Press, 1992), pp. 3–16.

25. Ruth Benedict, "Anthropology and the Humanities," 585–93.

26. Victor Barnouw, "Ruth Benedict: Apollonian and Dionysian," *University of Toronto Quarterly* 18 (April 1949): 242.

27. See Banner, *In Full Flower,* p. 165.

28. RFB to MM, Aug. 12, 1939, LC, R-7; RFB to "Chuck," Aug. 13, 1939, LC, R-16; MM to RFB, Oct. 5, 1939, LC, S-5; RFB, "Primitive Freedom," *Atlantic Monthly* 169 (1942), reprinted in Mead, *Ruth Benedict,* pp. 134–46.

29. See "Preface to the Fifth Edition," in *American Men of Science: A Biographical Directory,* ed. J. McKeen Cattell and Jacques Cattell, 5th ed. (New York: Science Press, 1933), p. viii. The starred rankings were determined by the answers to questionnaires sent to "several thousand" scientists.

30. MM to RFB, Dec. 2, 1932, LC, S-5.

31. RFB to MM, May 15, 1932, LC, S-4. Otto Weininger's work *Sex and Character,* published in English as well as German in 1903, was a best-seller both in Europe and the United States.

32. MM to RFB, Oct. 22, 1931, LC, S-3.

33. On Margery Loeb's suicide attempt, see RFB to Margery, summer 1929; Nov. 29, 1929, VC, 1.5.

34. RFB journal fragments, dated June 15, 1934, VC, 36.1.

35. RFB to MM, June 27, Oct. 22, 1931, LC, S-5.

36. RFB journal fragment, VC, 36.1.

37. RFB journal fragment, VC, 36.1.; Lurker, *Gods and Symbols of Ancient Egypt*, p. 65.

38. RFB to MM, Aug. 3, 1938, LC, S-5.

39. RFB to MM, Feb. 7, 1933, LC, S-5.

40. RFB to MM, Jan. 21, 1937, LC, S-5.

41. Bernard J. Paris, *Karen Horney: A Psychoanalyst's Search for Self-Understanding* (New Haven: Yale University Press, 1994), pp. 181–89, 214–22.

42. Mead reprinted the chapter in her brief biography of Benedict. See Mead, *Ruth Benedict*, pp. 146–59.

43. Edward Hoffman, *The Right to Be Human: A Biography of Abraham Maslow* (Los Angeles: J. P. Tarcher; New York: dist. by St. Martin's Press, 1988), p. 155.

44. Margaret Mead, "Notes on the Columbia University Biography," LC.

45. See clipping files, OC.

46. *AW*, p. 155.

47. T. George Harris, "About Ruth Benedict," pp. 51–52.

48. Benedict, *Patterns of Culture*, p. 18.

49. Ibid., pp. 1–20. On Mead's commitment to scientific rationality, see Mead, "The Meaning of Freedom in Education," *Progressive Education* 8 (Feb. 1931): 111.

50. Steven Biel, *Independent Intellectuals in the United States, 1910–1945* (New York: New York University Press, 1992); Richard Wightman Fox, "Epitaph for Middletown: Robert S. Lynd and the Analysis of American Culture," in *The Culture of Consumption*, ed. Fox and T. J. Jackson Lears (New York: Pantheon Books, 1983), pp. 103–41; M. C. Smith, *Social Science in the Crucible*; Cross, "Designs for Living"; and Ogburn and Goldenweiser, *Social Sciences and Their Interrelationships*.

51. Michael M. Sokal, "The Gestalt Psychologists in Behaviorist America," *American Historical Review* 89 (1984): 1240–63.

52. Alexander Goldenweiser, "Anthropology and Psychology," in Ogburn and Goldenweiser, *Social Sciences and Their Interrelationships*, p. 85; and *AW*, p. 14. See also Judith Modell, " 'It Is Besides a Pleasant English Word'—Ruth Benedict's Concept of Patterns," *Anthropological Quarterly* 62 (Jan. 1989): 27–40, and the updated version in Banner and Janiewski, *Reading Benedict/Reading Mead* (forthcoming).

53. Mead, "Retrospects and Prospects," p. 127.

54. Gardner Murphy and Friedrich Jensen, *Approaches to Personality: Some Contemporary Conceptions Used in Psychology and Psychiatry* (New York: Coward-McCann, 1933), pp. 335–405. On the history of the term "paranoia," see J. Laplanche and J.-B. Pontalis, *The Language of Psycho-Analysis*, trans. Donald Nicholson-Smith (New York: W. W. Norton, 1973), pp. 296–97.

55. On Freud's social psychology, see Louise E. Hoffman, "The Ideological Significance of Freud's Social Thought," in *Psychology in Twentieth-Century Thought and Society*, ed. Mitchell G. Ash and William R. Woodward (Cambridge: Cambridge University Press, 1987), pp. 256–61. The notion of a "primal horde" comes from *Totem and Taboo*. See also Freud, "Group Psychology and the Analysis of the Ego," *Standard Edition*, vol. 18, pp. 139–41. This 1921 work was translated into English in 1922. In "Ruth

Benedict: Anthropological Folklorist," *Journal of American Folk-Lore* 92 (1979): 453, Virginia Briscoe contends that Goldenweiser was the most psychoanalytically oriented of the Boasians and that he had a major impact on Benedict. Briscoe, however, conflates Freudianism, neo-Freudianism, and the non-Freudian psychological point of view.

56. Benedict, "Science of Custom," p. 647. See also Westbrook, *John Dewey*, p. 439.

57. Benedict, "Science of Custom," p. 649.

58. Benedict, *Patterns of Culture*, pp. 36, 271.

59. See Maslow, *Farther Reaches of Human Nature*, p. 200.

60. Victor Barnouw, "Benedict," in *Masters: Portraits of Great Teachers*, ed. Joseph Epstein (New York: Basic Books, 1981), p. 174.

61. See Silverman, *Totems and Teachers*, p. 156.

62. Lee, "Ruth Fulton Benedict," pp. 345–46. On modern science, Benedict recommended Alfred North Whitehead, *Science and the Modern World* (1925; New York: Macmillan, 1954), which includes a discussion of Planck and Einstein, pp. 165–98.

63. Evelyn Fox Keller, *A Feeling for the Organism: The Life and Work of Barbara McClintock* (San Francisco: W. H. Freeman, 1983).

64. *AW*, pp. 317–18; Santayana, *Three Philosophical Poets*, p. 4.

65. See Mead, *Ruth Benedict*, p. 171.

66. Santayana, *Three Philosophical Poets*, p. 4.

67. Biederman, *Dictionary of Symbolism*, p. 353.

68. E. Wilson, *Axel's Castle*, p. 264.

69. ES to RFB, Oct. 6, 1928, *AW*, p. 193.

70. Clifford Geertz, "Us/Not-Us: Benedict's Travels," in *Works and Lives: The Anthropologist as Author* (Stanford, Calif.: Stanford University Press, 1988), pp. 106–7.

71. Benedict occasionally referred to Dante's *Inferno* in her writing. Thus in "Malvina Hoffman," unpub. speech, *AW* draft, LC, she wrote that some tribal people were "moved by suspicion and fear that remind us of Dante's Inferno, and some self-respecting and unafraid as Dante dreamed the inhabitants of his Paradiso to be."

72. On the Plains men-women, Benedict relied on an unpublished manuscript by Ella Deloria, a member of the Dakota tribe who was a Ph.D. candidate in anthropology at Columbia. See Janet L. Finn, "Ella Cara Deloria and Mourning Dove: Writing for Cultures, Writing Against the Grain," in *Women Writing Culture*, ed. Ruth Behar and Deborah A. Gordon (Berkeley: University of California Press, 1995), pp. 131–47. In 1935 Benedict wrote to Robert Lowie that she feared that Deloria's account of the Dakota berdache was romanticized. (RFB to RHL, April 17, 1935, VC.) By 1939, Benedict revised her conclusions about the Dakota, noting that among them active (as opposed to passive) homosexuality was forbidden and that berdaches were regarded with ambivalence. Ruth Benedict, "Sex in Primitive Society," *American Journal of Orthopsychiatry* 9 (1939): 572.

73. Lang, *Men as Women*, p. 20.

74. Alfred L. Kroeber, "Psychosis or Social Sanction," *Character and Personality* 3 (1940): 210. Robert H. Lowie was ambivalent toward homosexuality; in *Primitive Religion* (1924; London: Allen Lane, 1973), pp. 181, 243–46, he called it a "perversion," while expressing admiration for its connection to spirituality in some tribes.

75. Quoted in Bowles, *Louise Bogan*, p. 103.

76. At least one biography of Bogan has been written (by Elizabeth Frank), as have many analyses of her poetry. There is no biography of Léonie Adams, however, and little recent analysis of her poetry. I have traced her life through her papers, those of Edmund Wilson at Yale, and those of Mead at LC.

77. Margaret Mead, introduction to her *From the South Seas: Studies of Adolescence and Sex in Primitive Societies* (New York: William Morrow, 1939). See also Klineberg, "Historical Perspectives," pp. 37–38.

78. *AW,* p. 320.

79. Ibid., pp. 335–36. In a 1936 letter to a Dr. Folsom, Benedict stated that, like him, she didn't like the word "pattern" in her title. But the publisher didn't like "ethos" or "configurations," and she couldn't think of anything else. RFB to Dr. Folsom, Feb. 29, 1936, VC, 2.8.

80. Benedict, "Configurations of Culture," p. 83. See also Benedict, "Folklore," "Magic," and "Myth," in *Encyclopaedia of the Social Sciences,* vol. 6, pp. 288–93; vol. 10, pp. 39–44; vol. 11, pp. 178–81.

81. Ruth Benedict, "Religion," in *General Anthropology,* ed. Franz Boas (Boston: D. C. Heath, 1938), pp. 641–59.

82. On monsters and the movies, I have used Thomas Doherty, *Pre-Code Hollywood: Sex, Immorality, and Insurrection in American Cinema, 1930–1934* (New York: Columbia University Press, 1999), especially pp. 221–318.

83. Lois Scharf, *To Work and To Wed: Female Employment, Feminism, and the Great Depression* (Westport, Conn.: Greenwood Press, 1980), pp. 673–83; and Banner, *Women in Modern America,* pp. 179–205.

84. On the reassertion of aggressive masculinity, see chapter 12 of the present book. For homosexuality in the 1930s, I have relied on Terry, *An American Obsession,* pp. 268–96, and Carlston, " 'A Finer Differentiation.' " On the "sex crime panic," see Estelle Freedman, " 'Uncontrolled Desires': The Response to the Sexual Psychopath, 1920–1960," in Peiss and Simmons, *Passion and Power,* pp. 199–225.

85. Richard Chase, "Ruth Benedict: The Woman as Anthropologist," Columbia University *Forum* 2 (1959): 19–22.

86. Benedict, *Patterns of Culture,* p. 276.

87. Ibid., pp. 245, 259.

88. Ibid., pp. 260, 277. Havelock Ellis printed Josiah Flynt's work, "Homosexuality Among Tramps," as an appendix to *Sexual Inversion,* beginning with the 1902 edition of his work.

89. *Webster's Encyclopedic Unabridged Dictionary.*

90. Benedict, *Patterns of Culture,* pp. 42–43, and "Science of Custom," p. 648.

91. Myrna Garvey Eden, "Malvina Cornell Hoffman," in *Notable American Women: The Modern Period; A Biographical Dictionary,* ed. Barbara Sicherman and Carol Hurd Green (Cambridge, Mass.: Harvard University Press, Belknap Press, 1980), pp. 343–45; and Malvina Hoffman, *Heads and Tales* (New York: Charles Scribner's Sons, 1936).

92. Benedict, "Malvina Hoffman," in typescript, *AW,* LC; memorandum from RFB to Ruth Aimes, April 9, 1945, VC.

93. See Margaret Mead, ed., *Cooperation and Competition Among Primitive Peoples* (1937; Boston: Beacon, 1961).

94. Irving Goldman, "The Zuñi of New Mexico," in Mead, *Cooperation and Competition*, pp. 313–53.

95. Ruth Benedict's "Handbook of Psychological Leads for Ethnological Field Workers" was never published. I found a mimeographed copy in the Geoffrey Gorer Papers, SU.

96. Pandora, *Rebels Within the Ranks*, pp. 160–63.

97. Gregory Bateson, *Naven* (Cambridge: Cambridge University Press, 1936), vii.

11 / The *"Squares" on the Sepik:* Sex and Temperament, *Part 1*

1. On their difficulties in Manus, see MM to RFB, Dec. 7, Dec. 30, 1928; Feb. 21, 1929, LC, S-3. On March 25, 1929, Mead wrote: "We are gloriously happy," and regretted telling Ruth about their conflicts (LC, S-3). She defines "event analysis" in *BW,* p. 197.

2. In articles, Mead addressed the thinking process of Manus children (her original project), the structure of kinship in the society, how fathers reared children, and the meaning of child rearing on Manus for Western progressive education. In other words, Mead's multifaceted imagination was in operation on this project, as in much of her work, and she published much of her research in places other than *Growing Up in New Guinea.* See Margaret Mead, "Meaning of Freedom in Education," 107–11; "An Investigation of the Thought of Primitive Children, with Special Reference to Animism," *Journal of the Royal Anthropological Institute* 62 (Jan.–June 1932): 173–90; and "Kinship in the Admiralty Islands," *Anthropological Papers of the American Museum of Natural History* 34, no. 2 (New York, 1934), 183–358.

3. Interview with Barter Fortune, CU.

4. See MM to RFB, April 9, 1933, LC, R-7.

5. On Mead and the Omaha berdache, see Margaret Mead, "Summary Statement of the Problem of Culture and Personality," March 1933, New Guinea Field Notes, Tchambuli, LC, N-102; handwritten, untitled comments by Gregory Bateson on the Omaha berdache, undated, unsigned, in Bateson's letters in the R file, LC; Mead, *Sex and Temperament,* p. 295; MM to George Devereux, July 26, 1938, LC, R-10; and Mead, "Cultural Determinants of Sexual Behavior," pp. 1452–53.

6. Mead, *Coming of Age in Samoa,* p. 95, and *Growing Up in New Guinea,* pp. 166, 193, 198–99.

7. On Mead's definition of transvestites as either homosexual or heterosexual, see Bettie Wysor, *The Lesbian Myth* (New York: Random House, 1974), p. 108. Havelock Ellis had noted that identification in "Eonism," in *Studies of the Psychology of Sex,* vol. 3, pp. 1–110, citing the definitive work by Magnus Hirschfeld, *Transvestites: The Erotic Drive to Cross-Dress,* published in 1910. Over time Mead changed her opinion about the importance of transsexuals to definitions of gender. In her "Background Statement About Homosexuality" (see prologue, n. 19), she cited the case of a hermaphrodite child who had been misidentified as a girl and, when she developed male genitalia at puberty, decided to remain a girl, as proof that environment predominated over biology in gender identity. In *Male and Female,* p. 131, however, she stated that research on

hermaphrodites had shed little light on the relationship between endocrine balance and homosexual identity.

8. The Navajo had a strong berdache tradition. In 1934 Willard Hill found them celebrated as spiritual beings. W. H. Hill, "The Status of the Hermaphrodite and Transvestite in Navaho Culture," *AA* 37 (1935): 273–279.

9. Mead noted in *BW,* p. 228, that she didn't apply for a research grant for this trip, so she didn't have to spell out precisely what she intended to do.

10. *Sex and Temperament,* p. xiv.

11. *BW* draft, "Sex and Temperament," p. 13.

12. Sigmund Freud, "The Psychogenesis of a Case of Homosexuality in a Woman," 1920, reprinted in Freud, *Sexuality and the Psychology of Love,* ed. Philip Rieff (1963; New York: Simon & Schuster, 1983), pp. 123–49.

13. V. F. Calverton reprinted Westermarck's chapter in a compilation of the basic writings of anthropologists, which included a chapter from Mead's *Coming of Age in Samoa;* see Calverton, *The Making of Man,* pp. 529–64. According to Mead, Westermarck was basic reading for anthropologists. JH, p. 143.

14. William McDougall, *Outline of Abnormal Psychology* (New York: Charles Scribner's Sons, 1926), p. 353; Mathilde and Mathias Vaerting, *The Dominant Sex: A Study in the Sociology of Sex Differentiation* (New York: G. H. Doran, 1923). On the male/female binary in the 1930s, see Meyerowitz, *How Sex Changed;* Stephanie Hope Kenen, "Scientific Studies of Human Sexual Difference in Interwar America" (Ph.D. diss., University of California, Berkeley, 1998); Henry Minton, "Femininity in Men and Masculinity in Women: American Psychiatry and Psychology Portray Homosexuality in the 1930's," *Journal of Homosexuality* 13 (fall 1986): 1–21; and Joseph Pleck, "The Theory of Male Sex Role Identity: Its Rise and Fall, 1936 to the Present," in *In the Shadow of the Past: Psychology Portrays the Sexes; A Social and Intellectual History,* ed. Miriam Lewin (New York: Columbia University Press, 1984), pp. 205–25.

15. Benedict, *Patterns of Culture,* p. 262.

16. In "Tamberans and Tambuans in New Guinea," *Natural History* 34 (May/June 1934): 234–36, Margaret Mead presented the Tamberan cult as oppressing women. On reports of homosexuality, see H. Ellis, *Studies in the Psychology of Sex,* vol. 2, pp. 20–21, and C. G. Seligman, "Sexual Inversion Among Primitive Tribes," *Alienist and Neurologist* 23 (Jan. 1902).

17. H. Ellis, *Psychology of Sex,* vol. 4, p. 20; CTK to MM, undated letter, 1930s, LC, N-12.

18. Margaret Mead, quoted in Golde, *Women in the Field,* pp. 319–20.

19. Mead, *Sex and Temperament,* pp. 140, 149.

20. Ibid., p. 179. In her restudy of the Mundugumor in the early 1980s, Nancy McDowell found that Mead's description of the tribe was exaggerated, but it wasn't inaccurate. They were aggressive, but they were also caring, and their caring behavior was more than just "deviant." From reading Mead's field notes at the Library of Congress, McDowell concluded that she was a brilliant observer. Had she used a more complex framework than Benedict's configurationist one, which drew a dichotomy between normal and deviant individuals, she might have arrived at more nuanced results. See Nancy McDowell, *The Mundugumor: From the Field Notes of*

Margaret Mead and Reo Fortune (Washington, D.C.: Smithsonian Institution Press, 1991).

21. *BW* draft, "Sex and Temperament," p. 6.

22. RFF to MM, Feb. 14, 1948, LC, R-6.

23. RFB to MM, Feb. 10, 1933, LC, S-5.

24. MM to RFB, Jan. 16, April 23, July 31, Dec. 2, 1932, LC, S-3.

25. MM to RFB, Oct. 21, 1932, LC, S-4; RFB to MM, Feb. 7, 1933, LC, S-5.

26. Mead, *Male and Female*, p. 147.

27. Ibid., p. 67.

28. MM to RFB, Sept. 23, 1932, LC, S-3.

29. MM to RFB, March 29, 1933, LC, R-7.

30. The classic analysis of the "intellectual aristocracy" is Noel Annan, "The Intellectual Aristocracy," in *Studies in Social History: A Tribute to G. M. Trevelyan*, ed. J. H. Plumb (New York: Longmans, Green, 1955), pp. 243–87. My discussion of Bateson's background is drawn from David Lipset, *Gregory Bateson: The Legacy of a Scientist* (Englewood Cliffs, N.J.: Prentice-Hall, 1980); from "Case History," attached to a letter, MM to Erik Erikson, April 27, 1947, R-8; and from the Gregory Bateson Papers, LC.

31. GB to MM, May 11, 1934, LC, R-2.

32. MM to RFB, March 29, 1933, LC, R-7.

33. For the life of Noel Teulon Porter, I have used his long obituary in the *Cambridge News*, Dec. 18, 1962, p. 6, written by Lance Sieveking, Cambridge Public Library, Cambridge, England, and Porter's seven-volume typescript autobiography, "As I Seem to Remember," Special Collections and Manuscripts, Cam-U.

34. The lecture is contained in the final volume of the autobiography.

35. GB to MM, [Sept.], Oct. 8, 1933, LC, R-2.

36. GB to RFB, Nov. 16, 1933, LC, S-1. Noel Porter wrote to Margaret that Gregory had "an appealing tender wistful touchingness" to which maternal people of either sex responded, and he described himself as something of a mother to Gregory. Nov. 1933, LC, R-10, unidentified file.

37. GB to Johnny, Nov. 24, 1930, LC, O-1.

38. GB to MM, Half Moon, n.d. [Oct. 1933], LC, R-2.

39. Lipset, *Gregory Bateson*, p. 93.

40. Geoffrey Gorer, "The Adventures and Travels of Mr. Roderick Cantilever," SU. Gregory Bateson, "Morale and National Character," in *Steps to an Ecology of Mind: Collected Essays in Anthropology, Psychiatry, Evolution, and Epistemology* (1972; Northvale, N.J.: Jason Aronson, 1987), p. 96. See also *Charterhouse: An Open Examination, Written by the Boys* (London: K. Mason, 1964), pp. 82–90, 105–6.

41. *BW*, p. 234.

42. GB to MM, Feb. 6, 1934, LC, R-2.

43. RFF to MM, March 9, Sept. 12, 1933, LC, R-4. See also interview with Ian Hogbin, CU.

44. GB to MM, Feb. 6, 1934, LC, R-2.

45. MM to RFB, March 9, 1933, LC, S-4.

46. Interview with Barter Fortune, CU.

47. *BW*, p. 234.

48. References to the "episode of the second goats" occur in letters between Margaret and Gregory, and Margaret notes its importance in her "Notes for GCB" (see ch. 3, n. 31). By goats, I think they meant "ghosts." Gregory had confused the two words as a child. See Lipset, *Gregory Bateson*, p. 47. In "Summary Statement on Culture and Personality" Mead contended that passive individuals, left alone without mental stimulation, would "see ghosts." But when two passive individuals came together and exchanged ideas, deep spirituality would result. The episode of the "first goats" would have been their first meeting, when she and Reo picked up Gregory to take him to the Christmas celebration at Ambunti, and she and Gregory were immediately attracted to each other.

49. Elizabeth Brown to GB, April 15, 1932, O-1. Letters from Bett to Gregory are in the Gregory Bateson Papers, LC. Hortense Powdermaker, in *Stranger and Friend*, p. 36, identifies her as attending Malinowski's seminar. In *Naven*, Bateson acknowledges her assistance to him among the Iatmul and that of her husband, as Mr. and Mrs. Mackenzie of the *Lady Betty*.

50. GB to MM, Sept. 23, Dec. 2, 1933, LC, R-1; "Kreegery" to GB, Nov. 1, 1933, LC, O-1.

51. MM to RFB, Jan. 16, June 29, 1933, LC, S-4.

52. On Steve, see MM to CTK, Jan. 29, 1937, LC, B-9; letter from Steve to MM, undated, 1930s, located in the middle of MM's letters to Carrie Kelly (CTK), B-9; Steve's letters to Mead, including diary entries, are mostly in LC, R-9, general correspondence file; unsigned, undated letter to GB, LC, O-1, identifiable by handwriting.

53. Margaret Mead, *Letters from the Field, 1925–1975* (New York: Harper & Row, 1977), p. 140; *BW*, p. 242.

54. *Sex and Temperament*, p. viii.

55. *BW* draft, "Sex and Temperament," pp. 13–14.

56. In constructing what happened at Tchambuli, I have used *BW* draft, "Sex and Temperament," as well as the notes Margaret and Gregory wrote to each other (they called them "slips"), which are located in LC, mostly in the R-1 and R-2 files, with some in the S addition. I have also used letters, especially in the R file, between Reo, Gregory, and Margaret that refer to events on the Sepik—as well as information from the "Summary Statement on Culture and Personality," which Mead wrote in March, based on work they did during the previous months. There is also material in JH, especially p. 345, and in Mead's "Notes for GCB." I have also relied on Gerald Sullivan, "Of Feys and Culture Planners: Margaret Mead and Purposive Activity as a Value," in Banner and Janiewski, *Reading Benedict/Reading Mead* (forthcoming).

57. It sounds as though they were influenced by the "masculinity" and "femininity" scales then widely used in educational and employment testing. Lewis Terman and Catherine Cox Miles of Stanford University designed the scales, which were weighted to prove that extreme differences between masculinity and femininity equaled normalcy for men and women. See Pleck, "Theory of Male Sex Role Identity," and Miriam Lewin, "Rather Worse than Folly," in Lewin, *In the Shadow of the Past*.

58. Their perspective on Christ is mentioned in Mead's "Summary Statement."

59. MM to RFB, March 29, 1933, LC, R-7.

60. MM to RFB, March 9, 1933, LC, S-4.

61. RFB to MM, Oct. 16, 1932, *AW*, p. 324.

62. Mead discusses the development of their thinking, including their turning to Mendel and Jung, in the *BW* draft chapter, "Sex and Temperament."

63. *BW,* p. 256.

64. GB to Rhoda Métraux, May 1, 1967, Gregory Bateson Papers, U-Cal, Santa Cruz (UCSC), 956–58. On Diaghilev and Nijinsky, I have used Peter Ostwald, *Vaslav Nijinsky: A Leap into Madness* (New York: Lyle Stuart, 1991). In her *Achievement in American Poetry*, p. 54, Louise Bogan, echoing many others, called the Ballets Russes the most important aesthetic influence in France and England in the years immediately before World War I. See also Gaylyn Studlar, *This Mad Masquerade: Stardom and Masculinity in the Jazz Age* (New York: Columbia University Press, 1996), pp. 155–56.

65. On their derivation of "fey," see Mead, "Retrospects and Prospects," p. 132. In this source Mead defined "fey" as a "temperamentally dictated aesthetic detachment." In JH, p. 345, she defined the Turk as the person who stood in the center and manipulated everyone else. On Gregory's identification with Diaghilev, see MM to GB, June 1–3, 1934, LC, R-2.

66. Mead, *Letters from the Field*, p. 133.

67. GB to MM, Friday, undated, R-2.

68. "Monday the Third [1933]." Many of the slips are undated.

69. MM to GB, undated note, Tchambuli, LC, R-1; RFF to Luther Cressman, April 9, 1933, LC, R-4. Perhaps Reo never sent the letter; a handwritten draft of it is in the R-4 file, among letters from Reo to Margaret.

70. MM to RFB, March 14, 1933, LC, S-4.

71. These comments of Mead's about herself, Reo, Gregory, and Ruth, as well as her complaints about their living situation, are in letters she wrote to Benedict in the late winter and spring of 1933. See MM to RFB, Feb. 23, March 9, March 19, 1933, LC, S-4; and MM to RFB, April 9, 1933, LC, R-7.

72. MM to RFB, April 9, 1933.

73. This standard belief of the age can be found in Ruth Benedict's college paper on Shakespeare's *Othello*, in which she concluded that Othello's emotions were simply a stronger variation of the emotions of the "cold" Northern race. Extending these beliefs, the famed explorer Sir Richard Burton believed in the existence of a so-called Sotadic zone, of rampant sexuality, gender crossing, and homosexuality, existing throughout the Southern Hemisphere, from the Mediterranean region through India and the Pacific Islands to South America and the southern states of the United States. See Sir Richard Francis Burton, *The Erotic Traveler*, ed. Edward Leigh (New York: Putnam, 1967).

74. Undated, unidentified slips; *BW* draft, "Sex and Temperament"; MM to GB, July 7, 1934, LC, R-1.

75. Sylvia Nasar, *A Beautiful Mind: The Life of Mathematical Genius and Nobel Laureate John Nash* (New York: Simon & Schuster, 2001), pp. 83–84.

76. Definitions and redefinitions of the categories run throughout the letters between Mead and Bateson in 1933 and 1934. Cf. MM to GB, Oct. 3, Oct. 6, Nov. 6, Dec. 19, 1933; Jan. 5, Apr. 11, 1934, LC, R-1.

77. J. L. Moreno to MM, March 25, 1941; MM to J. L. Moreno, Apr. 8, 1941, misc. correspondence, 1941, LC, I-20.

78. Mead, "Cultural Determinants of Sexual Behavior," p. 1452.

79. MM to RFB, March 29, 1933, LC, R-7.

80. RFB to MM, Feb. 7, March 25, 1933, LC, S-5.

81. My description of Naven is taken from Gregory Bateson's descriptions in *Naven*. See also Mead, *Sex and Temperament*, pp. 256–57, 263. In "The Tchambuli View of Persons: A Critique of Individualism in the Works of Mead and Chodorow," *AA* 86 (1984): 615–29, Deborah Gewertz notes that when Mead worked among the Tchambuli, 52 percent of the men between the ages of fifteen and forty-five were away from the villages, working elsewhere. She praises Mead for her research design, but faults her for failing to address the history of the Tchambuli and for using Western categories for reality, not native ones. She doesn't address Mead's conclusions about homosexuality.

82. On the separate societies and colors, see MM to GB, May 30, 1934, LC, R-1. I base my description of the colors on *Sex and Temperament*, p. 283. On the various figures they identified with, see MM to GB, June 12, June 13, 1934, R-1. Reo probably meant the disciples of Jesus in his identification with the apostles, but it is possible that his identification was with the Cambridge Apostles, a student group at Cambridge University known for their homosexuality.

83. *BW* draft, "The Field," pp. 8–9; and Howard Langer, audio interview with Dr. Margaret Mead on Social Anthropology, American Character, Primitive Societies, Folkways Records, c. 1953.

84. Reo's hiding the paper is described in a letter from Barter Fortune to A. G. Bagnall, head, Turnbull Library, Victoria University, Wellington, New Zealand, Jan. 27, 1980, VU. Reo discusses his annoyance over Gregory's hiding the gun in RFF to MM, Sept. 12, 1933, May 17, 1934, LC, R-4; Mead describes the miscarriage, her reactions to it, and Reo's anger in her "Notes for GCB" and in JH, p. 347. See also MM to GB, May 30, 1934, LC, R-1; and *BW* draft, "Having a Baby," p. 4. In this source she suggests that it was an "early" miscarriage.

85. Reo's accusations of sadism are contained in RFF to MM, May 17, 1934, LC, R-4. A. G. Bagnall, in his letter to Barter Fortune, discusses Barter Fortune's account of a malarial episode that Reo had when he stayed with Barter after leaving the Bonaro. Reo described to Barter an incident soon after the Easter scene, when Margaret declared that a rash on her leg was a map of Australia. They decided that also must have been a malarial hallucination.

86. MM to RFB, June 16, June 19, 1933, LC, S-4. She refers to the scorpion bite in MM to GB, Oct. 23, 1933, LC, R-1.

87. CTK to MM, [undated letter], April 6, 1934; Oct. 1, 1935, LC, B-9; MM to GB, Feb. 10, 1934, R-2. Mead describes Kelly in a letter to Jane Belo, undated, LC, R-7.

88. RFF to MM, [c. 1933]; May 17, 1934, LC, R-4.

89. CTK to MM, n.d. [1933], LC, B-9.

90. MM to GB, July 6, 1934, LC, R-1; Aug. 26, 1933, S-3; MM to RFB, July 5, Aug. 26, 1933, LC, S-4; RFB to MM, Aug. 19, 1933, S-5.

91. RFB to MM, July 19, 1933, LC, S-5.

92. MM to GB, n.d., Oceanic line, Monday night; Sept. 23, Dec. 5, 1933, LC, R-1; Oct. 25, 1933, LC, B-1; MM to RFF, Sept. 4, 1933, LC, R-4.

93. MM to GB, Oct. 15, Dec. 15, 1933, LC (slips); MM to GB, April 8, 1934, LC, R-2; Edward Mead to MM, Dec. 13, 1933, LC, A-4.

94. MM to GB, Oct. 23, 1933, LC, R-1.

95. MM to GB, March 19, 1934, LC, R-1.

96. MM to GB, Oct. 9, Oct. 23, Nov. 11, 1933, LC, R-1.

97. GB to MM, Feb. 16, 1934, LC, R-2.

98. MM to GB, Dec. 13, 1935, LC, S-1. On Dollard, see Nadine Weidman, "John Dollard," in *American National Biography*, ed. John A. Garraty and Mark C. Carnes (New York: Oxford University Press, 1999), pp. 708–10.

99. MM to CTK, July 28, 1934, LC, B-9; MM to GB, Jan. 27, Feb. 16, 1934, LC, R-1.

100. MM to GB, July 28, 1935, LC, R-2.

101. MM to CTK, July 28, 1934, LC, B-9; Lee (Leah Josephson Hannah) to MM, undated, unidentified correspondence file, LC, B-12.

102. Ann McLean, "In the Footprints of Reo Fortune," in *Ethnographic Presents: Pioneering Anthropologists in the Papua New Guinea Highlands*, ed. Terence E. Hays (Berkeley: University of California Press, 1992), pp. 37–67. Fortune initially called the tribal society the Purari.

103. GB to MM, Jan. 3, May 11, 1933, LC, R-1; MM to GB, Oct. 3, Oct. 6, Oct. 25, Nov. 6, 1933; Jan. 3, March 19, 1934, LC, R-1; Oct. 23, 1933, LC, B-1.

104. Some psychoanalysts who knew Benedict and Horney suspected that they were lovers, but there isn't anything in their papers (or those of Mead) to support the suspicions. Bernard Paris, Horney's biographer, mentioned them to me in a telephone conversation in October 1998, although he said he hadn't been able to verify them. On their evening interactions, see "Oral interview with Margaret Mead," Karen Horney Papers, YU. In this source, Mead also states that she and Horney didn't get along well. (Horney could be as forceful as she.) On Mead's closeness to Fromm, see his letters to her in LC, C-files. The letters from Mead in the Erich Fromm Papers, NYPL, pertain to business matters.

105. Mead, "More Comprehensive Field Methods," *AA* 35 (1933): 37–53.

106. Margaret Mead, "The Use of Primitive Material in the Study of Personality," *Character and Personality* 3 (Sept. 1934): 3–16; Mead, review of *The Riddle of the Sphinx*, by Géza Róheim, *Character and Personality*; Mead, *Cooperation and Competition Among Primitive Peoples*.

107. Mead discusses Scott in *BW*, pp. 215–18. Additional material is in *BW* draft chapter, "The Years Between Field Trips." Information on him can also be found on the World Wide Web under Technocracy, an organization still in existence.

108. There is no biography of Geoffrey Gorer. For biographical details, I have used the autobiographical information in his introductions to his *Hot Strip Tease and Other Notes on American Culture* (London: Cresset Press, 1937); *American People: A Study in National Character*, rev. ed. (New York: W. W. Norton, 1964); "I Speak for Myself," typescript, Geoffrey Gorer Papers, SU; and his extensive correspondence with Mead. Most of that correspondence is in LC, with duplicates in SU, although some key letters from Mead to Gorer are only in SU.

109. A number of individuals whom Jane Howard interviewed expressed this opinion. See interviews with Esther Goldfrank Wittfogel, Lola Romanucci-Ross, Percy Lee Langstaff, and Wilton Dillon, CU. For Gorer's work, see *Bali and Angkor: A 1930s Pleasure Trip Looking at Life and Death* (1936; New York: Oxford University Press,

1986); *Africa Dances: A Book About West African Negroes* (New York: Knopf, 1935); and *Himalyan Village: An Account of the Lepchas of Sikkim* (London: M. Joseph, 1938).

110. Interview with Edith and Philleo Nash, CU; MM to GB, Jan. 9, 1935, LC, S-1; MM to GG, May 31, 1936, LC, B-4. For their letters about love and artistic production, see MM to GG, Apr. 4, May 31, Aug. 20, Oct. 1, 1936, LC, B-4, B-5, and N-5; GG to MM, Apr. 23, Oct. 16, Dec. 5, 1936, LC, B-4. For Mead's response to *Hot Strip Tease*, see MM to GG, Dec. 4, 1936, LC, B-5. For Mead's realistic attitude toward Gorer, see MM to John Dollard, July 26, 29, 1936, LC, N-5; MM to GG, May 31, 1936; July 4, 1937, LC, B-4, and N-5.

111. MM to GB, Nov. 14, 1933, LC, R-1; GB to MM, June 4, 1933, LC, R-2.

112. GB to MM, Jan. 3, Aug. 21, 1933; Jan. 3, 1935; LC, B-3; Mead, *Ruth Benedict*, p. 49; *BW* draft, "Sex and Temperament," p. 22; and Charles Montagu Doughty, *Arabia Deserta* (1888; London: Jonathan Cape, 1926).

113. M. C. Bateson, *With a Daughter's Eye*, p. 61.

114. MM to RFB, Apr. 9, 1933, LC, R-7; MM to RFB, March 9, 1933, S-4.

115. MM to GB, Dec. 13, 1933, LC, slips.

116. MM to Elizabeth Hellersberg, Aug. 4, 1947, LC, R-10; MM to Erik Erikson, April 27, 1947, LC, R-8; MM to GB, Nov. 27, 1948, LC, R-3.

117. Margaret Mead, "The Sex Life of the Unmarried Adult in Primitive Society," in Wile, *Sex Life of the Unmarried Adult*, pp. 53–74.

12 / *From the Hanover Conference to the Witches of Bali:*
Sex and Temperament, *Part 2*

1. Obituary, Lawrence Kelso Frank, *New York Times*, Sept. 24, 1966.

2. Lawrence J. Friedman, *Identity's Architect: A Biography of Erik H. Erikson* (New York: Scribner, 1999), p. 125; MM to GB, March 10, 1933, LC, R-2. On Frank, see Stephen J. Cross, "Frank," and Mead, Letter, in "Tributes to Larry Frank on his 75th Birthday," mimeo. volume, LC, B-5.

3. This material on homosexuality is located in the Hanover Conference File, LC, F-31 and F-32. Mead seems also to have attended the Hanover Conference in the summer of 1935. I have been unable to locate the transcripts of these conferences, although in her 1935 "Report for the Commission on the Revision of the Curriculum of the Secondary Schools," LC, I-7 and I-8, Mead called for integrating the social sciences around a life history approach, including studying the categories of male and female. She didn't include the topic of sexual orientation.

4. MM to GB, Dec. 14, 1934, LC, R-2.

5. Mead, *Sex and Temperament*, p. ii. See also Lois W. Banner, "Mannish Women, Passive Men, and Constitutional Types: Margaret Mead's *Sex and Temperament in Three Primitive Societies* As a Response to Ruth Benedict's *Patterns of Culture*," *Signs: Journal of Women in Culture and Society* 28 (spring 2003).

6. MM to GB, Feb. 7, 1934, LC, R-2.

7. In Mead's review of *Patterns of Culture* in *The Nation*, Dec. 12, 1934, 686–87, she blandly praised it as "a counsel of hope," showing individuals' possible configurations to follow. She described it to Bateson as "lightly, casually done." Nov. 3, 1934, LC,

R-2. In her friend-of-the-court brief for Walter Spies, Mead implicitly attacked even Benedict's praise of the hobo. She noted a study showing that older male hobos (called "wolves") forced younger boys (called "lambs") into active/passive homosexuality.

8. Mead, *Letters from the Field*, p. 108.

9. Vern L. Bullough, in *Science in the Bedroom: A History of Sex Research* (New York: Basic Books, 1994), p. 210, traces the first usage of "gender" in the present-day sense of socialization to John Money of Johns Hopkins University. The OED traces the first use to Ann Oakley, *Sex, Gender, and Society* (San Francisco: Harper & Row, 1972), although Oakley traces it to Money. According to Suzanne J. Kessler and Wendy McKenna, *Gender: An Ethnomethodological Approach* (New York: John Wiley & Sons, 1978), p. 7, "until recently the word gender was not used in everyday life." By 1971, Mead noted that she was using it to mean male or female, and "sex" to mean sexuality, although that usage seems to me to be still grounded in the older definitions. Mead, "Temperamental Differences and Sexual Dimorphism," p. 180.

Mead did use the term "gender" in the original meaning related to language structure, and the variety of gender classifications in the Arapesh and the Tchambuli languages, including a large number of neutral categories, may have influenced her in breaking down the fixed male/female binary. Gregory Bateson cautioned her not to use the word "gender" because it was too "snaky." Jan. 3, 1933, LC, R-1.

10. Allport, *Personality*, pp. 25–40; Roback, *Psychology of Character*, p. xi.

11. Mead, "Preface to the 1950 Edition," *Sex and Temperament*, n.p., and "Temperamental Differences," p. 108.

12. *BW* draft, "Sex and Temperament," p. 33. Thompson was the first American correspondent to interview Hitler, and she published a series of articles on him in the *Saturday Evening Post* in which she dismissed him as bizarre. See Peter Kurth, *American Cassandra: The Life of Dorothy Thompson* (Boston: Little, Brown, 1990), pp. 161–63.

13. Benedict, *Patterns of Culture*, p. 234.

14. Mead, *Sex and Temperament*, pp. 280, 284.

15. Allport, *Personality*, p. 122; Mead, *Sex and Temperament*, p. 284.

16. Mead, *Sex and Temperament*, pp. 283–84.

17. Mead, "Cultural Determinants of Sexual Behavior," p. 1452.

18. Mead, *Sex and Temperament*, p. xxvii.

19. Idem. Mead refers to Willard Hill's *AA* article idealizing the Navajo nadle in Mead, "Some Relationships Between Social Anthropology and Psychiatry," in *Dynamic Psychiatry* ed. Franz Alexander and Helen Ross (Chicago: University of Chicago Press, 1952), p. 417. By 1938 Benedict revised her position to propose that the men-women were sometimes ridiculed and that they never took the active role in active/passive sex.

20. Mead, "Background Statement About Homosexuality," p. 8, and "Walter Spies of Bali," LC, N-30.

21. Geoffrey Gorer discussed these matters in the first draft of his book on the Marquis de Sade; see Gorer, preface, *The Life and Ideas of the Marquis de Sade* (London: Peter Owen, 1953).

22. Mead, *Sex and Temperament*, p. 271.

23. Ibid., p. 105.

24. Ibid., p. 101.

25. Ibid., pp. 296–306.

26. Ibid., p. 297.

27. Ibid., pp. 301–2, 296–302.

28. Ibid., p. 296; Mead, *Male and Female*, p. 348.

29. John Farley, *Gametes and Spores: Ideas About Sexual Reproduction, 1750–1914* (Baltimore: Johns Hopkins University Press, 1982), pp. 189–203.

30. Mead, *Sex and Temperament*, p. 298. Margaret Mead, "Sex and Achievement," *Forum* 94 (1935): 301–3.

31. Mead, "Cultural Determinants of Sexual Behavior."

32. Mead, *Sex and Temperament*, p. 316.

33. Mead, *Male and Female*, pp. 68, 74.

34. Mead, *Sex and Temperament*, pp. 292–95.

35. Mead, draft essay on lesbianism for *Redbook*, typescript, Feb. 15, 1971, LC, I-98.

36. Mead, Spies brief; "Background Statement About Homosexuality," p. 8; and *Male and Female*, pp. 78–104. The first author to advance the "womb envy" thesis was Karen Horney, in 1926. See Janet Sayers, *Mothers of Psychoanalysis* (New York: W. W. Norton, 1991), pp. 100–5.

37. MM to GB, Feb. 21, 1935, LC, S-1.

38. MM to John Dollard, Sept. 19, 1938, LC, N-5.

39. Mead, *Sex and Temperament*, p. x, and *Male and Female*, p. 155. On masculinity in the 1930s, cf. Christopher David Breu, "Hard-Boiled Masculinities: Fantasizing Gender in American Literature and Popular Culture, 1920–1945" (Ph.D. diss., University of California, Santa Cruz, 2000); and Barbara Melosh, "Manly Work: Public Art and Masculinity in Depression America," in *Gender and American History Since 1890*, ed. Melosh (New York: Routledge, 1993), pp. 155–81. For studies of unemployed men, see Banner, *Women in Modern America*, p. 214.

40. Mead, *Sex and Temperament*, p. 310.

41. MM to Emily Fogg Mead, March 29, 1938, LC, R-6.

42. Idem.

43. Geoffrey Gorer, "Margaret Mead," 1949, unpub. typescript, Geoffrey Gorer Papers, SU. See also Mead, "Chi Omega Acceptance Speech."

44. The history of feminist ideology in the 1920s and 1930s remains mostly unstudied. Nancy Cott, in *The Grounding of Modern Feminism*, deals mainly with organizations, and the account ends in 1930. Mari Jo Buhle, *Feminism and Its Discontents: A Century of Struggle with Psychoanalysis* (Cambridge, Mass.: Harvard University Press, 1998), covers only feminist psychoanalysts. In *Inventing Herself: Claiming a Feminist Intellectual Heritage* (New York: Scribner, 2001), a brief survey, Elaine Showalter identifies Benedict and Mead as the major feminist thinkers of this era.

In the 1920s Charlotte Perkins Gilman complained that her books weren't being read and that she wasn't invited to speak anywhere. See Charlotte Perkins Gilman, *The Living of Charlotte Perkins Gilman: An Autobiography* (New York: D. Appleton-Century, 1935), pp. 332–33. Judy Weiss, "Womanhood and Psychoanalysis: A Study of Mutual Construction in Popular Culture, 1920–1963" (Ph.D. diss., Brown University, 1990), contends that the absence of a strong feminist movement and ideology from the 1920s on permitted the psychoanalysts in the 1930s and 1940s to restructure female roles around motherhood and domesticity.

45. Mead, preface to the 1950 edition of *Male and Female*, reprinted in the 1963 edition, n.p.

46. Mead, *Male and Female*, p. 155.

47. Benedict, "Sex in Primitive Society."

48. L. Friedman, *Identity's Architect*, pp. 136–39; MM to GB, Sept. 16, 1939, LC, S-1.

49. MM to Erik Erikson, July 12, 1936, LC, N-5. On Mead and Bateson on Bali, I have used Margaret Mead, "On the Concept of Plot in Culture" (1939), in Mead, *Anthropology, a Human Science*, pp. 37–40; Mead, "Balinese Character," in Gregory Bateson and Margaret Mead, *Balinese Character: A Photographic Analysis* (New York: New York Academy of Sciences, 1942); Mead, *Letters from the Field*, pp. 159–238; *BW* and *BW* draft, "Bali." I have also relied on Gerald Sullivan, *Margaret Mead, Gregory Bateson, and Highland Bali: Fieldwork Photographs of Bayung Gede, 1936–1939* (Chicago: University of Chicago Press, 1999), and on the letters in LC, R-10 and N-5.

50. GB to MM, June 19, 1934, LC, R-2.

51. On Spies and the European community on Bali, I have used James A. Boon, "Between-the-Wars: Rereading the Relics," in Stocking, *Malinowski, Rivers*, pp. 218–45; and Hans Rhodius and John Darling, *Walter Spies and Balinese Art* (Zutphen, Netherlands: Terra, 1980).

52. MM to John Dollard, Sept. 19, 1938, LC, R-10; MM to Gardner Murphy, Sept. 27, 1938, R-10; MM to Marie Eichelberger, Sept. 16, 1938, LC, R-7. Sociologists were also critical of Mead's work. See Stephen O. Murray, "The Reception of Anthropological Work in Sociological Journals, 1922–1951," *Journal of the History of the Behavorial Sciences* 24 (April 1988): 135–47.

53. Mead, "Balinese Character," pp. xi–xii.

54. Margaret Mead, "Memo for Ruth Fulton Benedict on an Exploration into the Problem of the Personal Equation in Field Work," 1941, LC.

55. Mead, "The Cultural Dimension in the Study of Personality," 1946, LC, I-31.

56. Mead, "On the Concept of Plot in Culture," pp. 37–40; *Male and Female*, p. 52; Roback, *Psychology of Character*, p. xv.

57. MM to Marie Eichelberger, Sept. 16, 1938, LC, R-7.

58. Margaret Mead, "Children and Ritual in Bali," in *Childhood in Contemporary Cultures*, ed. Mead and Martha Wolfenstein (Chicago: University of Chicago Press, 1955), p. 44.

59. MM to Erik Erikson, July 12, 1936, LC, N-5.

60. Mead, "Cultural Determinants of Sexual Behavior," p. 1453.

61. MM to Noel Porter and Muss, April 13, 1938, LC, O-2.

62. MM to RFB, June 24, July 11, 1936, LC, S-4; MM to GG, Oct. 1, 1936, LC, N-5; GG to RFB, Sept. 5, 1936, VC, 72.

63. MM to Gardner Murphy, Feb. 4, 1937, R-10.

64. Mead, "Some Relationships Between Social Psychology and Anthropology," in Alexander and Ross, *Dynamic Psychiatry*.

65. MM to John Dollard, Jan. 20, 1938, LC, N-5; Sayers, *Mothers of Psychoanalysis*,

on the psychoanalytic focus on mothering; Kathleen W. Jones, " 'Mother Made Me Do It': Mother-Blaming and the Women of Child Guidance," in *"Bad" Mothers: The Politics of Blame in Twentieth-Century America,* ed. Molly Ladd-Taylor and Lauri Umansky (New York: New York University Press, 1998), pp. 99–124; and Buhle, *Feminism and Its Discontents,* pp. 125–64. Margaret Mead first advanced the "mother-blaming" thesis in "The Institutionalized Role of Women in Character Formation," *Zeitschrift für Sozialforshung,* Jahrgang 5 (Paris: Librarie Félix Alcar, 1936), a publication of Max Horkheimer's Institute for Social Research.

66. M. C. Bateson, *With a Daughter's Eye,* p. 36.

67. MM to CTK, Jan. 27, 1937; CTK to MM, Feb. 10, 1937, LC, B-8.

68. Jane Belo to MM, 1939; MM to Jane Belo, Feb. 2, 1939, LC, R-7.

69. MM to GG, Jan. 17, 1939, SU.

70. MM to RFB, Jan. 7, 1929, LC, B-1; MM to GG, Jan. 17, 1939, SU; John Dollard et al., *Frustration and Aggression* (New Haven: Yale University Press for Institute of Human Relations, 1939). For Mead's break with Dollard, see JH, p. 154.

71. MM to RFB, Jan. 12, 1939, LC, B-1. In 1944, speaking at the annual conference of the Superintendents of Correctional Institutions for Women and Girls in New York, Mead referred to male homosexuals as dangerous because they formed "exploitative and promiscuous relationships." Estelle B. Freedman, *Maternal Justice: Miriam Van Waters and the Female Reform Tradition* (Chicago: University of Chicago Press, 1996), p. 263.

72. Mead, "Cultural Determinants of Sexual Behavior," p. 1471.

73. In making this case, she relied on Frank A. Beach, *Hormones and Behavior: A Survey of Interrelationships Between Endocrine Secretions and Patterns of Overt Response* (New York: Paul B. Hoeber, 1948), pp. 69–70.

74. Margaret Mead, "Fifteen Years Later," introduction to the Pelican edition of *Male and Female,* 1962.

13 / *Race, Gender, and Sexuality*

1. I discuss the female iconography at Columbia in my *Finding Fran: History and Memory in the Lives of Two Women* (New York: Columbia University Press, 1998), pp. 133–34.

2. In describing the entrance, I have relied on Donna Haraway, *Primate Visions: Gender, Race, and Nature in the World of Modern Science* (New York: Routledge, 1989), pp. 26–50.

3. Robert Lynd, "Ruth Benedict," in *Ruth Fulton Benedict: A Memorial,* prepared by the Wenner-Gren Foundation for Anthropological Research (New York: Viking Fund, 1949), p. 23; and Sidney Mintz, "Ruth Benedict," in Silverman, *Totems and Teachers,* p. 61.

4. Ralph Linton, *The Study of Man: An Introduction* (New York: D. Appleton-Century, 1936), pp. 92–112.

5. Linton and Wagley, *Ralph Linton,* pp. 6–12.

6. RFB to MM, Aug 3, 1938, LC, B-1; RFB to MM, April 7, 1939; Jan. 22, 1940, LC, S-4.

7. Interview with Robert C. Suggs, CU. Suggs was the major critic of Linton's ethnography of the Marquesans; he charged that Linton's finding that the society practiced polyandry, with women sexually aggressive, was derived from one informant and was inaccurate. Suggs, "Sex and Personality in the Marquesas: A Discussion of the Linton-Kardiner Report," in *Human Sexual Behavior: Variations in the Ethnographic Spectrum*, ed. Donald S. Marshall and Robert C. Suggs (New York: Basic Books, 1971), pp. 163–68.

8. Mintz, "Ruth Benedict," pp. 156–57, 161.

9. On Linton and Kardiner's seminar, see MacMillan, "Columbia Department"; Friedman, *Identity's Architect*, pp. 135–36; William C. Manson, *The Psychodynamics of Culture: Abram Kardiner and Neo-Freudian Anthropology* (New York: Greenwood Press, 1988), and "Abram Kardiner and the Neo-Freudian Alternative in Culture and Personality," in Stocking, *Malinowski, Rivers*, pp. 72–94; and Abram Kardiner, *The Individual and His Society: The Psychodynamics of Primitive Social Organization* (New York: Columbia University Press, 1939), p. xiii.

10. RFB to MM, Oct. 1, 1936, LC, S-3.

11. Abram Kardiner and Edward Preble, *They Studied Man* (Cleveland: World, 1961), pp. 211–12; and Abram Kardiner oral interview, CU-Oral.

12. Abram Kardiner, *Sex and Morality* (Indianapolis: Bobbs-Merrill, 1954), p. 83. See also Abram Kardiner, *My Analysis with Freud: Reminiscences* (New York: W. W. Norton, 1977).

13. See the following brief biographies in Gacs et al., *Women Anthropologists*: George Park and Alice Park, "Ruth Schlossberg Landes," pp. 208–14; Joyce Griffen, "Ruth Murray Underhill," pp. 355–60.

14. Ruth Landes to RFB, Nov. 11, 1939, VC, 31.3.

15. RFB to MM, July 26, 1936, S-4; RFB to MM, Aug. 28, 1938, LC, B-1.

16. Mead, *Ruth Benedict*, p. 29; Ruth Benedict, "Women and Anthropology," in *The Education of Women in a Democracy*, prepared by the Council on the Education and Position of Women in a Democracy (New London, Conn.: Institute of Women's Professional Relations, 1940); David M. Fawcett and Teri McLuhan, "Ruth Leah Bunzel," and Ruth E. Pathé, "Gene Weltfish," in Gacs et al., *Women Anthropologists*, pp. 32, 372–81.

17. Briscoe, "Ruth Benedict," p. 471.

18. Marie Eichelberger to MM, July 12, 1938, LC, B-4.

19. RFB to MM, Jan. 21, 1937, LC, S-4.

20. RFB to MM, Aug. 4, 1938, LC, B-1.

21. RFB to Dr. Oliver Cope, Feb. 27, 1943, VC, 11.2. The article to which she referred is Ruth Benedict, "We Can't Afford Race Prejudice," *Frontiers of Democracy*, Oct. 9, 1942, p. 2.

22. RFB to Amram Scheinfeld, Feb. 9, 1943, VC, 11.2. Scheinfeld's book was published as *Women and Men* (New York: Harcourt, Brace, 1944).

23. Pearl S. Buck to RFB, Oct. 24, 1940; RFB to Pearl Buck, Nov. 11, 1940, VC, 11.2. Benedict's speech is "Anthropology and Some Alarmists," March 10, 1941, unpub. speeches, VC, 58.6.

24. Benedict noted these influences in a biographical statement she wrote for

her publisher for *The Chrysanthemum and the Sword*. RFB, biographical statement, 1946, VC.

25. Jack Harris to Melville Herskovits, Oct. 29, 1936, in "An Ethnographer at Work: Inside the Department of Anthropology at Columbia University, 1936–37," typescript mss., Melville Herskovits Papers, NU.

26. On the polarization and the radicalism among the students, see McMillan, "Study of Anthropology." According to Esther Goldfrank, *An Undiscovered Life*, p. 111, the junior faculty and the more advanced graduate students supported Benedict, while the more recent graduate students supported Linton. See also R. Murphy, "Anthropology at Columbia."

27. Andrea Walton, "Women at Columbia: A Study of Power and Empowerment in the Lives of Six Women" (Ph.D. diss., Columbia University, 1995), p. 254.

28. George W. Stocking Jr., "Franz Boas and the Culture Concept," in *Race, Culture, and Evolution: Essays in the History of Anthropology*, ed. George W. Stocking Jr. (New York: Free Press, 1968), pp. 214–29. On the Boasians and race, I have also used Lee D. Baker, *From Savage to Negro: Anthropology and the Construction of Race, 1896–1954* (Berkeley: University of California Press, 1998); Matthew Frye Jacobson, *Whiteness of a Different Color: European Immigrants and the Alchemy of Race* (Cambridge, Mass.: Harvard University Press, 1998); and Barkan, *Retreat from Scientific Racism*.

29. Goldenweiser, *Anthropology*, p. 20.

30. Benedict, *Patterns of Culture*, pp. 13–16.

31. On Herskovits, see Simpson, *Melville J. Herskovits*. He had been in Parsons's and Goldenweiser's courses at the New School along with Ruth Benedict, and they had recruited him to the Columbia program. For the Boasians on race, cf. Alfred L. Kroeber, *Anthropology* (New York: Harcourt Brace, 1923); Robert H. Lowie, *Are We Civilized?* (New York: Harcourt, Brace, 1929); Paul Radin, *The Racial Myth* (New York: McGraw-Hill, 1934); and Edward Sapir, "Language, Race, and Culture," in Calverton, *Making of Man*, pp. 142–54.

32. Otto Klineberg, *Race Differences* (New York: Harper & Bros., 1935), p. 1.

33. Benedict, *Race*, pp. 103, 106–7, 127.

34. Ibid., p. 111; Julian S. Huxley and A. C. Haddon, *We Europeans: A Survey of "Racial" Problems* (New York: Harper & Bros., 1936), pp. 110–43; Magnus Hirschfeld, *Racism*, trans. Eden and Cedar Paul (London: Victor Gollancz, 1938), pp. 57–58; Ashley Montagu, *Man's Most Dangerous Myth: The Fallacy of Race* (New York: Columbia University Press, 1942), pp. 71–74.

35. Benedict, *Race*, p. 35.

36. Ibid., p. 119.

37. For the disagreement between Benedict and Herskovits, see Walter Jackson, "Melville Herskovits and the Search for Afro-American Culture," in Stocking, *Malinowski, Rivers*, pp. 95–126.

38. Benedict, *Race*, pp. 87, 154.

39. Frederic A. Lucas, ed., *General Guide to the Exhibition Halls of the American Museum of Natural History*, rev. ed. (New York: American Museum of Natural History, 1928).

40. John Michael Kennedy, "Philanthropy and Science in New York City: The

American Museum of Natural History, 1868–1968" (Ph.D. diss., Yale University, 1968), p. 163.

41. Howard, *Margaret Mead*, pp. 132, 253–54; Dallas *Times Herald*, March 29, 1929, Clipping File, LC, L-3.

42. Clark Wissler, quoted in Kennedy, "Philanthropy and Science," p. 242.

43. Torrey, *Freudian Fraud*, pp. 69–70.

44. Clark Wissler, *Man and Culture* (New York: Thomas Y. Crowell, 1923), pp. 281–313.

45. Freed and Freed, "Clark Wissler," p. 808; MM to GB, Nov. 6, 1933, LC, R-1.

46. Robert Lowie to Risa Lowie, June 11, 1923, Robert H. Lowie Papers, UCB.

47. Henry Fairfield Osborn, *Fifty-two Years of Research, Observation, and Publication, 1877–1929* (New York: Charles Scribner's Sons, 1930).

48. Robert Lowie to Henry Fairfield Osborn, June 19, 1922, Robert H. Lowie Papers, UCB.

49. MM to RFB, summer 1931, LC, S-3.

50. MM to W. E. B. Du Bois, Oct. 18, 1935, LC, C-2.

51. Lenora Foerstel and Angela Gilliam, "Margaret Mead's Contradictory Legacy," in *Confronting the Margaret Mead Legacy: Scholarship, Empire, and the South Pacific,* ed. Foerstel and Gilliam (Philadelphia: Temple University Press, 1992), pp. 104–9; Haraway, *Primate Visions,* p. 58.

52. Goldenweiser, *Anthropology,* p. 20.

53. These comments are contained in the mimeographed bulletins from the field that Mead sent to her family and close friends, dated August 31, Sept. 14, Sept. 27, Dec. 11, 1925, LC, R-15.

54. MM to Elizabeth Mead, Nov. 19, 1925, LC, Q-10; MM to Eda Lou Walton, March 26, 1926, LC, R-4.

55. Jean Walton, *Fair Sex, Savage Dreams: Race, Psychoanalysis, Sexual Difference* (Durham: Duke University Press, 2001), pp. 144–89. Mead describes the incident in *BW,* p. 184.

56. Rogin, *Blackface, White Noise,* p. 49.

57. Mead and Baldwin, *Rap on Race,* p. 19.

58. Mead's most critical discussion of the male administrators is in *Letters from the Field,* p. 64.

59. MM to RFB, Dec. 2, 1932, LC, S-5.

60. The reference is contained in the mimeographed copy of the bulletin in the Arapesh field notes, Sept. 13, 1932. For Mead's request to remove the word, see correspondence file, *Letters from the Field,* LC, I-277.

61. Otto Klineberg oral interview, CU-Oral.

62. Louise M. Newman, "Coming of Age, but Not in Samoa: Reflections on Margaret Mead's Legacy for Western Liberal Feminism," *American Quarterly* 48 (June 1996): 233–72. See also Louise M. Newman, *White Women's Rights: The Racial Origins of Feminism in the United States* (New York: Oxford University Press, 1999), pp. 158–80, and Micaela di Leonardo, *Exotics at Home: Anthropologies, Others, American Modernities* (Chicago: University of Chicago Press, 1998). For a more balanced view of Mead as subjected to criticism both as a woman and as a popularizer in an academic discipline, see Nancy C. Lutkehaus, "Margaret Mead as Cultural Icon and Anthropol-

ogy's Liminal Figure," in Banner and Janiewski, *Reading Benedict/Reading Mead* (forthcoming).

63. Mead and Baldwin, *Rap on Race*, p. 17; Malinowski, *Argonauts of the Western Pacific*, p. 7.

64. Lola Romanucci-Ross, "Anthropological Field Research: Margaret Mead, Muse of the Clinical Experience," *AA* 82 (1980): 306, and *Mead's Other Manus: Phenomenology of the Encounter* (South Hadley, Mass.: Bergin & Garvey, 1985).

65. MM to Herskovits, [1925], NU; Louise J. Schlichting to Jane Howard, Jane Howard Papers, CU.

66. File on *A Rap on Race*, Sept. 1971, LC, I-200.

67. Margaret Mead, "Introductory Remarks," in *Science and the Concept of Race*, ed. Mead et al. (New York: Columbia University Press, 1968), pp. 3–9.

68. The "squares" test she devised is located in LC, Q-35.

69. GB to RFF, Jan 22, 1935, LC, R-2.

70. Benedict, "Toward a Social Psychology," pp. 50–51; G. Murphy and F. Jensen, *Approaches to Personality*, p. 25. For a classification by types of glands, see Louis Berman, *The Glands* (New York: Macmillan, 1928). On Allport's classification, see MM to GB, April 22, 1934, LC, R–4. See also W. A. Willemse, *Constitution-Types in Delinquency: Practical Applications and Bio-Physiological Foundations of Kretschmer's Types* (London: K. Paul, Trench, Trubner, 1932), pp. 1–2.

71. Barkan, *Retreat of Scientific Racism*, p. 94. See also Frank Spencer, ed., *A History of American Physical Anthropology, 1930–1980* (New York: Academic Press, 1982).

72. Victor Barnouw, *Culture and Personality* (Homewood, Ill.: Dorsey Press, 1963), pp. 18–19; J. M. Tanner, "Growth and Constitution," in *Anthropology Today: An Encyclopedic Inventory*, ed. Alfred L. Kroeber (Chicago: University of Chicago Press, 1953), pp. 750–70; Klineberg, *Race Differences*, pp. 54–67; Roback, *Psychology of Character*, pp. 98–100; and Allport, *Personality*, pp. 72–78.

73. Ernst Kretschmer, *Physique and Character: An Investigation of the Nature of Constitutional Types and of the Theory of Temperament*, trans. W. J. H. Sprott, 2d ed. rev. (New York: Cooper Square, 1970). For the early history of constitutional typologists, see W. H. Sheldon et al., *The Varieties of Human Physique: Introduction to Constitutional Psychology* (New York: Harper & Bros, 1940), pp. 10–29.

74. Ernst Kretschmer, *The Psychology of Men of Genius*, trans. R. B. Cattell (New York: Harcourt Brace, 1931).

75. Benedict, *Race*, p. 173.

76. Edward Sapir, "Personality," in *Selected Writings of Edward Sapir*, p. 562. Constitutional-type theorists didn't disappear with Hitler's takeover of power in Germany. In the early 1940s W. H. Sheldon did a famous study, observing the photographs of four thousand college students and classifying them as mesomorph, endomorph, and ectomorph—again using the classic categories of athletic, fat, and thin. In his textbook *Culture and Personality*, Barnouw discusses many other constitutional-type theorists from the 1940s and 1950s.

77. Willemse, *Constitution-Types*, p. 42.

78. G. Bateson, *Naven*, p. 160.

79. A. L. Kroeber, *Anthropology*, p. 36.

80. Montagu, *Man's Most Dangerous Myth*, pp. 177–80.

81. Margaret Mead, "People of Melanesia and New Guinea," LC, I-131.

82. Mead, *Sex and Temperament*, p. xiii.

83. See "Squares Test, Diagrams and Notes," LC, S-11.

84. Nancy Lays Stepan, "Race and Gender: The Role of Analogy in Science," in *Anatomy of Racism*, ed. David Theo Goldberg (Minneapolis: University of Minnesota Press, 1990), pp. 39–47; and Cynthia Eagle Russett, *Sexual Science: The Victorian Construction of Womanhood* (Cambridge, Mass.: Harvard University Press, 1989), pp. 11–31.

85. Gunnar Myrdal, *An American Dilemma: The Negro Problem and American Democracy*, vol. 2 (1944; New York: Pantheon Books, 1972), 1073–78.

86. Ruth Feldstein, *Motherhood in Black and White: Race and Sex in American Liberalism, 1930–1965* (Ithaca: Cornell University Press, 2000), pp. 28–52; Kate Weigand, *Red Feminism: American Communism and the Making of Women's Liberation* (Baltimore: Johns Hopkins University Press, 2001), p. 99.

14 / *Ripeness Is All*

1. MFF, "Family Life of Ruth Fulton Benedict," p. 8, OC.

2. MFB to MM, Sept. 10, 1939, LC, S-5.

3. Mead, *And Keep Your Powder Dry*, p. 3.

4. RFB to MM, Dec. 4, 1939, LC, B-1.

5. Mead, "What Are We Doing About the Psychological Front?" typescript, Dec. 24, 1941, LC, I-20. To understand the Committee for National Morale and the background to Mead and Benedict's involvement in World War II, I have used Modell, *Ruth Benedict*; Caffrey, *Ruth Benedict*; L. Friedman, *Identity's Architect*; Ellen Herman, *The Romance of American Psychology: Political Culture in the Age of Experts* (Berkeley: University of California Press, 1995); Carlton Mabee, "Margaret Mead and the Behavioral Scientists in World War II: Problems in Responsibility, Truth, and Effectiveness," *Journal of the History of the Behavioral Sciences* 23 (Jan. 1987): 3–13; and Virginia Yans-McLaughlin, "Science, Democracy, and Ethics: Mobilizing Culture and Personality for World War II," in Stocking, *Malinowski, Rivers*, pp. 184–217. Mead discussed their efforts in *Ruth Benedict*, and in *BW* draft, "War and Postwar Years," which she omitted from *Blackberry Winter* but published as "Anthropological Contributions to National Policies During and Immediately After World War II," in *The Uses of Anthropology*, ed. Walter Goldschmidt (Washington, D.C.: American Anthropological Association, 1979), pp. 145–57. See also Gregory Bateson and Margaret Mead, "Principles of Morale Building," *Journal of Educational Sociology* 15 (1941): 206–20.

6. L. Friedman, *Identity's Architect*, p. 164.

7. Lynd and Lynd, *Middletown*; and John Dollard, *Caste and Class in a Southern Town* (New Haven: Yale University Press, 1937).

8. MM to RFB, Oct. 9, 1939, LC, S-4.

9. Margaret Mead, "The Comparative Study of Cultures and the Purposive Cultivation of Democratic Values" (1942), in *Anthropology; a Human Science*, pp. 92–104. See also Margaret Mead, "National Character," in A. L. Kroeber, *Anthropology Today*, pp. 652–53.

10. Benedict, typescript, Department of Agriculture lecture in Washington, D.C., Feb. 25, 1938, VC, 55.

11. Geoffrey Gorer, "Themes in Japanese Culture," *Transactions of the New York Academy of Sciences* 5 (1943): 106–24.

12. MM to GB, Apr. 23, 1943, LC, R-3.

13. Margaret Mead, "The Mountain Arapesh, II: Supernaturalism," *Anthropological Papers of the American Museum of Natural History* 37 (1940): 319–451.

14. Edward Montgomery and John Bennett, "Anthropological Studies of Food and Nutrition: The 1940s and the 1970s," in Goldschmidt, *Uses of Anthropology*, pp. 124–44.

15. *BW* draft, "War and Post-War," p. 2.

16. Margaret Mead, "Cultural Contexts of Nutrition Problems," in *Anthropology, a Human Science*, pp. 175–93; Nina Swidler, "Rhoda Bubendey Métraux," in Gacs et al., *Women Anthropologists*, p. 263.

17. *BW* draft, "War and Post-War," p. 4.

18. Mead describes the work on this film in her introduction to Edith Cobb, *The Ecology of Imagination in Childhood* (New York: Columbia University Press, 1977), p. 3.

19. C. Douglas Lummis, "Ruth Benedict's Obituary for Japanese Culture," in Banner and Janiewski, *Reading Benedict/Reading Mead* (forthcoming).

20. John W. Dower, in *War Without Mercy: Race and Power in the Pacific War* (New York: Pantheon Books, 1986), pp. 24–40, analyzes the writings of social scientists about Japan during World War II. He notes that Benedict's *Chrysanthemum and the Sword* differed from most of the other writings on the subject, but he doesn't analyze her book.

21. Ruth Benedict, *The Chrysanthemum and the Sword: Patterns of Japanese Culture* (Boston: Houghton Mifflin, 1946), p. 197.

22. Geoffrey Gorer, "Japanese Character Structure and Propaganda," in *The Study of Culture at a Distance*, ed. Margaret Mead and Rhoda Métraux (Chicago: University of Chicago Press, 1953), pp. 401–2.

23. Benedict, *Chrysanthemum and the Sword*, pp. 54, 186, 187–88. On the background to the writing of this book, including the important conference on Japan in New York City in December 1944, which influenced Benedict, see Nanako Fukui, "Reading Benedict: A Lady of Culture," in Banner and Janiewski, *Reading Benedict/Reading Mead* (forthcoming).

24. Ruth Benedict, "Male Dominance in Thai Culture," in Brockman, *About Bateson*, pp. 215–31; and preface to Rebecca Hourwich Reyher, *Zulu Woman* (New York: Columbia University Press, 1948), pp. i–xi.

25. Mead, *Ruth Benedict*, p. 64.

26. Margaret Mead, "The Book I Tore Up," unpub. mss., LC, I-273.

27. Lapsley, *Margaret Mead and Ruth Benedict*, p. 292.

28. Joy Hendry, "The Chrysanthemum Continues to Flower: Ruth Benedict and Some Perils of Popular Anthropology," in *Popularizing Anthropology*, ed. Jeremy MacClancy and Chris McDonaugh (London: Routledge, 1996), pp. 106–21.

29. Paul S. Boyer, *By the Bomb's Early Light: American Thought and Culture at the Dawn of the Atomic Age* (New York: Pantheon Books, 1985), pp. 205, 274, 286; Ruth Benedict, "The Past and the Future: *Hiroshima* by John Hersey," *Nation*, Dec. 7, 1946, p. 656.

30. According to Gregg Harken, in *Brotherhood of the Bomb: The Tangled Lives and Loyalties of Robert Oppenheimer, Ernest Lawrence, and Edward Teller* (New York: Henry Holt, 2002), Oppenheimer feared what might happen to his scientist brother, not himself, while he had an affair with Ruth Tolman. Harken mentions the affair on p. 290.

31. *AW*, p. 354.

32. Mead, "What Are We Doing About the Psychological Front?"

33. Margaret Mead, "Has the Middle Class a Future?" *Survey Graphic* 31 (Feb. 1942): 64–67, 95.

34. Mead, *And Keep Your Powder Dry*, p. 167.

35. Margaret Mead and Paul Byers, *The Small Conference: An Innovation in Communication* (The Hague: Mouton, 1968), p. 167. Yans-McLaughlin, in "Science, Democracy, and Ethics," stresses Mead's commitment to democracy and small groups as key to her thinking during World War II. See also Margaret Mead and Muriel Brown, *The Wagon and the Star: A Study of American Community Initiative* (New York: Rand McNally, 1967).

36. I base my analysis of Mead's attitude toward ethnicity in the World War II period on *And Keep Your Powder Dry*.

37. Ruth Benedict, "Review of Fromm, *Escape from Freedom*," typescript, VC, 54.18; cf. Ruth Benedict, "Recognition of Cultural Diversities in the Postwar World," *Annals of the American Academy of Political and Social Science* 128 (July 1943), 101–7, reprinted in *AW*, pp. 439–48.

38. Margaret Mead, "The Comparative Study of Cultures and the Purposive Cultivation of Democratic Values" (1942), in *Anthropology, A Human Science*, pp. 92–104.

39. Maslow, *Farther Reaches of Human Nature*, pp. 192–93. Benedict's scheme can be found in Benedict, "Synergy: Some Notes of Ruth Benedict," selected by Abraham Maslow and John J. Honigmann, *AA* 72 (1970): 320–23; and T. G. Harris, "About Ruth Benedict," p. 52.

40. See Ruth Bunzel, "The Economic Organization of Primitive Peoples," in Franz Boas, *General Anthropology*, pp. 327–408.

41. Benedict, "Primitive Freedom," *Atlantic Monthly*, 1942; *AW*, pp. 386–98.

42. See Lary May, *The Big Tomorrow: Hollywood and the Politics of the American Way* (Chicago: University of Chicago Press, 2000), p. 6.

43. Margaret Mead, "The Idea of National Character," in *The Search for Identity: Essays on the American Character*, ed. Roger Shinn (New York: Harper & Row, 1964), pp. 17–27, and "Anthropological Techniques in War Psychology," *Bulletin of the Menninger Clinic*, July 7, 1943, p. 137, LC, I-24.

44. Benedict, "Synergy," p. 327.

45. Mead, *And Keep Your Powder Dry*, p. 235.

46. RFB to MM, June 4, 1936, S-4; Apr. 23, June 9, 1938, LC, S-5; MM to GB, Sept. 16, 1939, S-1.

47. RFB to MM, June 9, 1930, LC, S-5.

48. Marie Eichelberger to MM, July 12, 1938, LC, B-4; RFB to MM, March 2, 1940, R-7.

49. MM to RFB, Feb. 29, 1940; Mar. 2, 1940, LC, S-5.

50. MM to GB, Feb. 27, 1940, LC, S-1.

51. RFB to MM, Mar. 2, 1940, LC, R-7.

52. RFB to MM, June 4, 1936, LC, S-5.

53. Interviews with Sherwood Washburne and Gregory Bateson, CU.

54. MM to CTK, July 13, 1947, R-8; "Copy of Gregory's Letters After He Went to Bed," night of June 13, 1948, LC, R-3.

55. MM to Milton Erikson, Jan. 27, 1948, LC, R-8.

56. GB to MM, Aug. 29, 1949; MM to GB, Feb. 22, 1951, UCSC, 942-3, 942-4.

57. MM to E. P. Chinnery, Feb. 28, 1939, LC, N-4. Chinnery's résumé is in LC, R-12.

58. In describing these developments in anthropology and in the Columbia department, I have relied on A. Linton and C. Wagley, *Ralph Linton;* Robert Caneiro, "Leslie White," and Robert Murphy, "Julian Steward," in Silverman, *Totems and Teachers.*

59. Caneiro, "Leslie White."

60. Manson, *Psychodynamics of Culture,* p. 103; *AW,* p. 428.

61. On the project, see Manson, *Psychodynamics of Culture;* Margaret Mead and Rhoda Métraux, *Study of Culture at a Distance,* p. 8; and Margaret Mead, "Research in Contemporary Cultures," in *Groups, Leadership, and Men: Research in Human Relations; Reports on Research Sponsored by the Human Relations and Morale Branch of the Office of Moral Research, 1945–1950,* ed. Harold Guetzkov (Pittsburgh, Pa.: Carnegie Press, 1951), pp. 106–18.

62. Mead dressed him down for using the title; she thought that it would annoy his colleagues at Yale. MM to GG, Dec. 4, 1936, LC, B-5.

63. Mead and Métraux, *Study of Culture at a Distance,* p. 8.

64. Geoffrey Gorer and John Rickman, *The People of Great Russia: A Psychological Study* (1949; New York: W. W. Norton, 1962), p. 211.

65. Robert Endleman, "The New Anthropology and Its Ambitions: The Science of Man in Messianic Dress," *Commentary,* Sept. 1949, 284–90. In his history of anthropological theory, Marvin Harris was vitriolic. "The meeting of the two disciplines [anthropology and psychiatry] tended to reinforce the inherent tendencies toward uncontrolled, speculative, and histrionic generalizations which each in its own sphere had cultivated as part of its professional license." Marvin Harris, *The Rise of Anthropological Theory: A History of Theories of Culture* (New York: Thomas Y. Crowell, 1968), p. 448.

66. Margaret Mead, "The Swaddling Hypothesis: Its Reception," *AA* 56 (1954): 395–409.

67. K. A. Cuordileone, " 'Politics in an Age of Anxiety': Cold War Political Culture and the Crisis in American Masculinity, 1949–1960," *Journal of American History* 87 (2000): 1–31.

68. MM to GG, Dec. 19, 1950, LC, B-6.

69. Mead, *Continuities in Cultural Evolution,* pp. vi, 18, 35; Mead review of T. H. Huxley and Julian Huxley, "Touchstone for Ethics," *New York Times Book Review,* Nov. 16, 1947, p. 8.

70. Ibid., p. 35.

71. Mead, "Research in Contemporary Cultures—Eighteenth General Seminar, May 26, 1948," mimeo. ms., LC, G-14.

72. Margaret Mead, "An Anthropologist Looks at the Report," in *Problems of Sex-*

ual Behavior: Proceedings of a Symposium on the First Published Report of a Series of Studies of Sex Phenomena by Alfred C. Kinsey, Wardell B. Pomeroy, and Clyde E. Martin (New York: American Social Hygiene Association, 1948), pp. 58–69.

73. Cf. Margaret Mead, "Toward a New Role for Women," in *Women Take Stock of Themselves* (New York: Woman's Press, 1940), pp. 11–16, "Women's Social Position," *Journal of Educational Psychology* (April 1944): 453–62, "Some Aspects of the Role of Women in the United States," unpub. typescript, 1946, for *Esprit*, LC, "What Women Want," *Fortune* 249 (Dec. 1946): 171–75, 220–24, and "Setting New Patterns of Women's Work," *Responsibility* (for the National Association of Negro Business and Professional Women's Clubs) 5 (1947): 13–14.

74. She later defended herself by contending that it wasn't until after the Korean War that women's return to the home became apparent. Mead, introduction to the Pelican edition of *Male and Female*, 1962, p. 14.

75. MM to RFB, July 7, 1947, LC, R-7.

76. *BW* draft, "Perry Street and Waverly Place," p. 8.

77. Lindzey, p. 315.

78. Mead, *Male and Female*, pp. 20–21.

79. Margaret W. Rossiter, *Women Scientists in America: Before Affirmative Action, 1940–1972* (Baltimore: Johns Hopkins University Press, 1995), p. 316.

80. G. E. Hutchinson, *The Itinerant Ivory Tower: Scientific and Literary Essays* (New Haven: Yale University Press, 1953), p. 130; Erik Erikson, in *Ruth Fulton Benedict—a Memorial*, p. 15.

81. MFF, "Family Life of Ruth Fulton Benedict," p. 9.

82. Mead, "Research in Contemporary Cultures," mimeo. ms., Sept., LC, G-14.

83. MFF to RFB, Sept. 7, 1948, VC, 31.3.

84. Margaret Mead, "Ruth Fulton Benedict, 1887–1948," *AA* 51 (1949): 457–62.

Index

A NOTE ABOUT THE AUTHOR

LOIS BANNER received her B.A. from the University of California at Los Angeles and her M.A. and Ph.D. from Columbia University. She has taught at Rutgers University, Princeton University, the University of Scranton, Hamilton College, the University of Maryland, and George Washington University. She is currently Professor of History and Gender Studies at the University of Southern California, and is a Past President of the American Studies Association and the Pacific Coast Branch, American Historical Association. Her previous books include *American Beauty; In Full Flower: Aging Women, Power, and Sexuality;* and *Finding Fran.* She and her husband live in Santa Monica, California.

A NOTE ON THE TYPE

THIS BOOK was set in Janson, a typeface long thought to have been made by the Dutchman Anton Janson, who was a practicing type-founder in Leipzig during the years 1668–1687. However, it has been conclusively demonstrated that these types are actually the work of Nicholas Kis (1650–1702), a Hungarian, who most probably learned his trade from the master Dutch typefounder Dirk Voskens. The type is an excellent example of the influential and sturdy Dutch types that prevailed in England up to the time William Caslon (1692–1766) developed his own incomparable designs from them.

Composed by North Market Street Graphics,
Lancaster, Pennsylvania
Printed and bound by Berryville Graphics,
Berryville, Virginia
Designed by Virginia Tan